OF
MICE AND
MAGIC

Other books by Leonard Maltin

Movie Comedy Teams

The Art of the Cinematographer (originally published as
Behind the Camera: The Cinematographer's Art)

The Great Movie Shorts

The Disney Films

Carole Lombard

Our Gang: The Life and Times of the Little Rascals *with Richard W. Bann*

The Great Movie Comedians

Edited by Leonard Maltin

TV Movies

Hollywood: The Movie Factory

Hollywood Kids

The Laurel and Hardy Book

Real Stars, Vols. 1–3

To Rosemary Courtney —
With animated greetings
from
Leonard
Maltin

February
1981

OF
MICE AND
MAGIC

A History of American Animated Cartoons

Leonard Maltin

Research Associate: **Jerry Beck**

McGraw-Hill Book Company

New York St. Louis San Francisco Auckland Bogotá
Hamburg Johannesburg London Madrid Mexico
Montreal New Delhi Panama Paris São Paulo
Singapore Sydney Tokyo Toronto

To my loving wife,
Alice,
who brings such joy
to my life

Library of Congress Cataloging in Publication Data

Maltin, Leonard.
Of mice and magic.

Includes index.
1. Moving-picture cartoons—United States—History
and criticism. I. Title.
PN1997.5.M3   791.43'3   79-21923
ISBN 0-07-039835-6

1 2 3 4 5 6 7 8 9 0 VHVH 8 9 8 7 6 5 4 3 2 1 0

The editors for this book were Robert A. Rosenbaum
and Esther Gelatt, the designer was Elliot Epstein, and
the production supervisor was Thomas G. Kowalczyk.
It was set in Palatino by University Graphics, Inc.

Printed and bound by Von Hoffmann Press, Inc.

Contents

Preface   vii

1. **The Silent Era**   1

2. **Walt Disney**   29

3. **Max Fleischer**   79

4. **Paul Terry and Terrytoons**   121

5. **Walter Lantz**   155

6. **Ub Iwerks**   185

7. **The Van Beuren Studio**   195

8. **Columbia: Charles Mintz and Screen Gems**   205

9. **Warner Brothers**   219

10. **MGM**   275

11. **Paramount/Famous Studios**   305

12. **UPA**   317

13. **The Rest of the Story**   337

Filmographies by Studios   343

The Walt Disney Cartoons, 343
The Max Fleischer Cartoons, 356
Terrytoons, 366
The Walter Lantz Cartoons, 379
The Ub Iwerks Cartoons, 391
The Van Beuren Cartoons, 392
The Columbia/Screen Gems Cartoons, 397
The Warner Brothers Cartoons, 404
The MGM Cartoons, 425
The Paramount/Famous Studios Cartoons, 432
The UPA Cartoons, 444

Academy Award Nominees and Winners   447

Sources for Renting and Purchasing Cartoons   453

Glossary of Animation Terms   451

Index   456

Preface

I love cartoons.

I always have; as a child of the TV generation, I grew up with Farmer Al Falfa, Porky Pig, Mickey Mouse, and dozens of other cartoon characters. I had no idea they were twenty to thirty years old at the time. They were new to me.

As an adolescent I was told that cartoons were for kids—but I never outgrew my love for these films and their stars. Instead, I became curious to know more about them; when they were made, who created the characters, why some series were funnier than others, and why there seemed to be three thousand mice in every Paul Terry cartoon.

All I could find at the library were several books on Walt Disney. General histories of film barely mentioned animation, reserving what little space there was for Disney and the pioneers of experimental animation (Len Lye, Lotte Reiniger, Norman McLaren, and others). In these surveys, Bugs Bunny did not warrant so much as a passing nod, and neither did his creators.

For several decades there was a snob barrier that prevented the Hollywood cartoon from receiving serious attention. A sly distinction arose between the "cartoon" and the "animated film," the latter term connoting an independent, nonstudio endeavor, which earned respectability in museums, schools, and publications because it was "artistic."

Perhaps Hollywood cartoons were too successful in the commercial marketplace to overcome such feelings. Perhaps their unpretentiousness worked against them. Certainly the fact that the film industry ignored these cartoons—when they were still being made—didn't help their bid for prominence or posterity.

Only in recent years, as young people weaned on these cartoons began to infiltrate the world of film study, has the Hollywood cartoon come into its own. More attention has been focused on cartoons in the past five years than in the previous twenty-five combined. People who once took cartoons for granted are beginning to discover what remarkable films they are—and that the great animation directors and artists were outstanding *filmmakers*, who knew how to use their medium to its fullest potential. Their mastery of cinematic technique was equaled only by their ability to entertain. My friends and colleagues Joe Adamson, Mike Barrier, John Canemaker, and Greg Ford have been pioneers in this "new wave" of recognition.

Still, there is much work to be done. When I set out to write this book, I discovered that it would involve a great deal of "primary research." There were no sources to consult for some of the simplest details about American cartoon studios. Trade magazines of the twenties, thirties, and forties had little to offer, since news of cartoon production was not considered important. Cartoon departments of major Hollywood studios were so far removed from the mainstream of daily operations that a spokesman for one company I contacted swore he didn't know such a department ever existed.

Compiling this history was something like assembling a giant jigsaw puzzle. Fortunately, many of animation's most distinguished veterans are still alive and were kind enough to share their memories. Many opened their files to lend me valuable documents and illustrations.

As this book started to take shape, I decided to confine its boundaries to the American theatrical cartoon, in order to do as thorough a job as possible. A global history of animation, and an American history encompassing independent, sponsored, industrial, and television work, deserve book-length studies of their own.

For their help and encouragement I am deeply indebted to Al Eugster, the late Dick Huemer, Shamus Culhane, Chuck Jones, Friz Freleng, I. Klein, Bob Clampett, Jack Hannah, Walter Lantz, Jack Zander, Preston Blair, Jules Engel, Michael Lah, Myron Waldman, Dick Lundy, Zack Schwartz, Phil Klein, Ray Patterson, Bill Hurtz, Ed Cullen, Emery Hawkins, Grim Natwick, Harry Love, Sid Marcus, Irv Spence, Bill Littlejohn, Dave Hilberman, Eli Bauer, Al Kouzel, Otto Messmer, Bill Hendricks, Hal Elias, Steve Bosustow, Bill Melendez, Lu Guarnier, Tissa David, Howard Beckerman, Adrian Woolery, Howard Post, Willis Pyle, Paul Sommer, and Jules Feiffer. Earlier conversations with Ward Kimball, Frank Thomas, Ernie Pintoff, Gene Deitch, Richard Williams, and the late John Hubley were also extremely helpful.

Many other people helped me realize this project by finding information, loaning research materials, making films and illustrations available, and offering moral support: Alan Greenfield, Mark Mayerson, Will Timbes Friedwold, Gordon Berkow, William K. Everson, Ron Schwarz, Mark Langer, Leslie Cabarga, Joe Adamson, Ron and Chris Hall, Mark Kausler, David and Kathy Mruz, Gary Terry, Jeff Missinne, Burt Shapiro, Ron Billen, Bob Smith, Steve Schneider, Jerry Haber, Don Krim, Seth Willenson; Charlie Pavlicek and Milton Menell of Select Film Library; George Nelson, Stanley Solson, Sue Henderson, Rita Moriarty, and Hal Geer of Warner Brothers; Bill Theiss of Viacom; Bill Kenly of Paramount Pictures; Gary Bordzuk and Hal Cranton of MCA-Universal; Susan Dalton and Maxine Fleckner of the Wisconsin Center for Film and Theater Research; and the staff of the Department of Film at the Museum of Modern Art.

Harvey Deneroff generously loaned me his interviews with the late Paul Terry, and with Terry associates Tommy Morrison and Mannie Davis.

David R. Smith of the Walt Disney Archives patiently answered dozens of questions and made valuable information available to me. His thoroughness sets a high standard for all film historians.

Jan Kucik shared his knowledge and animation materials with equal enthusiasm.

Phil Johnson proved that frame enlargements don't have to be blurry, and made it possible for me to illustrate important moments from many cartoons.

In 1973 Michael S. Engl gave me the opportunity to develop and teach a class on the history of animation at the New School for Social Research in New York. This experience laid the groundwork for my book, and I will always be grateful to Mike for his kindness and support. Donald Spoto continues to encourage and nurture this class.

In my class I met Jerry Beck, whose tireless devotion to cartoons made him a valuable colleague on this book. His diligence in research is exceeded only by his love for Bosko, which I shall not attempt to explain.

My acknowledgments could not be complete without a sincere thank you to Barry Lippman, who initiated this project and stood by patiently while I missed several deadlines, and to John Thornton and Gerry Howard, who nurtured it to life.

Finally, I would like to thank my wife, Alice, who not only transcribed most of my interviews and typed much of the manuscript, but put up with creeping cartoonitis for well over a year. Without her love and support this book would not exist.

The Silent Era

OWARD THE END of the 1920s, a large group of New York animators held a testimonial dinner for Winsor McCay, whom most considered to be their mentor. As I. Klein recalls it, McCay concluded his brief remarks with a candid and unflattering appraisal: "Animation should be an art, that is how I had conceived it. But . . . what you fellows have done with it is [make] it into a trade . . . not an art, but a trade . . . bad luck."

McCay was only half right. Animation *had* become a trade, but that did not obliterate its potential as an art. Like the comic strip, the animated cartoon became a popular art form. What held it back in the silent era was economic pressure to make the cartoon a screen equivalent of the comic strip—and produce it nearly as often. Animators who had to crank out one film a week had little opportunity to analyze their medium, and no time for experimentation or improvement except on the job. That the medium progressed as far as it did by the 1920s is a tribute to the early animators' dedication and spirit.

But animation developed only so far in the silent era and then marked time. There was nowhere else to go within the rigid boundaries of silent black-and-white gag cartoons, it seemed. Creative men continued to turn out entertaining films, but a treadmill effect started to set in until sound lifted animation out of the doldrums.

That considered, it's astonishing to see how many major developments came about *prior* to 1920, when the motion picture itself was still in its infancy.

The century began with J. Stuart Blackton's THE ENCHANTED DRAWING, a short Edison film based on that newspaper cartoonist's "chalk-talk" vaudeville act: On a large pad of paper Blackton draws a man's face with a bottle and glass above his head. Then he reaches toward the easel and "lifts off" the bottle and glass—now actual three-dimensional objects—to pour himself a drink. This displeases the cartoon man, whose facial expression turns sour at the same moment the bottle and glass are removed.

There is no animation in this 1900 short, but there is imaginative use of the motion-picture medium. Blackton understood that

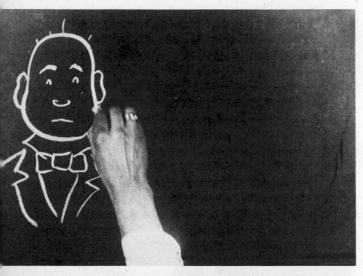

J. Stuart Blackton brings drawings to life in HUMOROUS PHASES OF FUNNY FACES (1906).

years later in the film that is often cited as the first animated cartoon, HUMOROUS PHASES OF FUNNY FACES. Here, letters, words, and faces come to life, drawn by an *unseen* hand. This indeed was "movie magic."

Of course, creating the illusion of movement through animated drawings predated the motion picture by many years. Sequential drawings were made by cavemen, and numbered illustrations traced the development of many later civilizations. The discovery of "persistence of vision" in the 1800s led to the invention of such devices as the zoetrope, or "wheel of life." This was a cylinder that spun on an axis; inside the open drum was a strip of drawings, each slightly different from the one preceding it. The drum was perforated with tiny slits through which the eye could see when the cylinder revolved. The effect of "moving pictures" was created by the human eye, which held one image intact until the next one appeared. The succession of slits acted something like a shutter on a projector. The zoetrope was a direct forerunner of the motion picture, and the men who created drawings for it were in fact the first animators.

But the zoetrope, and machines like it, were considered little more than novelty toys—a more sophisticated version of the "flip-books" that were also popular at this time. Perhaps it was the simplicity of the drawings that inspired such feelings. The actions depicted in this kind of animation were basic and brief: a girl skipping rope, a man jumping through a hoop, and the like.

Even so, these devices established the elementary procedures by which animated films could be made. One must speculate that the reason no one attempted to make animated cartoons for so many years *after* the introduction of film was the tremendous amount of labor involved. At sixteen frames per second, it would take nearly a thousand drawings to create one minute of an-

since film is a sequence of individual frames, one could simply halt the movement of film through a camera, make appropriate changes in props and drawings, and continue—leaving the motion-picture audience to challenge the credo that "seeing is believing."

Blackton advanced his experiments six

imation—a far cry from the demands of a flip-book. There were also technical questions to be answered, and no one with experience to consult.

Two men overcame these obstacles in their pioneering efforts and produced animated films that can stand today as models for all to follow. One was a Frenchman, Emile Cohl; the other was an American, Winsor McCay.

While this book is concerned with American animation, it would be irresponsible to ignore the accomplishments of Emile Cohl. Several years before McCay made his first short subject, Cohl produced a series of animated films that embrace sophisticated concepts of movement, design, humor, and format. They have every ingredient one expects to find in a modern cartoon except for sound and color.

Cohl's comic vignettes are played in pantomime by a cast of stick figures, drawn in white against a black background. The settings materialize, and change, by "metamorphosis," evolving from one to the next in a continuous flow as if their lines were made of clay, to be reshaped at the artist's whim. The ingenuity of a film like DRAME CHEZ LES FANTOCHES (1908) is matched only by its charm.

McCay never mentioned Cohl's work, so it isn't known whether he had the opportunity of seeing these films before embarking on his own movie projects.

Winsor McCay was a newspaper cartoonist whose efforts during the first ten years of this century are widely considered to be the pinnacle of American comic art. McCay combined the abilities of a superb draftsman with the imagination of a master storyteller. Such comic strips as *Little Nemo in Slumberland* and *Dreams of a Rarebit Fiend* are still celebrated today.

McCay credited his son's acquisition of several flip-books as the inspiration for the first film effort. J. Stuart Blackton's work may have been another influence; it was Blackton who directed the live-action sequences of McCay's first film. Whatever the case, McCay plunged into this experiment with typical enthusiasm—and stamina. He worked as much as four years on LITTLE NEMO, which finally debuted in April 1911. After laboriously animating four thousand drawings, McCay hand-colored the 35mm frames to achieve a particularly striking effect in his vaudeville act, where the short subject was first unveiled. (This color footage still exists.)

There is no story line to the animated film. The stars of McCay's comic strip exclaim via comic-strip balloons, "Watch us move!" and that's exactly what they do—in a continuous parade of movement, metamorphosis, and exaggeration. Characters flip upside down and stretch as if in a fun-house mirror. The

Walt Disney examines a praxinoscope, a close cousin to the zoetrope. Sequential images appear on the inner lining of the cylinder; when the cylinder is spun, one looks in the mirrors at the core of the machine to get the illusion of moving pictures.

GERTIE THE DINOSAUR **(1914) devouring a treetop.**

effect is dreamlike, and the animation precise: Perfectionist that he was, McCay made sure that his use of perspective was exact and that the drawings remained true-to-character no matter how the figures moved around.

LITTLE NEMO was well received, and McCay set to work on a second animated film, THE STORY OF A MOSQUITO. This one took a year to complete and went beyond the pyrotechnics of LITTLE NEMO to tell the comic story of a mosquito's encounter with a drunken man. McCay later wrote: "While these films made a big hit, the theatre patrons suspected some trick with wires. Not until I drew GERTIE THE DINOSAUR did the audience understand that I was making the drawings move." This may sound hard to believe, but it's true. Most movie audiences were naive and still trying to accustom themselves to the idea of motion pictures per se.

Thus, the notion of a *drawing* coming to life was astonishing; that a dinosaur could be the subject of such a drawing was positively awesome. Advertisements for GERTIE proclaimed, "She eats, drinks, and breathes! She laughs and cries! Yet, she lived millions of years before man inhabited this earth and has never been seen since!"

McCay incorporated the animated Gertie into an ingenious vaudeville routine in which he appeared as her trainer and bantered with her onstage. She would seem to obey his commands, react to his remarks, and even catch a pumpkin thrown into her mouth as a snack. For a finale, McCay would appear to walk right onto the screen and be carried away on Gertie's back.

GERTIE had a galvanizing effect on audiences. Those who could not see McCay in person enjoyed a one-reel film reminiscent of LITTLE NEMO in which the cartoonist accepted a bet from fellow cartoonists (including George McManus) that he could make a dinosaur come to life. The audience was then given a brief idea of how the film was made, with towering stacks of drawings, each different from the one preceding it. Finally, McCay's dialogue with the dinosaur was reproduced as a series of title cards.

There were ten thousand drawings in this one-reel film, each one inked on rice paper and mounted on cardboard. The entire picture—Gertie plus background—was redrawn for each individual frame of film. McCay did all the drawings of Gertie, while his assistant John A. Fitzsimmons traced the backgrounds. This accounts for the unstable quality of the line drawings, which "shimmer" throughout the film; for all his ingenuity, McCay wasn't able to lick this problem.

The artist—who was known for his speed and accuracy—set up a primitive machine to flip his finished animation. This enabled him to study his own work and redo whatever sequences he found unsatisfactory.

But McCay had no one to consult for guidance in the art of animation. It was virgin territory, and he set his own precedents. When Gertie uproots a tree trunk and devours it for lunch, McCay painstakingly animates the roots coming up through the surface, and illustrates the particles of dirt that fall from the trunk as Gertie hoists it aloft. He shows Gertie chewing, swallowing, drinking, breathing, dancing, crying—and somehow, we ignore the shimmering lines, the dim quality of most surviving prints. Gertie *lives*. She has *personality*, and she exudes the same impish charm today that captivated audiences in 1914. Gertie is an overgrown child, playful and mischievous. When McCay scolds her, she begins to cry, and even contemporary audiences react audibly to this comic-poignant scene.

Winsor McCay breathed life into an inanimate character, and this was his greatest achievement. It did not go unnoticed. GERTIE was so successful that it made people forget the animated films that preceded it—even McCay's. For years GERTIE has been named in film histories as the first animated cartoon. With all its impact, it might as well have been.

Many men who started working in animation during the teens were inspired to do so by this one film. One might say that GERTIE launched an entire industry.

Oddly enough, McCay had no desire to be a part of that industry. He preferred to continue his vaudeville appearances, keep up with his newspaper strips, and work on films at his own pace.

His post-GERTIE efforts are distinguished by the same graphic precision he brought to his newspaper work. Perspective and anatomical detail were of paramount importance to McCay. His naturalistic animation in THE CENTAURS and THE SINKING OF THE LUSI-

TANIA surpass anything attempted along these lines for the next thirty years. His lifelike treatment of the human form, in detail (CENTAURS) or en masse (LUSITANIA), would make any animator proud today.

By the early 1920s McCay drifted away

Original advertisement for GERTIE THE DINOSAUR.

Winsor McCay draws Gertie for his cartoonist friends (including *Bringing Up Father's* George McManus, seated at left) at Riesenweber's Restaurant in New York, as part of the filmed introduction for his animated cartoon.

from animation altogether, but he proudly called himself the "creator of animated cartoons," and in a very real sense he was.

Other comic artists tried to capitalize on McCay's success by making animated cartoons. Henry (Hy) Mayer, prolific illustrator, author, and onetime editor of PUCK, drew comics on-screen for the Universal Weekly as early as 1913 and soon took on young Otto Messmer—later to be animator of Felix the Cat—as his assistant. He also had a popular series that appeared on screen magazines as TRAVELAUGHS. Bert Green, who worked with Mayer at one time, provided brief cartoons for the weekly PATHÉ NEWS and in 1921 produced a special short subject on the making of animated films.

Rube Goldberg pursued the animated cartoon with characteristic zeal. Pathé signed a lucrative contract for him to turn out a newsreel spoof called THE BOOB WEEKLY, and Goldberg opened his own tiny studio to churn out the films while keeping up with his newspaper assignments. The series was a great success, but after a year Goldberg was exhausted and had to quit. Biographer Peter C. Marzio reported that Rube netted $75,000 from his year of labor. This was a hefty sum in those days, especially for animated cartoon work; it gives some measure of Goldberg's popularity. The two surviving entries from this series, NUTTY NEWS and LEAP YEAR, are downright hilarious, the latter chronicling the story of "Miss Ophelia Fadeout, whose face had frightened all the children in the neighborhood, but who, nevertheless, still hopes to chloroform some poor simp into matrimony."

George McManus, Milt Gross, and Sidney Smith were other comic strip men who tried their hand at animation, but they lacked the dedication or interest to stay with it. It remained for others to shape the animated cartoon into a continuing commercial format.

John Randolph Bray was a successful newspaper cartoonist who became intrigued with animation around 1910. "I thought there was something new and original that would get over big," he told Harvey Deneroff in a 1972 interview. (He also admitted, "I thought there was good money in it.") But Bray was convinced that there had to be a simpler way to make a cartoon than drawing every picture in its entirety over and over again. He abandoned his newspaper work to concentrate on this problem and turned out a charming one-reel short called THE DACHSHUND AND THE SAUSAGE (also known as THE ARTIST'S DREAM).* The premise of the film

*While this film is often dated 1910 by film historians, it was not announced for release by Pathé until June 1913.

was simple: An artist is interrupted while finishing a drawing. When he's out of the room, his cartoon dog eats a plate of sausages sitting on top of a bureau. The artist returns and can't believe his eyes.

When Bray showed his finished film to Charles Pathé, the producer-distributor encouraged Bray to make others and offered to distribute these cartoons. Bray's second film introduced a character called Colonel Heeza Liar, based on the tale-spinning Baron Munchausen. COLONEL HEEZA LIAR IN AFRICA (1913) opened with a stanza that announced its topical premise: "Heeza Liar was his name/And Colonel was his handle./ He roamed the desert seeking fame/To snuff out T.R.'s candle." T.R. was, of course, Teddy Roosevelt, whose African hunting exploits had been front-page news and the inspiration for several live-action films. (A subsequent HEEZA LIAR episode caricatured Woodrow Wilson.) In Bray's cartoon, a kangaroo hops into the foreground from the distant horizon; the Colonel emerges from the kangaroo's pouch and tips his hat to the camera. The balance of the film consists of Heeza Liar's escapades with various jungle animals such as a playful chimpanzee and an enthusiastic bear who likes to hug. All the commentary is written in rhyming verse.

Technically the film is adequate. Bray is true to perspective and proportions; when the character runs in circles, his drawings remain consistent and accurate. Movement is not smooth, but it's more than adequate to put over the simple story and gags. One minor flaw, common to many silent cartoons, is that the camera picks up wrinkles in the animation paper.

COLONEL HEEZA LIAR IN AFRICA is considered the first commercial-cartoon release; it was neither part of a vaudeville act nor a one-time endeavor. It was the beginning of a film *series*, and this marked a turning point in animation history.

Bray was responsible for other milestones as well. In January 1914 he applied for a patent, which was granted on August 11 of that year, for a labor-saving method of making animated cartoons. Bray would print many copies of a background setting on translucent paper. On different sheets, specific portions of the settings would be blocked out. Then these could be laid over blank paper on which the artist would animate *only the part of the scene that had to move*. The translucent sheets would blend together under the camera lens and appear to be one finished drawing.

In his patent application, Bray used COLONEL HEEZA LIAR IN AFRICA to illustrate this method and showed how a scene could be broken down to such specifics as having the character and background printed in their entirety except for the Colonel's head, which was to twist around. He admitted that there were times when it was easier to simply redraw the whole figure instead of spending the time and effort to print so many component sheets. He also outlined his ability to replace the drawn character in some sequences with a paper cutout in order to achieve a certain effect.

John R. Bray's COLONEL HEEZA LIAR IN AFRICA **(1913).**

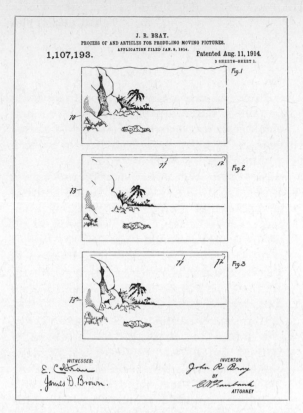

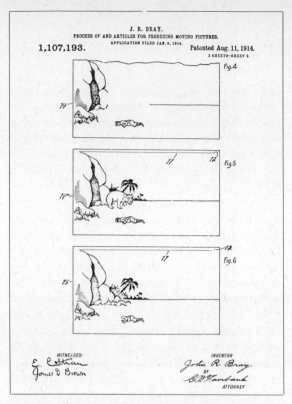

Illustrations from Bray's patent application, using this scene from COLONEL HEEZA LIAR IN AFRICA **to show his "assembly line" method of preparing each frame of the cartoon.**

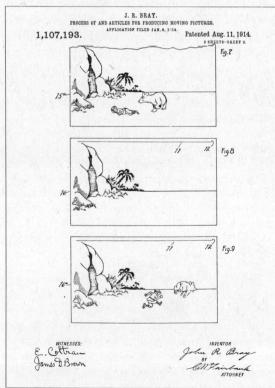

In other words, Bray endorsed any technique that would save the artist time in making his animated cartoon—particularly since most of these corner-cutting ideas were undetectable to an audience watching the finished product.

In July 1914, Bray applied for a second patent, which was not granted until November 9, 1915. In this application, Bray described a simple method for applying a range of gray tones to animated films—which until this time had been mostly black-and-white line drawings.

He wrote:

By means of my present invention, I am able to give to different parts of the picture, a different tone or shade in a very simple and inexpensive manner. . . . Not only does the varying of the shade or tone in different parts of the picture render the latter much more attractive and effective, and cause desired parts of the picture to stand out more distinctly, but at the same time . . . [it] softens the otherwise objectionable white glare and makes the picture less trying to the eyes of the observer. Furthermore, the picture, if appearing upon the screen as black lines upon a white surface, will also show as black lines any scratches which may be on the film due to repeated use and careless handling. By means of my invention, I am able to render these far less conspicuous and thus greatly increase the number of times which the film may be used and give satisfactory results.

The method that Bray proposed was a variation of his earlier process: breaking down the scene into all its basic components, then filling in various parts of the scene—both character and background—with black, white, and gray-tone paints on the back side of translucent sheets, producing as many as five layers for each shot. Some, of course, would remain stationary during the animation process, and others would move and change.

Obviously, this technique approaches the development of a modern system of animation. But Bray was unable to refine his process to its simplest form. He came close, and even mentioned the one word that would later revolutionize the animation industry— but only as an afterthought:

In carrying out my invention, the pictures are made in any suitable manner on separate sheets of material having such a degree of translucency or transparency as will permit the tone or shade producing layer to be seen through the sheet with the desired degree of distinctness. In practice, I preferably employ tracing paper, but it is evident that other material having a different degree of translucency, might be employed under other conditions to secure the same results. For instance, the sheet may be of such material and thickness as to be ordinarily considered opaque,

but still be sufficiently translucent for the present purposes if a light be placed in the rear. The sheet may be even more nearly transparent than tracing paper, as for instance celluloid.

Celluloid. This was the word—familiarly shortened to "cel"—that effected the single greatest change in cartoon production.

While Bray came near the target with his detailed and well-organized ideas, it was another former newspaper cartoonist, Earl Hurd, who hit bull's-eye. On December 19, 1914, he applied for a patent on the process that is still used today in the production of animated cartoons. Hurd proposed the drawing of a complete, stationary background on paper, with the characters inked and painted on clear celluloids laid on top. "I believe I am the first to employ a transparent sheet or a plurality of transparent sheets in conjunction with a background which is photographed therethrough upon the negative film," he stated in his patent application. He went on to explain:

In my process a single background is used for the entire series of pictures necessary to portray one scene. The background shows all of those portions of the scene that remain stationary and may conveniently be drawn, printed, or painted on cardboard or other suitable sheet. I prefer to paint the figures of the background in strong blacks and whites upon a medium dark gray paper and when the transparent sheet carrying the movable objects is placed over this gray tone of the background, the objects on the transparent sheet appear to stand out in relief, giving what may be termed a "poster effect."

It is important to note that Hurd was not only interested in placing his characters on cels, but he was—like Bray—interested in using this technique to save work. A crucial feature of Hurd's patent was the use of several cels together. The example in his patent papers shows a woman spanking her little boy. In this action, only her right arm and

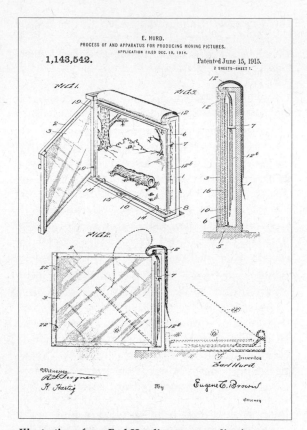

Illustrations from Earl Hurd's patent application.

his legs actually move, so these components are on separate cels, while another stationary cel shows the woman's body and the boy on her lap. Thus it was not Hanna and Barbera who discovered assembly-line animation in the television era; J. R. Bray and Earl Hurd preceded them by forty years.

Ironically, Hurd's cel-and-background process was not immediately taken up as standard procedure. Most early animators preferred to work on paper and saw no reason to complicate matters by inking those drawings onto cels. While Hurd's method had its supporters, it was not until the sound era that production was standardized that way.

Oddly enough, it was *another* patented process of Bray's that became the favored method in early animation studios. This method, filed on July 30, 1915, and patented April 11, 1916, proposed that the stationary objects of a scene be drawn on a translucent sheet and laid *over* a piece of paper where characters and objects would be animated. The end result was much the same as with Hurd's procedure—the background was drawn only once—but, as Bray pointed out, in this method one could show characters walking behind objects in an utterly simple and realistic fashion because they actually were being photographed "underneath" those objects.*

The next major steps came from an organization credited as being the first full-fledged animation studio. Its founder was Raoul Barré, a French-Canadian artist who, like so many newspaper cartoonists, became intrigued with the possibilities of animation during the teens. He and Bill Nolan made primitive animated advertising films as early as 1912; two years later, Barré opened his own studio in the Bronx, with Nolan at his side. Here, three important developments emerged within a year's time.

The first was a "peg system" invented by Barré. Until this time, animators had to use various makeshift methods to "register" their drawings, so that each successive tracing was in perfect alignment with the one before.

In his brochure "In Search of Raoul Barré," published in 1976 by the Cinematheque Quebecoise, Andre Martin has written: "Winsor McCay . . . used a paper cutter to give perfectly straight edges to the sheets of paper and right-angle forms to keep them

exactly superimposed, one on top of another. Bray made use of a system of crosses in the four corners of the drawing, a form of registering borrowed from color printing techniques.

"In 1914 Barré resolved the problem of registration and superimposition by creating the 'peg system.' Each drawing could now be mechanically perforated. These holes in the sheets of drawings allowed them to be perfectly aligned on a peg board. In this way the successive phases of the animation process were assured of exact correspondence."

Barré's next development was the "slash system," a variation on Bray's methods in which the animation paper was cut or "slashed" at the dividing line between stationary objects and movement. One character might remain on the first piece of paper standing still while another moving character was animated on successive sheets laid underneath. This system was used at several studios through the 1920s.

The last great breakthrough came from Bill Nolan, who was soon to achieve fame as one of animation's finest practitioners. He discovered that if a background was drawn on long sheets of paper, it could pass "underneath" a character and provide the illusion of horizontal (or even vertical) movement, even though the character was walking in place. This device became a vital part of animated film making.

There were other ideas and inventions, of course, in the early days of animation. Barré experimented with new techniques, such as animating "special effects" on glass, overlaid on the pen-and-ink drawings. Veteran animator Grim Natwick feels that one of the most important steps was the invention of "the glass disk in the center of the drawing board, in the 1920s. That facilitated better drawing because you could always swing the disk around to make a nice line on things.

---

*Walter Lantz recalls using a variation of this process when he started working at the Hearst International Studio in 1916. Matters were simplified somewhat because the "backgrounds" were incredibly sparse. "Usually, we'd have the horizon lines very high," Lantz recalls, "and then we'd cut out that sheet of paper right below the horizon line and use that as an overlay on the drawing. Then, if we had a chair or any object that the character had to walk in front of, we had to trace that chair *with* the character as he went by it. It would wiggle all over the place, but that's how we did it."

Paul Terry developed another method that involved double-exposure. "I'd photograph the background first, and then I would reverse the film and make a male and female of it," he explained to Harvey Deneroff. In other words, a matte process. But Terry soon abandoned this modus operandi in favor of Hurd's cel method.

Rather than obstructing with your hand, you could see what you were doing." Credit for this advancement goes to animator George Stallings.

But the biggest advancement during the teens was the development of animation itself: as an art, as an industry, as a profession.

Animation, like live-action film making, was centered in New York in the teens, and three main cartoon studios emerged: Raoul Barré, Hearst International, and J. R. Bray.

Barré's is credited with being the first. He set up shop in the Bronx, and hired two young cartoonists, Gregory LaCava and Frank Moser. Their first assignment was a series of films called ANIMATED GROUCH CHASERS, produced and released by Edison in 1915–16. These shorts opened with live-action footage and segued into animation.

It was a landmark series. Andre Martin writes:

The ANIMATED GROUCH CHASER series developed examples of logically structured metamorphosis and nonsense that defined the standard of carica-

Advertisement for Raoul Barrés first cartoon series.

ture in American animated drawing for the next thirty years. In CARTOONS ON THE BEACH, Mr. Hicks gets lost in the sky and casually takes a bite out of a cloud, as a result of which he suddenly sprouts wings. In CARTOONS IN THE HOTEL, a cow eats Silas Bunkum's beard, immediately grows a beard of its own and heads for the barbershop; a chicken eats ostrich feed, grows to gigantic proportions and lays an enormous egg from which hatches a small car. It is obvious that Barré consciously introduced surreal elements into his animation. A young girl's chaperone is literally transformed into a dragon in an episode of CARTOONS IN THE PARLOUR. In BLACK'S MYSTERIOUS BOX, two hairy arms emerge from a fantastic box, drag the hero inside and end up grabbing anything within reach.

In 1916 newspaper tycoon William Randolph Hearst, who was then enjoying great success publishing and syndicating comic strips, decided to open an animation studio to bring these cartoon properties to the screen. He called his company International Film Service and hired LaCava, Moser, and Bill Nolan away from Barré. LaCava was put in charge, and, possibly through his intervention, some of this studio's work load was "farmed out" to Barré. In particular, Barré animated a number of the PHABLES series based on Tom E. Powers's clever comic drawings.

Barré's association with Hearst was short-lived, however. In that same year he joined forces with another cartoonist, Charles Bowers, who had acquired the screen rights to Bud Fisher's popular comic strip MUTT AND JEFF, and made the initial shorts. Peter Milne wrote in the *Motion Picture News* of April 15, 1916:

If we were in the exhibiting line we would instantly seize upon JEFF'S TOOTHACHE and THE SUBMARINE, the first two animated cartoons drawn by Bud Fisher. . . . [They] are excellent animated cartoon comedies containing funny drawings and funny plots and real plots. . . . Mr. Fisher has mastered whatever difficulties confronted him when he decided to draw for the camera, in exhaustive style. His cartoons are rapid in action, smooth in execution, void of eye-straining jumpiness, and, what is superfluous to add, they picture the same Mutt and Jeff that cavort in the papers.

Fisher, already wealthy from the comic strip, which ran in more than one hundred newspapers, launched The Mutt and Jeff Film Company with Bowers in charge, but within the year Bowers moved in with Barré at his studio. Fisher's original idea to distribute the shorts himself gave way to the more practical method of having an established company—Fox Films—handle that chore.

One thing Fisher never surrendered was his public image. At no time were the names of Barré or Bowers mentioned in connection with these animated films. If one believed the considerable publicity that surrounded this series, Bud Fisher did it all himself. In a 1919 press release Fisher was "interviewed" and spoke of his recent travels in Europe. "First of all," he began, "I am mighty glad the war is over. It kept me pretty busy over there drawing for the animated screen and directing the productions by cable. I picked up a great many ideas in my travels and have been putting Mutt and Jeff through the paces since my return."

This must have come as news to Barré, Bowers, and their staff, who seldom saw Bud Fisher on the studio premises even when he wasn't traveling abroad. Animator I. Klein recalls that he occasionally visited and: "On those occasions he always arrived with two tall show-type girls. Never with the same two. He'd stroll around the studio with his hat on, thumbs in the armpits of his vest, the girls holding on to his elbows, his head tilted back in regal fashion. From his Olympian height he couldn't see the hired help."

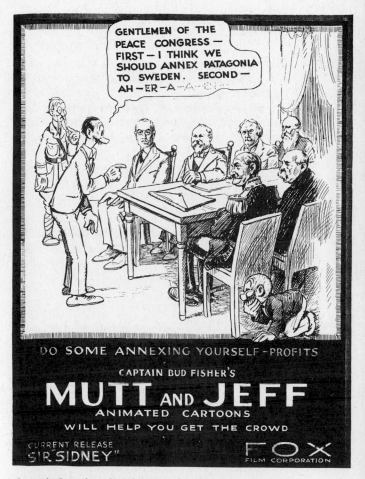

A topical trade advertisement for the MUTT AND JEFF series from 1918.

Far from relying on Fisher, the studio gathered some promising young talent over the next few years: Dick Huemer, Burt Gillett, Mannie Davis, Ben Sharpsteen, Vladimir (Bill) Tytla, Albert Hurter, I. Klein, Ted Sears, George Rufle, Ben Harrison, Manny Gould, George Stallings, and Frank Moser—every one a name to reckon with in the continuing development of animated cartoons. "Vet" Anderson, a well-known editorial cartoonist, also joined the staff, and reportedly Milt Gross did a brief stint there.

Huemer, who started at the studio in 1916, later wrote:

Barré was a good man to work for. An artist himself, a fine arts painter rather than a cartoonist, he had a deep devotion to the nascent business. And it was just barely that, especially from an economic standpoint. You certainly couldn't in those days call it an art form. But long before Disney, he had the idea of plowing back what profits he made (and they were indeed minuscule) to produce better pictures, create a demand for them, and thus make more money for all concerned, artist as well as producer.

In his extremely limited way, he did what he could to further this end. For instance, he organized art classes for after-hours studies, where the animators could improve their skills by drawing from the live models which he supplied free of charge. This is something which Disney also did so many years later. . . .

At best, very little time could be allotted to the story phase of the operation, since the most important thing was how much footage could be ground out every week. But he did what he could, and saw to it that there was at least some delineation of the action and plot before animation was begun instead of leaving the whole thing up to each animator to invent and improvise as he went along.

The MUTT AND JEFF films were snappy, entertaining cartoons. Their humor was not so much Bud Fisher's as that of the Barré-Bowers staff—earthy at times and ethnic, reflecting its New York origins.

More importantly, the films revealed the enthusiasm that went into their creation. To be sure, the young staff had no pretense about art, and turning out a new short every week took its toll. But the potential tedium was relieved by the freedom everyone had to experiment and try new ideas. In one famous short, SOUND YOUR A, Jeff appeared to converse with the conductor of the orchestra which was a standard feature of movie theaters of the day, and then proceeded to lead the band himself—his baton keeping perfect time for the tune being played.

A later film, ON STRIKE, was enthusiastically described by F. C. "Wid" Gunning in the trade magazine *Wid's Daily* on January 18, 1920:

Following the course so common now, Mutt and Jeff decide to go on strike in this Fox animated cartoon. Observing the ease and comfort of their creator, Bud Fisher (the reel includes several shots of the caricaturist), they decide to turn out their own production, which is a fizzle, and the failure of which causes them to return to the fold. The idea is novel and the offering should fit in on any program.

Everyone in the studio looked up to Albert Hurter, a Swiss artist who somehow drifted into animated cartoons. "He was the one good, real artist there," says I. Klein. "He was trained in Europe; he knew about fine arts. The first time I heard of Van Gogh was through him. He was a great admirer of the fine arts, particularly Heinrich Kley, the German graphic artist. His animation was realistic; whenever they needed something real, they gave it to Hurter." His most famous accomplishment at the Mutt and Jeff studio was the animation of an American flag waving in the breeze; he studied the real thing and then reproduced it in meticulous detail. Hurter later became a renowned sketch artist at the Disney studio.

In 1918 Raoul Barré left his studio and gave up animation—at least for a while. There was friction between him and Bowers, and stories circulated that Barré had actually gone crazy. Whatever the case, Bowers took control of the studio and supervised the stories, as Barré had done before him. "The most frequent word in his scripts was 'ad lib,'" I. Klein recalls. "'Mutt walks into a scene . . . ad lib' . . . meaning that the animator should improvise some funny business at that point. In other words, the stories were only outlines of a general theme. The humor within the scenes depended on the individual animators." A talented cartoonist, Bowers also provided thumbnail sketches for his animators to work from.

His reign as studio head was short. In 1919 he was fired by Bud Fisher for financial improprieties, but he wasn't idle very long. Less than one year later, he persuaded Fisher to let him produce MUTT AND JEFF cartoons as an independent contractor. He opened a tiny studio in Mount Vernon, New York, and hired many animators who had worked at the Bronx shop; in late 1921 he decided to pursue other ventures and discontinued production, only to resume three years later with a new setup in Astoria and a new contract with Bud Fisher. This time he was ousted by an animators' cooperative that negotiated with Fisher to do MUTT AND JEFF, and Bowers faded from the animation scene forever.

During these adventures the former Barré-Bowers studio continued to operate, first under animator Dick Friel, and then with Burt Gillett in charge. After Bowers abandoned MUTT and JEFF in 1921, Friel continued its production under the banner of Jefferson Film Corporation.

All in all, Archibald J. Mutt and Edgar Horace Jeff were animated by more different people in more different places than any other characters in cartoon history. Their ongoing popularity in the funnies assured them a place on theater screens no matter how often the flow of production was interrupted.

Comic strip characters were the mainstay and raison d'être of Hearst's International Film Service, established in 1915. Hearst's King Features Syndicate owned the rights to such popular "stars" as Krazy Kat, Happy Hooligan, and the Katzenjammer Kids. It seemed to Hearst that animated counterparts could only increase their popularity—and if he made a profit on the films themselves, so much the better. In a further corporate tie-in, these cartoons were limited to one third of a reel in length, so they could be released as part of Hearst's weekly newsreel.

As previously mentioned, Hearst hired Gregory LaCava and Frank Moser away from the Barré studio to head this new operation. The reason for this was simple: He needed someone with experience, and there was nowhere to turn except the few established animation studios. LaCava was a proficient cartoonist, but his real talent lay in the field of comedy. In the 1920s he left animation to try his luck in live-action films and soon became one of the top directors in Hollywood; he is best remembered for the classic screwball comedy MY MAN GODFREY.

Frank Moser had no such ambitions, but he possessed a quality that was equally important in these early days. Fellow animator Bert Green called him "the most rapid animator in the game." Green added, "Moser literally shakes them out of a hat. I have seen Moser take a scenario of HAPPY HOOLIGAN and in thirty days hand you a pile of between two and three thousand drawings that you couldn't jump over and live through it. Yes, and catch the 5:15 for Hastings 'nine times running.'"

Raiding rival studios for talent was a way of life for the next twenty years; one could fit all the experienced animators in the United States into a subway car and still have seats left over. "There weren't any animators and that was the fact," declares Grim Natwick. "And nobody was developing animators; that's why Walt Disney started [doing that] later. I happened to be a functioning animator and there were periods when I'd be offered a job at another studio on an average of every two weeks or so."

Yet Natwick started out on the ground floor of this business, just like everyone else. There were no animators with seniority in 1916 because the medium was brand new and everyone was still learning. The only "seniority" occurred when newspaper cartoonists of some repute moved into animation studios; the rest of the staff filled in with young men, many in their teens, some of whom had been to art school and others who simply liked to draw.

In Natwick's case, he and Gregory LaCava had gone to art school together in Chicago. While LaCava pursued the new motion-picture medium, Natwick made a good living illustrating sheet-music covers. When Natwick moved from Chicago to New York, he looked up his old friend, who was now running the International studio at 729 Seventh Avenue. "I was having lunch with LaCava one day and he said, 'Why don't you

Krazy Kat and Ignatz Mouse in a scene from KRAZY KAT, INVALID (1916), animated by Leon Searl.

try this thing?' He found it very hard to get artists to do this; nobody knew how to animate. They would come in and see somebody drawing a hundred drawings a day and it would frighten them. We knew each other well, and I had apparently shown a knack of drawing humorous drawings, so he persuaded me to try it for a couple of weeks. That lasted about fifty years. I was what they call a natural animator, and I don't know why; I have always attributed it to the fact that I was interested in athletics. I found that almost all the good animators were either devotees of athletics or athletically inclined. That may not be so true now, because the kids come up through art school. In those days, I was about the only animator, even at the Disney studio, who had had several years of real, sincere, earnest art education."

Among the younger element there were those who had taken art courses, but once they found full-time employment at studios like Hearst's there was neither time nor incentive to continue such studies. Some of the older, uneducated cartoonists intimidated them as well. Shamus Culhane recalls that when he worked at Harrison and Gould studios in the 1920s, as an inker: "I was an oddball. In the first place, I brought books in to read at lunch—amazing! Then, when I happened to mention that I was going to the Art Students League to take a course in etching, one of the animators took me to one side and said, 'Don't learn all that shit, it will stiffen you up.' To quote him verbatim."

Mostly, it was on-the-job training. Walter Lantz, later to be the creator of Woody Woodpecker, started at Hearst's at age sixteen and progressed from cameraman to inker and finally to animator. He explains: "I would take the old Charlie Chaplin films and project them one frame at a time, make a drawing over Chaplin's action, and flip the drawings to see how he moved. That's how most of us learned to animate." This very form of "action analysis" became a mainstay of Disney's studio art courses many years later.

Just as Bud Fisher was the figurehead "creator" of his MUTT AND JEFF cartoons, Hearst cartoonists like George Herriman, Rudolph Dirks, and Frederick Opper had no contact with the animators who brought their characters to life. At this studio, the animators did receive screen credit, though in such a way as to give the impression that the film was a "collaboration." A sample title card read: "KRAZY KAT AND IGNATZ MOUSE— AT THE CIRCUS—A Cartoon By George Herriman"; then in smaller letters: "Animated by Leon Searl."

Herriman's brilliant comic strip suffered at the hands of the Hearst animators, who were forced to simplify the complicated drawing style and all but eliminate backgrounds in order to turn out their cartoons on a production-line basis. The humor was somewhat diluted as well. THE KATZENJAMMER KIDS made the transition to motion pictures much better than KRAZY KAT. Here the animators could concentrate on simple reproduction of the familiar characters and devise endless variations on the enduring theme of childhood mischief.

Other adaptations included George McManus's BRINGING UP FATHER, Tad Dorgan's SILK HAT HARRY and TAD'S INDOOR SPORTS, Walter Hoban's JERRY ON THE JOB, and Jimmy Swinnerton's LITTLE JIMMY. T. E. Powers's PHABLES, perhaps the most unusual, were executed in the artist's stylishly simple fashion and permeated by his impish sense of humor. As various human foibles are illustrated, Powers's miniature Greek-chorus characters, the Joys (stick-figure females, with bright smiling faces and wide skirts) and the Glooms (with pointed caps, pointed noses, pointed beards) com-

ment metaphorically from the bottom of the film frame.

Visually the Hearst cartoons were primitive. Gray tones were unheard of; characters and backgrounds were rendered in simple line drawings, animated and inked on paper. Movement was spare, dialogue (in comic strip balloons) was at times overabundant, and cinematic innovations were few. They were "living comic strips" in the truest sense, but without the graphic styling that made the better comics of the day so striking.

Hearst closed his studio in July 1918, but continued to finance and license cartoon production with his newspaper characters. John Terry (Paul's brother, and an early experimenter with animation in his native San Francisco) opened a studio in New York's Greenwich Village, apparently with Hearst's backing, and hired most of the Hearst International staff—LaCava, Nolan, Gillett, Natwick, Sharpsteen, Lantz, and Jack King— to continue making PHABLES, HAPPY HOOLIGAN, BRINGING UP FATHER, and JUDGE RUMMY cartoons.

In 1919 other films bearing the name International Film Service were released by Bray studios, and soon Bray was actually producing new cartoons with such Hearst characters as Krazy Kat and Jerry. This came about, according to Bray, because Hearst was infringing on Bray's patents. "We were going to sue him," he later explained. "Then I figured he was too big for us. He could tie us up in a knot; keep us on a string for ten to twelve years and run us ragged. So I took over the distribution of his cartoons. . . . But we found out they weren't successful. They were poorly done."

Bray fared much better making new cartoons himself with the established characters. At least one surviving KRAZY KAT—THE

Some top New York animators in a rare moment of recreation. Front row, left to right, Sammy Stimson, John Foster, George Stallings, Grim Natwick, unknown, Jack King, an office worker; back row, Ving Fuller, Joe Armstrong, Guy Gaston, Frank Sherman, Clyde (Gerry) Geronomi, Bill Nolan, Walter Lantz, unknown.

GREAT CHEESE ROBBERY (directed by Vernon "George" Stallings)—shows tremendous improvement over the earlier KRAZYS produced by Hearst. Not only is the film-making technique more sophisticated, but the story is clearly defined and well developed. In this episode, Ignatz Mouse steals some cheese; Krazy is accused of the theft, but all that Ignatz knows is that an innocent party is being held by the cops. His conscience starts to bother him and soon guilt overtakes him as all the objects in his house—the newspaper, the bed sheet, and everything else—become specters pointing accusing fingers at him. Finally he goes to bail out the poor sap, only to discover that it's Krazy! Basic as this story may seem, it's a far cry from the static parrying of dialogue that filled so many earlier KRAZY KAT cartoons.

If John R. Bray was particular about the quality of films he released, he had good reason. His studio had pioneered and developed some of the most sophisticated cartoons of the teens.

Bray was the first successful cartoonist to become an even more successful cartoon producer. After the success of his COLONEL HEEZA LIAR, and the granting of three important patents, Bray set up shop and hired other cartoonists to animate for him. The first was Earl Hurd, who brought not only his talent and imagination but his patent on the use of cels to Bray's studio. Together they formed the Bray-Hurd Patent trust and demanded license fees from every studio that used their techniques. (Most of the New York studios in the 1920s animated on paper and avoided such tariffs, but in the early 1930s practically everyone used cels and paid Bray and Hurd for their use.)

Hurd may be best known as the inventor of cels, but in the teens he made an equally significant contribution with his BOBBY BUMPS cartoons. The first of these were made for Universal in 1915, and perhaps their success led to Bray's production offer. They are among the most mature, most well-conceived cartoons of the silent era—certainly the best work done in the mid- to late teens. The films use a full range of gray tones in characters and backgrounds, with pleasing effect. The animation, if not fluid, is workmanlike and functional. The characters Bobby Bumps and his dog Fido are likable as well and can be said to have personality—derived more through dialogue, stories, and facial expressions than from any sophisticated animation, but personality just the same. Most important, however, is the substance of the films, and this is where they leave the competition behind. Hurd's BOBBY BUMPS cartoons have a beginning, a middle, and an end. They are well thought out, like a good comic strip, with clever story ideas and gags. Ingenious cinematic devices add to their appeal.

Example: BOBBY BUMPS—BEFORE AND AFTER opens as Bobby finds a bottle in a garbage bin. The picture *dissolves* (an unusual technique to find in cartoons of this period) to a close-up showing the contents to be a hair restorer. Bobby tries it out on Fido, and the picture cuts to an iris close-up of Fido's posterior. Above the iris is the headline

"What Bobby Expected," followed by animation of hair growing on the dog. Then another headline announces, "What Came Up," and from the dog float the letters N-O-T-H-I-N-G.

The story proper has Bobby selling the bottle of hair restorer to his father, who imagines hair growing on his bald pate—and is duped by Fido's scheme of having two dogs, one short-haired, the other long-, pretending to be the same dog before and after treatment. During the night, when Pop is asleep, Bobby and Fido glue feathers to his head. In the morning, the unamused father punishes his son by letting his scalp-massaging machine spank the boy.

The range of visual ideas in Hurd's repertoire is amazingly broad. In BOBBY BUMPS SETS OUT TO SCHOOL, the youngster's attitude toward education is illustrated by showing him walking with oppressively oversized school books on his back; no dialogue is necessary to make the point. In BOBBY BUMPS

Animator Earl Hurd writes a message to his juvenile star in BOBBY BUMPS PUTS A BEANERY ON THE BUM (1918).

PUTS A BEANERY ON THE BUM, Fido gets into a fight with a cat who calls him a cur. "I'm going to make him eat those words," declares Fido as he dares the cat to speak again. "You dirty cur," says the cat. Fido grabs the dialogue balloon, crumples it up, and stuffs it down the cat's throat!

The BEANERY cartoon is full of interaction with the unseen animator, a device one usually associates with Max Fleischer's later INKWELL series. An artist's hand draws Bobby in silhouette, lying down. Bobby gets up and the animator says, "hat off," so he can ink in his hair, the rest of his features, and clothing. The rest of the cartoon maintains this playful banter, culminating in a *deus ex machina* finale, in which the animator responds to Bobby and Fido's cries for help by drawing a ladder, which they climb to escape from the clutches of an angry cook; the animator then erases the drawing so the chef cannot follow and hands Bobby his inkwell, so Bobby can douse his adversary.

Earl Hurd's cartoons set a standard that was difficult for his colleagues to match. Among the other cartoonists to join him at Bray's studio were Leighton Budd, who created LUNYLAND; F. M. Follett, known for his newspaper cartoons* *Private Conscience* and *The See-See Kid*, who animated THE QUACKY DOODLES FAMILY; and Wallace Carlson, whose creations included DREAMY DUD, OTTO LUCK, and GOODRICH DIRT, which owed a lot to BOBBY BUMPS in format and design.

But Bray's most important finds were Max Fleischer, Paul Terry, and Walter Lantz. All three made their mark at Bray and went on to open their own successful studios.

With this kind of talent on hand, Bray was able to accept a commitment for one cartoon a week, which appeared as the final portion of THE PARAMOUNT-BRAY PICTOGRAPH, a screen magazine (like Hearst's) with several live-action segments per issue. Each artist had one month to complete his cartoon, and the deadlines were staggered so that one would be ready every week. When one of these key cartoonists left the studio (as Fleischer and Terry did during World War I), it was necessary to find an immediate replacement to maintain the regular output.

Bray's operation was essentially that of a modern cartoon studio. "We had about thirty or forty . . . artists working in our studio," he recalled in 1972. "We worked out a system of the original cartoonist laying out the thing in pencil. Then another fellow would ink in certain parts of it. Then another girl or boy would put on color on the back of the picture. . . . Of course, it was fairly crude when we started in. But it got more perfect, until finally it got as good, I guess, as most of the cartoons you see. . . ."

Bray started another less formal tradition in animation when he graduated from the drawing board to the executive office. After several COLONEL HEEZA LIAR cartoons in 1914 and 1915 (which modestly credited him as "the world's greatest motion picture cartoonist"), he stopped drawing, in order to supervise his rapidly expanding business. A commitment with Paramount for the weekly PICTOGRAPHS in 1916 necessitated live-action filming, while the arrival in 1917 of J. F. Leventhal, a mechanical draftsman, prompted Bray's first instructional films for use in World War I.

Bray was a man of vision who was always ready to try something new. When magazine illustrator C. Allen Gilbert came to him with a proposal for making films combining sil-

*Some newspaper cartoonists adapted to the rigors of animation, while others didn't. Carl Anderson animated Bray's POLICE DOG series, but enjoyed greater success with his *Henry* comic strip. Louis Glackens, brother of the well-known artist William Glackens, tried his hand at animation for a short time, as did editorial cartoonist "Vet" Anderson.

houette animation and live action, Bray sponsored him in the short-lived experiment. When he heard about a process called Brewster Color, he tried it out in one short (THE DEBUT OF THOMAS CAT, 1920), but didn't use it again because the double-emulsion film was too susceptible to scratches.

He also sponsored another experiment, which was described by *Wid's Daily* on November 30, 1919:

Over at the Rialto they showed an unusual short recently—an animated cartoon idea of Leventhal of the Bray organization showing Dr. (Hugo) Riesenfield leading his orchestra and directing a waltz. The orchestra was synchronized perfectly and it made a big hit when run off. Whether or not the Doctor is well known enough outside of New York to play the reel is questionable, but if it comes down to that you needn't run it as a Riesenfield stunt, but put the name of your own musical director to it and let it ride . . .

Bray's biggest move was into the field of instructional films. J. F. Leventhal impressed Bray with his realistic animation, and this set the producer onto a new course, that of pioneering the largely untapped educational film market. Bray developed the prototype for filmstrips and filmstrip projectors; when 16mm safety film was introduced, he released the entire backlog of live-action footage from his PARAMOUNT (and later GOLDWYN) PICTOGRAPHS with great success. Bray's educational film division prospered long after the theatrical business failed, and the studio bearing his name is still going strong today.

When Bray turned his attention to these new pursuits, he looked for someone to supervise the continuing production of cartoons for theaters. The task fell to George Stallings, who at this time was using the first name of Vernon. A talented animator, Stall-

ings joined the studio during a fallow period. Paul Terry had started his own studio after World War I. Max Fleischer left in 1921, taking his very popular OUT OF THE INKWELL cartoons with him, while Earl Hurd moved to Paramount with BOBBY BUMPS. Milt Gross, on the verge of great success as a newspaper cartoonist, made some films for Bray in 1920 (including one typical reel called FRENCHY DISCOVERS AMERICA), but left after a very short time. New ideas were scarce; KRAZY KAT and JERRY ON THE JOB were losing steam, and, for want of a better idea, COLONEL HEEZA LIAR was taken out of mothballs.

Then Stallings was replaced by an ambitious young animator named Walter Lantz. Lantz was full of fresh ideas, and the studio's product improved. His DINKY DOODLES, combining live action and animation, rekindled the kind of interest that Fleischer's OUT OF THE INKWELL series had evoked several years before. Lantz's follow-ups—UNNATURAL HISTORY, and HOT DOG cartoons with Pete the Pup—met with similar success. Also on the Bray staff at this time was a nucleus of animators who just ten years later would help shape the destiny of the Walt Disney studio: Jack King, David Hand, Clyde "Gerry" Geronimi, and, in the educational division, Cy Young and Alec Geiss.

Another young man who started his animation career with Bray in the 1920s was Shamus Culhane, who recalls some of the mundane—but formidable—problems at that time: "The cels were a disaster. In the first place, they were nitrate. It was phenomenal how people handled those damn things. Why we weren't blown up and burned to hell, I don't know." No one ever gave a second thought to dangling a cigarette over his work—even though the celluloids were highly flammable.

"The biggest problem was the paint," he continues. "You would work all day and finish a shot, with a pile of drawings you'd been working on, cels all done. All of a sudden, as the weather changes here, you'd get up one morning and it would be blazing hot. I'd run down to the studio and everything was stuck to the next drawing. Or in the winter time they'd turn the heat off in the building for Saturday and Sunday and it would be very, very cold. You'd come in, in the morning, you'd take some cels and all the paint would fall on the table. It would crack. It looked terrible and it had to be scraped off and done all over again. We did all kinds of things, like trying to put cornstarch on the back to see if it would absorb the moisture. Sometimes it did, but mostly it didn't. It was a pain in the ass; you got cornstarch all over yourself and the drawings. What a way to work."

But, as Jimmy Durante would have said, them's the conditions that prevailed—at least until 1927, when Bray suddenly closed his animation studio. The market for cartoons was shaky, and after losing his distribution deal with Goldwyn, the income level dropped. Bray continued making educational films, but the theatrical cartoon staff looked elsewhere for work.

Bray's was the last of the teens' three major studios to close; Hearst's International Film Service had not lasted the decade, nor had Barré's, although his successors continued to run that shop into the early 1920s. It was Fleischer and Terry, Bray alumni, who headed New York's most successful animation studios in the 1920s, and who survived for many years to come. They were joined by another cartoonist, Pat Sullivan, to form a new triumvirate that dominated the cartoon industry for the rest of the silent film era.

Sullivan, born in Australia, had led a colorful and checkered life before finding steady employment as a newspaper cartoonist in America. As assistant to the popular William F. Marriner, he inherited that cartoonist's comic strips when Marriner died in a 1914 fire. Sullivan subsequently turned one of them, *Sambo and his Funny Noises*, into an animated cartoon series called SAMMY (or SAMMIE) JOHNSIN in 1916.

Sullivan photographed his work at the Universal studio in Fort Lee, New Jersey, where he met a young artist named Otto Messmer who had just started learning the rudiments of animation. Messmer went to work for Sullivan in New York, and, except for Messmer's active duty in World War I, the two were together until Sullivan's death.

Their association ran deeper than mere collaboration, however. As Messmer grew increasingly proficient, Sullivan gave him more responsibility for the films, until Messmer was doing all the work, with the help of a few assistants. Sullivan never drew a line again, but took all the credit for Messmer's work.

Besides SAMMIE JOHNSIN, Sullivan produced a series of Charlie Chaplin animated cartoons, which Messmer recalls the comedian enjoyed. This series gave Messmer the opportunity to study Chaplin's pantomime and body movements, which profoundly affected his future work. Another Sullivan series was BOOMER BILL. But Messmer is proudest of a onetime short called 20,000 LAUGHS UNDER THE SEA, inspired by Universal's release of a feature film based on the Jules Verne story.

In 1919 John R. Bray left Paramount to release his films through Goldwyn, forcing Paramount to create its own screen magazine, with a weekly animated feature. A group of animators under the leadership of Paul Terry turned out most of the weekly entries, but Paramount producer John King also called on Pat Sullivan for contributions.

Otto Messmer recalls an important moment in animation history: "The studio

The Five Senses as Interpreted by "FELIX"

SEEING	HEARING	SMELLING	TASTING	FEELING

SINGLE REEL NOVELTY
Animated by
PAT SULLIVAN

WORLDS RIGHTS
M. J. WINKLER
220 West 42nd Street, New York

A 1921 trade advertisement shows the earliest design of Felix the Cat.

being busy, Sullivan asked me to do one in my spare time, at home. I did a quick one showing a black cat being outwitted by a mouse. I used plenty of picture gags. Paramount liked it and signed it up for their PARAMOUNT SCREEN MAGAZINE. It made a hit with the public. I wrote and animated it alone with studio assistants. It grew in popularity, and as the demand became more urgent, Sullivan took on more animators, at various times, to help."

The name Felix was coined by John King, who liked the contrast of "felix," for felicity, with the traditional superstition about black cats. Messmer had made Felix black because "it saves making a lot of outlines, and solid black moves better."

As Messmer remembers it, the name of the first episode in 1919 was FELINE FOLLIES; and the second, after which Felix was officially named, was MUSICAL MEWS. The design of the character was quite different then from the one that evolved in later years. John Canemaker has described this early version as looking like an "angular dog."

Angular or not, Felix was successful enough for Sullivan to think about branching out on his own. At the end of 1921 he left Paramount and signed a deal with M. J. (Margaret) Winkler, who would distribute the films worldwide. Sullivan committed himself to a monthly schedule, and the first one-reel subject, FELIX SAVES THE DAY, appeared at the beginning of 1922. Oddly enough, this remains Messmer's favorite film from the series, perhaps not so much for its story line (in which Felix is a lucky mascot for the New York Yankees) but for the fact that he made it virtually alone.

Sullivan was a wily showman, and he set to work promoting his character. He soon discovered that Felix was even more popular in England than in the United States, and his fame grew with each passing year. Felix merchandise started to appear, and Sullivan (like Disney a decade later) reaped considerable rewards from the licensing of his character. Later a comic strip was launched, which Messmer drew for many years.

As production continued on the series, Messmer made an important discovery: "I found that I could get as big a laugh with a little gesture—a wink or a twist of the tail— as I could with gags." This was the key to

Felix's success. The stories were generally good, and the gags quite ingenious, but it was the development of a distinctive *personality* that made Felix the greatest cartoon star of the silent era.

Felix had a mind, and he used it to think his way out of a tough spot. From this foundation came the trademarks of this series: Felix's pensive walk, with head down in a thoughtful position and hands clasped behind his back, and his unique gift for turning his tail into any implement necessary at the moment—an oar, a baseball bat, a fishing hook, a telescope. This talent was complemented by Felix's frequent excursions into unreality: He could jump into a telephone and squeeze himself through the wires; cross over a chasm on a "bridge" of question marks that emanated from his head; disguise himself as a suitcase in order to take a free trip, and so on.

Felix was sometimes called the Charlie Chaplin of cartoon characters. Mark Langer has written: "Like Chaplin, Felix is a loner in a hostile or at best indifferent world, who combines resourcefulness and a touch of viciousness in order to survive." In FELIX IN

HOLLYWOOD, he tours the movie studios and tries to impress a producer by imitating Chaplin, using his tail as a cane. Whom should he bump into but Chaplin himself, who snarls, "Stealing my stuff, eh?"

Felix's quick-wittedness impelled Messmer to find consistently clever ideas for stories and gags. Anything less would have been unworthy of the character—a sure sign that Felix's personality had taken root. If the episode with Chaplin, from 1923, sounds saucy, consider later entries in which we see Felix receiving his paycheck from Pat Sullivan studios (WHYS AND OTHERWISE), taking his children to the movies only to find "Daddy" on-screen (FLIM FLAM FILMS), or talking back to his animator (COMICALAMITIES).

Messmer's retelling of what lay behind the Felix formula is disarmingly simple: "I put emphasis on personality in Felix, eye motion and facial expressions, and started each cartoon with a theme to get the audience interested." That simple credo—backed by unlimited imagination—kept Felix going through several hundred adventures, as Sullivan upped his output from twelve to twenty-six cartoons a year.

By this time Otto Messmer had some help. While he still functioned as a one-man band—writing, directing, and partially animating every film—he was joined in 1923 by Bill Nolan, whom he characterizes as "a super animator who added a lot of class to the Felix films." Nolan's legendary speed was also a great asset.

Among the others who joined the tiny Sullivan studio at this time were Harold (Hal) Walker, Dana Parker, and a trio of young men who rose from the lowly position of "blackeners" (filling in Felix's outline) to become animators in the 1930s: Al Eugster, Rudy Zamora, and George Cannata.

When Nolan left to produce his own car-

Felix in his prime: an original animation drawing, inked on paper, from a 1926 short.

Pat Sullivan (far left) poses as an animator for this 1925 publicity photo. To his right are the men who really made the Felix cartoons: Otto Messmer, Raoul Barré, Dana Parker, Hal Walker, Al Eugster, Jack Boyle, George Cannata, Tom Byrne, and cameraman Alfred Thurber. This was the entire staff of the studio!

toons with KRAZY KAT in 1925, he was replaced by one of Messmer's idols, Raoul Barré. "He was a genius in animation, and had been out of the game for a few years, doing oil paintings and great art posters for an advertising agency," Messmer recalls. "It was a thrill to have this man work with me on FELIX. He had a great flair for gags and tricky effects which enriched the stories I outlined for Felix. I missed him when he left, around 1927."

Barré had created much of the animated-cartoon vocabulary in his earliest films of the teens. Now he returned to his métier and

contributed some wonderful ideas to the series. Andre Martin cites the memorable "drunken flowers" in TWO LIP TIME and the distorting movie lens in FELIX BUSTS A BUB-BLE as two sequences devised by Barré.

The Felix cartoons of the late 1920s are remarkably sophisticated, in humor and in film technique. Despite the handicap of having no voice, Felix is as recognizable and rounded a personality as any later cartoon star; his improved design not only makes him more appealing, but the enlarged white area around the eyes and mouth showcases his expressions all the better.

Max and Dave Fleischer engineered some clever interaction between Koko the Clown and the animator at his drawing board, and years later Chuck Jones made a definitive statement on the ephemeral nature of cartoon characters in his DUCK AMUCK—but none of these cartoons can overshadow the brilliance of Felix's COMICALAMITIES, made in 1928. Here Felix's creator forgets to blacken him in, causing Felix to fend for himself and use shoe polish. When the director tries to end the movie by closing in the iris, Felix stops the circle in midmotion and declares, "This picture isn't over by a long shot." For his own finale, Felix takes an eraser and pencil to change the face of a feminine cat from homely to beautiful. Expecting a big romance to start, he's astonished when she suddenly snubs him. But unlike his hero Charlie Chaplin, Felix doesn't take this lying down. He grabs the cartoon girl and tears her up!

The fluidity and imagination of these cartoons did not go entirely unnoticed. In 1929 Creighton Peet sang their praises in *The New Republic:*

When it comes to "pure cinema," "visual flow," "graphic representation," "the freedom of the cinematic medium," and all the other things learned foreign cinema enthusiasts talk about, nothing that Jannings or Lubitsch or Murnau or Greta Garbo or Rin Tin Tin can do has more than a roll of celluloid's chance in Hell beside Felix Cat and the other animated cartoons. . . .

Unhampered by any such classical limitations as dramatic unities, or even such customary necessities as the laws of gravity, common sense, and possibility, the animated drawing is the only artistic medium ever discovered which is really "free." And this in spite of the fact that it is only an eight-minute tidbit thrown in at the end of a love drama while the audience is being changed. . . .

Careening wildly through three dimensions of space—or even four or five for all I know—skating on the furthest edge of plausibility, the little black cartoon cat is undismayed by any of the facts of life which might worry a more substantial feline of fur and claws. Gaily, impertinently, he chins himself on the vacant air, hoisting himself into a world of innumerable and elastic dimensions, and limitless possibilities, in which every tree and stone has not only a potential life but a complete set of emotions.

Cartoons became more elaborate in the years to come—with color, sound, and increasingly sophisticated animation. But few, if any, later film makers were able to recapture the simple spark and buoyancy of Felix.

Sadly, Felix did not survive the transition to sound. Pat Sullivan was unimpressed with the possibilities of talking pictures and didn't want to invest the time or money to make the changeover. As a result, Felix declined in popularity and within a year was obsolete. Sullivan's alcoholism and failing health after the accidental death of his wife made it difficult to discuss any serious business matters, and when he died in 1933 his affairs were so disorganized that neither Messmer nor anyone else was able to carry on. Felix enjoyed a brief revival at the Van Beuren studio in 1935, but after just a few films this series expired as well, and the character was relegated to the comic pages for the next twenty-five years.

Otto Messmer divorced himself from animation when the Sullivan studio folded, returning briefly in the mid-1940s to do some story work for Famous Studios. It was not until 1967 that he received official recognition for his pioneering work with Felix, and in the ensuing years various institutions and film enthusiasts have tried to make up for the years of neglect by paying homage to this masterful creator of cartoon life.

As for the other silent-film animators, their world began to change in the late 1920s. For one thing, there was a new name to reckon with, not in New York but in California: Walt Disney. He and most of his staff came from Kansas City, where their major influence was Paul Terry's AESOP'S FABLES, and their only instruction was from Edward Lutz's 1920 handbook on animation. Yet they were forging a new, liquid style of cartooning that had some New Yorkers sitting up and taking notice. Walter Lantz and Bill Nolan set up shop in California, and this began a gradual migration west for much of the animation industry. For the first time young people recruited to work in this field would come from outside the world of New York newspapers.

Then Disney prodded his competitors into production of talking pictures with STEAMBOAT WILLIE, the landmark sound cartoon with Mickey Mouse. Many of the New Yorkers would have been content to release their silent films with music-and-effects sound tracks, as they did in 1929, but by 1930 there was no question that sound was vital to the continuation of cartoon production.

To some minds, it rescued animation from a slow death. "Without sound," says Dick Huemer, "animated cartoons in my estimation would have gone the way of the dinosaur and the trolley car." Sound opened new vistas to the animated cartoon and imposed discipline where once had been chaos.

Some motion picture people considered sound an important adjunct to cartoons long before the sound track itself was a reality. Industry Boswell F. C. "Wid" Gunning wrote in 1919:

In some of New York's biggest houses these cartoon subjects often get more laughs proportionate to their length than comedies of a different type.

This is particularly true in the Broadway houses—and mostly because of the work of the orchestra. But even with an organ and a few "effects," just as good results can be obtained.

If you don't overwork it, the old "groan" stuff, pulled in synchronism with the action of the cartoon, helps mightily. And then they use all sorts of other traps like the buzzing of mosquitoes, the willunous laughter of the willun, chicken squawks and all that sort of thing. This helps very much, as has been found by comparing this manner of running the cartoon with the usual stunt of "just running it."

It was precisely this kind of effect that Disney achieved in STEAMBOAT WILLIE—and abandoned just as quickly to seek more sophisticated and persuasive use of sound and music.

Looking back at cartoons produced in the teens and twenties, one greatly regrets that animators were unable, or unwilling, to retain the visual virtuosity that marked their best endeavors. Earl Hurd, Otto Messmer, and the Fleischers flirted with surrealism and the fourth dimension not through any artistic credo but from the simple necessity of expressing themselves in a purely visual manner and exploring new ways of doing so for humorous effect. In 1976 *New York Times* critic Vincent Canby reviewed a program of Felix the Cat cartoons and dealt with this very matter. He wrote that "the Messmer backgrounds are simple to the point of being philosophic statements (one tree is all trees, one house is all houses, etc.) . . ." and that in these films "the freedom of the form looks almost avant-garde."

How true, and how sad that animators, in their desire to "improve" and expand the medium, dismissed these qualities as limitations imposed by silence instead of seeing them as virtues that could have been enhanced by sound. With the addition of sound, color, and refined drawing techniques, it was thought atavistic and unnecessary to toy with space and dimension, and breathe life into inanimate objects for comic effect. These trends lasted a few years in the 1930s and then disappeared.

No one mourned the passing of the silent cartoon. Sound brought increased production, greater prosperity, and artistic and technical advances to the field.

But the cartoon without a voice had something to say, as well, and when it was speaking through creative artists, like Cohl, McCay, Hurd, and Messmer, it could be as eloquent as anything produced in the half century that has followed its demise.

2

Walt Disney

It IS IMPOSSIBLE to overstate the impact that Walt Disney had on the development of animated cartoons.

He did not invent the medium, but one could say that he *defined* it. Disney innovated and perfected ideas and techniques that dramatically changed the course of cartoon production. Some were utterly simple while others were awesomely complex.

He had no illusions about the way these advancements came about. In 1940 he declared, "The span of twelve years between STEAMBOAT WILLIE, the first Mickey with sound, and FANTASIA is the bridge between primitive and modern animated pictures. No genius built this bridge. It was built by hard work and enthusiasm, integrity of purpose, a devotion to our medium, confidence in its future, and, above all, by a steady day-by-day growth in which we all simply studied our trade and learned."*

Disney valued the contributions of every person on his staff and had a rare gift for orchestrating these talents. "He was a direc-

---

*This and most subsequent quotes from Disney are taken from a speech he delivered to the Society of Motion Picture Engineers in the Fall of 1940, later reprinted in the Society's *Journal*.

tor of men rather than a director of pictures," says animator Grim Natwick. Studio veteran Frank Thomas adds, "He had a talent to draw out of guys what they didn't have."

This is something that Disney's rivals were slow to realize. Sid Marcus, who was at the Charles Mintz studio in the early 1930s, recalls, "We were always trying to figure out why he was so successful, and we were usually wrong." Time and again, producers deluded themselves into believing that there was some unsung hero lurking in Disney's shadow, and if they could hire him their films would be as good as Disney's. That person didn't exist.

New York animators rushed to see each new Disney release in the 1930s. Al Eugster, then working for Fleischer, says, "That was frustration if there ever was one, because we'd look at the Disney films and, my God, there was no way of catching up artistically. I guess most animators were curious about how they made those cartoons . . . it was really like magic. And eventually a lot of animators ended up at Disney's for that reason. They wanted to find out what made it tick."

"I had never seen a storyboard until I came to Disney's in 1933," says Dick Huemer. "We outside of Disney's had always thought that he had some great secret that made his cartoons so perfect. When I saw the storyboards, I thought 'Aha! This is it!' Well, that was only *part* of it—the rest was his genius and perfectionism."

One can only speculate about the roots of this genius. Nothing in Disney's background would suggest a potential for greatness. But there is in the story of his severe midwestern upbringing a clue to some important character traits. He learned to work—and work hard—from the time he was a child. He never knew luxury. Drawing was more than just a pastime for him; it was an escape from the harsher realities of life. Disney's father was an itinerant ne'er-do-well. One could say that Disney's adult life was a reaction to these childhood experiences and situations. He became a workaholic, which led to clashes with employees who didn't share his obsessive zeal. Escapism and happy endings became the hallmarks of Disney entertainment, both in his films and in his amusement parks. As for success, Walt wasn't content simply to reverse his father's failure. He was determined to become the most successful man in his field, and he expended himself mentally and physically to attain that goal.

It all began in 1919 in Kansas City, where teen-aged Walt Disney found employment as a commercial artist and met another young draftsman named Ub Iwerks. Together they went to work for the Kansas City Film Ad Company, which produced short animated commercials for local merchants that appeared in Kansas City theaters. After absorbing the basic techniques of animation, Walt decided to strike out on his own. At first he did advertisements and comic

vignettes for the Newman's Theater in a series called NEWMAN'S LAUGH-O-GRAMS. Then in 1922 he moved on to full-blown theatrical cartoons in the LAUGH-O-GRAMS series, which spoofed famous fairy tales like "Cinderella" and "Puss in Boots."

From the very start Walt realized that animation was not a one-man business. He was a capable animator, but Ub Iwerks was much better, and Walt began to rely on him, and on other members of the small staff that he assembled—including Hugh Harman, Rudolf Ising, and Carmen "Max" Maxwell. The LAUGH-O-GRAMS cartoons weren't bad at all, and the few that survive show genuine charm and invention. While the animation itself is basic, there is a clear attempt to give the films a look of quality, particularly in PUSS IN BOOTS. A full range of wash tones and an unusual amount of background detail are among the signs that even then Disney was striving to make his films look good.

Walt also acquired a habit of spending more on his films than he was making, which—coupled with distribution problems—put him out of business within a year's time. But a "pilot" film for a new series called ALICE IN WONDERLAND gave him the impetus to go to Hollywood and start fresh. Distributor M. J. Winkler agreed to finance an ALICE IN CARTOONLAND series on the basis of this short, and Disney established a makeshift studio in California, with brother Roy as his tolerant business manager. Soon Iwerks, Ising, Harman, and Harman's brother Walker were there with him.

ALICE IN CARTOONLAND was an undisguised attempt to reverse the idea of Max Fleischer's OUT OF THE INKWELL series. Instead of having a cartoon clown frolic against a live-action background, Disney had a live-action girl living in a cartoon world. The amount of interaction between Alice and her animated friends varied from

Walt Disney, Ub Iwerks, Rudolf Ising, and Hugh Harman clown for the camera while filming an ALICE IN CARTOON-LAND short.

one episode to the next—depending, no doubt, on exigencies of time and money. In some entries Alice hardly appears at all, while in others there are ingenious devices that maximize the fantasy of live and cartoon figures interacting. In ALICE'S WILD WEST SHOW the live girl blows cartoon smoke rings; in ALICE'S EGG PLANT she is splattered with cartoon eggs; while in ALICE CHOPS THE SUEY there is a distinctly Fleischeresque opening in which an animated silhouette hops out of an inkwell, shakes off the ink, and reveals herself as Alice in live action.

Turning out these shorts at a rate of one every two or three weeks did not offer much opportunity for improvement. It was a dead-line situation in which Walt and the others simply did their best to produce an amusing short based on tried-and-true gag formulas. Many of these gags remain funny today.

The drawing and animation style of these shorts is simple; backgrounds are spare, and corner cutting is evident. Disney later acknowledged that Paul Terry's AESOP'S FABLES cartoons provided the basis for most of his character design during this period, while Alice's feline friend Julius seemed to be a second cousin to Felix. (One character in

A publicity still for the ALICE IN CARTOONLAND **series.**

ALICE SOLVES THE PUZZLE was a direct forerunner of Disney's own Peg Leg Pete; although he was pictured as a bear, the design and even the name, Bootleg Pete, were similar.)

The series was well received from the very start. *Moving Picture World* reviewed ALICE'S WILD WEST SHOW on May 10, 1924, and wrote: "In this reel, the first of a series produced by Walter Disney and distributed on the state right market by M. J. Winkler, clever use is made of photography and cartoon work in combination. There is considerable novelty in which this is handled, the photographed characters and cartoon characters working together against a cartoon background; there are also a number of scenes in which straight camera work is employed. A pretty and talented little tot, Alice, is the featured player, and she will make a hit with almost any audience. . . ."

Disney had stopped drawing by this time, giving rise to the popular notion that he *couldn't* draw. This is nonsense. He had earned his living as a commercial artist for

several years and was certainly proficient, if not inspired. But he was no match for Ub Iwerks, who was precise and lightning-fast, or Hugh Harman, who, along with the other men, found that his animation was improving with each passing year. Experience was the best teacher, and Disney was the best coach, urging his young employees to try harder every time at bat. Constant pressure from Winkler in New York to upgrade the series was another important factor in Walt's ongoing struggle for improvement.

By the time the ALICE series had run its course and Disney was producing a new series, OSWALD THE LUCKY RABBIT, the quality of his studio's animation was markedly higher. The trade press gave the series a solid endorsement, with *Film Daily* writing, "Introducing Oswald, a rival to the other animal cartoon stars. And Oswald looks like a real contender. Walt Disney is doing this new series. Funny how the cartoon artists never hit on a rabbit before. Oswald with his long ears has a chance for a lot of new comedy gags, and makes the most of them. Universal has been looking for a good animated subject for the past year. They've found it." Of equal importance to Disney was recognition within the cartoon business, and this too he received. Dick Huemer says, "His OSWALDS had something more in them than what we in New York were doing at the time. I remember seeking them out when they were playing at the Colony Theatre on Broadway and being considerably impressed and not a little jealous."

That "something more" was a rubbery kind of movement that tied into fresh and amusing gags. In OH, WHAT A KNIGHT Oswald wrings himself out to dry, and later, when kissing a fair maiden's hand, he pulls an endless length of arm from her sleeve in order to have more to kiss! In TROLLEY TROUBLES even Oswald's electric car is flexible, widening and flattening to accommodate the unpredictable changes in the tracks beneath it.

BRIGHT LIGHTS features this same kind of elasticity but takes it one step further—not only do Oswald's legs come off at one point, but the force of an impact smashes his body into ten pieces that are miniature replicas of the full-sized rabbit.

These cartoons also experiment with cinematic devices unseen in the earlier ALICE series. In OH, WHAT A KNIGHT the climactic sword fight is staged with shadows against a castle wall. BRIGHT LIGHTS is full of ingenious visual ideas. A trio of lions leap toward the audience, each one blackening the screen as its roaring mouth covers the camera lens. In an earlier scene, Oswald lifts a large man's shadow off the ground and slips underneath, to sneak into a show without paying admission.

Many of these visual innovations were suggested by Ub Iwerks; some were the impromptu inventions of Oswald's other animators, who in 1927 included Isadore "Friz" Freleng, summoned from Kansas City to replace Rollin "Ham" Hamilton. Walt was already assuming a position he was to maintain for many years, that of chief story man. The OSWALD cartoons were not formally plotted out; neither scripts nor storyboards were considered necessary yet. The basic ideas and specific gags came out of a bull session conducted by Walt during which everyone would make suggestions. Walt would then organize the cartoon and divide its action among his four animators, who were free to make comic embellishments as they went along—subject to Walt's veto.

Looking back on this period, Disney later commented: "The series was going over. We had built up a little organization. Roy and I each had our own homes and a flivver. We had money in the bank and security. But we

didn't like the looks of the future. The cartoon business didn't seem to be going anywhere except in circles. The pictures were kicked out in a hurry and made to price. Money was the only object. Cartoons had become the shabby Cinderella of the picture industry. They were thrown in for nothing as a bonus to exhibitors buying features. I resented that. Some of the possibilities in the cartoon medium had begun to dawn on me. And at the same time we saw that the medium was dying. You could feel rigor mortis setting in. I could feel it in myself. Yet with more money and time, I felt we could make better pictures and shake ourselves out of the rut."

Disney traveled east to meet his distributor in New York and ask for more money. The OSWALD series was a hit, he was putting more into each production, and he saw no reason why he couldn't get a raise. But Disney got the shock of his life when Charles Mintz (Margaret Winkler's husband, who

Disney's version of Oswald the Lucky Rabbit.

now operated their distribution company) told Walt that not only wouldn't they increase his $2,250 production fee, but if Walt wouldn't accept $1,800, Mintz was prepared to take the character and his key animators away from him. Disney knew he had no rights to Oswald, but he couldn't believe that his animation colleagues would desert him; an agitated phone call to Roy led to confirmation that everyone except Ub Iwerks had agreed to work for Mintz.

Dejected, Disney admitted defeat and told Mintz that there was no way for him to produce the cartoons for $1,800. He returned to California without any clear idea of what to do next. (Disney remained bitter about Mintz's double cross for many years, but enjoyed a certain satisfaction when in 1929 Universal Pictures pulled the rug out from Mintz just as Mintz had done with Walt.)

At this point Disney resolved never to

A look at the violent (but fun-loving) Mickey of STEAM-BOAT WILLIE (1928). © Walt Disney Productions.

relinquish ownership of his films or creations again. He and Ub discussed the possibility of a new character with which to launch another series, and Ub drew some sketches of the rodent who came to be known as Mickey Mouse. Walt liked them and devised a story spoofing the current Lindbergh mania called PLANE CRAZY. Ub animated the entire film by himself in less than two weeks! Then in the spring of 1928 a second Mickey Mouse cartoon, GALLOPIN' GAUCHO, was created. Preliminary screenings of these cartoons brought no response from potential distributors. They were good shorts, but there was nothing special or different about them. Mickey's movements and facial gestures were, in fact, precisely those of Oswald, as animated by Iwerks.

Then lightning struck. The enormous success of THE JAZZ SINGER in early 1928 had sent Hollywood into a furor over the prospects of talking pictures. Studios and theater owners were divided in their reaction to sound, but the voice of the public was clear—talkies meant big business. While many producers debated the merits of converting to all-sound production, Disney saw his opportunity to provide something unique: a synchronized sound cartoon.

A test was made of a scene for the third Mickey Mouse cartoon, STEAMBOAT WILLIE. "When the picture was half finished, we had a showing with sound," Disney later recalled. "A couple of my boys could read music and one of them [Wilfred Jackson] could play a mouth organ. We put them in a room where they could not see the screen and arranged to pipe their sound into the room where our wives and friends were going to see the picture. The boys worked from a music and sound-effects score. After several false starts, sound and action got off with the gun. The mouth organist played the tune, the rest of us in the sound department bammed tin pans and blew slide whistles on the beat. The synchronism was pretty close.

"The effect on our little audience was nothing less than electric. They responded almost instinctively to this union of sound and motion. I thought they were kidding me. So they put me in the audience and ran the action again. It was terrible, but it was wonderful! And it was something new!"

Exact details of this now-historic screening vary from one account to the other, but the effect was the same on every participant. Ub Iwerks later said, "I've never been so thrilled in my life. Nothing since has ever equaled it." The tiny Disney crew—which consisted of Walt, Roy, Ub, Les Clark, Johnny Cannon, and amateur musician Wilfred Jackson—had discovered the miracle of talking pictures.

Audience reaction to the completed STEAMBOAT WILLIE duplicated the excitement of that private test screening months earlier. The idea that make-believe cartoon characters could talk, sing, play instruments, and move to a musical beat was considered nothing short of magical.

In 1932 the distinguished critic Gilbert Seldes noted: "The great satisfaction in the first animated cartoons was that they used sound properly—the sound was as unreal as the action; the eye and the ear were not at war with each other, one observing a fantasy, the other an actuality. . . ."

And as late as 1935 John Grierson would write: "Out of the possibilities of sound synchronization a world of sound must be created, as refined in abstraction as the old silent art, if great figures like Chaplin are to come again. It is no accident that of all the comedy workers of the new regime the most attractive, by far, is the cartoonist Disney. The nature of his material forced upon him

something like the right solution. Making his sound strip first and working his animated figures in distortion and counterpoint to the beat of the sound, he has begun to discover those ingenious combinations which will carry on the true tradition of film comedy."

It was harmonica-player Jackson who had shown Walt a metronome and suggested that a pattern of musical beats could be mathematically related to film speed. This meant that the actual music score did not have to be composed before the film was made; only the meter had to be determined. The importance of this method was driven home when Disney added sound tracks to his unreleased silent cartoons PLANE CRAZY and GALLOPIN' GAUCHO. The finished products reveal their origins; because the animation was not done to a specific beat, and gags were not geared to particular sound effects or songs, there is no fusion between sound and picture.

To compose background music and supervise this aspect of production, Walt sent for an acquaintance named Carl Stalling, who had played organ accompaniment for silent pictures in Kansas City. He not only composed and arranged the music for STEAMBOAT WILLIE, but he proposed the idea for THE SKELETON DANCE and launched the SILLY SYMPHONY series.

SKELETON DANCE was a daring idea in several ways. First, it featured no familiar characters. Second, it was neither a story nor a vehicle for comedy gags, but a mood piece. Third, it was designed to conform to a particular music track. The finished film was a triumph for Disney, Iwerks, and Stalling—a conceptual work that achieves every one of its goals in brilliant fashion. Though fifty years have passed and endless changes have occurred in animation, it remains one of the best short cartoons ever made. From Iwerks's

(Top) **A classic moment from a classic cartoon:** THE SKEL-ETON DANCE **(1929).** © **Walt Disney Productions.**

(Bottom) **A scene from** MICKEY'S STEAMROLLER **(1934).** © **Walt Disney Productions.**

imaginative establishing shot of a graveyard at night to the atmospheric touches of black cats silhouetted against the moonlit sky, a skeleton leaping into the camera, and the disarming delight of watching four bony bodies dance as a precision chorus, the film is animated fantasy at its best.

The success of THE SKELETON DANCE inspired a continuing series of noncharacter cartoons that evoked settings, seasons, and events. Perhaps it was the challenge of ani-mating these ambitious films that first set Walt to thinking about the need to improve his staff's capabilities—or perhaps it was the sudden departure of Ub Iwerks in early 1930 that necessitated a long, hard look at his prospects for growth and expansion.

"I was ambitious and wanted to make bet-ter pictures," Disney later remarked, "but the length of my foresight is measured by this admission: Even as late as 1930, my ambition was to be able to make cartoons as good as the AESOP'S FABLES series."

Reaction from the public and from the trade should have bolstered Disney's confi-dence, for his Mickey Mouse cartoons were enormously popular. Within two years Mickey was a national celebrity, "with a big-ger screen following than nine tenths of the stars in Hollywood," according to columnist Louella Parsons. *Motion Picture Daily* wrote, "When you say it is up to the Disney Mickey Mouse standard, there is nothing left to be said." Such compliments were rare for ani-mated cartoons, but Mickey Mouse was not regarded as an ordinary cartoon star. His worldwide impact was unprecedented. Theater owners often advertised his new car-toon above the name of the feature film on their marquees. Mickey's fans ranged from little children to renowned intellectuals. In 1932 Disney received a special Academy Award for his creation.

With this success came problems, of course, one of which was noted by Terry Ramsaye in the *Motion Picture Herald* of February 28, 1931:

Mickey Mouse, the artistic offspring of Walt Disney, has fallen afoul of the censors in a big way, largely because of his amazing success. Papas and mamas, especially mamas, have spoken vigorously to censor boards and elsewhere about what a devilish, naughty little mouse Mickey turned out to be. Now we find that Mickey is not to drink, smoke, or tease the stock in the barnyard. Mickey has been spanked.

It is the old, old story. If nobody knows you, you can do anything, and if everybody knows you, you can't do anything—except what every one approves, which is very little of anything. It has happened often enough among the human stars of the screen and now it gets even the little fellow in black and white who is no thicker than a pencil mark and exists solely in a state of mind.

This merely aggravated a problem that already existed at the Disney studio: Mickey Mouse's nondescript personality. When created by Ub Iwerks, he was just another "funny animal" drawing; he had no characteristics to distinguish him from other cartoon performers. At no time did Iwerks or Disney consider him a full-bodied entity with individual traits or a mind of his own. But now Mickey was a star, and they had to create vehicles for him. Having to eliminate risqué or vulgar humor was just one more blow to the Disney staff; Mickey's early barnyard escapades were full of outhouse humor, and his treatment of fellow animals would never win applause from the Humane Society.

To solve this problem, Walt and his staff buoyed their star with elements that would keep his films afloat: gags, and plenty of them; supporting characters, who included Minnie Mouse, Peg Leg Pete, Pluto, Horace Horsecollar, and Clarabelle Cow; and music, which remained the backbone and raison d'être of these shorts for several years.

Still, Disney was not satisfied. Alone among animation producers, he realized that there had to be some development, a maturing process, or he would soon be on a treadmill. The first chore was to find talent. The number of skilled animators in 1930 was minuscule, so Walt and Roy spent considerable time wooing the top men from both coasts to join their staff. As the ranks swelled, Disney began to learn the particular strengths of his employees and channeled their energies into the areas where they could do the most good. This was the beginning of specialization in the cartoon field, and Disney was the first to understand its

Minnie Mouse in THE PET STORE (1933). © Walt Disney Productions.

importance. He assigned Ted Sears to head the new story department. Until then, animators had doubled as gagmen; now Disney assigned some of them to concentrate on story alone. As animators, they understood the necessities as well as the possibilities of the medium and were able to express their ideas visually.

Although the story department became a fixture at the studio, Disney never closed the door to ideas from outside it; it was standard operating procedure to circulate memos or scripts to the entire staff, and to offer bonus payments for gags and ideas that were usable for each new film.

Webb Smith is credited with being the first man to use a storyboard. As obvious as this procedure seems today, it was revolutionary at the time. Written notes, thumbnail sketches, even visual outlines had been used before, but this was the first time that a sequence of drawings was used to plot out a film *in its entirety*. Rough but expressive sketches were pinned on boards, enabling everyone involved to picture what the film would look like, and to coordinate all efforts toward one common goal. It was a practical and organized way to map out a story, and it gave Walt and his directors greater control than the former trial-and-error method allowed. Disney became well known for his ability to scan a storyboard and sense where the action was sagging or where it needed trimming. There is no question that this was an integral factor in making his shorts the best-crafted products of the early 1930s. Disney's cartoons had a beginning, a middle, and an end, at a time when other studios were just trying to find a way to fill six minutes.

The improvement in the Mickey Mouse series was marked. As Disney himself noted, "Each year we could handle a wider range of

story material, attempt things we would not have dreamed of tackling the year before." The 1929 outings like MICKEY'S FOLLIES or THE JAZZ FOOL are disjointed musicales with barnyard gags thrown in; by 1931 the studio was turning out beautifully constructed cartoons like THE DELIVERY BOY and BARNYARD BROADCAST, in which music is the centerpiece and gags are interwoven in such a way that the film builds to a climax.

In THE DELIVERY BOY Pluto's discovery of a stick of dynamite interrupts Mickey and Minnie's rendition of "The Stars and Stripes Forever," while in BARNYARD BROADCAST a pair of mischievous kittens running around Mickey's radio station with their mother causes Mickey to pursue them and crash through the roof for a raucous finale. The gags are funny, the music is ebullient, and the animation is better than ever before.

Disney knew that whatever improvements he wanted would cost money; this was a continuing source of discord between the producer and his distributors, who financed the cartoons. When he was desperate to find a distributor with sound equipment who could both legally record and then distribute STEAMBOAT WILLIE, he signed with producer Pat Powers. When his cartoons became successful and Powers was earning the lion's share, Disney was bailed out by Columbia Pictures, which agreed to purchase the Powers contract. Then Disney and Columbia parted company because the studio was unwilling to advance more money for Disney to make his films.

"By 1931, production costs had risen from $5,400 to $13,500 per cartoon," he explained. "This was an unheard-of and outrageous thing, it seemed. And a year later, when we turned down Carl Laemmle's offer to advance us $15,000 on each picture, he told me quite frankly that I was headed for bankruptcy. This was not shortsighted on his part. He had no way of seeing what we saw in the future of the medium.''

Disney found an ideal home at United Artists, where he joined such notable producers as Charlie Chaplin and Samuel Goldwyn, and received a highly favorable distribution deal. This arrangement left him free to concentrate on production instead of the distribution dilemmas that had plagued him so long.* Through it all, brother Roy remained his supportive business manager and confidant.

Walt's next important step was color production. By the early 1930s, several studios had experimented with cartoons in Technicolor's two-color process—using colors from only the red and green portion of the spectrum—but the results did not justify the additional work and expense. Now the Technicolor company approached Disney with its latest tests on a three-color process that encompassed all the colors of the rainbow.

In what would become a familiar situation throughout his career, Disney was the only one convinced that Technicolor would be a real asset to his films; even Roy tried to discourage the idea. But Walt signed a deal with Technicolor based on three-year exclusivity in the animation field. Disney's folly turned into another jackpot for the young producer when his first color short, FLOWERS AND TREES, became a nationwide sensation and won the Academy Award as best animated short subject of the year.

FLOWERS AND TREES gathers all the best elements of the SILLY SYMPHONIES into an archetypal story. At dawn the forest comes to life. Trees, flowers, and other flora stretch,

*Disney left United Artists in 1937 to sign with RKO at more favorable rates. His next move, in the 1950s, was to establish his own distribution company, Buena Vista.

Congratulations Mickey on your Seventh Birthday!

ON September 28th, 1935, Mickey Mouse will be exactly seven years old. Already this event is receiving unlimited enthusiastic publicity in newspapers and magazines; famous band-leaders are broadcasting Walt Disney tunes over the air; manufacturers of all types of Mickey Mouse merchandise are giving Mickey thousands of window displays. International broadcasts will encircle the globe with London, New York, Paris and Hollywood joining the celebration.

Smart showmen have already jumped on the band wagon by scheduling "Walt Disney Revues" for their theatres. Other exhibitors anxious to capitalize on the tremendous public interest being aroused, are booking every available Silly Symphony and Mickey Mouse subject.

Don't be left out in the cold. Visit your United Artists Exchange today and get your share of prosperity.

SEPTEMBER 28th to OCTOBER 4th
7th Anniversary Week!

A self-explanatory trade advertisement from 1935.

shake their heads, and greet the day. The romance of two young trees is interrupted by the sinister advances of a craggy tree trunk who tries to kidnap the female tree. Defeated, he seeks revenge by setting the forest on fire. Bluebells sound an alarm, and the forest is panic-stricken until a group of birds poke holes in the clouds above, to provide rain that will douse the deadly blaze. The tree trunk has been killed by his own fire, and now two vultures swoop over his corpse. The tree lovers are reunited in marriage and the forest rejoices, calm and happy once more.

The qualities of anthropomorphism and personification that run throughout the SYMPHONIES are seen to best advantage in this short. Trees, flowers, and plants are given human features and characteristics that somehow seem natural and appropriate—so much so that the story can be told entirely in pantomime. Music, of course, both complements and enhances the action on-screen as strains from Rossini and Schubert evoke the various moods of the film.

The use of color is particularly impressive, since the Disney artists went beyond mere color keying to find expressive and challenging ways to use the new medium. Different tones are used to create shading on the various characters, and when the female tree observes her reflection in the water, she sees herself and the backdrop in paler hues. Right from the start Disney was concerned with creative use of color, not just color itself.

FLOWERS AND TREES set the SILLY SYMPHONIES onto a course of success that lasted for more than six years. The addition of color ensured box-office success, but Disney had other things in mind for this series. While the Mickey Mouse cartoons eased into a comfortable niche at the studio, Disney looked to the SYMPHONIES as a proving ground for fresh ideas and new talent.

One of Walt's most important pursuits was the development of personality in cartoons. He wanted audiences to respond with a variety of emotions, and he knew that character credibility was a major ingredient for this kind of success. "After all," he remarked, "you can't expect charm from animated sticks."

When it came time to prepare a cartoon called THE THREE LITTLE PIGS, he emphasized his desire to project strong personalities for the main characters. Some of his animators understood what Walt was getting at, and so did the short's director, Burt Gillett. The result was a cartoon that broke new ground in animation history.

"That was the first time that anybody ever brought characters to life," says Chuck Jones, who remembers his reaction to the Disney short in 1933. "There were three characters who *looked* alike and *acted* differently; the way they moved is what made them what they were. Before that, in things like STEAMBOAT WILLIE, the villain was a big heavy guy and the hero was a little guy; everybody moved the same. Even in Fleischer's stuff, the basic difference between Popeye and Bluto was the size difference, not the action difference."

By this time the collaborative efforts of the Disney studio were coming into full bloom. Disney had veteran animator Albert Hurter working exclusively on preliminary sketches for films. His expressive drawings helped develop characters that the animators would then bring to life. It was Hurter who created the Three Little Pigs and the Big Bad Wolf. Studio musician Frank Churchill fiddled around with a theme song for the movie, and story man Ted Sears provided the lyrics "Who's Afraid of the Big Bad Wolf?"* Pinto Colvig, a story man who doubled in the voice department (most notably as Goofy), pitched in on the song's composition. Burt Gillett, the short's director, was another veteran with a keen mind, whose credits included FLOWERS AND TREES and some of the best Mickey Mouse cartoons.

The animators were beginning to display

*The complete song lyric was written by Ann Ronell.

specialties and individual talents that helped determine who should be responsible for what in this cartoon. Norman "Fergy" Ferguson, who became a legend in the animation industry for his rough but vivid animation of Pluto, was assigned the Big Bad Wolf. Dick Lundy, who had a particular knack for animating dances, did all of the scenes in which the pigs danced to the perky theme song. Fred Moore, one of the youngest animators at the studio, who showed a tremendous gift for personality animation, handled most of the pig footage. And a relative newcomer from the East Coast, Art Babbitt, filled in some of the remaining scenes.

THE THREE LITTLE PIGS was released in May 1933. "It caused no excitement at its Radio City premiere," Disney later recalled. "In fact, many critics preferred FATHER NOAH'S ARK, which was released about the same time. I was told that some exhibitors and even United Artists considered THE PIGS a 'cheater' because it had only four characters in it. The picture bounced back to fame from the neighborhood theaters." Whether or not the general public consciously responded to the personality animation in this short is difficult to know; but the "message" of the film as delivered in its happy theme song was a welcome tonic to Depression audiences. "Who's Afraid of the Big Bad Wolf?" was Disney's first song hit and helped THE THREE LITTLE PIGS to become the most popular animated short subject of all time.

THE THREE LITTLE PIGS was just the beginning for Walt; he knew that he had just scratched the surface of animation's possibilities. From this point on, the SILLY SYMPHONIES revealed an ever-growing mastery of the film medium; Disney searched for stories with "heart" that would inspire his staff. "By 1935 even THE THREE LITTLE PIGS looked dated and a bit shabby in comparison with the newer SYMPHONIES," he later boasted.

A good example of this growing sophistication could be seen in the 1934 release THE FLYING MOUSE. The story concerns a little mouse who lives with his family and friends in the forest and wants more than anything else to be able to fly. When he bravely rescues a butterfly from the clutches of a spider, the butterfly turns into a fairy princess who grants him one wish. He says he wants to fly. "A mouse was never meant to fly," she tells him, but he is persistent and she finally agrees. The mouse grows wings and is jubilant at his newfound skill, but he soon encounters unexpected problems. The birds regard him as a freakish intruder and refuse to play with him. The shadow he casts on the ground resembles that of a bat or vulture, and scares his mother and three brothers away.

He flies toward a cave and is met inside by four greasy-looking bats, who greet him as a "brother." When he protests that he's a mouse, they reply that he's neither a bat nor a mouse and dance around him as they sing a taunting refrain, "You're Nothing but a Nothing." The frightened mouse flees from the cave and bemoans his fate. One of his teardrops turns into the fairy princess, who agrees to restore him to mousehood, advising, "Do your best . . . be yourself . . . and life will smile on you." The mouse gladly accepts her advice and runs home to be greeted by his happy mother and family.

The emotional impact of this fairy tale is realized not just by fine animation and story work but by remarkable use of color. The story takes place from morning till night, and the *light changes* in each successive sequence. The film opens brightly, with soft pastel colors; the sky is not a deep blue as yet. The colors become more intense as the story progresses, and when the mouse heads for the cave the colors deepen around him. The cave itself is dark; when the bats sing their song to the frightened mouse, the entire frame is jet black except for the characters in center frame. Outside the cave, the sky is still rich with color, but darkening. As the mouse sees his reflection in a pond, the sun is going down; rays of yellow and gold still light the horizon, while a deeper blue settles in above. When the princess transforms our hero back into an ordinary mouse and he heads for home, he casts a long shadow along the ground; by the time he reaches his front gate it is dark outside and there are stars in the sky. His mother stands in the open doorway, bathed in a warm glow of light, awaiting her son's return.

Seventeen years later when UPA "introduced" psychological use of color in GERALD MCBOING BOING, it was hailed as a breakthrough in animation; but Disney had the idea in 1934 and used it to brilliant effect in this cartoon.

For all its success, THE FLYING MOUSE has flaws as well. To differentiate the hero of this film from studio star Mickey, he and the other mice were designed in a moderately realistic fashion. They have snouts, whiskers, beady eyes, and long tails. Thus, when a conspicuously cartoony spider is introduced, the effect is somewhat jarring; he is a visual incongruity in this particular film. The transformation of the butterfly into a fairy princess is well done, but the princess herself is stiff and unappealing. Even the Disney artists, with all their training, had difficulty animating a believable human form.

Critics and audiences were unmindful of these shortcomings, but Disney recognized them and searched for new ways to improve the quality of his cartoons. One revolutionary idea was the institution of pencil tests—actually photographing the rough animation drawings before proceeding with cleanup, inking, and painting.

"I think it is astounding that we were the first group of animators, so far as I can learn, who ever had the chance to study their own work and correct its errors before it reached the screen," said Walt. "In our little studio on Hyperion Avenue, every foot was drawn and redrawn until we could say, 'This is the best that we can do.' We had become perfectionists, and as nothing is ever perfect in this business, we were continually dissatisfied."

Costs soared on the SILLY SYMPHONIES. THE THREE LITTLE PIGS cost $60,000, and some later entries in the series approached $100,-000. But Disney chalked it up to "research and development" and continued to pour most of his meager profits back into production.

The period of 1934–35 marked a turning point in the Disney saga. Not only were there such exciting new films as THE GRASSHOPPER AND THE ANT, THE TORTOISE AND THE HARE, and THE BAND CONCERT, but the studio was moving in a new and exciting direction.

Walt wanted to make a feature film. In 1933 there had been rumors of a Mickey Mouse feature, and that same year plans were made to produce ALICE IN WONDERLAND with Mary Pickford in the lead. Pickford had agreed to finance the film, and preliminary work was under way when Paramount Pictures made its own version of ALICE and the Disney project folded. Will Rogers was similarly interested in a combination live-action/animation feature that would star himself as Rip Van Winkle, but this project also failed to materialize.

Now Disney was determined to move forward. His ambition embraced both practical and personal goals. He was spending more and more money for short subjects, while the profit potential had reached a ceiling. Theater owners would not pay more than a fraction of their feature-film rental for a short, no matter how good it was. Disney felt that he was approaching a dead end. He also knew that expansion was the lifeblood of his business, and feature-film production was not only logical but inevitable.

Having sweated out the long, hard road from STEAMBOAT WILLIE to THE THREE LITTLE PIGS, Walt knew that it would take tremendous training, preparation, and trial and error to make a feature-length animated film. He knew that it would mean hiring more talented people to work on staff.

When he was hampered by a lack of capable artists in the early 1930s, Disney had sent some of his young animators to night classes at the Chouinard Art School in Los Angeles. He furthered this staff's development by hiring Chouinard instructor Don Graham to conduct night classes at the studio beginning in November 1932.

Now, as his demand for talent increased—and his plans for a feature film solidified—Walt hired Graham to work at the studio full-time. The purpose was not just to train young animators, but to get every artist on the staff to sharpen his skills and better understand the nature of animation.

"Many men do not realize what really makes things move," Walt wrote in a lengthy memo to Graham at the outset of this training program. "Why they move—what the force behind the movement is. I think a course along that line, accompanied by practical examples of analysis and planning, would be very good. In other words, in most instances, the driving force behind the action is the mood, the personality, the attitude of the character—or all three. Therefore, the mind is the pilot. We think of things before the body does them.

"There are a number of things that could be brought up in these discussions to stir the imagination of the men, so that when they get into actual animation, they're not just technicians, but they're actually creative people."

Walt summarized his qualifications for a good animator: "The list would start with the animator's ability to draw; then, ability to visualize action—breaking it down into drawings and analyze the movement, the mechanics of the action. From this point, we would come to his ability to caricature action—to take a natural human action and see the exaggerated funny side of it—to anticipate the effect or illusion created in the mind of the person viewing that action.

"It is important also for the animator to be able to study sensation and to feel the force behind sensation, in order to project that sensation. Along with this, the animator should know what creates laughter—why do things appeal to people as being funny."

Graham conducted life-drawing classes, seminars, field trips to the local zoo, and training sessions for various specialists at the studio—but his most important work, as Walt had predicted, was in the action analysis classes. Here, animators and their assistants studied live-action film (including the work of Charlie Chaplin and other silent comedians), as well as studio cartoons, to explore the dynamics of movement. At first there was some resentment from the older animators, who felt that they already knew their craft. But the younger corps of Disney animators, many of whom had gone to art school, were stimulated by this experience, and soon there was a remarkable esprit de corps at the studio.

"It was like a marvelous big Renaissance craft hall," said John Hubley. "We were just all so excited about anything that happened; almost every day, something was new," says Jack Hannah. Ward Kimball recalls, "You

The title character in THE COUNTRY COUSIN (1936), hiccups after drinking champagne in two expressive animation drawings from a famous sequence by Art Babbitt. © Walt Disney Productions.

were a real student of animation then . . . spent your noon hour running film on movieolas, and talked about it, and you worked late at night—no unions, of course—and you had a much different attitude than the animators have today. It was a whole new world, and the new world was at Disney's."

It is important to remember that this was during the Depression, when jobs of any kind were scarce, let alone jobs in the field of art. This worked to Disney's advantage when in 1934–35 he embarked on a major expansion project; hundreds of applicants came to him from around the country, most of them young and fresh from art school. Among this group were the men who (along with veteran Les Clark) formed the nucleus of his feature-film crew, later referred to as the "nine old men": Frank Thomas, Ollie Johnston, Milt Kahl, Marc Davis, Wolfgang (Woolie) Reitherman, Eric Larson, John Lounsbery, and Ward Kimball.

These were just a few of the many talented people who joined the studio during this unforgettable period. Others included men who achieved fame in the world of comic art (Walt Kelly, Virgil "Vip" Partch, Hank Ketcham, Claude Smith, Sam Cobean) and many more who went on to such studios as Walter Lantz, MGM, Screen Gems, and UPA.

Not everyone who came to Disney's at this time was unschooled in animation. Many artists who had been working for Ub Iwerks, Charles Mintz, and Walter Lantz gravitated to Disney during this period of expansion. Some of them found that they had to unlearn bad habits and develop a fresh approach to animation, and many wished that they had come to the studio with no experience whatsoever. Al Eugster voices this opinion and adds, "Before I went to Disney I was working for Iwerks. I was making $135 there and I went to Disney for $50. I figured that it was my tuition fee, and that's what it amounted to—a four-year course in animation. I think it was worth it."

Even among this talented group there were obvious "stars," and one of them was Bill Tytla. Zack Schwartz, who became an art director at the studio in the late 1930s, echoes a popular sentiment when he says, "Bill Tytla was the greatest draftsman I've ever known—in animation or anywhere else. He was not a cartoonist; he was a sculptor, and his work had tremendous power and sense of form."

Because of this reputation, Tytla was a frequent guest lecturer in Don Graham's classes; his keen understanding of animation as an art, coupled with an utter lack of personal pretense, made him an ideal teacher. Graham often called on him to talk to assistant animators and cleanup men, who didn't have the benefit of creative freedom but whose work was all-important to the studio's success.

"You fellows possibly may think that just because you are doing a bunch of Ducks and Mickeys, that all you must do is learn how to draw well enough to draw a Duck and a Mickey," said Tytla in one of those sessions in 1937. "But the funny thing is that the more you know about drawing, the more ably you will handle the Duck and other characters. And, besides, five years from now you won't be doing Ducks anyway. The type of stuff we have been doing here the last few years has been a change from what preceded it, and will be different from what is about to follow. You men who have animated before . . . will agree that there has been quite a bit of change since you started to animate. In those days we never had a problem of animating characters that were similar and yet markedly different. Today we are not merely trying something—we are really on the verge of something that is new. It will

take a lot of real drawing—not clever, slick, superficial, fine-looking stuff, but really solid, fine drawing—to achieve those results, and those results will have to be achieved by the fellows who have absolute control of what they are trying to do. These animators will have to be able to not only draw, but to take a figure, and no matter how they twist, distort, slap, or extend that figure, that figure will still have weight. Those animators will have to be able to put across a certain sensation or emotion—for that is all we are trying to do in animation."

Don Graham's lectures to the working animators often dealt with the problem of laziness—taking the easy way out of a problem instead of meeting a new challenge. "Suppose the Duck walks into a room," he told one group. "The animator may have a stock walk for him—or five stock walks for him—but none of them fits the mood exactly, so he uses the one that's closest to the mood. Possibly, if he went back and looked at the problem differently and said, 'What's the feeling I am trying to get over?', a whole new walk might evolve. It would be a real contribution to the industry because it would give other fellows courage to go ahead and think things out on their own. It is a matter of courage—the animator may not have drawn his concept of the action as well as he hoped, the director will say it's rotten—it isn't the Duck, it isn't Pluto—but if he keeps on attempting to get ideas or feelings over with his actions, although no one has ever seen that type of handling before, and if he doesn't lose the character of the actor, he can't help but win in the end. That is the way every animator has gotten ahead here—by trying something new and seeing how it works."

The atmosphere of self-examination spread beyond Don Graham's classes. From the outset of his studio's existence, Disney had followed a practice of writing things down. He believed in memos, and hired stenotypists to transcribe what was said at story meetings, so that every participant could have a copy. Now he transcribed all of Graham's classes for the staff and encouraged his directors and department heads to issue lengthy memos on various aspects of production.

In 1935 story department head Ted Sears composed detailed analyses of the key Disney characters, outlining their established personality traits and citing specific scenes that best captured these elements.

Of Mickey Mouse he wrote, "Mickey is not a clown . . . he is neither silly nor dumb. His comedy depends entirely upon the situation he is placed in. Mickey is most amusing when in a serious predicament trying to accomplish some purpose under difficulties or against time. [A] good Mickey role was as leader in THE BAND CONCERT. Here . . . he kept at his job with a serious determination despite all the troubles and interruptions. When Mickey is working under difficulties, the laughs occur at the climax of each small incident or action. They depend largely upon Mickey's expression, position, attitude, state of mind, etc., and the graphic way that these things are shown. Mickey is seldom funny in a chase picture, as his character and expressions are usually lost."

Concerning Pluto: "Pluto is best appreciated when he is not too smart. His character should always be that of a real dog, with just enough exaggeration to make him a comic. Pluto's dumb thoughtfulness or reasoning is also funny. This was shown clearly when he listened to the devil character in MICKEY'S PAL PLUTO, also in the way he responded to Mickey's lecture on cats in PLUTO'S JUDGMENT DAY. Pluto is nervous and sensitive—easily startled. His feelings are easily hurt when scolded. He is foolhardy rather than brave.

Pluto might show real bravery when Mickey is in danger . . . otherwise his courage is 90% bluff. He might be described as a likeable coward."

Goofy was always referred to at the studio as the Goof. "The Goof's dumbness is of a different type from Pluto's," Sears wrote. "He is on the silly side, and always harmless. He tries to do things in a way he considers clever. He always does them wrong, and ends up with a foolish apologetic laugh. He seldom loses his temper. This makes him a good foil for the hot-headed duck. In handling the Goof, we can take liberties . . . inanimate objects can have more life—they may be exaggerated and humanized when connected with the Goof, as we feel he sees them that way."

Sears was able to delineate these characters quite clearly, but his conclusions were based on several years of development by Walt, story men, directors, and especially animators. While many people worked on Disney's star characters in the 1930s, there was no question that Norman Ferguson really established Pluto, Fred Moore reestablished Mickey Mouse, and Art Babbitt gave definition and direction to Goofy for the first time.

Ferguson, as noted before, became something of a legend—a man who commanded universal respect in the animation business. Yet he could barely draw, in the common sense of the word. Says Shamus Culhane, "I liked the way he drew; it was very rough, but oh my, was he accurate. At first it didn't look like anything. But when you looked through this barbed wire that he had concocted, there was a really good drawing there, and funny." Ferguson was one of the first men to realize that animation was *movement* and *expression,* not just a series of drawings. He may have been the original inspiration for Disney's platoon of assistant

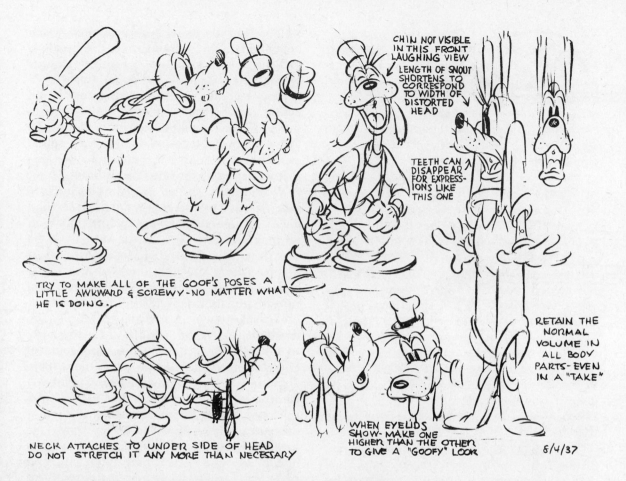

Detail from a model sheet of Goofy from 1937. © Walt Disney Productions.

animators, in-betweeners, and cleanup men; Walt realized that it was easy to find people who could draw, but it was rare to find someone who could animate. So he left the animation—the working out of movement, position, and personality—to men like Fergy, and then turned over those rough drawings to assistants who could clean them up and fill in the detail that the animator had only indicated. This eventually became standard procedure at all studios, but Fergy's drawings provided a unique challenge for his assistants. Jack Hannah started out as an in-betweener and assistant to Ferguson, and he recalls, "When you had to in-between those (drawings), oh boy!" Walt knew that the additional labor involved in cleaning up after Fergy was worthwhile, not only because he was so good, but because he worked so fast.

It was Ferguson who first animated the character of Pluto as a bloodhound in the 1930 Mickey Mouse cartoon THE CHAIN GANG. While it took time for Pluto's character to evolve, as he became Mickey's playful pet, it was Ferguson who immediately under-

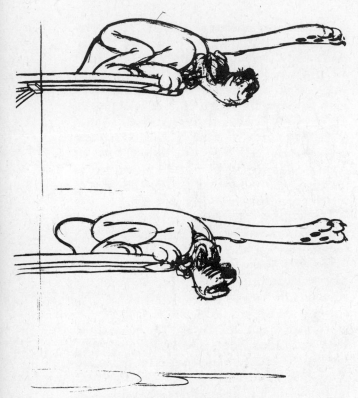

Two animation drawings of Pluto from PANTRY PIRATE
(1941). © **Walt Disney Productions.**

stood the importance of giving the character a *mind* if he was to succeed as a pantomime personality. He realized that facial expressions were meaningless unless there were thought processes behind them.

No matter how precise and organized the studio became, Fergy maintained that animation was basically an instinctive art. In the case of Pluto he felt it was almost impossible to preplan the timing of a given scene. "It is hard to anticipate the necessary feeling in certain spots where expressions will be used," he wrote. "This sometimes means it will be necessary to add footage when such spots are reached in animation. For example, in the flypaper sequence (PLAYFUL PLUTO) as

well as Pluto on ice skates (ON ICE), so much depended on the building up of the situation and the pauses for Pluto to think about different ways of getting rid of the flypaper or getting up on his feet on the ice. Good expressions were necessary in these spots to build the gag or situation to a climax. To arrive at the footage needed for such spots, as well as the follow-up in action, the animator has to feel the situation himself."

Fred Moore joined the studio in 1930 when he was eighteen years old. He too had a flair for personality animation that Walt soon recognized, and in the mid-1930s he was the man in charge of Mickey Mouse. At a time when Mickey's thunder was being stolen by other characters, Moore redesigned him to give him more flexibility and a modern facial styling. According to Moore, "In some pictures he has a touch of Fred Astaire; in others of Charlie Chaplin; and some of Douglas Fairbanks, but in all of these there should be some of the young boy." Nobody captured this feeling better than Moore.

Goofy began life in the early 1930s as a stringbean character called Dippy Dawg. He had a silly laugh, provided by Pinto Colvig, and a silly manner to match. But he never came into focus as a star personality until Art Babbitt set to work on him. Near the end of 1935 Babbitt wrote, "In my opinion the Goof, hitherto, has been a weak cartoon character because both his physical and mental make-up were indefinite and intangible . . . the only characteristic which formerly identified itself with him was his voice. No effort was made to endow him with appropriate business to do, a set of mannerisms or a mental attitude. . . .

"Think of the Goof as a composite of an everlasting optimist, a gullible Good Samaritan, a half-wit . . . and a hick. He is loose-jointed and gangly, but not rubbery. He can move fast if he has to, but would rather avoid any overexertion, so he takes what seems the easiest way. He is a philosopher of the barber shop variety. No matter what happens, he accepts it finally as being for the best or at least amusing. . . . He very seldom, if ever, reaches his objective or completes what he has started."

Babbitt, like his colleagues, also determined a definite set of physical characteristics for the Goof: "His posture is nil. His back arches the wrong way and his little stomach protrudes. His head, stomach, and knees lead his body. His neck is quite long and scrawny. His knees sag and his feet are large and flat. He walks on his heels and his toes turn up. His shoulders are narrow and slope rapidly, giving the upper part of his body a thinness and making his arms seem long and heavy, though actually not drawn that way. His hands are very sensitive and expressive and though his gestures are broad, they should still reflect the gentleman. His shoes and feet are not the traditional cartoon dough feet. His arches collapsed long ago and his shoes should have very definite character."

No group of animators ever knew their characters as well as Disney's did, but this was not without its drawbacks and problems. As characters like Pluto and Goofy ripened into maturity, older one-dimensional creations like Horace Horsecollar and Clarabelle Cow had to be retired. They offered no potential for development and looked archaic alongside the new, full-bodied Disney stars.

There was also the ongoing dilemma of what to do with Mickey Mouse. Mickey remained a short-subject star for twenty years to come and will always be the corporate symbol of the Disney organization. But, in truth, Mickey's death knell was sounded in 1934, in the form of a squawk. The squawk belonged to Clarence Nash, and the character who voiced it was Donald Duck.

Donald was unique in that his voice preceded the creation of the character. Disney had heard Clarence Nash reciting "Mary Had a Little Lamb" as a flustered duck on a Los Angeles radio show and recognized the cartoon potential for such a voice. Donald made his debut as a supporting character in THE WISE LITTLE HEN, one of the SILLY SYMPHONIES series, and then was showcased in ORPHANS' BENEFIT, in which he attempted to do his recitation before a jeering audience of mischievous mice-children.

Donald's screen personality was largely the creation of animator Dick Lundy, who recalls working on THE ORPHANS' BENEFIT: "I listened to the dialogue track and decided that he was an ego show-off. If anything crossed him he got mad and blew his top. For this I had him lean forward, chin out, arm straight out and fisted. The other arm, with fist, was swinging back and forth. His one foot was out straight, heel on floor, the other foot under him as he hopped up and down, quacking. This action was fairly violent for that time."

In 1935 animator Fred Spencer composed a character analysis of Donald Duck that read, in part, "Donald has developed into one of the most interesting screen comics. The audience always likes him, provided he plays true to his own character. His best features are his cocky, show-off, boastful attitude that turns to anger as soon as he is crossed; his typical angry gestures with which the audience is familiar, especially his fighting pose and his peculiar quacking voice and threats when angry.

"The Duck gets a big kick out of imposing on other people or annoying them; but immediately loses his temper when the tables are turned. In other words, he can 'dish it out' but he can't 'take it.'"

Donald's aggressive character was an immediate sensation with audiences, which until then had seen only happy-go-lucky, mild-mannered characters in starring roles. Even in THE BAND CONCERT, in which the animation of Mickey Mouse was superbly expressive, Donald managed to steal the show with his bombastic personality.

Donald's overnight success, coupled with the development of Goofy and Pluto, made it clear that Mickey Mouse's days as a solo star were numbered.

Competition from other characters was not the only reason for Mickey's decline. Ward Kimball feels that there were other subtle factors at work. "The more we got into reality, the more Mickey became an abstraction," he told animation historian Mike Barrier in the early 1970s. "In the old days of cartooning the characters didn't have much relationship to reality. You could put almost anything into animation and the public accepted it. But who ever heard of a four-foot-tall mouse? That was the problem. Donald Duck, Goofy, Pluto, Clarabelle Cow, and all the rest were drawn to scale. They were believable because they were of a relative size. Then along comes a mouse as big as they are and it stopped working."

"There's another subliminal thing that probably contributed to the demise of Mickey," he continued. "Whereas we were drawing in THE FLYING MOUSE, for instance, ears that really turned in perspective, Mickey had these round bowling balls up there, and no matter how you turned him, they would keep their shape. This is another thing that might have contributed to questioning his reality. As our pictures got more 'real' and the stories more complicated, his ears, along with his size, contributed to the demise of Mickey Mouse."

Walt Disney had no intention of retiring Mickey at this time. Mickey was, after all, a worldwide celebrity, a merchandising king-pin, and the cornerstone of Disney's growing studio. Mickey was close to Walt in many ways; Disney had even done Mickey's voice since the earliest days of sound.

The solution was to co-star Mickey with other characters from this point on, and, with occasional exceptions, this is how the mouse spent the rest of his years on-screen. (Those exceptions included two of Mickey's most elaborate and enjoyable films: THRU THE MIRROR, a Lewis Carroll-like fantasy in which Mickey is caught in a strange, surreal Wonderland, and THE BRAVE LITTLE TAILOR, a vivid retelling of the classic fairy tale in which Mickey battles a monstrous and quite menacing giant.) Most successful of all were the early "trio" shorts with Mickey, Donald, and Goofy—MICKEY'S SERVICE STATION, MICKEY'S FIRE BRIGADE, MOVING DAY, CLOCK CLEANERS, LONESOME GHOSTS, and MICKEY'S TRAILER, to name a few. These superbly animated shorts featured the characters as a

One of Mickey Mouse's most ambitious short subjects, THE BRAVE LITTLE TAILOR (1938). © Walt Disney Productions.

team that approached a given situation, then split up for solo episodes before coming together again at the finale. While the formula began to wear thin toward the end of the 1930s, the above-named shorts presented the Disney machinery working at full steam: wonderful characters in funny, fantastic situations.

The only criticism one could make of these shorts is that they were becoming *too* refined, too concerned with characterization and not enough with gags and movement. This development was almost inevitable as animators who had been weaned on story-thin, fast-moving musical cartoons stretched out and put their accumulated knowledge and skill to work. No one except the Disney crew could have milked "character gags" the same way—but this tended to make the cartoons "soft" and introspective instead of funny. A story would stop dead in its tracks in order for Pluto to sniff around a magician's hat in MICKEY'S GRAND OPERA, and Goofy could play hide-and-seek with an almost-human piano for endless footage in MOVING DAY.

Even within the studio there was a feeling that the new cartoons lacked the spirit of the early 1930s, when Mickey and his cohorts projected such a carefree attitude, and the animators were unencumbered by endless detail and an enormous assembly-line operation. This was all part of growing pains.

While refinement of the Disney "stars" was occupying some members of the staff, others were making advancements of a different kind on the SILLY SYMPHONIES. As work began on a feature film project, Walt relied more and more on the SYMPHONIES to give his crew a chance to develop new techniques. Greater sophistication in layout, backgrounds, and the like were matched by the ability to create new and sympathetic characters in each seven-minute short. Spe-

cific achievements, such as the first successful animation of speed in THE TORTOISE AND THE HARE, were hailed not only within the studio but throughout the animation industry. Other films, like WHO KILLED COCK ROBIN?, MUSIC LAND, THE COUNTRY COUSIN, LITTLE HIAWATHA, FERDINAND THE BULL, MOTHER GOOSE GOES HOLLYWOOD, and THE UGLY DUCKLING brought additional praise and prestige to the Disney crew.

THE OLD MILL, released in 1937, marked yet another milestone for the studio; aside from being an outstanding cartoon, it introduced Disney's latest technical marvel, the multiplane camera. Built at a cost of $70,000 and standing fourteen feet high, this invention enabled the camera to look through a series of animation "planes" instead of just one, so that the finished picture would have a feeling of depth and dimension. The famous establishing shot of THE OLD MILL was layer upon layer of landscape—from reeds and thistles in a pond in the foreground (with ripples in the pond) to the mill itself, to a procession of cows walking behind the structure, to the clouds passing in the sky.

Ub Iwerks had developed something similar in the mid-1930s, but he never carried it to this degree of intricacy. Maintaining sharp focus and controlling illumination on seven levels was just part of the challenge. William Stull described the awesome operation of the multiplane camera in an article for *American Cinematographer* in February 1938:

The problems of perspective, proportions, and timing in these multiplane scenes can be incredibly complex. Picture, for instance, a traveling shot in which the camera "follows" an animated character walking through a landscape.

In one plane the drawings (on celluloid) of the character would animate, following one scheme of perspective and timing. Behind him, the back-

Disney's famous multiplane camera setup. The camera (*top*) looks down through several layers of drawings, each one separately illuminated from the side.

stages is adjustable up and down along the camera's optical axis, and may as well be swung in any direction laterally—north or south, east or west, as the Disney engineers phrase it.

The camera itself is susceptible to all these adjustments, and may be rotated through to a full 360 degree circle about the lens' axis, as well. In all, camera, backgrounds, foregrounds, and animated action are capable of *no less than 64 separate and distinct adjustments for every frame exposed!*

Two engineering graduates of the California Institute of Technology are kept constantly busy figuring out the mathematics involved in drawing and photographing these multiplane scenes. Thanks to their efforts, the problems of actual photography are minimized.

Of course, this camera was merely a tool, not an end in itself. It remained for Disney and his creative staff to devise sequences worthy of multiplane treatment—material that would be enhanced by the dramatic possibilities this device offered them.

Complementing the development of this camera was Disney's establishment of an effects department. Animators had been informally classified by specialties before, but this was the first time anyone was ever designated to handle nothing but effects. Now character animators were free to concentrate on their "actors," while a separate department that included Joshua Meador, Cy Young, Don McManus, and George Rowley, added clouds, rain, rippling water, reflections, or whatever elements a sequence called for.

This development must have come as quite a shock to veteran animators who could remember a time when they were responsible for everything connected with a scene— the characters, the backgrounds, the layout, the gags, and even the inking. I. Klein recalls that there were so many embellishments added to his animation on WYNKEN, BLYNKEN AND NOD (including multiplane footage) that

ground would move past, not only in a different physical plane, but timed to an entirely different but necessarily rigidly proportioned degree of movement between exposures.

In the foreground might be one, two, or three sets of celluloids, perhaps animated, perhaps merely moving past, but proportioned and timed still differently.

The range of adjustments permitted by this intricate photographic set-up is incredible. Each of the

he did not recognize his own work when it came on the screen.

The culmination of all this technical and talent development was the production of Disney's first feature-length film, SNOW WHITE AND THE SEVEN DWARFS.

Looking back, Disney once said, "Webster sums up the spirit of the SNOW WHITE enterprise in his definition of 'adventure': 'risk, jeopardy; encountering of hazardous enterprise; a daring feat; a bold undertaking in which the issue hangs on unforeseen events.'"

Disney *was* venturing into the unknown, in more ways than one. He had proved it possible for an animated cartoon to involve an audience emotionally for seven minutes, but there was no way of knowing whether this involvement could be sustained for seventy minutes or more. People in the film industry predicted that no adult would *want* to see a feature-length cartoon. Disney recognized these obstacles and believed that he could overcome them.

The biggest problem was developing an approach to the construction of a feature. "You couldn't possibly realize all the things we had to learn, and unlearn, in doing SNOW WHITE," Disney told reporter Paul Harrison when the film was completed. "We started out gaily, in the fast tempo that is the special technique of short subjects. But that wouldn't do; we soon realized there was danger of wearing out an audience. There was too much going on."

Simplicity was one of the keys to a successful cartoon feature and, as Disney learned, one of the most difficult things to achieve. Relying on a classic story like SNOW WHITE was both an advantage and a problem. Told in its most basic form, the plot was too thin (and too brief) to sustain a feature, but fleshing it out might add unnecessary clutter and diffuse the impact of this famous tale.

What Disney needed was a cohesive script in which one sequence would flow into the next and comic or musical interludes would not seem like padding. He got his wish, but it involved some difficult decisions along the way. "A lot more than just experimental shots and drawings went into the wastebasket," said one contemporary report. "Two long completed sequences, one where the dwarfs had a soup concert and another where they build a bed to give to Snow White, were reluctantly snipped out to save running time. One night, two thousand feet went at one whack. Disney had to order it, and it hurt him a lot more than it did you." Actually, running time was not the main reason the footage was cut; Walt felt these entertaining but extraneous scenes hindered the progress of the story.

When THE THREE LITTLE PIGS had presented a trio of similar characters with distinctly different personalities, it had been hailed as a major step forward. Now Disney topped himself by creating *seven* wholly individual personalities, each with physical characteristics all his own and a point of view to match. There was no mistaking Doc for Grumpy, or Dopey for Bashful, in the finished film—and that was the result of painstaking attention to detail by everyone on the Disney staff.

"It is still difficult, if you draw one character and then switch to another," said Bill Tytla at one of Don Graham's classes, "because the spacing on them is different, the way they handle their hands is different . . . and their timing in a certain situation. If Doc would say something, they wouldn't all turn and look at him at the same time. Happy would probably be first, and Sleepy would probably be last in his reaction to a sentence, and by the time Sleepy was turned, the other

Model sheets from SNOW WHITE AND THE SEVEN DWARFS **emphasizing relative size, proportions, and posture.** © Walt
Disney Productions.

fellow would anticipate into his business. [There is] never any mechanical mass movement."

Every individual scene in the film became an intricate project. Shamus Culhane animated the dwarfs' march home from their mine while they sang "Heigh Ho." "I worked six months on that goddamn thing and I don't think it's a whole minute [in the film]," he says. What took six months? "Well, in the first place the proposition was very difficult. Each Dwarf had a different style of walk. They were always in a row, and

they had to stay even. And they often walked in perspective, sharp perspective in some cases, which meant that you had to sit down and map out every damn walk with a blue pencil and a ruler. In perspective you would diminish these steps so that everybody diminished properly, even if they had a different step—with Dopey *out* of step. I had two assistants and one in-betweener and we all worked about six months. There was that much work."

Just getting it right wasn't enough. It had to be *good*, and no one was a tougher critic

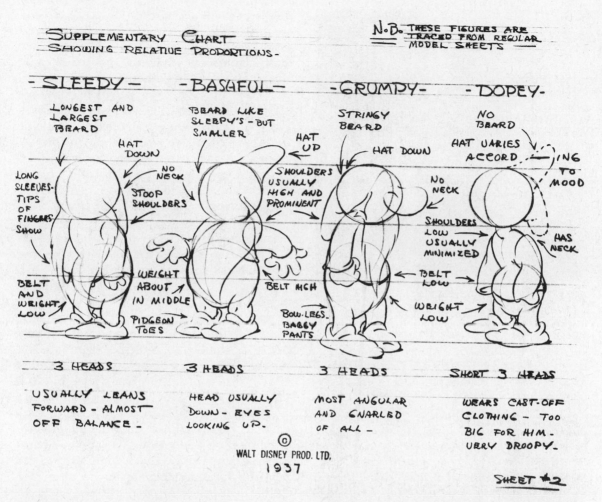

SUPPLEMENTARY CHART —
SHOWING RELATIVE PROPORTIONS-

N.B. THESE FIGURES ARE TRACED FROM REGULAR MODEL SHEETS —

-SLEEPY-   -BASHFUL-   -GRUMPY-   -DOPEY-

LONGEST AND LARGEST BEARD
BEARD LIKE SLEEPY'S - BUT SMALLER
STRINGY BEARD
NO BEARD

HAT DOWN
NO NECK
HAT UP
HAT DOWN
HAT VARIES ACCORD——ING TO MOOD

LONG SLEEVES - TIPS OF FINGERS SHOW
STOOP SHOULDERS
SHOULDERS USUALLY HIGH AND PROMINENT
NO NECK
SHOULDERS LOW USUALLY MINIMIZED
HAS NECK

WEIGHT ABOUT IN MIDDLE
BELT HIGH
BELT LOW

BELT AND WEIGHT LOW
PIDGEON TOES
BOW-LEGS. BAGGY PANTS
WEIGHT LOW

3 HEADS   3 HEADS   3 HEADS   SHORT 3 HEADS

USUALLY LEANS FORWARD - ALMOST OFF BALANCE -
HEAD USUALLY DOWN - EYES LOOKING UP.
MOST ANGULAR AND GNARLED OF ALL -
WEARS CAST-OFF CLOTHING - TOO BIG FOR HIM. VERY DROOPY.

© WALT DISNEY PROD. LTD,
1937

SHEET #2

than Walt. As he viewed preliminary footage in the ''sweatbox'' (the studio's colloquial term for screening room), he dismissed a lot of capable work as being good enough for shorts but not good enough for SNOW WHITE.

Bill Tytla tried to impart this feeling to in-betweeners and cleanup men in a lecture given in Don Graham's class. "We have tried to get an entirely different type of drawing into the characters than in the shorts," he said. "In the shorts everything is based more or less on a ball, and when it is inked every-

thing has a sharp, hard, incisive line without any feeling of texture, as in Mickey, the Duck, or the Goof. The problem in this stuff is to try to get the feeling of various kinds of texture—texture of the flesh, the jowls of the dwarfs, the drawing into the eyes, the mouth, the texture of the hair and of old cloth, so that it feels heavy, unwashed for a couple of hundred years, according to the story. . . .

"We are trying to stress the use of hands in the dialogue; dialogue can go awfully dry if something isn't done to relieve it." And,

Part of the finished product: the heart-rending climax of
SNOW WHITE AND THE SEVEN DWARFS (1937). © Walt Disney Productions.

most importantly, Tytla said, "We are trying
to keep animation simple, which is a very
hard thing to do."

Of all the problems this film presented,
perhaps none was so great as the animation
of realistic human characters. Some critics
found this the film's major shortcoming, particularly in the drawing of the Prince. People
in the animation industry had too much
respect for Disney's achievement to dispar-
age the "human" animation, but many of
them passed it off as mere *rotoscoping*.
(Rotoscoping is the practice of tracing the
movements of live actors onto animation
paper, and Disney publicity made no effort
to hide the fact that live footage was used for
this feature. The woman who posed for
Snow White, then married to animator Art
Babbitt, later became famous as dancer
Marge Champion.)

But Grim Natwick, the man chiefly
responsible for animating Snow White, clar-

ifies the stories about techniques used to create this character. "We went way beyond
rotoscope," he says. "And even when we
took a rotoscope drawing, her chin came
almost as far down as her bosom would be,
so we had to reconstruct the entire body; we
did that by making her very short-waisted.
You see, Snow White was really only about
five heads high. [A realistic human form is
usually six.] So if the leg motion was nice,
we could get some [use out of it] . . . but it
all had to be redrawn, of course.

"I remember one scene I had where there
were 101 rotoscoped tracings; that would
mean that they traced every second frame on
the film. I used drawing one and drawing
one hundred and one, and I filled in the rest,
because there wasn't enough in it to give us
anything to animate.

"Let me say something about realism,"
Natwick continues. "She was not actually
that real. There were probably two thousand
different drawings made trying to develop
Snow White's character. She started out as a
little fairy-book character and that didn't
seem right. As the character changed, they
gave us two complete months to practice
animation on Snow White before we had to
make a single scene that would go into the
picture. So if a model came in from the
designing department that we animated, and
we found things we didn't like, we simply
went back and told them. As a matter of fact,
every model that came to an animator at Disney's did not have to be animated until the
animator wrote his okay on it."

Natwick had no less than *five* assistants
on SNOW WHITE, and with good reason:
"Each drawing was complicated, and was
virtually an illustration. I've always had tremendous respect for Marc Davis and Les
Novros and the other fellows that worked
with me. They had to be excellent. Those
drawings were as good as you saw in the

average illustrated children's book in those days, or even today. The dwarfs were much easier to draw, because you tied the nose, eyes, and whiskers together, and if it wasn't a perfect in-between, you wouldn't notice it. But you could not have an imperfect in-between on Snow White, because the eyes were in an open space; the eyes and other elements like the mouth had to follow through *perfectly*, otherwise you'd get a jitter or a dance, as happened with some prints, even though we used every trick we could think of to avoid it."

The amount of work involved in Snow White's creation was so enormous that no one could have calculated it ahead of time. "We considered changing the name of the picture from SNOW WHITE to FRANKENSTEIN," Disney once remarked, referring not only to the never-ending work but to the ever-mounting costs. He had originally hoped to produce the feature for $250,000, but by the time he was finished the figure was six times that amount. Along the way, tremendous strides were made in the development of animation techniques, at both the creative and technical levels. While this was a source of great satisfaction to Disney, he rued the fact that so many things were discovered while the picture was in progress: "You see, we've learned such a lot since we started this thing, I wish I could yank it back and do it all over again."

All that mattered now was the public's reaction. None of the technical achievements or discoveries would have counted for much if the finished product hadn't delivered the goods.

Variety's reviewer summed up the worldwide response as well as anyone when he wrote, "There has never been anything in the theatre quite like Walt Disney's SNOW WHITE AND THE SEVEN DWARFS, seven reels of animated cartoon in Technicolor, unfolding an absorbing, interesting, and at times thrilling entertainment. So perfect is the illusion, so tender the romance and fantasy, so emotional are certain portions when the acting of the characters strikes a depth comparable to the sincerity of human players, that the film approaches real greatness."

What impressed people most was the film's ability to evoke a *variety* of emotions: from the unrestrained happiness of Snow White's frolics with the dwarfs to the vivid horror of the Queen's transformation into a wicked witch, the infectiously cheerful renditions of songs like "Heigh Ho" and "Whistle While You Work" to the overwhelming sadness of Snow White's apparent death. That any film, let alone an animated cartoon, could elicit such a remarkable range of responses from adults and children alike was astonishing.

All the love, dedication, and hard work that went into SNOW WHITE paid off. The film was a tremendous hit in 1937–38, earning more than eight million dollars around the world. Its songs became not only hits, but standards, and the characters enjoyed the same merchandising success that Mickey and his friends had known since the early 1930s.

For Walt and his staff there was great satisfaction. No other project ever recaptured the special excitement of this, the first feature film. There would be other challenges ahead, but SNOW WHITE remained a unique experience for the many people who worked on it.

Not that anyone was resting on laurels. No sooner was SNOW WHITE completed—after months of back-breaking work to meet a Christmas premiere date—than full-scale production commenced on PINOCCHIO.

"The two years between SNOW WHITE and PINOCCHIO were years of confusion, swift expansion, reorganization," said Disney.

"Hundreds of young people were being trained and fitted into a machine for the manufacture of entertainment which had become bewilderingly complex. And this machine had been redesigned almost overnight from one for turning out short subjects into one aimed mainly at increased feature production."

One by-product of this expansion, which had begun in the mid-1930s, was Walt's increasing reliance on intermediaries to supervise the ever-growing output at the studio. These directors were former animators whom Disney had promoted. Most were capable men, but some of them feared for their position and wanted to avoid displeasing Walt at all costs. Consequently, they bore down on animators and artists and discouraged invention and new ideas that Walt himself would have approved. When the animators got to deal with Walt directly and saw this to be the case, their frustration only increased.

"I had more luck with Walt in sweatboxes than I did with the directors," affirms animator Al Eugster. "Walt himself knew what he wanted, but the directors had to guess at what he wanted, so they were in a tough spot. I got the feeling that if I'd always worked with Walt, I would have made out a lot better."

"It was a very harsh place to work in," says Shamus Culhane, "but harsh with every kind of advantage. Even in those days, a movieola [a film-editing and viewing machine] cost twelve hundred bucks or something, but everyone had one. You could shoot stuff over as long as you wanted." At every other studio, animators worked at drawing boards with wooden disks over the light-box. Disney's disks were cast aluminum.

"The marvelous thing about the studio," Culhane adds, "was that you could work all day, the whole eight hours, and at the end of the day look at what you did and put it in the wastepaper basket with no compunction. Nobody would ask you why you did it; they would ask if you *didn't*."

Despite financial pressures, Disney refused to compromise with quality, and he was determined to incorporate into PINOCCHIO all the lessons he had learned during the production of SNOW WHITE. Plans took shape to make this second feature even more elaborate than the first. Disney later declared, "PINOCCHIO might have lacked SNOW WHITE's heart appeal, but technically and artistically it was superior."

Story concept remained the biggest obstacle. One day Walt made the difficult decision to scrap five months' work—including animation—because it just wasn't right. The PINOCCHIO team started from scratch and built a much better film.

The cast of characters in PINOCCHIO provided Disney's animators with a new set of hurdles. Pinocchio had to project the likable qualities of a little boy while remaining a wooden puppet. Jiminy Cricket had to register as an important character even though his size was a fraction of the others'. The Blue Fairy had to be a beautiful woman, yet ethereal and not a "glamour girl." The two heavies, Stromboli and J. Worthington Foulfellow (the fox), were designed as completely different types of villains—the former, a flamboyant personification of evil, and the latter, a roguish kind of con man.

Animating Monstro the whale presented an entirely different problem, as described in a *Popular Mechanics* article from January 1940:

The creation of Monstro the whale lay rather equally between the regular character animators, the effects animators, and the layout men. For months they experimented with some way to fix up Monstro so that his big bulk took on depth, perspective and highlighting. The whale was first drawn in pencil on regular animation paper. Then the drawing was traced to a special type of colored paper and the highlights rendered in chalk.

From this point, the drawing went through a tracing-dyeing-photographing process on a newly developed type of sensitive film. In this way, subtleties of highlights and perspective were obtained, as well as nuances and shades of coloring impossible with regular paints. Whale models created within the studio also helped the animators and layout men with their project. A miniature whale skeleton some five feet long was made, which the artists could twist and turn at will. The model department fashioned a rib cage and lungs which could be pumped to simulate actual breathing. Clay models were made and painted in oil so that the artists could study probable highlights and light changes on Monstro's skin.

The layout men discovered the illusion of great size could only be carried out by paying minute attention to perspective. They drew him to approximate the scale of a three-story building. Wherever possible, the whale filled up most of the camera field.

Even the sound effects accompanying Monstro required extra work and experimentation, most of which was in the capable hands of sound wizard Jim Macdonald.

The finished film was more sophisticated than SNOW WHITE in terms of story and imagery as well as technique. If SNOW WHITE was a fairy tale laced with moments of terror, PINOCCHIO was an extended nightmare with occasional humorous interludes. Many of its major sequences—the abduction of Pinocchio by Stromboli, the transformation of Lampwick into a jackass on Pleasure Island, the chase at sea to elude Monstro the whale—rank among the most terrifying moments in screen history. It was this full-bodied sense of drama that made PINOCCHIO so powerfully effective.

A series of sketches showing the preliminary version of Pinocchio, which was later scrapped. © Walt Disney Productions.

PINOCCHIO marked Disney's second feature success. Critics outdid themselves in singing his praise, and skeptics who had thought that SNOW WHITE could never be topped were silenced. Many people feel that PINOCCHIO was Disney's finest achievement in the feature-film category.

But now Disney surprised everyone by turning to a project so different, so unusual, that it would never be duplicated—by Disney himself or any of his rivals. The original title of the film was CONCERT FEATURE, but it was later changed to FANTASIA.

The genesis of this film was a SILLY SYMPHONY illustrating Paul Dukas's famous musical piece "The Sorcerer's Apprentice," with Mickey Mouse in the leading role. A chance meeting between Walt and Leopold Stokowski led to the great conductor's partic-

Mickey Mouse, as the Sorcerer's Apprentice, struggles against the tide of water he has magically created, in these animation drawings by Preston Blair from FANTASIA (1940). © Walt Disney Productions.

ipation in the film. Disney was exuberant, and his expectations for the short were realized by an enthusiastic crew.

The crew's enthusiasm, and the necessity of recording Stokowski with one hundred musicians at an outside studio, ran the cost of this short subject up to $125,000. At this point Roy Disney admonished Walt that there was no way to recoup their investment on such an expensive short. So, in the spring of 1938 (while PINOCCHIO was still in progress), Walt set in motion the idea of reengaging Stokowski for an entire feature, of which THE SORCERER'S APPRENTICE would be a part. Once struck by this idea, Disney plunged into the project with his usual fervor, telling chief engineer Bill Garity that he wanted a completely new projection and sound system for this film.

The next chore was selecting other pieces of music that, like "Sorcerer," would lend themselves to visual adaptation. The final selection included "Toccata and Fugue in D Minor" by Bach, "The Nutcracker Suite" by Tchaikovsky, "The Rite of Spring" by Stravinsky, "Pastoral Symphony" by Beethoven, "Dance of the Hours" by Ponchinelli, "Night on Bald Mountain" by Mussorgsky, and "Ave Maria" by Schubert. Debussy's "Claire de Lune" was recorded but not used in the film.

Each segment was designed to create a different mood and feature an individual animation style. "Toccata and Fugue," with its visual impressions of the sound track, was inspired by the experimental films of Oskar Fischinger. Ironically, Fischinger himself had proposed a collaboration with Stokowski in 1936; the project had never come to fruition, and now, three years later, Fischinger was on the Disney staff, helping to create this unusual sequence. But the committeelike atmosphere of the studio was stifling for an artist like Fischinger; moreover, both Disney and his artists have grave suspicions about and a certain contempt for the word "abstract."

In a studio newsletter, effects animator Miles Pike recalled the initial discussion of this sequence, when reference was made to Fischinger's work as "pretty good stuff." But he also recounted one of the other participants snapping, "We don't want anything like that, do we?" and someone else replying, "Hell, no!" Yet the whole idea of the sequence *was* the depiction of musical sounds as abstract figures, and the animators did take their cue from Fischinger's preliminary work. (Fischinger later left the studio, frustrated and unhappy.)

According to the studio newsletter, "One of the most arduous tasks in developing an overall style for the 'Nutcracker' was that of getting away from a ten-acre-lot type of staging, and finally achieving a tiny and intimate world as a stage. In this gnat's-eye view of things was fantasy finally found." The most memorable portion of this segment was the dance of the mushrooms, a disarmingly simple and eloquent piece of work.

Jules Engel recalls: "When I went to work on the Chinese Dance, the mushroom characters were already there, but the people who were working on that material had never seen a ballet in their life, and I don't think they ever went to the theater. One member of the group, Elmer Plummer, was a very fine colorist and drew extremely well. But he had never been exposed to the ballet, nor had the director who was running the unit. For me it was very simple, because I not only had animation background but I was already familiar with the world of dancing; there was no problem to take that thing and put it into continuity. Then Art Babbitt did the animation."

"The Rite of Spring" was chosen to depict the creation of the world. Walt wanted the result to look "as though the studio had sent an expedition back to the earth 6,000,000 years ago," and, to that end, his staff busied itself with extensive scientific research. Some of the practical solutions to animation problems had little to do with science, however. Bill Roberts told his colleagues: "Draw a twelve-story building in perspective, then convert it into a dinosaur and animate it." And art director Dick Kelsey composed a poem that expressed his particular dilemma in styling this segment: "The Rite of Spring is a moody thing/So make it dark as night,/With lots of jets and black silhouettes/But be damn sure it's light."

Personality animation was one of the key factors contributing to Mickey Mouse's success in THE SORCERER'S APPRENTICE. Fred Moore supervised the treatment of Mickey and redesigning him provided eyes with pupils for the first time on-screen. But the SORCERER depended on effects animation as much as any segment of FANTASIA, and art director Zack Schwartz recalls one particular achievement in this area: "Ugo D'Orsi animated the water in THE SORCERER'S APPRENTICE alone, by himself. He did the *cels* himself. He did it in pencil first, but then instead of handing it to someone in ink and paint, he did it all." D'Orsi shot film of water and studied it frame by frame—not to trace it, but to find the quality of water he could seize upon and animate.

The PASTORAL SYMPHONY is notable chiefly for the stir it created when the Hollywood Production Code office insisted that the "centaurettes" created by Fred Moore would have to wear brassieres. Artistically, its most interesting achievement lay in the attempt to create stylized backgrounds. "Forms were suggested rather than realistically presented," stated the staff newsletter.

DANCE OF THE HOURS was one of the film's best-received numbers, because it combined elements of music, dance, and comedy in such a delightful and unpretentious manner. The idea of alligators, ostriches, and hippopotamuses executing elegant and accurate ballet steps was irresistible, and the Disney artists gleaned valuable pointers from the drawings in this fanciful mode by Heinrich Kley. In addition to having actual choreog-

de force, with particularly memorable work from Howard Swift (on the ostriches) and Preston Blair (on the hippos). Says Blair, ''When directors like [Norm] Ferguson and T. Hee have animators that continue the creative process into their animation, instead of just grinding the stuff out, they deserve great credit for encouraging instead of stifling the animators' creative processes. Walt Disney felt very strongly on this point, and in FANTASIA it shows, as a production where the creative machine was tuned at full speed and running on every cylinder.''

Detail and more detail: Betty Reynolds adds finishing touches to a ''centaurette'' cel for FANTASIA.

raphy (which was inspired in part by live-action film of leading ballet dancers) the sequence had movement that was dictated by graphic considerations.

''Prior to rough layout we adopted a linear motif for each sequence,'' wrote art director Ken O'Connor. ''In the first sequence our motif was vertical and horizontal in design. This tied in with the vertical necks and legs of the ostriches, and as far as possible the birds were kept moving horizontally and vertically. . . . In the second sequence . . . we adopted the ellipse as a motif. This was more active than the previous one and tied in with the rotund hippos and their circular ballet movements. . . . For the sequence involving the crocodiles, we introduced a zig-zag motif as being most violent. It was related to the angular reptilian construction and carried out by diagonal paths of action.'' Similar thoroughness was evident in the decisions about use of color.

The animation in this sequence was a tour

One of the most famous single pieces of animation in FANTASIA is Bill Tytla's rendering of the Black God in NIGHT ON BALD MOUNTAIN. Disney knew that Tytla was the right man to tackle this weighty assignment and gave him all the help in the world to get the job done. Kay Nielsen's storyboard illustrations for this sequence pinpointed the crucial visual elements and movements, and Bela Lugosi was hired to enact the role of the Black God in live-action footage, which Tytla then studied. The result was a sequence that many feel has never been surpassed for sheer power of movement.

The BALD MOUNTAIN segment and its expression of evil are contrasted with the purity of the AVE MARIA segment for the film's finale. While this last section may not seem as intricate or expressive as Tytla's work, staffer Ed Gershman wrote in 1940, ''Some of the closest animation ever attempted by any animator in the studio was the animation of the nuns in the long pan. So close was this animation that the difference in the width of a pencil line was more than enough to cause 'jitters,' not only to the animation, but to everyone connected with the sequence.''

The technical problems in making FANTASIA must have seemed insurmountable at times. Sound engineer Robert Cook discovered that the studio's raw-film supplier had used a new kind of ink to edge-number the film, and it was flaking off and sending particles all over the film frame, which interfered with sound quality when the footage was reprinted. No cleaning solution seemed to work, and technicians had to actually paint out the almost-invisible specks.

In the camera department there were other headaches. "FANTASIA was the first feature to make use of the studio's two new multiplane cranes," according to the studio newsletter. "Of the over 8,000 feet shot, 3,500 feet was multiplane footage, more than in SNOW WHITE and PINOCCHIO combined. Due to an unprecedented amount of multiple exposure, the average exposure per frame ranged around the 2½ mark (20,527 feet of negative passed beneath lenses in order to produce 8,000 final screen feet)."

Adding to the technical challenges were the problems that Disney faced with Fantasound, a multitrack, multispeaker sound system that was stymied because of war priorities, which made mass installations of the equipment unfeasible.

When all was said and done, was this tremendous effort worthwhile? Some critics thought so, while others charged Disney with musical blasphemy. The public was equally divided in its reaction, with the masses who comprised Disney's major audience staying away, put off by the movie's highbrow connotations.

For the artists and technicians involved, FANTASIA was probably the greatest challenge of their careers. And Walt was unswerving in his sentiments about the project. "FANTASIA merely makes our other pictures look immature," he said at the time of the film's release, "and suggests for the first time what the future of this medium may well turn out to be. What I see way off there is too nebulous to describe. But it looks big and glittering. That's what I like about this business, the certainty that there is always something bigger and more exciting just around the bend; and the uncertainty of everything else."

Uncertainty was most assuredly the right word to describe Disney's prospects at this juncture, for the next few years held in store a series of events he never could have predicted.

The first blow was World War II. The outbreak of war in Europe cut off Disney's highly profitable foreign market at a time when he badly needed that revenue. All the profits from SNOW WHITE were poured back into studio expansion (and the construction of a modern new plant in Burbank), as well as into production costs on PINOCCHIO and FANTASIA. The inconvenience of being denied materials for Fantasound systems in 1940 was just the beginning of things to

Deems Taylor, Leopold Stokowski, and Walt Disney at a recording session for FANTASIA.

come. America's participation in the war, beginning in December 1941, stripped Disney of staff and vital supplies, such as color film stock, and then the government enlisted his all-out support for the production of wartime films. He was forced to give to government demands priority over those of paying audiences.

Another problem was the commercial failure of FANTASIA, coupled with heavy criticism in many quarters. This discouraged Disney, who had believed that his innovation would signal a new dawn for the animated cartoon. He could have taken the easy route and made a simple follow-up to SNOW WHITE AND THE SEVEN DWARFS, but instead he decided to venture into new and unexplored territory. He learned that such creative experimentation has its price tag. Plans to update FANTASIA on a yearly basis by inserting new musical selections were never realized.

The cruelest blow, many feel, was the bitter studio strike that occurred in mid-1941. Disney was a visionary, and a genius, but he was also a self-made man. His painful experiences with crooked distributors and disloyal employees during his first years in business helped to shape his views on success and turn him into a kind of benevolent despot.

No expense was spared when it came to production at the studio; Disney even instituted a bonus payment plan for what was deemed top-quality animation. But because Walt drove himself so hard, he expected the same degree of dedication from everyone in his employ. Many people worked nights and weekends to finish SNOW WHITE on time, with no such thing as overtime salaries to compensate them.

Disney felt the personal glow of success and thought his co-workers would share that feeling. But by 1940 the studio had grown to factory proportions, an analogy that seemed particularly appropriate to the new Burbank facilities, which lacked the ramshackle hominess of the Hyperion shop. Fewer people on the staff had direct access to Walt and consequently had no particular compassion for his dedication to the cartoon medium. They merely felt neglected and underpaid.

Disney's naive but stubborn attitude to unionism added fuel to the fire and inspired many upper-echelon artists to join the labor movement. Walt issued statements in which he spoke of union organization as a legal and proper procedure, but privately he was distraught that his workers would want to "band against him" after he had given so much to them and to the animation industry in general. His ill-advised attempts to quell the tide by firing union activists only made matters worse. On May 28, 1941, some five hundred picketers were lined up outside the studio.

The Disney strike is a complicated subject, with many serious questions to be considered on both sides of the fence, but one thing is clear: It seriously changed the atmosphere of the studio and affected the work produced there in years to come.

For one thing, Disney lost many of his finest men, including Art Babbitt and Bill Tytla, along with a younger group that eventually formed the nucleus of UPA—John Hubley, Dave Hilberman, Steve Bosustow, Adrian Woolery, Bill Hurtz, and others. For some of the people who stayed, the communal feeling and spirit of adventure were never recaptured. Certainly Walt was never quite the same in his attitude toward the staff.

It is ironic that in the midst of the strike RKO released THE RELUCTANT DRAGON, a live-action tour of the Disney studio showing the humor and harmony among the workers as they created cartoon entertainment. The most interesting and important section of this lightweight film, however, is the BABY WEEMS segment, a charming story about an infant with a genius IQ, which is told as a series of storyboard sketches, with minimal animated movement. At the time it was seen merely as something different; perhaps to some it was a "cheater" because it required so little work. But, in retrospect, BABY WEEMS foreshadows the stylization and "limited animation" of UPA. Whether consciously or not, some of the Disney artists were eager to show, as early as 1941, that there was more than one way to approach the animated cartoon.

Phyllis Bounds paints cels of Timothy the Mouse for DUMBO; a cel of the black crows rests on her desk.

The last Disney features to emerge unscathed by the problems of the strike or the war were DUMBO and BAMBI.

Says Dick Huemer, "The saga of DUMBO is a complicated one indeed, and not at all an easy, clear-cut one to delineate. All Disney's features started with a book, or establishing story. From there on it was worked up on storyboards by sections of story men and presented to Walt. Here at story meetings much was added and subtracted, by Walt and others. Many such meetings finally produced a result with which Walt would be satisfied. So much for this stage. Now the okayed sequence was moved into the director's room, where it was timed, broken down into scenes, and layouts for the animators, and moved into actual animation. Sweatboxing honed the sequence to as near perfection as Walt the arch-perfectionist could bring it. So much for the normal procedure.

"With DUMBO, however, there was an added step which had never occurred before. Step Two with storyboards and meetings had been taken and the original story idea (which in effect was all it really was) expanded, embellished, many of the new elements like Casey Junior arrived at—and

then, Walt dropped it. I don't know why.

"What happened some time later is what constitutes the unusual step. Joe Grant and myself, who had established ourselves as a writing team, took what had been done so far, and decided to see if we could rekindle Walt's enthusiasm for Dumbo. This was accomplished by putting the whole story line on paper, straightening out what appeared to be stumbling blocks, adding new material (such as pink elephants), submitting this a chapter at a time for Walt to read as a sort of continued novel. Walt was very enthusiastic about this way of operating (although it was never done again) and immediately put the picture back into production. Here it followed the normal procedure, where much, much more was added—gag, action, and dialogue. Despite the above aberration, DUMBO remains no less the characteristic community effort, common to all that goes onto the big screen."

Perhaps because of Huemer and Grant's groundwork, DUMBO was one of the easiest features the Disney staff ever tackled. Changes and problems were minimal once the film went into production, and everyone was imbued with the wonderful spirit and *simplicity* of the story about a flying elephant. Production time was short, and the cost was lower than for any of the features that preceded it.

Critic Cecelia Ager wrote, "DUMBO's the most enchanting and endearing of their output, maybe because it's the least pretentious of their works, the least self-conscious. It tries only to be a wonderful example of a form they themselves created—the fable expressing universal human truths in animal guise."

Besides heart and humor, DUMBO also boasted the studio's first surrealistic sequence, PINK ELEPHANTS ON PARADE. Later shorts, including DER FUEHRER'S FACE and PLUTOPIA, would draw on this sequence for inspiration, and segments of such features as THE THREE CABALLEROS, MAKE MINE MUSIC, and MELODY TIME would try to extend its principles, but PINK ELEPHANTS remains unique and unforgettable. Depicting Dumbo's psychedelic visions after he has swallowed a basinful of champagne, it perfectly captured the fantasy of the situation in a way no live-action film ever could. This was the animated cartoon at the height of its powers.

The naturalistic beauty of BAMBI was quite a contrast to the high-flying fantasy of DUMBO. Disney had purchased rights to Felix Salten's lyrical book about forest life in 1937 and realized that it would require a completely new stylistic approach. He assigned a special crew to work on BAMBI while the rest of the staff continued its chores for PINOCCHIO, FANTASIA, and other films. With occasional interruptions, this team spent five years perfecting the story, characters, and animation techniques for BAMBI.

Never before had Disney artists studied nature so closely. They knew that Bambi's story could only play against a backdrop that was completely credible, and that the characters themselves had to give the impression of being real animals. Caricature, exaggeration, and stylization were encouraged, but only as embellishments of reality.

The story, too, presented a different set of principles than those the Disney staff was accustomed to. There is humor in BAMBI, but the film is basically serious—a visual poem extolling the glory of nature, as seen in the cycle of seasons, and the unchanging pattern of life for the forest animals, from birth to maturity. One false step could have turned this delicate story upside down: a piece of comedy at the wrong moment, a heavy-handedness in the depiction of a new season.

But BAMBI stays on course from beginning to end and ranks as Disney's loveliest film. Its sentiment is honest, not cloying, and its visual evocation of nature is a tasteful compromise between an artist's fancy and a naturalist's authenticity.

Unfortunately, BAMBI was Disney's last major animated feature for a number of years. The financial burden of the war and the need to stimulate cash flow caused Disney to keep the pot boiling with less ambitious projects for the balance of the decade. None of these endeavors cut corners in any way, but they were simply less arduous and less time-consuming than SNOW WHITE, PINOCCHIO, FANTASIA, and BAMBI had been.

VICTORY THROUGH AIR POWER drew on realistic animation techniques the staff had refined while making training films for various branches of the armed forces. It impressed people with the propagandistic power of animation as it put into visual form

A DAY WITH MR. DISNEY

In which Motion Picture Herald gets a cover

Walt, arriving at the studio, is greeted by a reception committee bearing messages. . . .

The army and navy join Walt at the conference table. . . .

Joe Grant, offering an idea to Walt, holds him with his electric eye while Dick Huemer prays hopefully. . . .

—gives careful consideration to Donald Duck's comments about his work for the day. . . .

—eats lunch, talking to three tables at the same time. . . .

—enjoys a quiet cigarette while his mind roves. . . .

—answers fan mail. . . .

—speaks Mickey Mouse's voice, an assignment which has always been his exclusively. . . .

—journeys into the hall, where he is approached by persons having problems. . . .

—listens to the gang "selling" a gag in "Victory Through Air Power." . . .

Walt comes off the nest with Motion Picture Herald's Fourth of July cover idea. . . .

—hitches a ride with a car pool.

The drawings by Roy Williams, the words by Ralph Parker, from Disney's "Dispatch"—with variations.

A cartoon chronicle of Walt Disney's typical day at work, drawn by Roy Williams and written by Ralph Parker in 1943. It probably wasn't far from the truth.

the wartime theories of aviation expert Major Alexander de Seversky.

SALUDOS AMIGOS was merely a string of four short subjects linked by some live-action footage and the overall theme of America's "good neighbor policy." It served, in some ways, as a blueprint for the more extensive feature film, THE THREE CABALLEROS. This film had more of a story thread, although its segments were actually just as arbitrary and disconnected as the earlier efforts. But THE THREE CABALLEROS ventured beyond the realm of short-subject predictability with its bold and dazzling animation techniques. Some of the cartoon material resembles an early version of the Peter Max psychedelic style so popular in the 1960s; other moments, particularly in the title number animated by Ward Kimball, transcend the normal Disney boundaries and head toward lunacy by virtue of comic imagination and hairbreadth timing.

THREE CABALLEROS also boasted some of the most ingenious photographic processes seen to date in any Hollywood film. Most of them were developed by Ub Iwerks, who returned to Disney in 1940 to concentrate on such technical matters. An article in *Popular Science Monthly* explained:

This cartoon-over-live-action effect was achieved through a further development of the "process projection" already used by all major studios to place actors in front of previously filmed backgrounds. Disney's small projection outfit could place cartoon characters in the foreground, but live actors couldn't perform before a screen about twice the size of this magazine, and so several crews got busy on large-scale projections. Music and songs were recorded, and the cartoon action was timed to fit them. Optical experts designed and ground special quartz lenses to deliver maximum light from the projector. The sound crew set up a translucent plastic screen measuring 14 by 20 feet, placed the projector 50 feet distant on one side and the camera 25 feet away on the opposite side. The arrangement provided for the living actor to perform on the stage in front of the projected action of the cartoon, and for the Technicolor camera to record both. . . .

When cartoon characters are to appear in front of living actors, the job is easier than when it is the other way around. A movie of the live action is projected onto a front-surface mirror, which reflects the image onto a small screen. Transparent "cels" of cartoon characters are photographed against the screen by a camera mounted above.

THE THREE CABALLEROS marked the first time Disney had made extensive use of a combination of live-action and animation since the Alice cartoons of the 1920s. But the effects in this film were downright primitive in comparison to Iwerks's further develop-

ments for SONG OF THE SOUTH. The eye-popping sequences in this film weren't topped for nearly twenty years, when MARY POPPINS achieved the ultimate in live-and-cartoon juxtaposition.

The live portion of SONG OF THE SOUTH didn't impress anyone in 1946, but the cartoon segments were greeted as Disney's finest work in years. Indeed, these vivid retellings of Joel Chandler Harris's famous moral lessons, with Brer Rabbit, Brer Fox, and Brer Bear, are as close to perfection as one could possibly hope for. Here, for the first time in several years, outstanding character animation was combined with compelling story treatment—and audiences responded.

ICHABOD AND MR. TOAD, released three years later, maintained that standard in its presentation of Kenneth Grahame's *The Wind in the Willows*, one of the studio's neatest cartoon efforts. Like all great Disney films, this one artfully built a believable set of characters and situations on a fantasy foundation. What's more, the film adhered to a consistent *point of view*, telling the story of J. Thaddeus Toad and his adopted horse, Cyril, with wit and imagination.

The second half of this feature, "The Legend of Sleepy Hollow," is more conventional in outlook and treatment, but well crafted and very entertaining. All in all, ICHABOD AND MR. TOAD fared much better as a double entity than Disney's earlier pastiches of the 1940s—MAKE MINE MUSIC, FUN AND FANCY FREE, and MELODY TIME. Lacking the thematic unity of FANTASIA, these features rose and fell on the merits of each individual sequence, which ran the gamut from excellent to ordinary to downright bad. There was no way to rate them as cohesive units, and today it is academic to discuss their merits since most of the better segments (WILLIE THE OPERATIC WHALE, JOHNNY APPLESEED, and others) are shown as short subjects and no longer connected with the surrounding material.

Walt Disney's preoccupation with feature films and other projects turned the studio's short-subject department into a sort of stepchild. Whereas ten to fifteen years before seven-minute cartoons had been the company's bread and butter, its training ground, and its vehicle for new developments and ideas, by the 1940s this was no longer the case.

There was never any great profit in shorts, particularly as Disney spent more time and money on them than any other studio. But they created a valuable inventory, promoted and propagated the studio's starring characters, and kept the factory humming at a more consistent pace than features ever could. Disney always knew that when a feature animator was between assignments, he could put him to work on shorts to fill the time.

Like everything else at the studio, short subjects became a specialty, and from the late 1930s onward there was very little crossbreeding of talent from the feature-film staff. The shorts had their own directors, animators, writers, and artists. "Walt would get you into a position where the wheels were going smoothly where you were, and he was very reluctant to break up that situation," one employee recalls. This caused some resentment among talented people who had the ambition to move on to other things, and it also created a caste system within the studio.

Working on the shorts did offer one advantage over feature films, however, and that was a liberal amount of creative freedom for the director. Even though Walt kept tabs on the shorts and approved every film before

it went into production, the actual creation was in the director's hands.

Most of the short-subject directors of the 1930s—David Hand, Wilfred Jackson, Ben Sharpsteen—graduated to features by the end of the decade. Others, like Dick Huemer and Clyde Geronimi, later followed the same path, while Burt Gillett and Dick Lundy left the studio. This cleared the way for a new team of directors, all of whom had come up through the ranks; first four, then three in number, they were responsible for virtually all the short-subject output through the 1950s, and their personal styles developed in a way that working on feature films never would have permitted.

Senior member of the team was Jack King, who had been with Disney in the earliest days of Mickey Mouse, but left in the mid-1930s to direct for Leon Schlesinger. When he returned, it was to direct Donald Duck in his new starring series, which he did from 1937 to 1947. King was a capable, if uninspired, director who seemed to rely more on his story men than on his own comic or visual imagination. Many of his cartoons suffered from unimaginative presentation, and his unwillingness to "break loose" was a great frustration to one writing team in particular—Carl Barks and Jack Hannah. Barks went on to become the highly respected artist-writer of the Donald Duck/Uncle Scrooge comic books, while Hannah moved into the director's chair himself. When their work was good, it stimulated King, just as Roy Williams did much later with the stories for two excellent shorts, DONALD'S DILEMMA and DONALD'S DREAM VOICE, both released the year that King retired, in 1947.

Animator Jack Kinney made an impressive directing debut in BONE TROUBLE, one of the best Pluto shorts of all time, which has a memorable fun-house mirror sequence. But there were already several Pluto experts on the lot and no one to handle Goofy since Dick Huemer had launched him on his solo career in GOOFY AND WILBUR. There was also a logistical problem, as Pinto Colvig, the voice of Goofy, had moved to the Fleischer studio in Miami. The solution was found in a new format for the Goof devised by Ralph Wright and introduced in a segment of THE RELUCTANT DRAGON entitled HOW TO RIDE A HORSE. The only voice on the sound track was that of a narrator, as Goofy pantomimed the wrong way to achieve expert horsemanship, with highly amusing results. The success of this sequence led to a long series of Goofy sports cartoons, almost all of which were directed by Kinney.

Jack's brother Dick Kinney wrote the stories for some of these shorts and had a lot to do with the evolution of Disney humor during the 1940s. Both Kinneys sensed a changing approach to comedy in the contemporary cartoons of such rival studios as Warner

Violence about to erupt in HOCKEY HOMICIDE (1945). © **Walt Disney Productions.**

Brothers and MGM. While Disney had dominated the field in the 1930s, Bugs Bunny and Tom and Jerry were now the major stars, in brashly funny, fast-paced, often violent cartoons—a far cry from the Disney norm. The Kinneys worked to close that gap, reaching a peak of perfection in HOCKEY HOMICIDE (1945), a frenzied, furious satire in which the violence of a hockey game accelerates to the point where rapid-fire images of completely extraneous material (including a shot of Monstro the whale from PINOCCHIO) are hurled at the viewer to simulate sheer chaos.

Kinney also directed Disney's most famous wartime short, DER FUEHRER'S FACE, in which Donald Duck is an unwilling assembly-line worker in Naziland. Kinney's broad, brisk approach to comedy made him the ideal person to pilot this short, which had no use for cuteness or subtlety; it had to score a direct hit on the audience with its spoof of Hitler's overbearing government, and it did.

Like Kinney, Charles "Nick" Nichols was a staff animator whose promotion to the director's chair came about when someone else vacated the job. In this case, it was Clyde Geronimi, who'd been specializing in Mickey and Pluto. Nichols's affinity for these characters made him an obvious successor, although he lacked Geronimi's versatility. Nichols was soft on action and slapstick gags, but he continued the tradition of Pluto pantomime and guided Mickey through the last phase of his screen career in some pleasant low-key cartoons. His most unusual endeavor was Pluto's surrealistic nightmare in PLUTOPIA (1950), which echoed earlier dream sequences in DUMBO and DER FUEHRER'S FACE.

The last director to join the short-subject ranks—in 1944, the same year as Nichols—was Jack Hannah, who had gone from being an in-betweener to animator to story man.

Since his specialty in the story department was Donald Duck, he was given mostly Donald assignments and worked in tandem with Jack King until the latter's retirement. Hannah also developed Chip 'n' Dale, the mischievous chipmunks with high-pitched voices, who became ideal adversaries for Donald Duck. Hannah shared with Kinney a fondness for fast pacing and vigorous gags, as evidenced in some of his earliest shorts like NO SAIL (1945), in which Donald and Goofy are adrift at sea, and the excellent Goofy sports reel, DOUBLE DRIBBLE (1946).

Perhaps to avoid stagnation setting in, a pool system of writers and animators was used, with directors selecting each new story from various ideas submitted to them, then signing up four or five animators. Normally, certain people like to work together, but there was just enough variety through this method to keep the staff on its toes.

Walt Disney's first contact with a short was upon completion of a storyboard. He would come by and make comments or suggestions; when he approved, the film went into production. After the sound track was recorded, and animators finished the rough pencil tests of the action, a composite reel was assembled. "We would call a group of the younger people—the inkers, the painters, the ones most removed from production—and have a showing," Jack Hannah explains. "Then we'd have a written questionnaire about how they enjoyed it, what they didn't like, etc. Walt always sat in on those. When the people left, we'd all meet out in the hall and Walt would go over the short and the reactions. He wanted to hear the audience react, where the laughs were and weren't. There would be some discussion of changes, or a go-ahead, and that's the last time he would see it."

There were no rigid schedules, but directors, writers, and others came to know about

A storyboard sketch from DER FUEHRER'S FACE (1943). ⓒ Walt Disney Productions.

how much time they would have for each phase of production. A director might have as many as six shorts in the works at one time, each in a different department of the studio.

There is no question that the Disney shorts were beautifully packaged and expertly animated, but by the late 1940s they were, on the whole, routine. There are very few outright clinkers, but at the same time there are hardly any one can pinpoint as being special or outstanding. None of them recapture the flavor or impact of the great 1930s cartoons; at best they achieve a consistent level of formula comedy.

Perhaps this was inevitable. Despite Disney's large staff of writers, he could not avoid the problem every cartoon studio faced of finding fresh ideas and new approaches to starring characters after ten to twenty years. After a while, Jack Hannah says, "I got so damned tired of that duck's voice, I just could not stand having to work with it all the time," and one can assume that his colleagues harbored similar feelings toward their longtime "stars."

A partial solution came in the early 1950s when the short-subject writers and directors started branching out with one-shot cartoons—a latter-day return to the SILLY SYMPHONIES idea. At the same time, feature animators and directors like Ward Kimball, Wilfred Jackson, Clyde Geronimi, Hamilton Luske, and Woolie Reitherman returned to the short-subject field for special projects that departed from the character series.

Among the best of these were MELODY and TOOT, WHISTLE, PLUNK, AND BOOM, part of a projected series on aspects of music devised by Dick Huemer, and co-directed by Ward Kimball and Charles Nichols in a flat, stylized approach reminiscent of UPA; PIGS IS PIGS, another graphically stylized cartoon, by Jack Kinney; and BEN AND ME, a delightful featurette directed by Hamilton Luske about

Disney goes modern, with a vengeance: a scene from MELODY (1953). © Walt Disney Productions.

a Colonial mouse who inspires Benjamin Franklin.

Jack Hannah also hit his stride in the mid-1950s with the development of two new characters: a big, dumb, hungry bear named Humphrey and a fastidious forest ranger. The bear, animated in most cases by Bob Carlson, was introduced in a Donald Duck cartoon called RUGGED BEAR and then became part of the ranger series with Donald in 1954 and 1955. These cartoons, particularly GRIN AND BEAR IT and BEEZY BEAR, are belly-laugh comedies that can hold their own against the best of MGM and Warner Brothers, which seemed to corner the market in gag cartoons at this time. Humphrey and the ranger were successful enough to star in some of their own films, as well, without having to rely on the marquee value of Donald Duck.

Unfortunately, these entertaining films marked the end of an era at Disney's, for despite the modern accouterments of CinemaScope, stereophonic sound, and even 3-D, the market for shorts was shrinking. Disney could no longer justify spending as much as $75,000 for each seven-minute film, and at the end of 1955 he phased out his short-subject units, laying off some employees and reassigning others to work on the new *Disneyland* television series.

The studio continued to produce extra-length short subjects on an unpredictable schedule through the early 1960s. Some of them were quite good—ranging from Bill Justice's imaginative A COWBOY NEEDS A HORSE and NOAH'S ARK (done with puppet animation) to the tall tale PAUL BUNYAN. But for all intents and purposes the Disney short, as audiences had known it for thirty years, was dead.

While the 1950s saw the demise of short cartoons at the studio, it was also the decade that feature-film production took a giant step in the right direction. Since the mid-1940s critics had complained that Disney was off the track—that somehow he had lost the magic touch so evident in films like SNOW WHITE and DUMBO. It was difficult to muster the same enthusiasm for SALUDOS AMIGOS or FUN AND FANCY FREE that characterized the reactions to PINOCCHIO or BAMBI. These multi-episode films lacked solid story lines, and, consequently, they lacked heart and warmth, the qualities people liked best in Disney features.

With World War II and the labor tumult now part of the past, Disney vowed to return to bigger, better feature-length cartoons, and, as before, declared his intention to release a new feature every year. He made good his vow for three years running, thanks to overlapping production and juggling of talents.

The first new film in the "classic" tradition was CINDERELLA, released in 1950. Comparisons to SNOW WHITE were expected, but Disney had nothing to fear, for the new film could hold its own in any company. As before, the story crew created comic supporting characters (Jacques and Gus, the mice) to provide a balance with the human heroine and her adventures. Again, catchy and tuneful songs helped propel the story and endear the film to audiences. The film enhanced a traditional fairy tale with music, comedy, visual imagination, and charm. Not surprisingly, CINDERELLA was one of Disney's biggest cartoon successes at the box office.

ALICE IN WONDERLAND, released one year later, did not fare so well. Critics resented Disney's tampering with the Lewis Carroll classic, and audiences apparently found this story less appealing than the fairy tales associated with Disney. The episodic nature of ALICE and its hard-edged humor made it difficult to generate any empathy for the char-

acters. It emerged as a film with parts that outshone the whole; the animation of the Cheshire Cat, the procession of the cards, and the brassy tea party stand out. As CINDERELLA had yielded a hit song ("Bibbidi Bobbidi Boo") so did ALICE ("I'm Late").

Another year passed and another cartoon feature was completed: PETER PAN. This handsome, sure-footed retelling of the James Barrie fantasy, with its durable characters like Tinker Bell and Captain Hook, and consistently attractive production design, was one of the studio's most likable films.

Because films like CINDERELLA and PETER PAN did not startle the viewer with awesome visual innovations, there was a tendency to take the efforts of Disney's crew for granted. In fact, what had occurred between the time of SNOW WHITE and the release of these films was that the Disney staff had achieved that standard of perfection they sought so desperately in the 1930s. By the 1950s they reached the point many performing artists strive for: making what you do look easy.

Animation was no longer a novelty, to audiences or critics, and everyone was so accustomed to the impeccability of Disney's work that these films seemed facile and glib. In the case of PETER PAN, nothing could be further from the truth.

Creating a feeling of weightlessness in two-dimensional animated characters was quite a challenge, according to animator Milt Kahl, who declares, "There's nothing harder to do in animation than nothing. *Movement* is our medium."

Pinpointing the characterizations was no snap, either. Animator Frank Thomas told John Canemaker: "I had a particularly bad time getting started on Captain Hook. It was one of the low points of my life. These are the first scenes of him where he's walking, pacing the deck, saying, 'That Peter Pan! If I get my hook on him!', or whatever. I had four scenes. He was neither menacing nor foppish. This was because of the confusion in the minds of the director and story people. In Story, Ed Penner had always seen Hook as a very foppish, not strong, dandy-type of guy, who loved all the finery. Kind of a con man. Gerry Geronimi, who was the director, saw him as an Ernest Torrence: a mean, heavy sort of character who used his hook menacingly.

"Well, Walt could see something in both approaches, and I think he delighted in thinking, 'I wonder what the hell Thomas is going to do when he gets this.' If Walt would have ever said, 'Aw, I don't know,' fifty people would jump up thinking, 'Here's my chance to impress Walt.' They'd say, 'I think his head's too big. I think his feet are too small. I think he's too this. I think he's too that,' hoping Walt would say, 'Yeah, I think you're right.' This time Walt came to my aid, fortunately. He said, 'Well, that last scene has something I like. I think you're beginning to get him. I think we better wait and let Frank go on a little further.'"

None of these films was put together on the spot. Disney had begun preparations for PETER PAN as early as 1935. During the studio tour in THE RELUCTANT DRAGON (1941) one can see that figurines had already been cast of Captain Hook for use by animators. A tremendous amount of thought went into every animated feature before any footage was shot.

LADY AND THE TRAMP, Disney's next feature, was released in 1955, but Frank Tashlin recalled working on the story with Sam Cobean as early as 1940. LADY was something of a departure for the studio in that it presented a modern-day story (though technically set in the early part of the 1900s) and was not based on a well-known book. The staff created strong and likable characterizations for its canine cast and built an engaging film that

relied neither on strong story elements nor broad comedy. LADY AND THE TRAMP was a film of *personality* and low-key charm. It was also the studio's first feature in Cinema-Scope, the wide-screen process that caused considerable changes in the studio's approach to layout and editing, as well as requiring extra-length cels and backgrounds.

Disney made just one more feature in the wide-screen process and planned it as his masterpiece: SLEEPING BEAUTY. Released in 1959, SLEEPING BEAUTY was actually in progress for most of the decade. It was Walt's most expensive cartoon feature (six million dollars), and he wanted every dollar to show on-screen. The wide-screen Technirama process and stereophonic sound enhanced the animation, and helped make the film Disney's most elaborate and textured since PIN-OCCHIO. Another important departure for SLEEPING BEAUTY was its stylized, angular design for both characters and backgrounds, which replaced forever the soft, rounded figures of the thirties and forties that had gradually disappeared in the studio's work.

At the time of its release, SLEEPING BEAUTY came as a great disappointment to most critics, who made inevitable comparisons to SNOW WHITE and CINDERELLA, and accused the film of being heavy-handed. Much of this criticism was a backlash against Disney publicity, which touted the film as the ultimate in animation. Seen today, SLEEPING BEAUTY is an outstanding achievement in every respect, and if it lacks the jubilant spirit of SNOW WHITE AND THE SEVEN DWARFS, it has elements of maturity and sophistication that the earlier film did not have.

Production of SLEEPING BEAUTY revived the argument about Disney's use of live-action film. A full-length feature was filmed for the animators to study, and Disney told his artists to make the characters "as real as possible, near-flesh-and-blood." Some people, like Milt Kahl, rejected this method, calling it "a crutch, a stifling of the creative effort." "Anyone worth his salt in this business ought to *know* how people move," he added.

Almost as a reaction to the literalism in SLEEPING BEAUTY, the studio staff completely stylized the human characters in its next feature. Dogs were the nominal stars of 101 DALMATIONS (1961), but the most memorable character was the human villainess, Cruella de Vil, superbly animated by Marc Davis. In creating humans who were broad caricatures of reality, the Disney studio took a giant step in a new direction—and it did so in a completely disarming film that once more used the Disney specialty of playing fantasy against realistic settings.

101 DALMATIONS marked the first major use of a Xerox process that eliminated the process of hand-inking an animator's pencil drawings onto cels. This was a major time and money saver, but it also encouraged a roughness of line that completed the studio's move away from the 1930s style of drawing. Xeroxing had other benefits, of course, one of them being its duplicating potential; it is said, without exaggeration, that no one could have executed a film with 101 leading characters if Xerox hadn't existed.

By the 1960s the Disney animation team had consolidated into a tight-knit group, more uniform in its goals and consistent in its style than the large, broad-ranging teams that had collaborated on earlier films. Woolie Reitherman was named director, and Ken Anderson served double duty as art director and character designer. They steered the ship in collaboration with the studio's veteran "directing animators" Milt Kahl, Frank Thomas, Ollie Johnston, and John Lounsbery. (Ward Kimball, Les Clark, and Eric Larson—other members of the "nine old

men" team—left feature production to supervise other aspects of the Disney enterprises.)

It began to take longer to turn out each animated feature, since the crew was smaller than ever (with no short-subject talent pool to fall back on) and more responsibility was turned over to these six key men. THE SWORD IN THE STONE, released in 1963, took what seemed to be sure-fire material (E. B. White's account of young King Arthur's life) and fashioned it into a pat, unexceptional film with little of the Disney "magic" to recommend it.

THE JUNGLE BOOK, four years later, was the last animated film on which Walt Disney worked. One of Walt's major reasons for building a strong, reliable animation team was that he felt increasingly aloof from film production—both the live-action and animation departments. His mind was just as sharp as ever, and his ability to solve story problems and suggest simple solutions left even studio veterans in awe. But he sought new challenges and found them more in his amusement parks than in motion picture projects.

THE JUNGLE BOOK, released one year after Walt's death, was received with tremendous enthusiasm by critics and the public; it became one of the most successful cartoon features in the studio's history. But JUNGLE BOOK was less a great film than a showcase for great animation, and this has been a common factor in many of the studio's recent endeavors.

Animating full-bodied, expressive characters is what men like Thomas, Kahl, Johnston, and Lounsbery do best. Other artists provide a handsome backdrop and add dazzling animation effects. But breathing heart and soul into a film is not so easily accomplished. THE JUNGLE BOOK lacked this quality, and substituted for it a gallery of characters whose strongest identification was with the stars who provided their voices. The animators enjoyed working with people like George Sanders, Louis Prima, and Phil Harris, and incorporated elements of their performing personalities into the animated characters. Audiences naturally responded, so the animators felt justified in continuing this practice. "It is much simpler and more realistic than creating a character and then searching for the right voice," Reitherman contended.

But if referring to live-action film was a crutch in some people's eyes, using stars to provide actual characterizations was attributed to downright laziness. Phil Harris's breezy, bouncy manner as Baloo the Bear came across so well in JUNGLE BOOK that he was used again as Thomas O'Malley Cat in THE ARISTOCATS and Little John in ROBIN HOOD; all three were essentially the same

character, dictated by the same voice personality.

Using strong voices that communicate with an audience is a trick that Hanna and Barbera employed to overcome the lack of personality in their limited animation for TV. The same device didn't seem worthy of Disney.

Another trick, which was less perceptible to most viewers, was the reuse of old animation. The studio's methodical system of filing away old pencil sequences came in handy when someone wanted to consult a piece of animation from an earlier film to see how something was accomplished. But this procedure was taken one step further when, for example, a dance sequence in ROBIN HOOD was actually traced from original animation in SNOW WHITE.

In many ways the best Disney animation during the sixties and early seventies was not to be found in the full-length cartoon features, but in other less conventional assignments. Hamilton Luske directed the delightful animation in Disney's blockbuster hit MARY POPPINS, highlighted by the JOLLY HOLIDAY sequence in which farmyard animals sing of their affection for Julie Andrews and a quartet of penguins dance with Dick Van Dyke. Ward Kimball directed the equally engaging cartoon sequences in the less successful feature BEDKNOBS AND BROOMSTICKS.

A scene from Ward Kimball's Academy Award–winning short IT'S TOUGH TO BE A BIRD **(1969). © Walt Disney Productions.**

Kimball, who left features to supervise the Disney television show, also hit the bull's-eye with a half-hour featurette called IT'S TOUGH TO BE A BIRD, which defied every rule of Disney animation—and went on to win an Academy Award! This irreverent look at birds and flight incorporated cutout animation, clips from old Disney shorts, and a character that revealed its original pencil design through the Xeroxed cels.

The studio fared even better with a pair of

mini-films based on A. A. Milne's beloved
WINNIE THE POOH: WINNIE THE POOH AND THE
HONEY TREE and WINNIE THE POOH AND THE
BLUSTERY DAY. These cleverly conceived fea-
turettes managed to preserve the look of
Milne's original illustrations, while extend-
ing them into Disney territory. The half-hour
length effected an intelligent compromise
between short and feature, enabling the
story men and animators to build solid characterizations without either having to com-
press or protract their script. A third short,
WINNIE THE POOH AND TIGGER TOO, followed
in 1974; all three were directed by Woolie
Reitherman.

In the early days of the Disney television
show, Jack Hannah, Jack Kinney, and
Charles Nichols supervised the production
of new animation to link old shorts together
under various themes. There were no short-
cuts taken, and it was impossible to tell
where the old footage left off and the new
began. Other sequences combined live
action and animation, often showing Walt
talking to such characters as Donald Duck in
his studio office. But this kind of production
was costly and was generally discontinued in
the 1960s. Asked about producing cartoons
for television on a regular basis, Disney
replied, "We've developed our own cartoon
technique over a long period of years and it's
been pretty successful. Why should we
change? We could turn out a half-hour cartoon every week, sure, but it would be
cheating."

With Walt gone, and many of his veteran
animators dropping out of the picture, there
was a time in the late sixties and early seventies when it seemed that Disney animation
was going to die. Then a resurgence of interest in cartoons—and the phenomenal worldwide success of films like THE ARISTOCATS
and ROBIN HOOD—set the wheels in motion
so as not only to continue the animation

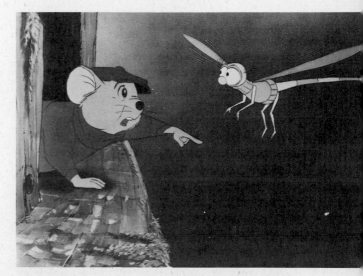

Bernard and Evinrude in the Disney studio's finest latter-day effort, THE RESCUERS (1977). © Walt Disney
Productions.

department, but find a way to keep it healthy
and growing. New artists were recruited
from colleges and art schools around the
country, and an apprentice/training program
was set up with California Institute of the
Arts, the university that Walt Disney was
instrumental in founding.

THE RESCUERS was the first feature to incorporate the work of studio newcomers with
contributions by the studio veterans. Whatever the resulting chemistry of such a combination, this unassuming feature about two
mice who set out to rescue a little girl who
has been kidnapped is the best cartoon feature to come from the studio since
101 DALMATIONS more than fifteen years
before. It has what so many other animated
films have lacked—heart.

It also has wonderful characters that come
from the imagination of their creators and
not from voice personalities. Madame
Medusa, Mr. Snoops, Evinrude, and Orville
the Albatross are figures that rank among the

richest in all of Disney cartoons; their existence is justified by a finely wrought script that holds the attention of the audience, making it a vicarious participant in the adventures of rescuers Bernard and Bianca.

THE RESCUERS carries on the great Disney cartoon tradition of fantasy treatment in its mouse-eyed view of the world. Every scene says, "This is an animated cartoon, not an imitation of live action."

What a good feeling it is to see this happen in a film that marks a watershed in the evolution of Disney animation—a swan song for some of the studio giants and a debut for some ambitious newcomers. One can only hope that as the younger men begin to shape the course of animation at the studio, they can assimilate the best of the past while embracing new and different ideas. No one would have wanted this more than Walt Disney himself.

"How very fortunate we are as artists," he said in 1940, "to have a medium whose potential limits are still far off in the future; a medium of entertainment where, theoretically at least, the only limit is the imagination of the artist. As for the past, the only important conclusion that I can draw from it is that the public will pay for quality, and the unseen future will take care of itself if one just keeps growing up a little every day."

Animation is still waiting for a new generation of Walt Disneys to follow this path of artistic growth and shape a full-fledged renaissance in this limitless medium.

Max Fleischer

3

MAX FLEISCHER'S CARTOONS were unique. In the silent era they sparkled with innovative ideas and technical wizardry, and during the 1930s their distinctive brand of humor put them in a class by themselves.

Still, Max Fleischer remains an unsung hero in the annals of animated cartoons. Two of his brothers, who contributed mightily to the success of his studio, are all but unknown. Even Fleischer's remarkable technical achievements have been largely ignored through the years.

Why?

First and foremost, Fleischer was not a good businessman. Although he held several important technical patents, he never retained ownership of his cartoons. He owned the rights to certain characters, but his biggest cartoon star, Popeye, was and is the property of King Features Syndicate.

Nor was Fleischer a good self-promoter. Animator Myron Waldman says, "I guess Disney had a better publicity staff and Max just cared about what he did rather than a lot of personal glory. I remember he wasn't too excited about merchandising. When he won a suit against somebody in Boston infringing on Betty Boop he remarked, 'I'm in the business of making cartoons, I'm not in the merchandising business.' Which I guess cost him a lot of money." This income was not superfluous; the profits from merchandising helped Disney defray the cost of making his sumptuous cartoons in the 1930s, and the continuing success of these products has helped to keep his name, as well as his characters, alive.

Another problem was Fleischer's modest outlook. He was more interested in mechanical innovations than artistic ones, and this hampered his studio at a time when Disney was setting a high standard for the competition to meet. During the twenties and early thirties, Fleischer had some of the most talented, and most promising, men in the animation field working for him, but most of them left the studio to go west and settle at Disney's. They recognized the challenge, and the potential for growth, that Max could not provide.

One New York animator who joined the migration but resettled in New York years later comments, "Those people who were quite content with the raw, peasant humor, the bad drawing, the kind of not-too-thought-out timing and the simpleminded stories . . . that bunch stayed here. The more adventurous, who really wanted to learn to do a better movie, left here. Every one of them. Nobody stayed who had that urge, because there was no way to make such a picture in New York. So, that marked a schism which exists to this day. And it's a very strange thing. The people in New York who later went down to Miami to work on GULLIVER and MR. BUG GOES TO TOWN [Fleischer's two feature films, made at his Florida studio], to a man they believed that any time that Max would give a little more time to work, they could have done all that stuff in SNOW WHITE AND THE SEVEN DWARFS easily, no problem. They had been self-hypnotized so they couldn't see the exquisite drawing which had nothing to do with their work."

This stunted artistic growth, which was curtailed completely when Fleischer lost control of his studio in 1942, cannot obscure the twenty-year period when he produced a series of ingenious and highly entertaining cartoons—cartoons that relied more on technical ingenuity and comical invention than artistic expertise to make them work. The Fleischer cartoons belong in a different context than Disney's; they create their own kind of magic.

Fleischer was born in Vienna, Austria, on July 19, 1883, and his life parallels that of many of his contemporaries. His parents emigrated to the United States when he was four, and Max grew up in Manhattan and then Brooklyn, New York. He had one older brother, Charles; three younger brothers, Joe, Lou, and Dave; and one sister, Ethel. At one time or another, all five brothers worked at the Fleischer studio.

Max studied at the Art Students League and Cooper Union in New York, but appar-ently he had no ambitions beyond putting his training to use in a steady job. He became a proficient cartoonist and commercial artist, and worked for a time as a photoengraver. While a staff artist on the *Brooklyn Daily Eagle,* he became acquainted with another, more established cartoonist named John R. Bray, who was later to play an important role in Max's film career.

Like his brother Joe, Max had great interest in mechanics, which helped him land a job as art editor of the magazine *Popular Science Monthly*. He later wrote, "While working with the *Popular Science Monthly,* I had an opportunity to write technical articles on the latest inventions and I began to wonder whether it wouldn't be possible for me to apply mechanics to the cartoons and make it a practical thing for producing motion picture cartoons by machinery. This was in 1915." Thus, Max's initial interest in animation was inspired by mechanics and not by artistic drive—an important factor in understanding his subsequent career.

Winsor McCay and John R. Bray had made animated cartoons by this time, but Max was intrigued with the idea of using a machine to create lifelike movement and take the guesswork out of animation. His idea was patented as the rotoscope, and this device was the raison d'être for his initial cartoon. The idea of the machine was elementary, although its construction was not: A camera projects a piece of live-action film, one frame at a time, onto a light-table, enabling an artist to trace the rear-projected image onto a piece of paper. The artist then turns a crank to proceed to the next frame and make his next drawing. Simply put, the rotoscope enabled an artist to trace live-action movements onto animation paper and achieve completely realistic results. Thus, a cartoon character could move and gesture just like a live actor.

For this experiment, Max worked with

brothers Joe and Dave. Joe was a wizard with machinery, but Dave filled an equally important function: He posed for the live-action film in a clown suit and was the initial model for Koko the Clown. (He also devised the scenario for this cartoon.)

"It was almost a year from the time we started that we got a piece of film a hundred feet long," Max later recalled. "A piece of film you could see on the screen in a minute. This represented a year's work but it proved that the theory was correct."

Max's next task was to sell someone the idea of producing cartoons with this process. The first man he went to see told the naive artist-inventor that the rotoscope was useless if he couldn't mass-produce films on a regular basis. Max thought it over and realized that it wasn't necessary to trace every single frame from scratch, since certain elements of the moving character remained stationary. With planning, observation, and experience, one could substantially reduce the amount of work and still produce a satisfactory cartoon. (Eventually, the rotoscope was to be reserved by Fleisher for use only in scenes requiring precise movement, and the balance of each cartoon was animated in freehand fashion.)

Fleischer went to show his sample reel to Paramount president Adolph Zukor and chanced to meet John R. Bray in the outer office. When Max explained his mission, Bray informed him that he had an exclusive contract to supply Paramount with short-subject product, but expressed interest in Max's film. Bray subsequently hired Max to produce one INKWELL cartoon a month, which appeared as part of his PARAMOUNT PICTOGRAPH screen magazine.

Production on this series was barely under way when the United States entered World War I, and Max was commissioned by Bray to work on training films for the Army at Fort Sill, Oklahoma, which he did until the time of the armistice near the end of 1918.

Meanwhile, brother Dave Fleischer had been gaining experience working as a film cutter, first for Pathé and then for the Army. This job gave Dave a fuller understanding of timing, which would prove all-important in his later work with Max. For a time Dave worked independently on his own cartoon projects.

After the war Max picked up where he had left off with Bray and introduced OUT OF THE INKWELL as a continuing feature of Bray's weekly screen magazine. Response was immediate. On April 21, 1919, an anonymous reviewer for *The New York Times* wrote, "One's first reflection after seeing this bit of work is, 'Why doesn't Mr. Fleischer do more?' After a deluge of pen-and-ink 'comedies' in which the figures move with mechanical jerks with little or no wit to guide them, it is a treat to watch the smooth motion of Mr. Fleischer's figure and enjoy the cleverness that animates it." Later that year the same reviewer wrote, "Mr. Fleischer's work, by its wit of conception and skill of execution, makes the general run of animated cartoons seem dull and crude."

About to switch affiliations from Paramount to Goldwyn in September 1919, Bray took a full-page advertisement in the trade publication *Moving Picture World* under the banner headline OUT OF THE INKWELL. It read: "In some of the past Bray Pictographs, we did a little experimenting with a brand new super-animated cartoon. We wanted to see how the public liked it. We wanted to see if they liked it as well as we did. They did. Already OUT OF THE INKWELL by Max Fleischer is the classic of animated cartoons. For humor, surprises, delicacy and accuracy of action, nothing has ever approached this feature. The little clown who grows right before your eyes out of the pen point and then shrivels up and flows back—just drops of ink—is known from Coast to Coast. He is going on with many new tricks, inspired by

A 1921 trade advertisement for OUT OF THE INKWELL.

Naturally, the fluid movement of Koko the Clown (referred to only as the Clown until 1923) attracted favorable attention, but the real novelty of Fleischer's films was the combination of live action and animation: Koko would materialize out of the cartoonist's inkwell or pen point and then interact with the live setting around his drawing board.

Max played himself in these films, posing as Koko's "master" and sometime nemesis. The endearing introduction of each film, in which Max seemingly drew the character and backgrounds right before the viewer's eyes, was accomplished by making a still photograph of Max's hand holding a pen and moving it frame by frame as the drawing was actually animated. The illusion was nearly perfect.

The Fleischers found that high-quality black-and-white still photographs could pass for "still life" in a moving picture quite well, and this was another major asset in the INKWELL's bag of tricks. To animate Koko hopping off Max's drawing board and shimmying down his chair, Dave Fleischer merely photographed the drawing-board setup and made a close-up of the chair. Koko was then inked onto cels that were laid over the black-and-white photos as if they were cartoon backgrounds. Again, the results were excellent.

Clever editing and juxtaposition could further enhance the live-and-cartoon combination. In MODELING (1923), for instance, a sculptor is working on a bust of a hook-nosed patron across the room from Max's drawing board. Koko has been making fun of the man, so Max tosses a wad of clay across the room, pinning Koko to the board. Now there is an actual piece of clay sitting on top of the cartoon clown as he struggles to move around and break loose. When he does, he hurls the ball of clay out of the frame; the picture cuts to live action as the

the genius of his creator and aided and abetted by the staff of Bray idea men."

Advertising hyperbole notwithstanding, this was unusual praise for a cartoon feature from its distributor, and provides some evidence of how highly Bray valued Fleischer's work. Before long he made Max a stockholder and officer in his corporation. But by 1921 Max felt he had outgrown his position in the company and decided to strike out on his own. Dave became his partner in a new company called Out of the Inkwell Films, Inc.

clay lands on the face of the unamused patron. Koko then sneaks off the drawing board and scurries across the room to climb onto the man's bust. Poking around the grotesque head, he eventually slips inside the mouth and disappears, only to astonish the patron, the sculptor, and Max as his journey beneath the clay surface causes the face to go through all sorts of weird contortions. A clay-covered Koko wriggles off the pedestal and down to the floor, hurrying back across the room in a delightful sequence of live stop-motion animation. The three men manage to grab him and hold on, but, unbeknownst to them, Koko squeezes out of his clay encasement and returns to Max's desk. Knowing he's in big trouble, he returns to safety inside the inkwell, pulling a stopper onto the well after him.

Without the aid of mattes, process screens, or elaborate devices, Max and Dave Fleischer presented an incredible variety of special effects in these films. Still dazzling after more than half a century is BEDTIME (1923), in which Koko seeks revenge on Max for stranding him atop a mountain peak on the drawing board—which for some reason is perched on Max's bedroom bureau. Koko hops off the bureau and goes to the edge of Max's bed. Balancing himself on the footboard, he breathes deeply, arms folded in a defiant position, and wills himself to grow larger. Before Max's very eyes (and ours, as well) Koko swells until he outgrows the tiny bedroom! Max runs outside in terror, and the next thing we see is a gargantuan Koko stalking the streets of New York in search of Fleischer. He towers over Manhattan's skyscrapers and, in one of the film's unforgettable moments, lifts the roof off a medium-sized building, sticks one arm inside, and pokes his fingers through the windows to see if a room is really empty. He finally traps his live-action master against a wall and peers

down at him with a ghastly leer. His giant hands reach forward (in a first-person shot from Max's point of view) and grab the frightened Fleischer, who squirms back and forth. At this point Max wakes up from what has been a terrifying nightmare—but, just to be safe, he runs to the drawing board and "pours" Koko off the easel back into his inkwell.

The shots of a giant-sized Koko amid New York's superstructures were accomplished by the simplest of means—animating Koko over a black-and-white still of the city—yet this kind of ingenuity was rare in films of the 1920s, and the sequence remains disarming and funny today. Special effects teams have rigged awesome sequences for recent Hollywood epics, but there isn't a scene in EARTHQUAKE or STAR WARS with the simple charm of Koko in BEDTIME.

The Fleischer studio was tiny (in 1923, the entire staff, ranging from Max to the office boy, numbered nineteen), but a wealth of

Max Fleischer puts Koko on the spot in SPARRING PARTNER (1924).

A giant-sized KoKo searches for Max Fleischer in downtown Manhattan; a highlight from BEDTIME (1923).

was assigned a sequence, with a vague notion of its leading to a particular point; another animator was to pick up the action at that juncture. In doing the scene, an animator might think of new ideas or be inspired to pursue a particular gag. This informal procedure accounts for the odd transitions—and frequent *lack* of transitions—from one sequence to the next. Since there was no rigid planning, animators might exceed or fall short of their estimated footage on the scene as well.

One of the first animators to join the Fleischers was Roland "Doc" Crandall, who stayed for many years. He was followed by Burt Gillett, Dick Huemer, Mannie Davis, and Ben Sharpsteen, all of whom came to the studio with some previous experience in animation. Because of this, it became unnecessary to rely so heavily on the rotoscope, and the device was held in reserve for special sequences.

However, Max devised a new invention called the *rotograph,* which gave the animators new flexibility in combining live action and animation. In this variation of the Rotoscope, a projector beams a strip of live-action film one frame at a time onto the underside of a translucent pane of glass. The animator then lays his clear cels of Koko on top of the glass, matching the cartoon to the live film, which is then photographed by a camera stationed above. This process enabled Koko to appear in a moving sequence instead of being limited to still photographs for his adventures in the real world. Unfortunately, the quality of the "sandwiched" elements was variable, since the live film was being rephotographed, but the results were more than adequate. It was a painstaking procedure, to be sure, and was used sparingly.

One of the most ingenious aspects of the INKWELL cartoons was always the initial appearance of Koko. Dave Fleischer tried to

inventive ideas emerged in its monthly INKWELL releases. Max had stopped animating to devote his time to running the business, which included seeking distribution for the films. They were parceled off to independent distributors around the country on a states' rights basis until the mid-1920s, when Fleischer formed his own short-lived distribution firm. Max continued to perform in the films, doing a creditable job because, in essence, he portrayed himself. There was no attempt on his part to be a Charlie Chaplin; he was just a benevolent figure at the drawing board sparring with his cartoon creation.

Meanwhile, brother Dave assumed the responsibility for directing the series. He initiated story ideas and worked with the animators to devise gags. All of this was accomplished on a highly informal basis. There was no storyboard, just a general idea of what the picture was about. Each animator

come up with a different way of presenting the character at the beginning of each cartoon, and it's impossible to find duplication in any of the surviving entries from the series. In SPARRING PARTNER Max draws Koko in pieces, all attached by a wire; when he pulls a string in Koko's stomach the clown consolidates into his lively self. In CONTEST he draws Koko in the process of walking—body first and then the head—for a remarkable effect. In MECHANICAL DOLL Max runs out of ink and can only fill in the top of Koko's suit in black, so Koko jumps up and down (this realistic motion was rotoscoped), letting the ink flow down through his costume. In KOKO'S CATCH Max draws a black ball, which bounces wildly around the screen; Max finally has to sprinkle salt on it to get the ball to stay put, then takes the squirming blob in his hands and stretches it out into the figure of Koko (a masterful illusion created by careful editing between live action and animated movements). Probably the wildest opening of all is that of KOKO GETS EGG-CITED, in which Koko takes pen in hand to "draw" the entire live-action background, including Max, as if it were a cartoon!

These tricks never wore out their welcome with audiences, but the cartoon sequences that comprised the "body" of many INKWELL entries left something to be desired. Here the disorganized nature of cartoon production at the studio showed through, and while no one could fault the actual animation, which was growing more fluid every year, the same could not be said for the scripts. The best subjects remained those that incorporated byplay between Koko and his live surroundings into the basic story concept.

In terms of gags, the Fleischer cartoons were certainly on a par with their competition, and this was due not only to the ingenious animators but to Dave Fleischer himself. Dave had shown artistic talent as a child, but never pursued it—or anything else, for that matter—too seriously. What he did develop was a fertile mind that learned to focus on gags, and this became his major contribution to the Fleischer cartoons. Dave left the business to Max, and the animation to his growing staff, but he kept the films stocked with a steady supply of laughs, which reflected his earthy and unpretentious sense of humor.

As for technique, the Fleischer staff used what was known as the "slash" system of animating first developed by Raoul Barré. This involved drawing and inking directly on paper (except in scenes with live back-

Koko the Clown and Fitz, as drawn by animator Dick Huemer in 1977.

grounds, in which cels were used), but retaining those elements of both character and background that remained stationary from one shot to the next. The cameraman would then "slash" the paper and join or overlap the appropriate pieces to create the completed picture. These would be held in place under a piece of glass while he would photograph it. Supposedly the use of high-contrast film eliminated the outlines of these paper fragments on the screen, but many surviving prints reveal them quite clearly.

Dick Huemer recalls that a heavy ink outline was adopted for these cartoons because of the film stock, so that the characters would remain bold and well defined against the stark white backgrounds. In the process, Huemer developed a remarkable skill with ink lines—a range, control, and subtlety he retains to this day. He also claims to have been the first animator to use an in-betweener. The Fleischers valued Huemer's work and reasoned that if someone assisted him by drawing in between his extreme poses, he could produce that much more. They were right; the in-betweener became a vital figure in the expansion of the cartoon industry. For the record, the first man to hold the job, working for Huemer, was Art Davis, Mannie's brother and later a respected animator and director himself.

Having established the INKWELL cartoons, Max Fleischer derived special satisfaction in the mid-twenties from a series of experimental projects. The first was a film explaining Einstein's theory of relativity, which ran four reels (about one hour). While not the first feature-length animated film, as some have claimed (except for some moving diagrams there is virtually no animation), it remains a milestone in Max's career.

For this endeavor, Fleischer collaborated with a respected science writer for the *New York American*, Professor Garrett P. Serviss, and enlisted the cooperation of some of Einstein's assistants. Max had already supervised a large number of factual and instructional films during World War I and understood how to communicate information simply and clearly to a general audience. When he and Serviss clashed over Fleischer's desire to use the phrase "stars twinkle," because of its scientific inaccuracy, the cartoon producer told Serviss, "Professor, perhaps this is the thing that you don't realize. I have read your articles for fifteen years and they always fascinated me, but when I got to the bottom of the column, if something I had read was not clear I went back and read that particular paragraph over again. Now, Professor, that's an advantage you have in writing which we do not have in motion pictures, because once we say something on the screen which is not clear, the audience cannot pull the film back to review it. We must tell our audience these facts in a language which they understand the first time. I agree with you that it is incorrect to say 'stars twinkle' but the audience will understand that and won't find it necessary to review the picture." Fleischer's pride in recounting this story in his 1939 studio autobiography was justifiable, for he truly understood the principles of producing successful educational films.

The reviewer for *Moving Picture World* was unqualifiedly enthusiastic.

Several months ago the scientific world was startled by a theory propounded by the German astronomer Einstein which was at considerable variance with accepted theories regarding the universe. . . . Because of the large amount of newspaper publicity accorded this revolutionary theory, considerable interest was aroused in the average person's mind as to what it was all about. This film, translated into non-scientific terms and with easily understood illustrations of the different points, is a commendable effort to satisfy this curiosity. The success achieved by the makers is greater than naturally would have been expected, and they have wisely confined themselves almost entirely to the more popular aspects of this complicated theory and have not attempted to delve deeply into the sections regarding the fourth dimension and the bending of light rays which Einstein himself is quoted as saying probably can only be clearly comprehended by about a dozen persons. . . .

There are two versions, one in two reels for theater use and one in four reels with drawings, examples, etc., that are a little more complicated and carries the explanations a little further, which is intended for schools and colleges.

Buoyed by the apparent success of this venture, Max made a second feature film EVOLUTION, in cooperation with the American Museum of Natural History. It ran five reels and, like its predecessor, combined live-action film, photos, diagrams, and rudimentary animation.

But Fleischer's most popular innovation was the creation of the BOUNCING BALL in 1924. Dave and Max have both taken credit for its invention, Max claiming that its antecedent was a pointer system he developed during the making of army training films in 1917. Whatever the case, the novelty device quickly became one of the studio's most durable assets.

It should be emphasized that the Fleischers in no way invented the sing-along film. Song slides showing the lyrics of well-known tunes were a staple in theaters long before movies were popular; a live singer or musician would invite the audience to join in song. Later, film producers adopted this idea, either committing the actual slides to motion picture film or illustrating lyrics with drawings and live-action footage.

The Fleischers were the first to bring movement to what had been a static presentation and to imbue the traditional sing-along with humor and invention. Furthermore, these animated cartoons created a unique bond between the film and its audience—a two-way communication that transcended the traditional active-passive roles of performer and viewer in a lively and entertaining manner. Dick Huemer, who animated the initial Song Car-Tune, OH MABEL, recalls that at its first showing in New York's Circle Theater the audience response was so strong that the theater manager immediately rewound the print and ran it again.

The distribution of these films sometimes caused anxious moments for organists like Harry J. Jenkins, who recalled in an article for *Theatre Organ Bombarde*, "I played for many bouncing ball song films in Boston theatres between 1924 and 1927. Sometimes they had been used in other theaters before coming to mine, and arrived with some frames missing—something I didn't discover until rehearsal—if we had one. It was a puzzle to follow the ball as it bounced completely past two words to a third, at the expense of a couple of measures of music. Somehow we still managed and the audience sang along."

These early sing-along films were framed by cartoon sequences with Koko the Clown, but the bouncing ball itself, which lit on each word of the lyric in time to the song, was not animated at all. It was live-action film of a Fleischer employee holding a long stick with a luminescent white ball on the tip, bouncing the ball by hand in time to music while another man turned a large drumlike cylinder on which the lyrics were printed. One line at a time was exposed to the camera, which filmed this action with high-contrast

A typical example of how the Fleischer animators brought a song's lyrics to life, from the advertising short IN MY MERRY OLDSMOBILE (1930).

film; the pointer itself was never visible. For further clarity, the film was processed in negative form: white letters on a black background.

In addition to the bouncing ball, these car-toons featured ingenious visual ideas during the second or third chorus, in which the ball would be replaced by a cartoon character hopping over the words. For instance, Fitz the dog grabs the "I" from the first line of "In the Good Old Summer Time" and uses it as an umbrella, bouncing over the words as it starts to rain; on the next line of the lyric, lightning bolts strike each word just as Fitz hops off, obliterating the words and clearing the screen for the next line to follow.

The brief cartoon introductions to these songs are quite amusing as well. Conductor Koko grabs Fitz at the beginning of IN THE GOOD OLD SUMMER TIME and shakes him into the shape of a tuning fork. He strikes the instrument against his music stand, it produces a note, the fork turns back into Fitz, and the dog promptly swallows the musical note! In DARLING NELLIE GRAY the clown introduces The Koko Kwartet, "full of harmony, melody, and chicken salad," to sing along with the audience.

But the greatest novelty of all came shortly after the introduction of these Song Car-Tunes, when orchestra leader and theatrical entrepreneur Hugo Riesenfeld introduced Max to Dr. Lee DeForest, who was then experimenting with talking pictures. DeForest had created a synchronization process that he displayed in a series of short subjects called *Phonofilms*. Unfortunately, the film industry was not prepared to embrace DeForest's idea as a practical reality, and both the films and his invention were largely dismissed.

DeForest was persistent, however, and he devoted much of his time to signing "name" performers to appear in his films, hoping to give the primitive shorts box-office value. Fleischer's sing-along series seemed to be a natural for this treatment, and Max responded to the idea with great enthusiasm—after all, it was one more step in the technological development of cartoons.

Thus, four years before Walt Disney's STEAMBOAT WILLIE, Max Fleischer produced a series of synchronized sound cartoons with DeForest. MY OLD KENTUCKY HOME, reportedly the first, was sung by the Metropolitan Quartet, with Jimmy Flora at the organ. A dog plays the "Anvil Chorus" on his teeth with a mallet, then "My Old Kentucky Home" on trombone. Finally he turns to the audience and says, "Follow the ball and join in, everybody." His lip movements are animated with great care, and the line is read on the soundtrack very deliberately—but at least in surviving sound prints the synchronization is just a bit off. The match-up on the earlier "Anvil Chorus" is much better.

Still, it was a beginning, and an ambitious experiment. Most subsequent song cartoons eschewed dialogue and stuck to the basic bouncing-ball formula; this was not only easier for all concerned, but it enabled Fleischer to release the same prints without sound tracks through his normal distribution channels.

In many ways 1924 was Fleischer's busiest year. He formed his own distribution firm, Red Seal Pictures, with Edwin Miles Fadiman, and filled a substantial release schedule with live-action films. Some were purchased from other independent producers, and some were filmed by the Fleischer studio. Red Seal released the ANIMATED HAIR cartoons by the noted caricaturist Marcus (not the well-known animator Sid Marcus, as often reported), in which celebrity caricatures cleverly evolved from one to another by the movement of a few basic lines. Max also became interested in a slow-motion film process developed by the Novagraph Company and co-produced a series of shorts called MARVELS OF MOTION that examined various familiar actions through the use of slow motion, still frames, and reverse motion. Red Seal advertised a total of 120 subjects for the 1924–25 season, only 35 of which were Fleischer cartoons.

However, Red Seal was plagued with problems, both financial and personal, and

after two years the Fleischers were broke. They were bailed out by a businessman named Alfred Weiss, who arranged for them to release their films through Paramount in 1927. Weiss turned out to be a crook, but the Fleischer association with Paramount endured.

The OUT OF THE INKWELL cartoons of the late 1920s show the same strengths and weaknesses as the earliest entries in the series. When they're good, they can stand alongside the best animated cartoons ever made, but the potboilers that filled out the yearly release schedule are just that—time fillers that coast on the amiability of the characters and INKWELL format. In order to meet increased demand for the cartoons and produce a new title every few weeks, it was necessary to cut back on the amount of live-and-cartoon interaction. Some 1927–29 titles have hardly any live footage and substitute constant movement for real imagination. But these alternate with INKWELL gems that rank among the series' all-time best.

The blending of live action and animation had not lost its appeal, and the Fleischers somehow found new ideas with which to show off their technique. In KOKO'S EARTH CONTROL, Fitz mischievously pulls a lever that bears the notice, "Danger/Beware—If this handle is pulled, the world will come to an end." The world doesn't actually expire, but through a variety of camera tricks, it seems to go crazy: Normal actions of walking and driving are accelerated to a terrific speed, buildings seem to fall as the earth is tilted, and pedestrians find themselves sliding along the sidewalk! Other films provided a national audience (not to mention latter-day viewers) with glimpses of 1920s New York, ranging from mid-Manhattan side-

A sample of metamorphosis, as seen in KOKO THE KOP **(1927).**

walks to Coney Island's renowned Cyclone roller coaster, which an animator rides in KOKO SQUEALS.

The introduction of Koko continued to be a highlight of each new effort. In KOKO THE KID a blob of ink emerges from Max's pen; he spins it around the paper for a while, then holds the pen in place as the blob dribbles down and "pours" into a silhouette of Koko. And the increasingly clever use of metamorphosis, involving Koko, his dog pal Fitz (who with Koko formed the newly named Inkwell Imps), and incidental characters, gave these films a unique quality among the by-now distinctive cartoon output of rival studios.

Metamorphosis—the evolution of one object into another—was not a new idea; it formed the foundation of Emile Cohl's earliest animation experiments at the turn of the century. But the Fleischer animators' use of this device bordered on the surreal, as in KOKO THE KOP. Constable Koko is chasing Fitz, who suddenly jumps onto a wall and becomes a window, complete with an attractive housewife inside! She flirts with Koko, he kisses her, and during the kiss she and the window metamorphose back into Fitz. This film continues its parade of bizarre visual ideas as Koko and Fitz keep pulling backdrops aside or lifting them up to reveal others behind, then running through previously undefined "holes" in them to continue the chase. Finally, Koko is pursuing Fitz on a straightaway. The camera then reveals Max Fleischer hand-cranking a roll of paper on which the background is drawn, with his characters blithely running along as he creates the treadmill effect. Max curtails the chase by taking a scissor and cutting the paper right between Koko and Fitz, to their great amazement. They hop off the paper onto his desk, Koko running his hand along the cut edge of the paper in wonderment before joining Fitz back in the inkwell.

Koko also figured in two decidedly non-surreal films around this time. The first was commissioned by the American Telephone and Telegraph Company in 1927 and explained in simple terms the complex workings of the country's major telephone system. It was called THAT LITTLE BIG FELLOW. Two years later, the Fleischers were given a similar assignment by the Western Electric Company, which wanted a film that would explain the mechanics of movie sound tracks; this successful effort was called FINDING HIS VOICE.

The addition of sound to Fleischer's cartoons in 1929 put the studio on firmer footing than ever before. Like most of the animation industry, the Fleischer brothers had gone just about as far as they could in the silent medium; certainly they had mastered its technical problems, and, artistically, there seemed nowhere else to turn in the mass production of short entertainment reels.

Sound presented the film makers with a new and exciting challenge and gave the moviegoing audience a breath of fresh air.

Max has his characters on a treadmill, in KOKO THE KOP.

Paramount enthused in a June 1929 trade advertisement: "Paramount TALKARTOONS are something entirely new and entirely different from anything ever seen and heard before. For the first time cartoons will be actual talking pictures, not merely cartoons synchronized after their creation. By a special process, the cartoon figures will actually talk. The novelty value alone of the TALKARTOONS will make them successful. But, in addition, they will tell complete stories and will be brilliantly entertaining."

The Paramount ad was correct in calling the series "actual talking pictures," but, ironically, the Fleischer brothers decided to synchronize the dialogue and music in their films *after* the animation had been completed. Thus, a low priority was placed on precise lip movement, and dialogue itself was kept to a minimum, letting peppy music carry the audio burden of the initial TALKARTOON releases.

In an attempt to emphasize the "newness" of this all-talking series, Koko the Clown was temporarily put out to pasture, and for the first time the Fleischer staff had to dream up cartoon ideas that didn't fit into a prescribed formula. Because they were no longer going to use a combination of live action and animation, it was decided to implement a full range of gray tones in the backgrounds. Consequently, the silent-era slash system of animating in the black-and-white line-drawing format was abandoned in favor of the more widely used cel-and-background technique. This change necessitated hiring a larger staff. Another important addition was brother Lou Fleischer, whose musical knowledge made him the ideal choice to supervise that aspect of the studio's productions. He also became the resident expert on sound and its application to the cartoons.

"The dialogue was what they called post-synched," animator Al Eugster recalls. "In other words, Lou Fleischer would give us some kind of a metrical breakdown on the dialogue, 'I am going to the store.' We'd work it from that and then they would dub it in later, which wasn't a good way to work, obviously. The dialogue was very stilted because of the metrical breakdown." At the same time, this technique enabled the voice performers to add their own ad-libs to the sound tracks under their breath, an aspect of Fleischer's early-thirties cartoons that gives them tremendous charm today.

There was not yet a musical director on staff, so for the earliest talkies Lou Fleischer would purchase the rights to an existing record, which would then form the basis for a cartoon and give the animators a definite sound track to match. Accounting for every change in tempo, mood, and sound on the record with coherent action on the screen was quite a challenge. "We got to be experts at throwing rolled-up pieces of paper with bad ideas into the wastepaper basket," says Shamus (at that time known as Jimmie) Culhane.

Amazingly enough, the Fleischer operation in the early talkie era was just as informal as it had been at the outset of the 1920s. "To begin with," says Al Eugster, "we didn't have a story department. Eventually, we got Bill Turner working on stories. From that evolved story meetings and Dave would be in on that, plus the animators. But I don't remember seeing a script there in the beginning.

"We were concentrating on animation, but in the meantime we were absorbing other functions like the layout and so forth, which was good experience. Then eventually they got into the head animator system, where the head animator would do those layouts and stage it, and give out the work to the animators, besides doing animation himself.

"We had about four groups going; one head animator with three animators repre-

These scenes from I'M FOREVER BLOWING BUBBLES *(top left and right)* **and** LA PALOMA *(bottom left and right)* **give a pretty good indication of the comic appearance of Fleischer's early talkies (both 1930).**

senting the group. I still don't remember typewritten scripts. There was just a rough idea of what the story was about. Dave would furnish the head animator with the story and the head animator would lay it out, stage it, and break it into scenes. There was no control of footage. Today, we have what you call bar sheets or music sheets, and we time out one scene after the next, so we have some idea of what the overall footage will be.

Here, we just sort of ad-libbed, especially when Dave came around adding gags. I know I usually ran over footage on a picture, never could control it.

"We didn't have pencil tests at that time. They did have Bill Turner and Nellie Sanborn, who would take the young animators' work, flip through it, and retime it. You see, they had more experience in timing than we did. All I could go by, at the time, was a cheap watch that had a loud tick. I figured four ticks a second, and each tick would be six frames. So I sort of worked out my timing on that basis, rather than with a metronome, which we also used. I'd go through an action, and count off one, two, three, four, five, and then break it up and get my basic timing. But even then I could misinterpret, like characters falling from the ceiling to the floor. I'd go one, two, three and that felt all right when I counted it out, but when we got it on the screen—or rather, when Bill Turner called it to my attention—he'd say 'That's too slow, they're *floating* down.' So Bill cut out some drawings and it worked pretty well. Then, of course, when we saw the work that we did on film, we would profit by our mistakes.

''Dave Fleischer would make the rounds every morning and say, 'Let's see now, what gag can we get into this scene?' He'd say, 'You need a gag here? The worm comes out and says "Oh, my operation!"' or something like that, some touch. Once in a while, Dave would mention something to me and I'd rub my chin—it didn't seem very funny to me—and he'd say 'OK, Al, we'll try another one.' Then he'd go on to the next animator and do the same thing. Once he sat down next to Shamus and said, 'Jimmie, we need a gag here,' and he rubbed his chin. Dave said, 'Don't do that, Eugster does that!' He didn't want everyone mulling over his gags that didn't go over.''

Shamus Culhane remembers, ''His favorite thing was some ad-lib, a crazy ad-lib he would just hang on the story like you would hang a banana on a Christmas tree—whether it went or not. I was working with Rudy Zamora on THE MAINE STEIN SONG, a bouncing-ball picture, and Dave came around. They used to make a tracing of the line of lettering, so that you could change it into some object, so I had this tracing that said, 'Shout till the rafters ring.' Dave came along and said in that great flat voice of his, 'You got a gag?' I said, 'No, I just started this.' He said, 'Wait a minute, I'll give you a gag.' He looked up at the ceiling, and he looked and he looked and he finally said, 'What the hell is a rafter?'''

Sometimes Dave's enthusiasm for shoehorning gags into already existing sequences would drive animators slightly batty. Having planned a scene for THE PEANUT VENDOR in which a monkey jumped from bar to bar leaving fleas behind, Myron Waldman found that Dave wanted him to work in a throwaway gag besides, in which one flea would fall to the ground and then two fellow fleas would come in with a stretcher and carry him off. Waldman managed to convince Fleischer that because they were animating to a prerecorded song, there wasn't time to slip in this piece of business.

It was not only the quantity but the quality of gags that made the Fleischer films unusual. Dave Fleischer's sense of humor was broad, direct, and somewhat vulgar; most of the animators working with him were able to respond to this kind of material and embellish it in like fashion. ''These were East Side Jewish kids or people like me, raised in very broad ethnic surroundings,'' Shamus Culhane says. ''So they had this very vigorous style . . . kind of earthy, certainly very crude, but honest . . . I mean, nobody was putting on anything, this is really how they were.''

Fleischer films of the early 1930s abounded with ethnic jokes, sexual humor, visual and verbal gags that were aimed at adults in the audience, and not at children. (Paramount liked that idea. Promotional copy for the Talkartoon DIZZY RED RIDING HOOD enthused, ''This one is wow-packed with smartness for the sophisticates, and fun-filled with rollicking humor for the plain-minded. Fleischer has done a Lubitsch here. What a show!'') At the same time, children could not help but be amused by the strange-looking characters that populated these cartoons. If they weren't cross-eyed, they might be wall-eyed or at the very least goggle-eyed. Their bodies were arranged in odd proportions, and deformities of every kind were common.

This went hand in hand with the visual flavor of the films. The ambiance (so to speak) was strictly New York–inspired, as opposed to the sunny barnyard settings and characters that abounded in cartoons produced on the West Coast, mainly by men who had grown up in the rural Midwest. The Fleischer crew not only grew up in New York, but lived and worked there; its gray canyons, seamy characters, and unique sensibilities permeated their work. There was no mistaking the gritty appearance of a Fleischer film.

The studio's first starring character of the talkie era was Bimbo, whose very name was derived from ethnic slang. Like so many characters at this time, Bimbo was nondescript—so much so that he changed appearance in virtually every cartoon during his first year on-screen. The most that could be said for him was that he bore no resemblance to Mickey Mouse—a major distinction in the early 1930s.

But the Fleischer cartoons didn't depend on characterization to put them across; they were fashioned on a foundation of music and gags. Sometimes the music itself would become a gag, as in GRAND UPROAR when four bizarre-looking mice sing the "Sextette" from *Lucia*, or YOU'RE DRIVING ME CRAZY, in which various jungle animals take turns mouthing the scat-singing vocal on the sound track. Fleischer's affiliation with Paramount Pictures enabled him to use Paramount songs, so the 1930s product is full of such tunes as "Mimi," "Isn't It Romantic," "Beyond the Blue Horizon," and "Love Me Tonight." It's a sure bet that songwriters like

Rodgers and Hart never dreamed their feature-film scores would wind up as background music for Bimbo!

Paramount also offered Fleischer the use of their newsreel recording studio in Manhattan, and access to certain performers who were contracted to appear in New York–filmed features and shorts. Thus, Fleischer was able to enhance the appeal of his "Screen Songs" series with the Bouncing Ball by adding live-action footage of such stars as Rudy Vallee, Ethel Merman, Lillian Roth, and The Mills Brothers. Cartoon footage would generally frame the appearance of these stars, who would invite the audience to join in song with the bouncing ball. Dave Fleischer made sure that the series did not go stale, even though the innovative "second chorus" animation was abandoned at this time. Often the introduction of these live performers was handled in a novel manner (The Mills Brothers are pieced together like a jigsaw puzzle, Rudy Vallee comes to life on a piece of sheet music, and so on), while other times the cartoon footage transcended its usual incoherence to come up with a solid gag structure. SHE REMINDS ME OF YOU, for instance, is a hilarious spoof of the Roxy Theatre with all its gilt-edged grandeur; THIS LITTLE PIGGIE WENT TO MARKET features a very funny takeoff on newsreels; and STOOPNOCRACY features radio humorists Colonel Stoopnagle and Budd with some ridiculous inventions.

At this time Paramount, like several other major studios, owned a chain of theaters, and in the early days of the Depression, the corporation engineered a new moneymaking scheme. Paramount offered advertisers the opportunity to exhibit an entertaining short subject which would carry a "soft-sell" promotion for their product in 100 theaters. The cost to advertisers was $15,000 (or $150 per theater), and Paramount tried to allot no more than half that amount to produce the short. Each film was seen by an estimated three to four million people. Max Fleischer produced a series of such films, including A JOLT FOR GENERAL GERM (on behalf of Lysol), IN MY MERRY OLDSMOBILE (Oldsmobile), SUITED TO A T (India Tea Company), STEP ON IT and TEX IN 1999 (both for Texaco). Since the idea was to plug the sponsor's product in an entertaining way, these films were conceived and created like any other Fleischer cartoon. Indeed, one surviving title, IN MY MERRY OLDSMOBILE, is a delightful short, with a bouncing-ball chorus, that ranks alongside any contemporary Fleischer cartoon in terms of quality and content.

The Talkartoons are an odd lot. Any semblance of a script in them is strictly coincidental ("Our story conferences might last as much as a whole hour," recalls Culhane), and many of the films veer off in two or three directions, coming to a stop, but never really to a conclusion. Others seem to find their own path and follow through with clever comic ideas—WISE FLIES, for example, and the excellent SKYSCRAPING.

The sixth Talkartoon of 1930 introduced the character that became Betty Boop. In DIZZY DISHES she was actually a hybrid of a dog and a sexy girl, with a voluptuous feminine body but dog ears and a canine nose. (Why make her a dog at all? To appeal to the natural instincts of Bimbo, himself a humanized dog.) This character was invented and drawn by Grim Natwick, a Fleischer veteran of several years with a substantial background not only in animation but in art. Animation historians, as well as Natwick's colleagues, agree that only he would have had the ability and the confidence to devise a female character with an even remotely realistic body. Hardly anyone else in the studio could animate it.

During the next year this character without a name turned up in other Talkartoons. Response to her was strong, but the Fleischer staff kept changing her appearance. Natwick had modeled her after popular singer Helen Kane, and various women who could imitate her cutie-pie voice and delivery were hired to do the sound track. Eventually, Shamus Culhane and Al Eugster joined Natwick as "specialists" in drawing this character. "Grim had a big advantage," Culhane says. "When he was about twenty-something, he went over to Germany and he painted for two years; he was a fine artist. So I really tried to do as he did. I tried to make an arm that was an arm, and not just a kind of stick with a hand on it. Most of the guys couldn't do that. They didn't get much of a feel for the impossible gracefulness of the character."

(The ongoing informality of the animation business is indicated by a story that longtime colleagues Culhane and Eugster relate about how they got to be animators. In mid-1930, as the studio was about to start on a picture called SWING YOU SINNERS, four or five of Fleischer's most experienced animators suddenly broke their contracts and left for California. "So," recalls Eugster, "Max called all the young fellas in; Rudy Zamora, Culhane, George Cannata and myself. He said, 'Now you're animators.' That's it. Before, we were just doing a scene here and there and doing the best we could." Culhane picks up the story: "Teddy Sears and Grim Natwick coached us through that movie. Both very nice guys. I remember, Grim would come over with a big cigar and he'd look down and say, "Wellll, you know that's pretty goddamn nice. I'll tell you, though. . . .' and then he'd fix the whole thing up. And Dave was nice. He used to come around and say, 'You're doing fine.' Doing fine? I think I lost about six pounds in a month." Says Eugster, "We were officially animators, but we had to struggle to make it work." Is it any wonder that the quality of drawing in Fleischer's cartoons was so inconsistent?)

Betty Boop remained a member of the

Fleischer repertory company through 1931, when she began to figure more prominently in the cartoons and establish her own personality. Koko the Clown was brought out of retirement to join Bimbo in "support" of the new star. The dog ears and nose were forsaken, and a model sheet standardized her appearance, although some animators continued to have trouble dealing with the oddly designed character (oversized head, no visible neck, small torso, but exaggerated hips and thighs). No matter that Betty didn't make sense anatomically: she was adorable.

She was also the first animated cartoon star to deal with sex. In one of her first starring Talkartoons, BOOP-OOP-A-DOOP, she's propositioned by her boss, a circus ringmaster. This lascivious lecher waits to get her alone (in a close-up we see his pounding heart licking its lips), proclaiming, "Ah, me beauty, at last!" "D'ya like your job?" he asks, following with a whisper in her ear. Betty recoils and says "You mean . . . ?" before slapping him. Betty sings "Don't take my boop-oop-a-doop away," but the ringmaster won't take no for an answer and engages in a violent tussle with the unwilling woman. Koko tries to rescue her, while the band plays "Just One More Chance." When the ringmaster is finally subdued and Bimbo and Koko ask if Betty's all right, she replies happily, "Nope, he couldn't take my boop-oop-a-doop away."

Betty Boop was, in fact, a holdover from the 1920s—the perfect flapper, who could flirt and tease but remain pure and innocent. She really had no other personality traits, but the sheer novelty of such a character in animated cartoons kept her afloat for several years. Mae Questel became the established voice for Betty and brought a wonderful combination of sweetness and sauciness to the role. Betty was supplied with a steady flow of spirited songs, some of them standards but most of them composed especially

Betty Boop and Bimbo in ADMISSION FREE (1932).

for the cartoons by Sammy Timberg and Sammy Lerner. These songs, and Mae Questel's performance, provide the series with some of its most endearing moments.

The first official Betty Boop cartoon, STOPPING THE SHOW, features Betty as a vaudeville headliner who does imitations of Fanny Brice and Maurice Chevalier with some coaxing from the off-screen voices of those stars, and receives such an ovation that the next act on the bill is unable to perform. (A tiny error in this film epitomizes the casual nature of cartoon production at Fleischer's: An easel board featuring a photo of the real Fanny Brice spells her name "Fanny" in long shots and "Fannie" in close-ups.)

But sex remains a major raison d'être for the character and her films. In IS MY PALM RED? Betty visits Professor Bimbo, palm reader, who turns out the lights in his room to get a peek at the silhouette of Betty and her "see-through skirt." In BETTY BOOP'S BIG BOSS our heroine answers an ad that declares "Girl Wanted—Female Preferred." When the boss asks, "What can you do?" Betty replies with a flirty rendition of "You'd Be Surprised." And in BETTY BOOP'S MUSEUM even a prehistoric fossil comes to life to chase after her!

It has been said that the essential difference between Fleischer's cartoons and Disney's is that Disney's deal with a child's natural fears while Fleischer's depict adult traumas and emotions. This distinction comes through in some of the early Betty Boop shorts, which might be classified in current cinema parlance as "cartoons noirs." The "darkest" of all is the Talkartoon BIMBO'S INITIATION, which Leslie Cabarga has accurately described as "a bad dream," in which Bimbo is pursued through an underground maze by bouncing, hooded figures who ask menacingly, "Wanna be a member? Wanna be a member?" When Bimbo says no, he finds himself in one harrowing predicament after another, caught in a nightmarish world from which he cannot escape. Finally, one of the ghostly figures removes its hood to reveal Betty Boop inside. Now Bimbo wants to be a

The Queen asks who's the fairest in the land and gets some bad news in SNOW WHITE (1933).

member—and all the hooded specters turn out to be duplicates of Betty!

Two of the most striking Betty Boops involved the participation of performer/ bandleader Cab Calloway: MINNIE THE MOOCHER and SNOW WHITE. Each film was built around one of Calloway's song hits, the first a title tune and the second featuring "St. James Infirmary Blues." In both cases, the "plot" was engineered to send Betty into a darkened cave, where a ghost would sing these songs. Not only was Calloway's voice used, but the animators rotoscoped his unique strutting movements and transposed them to the singing character for a particularly striking effect. In both films, the vocals are performed against truly startling backgrounds. These renderings dissolve from one subtle design to another, using the gray-black wash tones of rock formations to suggest such eerie sights as a skull, craggy teeth, and bony skeletal fingers.

SNOW WHITE is a mind-boggling film that warrants detailed description. When Salvador Dali and Luis Buñuel created UN CHIEN ANDALOU in 1929, their stated intention was to produce a surreal, completely nonlinear film in which one image had no logical link to the next. Their work was widely heralded. But Fleischer's SNOW WHITE, made four years later, achieves some of these same goals (though unstated and probably unintended) and no one ever took notice of it until recent years.

The film opens at the royal palace, where an ugly Queen looks into her mirror and sings, "Magic mirror in my hand, who's the fairest in the land?" The mirror, which has tiny arms as well as a comic face, replies in song, "You're the fairest in the land, you're the fairest in the land." Then, Betty Boop arrives at the palace and sings of her intention to see her stepmama the Queen. (Two icicles hanging in the doorway join her on the last few words of her song.) She is welcomed by armored sentries Bimbo and Koko, who immediately lose their hearts to the pretty visitor. The Queen is not so happy to meet Betty, however; as Betty sings about the looking glass, the Queen's scowling face turns into a frying pan with two sizzling eggs for eyes. Sure enough, the mirror names Betty the fairest in the land and enthusiastically hugs and kisses her. This infuriates the Queen, who orders, "Off with her head!" illustrating the command by using two fingers to "cut" another one off like a guillotine.

Outside in the snow, a heartbroken Bimbo and Koko prepare for the execution. Koko is sharpening his ax on a grinding wheel, but he gets so carried away that he grinds up the ax into sawdust. He and Bimbo then try to cover their tracks by throwing a tree stump into the grave intended for Betty, but they fall in instead, plummeting to the bottom of a chasm and knocking themselves unconscious. Betty, who's been tied to a nearby tree trunk, is freed when the tree's branches lift her out of the binding rope. Betty walks away but trips and falls into a large snowball, which then starts to roll down a hill. It passes through a wooden frame that cuts the ball into a flat box shape and then sails under an icy lake, emerging with Betty encased in a block of ice resembling a see-through coffin. The coffin slides into the cottage of the Seven Dwarfs (so labeled), who promptly lift it on their shoulders and ski with it toward the Mystery Cave.

Meanwhile, the Queen visits Betty's grave site and asks her mirror, "Am I the fairest in the place?" "If I were you I'd hide my face!" the mirror replies. With this, the Queen uses her mirror to perform magic. She passes it over her body to transform herself into an even uglier witch. She uses it as a shovel to dig the snow-top off Betty's supposed grave. And she sits on it like a magic carpet in order to descend to the bottom of

(Top) Two singing icicles help announce Betty's arrival at the palace.

(Bottom) Koko the Clown struts like Cab Calloway while Bimbo and the Seven Dwarfs carry Betty Boop into the "mystery cave" in SNOW WHITE.

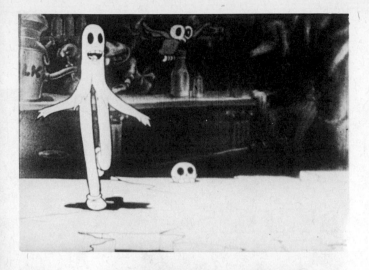

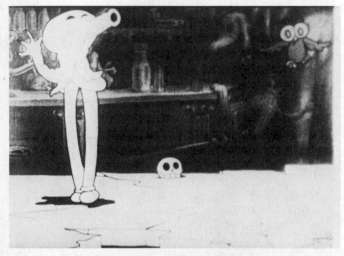

the hole, where she steps on the unconscious Bimbo and Koko, waking them up.

Now Koko springs to life and immediately begins singing, "Folks, I'm goin' down to St. James Infirmary," continuing his vocal rendition as he walks into the Mystery Cave, following close behind the Dwarfs and Betty's coffin. The Queen comes up behind and uses her mirror to turn him into a long-legged ghost, but he doesn't miss a beat of his song. As he struts along, the cave reveals eerie tableaux illustrating phrases of the lyric ("laid out on a long white table . . . have a chorus girl sing me a song" . . . and so on), and the ghost himself is transformed into visual symbols of the song. When he wails, "Put a twenty-dollar gold piece on my watchchain," he becomes a gold piece on a chain, and when he sings, "Hey boy! Hand me another shot of that booooze," his head becomes a bottle, from which he pours some booze into a glass and shoots that down his body!

When the song is over, the Witch passes her mirror over her body to become the Queen again, then slips it under Koko to create a pedestal and freeze him as a statue; this has a chain-reaction effect on Bimbo and Betty, who suffer a similar fate. Their pedestals grow high in the air, leaving the Queen alone with her mirror. Again she asks if she's the fairest in the land, and the mirror replies, "You're the fairest in the land," adding a Bronx cheer that is followed by a sudden explosion. The blast turns the Queen into a repulsive horny-faced dragon, and the cloud of smoke revives Betty, Bimbo, and Koko. The dragon gives chase, and the frightened three run for their lives toward the mouth of the cave. Right at the edge, Bimbo turns

"Hey boy!" sings the ghost of Cab Calloway-cum-Koko in SNOW WHITE, "hand me over a shot of that boo-oo-ze!"

around, yanks on the dragon's tongue, and manages to pull the entire monster inside out, leaving it to run in the opposite direction! Bimbo, Koko, and Betty rejoice outside in the snow.

SNOW WHITE is so full of bizarre images and crazy ideas that it's difficult to absorb it all in one or two viewings. Aside from the actions described above, every scene is replete with tiny throwaway gags—Dave Fleischer's touch—which cram even more into the six-minute extravaganza. When Betty arrives at the palace, Koko throws down a red carpet for her, and Bimbo follows with a suit of red-flannel underwear. As Betty walks away, a tiny mouse pops out of a flap in the underwear, tips one of its ears and calls, "Hiya!" Later, when the Dwarfs are skiing with Betty's coffin, a flowerpot resting on top falls off and suddenly grows hands to help itself back onto position. The action never stops, and the ingenuity seems limitless. Even the musical score is well conceived, making good use of such tunes as "Please" and "Here Lies Love" from Paramount's feature THE BIG BROADCAST.

No subsequent Betty Boop cartoon achieved this level of dark and mystic surrealism; it's quite possible that none of them aspired to it. But even the mildest Fleischer cartoons of this period remained engagingly off-center, springing innovative gag ideas that maintained the studio's reputation. In BETTY BOOP'S UPS AND DOWNS, the Moon auctions off Earth to the highest bidder, and when Saturn clinches the deal and removes a "For Sale" sign on the globe, it also removes the Earth's magnet, prompting a series of wild antigravity gags. BETTY BOOP'S CRAZY INVENTIONS climaxes with a runaway sewing machine sewing up the entire world—binding river banks together, seaming the land and the sky, and the like.

A compelling strain of silliness also runs through these cartoons, defying audiences not to laugh. In I HEARD, workers from the Never Mine strut through a shower to clean off soot before going to Betty Boop's tavern at lunchtime—and when lunch is over, they file back through the showers that replace the soot for their afternoon's work! These films abound with signs bearing such nonsensical slogans as "The Betty Boop Exposition—One Week—May 31–July 31."

It's interesting to note that Paramount Pictures, the distributors of Fleischer's cartoons, also heralded the screen debut of Mae West around this time. It has been said that the spicy Miss West bailed the company out of bankruptcy with the phenomenal success of her pictures in 1933 and 1934. But it has also been said that Mae West was single-handedly responsible for stirring "civil-minded" Americans to arise against verbal and visual indecency in Hollywood films. The result was the adoption of a new Production Code in 1934 that dictated morals and mores in American films for the next thirty years.

Cartoons were neither excluded from criticism nor exempt from the rules of this Code. In early 1933 a Georgia theater owner wrote to *Film Daily*, "The worst kicks we have are on smut in cartoons. They are primarily a kid draw, and parents frequently object to the filth that is put in them, incidentally without helping the comedy. The dirtiest ones are invariably the least funny." Although the exhibitor did not name names, the Fleischers were certainly guilty of this charge, more so than any other cartoon studio. Consequently, they were hardest hit by the new rulings of the Production Code.

The character of Betty Boop underwent substantial revision. Like Jane in the live-action Tarzan films, her body was immediately covered up; gone was the garter, the short skirt, the décolletage. The lechers who once lusted for Betty were retired and replaced by such all-American accouterments as a dog and a cute nephew. Betty became a bachelor girl with no interest in men whatsoever. Her character was transformed into a Goody Two-Shoes, and while she continued to sing, the tunes were no longer "That's My Weakness" and "You'd Be Surprised," but more on the order of "Be Human," which extols kindness to animals, and "Housecleaning Blues."

This new broom also swept clean most of the strange-looking animals that populated the films, not to mention Bimbo and Koko. As new supporting characters were introduced, Betty often took a back seat and became incidental to the stories. Animator Myron Waldman developed Betty's cute dog Pudgy, who carried the story of many cartoons himself, including one amusing entry (RIDING THE RAILS) that was nominated for an Academy Award.

Other cartoons paired Betty with established comic strip characters: Carl Anderson's Henry, Jimmy Swinnerton's Little Jimmy, and Otto Soglow's The Little King (who'd already starred in a series of his own for Van Beuren). None of these characters meshed particularly well with Betty Boop or with the Fleischer formula, except for Little Jimmy, who wasn't so far removed from a studio-created youngster.

The best character to emerge from these post-Code Betty Boop cartoons was Grampy, a cheerful inventor whose chosen profession inspired particularly engaging gags from the Fleischer crew. In his debut cartoon BETTY BOOP AND GRAMPY, he used his ingenuity to liven up a dull party; in GRAMPY'S INDOOR OUTING, he quells Junior's disappointment at having a carnival trip rained out by turning his apartment—and the entire apartment house—into a makeshift amusement park; and in HOUSECLEANING BLUES he tidies up Betty's house after a big party has left the place a shambles. Leslie Cabarga has speculated that the Fleischers showed special interest in this character because he reflected their fondness for mechanical tinkering, and it's a reasonable assumption. One can sense a certain wish-fulfillment as Grampy rigs a player piano to iron sheets and towels, creates party music by having a teakettle's steam blow through a flute, and fashions delightful Christmas toys from worn-out kitchen utensils.

Betty Boop served to introduce another more lasting character in the 1930s: Popeye. When Max Fleischer negotiated with King Features Syndicate to purchase the rights to bring this comic strip hero to the screen, he decided to test reaction to the first picture by making it officially part of the Betty Boop series. It's unlikely that Fleischer had no confidence in the new character; it was merely a

The beloved Grampy, in HOUSECLEANING BLUES **(1937).**

clever ploy to sneak the cartoon into hundreds of theaters that were already committed to play the Betty Boop series. Once people got a look at POPEYE THE SAILOR there was no question that they wanted to see more, and the series was officially launched a few months later.

Popeye was well known from his appearances in Elzie Segar's classic comic strip "Thimble Theatre," which originated in 1919. Originally, "Thimble Theatre" spotlighted Ham Gravy and his scrawny girl friend Olive Oyl. As the strip grew in popularity, Segar, who wrote all of his own material, began experimenting with longer continuities for his daily stories and adding new characters to his offbeat troupe.

Bill Blackbeard, in his introduction to the Nostalgia Press reprint volume of Popeye comics, noted that "Dickens could not have dwelt with more rapturous fascination on the activities his fancy furnished him for such of his creations as Pecksniff, Mrs. Gamp, Micawber, or Quilp, than Segar revealed in the escapades his muse brought dancing up for Popeye, Castor Oyl, Wimpy, or the Sea Hag."

The comparison to Dickens is particularly apt. Like the British author, Segar doted on colorful names, creating characters like Slink the Slicker and Chizzelflint. And like Dickens, his work appeared in serialized form, permitting and even encouraging a protracted form of narrative that would lead a story through an incredible maze before reaching its conclusion. Segar's stories in the 1930s often ran four months each and might devote as many as four days to one horse race or twelve to one prizefight, as in POPEYE AND THE JEEP.

Popeye made his debut in "Thimble Theatre" on January 17, 1929, as a gruff, straighttalking, hard-hitting sailor who captains Castor Oyl's ship to Dice Island. At the end

Popeye makes his screen debut with a sexy Betty Boop in POPEYE THE SAILOR (1933). Popeye © King Features Syndicate.

of that episode Popeye left the cast of characters, but he had already captured the fancy of Segar's loyal readers, and they demanded that he return to the strip. Segar obliged, and before long Popeye was the center of attention.

POPEYE THE SAILOR proclaims the character's screen debut with live-action footage of newspaper headlines announcing the event; a two-column picture of the sailor comes to life as he sings his expository theme song, "I'm Popeye the Sailor Man," illustrating his strength with such nonchalant gestures as punching a huge fish mounted on a plaque so hard that it splits into a cascade of tiny sardine cans.

(Dave Fleischer described the basic formula of the Popeye series, established in this first cartoon: "What I did was just show his strength . . . in the beginning of the picture. I'd have him walk under a pile-driver and the pile-driver would come down and the pile-driver would break and not his head,

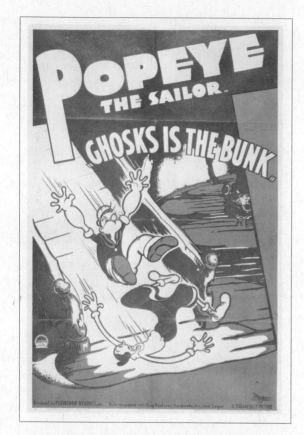

An original poster for GHOSKS IS THE BUNK (1939). Popeye
© King Features Syndicate.

titles in the series were derived from already-popular catch lines like BLOW ME DOWN, I EATS MY SPINACH, and Wimpy's LET'S YOU AND HIM FIGHT. These early Popeyes bear little resemblance to the character and format that evolved after about a year of production. Popeye's voice is different, and his manner gruff and even solemn. In this, he embodies some of the cruder aspects of Segar's concept; yet there is no real humor inherent in the character.

Even Olive Oyl's voice is different in some early episodes, borrowing many of ZaSu Pitts's mannerisms, although Mae Questel contends that she did Olive's voice from the start. She recalls that the first man to do Popeye's voice was William Costello, whose name in vaudeville had been Red Pepper Sam. "He did it for one year, that's all," she says. "Success went to his head so fast it was ridiculous." Costello was fired and at least one other man brought in (Dave Fleischer remembers hearing a man while buying a newspaper and hiring him on the spot) before Jack Mercer settled in the role. Mercer was an in-betweener at the studio who happened to do the voice just for fun. Little did he dream that his ambitions to become an animator would be replaced by a lifelong career as the voice of Popeye.

Mercer brought to the character an infectious sense of humor that did a great deal to soften the animated Popeye and make him more endearing. It is Mercer who created the memorable mutterings that make the 1930s cartoons so much fun, with Popeye constantly mumbling under his breath. Much of this dialogue was planned by Mercer ahead of time, but he and Mae Questel ad-libbed freely during recording sessions as well. A singer named Gus Wickie was the original voice of Bluto, while Mercer and Questel contributed many of the incidental characters' voices over the years. ("Believe it or

you see? It's a funny gag, but it establishes the strength of Popeye. Then we get to the Apparent Disaster, where Bluto has got the best of Popeye and Popeye doesn't want to fight. But he can't help it. Now, the audience is ready to push for Popeye, and hoping that he fights back, and when he does fight back, they're right with him.")

Betty Boop makes a brief appearance in POPEYE THE SAILOR as a hula dancer in a carnival sideshow, but there's no doubt whose cartoon this is. Two months after this "teaser," the first official Popeye cartoon was released, I YAM WHAT I YAM. Other early

not," says the actress, "during the war when Jack Mercer was overseas, we tried to get a guy to do Popeye. We got somebody, but he suffered from mike fright, and I did about six or seven cartoons as Popeye. I can still do the voice." And she does—amazingly well.)

The early Popeyes seem to be groping for a comfortable style, although they created a minor sensation when they were first released. Popeye quickly became one of Paramount Pictures' major properties, capturing newspaper attention, marquee billing, and fostering Popeye clubs and merchandise, just as Mickey Mouse had done a few years earlier.

In 1934, the Popeye we know and love came into focus, in classic shorts like A DREAM WALKING and the more typical entries THE DANCE CONTEST and WE AIM TO PLEASE. Contrary to popular belief—supported by the hack cartoons that finished off this series—no two Popeyes from the Fleischer era were quite alike. A DREAM WALKING, which has become a latter-day favorite at film festivals, makes wonderful use of perspective as Popeye follows Olive Oyl's sleepwalking excursion up, over, around, and through the dizzying heights of the city's houses, skyscrapers, and flagpoles. As with so many of Fleischer's technically impressive cartoons, this one simply follows the basic rules of perspective, but does so in such a disarming and hilarious fashion that audiences invariably respond with laughter and applause.

The timing of the cartoon is superb, with Olive's rock-steady sleepwalking tempo contrasted with Popeye's and Bluto's frantic and heated attempts to save her—and simultaneously do each other in. An extended sequence on the skeletal girders of a building-in-progress is memorable because it's such an impressive setting—realistically drawn and photographed in gray relief—for

An original poster for CUSTOMERS WANTED (1939). Popeye © King Features Syndicate.

the wiry, sharply defined characters who go shooting around its many levels. The Mack Gordon–Harry Revel song "Did You Ever See a Dream Walking?", from the Paramount feature SITTING PRETTY, provides a perfect foundation for the whole episode. Most of all, A DREAM WALKING is extremely funny, drawing its laughs not only from inventive situations but from the characters' reactions to them. (Even Wimpy gets into the act as the hamburger-chomping watchman at the construction site.)

The Popeye series eschewed the crazy look of the early Talkartoons but retained the city setting and expressive use of gray tones. These cartoons make better use of the full black-and-white spectrum than any others in film history. Many times, backgrounds are deliberately muted or blurred in order to make the characters stand out that much more; other times, establishing shots reveal a rich and creative use of blacks, whites, and varying shades of gray.

Sometimes, this gray shading was used to camouflage the fact that nothing was moving in the background, as in THE DANCE CONTEST, in which a hazy-looking crowd stands motionless in the ballroom as Popeye and Olive dance in the foreground. CONTEST also features Bluto with his hair slicked back as the local Romeo who sweeps women off their feet, until Popeye uses spinach to improve his dancing ability. Wimpy presides over the dance competition, blithely pulling a lever that sends fumbling couples through trap doors that appear on command.

J. Wellington Wimpy, whose fondness for hamburgers has become as much a part of American folklore as Popeye's penchant for spinach, was the series' most surreal character, a resolutely expressionless gentleman with a cultured tongue and a bland exterior that belied a supremely crafty mind. In WE AIM TO PLEASE, Wimpy impresses his friend Bluto by patronizing the diner run by customer-conscious Popeye and Olive, and telling them, "I'd gladly pay you Tuesday for a hamburger today." When they oblige him, Bluto gets in on the act, but oversteps his credit rating and pulls Popeye into a battle royal. Wimpy remained a die-hard opportunist throughout the cartoon series.

Bluto was one character who had not been a "Thimble Theatre" regular. He was adapted by Dave Fleischer as an all-purpose nemesis from a villain who had made a one-shot appearance in the strip during June and July 1932 and was billed as "Bluto the Terri-

ble! Lower than bilge scum, meaner than Satan, and strong as an ox." His original position as series heavy was modified to the point where he and Popeye were often friendly rivals.

Bill Blackbeard writes, "I think the Popeye cartoons hewed more closely to the strip images of the characters than was the case in any other strip adaptations on the screen. . . . Aside from the heavy emphasis on spinach as fuel for Popeye in the cartoons (an emphasis not at all echoed in the strip, where spinach figured importantly in only one Popeye narrative out of dozens, the Popeye–Kid Mustard prizefight of the 12/36–1/37 Sunday strip), and the fantastic chase and fight action almost mandatory in the animated medium of the period, the affinity of the films and strips was highly marked; even the characters' voices seemed likely."

Where Fleischer and Segar differed most prominently was in essential goals. Segar was a storyteller, with a great flair for melodrama; this quality, infused with his vivid sense of humor, made the continuing comic strip an incredible experience for devoted readers. The Fleischer cartoons, on the other hand, were out for one thing only: laughter. While the animated cartoons' ideas and imagery were as impressive in their own way as Segar's, they were totally different in concept.

The most admirable trait of the Fleischer Popeyes was their dogged refusal to fall into a formula trap. For every standard ingredient in the series, there is a film that shakes the idea right off its pedestal. In the very first Popeye cartoon, while the sailor man sings his theme song and demonstrates his "macho" strength, he hoists his shirt at one point and reveals a corset underneath!

Popeye and Bluto's constant fights are given a good ribbing in IT'S THE NATURAL THING TO DO, based on a song introduced by

Bing Crosby in DOUBLE OR NOTHING. The film opens with Olive in her kitchen as the two rivals battle it out in her backyard. A telegram arrives, reading, "Cut out the rough stuff once in a while and act more refined. Be like ladies and gentlemen. That's the natural thing to do. (Signed) Popeye Fan Club. P.S. Now go on with the picture." Popeye and Bluto take the advice to heart and call on Olive in their best Sunday clothes, outdoing Alphonse and Gaston in courtesy. During a genteel tea party, Olive advises, "Never dunk above your elbow," and Popeye notes, "Conversing breaks up the monopoly of talking." This delicate society is clearly foredoomed, however, and the three of them wind up in a massive brawl, proclaiming in song, "It's the natural thing to do!"

Nothing was sacred in these cartoons, not even Popeye's spinach. I LIKE BABIES AND INFINKS opens on a strange object surrounded by blackness, with crying on the sound track. Gradually the camera moves back to reveal that the object is little Swee Pea's tongue, inside his huge wide-open mouth as he bawls uncontrollably. Olive calls Popeye and Bluto to come over and cheer him up. They try everything and soon turn the chore into a competition; still nothing works. Finally Popeye reaches for his spinach, but he grabs a can of onions by mistake. Instead of the usual results, the onions make him cry. Soon the aroma fills the room and Bluto and Olive are crying too. At this, Swee Pea starts to laugh uproariously for the fade-out.

If the spinach could be made the object of a comic twist, so could Popeye's whole demeanor. In LET'S CELEBRAKE Popeye and Bluto call on Olive to take her out for New Year's Eve, but Popeye, being the kind-hearted soul he is, can't bear to leave Olive's sweet old grandma at home. He decides to be her escort for the evening and, later at a nightclub, peps her up with some spinach, which helps make Grandma and Popeye the liveliest couple on the dance floor! In this delightful cartoon, Popeye's interest in Olive takes a back seat to his good-naturedness, thereby reaffirming his good qualities, which detractors who paint him as a one-dimensional character fail to notice.

Olive's capriciousness was the basis of many shorts, such as FEMALES IS FICKLE, in which Popeye nearly kills himself trying to save her pet goldfish, which falls into the ocean—only to have Olive decide that she doesn't want to keep the poor little thing cooped up anyway.

It's difficult to find any 1930s entry in the series that conforms to a cut-and-dried pattern. LET'S GET MOVIN' opens with Olive singing "I'm Moving Today," as Popeye and Bluto try to please her by doing the best job moving her furniture. This short makes excellent use of perspective and height, with such shots as that of Bluto on the sixth floor of the apartment building looking down at Popeye on the ground, and the like. One delightful gag has Popeye throwing a piano out the window, then racing down six flights of stairs in time to catch it on the sidewalk below. Naturally, he outdoes Bluto in the end and sings, "And now I have proven/no one can do movin'/like Popeye the sailor man!"

Many cartoons were built around songs by Sammy Timberg and Sammy Lerner. One of the best is BROTHERLY LOVE, with Olive spearheading a campaign with a song that concludes, "Let every Tom and Dick and Otto/obey our golden motto/for what we need is brotherly love." Popeye tries to practice this policy, but he finds it necessary to pummel a street full of rowdies in order to get them to subscribe to the idea.

Various cartoons in the series would spotlight Olive, Wimpy, Swee Pea, or other Segar creations like Eugene the Jeep, Poopdeck Pappy, and the Goon (in the memorable GOONLAND), always with amazing fidelity to the comic strip. In the early 1940s, Fleischer introduced Popeye's nephews Peep-eye, Pip-eye, Pup-eye, and Poop-eye, miniature versions of their uncle, who split every conversation in quarters, with each carrying part of the sentence. These enjoyable newcomers were clearly inspired by Donald Duck's nephews, Hewey, Dewey, and Louie, and shared with them a mystery of parentage that only dyed-in-the-wool cynics tried to explore.

Popeye was so valuable a property to both Fleischer and Paramount Pictures that it seemed a shame to limit his potential to monthly black-and-white cartoons. Paramount encouraged the producer to make a Popeye "special," and the result was a two-reel Technicolor short released in November 1936. This was before Disney's SNOW WHITE had provided the industry breakthrough for feature-length cartoons, but Fleischer's POPEYE THE SAILOR MEETS SINBAD THE SAILOR was treated as if it were a feature. Many theaters advertised it as the main attraction and made the accompanying feature film seem like so much filler on the program.

SINBAD is a funny, imaginative, and well-animated short. Fleischer's men let their skill for drawing detailed backgrounds run rampant with a rainbow spectrum of colors. The story has Bluto as Sinbad, presiding over a remote island. When he spots Popeye's ship sailing by, with Wimpy and Olive aboard, he orders his pet condor to bring back the girl and destroy the ship. He doesn't reckon with Popeye, however, who swims ashore with Wimpy and before long makes mincemeat of the island despot.

If anything, Fleischer outdid himself the following year with his second Technicolor two-reeler, POPEYE MEETS ALI BABA AND HIS 40 THIEVES. With several original songs and a clever plot, this one featured even more visual innovations than SINBAD, with Bluto as Abul Hassan, the notorious desert thief who rides the sands with his band of rogues. (His name forms a pun later on when Popeye snatches his flannel underwear and remarks, "Abul hassan got 'em anymore.") Coastguardman Popeye is assigned the task of rounding up these thieves and brings Wimpy along on his seaplane. Olive stows aboard, and when the plane crashes in the desert, the three are stranded together. As they trudge through the desert, the camera shows their silhouettes in long shot, framed against the sun on the horizon, while the picture dissolves from sun into moon. They arrive in a desert town that is quickly and completely vandalized by Hassan's men. When the latter kidnap Olive and take her to their cave, Popeye follows in hot pursuit.

Bluto and Popeye square off in the two-reel Technicolor special, POPEYE THE SAILOR MEETS SINBAD THE SAILOR **(1936). Popeye © King Features Syndicate.**

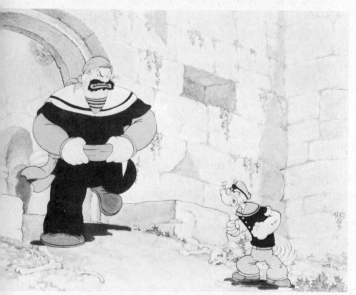

The cave door opens to his command "Open sesame." Once inside, Popeye uses his spinach, holding the can and ordering, "Open, says me!" and making short work of Abul Hassan and all forty of his cohorts. He brings back with him a truckload of stolen jewels to return to their rightful owners, singing, "I may be a shorty/but I licked the forty/I'm Popeye the Sailor Man!"

Again Paramount had a hit, with ALI BABA winning top-of-the-bill bookings around the country. A newspaper ad showed Popeye proclaiming, "Gable and Taylor is just amachures. I yam now the greatest lover in moovin' pitchers."

Actually, Popeye the lover was more evident in the last of these two-reel specials, POPEYE MEETS ALADDIN AND HIS WONDERFUL LAMP, released in 1939. An enjoyable cartoon, it is also the most ordinary of the three Popeye specials, lacking the inspiration and visual highlights that make the others so memorable. This one has Olive Oyl preparing a script for Surprise Pictures to star herself as a Princess and Popeye as Aladdin, who battles an evil wizard with the help of a Lew Lehrish genie.

Also missing from ALADDIN was any use of the studio's remarkable "3-D" process, used to great advantage in SINBAD and ALI BABA and so named for its startling illusion of depth. A Paramount press release explained at the time, "Ordinary cartoons today are drawn and the drawings are photographed. With the method which Fleischer has introduced for Popeye the cartoon studio looks like a duplicate in miniature of a regular Hollywood production camp. Sets are built and scaled down so that they will fit on a revolving turntable. This 'set' is within six feet of a special lens and camera. The machinery entailed in the new process weighs some three tons. It has trusses, movable tables, cranks, steel framework, gears

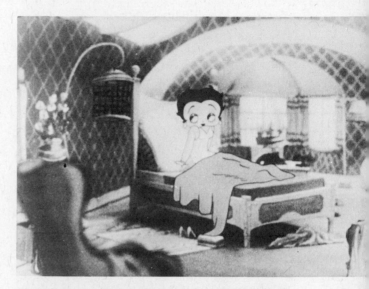

An example of Fleischer's "3-D" process, as seen in HOUSECLEANING BLUES (1937). This is actually a photographed set, with miniature props; only Betty and her blanket are drawn on a cel.

and gadgets enough to make a mechanical engineer dizzy."

Simply put, a horizontal animation camera and stand were attached to an enormous revolving turntable, on which miniature sets were built. The characters were inked and painted on celluloids as always, but the cels were then suspended upright in a steel frame that revealed the "live" backgrounds behind it. Special machinery enabled the background to turn a tiny bit at a time, just as one would move a traditional paper background for a panning shot. Fleischer and John Burks, who invented the system, further realized that placing some objects in the foreground, in *front* of the animated characters, would create an even greater feeling of depth and perspective.

The effect on screen was uncanny, but as good as it looked in black-and-white shorts like Popeye's FOR BETTER OR WORSER and

BETTY BOOP AND THE LITTLE KING, it was twice as good in color, when the added brightness and clarity of the characters made their appearance in these live-action settings all the more incredible. When Popeye walks through the jewel-filled cave of Sinbad, or when he, Olive, and Wimpy ride upon a cart filled with glittering gems at the end of ALI BABA, one can hardly believe one's eyes. Audiences who are not aware of the process usually don't recognize these scenes as a combination of live action and animation; all they know is that the backgrounds take on a dynamic quality and that the illusion of three dimensions is quite vivid.

What's toughest to understand is how this process was economically feasible, since miniature sets had to be constructed, alignment of the cartoon characters worked out ahead of time, and the photographing of these special sequences carried out in painstaking fashion. Often these "tabletop" scenes lasted no more than a half minute on screen.

Obviously, economic feasibility took a back seat to mechanical innovation in Max Fleischer's book of priorities. He took great pride in the many inventions he fathered and boasted of his fifteen separate patents in the animation field. But like so many other inventors, once he developed the machines he didn't know how best to implement and exploit them.

The Turntable camera preceded Walt Disney's much-publicized multiplane camera by several years, and one wonders why Fleischer didn't make as big a splash with his equally worthy invention. This injustice adds fuel to the fire of contention that Fleischer was really as much a pioneer as Disney, but simply not as recognized by the industry and the public in his time.

The irony is that Fleischer's fortunes began to sink at this time precisely because he began to imitate Disney. In 1934 Fleischer started a new series called COLOR CLASSICS, launched by (who else?) Betty Boop in an extra-long fairy-tale spoof called POOR CINDERELLA. Subsequent entries in the series had titles like THE LITTLE DUTCH MILL and SOMEWHERE IN DREAMLAND, and tried to emulate Disney's SILLY SYMPHONIES with gentle fables and atmospheric mood pieces. Some, like SONG OF THE BIRDS, were unadulterated tearjerkers. Because Disney had exclusive rights to three-color Technicolor, the earliest COLOR CLASSICS were filmed in two-color processes; SOMEWHERE IN DREAMLAND, a January 1936 release, was the first to boast full Technicolor hues.

The problem with the COLOR CLASSICS was a simple one: The Fleischer animators were trying to be something they weren't. Their attempts at sentiment were contrived, not sincere, and the results were some of the most treacly cartoons ever made. Although the staff worked hard to make these shorts attractive, they could never match the sumptuousness of Disney's contemporary product and failed on that count as well. Fleischer cartoons had their own charm, and when they tried to imitate Disney they succeeded neither as Fleischer creations nor as bogus Disneys.

The most interesting aspect of this series is its frequent use of the tabletop camera (as in SOMEWHERE IN DREAMLAND's kiddie paradise of ice-cream-cone fields and cookie carousels) and occasional character-design innovations (as in THE FRESH VEGETABLE MYSTERY). One of the most enjoyable COLOR CLASSICS features Grampy, who brings joy and cheer to a houseful of neglected orphans in CHRISTMAS COMES BUT ONCE A YEAR by turning their drab surroundings into a festive play park and using his ingenuity to cre-

Al Eugster, Pinto Colvig (best known as the voice of Goofy), Cal Howard, and Win Hoskins have fun in the courtyard of Max Fleischer's Miami studio.

ate dozens of toys out of household utensils. Here at least was a cartoon that bore the unique Fleischer stamp while doling out helpings of sentiment and comedy.

But if the COLOR CLASSICS suffered from Disneyfication, Max's next major venture all but suffocated from it. Before December 1937, no one in the film industry took the idea of a feature-length cartoon seriously. Cartoons, no matter how successful, were still a stepchild in the grand scheme of moviemaking, a filler for nighttime programs and a staple of the kiddie matinee. No one could possibly want to sit through an animated cartoon lasting more than an hour.

The enormous (and unexpected) success of Walt Disney's SNOW WHITE AND THE SEVEN DWARFS changed that thinking. Disney's gamble paid off, and subsequently other studios thought about the possibility of producing a feature film. In the case of the Fleischers, it was their distributor, Paramount Pictures, that encouraged them to make the move. After all, Paramount stood to gain much more from the worldwide release of a successful feature than it did from a handful of six-minute shorts. There is no evidence that the Fleischers would have tackled this ambitious enterprise if not for Paramount's prodding.

The feature project was ambitious in more ways than one. To produce the film the studio had to expand its staff from two hundred to nearly seven hundred, and to house this expanded troupe, Max Fleischer decided to build a new production plant in Miami, Florida. An equally important motivation for this move was to flee New York, which was the scene of a bitter labor strike by Fleischer employees in 1937. Fleischer figured—correctly—that the labor movement was not nearly as strong in Florida as it was in New York, and that he might escape many of his worst problems there. In addition, Miami offered Fleischer a short-term tax exemption on his studio. It seemed like an ideal setup.

The Fleischers claimed that after Paramount talked them into doing a feature, they mulled over various ideas for six months before deciding on Jonathan Swift's GULLIVER'S TRAVELS. If so, that would place their starting date somewhere in the spring of 1938; the film premiered in December 1939, some twenty months later.

Walt Disney spent the better part of four years making SNOW WHITE, but the comparison here is not one of how *much* time was spent, but *how* the time was spent. Disney knew that in order to create a feature film his staff had to grow, not just in numbers but in maturity. This was when he initiated art classes on studio time, encouraged specialization within his staff, and enabled his artists to experiment in a continuing search for perfection, regardless of cost. Fleischer had neither the time nor the interest to follow these procedures. He simply wanted to fulfill his commitment and try to make a good picture.

The first problem was one of enlarging the staff. In addition to his New York crew, Fleischer signed up as many California animators as he could lure away, including three valuable studio veterans who had since gone to Disney—Grim Natwick, James (Shamus) Culhane, and Al Eugster, all of whom had in fact worked on SNOW WHITE. But sheer desperation caused him to hire many others

sight-unseen, and a great many underqualified people joined the Miami payroll at this time. An east-west schism quickly developed, with New York veterans grumbling that some of their new colleagues were sloppy and uncaring. "They just didn't give a damn," Myron Waldman recalls. "It was just another job, a playground."

Furthermore, the studio needed a tremendous influx of lower-echelon workers—inkers, painters, and the like. Having nowhere else to turn, the studio set up classes and encouraged Miamians, particularly students from the Miami Art School, to attend in order to qualify for ready jobs. Needless to say, the quality of work that resulted was variable.

"Max moved down to this place in Miami where there was no material," Culhane remarks. "There were no actors to do tracks, no labs, there was nothing. If the camera broke down, there was no camera place. He might as well have moved to Peapock, Kentucky."

But the main problem with GULLIVER, that no amount of technical expertise could fix, was the script. After much discussion and a thorough rewrite, Dave Fleischer and his five story men fashioned a continuity that took its bare bones from Jonathan Swift and then went off on its own. Gone was the sly satire. Gone was the original feud between the kings of Lilliput and Blefuscu over which end of an egg to crack. Gone were episodes in the original book following Gulliver's arrival in Lilliput.

In their place was a gallery of cartoony characters, including King Little of Lilliput, King Bombo of Blefuscu, Bombo's spies Sneak, Snoop, and Snitch, carrier pigeon Twinkletoes, town crier Gabby, and, as love interest, Prince David and Princess Glory, united in love but separated by their royal fathers' feud.

There was just one thing missing from this newly minted brood: credibility. The crucial point that Disney understood and Fleischer's staff did not was that in a short subject an audience did not demand characterization; personality and gags were enough. But in a feature, one had to present a character with depth and feelings with which the audience could identify. Otherwise there was nothing to hold the viewer's interest for eighty minutes.

Fleischer's characters were strictly one-dimensional. Gulliver smiles a lot and says, "My, my." Prince David and Princess Glory speak not one word of dialogue until the final scenes, so it's impossible to feel any empathy toward them, even though David nearly kills himself in the story's climax protecting Gulliver from being shot. The remaining characters are buffoons, except for Gabby, who is just plain annoying—a character with all the frustrations of Donald Duck but none of his inherent humor.

This is just the beginning of GULLIVER's problems. The story, such as it is, takes forever to get started. There is nearly a half hour between the time Gulliver is washed ashore at Lilliput and the time he wakes up. In between, we must endure the tedious rantings of King Little and King Bombo, which finally culminate in an exposition of the key plot point: a conflict over their national anthems, "Forever" and "Faithful." (Resolution comes at the end of the film when Gulliver suggests that the songs be sung *together* at the wedding of David and Glory, symbolizing the union of the two countries.)

Since SNOW WHITE had a love story, and a musical score, it was clear that GULLIVER would have to include these elements as well, and they contribute strongly to the film's ultimate failure. The love story is barely a story at all, since the characters of David and Glory are all but ignored except

Seymour Kneitel, director Dave Fleischer, and Willard Bowsky go over a storyboard for GULLIVER'S TRAVELS.

when they sing. Furthermore, the drawing of these pint-sized humans is dull and unconvincing, particularly alongside Gulliver, who is meticulously rotoscoped throughout the film. The combination of ultrarealistic Gulliver, semirealistic David and Glory, and unrealistic cartoon types like Gabby and the two Kings just doesn't work.

For the music score, Paramount insisted that the Fleischers use studio songsmiths Leo Robin and Ralph Rainger; while they were certainly talented men with a great many hits to their credit, they did not provide GULLIVER with really worthwhile songs. Some, like

Ultrarealistic Gulliver and "cartoony" character Gabby in a scene from GULLIVER'S TRAVELS (1939).

"All's Well," work nicely within the context of the movie, but the major pieces, like "Faithful Forever," are pedestrian. Paramount did not achieve what it was after: a flock of hit-parade tunes that would help boost the film's popularity the way SNOW WHITE's score had done. Ironically, the one GULLIVER song that got the most mileage was not written by Robin and Rainger. "It's a Hap-Hap-Happy Day" was contributed by studio veteran Sammy Timberg, in collaboration with Al Neiberg and Winston Sharples; a cheerful if uninspired tune, it was used for years as background music in Paramount cartoons, particularly when Sharples became the studio's music director.

GULLIVER'S TRAVELS is not a terrible film by any means, but it isn't terribly good either. Artistically, its most interesting aspects are the opening storm at sea, which is masterfully animated, and the outstanding rotoscope work on Gulliver. To those who didn't know how these scenes were done,

they must have represented an impressive achievement. Gulliver's every move, every gesture, and every wrinkle in his clothing, are uncannily *right*—and so they should be, since they all were traced from live-action film of a man named Sam Parker, who acted out the role. One scene in which, his face lit by the torches below, he laughs and claps his hands at a dinnertime performance by the Lilliputians, is particularly good.

There is another impressive shot in GUL-LIVER'S TRAVELS: the main title sequence, in which the credits are superimposed over a three-dimensional sailing ship. This was, of course, one of Fleischer's live-action models, camouflaged as a drawing and providing the same memorable results as the tabletop animation of the earlier shorts. The question arises: Why didn't Fleischer use his unique tabletop technique in GULLIVER?

Why indeed. Perhaps it was too difficult to think of integrating the process into a film already overflowing with technical challenge for the staff. Perhaps it was considered too artificial for a feature film. Perhaps it was rejected because Disney hadn't done anything like that in SNOW WHITE.

Whatever the case, GULLIVER was doomed to unfavorable comparison with SNOW WHITE by everyone who saw it. Some critics were kind, and the public responded well, but the film simply wasn't the success Paramount had envisioned. What's more, it had the misfortune of being released after war was declared in Europe, cutting off that valuable foreign market. The most cutting reaction came from Walt Disney, who reportedly remarked, "We can do better than that with our second-string animators."

He was right, of course. If Fleischer had chosen to follow his own path and created something truly individual, he wouldn't have suffered so much from comparison with Disney. But he fell into the same trap as so many other cartoon studios of the 1930s—a trap he had avoided for many years. Paramount Pictures controlled the finances and distribution, and Paramount wanted Fleischer to be ''another Disney,'' whether he liked it or not. Perhaps they all would have been better off if someone's original idea to cast Popeye in the Gulliver role had been carried out. At least there would have been Jack Mercer's mutterings to liven up the slow spots.

When GULLIVER was completed—after months of harried and hurried production, with practically the entire studio on overtime in order to meet a Christmas release date—it was time to take stock of the studio's situation. The tail seemed to be wagging the dog, as Fleischer's enormous overhead now demanded that a second feature be initiated immediately, along with other short-subject series, to keep everybody busy.

Betty Boop had retired in 1939. Mae Questel claims that it was because she refused to move to Florida, but that wouldn't have been reason enough to drop a popular character. Betty's time had passed, and that seemed as convenient an excuse as any to pack her away. Good ideas for the series were at such a premium that one 1938 entry called OUT OF THE INKWELL revived Fleischer's silent-film format—and executed it with astonishing sloppiness.

Popeye was still the studio's number-one breadwinner, and the series remained entertaining even when the Fleischers started cutting corners in producing the monthly releases. The detailed, gray-toned backgrounds of the mid-1930s gave way to a much more streamlined approach—brighter, just as the studio's surroundings brightened from New York to Miami. The cartoons were still great fun, and Popeye was as amusing as ever, thanks largely to the creative contributions of Jack Mercer, who began to receive

story credit on many of the films. Cartoons like WIMMIN HADN'T OUGHTA DRIVE, WITH POOPDECK PAPPY, POPEYE PRESENTS EUGENE THE JEEP, and OLIVE'S BIRTHDAY PRESINK maintained the series' high standards of humor and imagination, even if the level of draftsmanship slipped a few notches along the way.

In the wake of GULLIVER, the studio inaugurated two new series and scheduled a pair of two-reel Technicolor ''specials'' for 1940. The first series, STONE AGE CARTOONS, predated THE FLINTSTONES by twenty years in transposing modern mechanical ideas to prehistoric times. (The idea wasn't original even then—it turns up in many silent comedies as well.) While pleasant and often quite funny, these cartoons were just gag collages that had no continuing hook to make them truly successful, and the series expired before the end of the year.

Twinkletoes and King Bombo, who starred in their own short subjects after making their screen debut in GULLIVER.

Fleischer's next idea was to try out the various supporting characters from GULLIVER'S TRAVELS in their own cartoons. GABBY was feted with a series of his own, while other cartoons grouped under the title ANIMATED ANTICS featured Twinkletoes and Sneak, Snoop, and Snitch. Since these characters generated limited appeal in the feature film, spotlighting them this way had little impact.

The two-reel special RAGGEDY ANN AND RAGGEDY ANDY presented much greater possibilities. Based on the characters and stories created by Johnny Gruelle, this cartoon comes closer to realizing its goals than most Fleischer attempts at "heart" and sentiment, but suffers from a different problem instead: it isn't long enough. The story follows Ann and Andy from their creation as dolls in Ragland, through their meeting the Camel with the Wrinkled Knees (whose Goofylike voice is provided by Goofy's own Pinto Colvig), and their journey to the Castle of Names, which is interrupted when Andy is lured away by a coy senorita doll. Ann reluctantly goes on alone, but collapses and becomes gravely ill. The problem is a broken heart, which can only be mended by Andy's timely arrival.

RAGGEDY ANN AND RAGGEDY ANDY has considerable charm—not the least because of its accurate animation of Gruelle's irresistible characters. The continuity, credited to Bill Turner, is solid and makes good fantasy sense, but it hurries by in twenty minutes and leaves no time to really develop the characters or milk the story for all it's worth. The plot accelerates with uncomfortable jerks, and Andy's sudden reappearance and burst into song is a bit jarring.

It's a shame that the Fleischers didn't select this property for feature-length treatment. The ingredients are all there, including the imaginative setting of Ragland, with its echoes of Oz, and more possibilities than

either Lilliput or Bugtown (in the studio's subsequent feature MR. BUG GOES TO TOWN) ever offered. The songs and score by Sammy Timberg aren't bad either. RAGGEDY ANN AND RAGGEDY ANDY could have been one of the Fleischers' crowning achievements if it had been handled with just a little more finesse.

Whatever its faults, RAGGEDY ANN AND RAGGEDY ANDY was far better than the studio's second two-reel special, THE RAVEN. Based on Edgar Allen Poe's famous poem, this hackneyed comedy stretched the story of an obnoxious door-to-door salesman (the title character) to protracted lengths with no noticeable rewards.

Having enjoyed only moderate success with these many and varied short-subject endeavors, the Fleischers had their next series foisted on them by Paramount. The company was intrigued by the tremendous popularity of Superman, who had been created just a few years earlier by Jerry Siegel and Joe Schuster in *Action Comics*. The story goes that a Paramount representative proposed a Superman cartoon series to the Fleischers, and Dave Fleischer replied that it would be virtually impossible to do. With the requirements of realistic animation and special effects, the cost of doing such a series would be prohibitive. When Paramount asked how much, Dave decided to quote such a high price that the studio would immediately say no. He said $100,000—four times the cost of an average cartoon. Suprisingly, Paramount said yes—and the Fleischers were obliged to produce a SUPERMAN series.

The first cartoon appeared in September 1941, backed by a tremendous Paramount promotional campaign, including coming-attractions trailers, unheard of for a cartoon short. The Fleischers didn't disappoint anyone. SUPERMAN, as the first episode was titled, delivered exactly what the customers wanted to see: an exciting, dramatic adventure with plenty of action and special effects.

Considering the difficulty Fleischer animators had with GULLIVER and other semi-realistic projects, the success of the SUPERMAN series is doubly impressive. Meticulous model charts captured the exact appearance of Clark Kent, Lois Lane, and Superman from contemporary comic books. Rotoscoping was used to a degree, but the animators had to rely on their own sense of proportion and perspective to make these human characters work. "Some animators fell right into it," recalls Myron Waldman, "and others couldn't do it, they couldn't draw that well. But we had some very good assistants; they weren't good animators but they were good figure men. They would follow up and clean up these drawings."

A tremendous amount of preparation went into the production of each Superman short. "They were very carefully laid out ahead of time, because the cost was so tremendous," says Waldman. "The stories were very complete. Then we had to keep that tempo going, and pick it up for the climax. Each scene had to have a dramatic look about it. That required quite a bit of thought. There were many more scene cuts [than usual]. And you had modeling,* too, on the characters . . . that meant somebody had to go back [and do it]. You'd indicate it on one or two drawings and then they would go back and put in all the modeling. You'd also indicate on your drawings where the light was coming from; all that was taken into consideration. In the settings, you'll notice, there's a lot of foreground stuff, to get different depths of perspective. We got an extra dimension that we didn't worry about too much in the other cartoons."

*Facial shadows.

Clark Kent and Lois Lane make an effective transformation from comic book to animated cartoon. © National Periodical Publications.

Pencil tests were made on these productions, a rare luxury for Fleischer shorts, and much of the elaborate gimmickry was handled by an effects department the studio had established during production of GULLIVER. Airbrush work, special paints, and double exposures were used to create some of the dazzling light rays and similar effects in the SUPERMAN series.

These cartoons are without question the most cinematically sophisticated the studio ever produced. The camera angles are indeed dramatic, and thoughtfully chosen. Each shot flows into the next, with a variety of pans, dissolves, and other linking devices. Effective use is made of shadows in practically every scene, and such qualities as speed, weight, and depth are vividly realized.

The biggest problem in conceiving the SUPERMAN series was striking a balance

Superman versus THE MECHANICAL MONSTERS (1941). ©
National Periodical Publications.

suited to a stylized and atmospheric
approach. These films are among the best
fantasy cartoons ever produced and feature a
gallery of spectacular and memorable highlights: the camera taking Superman's point
of view as he leaps into the air in THE BUL-
LETEERS; the Man of Steel grabbing both ends
of a disconnected wire and letting a surge of
power flow through his body in THE MAG-
NETIC TELESCOPE; using his X-ray vision in
MECHANICAL MONSTERS to find Lois trapped
inside a robot; or rescuing a passenger train
as it plummets off a trestle into a rocky canyon below in THE BILLION DOLLAR LIMITED.

The hard work that went into these films
shows on the screen, and SUPERMAN stands
as one of the Fleischer studio's finest
achievements. Unfortunately, it was also one
of its last.

Almost as soon as GULLIVER'S TRAVELS was
completed, work began on a second animated feature. Dave Fleischer favored Maurice Maeterlinck's *The Life of the Bee*, but
reportedly there was difficulty securing
screen rights, so the Fleischer staff developed
its own story along the same lines: life
among a colony of bugs that live in the garden of a home in the big city. Max and Dave
prided themselves on the fact that this was
the first animated feature not to be based on
a classic story or set in another time period.
The film was named MR. BUG GOES TO TOWN.

This time, the Fleischers had a wonderful
concept for a film, and they made the most of
it. The prime assets of MR. BUG are its
sequences showing life from a bug's eye
view. There is a dynamic opening sequence
showing Hoppity, the lead character, scram-
bling along a crowded city street, dodging
the path of human feet. Throughout the film,
humans are seen only in terms of hands and
feet—in other words, only as they relate to
the bugs.

between animated realism and cartoon fantasy. In the first short, action scenes are well
handled, and rotoscoping gives even some
casual sequences at the *Daily Planet* a
remarkably realistic look. But then Lois Lane
takes off in an airplane to visit the hideout of
a mad scientist, and the plane soars into
space like a rubbery bird. The animators
weren't accustomed yet to treating an entire
cartoon in realistic fashion. In fact, the scientist has a "comic relief" falcon that mimics
his every move. But these flaws are overrid-
den for the most part by the film's excellent
visual effects, especially at the point when
Superman repels the scientist's destruction
ray by flying toward it and punching each
lightning bolt into oblivion.

Subsequent entries in the series hammered out a more consistent format, emphasizing larger-than-life villains, mechanical
monsters, and futuristic equipment, all well

The problems with MR. BUG, however, are the same ones that plagued GULLIVER: shallow characters and a weak story line. Hoppity is a happy-go-lucky type with an insipid voice, and his girl friend Honey is a bland heroine. The plot elements—aristocratic C. Bagley Beetle using his wiles to win Honey's hand in marriage, and Hoppity's efforts to find the bugs a better place to live—are too hackneyed to enlist an audience's involvement. And, once again, the film is plagued with a passel of undistinguished songs. What emotions are stirred, after all, by lyrics like, "Boy, oh boy, oh boy, oh boy/We've got fun, we've got freedom, we've got joy"?

MR. BUG does have a fair share of favorable points, but there just aren't enough to give the overall film the impact it should have. The title sequence, like the opening of GULLIVER, is outstanding. The Fleischer shop devoted four months to the construction of a miniature three-dimensional set of New York City and worked out a complex choreography of camera movements to open the film and segue into animation of the big city, drawing closer and closer to street level, where the story begins.

The film's songs are by and large pedestrian. In contrast, however, there is a vivid, evocative music score by Leigh Harline, who did such outstanding work for Disney throughout the thirties.

Best of all is the film's most cinematic sequence, when the bugs try to relocate and unwittingly place themselves on a construction site. A skyscraper is going up, and to Hoppity and his pals it's the end of the world. As Hoppity runs about, his fellow bugs are suddenly hoisted into the air on a building girder. He tries to hop onto the ascending beam and leaps toward the camera in a game but futile effort.

Now the bugs are running for their lives, unable to comprehend the dizzy movement around them. As they rest for a moment, a bricklayer suddenly splashes a wad of mortar on their resting place and slams a brick on top; the insects dash away just in the nick of time, a microsecond away from being crushed. As they search for a safe place on another building girder, that particular stem of the building is riveted and the vibrations nearly shake them over the edge. There is tremendous movement, excitement, and realistic detail in this splendid scene, which, needless to say, has a happy ending.

Unfortunately, one great sequence cannot sustain a feature-length film, and that's exactly the problem with MR. BUG. Reviews of the film were mixed when it was released at Christmas time in 1941, and Paramount didn't have much faith in the cartoon feature, to judge from its treatment of the property. Possibly, the choice of insects as main characters was unwise, as indicated by the film's subsequent reissue under the title HOPPITY GOES TO TOWN.

Whatever the case, the Fleischer studio only got two turns at bat in the feature-film arena before Paramount Pictures made a harsh decision: to foreclose on Max and Dave

Honey Bee and Hoppity in HOPPITY GOES TO TOWN **(1941).**

and discontinue pumping money into their expensive studio. To say that the Fleischers were stunned would be a mild understatement. Although their personal relationship had deteriorated in recent years, they never dreamed that their studio might be in jeopardy. In fact, it wasn't. Paramount wanted production to continue on short subjects without interruption and contracted with three longtime studio employees—animator Seymour Kneitel (who had married Max's daughter Ruth), story man Isadore (Izzy) Sparber, and business manager Sam Buchwald—to run the operation.

But Max and Dave Fleischer were severed from the company in what was possibly, and even probably, an illegal maneuver; unfortunately, by the time Max tried to sue Paramount, the waters were too muddy, and too much time had passed, to achieve a fair resolution. The continuing feud between Max and Dave didn't help matters any.

So, after more than twenty years, the brothers were out of business. Their key employees stayed on the job for Paramount, which renamed the operation Famous Studios and moved the streamlined staff back to New York. But the magic was gone, and so was the creative spark in Max and Dave. They worked elsewhere, but never as well as they had in their own shop. Their days of pioneering contributions were past.

Max worked for the Jam Handy Company in Detroit making commercial and educational films, and later spent some time in the employ of his old colleague John R. Bray. By all accounts his actual work there was minimal, and he was regarded more or less as a figurehead. He continued to experiment with new film-related inventions, and was associated with various other projects during the next fifteen years, but none of them amounted to much in concrete terms. Max was always treated with the respect due an industry pioneer, but he was, after all, an old man (he turned seventy in 1953), and the film business has always thrived on youth. In 1961 he participated in production of one hundred new OUT OF THE INKWELL cartoons for television with a former employee, Hal Seeger. The pilot film featured Max on screen and made use of the venerable INKWELL format; there was even a Bouncing Ball sequence led by Koko. But the subsequent series abandoned these delightful vintage elements to concentrate on routine cartoon stories instead. They were no better or worse than other cheaply made assembly-line programs for the small screen, and the whole output couldn't hold a candle to any one INKWELL cartoon made forty years earlier by Max, Dave, and a handful of assistants.

Dave Fleischer found work at Columbia Pictures' cartoon studio. Relocated on the West Coast, he quickly discovered that animation people there didn't have much respect for his freewheeling approach to film making. Fittingly enough, he was most appreciated at Universal as a kind of troubleshooter for their live-action films and spent fifteen years there, working on everything from gags and story construction to special effects. He died in 1979 after a decade of retirement.

In the mid-1960s, Max and his wife moved to the Motion Picture Country Home, where he died in 1972 at the age of eighty-nine. As happens so often, it was just at this time that a nationwide revival of Fleischer cartoons was getting under way, focusing new attention on this long-neglected man and celebrating the innovations in his cartoons.

Max and his brother may have been neglected for many years, but the best films they made have stood the test of time, and that's as nice a compliment as one could pay any artist—or inventor.

Paul Terry and Terrytoons

SEVERAL GENERATIONS of Terrytoons employees came to know Paul Terry's oft-repeated motto: "Disney is the Tiffany's in this business, and I am the Woolworth's."

Terry's candid boast clearly revealed his attitude toward the cartoons he made. There was no love involved, and no artistic motivation. It was a product, which he manufactured on an uncompromising schedule . . . and sold with remarkable success. The chronicle of Terry's career is not one of artistic growth and achievement, but rather the story of survival and prosperity in the business of making animated cartoons.

Studio veteran Tommy Morrison explained, "We worked on volume and price. We would turn out twenty-six cartoons a year with a staff that was maybe *one fifth* the size of a Disney staff, who would turn out probably a lot less product. The Disney story departments, for instance, were divided up into units. And each unit would spend six to eight weeks on a story. And then if they weren't satisfied with it, they would shelve it and another unit could pick it up and try to develop it *further!* So many of their stories were developed over months of work, where we had a *schedule*. We had to knock out a

story every two weeks. *One* story department. As I say, we were a budget studio and we worked on volume and price. That, I believe, was Terry's theory."

"Every other Tuesday," Jack Zander recalls, "without fail, we would all get up and march into the projection room and see a new picture. He ground out a picture every two weeks, and I don't know how the hell he did it."

Terry's longtime partner, animator Frank Moser, had one answer: "We started with twenty people and sweat from morning until night to get the pictures out. I was there at eight thirty in the morning and kept working until five thirty, and when I went home I was tired out. I just did the best I could, and I sweat blood to deliver those pictures . . . every second week."

Hard work wasn't the only way Terry met his deadlines. He spent as little money on the films as possible; keeping them simple

121

made them easier and faster to produce. New and innovative ideas were frowned upon; Terry relied on formulas and repetition in his cartoons, and often reused animation from earlier films.

Outstanding creative talents could not survive at this studio, and the few who passed through its doors soon left for greener pastures. Terry leaned instead on his staff of "regulars," who stayed with him for twenty to forty years. They knew his routine by heart and were able to produce assembly-line cartoons almost in their sleep—which seems to have been the case on more than one occasion.

Terry's attitude may have been formed by some early experiences in the film business. His first encounter with indifference to animated cartoons came in 1915, when he tried to sell his first film, LITTLE HERMAN. He went to see Lewis J. Selznick, then a prominent producer/distributor, who watched his cartoon and offered him one dollar a foot for the finished product.

"Mr. Selznick," Terry explained, "the film I used cost me more than a dollar a foot."

"Well," said Selznick, "I could pay you more for it if you hadn't put those pictures on it!"

(Telling this story a half century later, Terry said he was never sure whether or not Selznick was pulling his leg. Nevertheless, the fact remains the distributor wasn't willing to offer him much for an ordinary animated cartoon.)

Another Terry recollection: "Way back in the early days, I remember one time I was talking to an exhibitor. He said, 'Well, yes, we use TERRYTOONS. We run the feature and then we put on a TERRYTOON and that drives the people out of the house.' So they have room for the line outside, so they can get in and get a seat. They used it as a cathartic."

The final blow to artistic ambition was probably struck by the business realities of running a cartoon factory. As Terry explained, "We'd start out to make a contract with the theaters, so you'd sign up a theater to use 26 pictures. When you get to December, you find that they'd only used 18, 15, or 20 because they didn't have room for them. Well, you couldn't insist upon them using them or paying for them. You'd have to cancel that contract to get them to sign a new contract for the following year. So the pictures that you put out in the first part of the season always did pretty well, and those that you put out at the end were not so good. The result was that the quality of the pictures didn't make any difference. The finest pictures may be released toward the end of the year; if they were, they wouldn't get any more consideration because they were good, bad, or indifferent. They're sold like ribbons."

Paul Terry wasn't always so cold-blooded about the animation field. In fact, he was one of the first working animators in the country. He came to this new medium through the same route that others followed at the time—newspaper cartooning—and did his fair share of experimentation and pioneering.

Paul Houlton Terry was born on February 19, 1887, in San Mateo, California. He was the youngest of five children (a sixth had died), and never got to know his mother, who died before he was one year old. His father was an auctioneer and apparently quite a flamboyant character. In later years Terry compared his household to the one in *You Can't Take It with You*. His brothers and sisters were all artistically inclined, and his father encouraged them to develop their talents. "It was a nice background to be raised in," he concluded.

The Terrys lived in the Richmond District

of San Francisco at the turn of the century. Paul was never much of a student. "I probably was a dreamer, more or less," he confessed, "and I applied myself to drawing more to the detriment of everything else."

He also idolized his older brother John and followed his example by quitting high school to work on a newspaper, the *San Francisco Bulletin.* He began as an office boy, but when he heard of a job on the *Chronicle* for a photographer, he spent one weekend learning the principles of photography and applied for the position on Monday. He was hired and was on the *Chronicle* staff at the time of the earthquake and fire of 1906.

Terry spent the next few years roaming the Northwest, working for various newspapers in Montana, Oregon, and eventually San Francisco again. Although he continued to draw, his principal occupation at this time was that of photographer. He returned to the drawing board when he made "the big move" to New York in 1911, and landed a job with the firm that controlled all subway and streetcar advertising in the city. He left them to work for the *New York Press* (which soon became the *Evening Sun*), illustrating stories in their Sunday supplement. He also drew a comic strip called *Alonzo,* which, in Terry's words, "didn't make any great mark in the world," although it was briefly syndicated by Hearst's King Features.

Then Terry shared a very special evening with many other budding artists in New York. "I went to a dinner one night, when I was on the *New York Press,* and that's where Winsor McCay showed us his picture GERTIE THE DINOSAUR. And all at once it consolidated, right there." After working in advertising agencies, and spending his time drifting from one newspaper to another, Terry knew what he wanted to do full-time. (His brother John was following a similar path; he had experimented with animation as early as

A sketch of Paul Terry by animator Jerry Shields.

1911 in San Francisco, in collaboration with Hugh (Jerry) Shields.)

He set to work on his first film, LITTLE HERMAN, a spoof of Hermann, a great magician of the day, doing his act. It was a one-man operation, and Terry provided his own gags and story. As he said, "See, 'way back in the early days, when I was going to high school, I got a job as an usher in a theater, in a vaudeville house. And of course I wasn't conscious of it, but I was absorbing gags and things that went on. And I learned a lot about show business."

He bought a secondhand camera and experimented with different techniques. At one time he devised an early matte system in which the background would be photographed separately and then the characters and action sandwiched together to make a print. His first film was animated on paper with the background overlaid on a cel.

Terry sold LITTLE HERMAN to the Thanhouser film company for $1.35 a foot; it was approximately three hundred feet in length. While waiting to see the boss, Terry screened his film for some neighborhood kids in the Thanhouser projection room. "When they ran the picture, these kids began to squeal. And that tipped me off to the idea to draw things that would appeal to kids; because if they laughed at it, the adults wouldn't have to know if it was funny, or whether it wasn't, because kids' laughter is so infectious. I decided right then and there, you make pictures for kids. I probably didn't know enough to make anything for adults, anyway."

Now Terry was prepared to devote all his energies to the making of animated cartoons. He contracted some work from William Randolph Hearst and then approached his friend

Bud Fisher, whom he had met back in San Francisco, with the idea of turning Fisher's popular *Mutt and Jeff* comic strip into a film series. Terry made a pilot film that Fisher used as part of a vaudeville act, much as Winsor McCay had done with GERTIE THE DINOSAUR.

Terry was anxious to arrange with Fisher to do a continuing series, "but he was a very difficult fellow to deal with because he was always too busy doing something else. You could never nail him down. So time went on, maybe six months, and I couldn't wait that long to do something, so I made a deal with J. R. Bray to make some Farmer Al Falfa pictures. And I'd just about signed up to make this series for a year or something when Fisher came around and said, 'Well, I'm all ready to go now.'" It was too late for Terry, and Fisher hired Charles Bowers instead.

Meanwhile, Terry became one of John R. Bray's staff animators and produced a monthly entry for Bray's screen magazine. It was at this time that he created an original character named Farmer Al Falfa, a bald, white-bearded old farmer who wore overalls and smoked a corncob pipe. Farmer Al Falfa didn't have much personality, but his constant skirmishes with barnyard animals kept him busy in these films for many years.

Terry was one of the first men to adopt Earl Hurd's cel process for his cartoons. Besides giving his films an impressive range of tones, which many competitors did not have at this time, the cel system enabled Terry to devise labor-saving methods of animating Farmer Al Falfa. "The drawing was made so that you could put the arm on a separate cel, and something else on another one," he later explained. "And the costume was designed so you could save a lot of labor, you wouldn't have to draw the whole thing." Already he was learning the secrets of assembly-line production.

A chubby-looking Farmer Al Falfa, in the silent days.

His work for Bray was interrupted by war service. In 1917 Terry was inducted into the Army and assigned to "record the medical history of the war, visually. Because in performing operations, they found that if the surgeon didn't tell you what he was doing you would never know from the photograph, because the blood photographed black. So they sent me to George Washington University and I studied under Dr. King about anatomy from a surgeon's angle. And my studio was right in the middle of the Army Medical Museum, which is the finest in the world."

The films covered a wide range of topics, from hernias to obstetrics, and used both live action and animation. Terry worked with a small staff, which included illustrator Frank Godwin, photographer Lucien Andriot, and director Sidney Franklin, for the balance of 1917 and 1918.

At the end of World War I, Terry returned to New York and formed a company with fellow animators Earl Hurd, Frank Moser, Hugh (Jerry) Shields, Leighton Budd, and his brother John Terry. This alliance was short-lived, and John Terry broke off to start his own studio with the staff and properties of Hearst's recently closed animation house. Paul continued making Farmer Al Falfa cartoons for Paramount release through 1920, at which time he stumbled onto an idea that would cement his reputation in the cartoon field.

One day just as Terry was leaving Paramount he received a call from a young actor-turned-writer named Howard Estabrook, who had an idea of making a series of animated cartoons based on *Aesop's Fables*. Terry later claimed that he'd never heard of Aesop, but he listened to Estabrook's idea and recognized something worthwhile. "Of course, by the time we got through with 'em, they didn't look like Aesop's Fables," he admitted, "but it's a foundation."

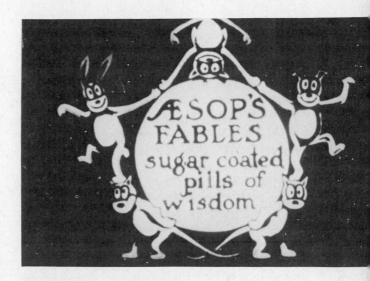

The fact that most of these fables depicted human foibles with animal characters was a perfect format for cartoons. Terry also learned that using animals in this way practically eliminated the possibility of offending anyone in the audience through ethnic stereotypes of human improprieties. This gave the series a good reputation with theater owners.

But the biggest novelty of the series was the idea of using an Aesop-type moral at the conclusion of each picture. Sometimes these sayings were closely intertwined with the film, but more often they were merely gag lines with only a slight relationship to the plot.

"The fact that they're ambiguous is the thing that made 'em funny," Terry contended. "Aesop said 2600 years ago that 'the race to the altar is run in laps,' or, 'Marriage is a good institution, but who wants to live in an institution?' If you put serious morals on, they wouldn't have gone at all, too heavy."

Mannie Davis, who later joined Terry as an animator and director, said, "They were funnier than the whole picture itself. Sometimes they were all that people remembered, the moral; they don't remember the pictures."

Terry cleverly kept his Farmer Al Falfa character alive by incorporating him into the fables, alternating between no-character cartoons and those that featured the farmer. The series was released by Pathé from its inception in 1921 and received immediate praise from the trade press. By 1924 *Moving Picture World* could write: "Reviewing one of Paul Terry's Aesop Fable cartoons is a matter requiring deliberation, simply because they maintain such a high standard of excellence that the reviewer fears repeating words of praise he has used often before, and digs into the dictionary to learn how to praise again without 'pulling the same old line.' The current fable, which is based on the saying ONE GOOD TURN DESERVES ANOTHER, is another work of art in the field of humorous imagination—let that suffice. Terry illustrates the idea by showing how a dog repays the kindness of a mouse by protecting it from a swarm of cats. The most remarkable bit of drawing is where two mice indulge in a game of handball."

Actually, the most remarkable thing about the Aesop's Fables is that Terry turned out *one a week* for eight years! That's a record unrivaled until the television era. To pull this feat off, Terry needed two things: a staff and financial backing. The staff numbered about twenty, with four or five director-animators: Frank Moser, Harry Bailey, John Foster, Fred Anderson, and Jerry Shields. They were joined later in the 1920s by Mannie Davis, and one of the studio neophytes was Bill Tytla.

"The artists, they all varied," Terry later commented. "When you had a situation, if it was a personality thing, you'd give it to a fellow like Tytla. If it was an action thing, you'd give it to a fellow like Moser. Moser was wonderful on waves, anything that had to do with mechanical subjects. But when he came to human beings, he wasn't the best. Other fellows were good. There was a fellow named Jerry Shields whose animation was very crude, but everything he did was funny."

Terry provided the basic stories. Many of his "morals" were borrowed from a short-subject series called TOPICS OF THE DAY, and others he devised himself. (Terry kept a gag file throughout his life, as a hobby as well as a business, and later bought out the gag collection of Joe Laurie, Jr.) He seldom participated in the animation of these films, preferring to run the business and work on story ideas.

"The story was very sketchy," Mannie Davis recalled in 1970. "The main thing was to get a laugh out of each little act. You know, a little piece of antic that a character would do. Today it wouldn't mean a damn thing; it's got to be acted out and it's got to have continuity of thought. [Then] we'd be springing all over the lot. But we would keep it . . . in the location it started out in. If it's an African story, everything would be down in the jungle, and then in the desert, and all that.

"I was my own director, my own story man, and my own animator. Each man did his own thing, his little reel [it was about five hundred feet], and we had, I think, one month to make them . . . there were five of us making them and [we] rotated."

The backing for this series came from an unusual source. The Keith-Albee Theatre circuit, then one of the largest chains of vaudeville and film theaters in the country, set up Terry in business as Fables Pictures Inc. The name later changed to Fables Studio, but the arrangement was the same: Keith-Albee, which eventually became RKO, owned 90 percent of the company and Terry owned the remaining 10 percent. The films were distributed by Pathé, but, in Terry's words, "the theater people assured its business."

The AESOP'S FABLES series chugged along throughout the 1920s, with no dramatic improvement or change in format. This could be said of the product of many silent-film cartoon studios, but in Terry's case the sheer volume of work, and the duration of his staff's tenure at the studio, worked against any opportunities for improvement.

Seen today, the silent FABLES have nothing distinctive or remarkable to recommend them. They are capably produced, if primitive in many ways, and the preponderance of mice as characters limits their novelty value from one reel to the next. There is none of the invention that distinguished the FELIX and the OUT OF THE INKWELL cartoons, and none of the personality that gave such characters as Mutt and Jeff their widespread appeal. At best, the FABLES are pleasant, fast-moving time-fillers, but, as Mannie Davis indicated, their story lines are virtually nil.

In 1928 the arrival of sound sent shock waves throughout the film industry, but Terry was reluctant to move into this new field. At the direction of his new boss, Amadee J. Van Beuren, whose Van Beuren Productions took over the Fables Studio for Keith-Albee, Terry released his first cartoon with a synchronized sound track in late 1928; its title was DINNER TIME. But Terry was content to continue adding simple sound tracks to silent product, and Van Bueren was not. This led to a clash between the men.

Frank Moser later recounted, during testimony for a trial, "When Disney came out with sound, I said to Terry, 'Paul,' I said, 'This fellow Disney is going into sound.

Typical Terry animals—and lots of them—in A CLOSE CALL (1924).

What are we going to do to keep pace with him?' And Terry told me that he wouldn't do anything for Van Beuren, and immediately thereafter Van Beuren fired him." It may well have been that Terry was looking for an excuse to go out on his own, but, whatever the case, Terry left the Fables company in 1929, while most of his staff stayed behind.

At this time, Terry approached Moser and asked if he'd like to become his partner in a new studio. Moser said yes, and the two shook hands. Then Moser went to a company called Audio Cinema for possible backing. There he met a Joseph Coffman, an expert on the new medium of talking pictures who was working as a consultant to various film companies; Coffman joined the two cartoonists to form Moser-Terry-Coffman. Audio Cinema agreed to finance the cartoons and provide space in their headquarters (the old Edison studio in the Bronx), but Terry and Moser were to work without pay until Audio had recouped its cost. Educational Pictures agreed to distribute the cartoons.

Allowing for the exigencies of producing cartoon with sound, Terry and Moser cut back on the FABLES schedule of one a week and contracted to make twenty-six a year instead. This timetable was no bed of roses, however, and the small studio had to work feverishly to meet its deadlines.

The task of integrating music into the cartoon stories and providing full-length scores fell to Philip A. Scheib. Scheib was a former child prodigy who had studied the violin in a Berlin music conservatory, returned to America to work in a more popular vein for Thomas Edison, and then found gainful employment orchestrating music for silent films. When talking pictures became a reality, it was a natural progression for Scheib to become involved with musical sound tracks.

"He had a lot of experience," Terry recalled, "but he relied upon his [music] library. So when he came to work for me, after the first picture I said, 'Listen, this won't work. You've got to write original scores. . . . I don't care how poor it is, or how good, but it's got to be written for this.'" Scheib stayed with Terrytoons for thirty years and saved the company many thousands of dollars in music rights by never once using a popular song, relying strictly on original material and tunes in the public domain.

Scheib also helped the Terry staff members conquer their initial fears of synchronizing animation to music, and enabled them to animate lip movement for song renditions from the very beginning in 1930. Terry later claimed that he was the first to completely prescore his cartoons.

Except for the musical element, these early-1930s Terrytoons are virtually indistinguishable from the 1920s AESOP'S FABLES. There is no discernible difference in story or animation values, although the company's first sound releases hewed to a theme, as described in a trade-paper advertisement: "Each subject is based on the popular music and customs of a different nation. CAVIAR starts the fun with more excitement than a Bolshevik riot. And after that there will be a new one every other week." Other titles included SPANISH ONIONS, HOT TURKEY, ROMAN PUNCH, CHOP SUEY, and SCOTCH HIGHBALL.

Paul Terry spent his time working on stories and coordinating his ideas with Philip Scheib. Frank Moser spent all of his time animating, and supervising the rest of the staff.

Tommy Morrison recalled, "In the early days, each animator made his own rough layout of the scene which he would hand to the background artist. And Moser acted just as any other animator, except that he was the boss. And he more or less supervised the giving out of scenes. He was a prodigious worker and probably could do twice as much as anybody else on the staff."

Bill Weiss confirms, "Moser was a prolific animator and he could on an average animate half the picture himself. And he would have a stock setup of backgrounds. Everything would move along at a tremendous pace, which is what kept the costs down."

But not everyone was so enamored of Moser's abilities. Said Mannie Davis, "He was a very clever guy with his pencil, but he wasn't funny. He was very, very fast, could make the stuff move nicely in those days. But he really had no sense of humor; he couldn't get a gag over. We were always at odds about that."

Two of Moser's young animators were equally upset about the lack of true quality in the studio's product. One of them was Art Babbitt, who left Terrytoons in 1932 to work for Walt Disney, and the other was Bill Tytla,

Babbitt's close friend, who stayed until 1934. Tytla had worked for Terry before, in the 1920s, and was familiar with Moser's work from that time. But he had gone to Europe in 1929 to study art and broaden his own horizons, and upon his return he had less patience with Moser's limited talents.

Tytla later spoke of this period in a lecture to Disney's animation class. Of Moser and other senior Terry artists, he said, "They couldn't do much if you took them off cats and mice. If there was a scene of an old man hit by a club and beautiful girls floated around him in his daze, the lead animators couldn't animate the girls—we would have to . . . It was just purely accidental that one or two of us liked drawing and went to art school because it was a lot of fun besides."

The atmosphere at Terrytoons was stifling for men like Babbitt and Tytla, and when Disney beckoned they gladly left. (Another Disney regular, Norman Ferguson, had been with Terry in the 1920s.) This left Moser and the Terry "regulars" who either didn't care about quality and innovation or trained themselves not to.

Moser and Terry parted company with Coffman early in the company's history, but stayed with Audio Cinema until 1932, when that firm hit the skids. Bill Weiss, then controller for the company, explained, "They made their money in engineering and wasted it in film production. When the sheriff moved in on Audio Cinema, Terry and Moser moved out." Weiss went with them as secretary and business manager as they relocated in the Harlem headquarters of Consolidated Film Laboratories. Then in 1934 Terrytoons moved to New Rochelle, New York.

Moser spent so much of his time on animation that he paid scant attention to the business of which he was half owner, but he did have certain concerns that caused deadlocks with his partner. One was the use of

color. Terry was dead set against it, just as he had been with sound, and for the same reason: higher costs. Another of Terry's beliefs was less pragmatic: He favored a variety of one-shot cartoons over the development of continuing characters.

On this point everyone argued with him. Says Weiss, "It was a constant battle with Terry for years and years—even on my part—until we came along with such characters as Puddy the Pup and Kiko the Kangaroo, which was certainly nothing to brag about. Kiko was the result of a discussion with Roger Ferri, the editor of the 20th Century-Fox house organ, who thought it would be a great idea if we had a kangaroo as a cartoon character. Puddy the Pup was, I think, one of the dogs that Terry's daughter had."

These characters were consistent with the overall personality of Terrytoons: genial and pleasant, but in no way memorable. At a time when Disney was making enormous

A posed shot of Farmer Al Falfa and Kiko the Kangaroo from FARMER AL FALFA'S PRIZE PACKAGE **(1936).** © **Terrytoons.**

strides in the development of animated film, Harman and Ising were trying to keep pace with Disney, Warner Brothers was pioneering a new kind of cartoon humor, and Fleischer was creating worldwide impact with his Popeye series, Paul Terry was content to just keep cranking out the same little time-fillers he'd always made.

In a short-term sense, Terry's attitude was sound. He and Moser were doing well, even though the average cost of making a cartoon had risen from the $4,000 range in the early 1930s to a range of $6–7,000 in 1935. The studio was working like a well-oiled machine. Production time was incredibly rapid. Once the story and sound track were completed, it was as little as two months from animation boards to theater screens for an average Terrytoon. But there was trouble brewing in this "perfect setup."

The cartoons were contracted to Educational Pictures Corporation, which in turn supplied short-subject product to 20th Century Fox. In 1935, Fox and Educational started receiving—and initiating—complaints about the quality of Terrytoons. Terry ignored these complaints and, in February 1936, was informed by Educational's president, Earl Hammons, that the company would not renew its contract for another season of cartoon shorts.

Moser and Terry were stunned. In the following week, they talked about possible solutions and examined the state of their business. Terry offered to buy out Moser's share in the company, hoping to find backing elsewhere to keep going. Moser agreed, sold his half interest, and, for all intents and purposes, disappeared from the animation scene. One week later, Terry signed a new two-year contract with Educational Pictures by making Hammons a major commitment to upgrade the quality of his cartoons. (Moser subsequently sued Terry, Hammons,

and business manager Weiss, claiming that they had conspired against him, and that the value of the business had been misrepresented to him. He lost his case.)

Tommy Morrison recalled: "Shortly after Moser left, Terry did expand our facilities and organized the story department so he no longer wrote all the stories. He started to buy new equipment, new cameras, and took more space in the building. The directors after that began to make the layout, rather than each individual animator making his own layout. The director would stage the picture. When Moser was there, you might have considered him a director although he didn't fulfill the complete function of the director."

Terry appointed Mannie Davis and George Gordon as directors at this time, and then found himself with a ready talent pool through a most fortuitous (and ironic) circumstance: the demise of Van Beuren Productions. With the closing of his former employer's studio, Terry was able to rehire not only some of his colleagues from the FABLES era, but a number of bright young men as well: Jack Zander, Dan Gordon, Ray Kelly, and Joe Barbera.

To the latter neophytes, the atmosphere at Terry's was little short of awesome. "He used to save drawings," says Zander. "Paul would file away runs, walks, actions, and so forth. He had an old guy working for him who knew where all this stuff was. If we had a mouse running across a scene, which most of Paul Terry's stuff did, he would go get that scene and we'd use the same mouse again. They might possibly opaque him a different color, but maybe not."

For one film, Dan Gordon devised a gag involving a typical Terry mouse. Paul Terry mulled it over and said, "Put two mice in." Gordon asked why, and Terry replied, "If one mouse is funny, two mice will be twice

DRAWING THE STORY

T HE story of a cartoon is not written, but drawn in a series of sketches showing the highlights of the picture, indicating the backgrounds, and giving the key for each sequence of action of the characters.

For example, a story calls for Kiko the Kangaroo to take the part of a fireman. Rough sketches numbers 1 and 2 show how one section of the burning building is to look and how Kiko will land on the ledge after flying over the street on a rope. Sketches 3, 4 and 5 indicate scenes in other pictures.

PAGES FROM A CARTOON SCENARIO
Paul Terry and staff executives discussing the story roughs for a Terry-Toon cartoon. Left to right George Gordon, chief animator for Mr. Terry; Mannie Davis, story director; Philip A. Scheib, musical director.

The evolution of a scene, as described by Terrytoons in a late-1930s publicity handout.

as funny." His word was law, and two mice were used.

But the most amazing part of the Terry operation, in Zander's eyes, was the preparation of the sound track. "Phil Scheib would have the most amazing recording session you ever saw in your life, and I know, because I participated in a lot of them. We would lay out a cartoon, a storyboard, and roughly time it. Then Phil would get his band in a recording studio and in one take the music and the effects and the voices would be recorded—everything at once."

Animators and others on the staff would participate. "You were there watching these music sheets and you'd hit something or you'd yell or whatever, and if it didn't come out exactly right, too bad. We made the animation fit the sound track."

Naturally, this hampered the freedom of the directors and animators, who had no chance to revise their thoughts or embellish a scene. Once the track was recorded there was no opportunity for changes to be made. Moser had proposed that Terry modify this system sometime earlier, but Terry wouldn't

The HEALTH FARM

A publicity drawing for THE HEALTH FARM (1936) with Farmer Al Falfa and Puddy the Pup. If only the animation had captured the spirit and energy of drawings like this. © Terrytoons.

budge. Now the studio newcomers found similar problems. "We tried some new ideas on him, but he wasn't really very receptive," says Zander. "He didn't want to experiment."

Terry's stubbornness cost him dearly. Zander got a phone call from Carmen "Max" Maxwell at MGM offering a job to him and any other talented fellows who were interested in joining the reorganized studio. Zander talked to Dan Gordon, Ray Kelly, Joe Barbera, and Terry's animator-turned-story man Carl "Mike" Meyer; they all quit at once, and, says Zander, "broke Paul's heart, because he had begun to like us and liked what we were doing." Terry was so miffed that he apparently removed their names from the credits of two cartoons that were about to be released. TRAILER LIFE and THE VILLAIN STILL PURSUED HER credited Paul Terry alone. George Gordon, who was one of Terry's particular favorites, was to leave a short time later. "If he had stayed," says Bill Weiss, "Terry had enough faith in him to let him run the place."

"This whole group went out and of course they didn't stay together . . . however, if this crew could have been kept together, I'm sure that the company probably would have been a lot more successful, both financially and certainly in prestige," Weiss concludes.

Initially, the loss of this bright young team left Terry unprepared. "So I guess in desperation," says Tommy Morrison, "he said to me, 'You always wanted to be a story man. Now you're head of the story department.' The only one who didn't go west who had an offer was George Gordon; he stayed on as director and he was the first one I worked with on a story. He came in to me—and I guess Terry had offered him a considerable amount of money to stay on, because he needed him badly—and said, 'My God, what are we going to do now?' You know, we had no story department.

"I said, 'Well, don't get excited, we'll work it out.' I started to dictate a story and he started to sketch it up. We put it up [on the board] and Terry came in and reviewed it, which he did with every story that the former story department worked on. And he seemed to think it was pretty good. I think it was THE DOG AND THE BONE. From then on I worked on stories."

Eventually, Terry appointed John Foster the head of his story department. Foster had worked with Terry back in the 1920s and had stayed with Van Beuren when Terry left. In the mid-thirties he returned to Terry's studio, as did Mannie Davis, who described Foster as "a homemade artist. He never studied, he just had a natural knack with comedy. He couldn't sit down to make an ink drawing, but he adapted himself to animation. It was very funny at times; he could draw enough to put it over." Terry took Foster away from animation and made him chief story man, which he remained for twenty years.

Terry also promoted animators Connie

Rasinski and Eddie Donnelly to director status, although they continued to animate throughout their long tenures at the studio. Davis, Rasinski, and Donnelly began directing in 1937 and with very few exceptions were the studio's only directors for the next two decades. Davis stayed on until 1961 and Rasinski worked for Terrytoons until he died.

Tommy Morrison, who had joined the studio in 1933 as an all-round apprentice (his father was a friend of Terry's), remained in the story department and eventually became story supervisor. His varied duties included writing lyrics for songs in the cartoons and supervising recording sessions. Morrison later did voices, and he too stayed with Terrytoons to the very end.

Having loyal employees who regarded the studio as their permanent home came in handy when Terry was faced with unionization in the 1940s. Most of his key men had been with Terrytoons for the best part of their adult life, and as senior employees they were well paid. "If they were there shorter than twenty-five years they were considered newcomers," Terry joked. "They stayed with me because I thought in terms of them. They were necessary to our success. And I gave them screen credit. . . . They all like to see their name in type or in lights or something. And I could never see why I should say it was just I that was doing it, because they were all so important."

Terry only bequeathed this honor to his key associates, however. To the day he sold his studio he never gave credit to his animators, let alone inkers, painters, and other technicians. In 1970 he evaluated the merits of some longtime employees:

"John Foster was the best, the most *brilliant*. They say, if you take a little out of this and a little out of that it's called research. That's very commendable. But if you take a big bite out of any one thing, that's plagia-rism and you're a thief. So, we used to have a saying, John Foster and I, 'Never steal more than you can carry.'

"Eddie Donnelly was a very hard worker. I remember we used to wash the cels and use them over again in [the 1930s], and Ed even used to do that at night so he could make a little extra money. [He started] at Fables, and he got to be a very good director. He was on a par with Connie Rasinski, and Connie was the best.

"He [Rasinski] came to work when it was Terry, Moser & Coffman. A friend of an old friend of mine named Litchfield, who was a painter, passed away, and his wife sent this kid over to get a job, and I gave him a job. And that's Connie. [His brother Joe worked for Terrytoons as a cameraman for many years, as well.] Connie, who came to work for me as a kid, developed very rapidly and he was with me practically all his life. He was fat and everything he drew was chubby and round and well fed."

The lower-echelon employees at Terrytoons who didn't feel so well fed easily succumbed to the idea of unionization when a West Coast organizer joined the staff in the early 1940s. "We were originally under the Brotherhood of Painters and Paperhangers," Tommy Morrison later recounted with some amusement, "because there was no other place to put us. And figuring that they use paints, it would be good if we were connected with them.

"But I resigned from the union because they were going to call a strike, which I knew would be deadly for everybody that worked here. The studio had piled up a backlog of films that could keep us going for a year or more. And I told the union that the strike would be disastrous, knowing . . . that Terry could just let everybody go and release these films.

"The studio operated with I guess what you might call scabs for a great many

A scene from G-MAN JITTERS, **with an early version of**
Gandy Goose (1939). © **Terrytoons.**

months. The strike lasted eight or nine
months. These people were out on the street
without jobs. And in the meantime other
people came in asking for jobs. It was a non-
union shop and they took the jobs of those
that had been out on the street.''

Eventually, Terry came to terms with
these workers, and sometime later they were
absorbed by the International Alliance of
Theatrical and Stage Employees and a more
legitimate union organization was formed.
But Morrison was right when he first warned
his fellow workers about striking. Terry virtually lost nothing during that nine-month
period.

In 1938, Terry bowed to commercial pressures and produced his first cartoon in color,
STRING BEAN JACK. The use of color was quite
good, and Terry's uncredited background
artists provided some truly attractive settings. Unfortunately, the character animation was less inspired than the backdrops,
with director John Foster designing his lead
character to look exactly like Jerry from the

Van Beuren TOM AND JERRY series of the early
1930s. They were following the ''Jack and the
Beanstalk'' story, which had one sequence
involving a harp, but Terry wasn't about to
hire a harpist to record this brief piece of
music, so Scheib used a piano on the sound
track instead! Fortunately, STRING BEAN JACK
had enough gags and peppy ideas to overcome these shortcomings.

Terry still wasn't prepared to absorb the
additional expense of full-color production,
however. He tried to postpone the inevitable
by releasing other cartoons in sepia tone,
sprinkling his output with a handful of color
entries each season until 1943, when black-
and-white finally bit the dust.

Terry also began to accept the idea of
developing more starring characters around
this time. Kiko the Kangaroo and Puddy the
Pup were put out to pasture and Farmer Al
Falfa disappeared. The first of Terry's new
''stars'' was christened Gandy Goose (after a
trial run as Willie) and was featured in his
own series beginning in 1938.

Gandy was inspired by Ed Wynn, whose
voice and fluttery mannerisms were imitated
by voice expert Arthur Kay. The success of
this character cued the Terry staff to a formula later adopted by Hanna and Barbera in
the television era: Copying the distinctive
voice of a popular entertainer can create
instant audience appeal. Gandy was really as
limited a character as any of Terry's earlier
creations, but his *voice* made him work. The
endearing silliness of Ed Wynn carried over
to Gandy Goose and gave the story men
something tangible to work with. They
adapted the story of Chicken Little and called
it DOOMSDAY, with Gandy as the bearer of
news that the sky is falling. In G-MAN JIT-
TERS they pictured him in anthropomorphic
terms as a little boy who smokes his father's
pipe and dreams that he's a Sherlock
Holmes–type detective.

Then they started to run dry. Someone

suggested a sidekick for Gandy, a straight man to offset his silly personality, so the studio resurrected a cat that had appeared in the one-shot cartoon THE OWL AND THE PUSSY-CAT and named him Sourpuss. Like Gandy, his voice and mannerisms were "borrowed" from someone else: Jimmy Durante.

Having come this far, the studio then fell into what became the "Terry trap" of the 1940s: the formula cartoon. The story department, in 1940, worked out a most enjoyable script for THE MAGIC PENCIL, which introduced Sourpuss as Gandy's friendly nemesis: Gandy acquires a pencil that makes drawings that come to life. Greedy Sourpuss takes advantage of the situation and eventually causes the destruction of the pencil. (This cartoon was directed by Volney White, who was at the studio for just one year before he moved to California.)

THE MAGIC PENCIL is an entertaining and imaginative cartoon. But seeing its success, the Terry crew, under pressure of turning out a new story every two weeks, decided that what worked one time would work again—and again—and again. For ten years they repeated the Gandy-Sourpuss formula with cookie-cutter precision. The specific details of each cartoon would change, but it was simply a matter of filling in the blanks. (During the war, the story men drafted Gandy and Sourpuss and created a subformula for their army antics.) Some of the later entries in this series such as DINGBAT LAND and COMIC BOOK LAND, have intriguing fantasy or dream premises, but they always revert to the same set pattern.

Unfortunately, this became the modus operandi of Terry's studio. Repetition was the byword, and that is why even the most avid cartoon buffs find it difficult to distinguish one Terrytoon from another in their minds. Even Philip Scheib's music sounds the same in every cartoon; because he was unable to use popular songs, as Carl Stalling

and Scott Bradley did, he had to rely on his own themes, which tended to sound alike and often *were* actual copies of earlier music.

Sometime around 1940, 20th Century Fox approached Terry with the idea of doing a feature-length cartoon. As Bill Weiss remembers it, "We went so far as to get a line of credit from a bank. And Mr. Terry and I went down to see PINOCCHIO. After we saw PINOCCHIO, our own personal feelings were that it wouldn't measure up to the success of a SNOW WHITE and forgot the venture." Terry recalled in 1970 that a more powerful reason for abandoning the idea was advice he received from his friend Dr. Giannini, President of the Bank of Italy and brother of Bank of America president A. P. Giannini. "He told me, 'Never make a cartoon feature,' because it was too hazardous. And maybe that's one of the reasons why I wouldn't. No, I would never make a feature. I wouldn't even today. If you had the money to make a feature, it'd be a whole lot better to make it in live action." Terry knew that making a feature-length cartoon was a gamble, and he never gambled on anything.

However, in 1942 Terry went against studio tradition by purchasing the rights to an established comic-strip character. Unfortunately the choice, Ernie Bushmiller's *Nancy*, was not well suited to animation. Only two cartoons were made with Nancy and her friend Sluggo, one of which, DOING THEIR BIT, was a paean to the good work of the USO, and the other, SCHOOL DAZE, a series of low-key vignettes strung together by schoolchildren trying to convince their teacher that *Nancy* comic books can teach them lessons better than textbooks. After this brief experiment, Terry reaffirmed his position against the acquisition of outside characters.

The war—which inspired the story for DOING THEIR BIT as well as one sequence in SCHOOL DAZE—offered natural story ideas for several years, and one of them, ALL OUT FOR

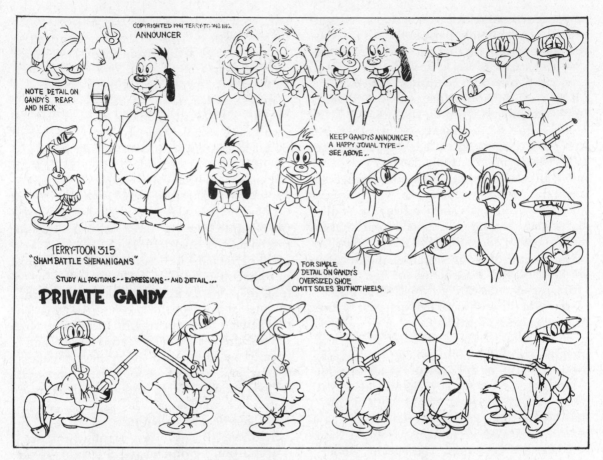

A model sheet from SHAM BATTLE SHENANIGANS (1941). © Terrytoons.

"v," won the studio its first Academy Award nomination. The studio also did a fair share of government-commissioned animation for the armed forces during World War II, although Bill Weiss remarks, "Sometimes we would work on a film that would be obsolete while we were working on it."

Back in the 1930s when Walt Disney tried to hire away Terry's "star" animator Bill Tytla, Terry resisted by offering Tytla a series of raises. Finally in 1934 Tytla left for California. Now, nine years later, Tytla was unhappy at the Disney studio, and Terry seized the opportunity to lure him back.

Tytla returned in mid-1943, but quickly grew discouraged at the lack of initiative and the assembly-line approach at the Terry studio. Terry, on the other hand, felt that Tytla had his limitations as a director. "He was one of the best animators that ever lived," Terry later said. "And he could render anything that you gave him to render very well. But he didn't seem to have the starting quality. He was lost unless somebody laid it out pretty well, and then he would embellish it." Tytla's only directing credit for Terry was on a Mighty Mouse cartoon called THE SULTAN'S DAUGHTER, and what impressed Terry was

Tytla's animation, not his direction. "I remember a dancing girl in that picture. [She] really made the picture. A beautiful piece of animation."

Tytla's frustration with the work atmosphere at Terry, combined with apprehensions over the growing labor problems there, caused him to leave the studio barely one year after rejoining its ranks. Again, an important talent went through Terry's revolving door.

Outside the studio, Terry was benevolent and sincerely friendly toward his employees. But within the confines of his New Rochelle offices he was a different person, and his major concern was the story department. In the early 1940s this unit consisted of John Foster, Tommy Morrison, Al Stahl, Donald McKee, and I. Klein, who came to work for Terry in the spring of 1940 after a stint with Disney on the West Coast. Klein later wrote: "Paul Terry took an active part in the story work not only by feeding his own gags to the stories but by a sort of assault-tactic on the story department. During my first two weeks Terry seemed to be a quiet soul, but soon enough his crash method of forcing a story out every two weeks became apparent. He considered himself Mr. Story Department for Terrytoons from whom all ideas originated. Other people's ideas were merely fillers. Nevertheless he expected and demanded support from the 'backfield.'"

Thus, any idea that was really good had to seem as if it came directly from Terry. So when Klein proposed a spoof of the newly popular Superman character using a fly, Terry heard him out and then dismissed the idea. A short time later he brought it up again, as if he'd conceived the whole thing, but in Terry's version the fly became a mouse. The story department set to work and

devised a cartoon called THE MOUSE OF TOMORROW.

In this cartoon the "origin" of Super Mouse is clearly chronicled. Cats of the city have imposed a reign of terror on the rodent community. The mice have barely a chance to live in peace, with endless traps and clever feline footwork sealing their doom. One mouse manages to escape from a particularly hungry cat and runs for shelter into an enormous supermarket. He examines the goods on the long lines of shelves and sets to work on a total transformation: He bathes in Super Soap, swallows Super Soup, munches Super Celery and plunges head first into an enormous piece of Super Cheese—from which he emerges in a flash as Super Mouse! He's no longer a tiny rodent, but a two-footed, humanized mouse with a massive chest and powerful biceps. His costume is like Superman's, with a flowing red cape, and his powers are similar, too: He can fly through the

The debut of Super Mouse (later Mighty Mouse) in THE MOUSE OF TOMORROW (1942). © Terrytoons.

air and repel bullets with his chest. Super Mouse soars to the rescue of his fellow mice and dispatches the neighborhood cats to the moon. Returning to earth, he is hoisted on the shoulders of his happy comrades, as the narrator declares, ''Thus ends the adventure of Super Mouse . . . he seen his job and he done it!''

The spoof element of THE MOUSE OF TOMORROW is mild at best. Beyond the basic concept—a super-powered mouse who saves his friends and foils the cats—there is no real embellishment or innovation. In short, it's a one-joke idea. But Paul Terry and his staff managed to turn this ''one-joke idea'' into the most successful property the studio ever had, doing nothing differently than they had done with any other character: repeating the same format over and over again.

Within one month of THE MOUSE OF TOMORROW's release to theaters, a second Super Mouse cartoon was unveiled. There was no doubt in Terry's mind that it was a solid idea to do so, and the reports from 20th Century Fox echoed that sentiment. But the character underwent at least one major change after a year in movie theaters: His name was switched from Super Mouse to Mighty Mouse. For years it has been assumed that the change came about because of legal action by the owners of Superman, but Bill Weiss says that isn't so. While the first cartoon was in preparation, a Terrytoons employee left the studio and took the idea with him. He went to work for a small publishing house and contributed *his* version of Super Mouse to a new comic book called *Coo Coo Comics*. The first issue appeared in October 1942, the same month that THE MOUSE OF TOMORROW was released to theaters.

By this time, the studio had already prepared other Super Mouse cartoons and had no intention of abandoning its idea because of a competitive comic book. But after a year

Terry decided that it would be foolish to promote a character with the same name as someone else's, and the change was made to Mighty Mouse. Years later, when the original cartoons were released to television, the main titles were refilmed and certain references to Super Mouse on the sound track were altered or eliminated.

Unfortunately, when the Terry crew lifted the idea of Superman for use in their cartoons, they also inherited Superman's major weakness: a one-dimensional personality. Mighty Mouse had no traits or characteristics; he didn't even speak—an off-screen narrator was the only voice heard in these cartoons. His sole raison d'être was to save mice in distress. Moreover, the appeal of Mighty Mouse was derived from his timely appearance at the last minute before hopelessness sets in. This meant that he could not appear until the climax of his own cartoons! For a brief time, the story crew experimented with casting him as ''a mysterious stranger'' who turns into the superhero, but this didn't work out. Mighty Mouse thus holds the distinction of spending less time on-screen than any other major cartoon star in history.

In trying to devise challenges for this character, the story department put Mighty Mouse into such famous disasters as THE JOHNSTOWN FLOOD, KRAKATOA, and THE WRECK OF THE HESPERUS. Paul Terry considered these cartoons failures, because he contended that the audiences didn't want to see Mighty Mouse battling the forces of nature; they wanted to see him lick a flesh-and-blood opponent. And he was right.

Terry also felt that the enduring success of Mighty Mouse was based in part on its religious theme. He explained, ''If you go back through history, when a person is down and there's no more hope, you say, 'It's in God's hands now.' . . . So, taking that as a basis, I'd only have to get the mice in a tough spot

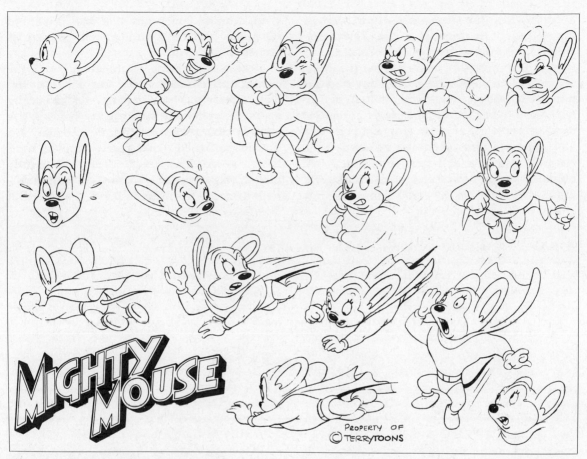

A Mighty Mouse model sheet drawn by Connie Rasinski. © Terrytoons.

and they say, 'Isn't there someone who can help?' 'Yes, there is someone; it's Mighty Mouse!' So down from the heavens he'd come . . . and lick the evil spirit, or whatever it was, and everything would be serene again. It was a pattern-made thing."

The most significant change in the Mighty Mouse series came in the late 1940s. For many years the studio had made musical spoofs of "mellerdrammers" with heroine Fanny Zilch, villainous Silk Hat Harry (aka Oil Can Harry), and a Nelson Eddy–type hero named Strongheart singing their dia-

logue in operetta fashion. The story men merely grafted Mighty Mouse onto this formula as the hero, who would save a mousy heroine from being sawed in two or from some other grisly fate. Tommy Morrison wrote most of the lyrics for these musicals with Philip Scheib, and vocalist Roy Halee was chosen as the singing voice of Mighty Mouse. The successful idea, put to work in such cartoons as LOVE'S LABOR WON, TRIPLE TROUBLE, and THE PERILS OF PEARL PURE-HEART, was milked dry by the usual Terry repetition.

Meanwhile, the studio was riding high on the success of another series that Terry considered the best they ever did: HECKLE AND JECKLE. As Morrison remembers it, these characters came about because Terry had the notion of doing something with twins or look-alikes. (In fact, he had made an earlier cartoon called ICKLE AND PICKLE.) The idea took root in a film called THE TALKING MAGPIES, the studio's first release of 1946. But unlike Mighty Mouse, these characters didn't have the early smell of success; it wasn't until November 1946 that a second film was released and an official series launched.

Heckle and Jeckle stand out among the Terrytoons characters for several reasons. First, Terry's "twin" idea was basically sound; no one else had tried it before. The choice of magpies was certainly unusual, and the design of the characters, coupled with likable voices (one New Yorkese, one slightly British falsetto), gave them a certain jauntiness unrivaled by other studio creations. But

A Heckle and Jeckle model sheet drawn by Connie Rasinski. © Terrytoons.

most importantly, Heckle and Jeckle were the first Terry "stars" who were basically antagonistic. Perhaps they were the studio's answer to the brash, bombastic cartoon stars at Warner Brothers, MGM, and Walter Lantz during the 1940s. Whatever the reason, their mischievous nature immediately set them apart from such gentle predecessors as Puddy the Pup, Gandy Goose, and even Mighty Mouse.

Heckle and Jeckle have several traits in common with Bugs Bunny. Nothing seems to faze them, and they survive risky encounters with enemies secure in the knowledge that everything will turn in their favor. Their saucy attitude extends to calling their adversaries names like "chum." And best of all, they express complete awareness of their pen-and-ink existence. In THE LION HUNT, Heckle (Or is it Jeckle? The two were never differentiated.) persuades his pal to go on a safari, and within an instant a car, then a boat, materialize under their feet to transport them to the jungle. "My," says Jeckle (Or is it Heckle?), "Things happen quickly in a cartoon, don't they?"

One entire cartoon, THE POWER OF THOUGHT, is based on the idea of animated unreality. "We cartoon characters can have a wonderful life," says one of the magpies, "if we only take advantage of it." He illustrates this by showing his friend how he can transform himself into anything at all, just by thinking about it—a mouse, a dog, a street lamp, and so on. Using this animated power, Heckle and Jeckle play havoc with a bulldog policeman's sanity, until the cop catches on and nabs both H. and J. by "doing some thinking of my own."

Unfortunately, this enjoyable aspect of Heckle and Jeckle's personalities became just one more formula ingredient to be repeated time and time again, with little or no variation. The difference here was that the char-

acters themselves brought an immediate appeal to each cartoon, making the repetition more endurable than it was with many other Terry stars. Dayton Allen, who did the magpies' voices for a long time, injected imitations of Groucho Marx and other favorites. In SNO FUN, in which Heckle and Jeckle play mounties, Allen has one of the magpies doing a Humphrey Bogart voice throughout the cartoon; in OUT AGAIN, IN AGAIN, they disguise themselves momentarily as Groucho and Harpo in order to evade a pursuing cop.

All in all, Terry's assessment was correct. Heckle and Jeckle were the best cartoons his studio ever did, and for a simple reason: The characters' likability overcame the films' other shortcomings.

Unfortunately, there was no such balancing factor in the studio's other films of the early 1950s. With the great success of Mighty Mouse and Heckle and Jeckle, Terry finally agreed that starring characters were more valuable and appealing than one-shot cartoons, and a parade of new "funny animals" made their debut. Some, like Dingbat, Nutsy, and Half Pint, disappeared after one or two cartoons. Others—like Little Roquefort, a buck-toothed mouse with oversized ears; the Terry Bears, rascally twins with an irascible father; and Dinky Duck, a winsome infant with a high-pitched voice—joined the studio roster of regulars. But these new characters had nothing distinctive to recommend them. At best their films were pleasant, but they suffered from the same rubber-stamp mentality that plagued all Terrytoons. The music was the same, the timing was the same, the drawing style was the same.

Perhaps the most remarkable thing about Terrytoons of the 1950s was that they hardly looked different than Terrytoons of the late

A theatrical poster circa 1950. © Terrytoons.

1930s. Most of the animators—Jim Tyer, Johnny Gentilella, Larry Silverman, Carlo Vinci—were the same. The character animation and design were as primitive as ever—sometimes downright poor. Only the backgrounds had some visual distinction. (Chief background artists Art Bartsch and Anderson Craig continued to work in watercolor long after other studios had turned to acrylics and other media, giving the Terrytoons an unusually attractive range of settings.) There was no way to "date" a cartoon from topical details in the stories, because Terrytoons existed in a vacuum. And they certainly sounded the same as they had twenty years

ago, because Philip Scheib's music scores hadn't changed a bit.

The first radical departure the studio made in decades was to film cartoons in Cinema-Scope, beginning in 1955. But just as with sound and color, Terry waited too long to make his move. Fox had the original license on the wide-screen process and could have booked Terrytoons with all its CinemaScope releases in 1953 and 1954. Theater owners playing other studios' wide-screen features would have wanted these cartoons as well. But by the time Terry finally took the plunge, the competition was keen, and the novelty was wearing thin. "We got into it too late," says Bill Weiss. "We could have made a lot of money by going right in when 20th Century Fox asked us to. Because there is no real problem in making a CinemaScope cartoon and 'unsqueezing' it for regular use, which we have done on every one that we made."

Of course, there was no reason for anyone at Terrytoons to want to make drastic changes, least of all Paul Terry; 20th Century Fox continued to distribute the studio's yearly output of twenty-six cartoons and, in the words of one observer, "couldn't get them fast enough." Whatever one's personal opinion of the Terry product, there is no question that these cartoons were among the most successful animated shorts ever made. Fox sold them around the world and insisted that Terry reissue a handful of shorts every year in addition to his prodigious output of new cartoons.

Then one day, without much warning, Paul Terry sold his studio and properties lock, stock, and barrel to CBS. He had been the first major cartoon producer to sell old cartoons to television, in 1952, and enjoyed great success, which culminated with a half-hour Mighty Mouse show on CBS. Prior to that time, Terry claimed, "We never made a great deal of money. The great boon, as far as

I'm concerned, was when television came along and made all this old stuff valuable again. Otherwise, you never would have heard of Terrytoons. It was just a hand-to-mouth business. You made a living. Sure, you paid your bills and had enough to go ahead for another year, like most businesses do. But we kept laying these negatives up, and then television came along; they were hungry for material. They've done better in television than they ever did in the theaters." When the network offered him $3,500,000 for all his assets in 1955, he quickly agreed and retired from the business, living comfortably to the age of eighty-four.

Terry shared his good fortune with no one. Twenty- and thirty-year veterans who thought they would eventually own a part of the business were left flat. "He got everything," said Mannie Davis in 1970. "He got all the money; he got all the glory; he had everybody's talent—he inherited all that for himself. He kept it; he's going to take it with him when he dies. I might sound a little bitter, but I am."

The irony is that Terry could have netted much, much more for his company. Bill Weiss, Terry's longtime business manager who took over as Terrytoons executive producer for CBS, says he recouped the network's investment in just two years. The library alone has earned millions more since that time, and so have the merchandising rights to Terry characters. This is an area that Terry barely touched, except for the licensing of his characters for use in comic books (which were often drawn by Terry staffers).

CBS retained the entire staff of Terrytoon veterans, anxious to have them continue making theatrical cartoons as well as launch new projects. But the company decided to hire an artistic supervisor and made a most unusual choice: Gene Deitch. Deitch had made his name in the New York office of UPA, working mostly on television commercials, including the highly successful Bert and Harry Piel campaign. He was about as far removed from the Terrytoons "image" as any man alive. CBS lured him with the idea of revitalizing the company and changing the image. (They also hoped to inherit the Piel's account.)

Deitch joined the studio in 1956 and stayed for two years. There was natural resentment of this thirty-one-year-old supervisor on the part of older staff veterans, and Deitch's radically new approach to cartoon production did not win him many friends among the Terry stalwarts. At times the air was so thick, according to one newcomer, "there was nothing to do but go into your own office and close the door." Deitch later

Little Roquefort in an all-too-typical scene, animated by Jim Tyer. © Terrytoons.

told Mike Barrier, "That studio must have surely ranked the next-after-last on any roster of cartoon studios. For thirty years they had been making the crassest of unadulterated crap. I was trying to make a renaissance of the most moldering foundation to be found anywhere."

Deitch was well suited to the role of creative director. He knew how to spot talent and hired bright young people to augment the existing Terry crew: Ernest Pintoff, Jules Feiffer, Tod Dockstader, Al Kouzel, and Eli Bauer. He encouraged designers like Kouzel to direct, and story men like Feiffer to lay out cartoons. "After all," explains Kouzel, 'Deitch came out of commercial studios, where the designers generally also did the storyboards, and very often did the layouts. In the large entertainment-type studios, you've got a story man on storyboards, and you've got somebody taking care of style, generally connected with the background department, and then you've got a layout man. What happened here was a mixing in of commercial-type categories into this old-time entertainment studio. And in a way this was quite good, because when you get down to it, an artist who has some vision of a storyboard should, if he's got the technical ability, do some fine layouts. To separate it in an artificial way is not good."

Pintoff brought with him an idea he had developed at UPA called FLEBUS, which he wrote, designed, and directed. (A former jazz musician, he also composed the music score, but contractually that credit had to go to Philip Scheib.) The film is an adult fable about a happy nebbish who gets upset when he encounters a man who resolutely doesn't like him. It was certainly the most cerebral cartoon the studio had ever released. Like many others to follow it, it resembled a UPA cartoon in visual style, point of view, and format. FLEBUS broke new ground in another

way as well: It won first prize in the short-subject category at the San Francisco Film Festival.

Unfortunately, Pintoff left the studio after this one endeavor, but the others stayed on. Deitch decided to abandon most existing Terry characters and start from scratch, so his young team developed such new characters as John Doormat, Gaston Le Crayon, Clint Clobber, and Silly Sidney. These largely unappealing creations almost made one long for the halcyon days of Dinky Duck and Little Roquefort.

Deitch was less interested in character appeal than he was in design and color styling, however, and these constituted the strong suit of his films. Suddenly, Terrytoons were among the most stylish and attractive cartoons on the screen, inheriting the praise and recognition that UPA had won in the early 1950s. But unlike the landmark UPA films, these Terrytoons had neither charm nor humor.

Clint Clobber (fully named DeWitt Clinton Clobber), superintendent of the Flamboyant Arms apartment building, was supposed to be a takeoff of Jackie Gleason, but he was merely bombastic, without the comic shading Gleason gave his Ralph Kramden character.

With his ability to draw or paint objects that would come to life, Gaston Le Crayon, a rubbery-limbed French artist, had greater potential for visual imagination. But neither he nor his films were inventive enough to overcome a basic absence of comedy.

The character of John Doormat, based on the trials and tribulations of a 1950s suburbanite, could have made for a great series, but the earliest entries like TOPSY TV and SHOVE THY NEIGHBOR were routine, earthbound gag cartoons. Later, director Al Kouzel teamed with writer Jules Feiffer to give the cartoons a more Thurberish feeling,

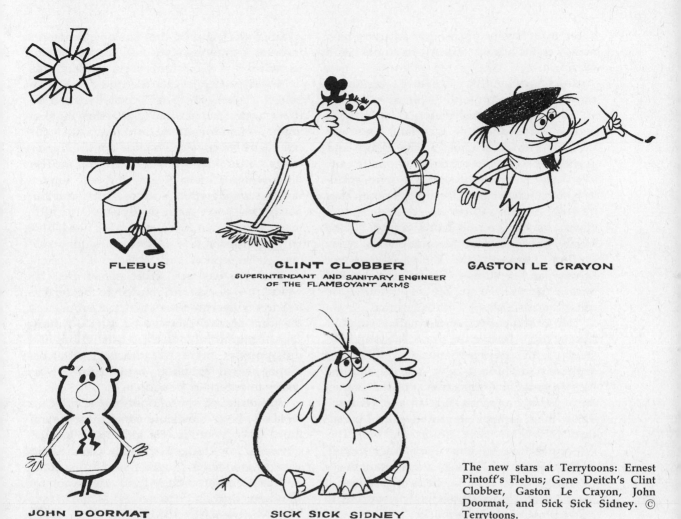

FLEBUS

CLINT CLOBBER
SUPERINTENDANT AND SANITARY ENGINEER
OF THE FLAMBOYANT ARMS

GASTON LE CRAYON

JOHN DOORMAT

SICK SICK SIDNEY

The new stars at Terrytoons: Ernest Pintoff's Flebus; Gene Deitch's Clint Clobber, Gaston Le Crayon, John Doormat, and Sick Sick Sidney. © Terrytoons.

like Feiffer's comic strips, which were just gaining popularity in New York's *Village Voice*. It resulted in one of the studio's best shorts, ANOTHER DAY, ANOTHER DOORMAT. This highly stylized cartoon was reminiscent of UPA at its best. In it, John Doormat is a mousy, henpecked husband who allows his Amazonian wife to browbeat him mercilessly—unaware that she longs for him to stand up and assert himself. As Doormat leaves his home to head for the office, how-

ever, his personality begins to change. He becomes more churlish and aggressive (denoted visually by a widening of the pupils in his eyes, formerly tiny and weak), running a tight ship at work and bossing his subordinates. He remains this way as he goes to replace a defective pipe at R. H. Remnant's Department Store, where his huffing and puffing attracts the attention of another customer—his wife. She can hardly believe her eyes and ears, but when she runs to him, eager to be swept up by this assertive new man, he shrivels up and reverts to his timid self.

Unfortunately, this clever and imaginative cartoon was the last John Doormat entry.

The final character created under Deitch's regime was Sidney the Elephant. This was the only "funny animal" of the group, and perhaps for that reason the only one to outlive Deitch's stay at the studio. But nevertheless the character bore Deitch's mark in that he was neurotic and frustrated. In SICK, SICK SIDNEY he sucks on his trunk and complains in a whiny voice that the jungle is too noisy for him to live in peace. Then a safari comes through and captures all the animals—except Sidney. Now the jungle is quiet—"*Too* quiet," wails Sidney. "I'm lonesome!"

The second cartoon in this series, SIDNEY'S FAMILY TREE, improves upon the original's story, with the elephant bemoaning his orphan status and getting himself adopted by two jungle chimpanzees. But the character of Sidney remains childish and neurotic. Still, this cartoon represented a breakthrough for the "new" studio and won Terrytoons its first Academy Award nomination in thirteen years. "It was a big moment for us," says story man Eli Bauer, "because it meant they [the industry] were starting to take the changeover seriously."

That same year, 1958, the studio produced its most famous cartoon, THE JUGGLER OF OUR LADY. R. O. Blechman had written and illustrated a book based on this ancient tale of a juggler who joins a monastery, and Gene Deitch persuaded him to help translate his book into an animated cartoon. Blechman collaborated with Al Kouzel on the project, which involved such simple drawings and backgrounds that the two men completed the production virtually by themselves. Deitch hired Boris Karloff to narrate the fable, thereby giving the film additional prestige.

Since the time of this short, Blechman's inimitable drawing style has become familiar to millions of television viewers through his work in commercials (such as the classic Alka Seltzer "talking stomach" spot), but in 1958 it was quite surprising to see this kind of animation on the screen, and THE JUGGLER OF OUR LADY won new acclaim for the Terrytoons studio. "I think that was one of the few films where CinemaScope was very important," says director Kouzel, "and unfortunately you don't see it in CinemaScope anymore. Using that big screen with these little wriggly characters was really something special, and it worked very well."

If there was any criticism of Deitch's work, it was that he tended to be heavy-handed. His characters were ponderous, and the kind of story he favored carried a message or buried its comedy in frustrations and unhappiness. Some co-workers felt that his emphasis on graphics overshadowed his desire to entertain an audience.

But none of these opinions applied to Deitch's first television project for Terrytoons, TOM TERRIFIC. He and his colleagues devised a low-budget series for use on CBS's *Captain Kangaroo* program that substituted imagination for money, and ingenuity for standard cartoon violence. Presented as a weekly five-part cliff-hanger, this series remains one of the finest cartoons ever produced for television.

Tom Terrific is an effervescent young boy with a funnel hat that enables him to turn into anything he wants to be. This makes Tom a mini superhero, who battles such foes as Crabby Appleton ("rotten to the core") with the aid of his faithful companion, a sleepy dog named Mighty Manfred.

The Tom Terrific stories are disarmingly simple. They do not talk down to their audience; instead, they create a double-edged effect by overdramatizing their simple plot

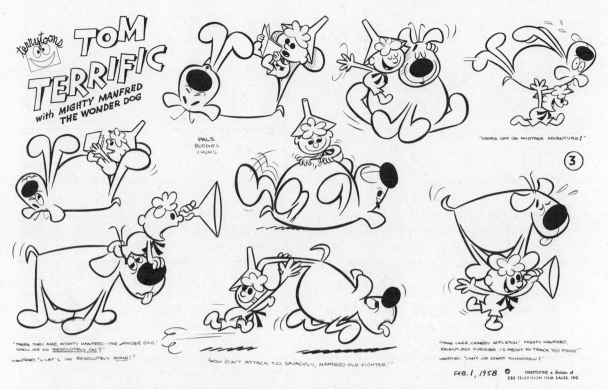

A model sheet of Tom Terrific and Mighty Manfred, drawn by Jim Tyer. © Terrytoons.

crises through Tom's emphatic dialogue and narration. The scripts are full of clever ideas as well, which enable children to respond on whatever level they can reach—the surface story line or the sly humor underneath. The laconic Manfred, misnamed a "wonder dog," perfectly synthesizes both elements.

Equally significant is the visual format of the cartoons: line drawings for the characters, with backgrounds as sparse as a horizon line with an occasional tree. Sometimes the characters weren't even opaqued! The sound track was just as lean: all voices by one man, Lionel Wilson, with music and occasional sound effects provided by a lone accordion. This utter simplicity enabled Deitch and his staff to concentrate on personality animation for the main characters and devote more time

to developing a strong script. What's more, Tom's powers of transformation made him a *visual* character, unlike so many static TV cartoon stars who followed.

For the series' second season on *Captain Kangaroo*, Deitch used tints and occasional colors. Unfortunately, the cartoons' long run on CBS expired when it was felt that no one would watch anything that wasn't in full color anymore.

Jules Feiffer, who contributed stories to TOM TERRIFIC, created a pilot for another children's television series called EASY WINNERS, but felt that the deck was stacked against him in this venture. When a CBS programming executive turned down the proposal as being "too *New Yorker*-ish," no one at the studio tried to help Feiffer revive the project. "I was

EASY WINNERS

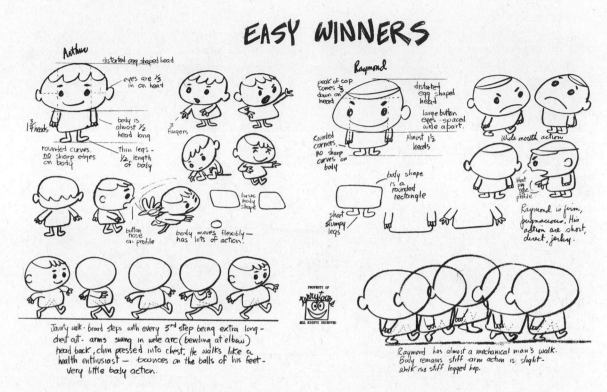

A rare model sheet, drawn by Jules Feiffer for EASY WINNERS, a television pilot that never sold. © Terrytoons.

getting paid to do stuff they had no intention of doing anything with,'' he says today, but every time he wanted to quit, they gave him a raise. When Feiffer's newspaper cartoons finally evolved from a part-time avocation to a full-time living, he left the studio.

In mid-1958, Bill Weiss fired Gene Deitch and assumed complete control of Terrytoons. Weiss knew something about animation from his thirty-year association with the studio, but he knew more about the nuts and bolts of running a business. He never liked Deitch's cartoons and knew that many others felt the same way. His first decision was to

drop most of the new characters and revive some of the old ones like Heckle and Jeckle and Mighty Mouse. He severed his connections with the Technicolor company and began filming and releasing his cartoons in DeLuxe color, a cheaper process that cut the budgets considerably. Weiss took other steps to reduce his costs, and the cartoons show it. No one ever praised the flowing animation in Paul Terry's HECKLE AND JECKLE series, but those shorts of the 1940s and early 1950s looked positively brilliant next to the alarmingly stilted cartoons of the 1960s. Heckle and Jeckle were still good characters, and story lines like the one for THOUSAND SMILE CHECKUP (1960) could have served them well if the primitive animation hadn't undercut the impact of each gag. Even Philip Scheib's music, now performed by what sounded like a three-piece band, spelled cheapness. (Scheib finally retired about this time, and was replaced by a man named Jim Timmens.)

Weiss was anxious to add new characters to the Terrytoons list and set his sights on television as well as the theatrical market. The cartoons his studio produced during the next ten years were all made with that dual purpose in mind. This is why supposed theatrical cartoons from this period often look like cut-rate television product.

Colonial-era character Hector Heathcoate was created by story man Eli Bauer for a theatrical cartoon called THE MINUTE AND A HALF MAN in 1959, the same year that veteran staffer Bob Kuwahara created a Japanese mouse named Hashimoto, whose debut film was HASHIMOTO SAN. Other theatrical cartoons were made with these characters, but when NBC bought a half-hour package called the HECTOR HEATHCOATE SHOW in 1963, new Heathcoate and Hashimoto cartoons were quickly produced to fill out the program. Some of these, in turn, were released theatrically many years later (such as BELABOUR THY NEIGHBOR, produced for TV in 1963 and released to theaters for the first time in 1970).

In a reversal of this situation, when THE DEPUTY DAWG SHOW premiered in 1960, Weiss actually received requests from 20th Century Fox exchange managers ("especially in Texas") to release these made-for-TV cartoons to theaters. As usual, much of the series' appeal was based on clever voice work, in this case by Dayton Allen.

DEPUTY DAWG represented the studio's first major encounter with the rigors of TV production. It must have resembled the Terry schedules of yore, as 104 episodes were cranked out over the next few years. Larz Bourne, the story man who created the series, wrote the scripts for practically every episode, but the pace was too much for him or any one else to handle alone. Consequently, this show brought significant changes to Terrytoons. For the first time, the studio hired freelance directors, animators, and writers, or contracted work from them. It is ironic to note that two of the director-animators who did work on this basis, for both DEPUTY DAWG and HECTOR HEATH-COATE, were Bill Tytla and George Gordon, Paul Terry's leading lights in years gone by. Stories for the two TV series were purchased from Jack Mercer, Cal Howard, Chris Jenkyns, and former Disneyites T. Hee, Dick Kinney, and Al Bertino.

TV production also gave a boost to young studio veteran Ralph Bakshi, who had joined

It looks like Mighty Mouse has been eating well in this 1960s still. © Terrytoons.

Deputy Dawg and his look-alike nephew in an episode from the successful TV series. © Terrytoons.

Terrytoons in November 1956 at age eighteen, as an opaquer. When the studio was desperate for animators in 1959, Bakshi volunteered and started working as a full-fledged animator, even though he had no practical experience in that role. By 1963 he was capable enough to direct several episodes of DEPUTY DAWG (DIAMONDS IN THE ROUGH, SHOW BIZ WHIZ, SAVE OLD PINEY).

Directing, however, was more a credential than a real job at this time. At Terrytoons the most important cog in the wheel was still the story department, and while many changes had been made in studio modus operandi, prescoring of cartoons was still the rule—only now, the nominal "director" was not in charge of this procedure. Tommy Morrison, billed as story supervisor, was.

This period also saw the gradual dissolution of the story department as it had existed for many years. Eli Bauer, who started there during the Gene Deitch regime, explains: "It was truly a story *department*, rather than three guys going their own route. We got together, we talked over, we threw gags in the pot, we were like gag writers in a sense. Tommy would say, 'Listen, we want a Heckle and Jeckle story,' or 'We want to do a story for Sidney.' Larz Bourne and I were both cartoonists, and we'd sit at the board drawing up the storyboard. We were visual writers.

"Since we were also capable of designing characters, if we had a new character, we'd design it and it would be ready for the story. When we'd pass it on, if it was such that either Larz or I would then do the layouts, it was because we were also capable layout men."

The exigencies of TV production, coupled with the departure of a strong creative director like Deitch, brought about unwelcome changes. "There was strong interaction with the director at first, but I think it became an assembly line later on," says Bauer. From a pattern of story sessions between the director and story crew, the studio got to the point where the so-called director might not even see the story until a recording was completed. Then he was obliged to follow the sound track precisely. He had no control over the cartoon's timing whatsoever, and his function was reduced to that of layout man and animation supervisor.

The studio continued to create new characters for theatrical cartoons, but now every cartoon was considered a "pilot" for possible TV use. ASTRONUT, featuring an outer-space gremlin who first appeared in a Deputy Dawg episode, followed a theatrical run with a TV half hour bearing the same title in 1965. That program was filled out with cartoons featuring Luno the Flying Horse (the most unappealing juvenile creation in recent studio history) and other existing characters. Later, the studio hatched another spinoff from DEPUTY DAWG called POSSIBLE POSSUM. These cartoons were directed and animated by such veterans as Connie Rasinski, Art Bartsch, Bob Kuwahara, Cosmo Anzilotti, and a relative newcomer to the studio, the talented Dave Tendlar.

The first person to upset the relative calm was Ralph Bakshi. He had talent and ambition in about equal parts and finally won the opportunity to direct his first theatrical cartoon, GADMOUSE THE APPRENTICE GOOD FAIRY, in 1964. The star was Sad Cat, perhaps the dreariest character ever created at Terrytoons, and this marked his debut. Story man Eli Bauer wrote the cartoon with Al Kouzel and remembers the finished product as extremely cluttered. "We said, 'Gee, Ralph, it looks good, but you lost the gag because there's so many things happening.' That's the kind of thing that works with FRITZ THE CAT and works with some of the other stuff theatrically, but it didn't work for the story Ralph was doing then."

Bakshi considered this a learning apprenticeship, and he wanted the chance to do *his* cartoons, the way he wanted. He began recutting the "finished" sound tracks Morrison handed him and experimented in other ways. After Sad Cat, Bakshi turned to another more topical series, JAMES HOUND. Whatever the faults of this series, it at least had more energy than most recent Terrytoons, and there is no doubt where the energy was coming from. CBS recognized this and decided to name Bakshi supervising director of Terrytoons in 1966. Fred Silverman, then in charge of children's programming for the network, saw in Bakshi the potential for many new and exciting ideas.

The one series to emerge under Bakshi's supervision was THE MIGHTY HEROES, which capitalized on the growing craze for superhero cartoons while spoofing them at the same time. The cast featured five defenders of justice: Diaper Man, Tornado Man, Rope Man, Strong Man, and Cuckoo Man, who joined forces to undo such self-descriptive villains as the Stretcher, the Shrinker, and the Enlarger. While hampered by the severe limitations of movement imposed by short schedules and tight budgets, Bakshi still managed to give these cartoons life and zest. The character design is quite good, and Bakshi's poses (familiar to anyone who has seen his subsequent work) are vivid and expressive.

After completing twenty-six episodes of this series, Bakshi left Terrytoons to become director of the Paramount Cartoon Studio in New York. This left Weiss with just the skeleton staff of Terrytoons veterans, who were dwindling in number. Connie Rasinski and Bob Kuwahara had died, and Mannie Davis had left the studio. Art Bartsch remained on staff, even though he was ill. Weiss considered him the most talented man he'd ever had and could not bear to fire him. "He was unreal, just fantastic," says the producer. "He could draw equally well with both hands. He could make a storyboard and you could use every drawing on the board as a layout." With Bakshi's departure, Weiss assigned Bartsch to direct additional cartoons with Sad Cat for theatrical release. Then Bartsch died.

Tommy Morrison stayed on with Weiss in New Rochelle, helping to plan new TV series. Proposals and pilots were made by animators and artists who were hired on a freelance basis, but none of the company's new ideas ever got on the air. (A proposed Charlie Chan series was later adapted for television by Hanna-Barbera.) There was no

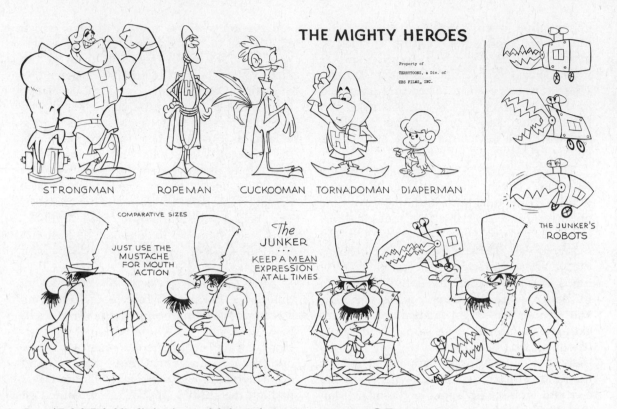

THE MIGHTY HEROES

Property of
TERRYTOONS, a Div. of
CBS FILMS, INC.

STRONGMAN   ROPEMAN   CUCKOOMAN   TORNADOMAN   DIAPERMAN

THE JUNKER'S ROBOTS

COMPARATIVE SIZES

JUST USE THE MUSTACHE FOR MOUTH ACTION

The JUNKER ... KEEP A MEAN EXPRESSION AT ALL TIMES

One of Ralph Bakshi's distinctive model sheets for THE MIGHTY HEROES. © Terrytoons.

serious thought given to producing new theatrical cartoons at this time, especially since 20th Century Fox was content to release Terrytoons' made-for-television product of the 1960s on a monthly basis.

Finally it became impractical to maintain a large, empty shop in New Rochelle, and the Terrytoons plant closed down. But activity did not cease at this time. Bill Weiss is still employed by Viacom, the company that inherited all of CBS Films' properties in the 1960s, and Terrytoons remains an important asset of that giant television distributor. Black-and-white cartoons are virtually worthless today, but the company's one thousand color cartoons, produced from 1938 to 1968, are still in active television distribution. Such characters as Mighty Mouse, Heckle and Jeckle, and Deputy Dawg command major licensing fees for everything from T-shirts to drinking glasses, while many of the films are sold for home use in 8mm and 16mm.*

Most surprisingly, 20th Century Fox continues to release twelve Terrytoons a year for the international market, deriving substantial income from theaters around the world that still play animated shorts as American theaters used to do. The cartoons do espe-

*Mighty Mouse and Heckle and Jeckle were revived in an all-new television series for the fall 1979 Saturday morning lineup, reaffirming their lasting popularity. The new series, licensed by Viacom, was produced and animated by Filmation in Hollywood.

cially well when Fox features are widely booked—which means that Terrytoons' fortunes for 1977 rose with the success of STAR WARS.

The irony of this ongoing success is the inescapable fact that Terrytoons were never very good. But time has worked in their favor: Television cartoon production in the sixties actually sank below the level of Terry's product of the forties and fifties, making the Terrytoons look good by comparison. Terry's basically nonviolent attitude and juvenile approach—at a time when cartoons were shown in theaters to adults as well as children—now fits television's defi-nition of what cartoons should be. As to repetition, kids seem to love formulas, making Terry's cartoon ideal TV fodder for the tiny tots.

Bill Weiss wisely followed in Terry's footsteps, helping to build a cartoon library that will yield rich rewards for many years to come. Like Terry, he harbored no illusions or aspirations about art or creativity. He continued his boss's tradition of turning out salable product, pure and simple.

And on that basis he and Terry have had the last laugh on a lot of creative, talented people who will never know the kind of success Terrytoons has enjoyed.

Walter Lantz

A DICTIONARY DEFINITION of the word "pioneer" is: "one of those who are first or earliest in any field of inquiry, enterprise, or progress." By that definition, Walter Lantz is not a pioneer.

But just behind every pioneer is a "second wave," which appreciates the pioneer's discoveries and learns how to implement them. Walter Lantz belongs to that group. He may also be called a survivor; anyone who operated a cartoon studio for forty-five years, well past the point of endurance for many of his competitors, has earned that designation.

Lantz survived for many reasons. An ambitious young man, he knew how to get ahead in the early days of animation when others were disorganized or ineffectual as businessmen. When he became head of his own studio, he claims that he left administrative details to others, but in one important area he remained alert and active: personnel acquisition. Lantz's studio was never known to launch great talent, although some prominent animators started there; it became better known as a place people came *to* after peaking elsewhere. Lantz never raided any rival studio. He didn't have to. In his words, "People worked for me who didn't want to work for Disney anymore." Over the years, he employed such notable figures as Tex Avery, Grim Natwick, Hugh Harman, Sha-

mus Culhane, Dick Lundy, and Jack Hannah, each of whom brought his special skills and expertise to the Lantz shop and upgraded the cartoon quality by a notch or two.

Lantz was never an innovator. He broke no new ground. But he was not a stifler, either, and he wanted his cartoons to be as good as they could be—within the boundary lines of a budget. He hired good people whenever they were available in order to achieve that goal. If they did, he was delighted, and if they didn't, he pressed onward, undaunted. A survivor.

Walter Lantz learned to survive early in life. Born in New Rochelle, New York, on April 27, 1900, he found himself with serious responsibilities as a young man. His mother died giving birth to a younger brother, Michael, and, besides helping to raise him, Walter worked in the grocery store run by his invalid father.

When he was fifteen, he went to work as

an office boy in the art department of William Randolph Hearst's *New York American*. He lived at the YMCA in Manhattan, took night classes at the Art Students League, and enrolled in several correspondence-school art courses. Shamus Culhane, who was friendly with Michael Lantz, remarks, "Walter was a very good artist. He won a couple of medals in Art Students League and was considered a very promising student. But he veered off into the cartoon." (Brother Michael went on to become a world-renowned sculptor.)

Walter's dedication and ambition won the respect of the *American*'s famous editor Morrill Goddard, who recommended Walter for a job in the new Hearst animation studio in 1916, reasoning that there would be more opportunity for advancement there than on the newspaper staff. He was right. Lantz started working as a camerman at the Hearst International Studio and within two years, at age eighteen, he was a full-fledged animator.

Gregory LaCava was production chief of the studio, and Lantz worked alongside such stalwarts as George Stallings, Jack King, George Rufle, I. Klein, Grim Natwick, Burt Gillett, Ben Sharpsteen, and Bill Nolan. Several of these men later worked for Lantz, and Nolan became his partner. The studio produced animated films of comic characters owned by the Hearst newspapers: Krazy Kat, Happy Hooligan, The Katzenjammer Kids, and others.

Lantz learned to animate by watching the others, and experimenting on his own. He was doing well when the studio suffered a series of upheavals. "World War One came along and most of the boys were drafted," he recalls. "I was young enough so I wasn't drafted, and I stayed on with Hearst another year animating a series called JERRY ON THE JOB." When Hearst closed his studio in 1918, Lantz worked on MUTT AND JEFF at the Barré/Bowers Studio for a year, then signed up with John R. Bray.

Lantz's first assignment was animating on Bray's COLONEL HEEZA LIAR series, which he did for several years. Bray was extremely pleased with Lantz's work, and when his general manager, George Stallings, took ill, he promoted Lantz to the position of studio manager. Lantz was now responsible for supervising all of Bray's output as well as developing his own cartoon series.

Lantz's first creation was Dinky Doodle, a little-boy character with a canine pal named Weakheart. Expanding on the format of Fleischer's OUT OF THE INKWELL, Lantz appeared in the DINKY DOODLE films and combined live action with animation. Whereas Fleischer appeared as himself, and the characters were a product of his pen and drawing board, the DINKY DOODLES series had no set format, and Lantz's role was never clearly identified. He was just a human friend of the cartoon characters.

"We'd go to the beach, we'd go to the woods, we went everywhere. We didn't just confine it to a studio," Lantz says of his first film series, citing this as a major distinction between these films and Fleischer's. But the biggest difference was in technique. "We would photograph me first going through a pantomime action with the character. Then we'd take the negative of my actions and make a series of 8 × 10 prints, bromides we call them, and we'd punch these stills [with peg holes] the same as we did the drawings. Then we'd place our paper over the still and animate the character to fit my live action. Then, that animation was traced on celluloid and painted, and we'd photograph each celluloid with each photographic frame of the action. It sort of made a composite picture of the celluloid and the photograph." In other words, every other frame of Lantz's action was turned into a separate black-and-white photo and was then exposed twice—accounting for thousands of still photos on each new production. The man in charge of the studio's darkroom was Anton Bruehl, later to become a well-known photographer, and one of his assistants was teen-aged James (Shamus) Culhane.

This method, painstaking though it was, offered tremendous flexibility to Lantz and his chief animators, Clyde Geronimi and David Hand (both of whom became key Disney artists in the 1930s). While the cartoons themselves remained somewhat prosaic, the gimmickry was superb. When an animal bites Lantz on the finger in LITTLE RED RIDING HOOD, he goes spinning in circles from the pain—achieved by animating photographic cutouts of Lantz against the photographic backgrounds.

After the success of DINKY DOODLES, Lantz developed two other series for Bray: HOT DOG, which featured Pete the Pup in a live-action/animation format, and UNNATURAL HISTORY, which was more in the line of Aesop's Fables.

In 1927 John R. Bray closed his cartoon studio. Lantz decided to move to California, where he got a job as a gag writer at the Mack Sennett studio. He quickly became, in his words, "the fair-haired boy," because he devised gags that used animation tricks. To accompany an explosion in a Ben Turpin comedy, he animated photographic cutouts of Turpin flying in the air, which delighted Sennett.

Lantz feels that he learned a lot during his short stay at this comedy studio. "When I was at Bray, we did everything cute . . . birds-and-bees type of stories," he says, but the Sennett experience changed his outlook on comedy. Sennett, he says, "was quite a guy . . . very rough, but a wonderful person. He's the one who knew how to use broad comedy. For instance, if he had a barrel of dynamite, he'd *label* the barrel."

After Sennett, Lantz worked briefly for

Animator-actor Walter Lantz with his characters Weakheart and Dinky Doodle, circa 1924.

Hal Roach and then did a short stint as gagman on the ANDY GUMP series at Universal. Again he was contributing animation gags, and through this series he came to meet Universal's legendary founder and president, Carl Laemmle. Young Lantz impressed the paternal president, who asked him about setting up a cartoon studio on the Universal lot. Lantz told him what he would need, and Laemmle gave the go-ahead.

Universal had been buying distribution rights to a series of cartoons featuring Oswald the Lucky Rabbit from producer Charles Mintz for several years. But Mintz was just a middleman. The cartoons were originally created by Walt Disney, who supplied them to Mintz. When Disney tried to get more money for his efforts, Mintz pulled the rug out by telling Disney that Universal controlled rights to the character and would hire someone else to do the series rather than pay more money. At that point, Mintz's brother-in-law George Winkler set up his own staff, comprised of ex-Disney people like Hugh Harman, Rudolf Ising, and Friz Freleng.

Now the tables were turned on Mintz and Winkler: Carl Laemmle informed them that Universal was setting up its own cartoon department with Walter Lantz in charge. The Winkler studio was suddenly out of business.

Universal issued a press release on April 9, 1929, which read, "Walter B. Lantz, animated artist, has arrived at Universal City to draw a series of pictures for Universal, featuring the pen and ink character 'Oswald, the Lucky Rabbit.' William C. Nolan has been signed to assist Lantz."

Lantz's first job was to add sound to six unreleased cartoons Winkler had completed. "It was funny how we did it," Lantz recalls. "We'd project a cartoon on the screen and all of us would stand in front of the cartoon. We had a bench with all the props on it—the bells, etc. As the action progressed on the screen, we'd time to it and make the sound effect, dialogue and all. Nothing was prescored. We did it as we watched the picture."

Lantz's next important encounter with sound came when Laemmle asked him to contribute an introductory sequence to the studio's all-talkie extravanganza THE KING OF JAZZ, starring Paul Whiteman. Universal spent (and subsequently lost) an enormous amount of money on this film, which was photographed entirely in the two-strip Technicolor process. Lantz's job was to create a sequence showing how Whiteman was crowned the King of Jazz. The bandleader was caricatured and portrayed as a big-game hunter stalking wild animals; his singing voice was provided by a member of the Whiteman Rhythm Boys trio named Bing Crosby. Even Oswald the Rabbit got into the act in this lively sequence full of rubbery characters and jaunty gags. For the finale, a lion conks Whiteman on the head, and his bump grows into a crown—officially designating him the King of Jazz.

Among its other distinctions, this was the first color sound cartoon, and it presented Lantz with a fair amount of challenges. First, there was the matter of dealing with Technicolor's limited color range within the red and green spectrum. Then the artists discovered that the paints they used did not adhere to cels—sometimes chipping off before the cameraman could commit a scene to film.

Finally, there was the music synchronization. Lantz rigged up a "visual metronome" system on film to give Paul Whiteman the proper beat to follow, but the bandleader balked at using this device. "Let me tell ya, sonny, I can keep a rhythm on anything," Lantz remembers him saying. "So you tell me how long the picture's going to be—three minutes, four minutes, whatever—and I'll give you the rhythm you want."

"I said we wanted four minutes," Lantz continues, "and I'll be darned if he didn't beat this thing out. It came to four minutes at 2/12 [two beats per second, or one beat every 12 frames]." The finished segment gets THE KING OF JAZZ off to a fine start and stands as one of Lantz's most engaging pieces of work.

After this special project, it was back to the grind—and a considerable grind it was: Universal wanted twenty-six Oswalds a year. Lantz took in veteran animator Bill Nolan as his partner in order to meet this heavy demand and then hired a staff. A member of Paul Whiteman's band, James Dietrich, became the young studio's music director.

The inconsistency of the Lantz-Nolan product was understandable, given these time demands, and appropriate verdicts were handed down in watchful trade-magazine reviews month by month. In January

1931 the *Motion Picture Herald* praised MARS: "When Oswald and Peg Leg flirt with a girl in the park, Oswald receives a kick that perches him on Mars. Oswald sings the 'Lucky Rabbit' number, while some particularly unique and unusual effects are achieved in cartoon work. The theme song idea for the shorts is one of the most striking ideas yet introduced into animated cartoons." But the *Herald* had harsh words for such March and May releases as THE FARMER and COUNTRY SCHOOL: "There aren't enough new touches in this number of the Oswald Rabbit series to make it rate more than just a fair cartoon" and "Situation in this one is decidedly not new, and the lines weak."

Criticism was also leveled at COUNTRY SCHOOL for its vulgar barnyard humor: "It may be merely a substitution for lack of good and original comedy ideas, but if it is, it fails to get by."

These hit-or-miss results did not come about for lack of effort. The Lantz-Nolan team was trying its best, but tight schedules and a character of limited possibilities made it difficult to score every time out. Lantz says that the average budget at this time was $4,000 a short.

Preston Blair has vivid memories of the cartoon operation in the early 1930s: "We were part of the big studio. We entered through the studio time-clock, and were paid through the Universal bookkeeping system. In fact, we were just across the studio green from the main offices.

"I remember it as a small, happy outfit. We all used to go into Lantz's little office at the start of each picture, and have a story conference to try to suggest gags and situations. So, as a rank in-betweener, I participated in suggesting gags with all the animators. Bill Nolan and Walt Lantz argued with me and the others in these meetings.

"George Moreno was a star animator with

The "new" Oswald of the late 1930s, left, and the original Oswald. © Walter Lantz Productions.

Lantz and had a particular style effective with Oswald's personality animation. Nolan was a great 'straight-ahead' animator. I should say animation has roughly two approaches to drawing a scene. In straight-ahead, you simply grow one drawing out of another with no exact position where you are going to end up, like a plant grows, or, as in the pose-and-in-between method, you draw first the 'extremes' of an action, and then go back and put in the in-between drawings. Each method has its virtues and drawbacks. Moreno was a pose-and-in-between animator—this is wise with personality. In action there is just nothing like pure straight-ahead art, and Nolan was a master with the pencil. I put him in the same category as the other famous draftsmen Fred Moore and Bill Tytla."

Lantz and Nolan headed separate units in order to maintain the production schedule, but, as Blair indicates, everyone participated in story conferences, and with good reason. This was the crucial stage of production for the studio. Oswald was one of those happy 1930s characters with no distinctive personality traits whatsoever; therefore, gags or story concept had to shoulder the responsibility for putting over each new short. There

Oswald serenades a receptive audience in the operetta cartoon KINGS UP (1934). © Walter Lantz Productions.

still pretty freewheeling in manner; almost anything seemed to be acceptable if one could fill up a reel in time to meet the deadline. Avery told Joe Adamson, "They gave me a scene to animate once: Oswald was on board ship with some guy with a peg leg, and I was supposed to show this guy firing a cannon. Well, I had the cannon droop and the ball roll out, then the cannon pointed straight up, then he went to light the fuse and it went out. I built it up from ten feet to sixty feet. The drawings kept stacking up! . . . We had no footage limit, and Walt said, 'Heck, yeah, we'll leave it in.'"

In 1932 the studio introduced its second star character, Pooch the Pup. More compact in size than Oswald, he seemed to be a peppier character but in reality was just another happy type who added nothing to the personality of the cartoons in which he starred.

Gags, situations, and music were the most important ingredients for a successful Lantz cartoon. MERRY OLD SOUL (1933) incorporates some delightful movie-star caricatures and marks the first time a Lantz cartoon was nominated for an Academy Award. CONFIDENCE (1933) is a wonderful concept-cartoon that shows Depression rising out of a city dump as a skeletal specter. That night it circles the globe (filmed in live action), spreading its poison, and in the morning the world reacts accordingly: There's a bank scare, a stock market crash, and general lethargy even on Oswald's normally happy farm. Oswald goes running to Dr. Pill for a cure, only to be told, "*There's* your doctor!" as the local M.D. points to a picture of Franklin D. Roosevelt on the wall. Accordingly, Oswald flies to Washington and asks FDR for the cure. The President sings "Confidence," and our rabbit hero gets the message. He returns home and injects the local citizens and farmyard animals with Confidence from a hypodermic needle. That does the trick and

were no strong characterizations or distinctive voice personalities to carry weak material.

The animation in these films was rudimentary, and wildly inconsistent. Some shorts were quite good in terms of solid, flowing animation while others presented alarmingly awkward sequences and character movement. The reason for this is simple: There weren't enough experienced animators to go around.

Tex Avery recalls, "I met a fella who knew a girl who was head of the inking and painting at Walter Lantz's, so I inked and painted for a while. . . . Then I worked up into inbetweens, then about that time Disney raided the whole West Coast for talent. And the three quarters of us who were left knew nothing of animation. We had just been inbetweening." But Avery and the others had to sink or swim as animators.

Production of the OSWALD cartoons was

Depression is defeated. This likable cartoon relies almost entirely on its story to put it over; the animation itself is uninspired, and the timing lacks vigor and precision. Characters float along, as so often happens in Lantz cartoons of this vintage—apparently due to the studio's casual attitude toward exposure sheets and exacting preparation of each scene.

The use of songs imposed definite timing on a cartoon, and this helps make HOT AND COLD (1933) with Pooch the Pup an enjoyable entry. The entire film is built around a song called "Turn on the Heat," from the 1929 Fox feature SUNNY SIDE UP. As it happens, Lantz's cartoon is not as imaginative or outlandish as the 1929 production number, but the peppy song does inspire an amusing story line with a weather king at the North Pole controlling the local climate. Rather than animate snow, Lantz blew a snowlike substance in front of the camera and double-exposed this with the cartoon action (a device repeated in other studio shorts of the 1930s).

An even more effective use of music occurs in KINGS UP (1934), which is performed as a light opera! Every bit of exposition and dialogue is sung from start to finish, giving a special lift to what would otherwise be a routine story line and format. (Oswald is a medieval balladeer who hopes to be knighted by the Queen, but is challenged instead by the villainous Black Knight; Oswald defeats him and wins the Queen's hand in marriage.) Another 1934 entry, THE TOY SHOPPE, borrows the Disney/Harman-Ising format of a toy shop coming to life at night, with pleasing results. It's a reasonably elaborate cartoon for the Lantz studio, with plenty of movement and effective backgrounds. As in a growing number of Oswald cartoons, however, the star character hardly appears at all. Oswald has some token scenes

at the beginning and end to justify having his name on the main title, and that's all. The same is true of GOLDIE LOCKS AND THE THREE BEARS and others that followed. One 1936 short, THE PUPPET SHOW, is actually a live-action puppet film, with periodic cutaways showing Oswald supposedly controlling the strings.

Both as an outlet for new ideas and a competitive move to keep up with the expanding cartoon market, Lantz initiated a new series in 1934 called CARTUNE CLASSICS. These were produced in the two-color process and hewed to the SILLY SYMPHONIES formula, with such titles as JOLLY LITTLE ELVES, TOYLAND PREMIERE, and CANDY LAND. Lantz produced only six of these shorts before returning to black-and-white series on a full-time basis.

The growing staff in 1934 included George Nicholas, Sid Sutherland, Ray Abrams, Steve Bosustow, George Moreno, Tex Avery, Ed Benedict, La Verne Harding, Virgil Ross, Fred Kopietz, Cecil Surry, Cal Howard, Victor McLeod, George Grandpre, and Manuel Moreno, many of whom would soon leave for greener pastures—and some of whom would return to Lantz years later.

In 1935, Lantz and Bill Nolan parted company, and a year later Lantz made another move to establish himself as an independent producer. Universal Pictures underwent a series of corporate and executive upheavals in late 1935 and 1936; a major result was the departure of Carl Laemmle. Lantz seized the opportunity to inform Universal that he no longer wanted to work for them, but rather wished to act as his own producer and sell the distribution rights to Universal on a contractual basis. The company agreed, and even helped Lantz finance his own studio setup. He at first remained on the Universal

Baby Face Mouse is threatened, in CHEESE NAPPERS (1938). © **Walter Lantz Productions.**

lot, but then moved in the 1940s to a Seward Street building that had formerly housed the Columbia cartoon studio.

In 1936 Lantz made another, inexplicable move: He completely redesigned Oswald, changing him from a Mickey Mouse–like black rabbit to a more realistically inspired white rabbit. Whether the cartoons simply lost some of their pep at this time or whether the change in design actually affected the personality of the cartoons is hard to say. But the problem was clear, even to Lantz: The studio needed fresh ideas and new characters.

First to arrive were a trio of monkeys named Meany, Miny, and Moe; they lasted one year. Then came such assorted animals as Snuffy the Skunk and Baby Face Mouse* (the latter bearing some resemblance to Sniffles at Warner Brothers) and a flurry of one-

*Renamed Willie Mouse by home-movie distributor Castle Films.

shot cartoons and potential series that didn't quite click. VOODOO IN HARLEM resurrected the combination live-action/animation technique Lantz hadn't used in years, while NELLIE, THE SEWING MACHINE GIRL launched a short-lived series of Gay Nineties melodrama spoofs that wrung every drop out a one-joke idea.

Then Lantz announced his most ambitious project to date: a feature-length cartoon. This was in the wake of SNOW WHITE AND THE SEVEN DWARFS' phenomenal success, and an unidentified newspaper clipping of the time tells the story:

Walter Lantz is one cartoon producer who declines to be panic-stricken by Walt Disney. Lantz has received $750,000 from Universal to make a cartoon feature, ALADDIN AND HIS WONDERFUL LAMP. With this, he says, he will make a feature that will compete with SNOW WHITE but in no sense imitate it. He says that no one can compete with Disney on shorts, because Disney has no desire to make any money on them. His profits come from royalties for the use of his name and characters.

Lantz says that the whole industry has profited by Disney's experiments, and that much of the cost of SNOW WHITE was spent in developing methods for its making. These advancements are available to the industry, and by figuring all problems out in advance, Lantz anticipates no difficulties with ALADDIN. He is going Disney one better in using human figures, and he feels that the result will be more acceptable.

The prince and princess of Disney's fable were drawn by means of a rotoscope, by which real humans were photographed going through the required action. Then, frame by frame, the images were projected on a transparent panel, through which they were traced by animators. Lantz feels that this literal system resulted in two faults—a jittering movement that contrasted with the fluidity of the animals and the fact that the human characters were too accurate to be seen beside the caricatures. Lantz says that he will use the rotoscope for timing, and then will reanimate the figures to get a convincing element of unreality in them. He has placed Frank Churchill, who did the music for SNOW WHITE, under contract, and the composer will prepare the score for ALADDIN.

ALADDIN was never made. Lantz got as far as the storyboard stage and then threw in the towel. Why? "Too costly and too much of a risk," he says. "If you miss, like everybody has outside of Disney, you can take an awful loss on it." It seemed that in features, just as in shorts, Lantz felt he could not effectively compete with Disney. He revived the idea of a feature in the 1940s, and hoped to use a combination live-action/animation format with Universal's top comedy stars Abbott and Costello. This could have been a wonderful film, following a path completely different from Disney's, but, as Lantz tells it, he could never make a deal with Abbott and Costello's agents, and the idea was dropped.

While composer Frank Churchill was on staff, he wrote the score for another ambitious film, BOY MEETS DOG, that almost went unseen. Lantz produced the short as an elaborate soft-sell commercial for Ipana Toothpaste. "I think it cost around nine thousand dollars to produce," he says. "They were going to give the theaters fifty cents a seat to run it, but something happened and it never came about. Then Gene Castle, who was the head of Castle Films, bought it from Ipana." Thus Lantz's elaborate color cartoon first saw the light of day on the home-movie market—with the actual plugs for Ipana removed.

Based on characters from Gene Byrnes' *Reg'lar Fellers* comic strip, the film combines unsubtle health tips (like instructions to massage your gums and brush your teeth) with a tearjerker tale of a villainous father (voiced by the ubiquitous Billy Bletcher) who denies his little boy any and all pleasures—including the adoption of a cute puppy—

until a nightmarish trial in the Land of Gnomes brings him to his senses. The backgrounds in this cartoon are unusually handsome for a Lantz effort, and the music score by Churchill (conducted by Nathaniel Shilkret) is robust and effective. It could be that the backgrounds were rendered by Willy Pogany, a once-prominent illustrator on the *New York American* and cover artist whom Lantz hired when he was out of work. Pogany designed a subsequent short with an elflike character named Peterkin, which Lantz still fondly recalls. "I don't think I've ever had such beautiful backgrounds in my cartoons," he says.

Lantz stopped directing around this time, although he resumed for a brief time in the early 1940s. Instead, he started looking out for available talent—within his studio as well as outside—and offered directing credits to others for the first time. He also gave his new directors the opportunity of working in color on a full-time basis, beginning mid-1939.

Burt Gillett, hired by Lantz after his second stint with Disney, created a stereotyped black youngster named Li'L Eightball, whose screen life was short but who resurfaced in Lantz's comic books of the 1940s. Veteran studio animator Les Kline tried his hand at directing for a while. But the most important graduation within studio ranks was that of Alex Lovy, who became a director in 1938 on the Willie Mouse cartoons and carried his affinity for cute characters into another project that happily took off: the creation of Andy Panda.

Lantz was constantly searching for animals that had not been used as cartoon stars before—over the years he succeeded with a woodpecker, a buzzard, a walrus, and a penguin. The panda was a novel idea, sparked by national attention given the donation of a panda to the Chicago Zoo. In fact, this event spawned the first story line, with Andy's father warning him, ''Don't leave the forest—panda hunters will capture you and put you in the newsreel,'' and little Andy scampering away, declaring, ''I'm gonna be in the newsreel!'' Andy's father is a lumbering type with a voice to match, while his son provides a spunky contrast. Their relationship seems to have been inspired somewhat by Fanny Brice's Baby Snooks radio skits, with innocently mischievous Andy always getting his thick-witted father in trouble, while the title of their first film, LIFE BEGINS FOR ANDY PANDA, was a neat switch on the similar name of a popular Andy Hardy feature. Sara Berner, who played the switchboard operator on Jack Benny's radio show, did the voice of Andy during his formative years.

Follow-up films with Andy and his pop stick to the pattern established in their first short, with pleasant if predictable results. In GOODBYE MR. MOTH (1942) Andy became a solo-star character, no longer a little boy. But before that graduation, he helped to introduce another Lantz star, in the 1940 cartoon KNOCK KNOCK. Ben ''Bugs'' Hardaway had recently joined the staff after a long stint at Warner Brothers, where he wrote or directed the cartoons that introduced the studio's looniest characters, Daffy Duck and Bugs Bunny. Now he set to work designing a similar character for Lantz and found the father-and-son Pandas perfect foils for his creation: Woody Woodpecker.

(Lantz has made a legend out of the story of his honeymoon at Sherwood Lake, California, when a woodpecker hammered away at his roof and inspired the creation of this character. This delightful story has apparently undergone some showmanly embellishment, since the honeymoon occurred one year after the production of the cartoon.)

KNOCK KNOCK opens with Andy asking his pop if it's really true that you can catch a bird by putting salt on its tail. Pop evades the question, but its relevance is quickly realized in the knock-knock-knocking that sounds like someone at the door, but turns out to be ''that woodpecker again,'' hammering on the roof. Pop braces himself along a beam under the roof awaiting the bird's entry through an ever-widening hole. Sure enough, the bird's head pops through, but he isn't fazed by the waiting hunter. ''Guess who?'' he says impishly, giving Pop's nose a tweak before retreating to the roof to issue his ''ha-ha-ha-HA-ha'' laugh for the first time on-screen. The balance of the film concerns the frantic efforts of Andy and Pop to capture the wily bird, who's at least one step ahead of them at every turn. Finally Andy catches him off-guard and empties an entire shaker of salt on his tail. The woodpecker laughs at this feeble effort, but finds that he can't run away. ''It works,'' he gasps in horror. ''It *works!* Help! Let me outta here!'' Just then, a pair of fellow woodpeckers in white coats arrive in an ambulance to take their feathered friend away. ''Confidentially, this guy's crazy,'' says one to Andy's pop. But in a moment it turns out that they're just as batty, and they join their wacky pal in hopping all over the place in a fit of raucous laughter.

Woody bears a strong character resemblance to Hardaway's earlier Daffy and Bugs. He is brash, he is nutty, he is overdramatic, and he is blessed with a gift for loony magic. He foils one of Andy's early attempts to sprinkle salt on his tail by suddenly producing a stein of beer, allowing Andy to pour his salt onto the head before blowing it in his face. Another time, he spins around to insult Andy for having the nerve to try and catch him, huffing and puffing as he swells in size from this temperamental outburst. Then, just as suddenly, he turns around and exhales the hot air as one would with a bagpipe! The similarity to earlier Warners' characters is enhanced by the fact that Woody's voice is that of Mel Blanc, who did the character for a couple of years until Warner Brothers signed him to an exclusive contract. (When he left, several people tried doing Woody, including Hardaway himself, until Lantz's wife, Grace Stafford, became the permanent voice in 1951.)

Woody's appearance was certainly more grotesque than any previous starring character in Lantz's repertoire. The components of his body seemed to have been stuck together like clumps of clay. He was skinny, with stumpy legs and disproportionately large feet; his long bill created a kind of symmetry with his pointed comb. Two lone teeth were revealed when he opened his mouth, giving him a particularly goofy look. This early Woody boasted a garish rainbow design, as well: His back was blue, his belly was red, his eyes were green and purple, his beak and feet bright yellow.

Needless to say, it would have been difficult for this character to go unnoticed, and half a year after the release of KNOCK KNOCK, Lantz brought forth a second cartoon called WOODY WOODPECKER, which officially acknowledged his newest star. In this one, Woody's fellow forest animals observe his behavior and decide that he's really nuts. They intimidate Woody into seeing a psychiatrist, and he does. But Dr. Fox is no mental giant himself, and the woodpecker soon has him ready for commitment to the nearest asylum.

Woody was unlike any character ever seen in a Lantz cartoon, and the nature of his personality inspired a change in tempo as well as a change in gag content. Woody is a hyperactive and often violent character—quite in tune with the brassy 1940s—and he simply wouldn't have come across in a measured or leisurely format. Lantz directed most of the early Woodys himself, and it's

The evolution of Woody Woodpecker, as recalled in a recent drawing by Walter Lantz. © Walter Lantz Productions.

interesting to compare them to Alex Lovy's first, ACE IN THE HOLE. The story and gags in this cartoon are pretty good, but Lovy treats them in an even-paced, mild-mannered fashion, which simply doesn't suit Woody's character. The cartoon has no punch, a pattern that continued in Lovy's other endeavors with Woody.

The best thing that happened to Woody, and to Lantz, in the early 1940s was the arrival of James (Shamus) Culhane as director. Lovy left the studio in 1942, and Lantz was desperate for talent. What with the draft and the pressure of making government-commissioned films, it was difficult to maintain a theatrical release schedule. (Lantz was more fortunate than most regarding the draft, in that one of his top animators was a woman, La Verne Harding.) That year he teamed animator Emery Hawkins with Ben Hardaway and then with writer Milt Schaffer to direct two cartoons.

Then Culhane arrived, to shoulder major directing chores for the next few years. Having worked for Fleischer, Iwerks, Disney, and Warners', Culhane came to Lantz with ample experience under his belt and a flurry of original and dynamic ideas.

Culhane started with some SWING SYMPHONIES and then turned to Woody Woodpecker. Looking back, he says, "It was a good character. It was a funny character. The shape and design of it was excellent and that trick voice was very smart. But he was not an actor. I like pantomime, and he's a real action character." That being the case, Culhane decided to concentrate on action to such a degree that "it should take you on a roller-coaster ride, really give it to you." And he found a perfect vehicle for this approach in his very first Woody cartoon, THE BARBER OF SEVILLE, which incorporated some of Rossini's music into the score.

"The story department did not do what I finally did with it," he explains. "They had him shave the guy in the chair . . . and that was it. But I, being a musician, began to hear what this was. I suddenly found myself doing lead sheets according to the music and I couldn't believe what was coming out: twelve-frame cuts, eight-frame cuts. 'Figaro, Figaro, Figaro, Fi-ga-ro'—I realized that if I did the thing once around at normal speed, when it came back to the 'Figaro, Figaro' part, I could go like a sonofabitch because the audience knew what the action was; they would retain the memory of it and be able to read a shot which they normally would not. It worked fine."

THE BARBER OF SEVILLE is an excellent cartoon in which Woody takes control of Tony's barbershop and puts a pair of unsuspecting customers through the wringer. The second, a construction man, asks for "the whole works" and Woody obliges, getting into the mood for a shave and haircut by singing the "Largo el Factotum" from *Barber of Seville*. His vigorous rendition of this familiar aria sets the pace for the gags. Woody's actions grow faster and more furious as the music accelerates; it's a perfect blending of sound and picture. While trying to find his customer, who's run away in terror, Woody splits into three, then four, then five images of himself as he cries for Figaro in the aforementioned sequence, in which the cuts come as fast as five and six frames each (one quarter of a second!).

Culhane's desire to draw pantomime from his character was not abandoned, either. Woody is a rich and visually expressive character in this cartoon. His facial expressions, as well as his actions, are beautifully keyed to the music.

One more vital point: Woody is better-looking than ever before. Layout man and color stylist Art Heinemann suggested that he be redesigned to make him less grotesque and more appealing. Lantz agreed, and Heinemann replaced the many garish colors with a simple combination of red hair, white belly, and yellow beak.

Culhane followed up his BARBER OF SEVILLE triumph with other good Woody Woodpecker cartoons, including one that again spotlighted his musical talents, SKI FOR TWO (in which he sings "The Sleigh" while skiing to Wally Walrus's Swiss Chard

Lodge). That cartoon, which circulated for many years under the title WOODY PLAYS SANTA, also features an incredible bit of camera movement, in a scene in which Wally gorges himself on a mid-day meal. As he reaches for food from his well-stocked table and stuffs it in his mouth, the camera actually pans back and forth with his hand at table level to emphasize Wally's gluttony.

The search for food became a dominant theme in the Woodpecker cartoons of 1945–46. In WOODY DINES OUT, our hero is "in the mood for food," but can't find a restaurant that's open. When he spots a sign in a window that boasts, "We specialize in stuffing birds," he marches in, but unbeknownst to him the proprietor is a taxidermist with a special interest in woodpeckers. The man offers Woody some "blackout borscht" full of knockout drops, and Woody's reaction to the potion is incredible: His head elongates and spins; his eyes cross; his comb and neckpiece become fright wigs; and Woody turns a succession of ghastly colors. Fire comes out of his mouth—his head shoots thirty feet in the air as his neck stretches the distance, and lightning bolts flash on his brain just before he passes out.

In WHO'S COOKIN' WHO? Woody scoffs at the story of the Grasshopper and the Ants, but when winter comes he finds himself without food. Embarrassed, he turns to the camera and says, "Pardon me, would one of you step in the lobby and get me a candy bar?" In a reprise from the 1941 PANTRY PANIC, starvation literally stares Woody in the face, until a wolf comes by and Woody conspires to cook him. The violence of this cartoon —Woody sticks the wolf's face into a waffle iron—is repeated in the follow-up FAIR WEATHER FRIENDS, as Woody and the wolf actually bite into each other's legs, and Woody puts the wolf into a meat grinder. All that can be said of these cartoons in contrast to the earlier PANTRY PANIC is that Culhane's films carry their violence to such an outrageous extreme that the potential pain is tempered by sheer absurdity.

Culhane also did a few cartoons with Andy Panda, and maintained the gentle nature of that character while enlivening the cartoons in which he starred. One of the best is FISH FRY, which was nominated for an Academy Award. Andy sees a cute-looking goldfish in the window of a pet store and decides to buy him; the fish is elated and swims happily in the goldfish bowl that Andy perches atop his head to walk home. Along the way, a scrawny alley cat sees the fish and tries to snatch it behind Andy's back. The fish bites the cat's finger, and then, in the film's funniest moment, atones for his violent attack. The adorable goldfish pets the injured paw and says, "Poor little pussycat!" He reaches for a tiny Red Cross doctor's bag and pulls out an *enormous* set of false teeth, which he places in his mouth to bite the cat again! At the moment of impact Culhane cuts to a shot hundreds of feet in the air as the cat soars upward in pain, with a police siren on the sound track. The gag is meticulously executed—and, being unexpected, a real laugh-getter.

Lantz's third series of the 1940s was called SWING SYMPHONIES, which crystallized in 1941 after the studio did a couple of one-shot cartoons based on popular songs like THE BOOGIE WOOGIE BUGLE BOY OF COMPANY B. These cartoons had no running characters, although the boogie-woogie episodes tended to concentrate on black stereotypes, with varying degrees of humor.

Few of these cartoons were truly inspired, but the sound tracks were usually first-rate, thanks to Lantz's musical director Darrell Calker. "He knew all the musicians," says Shamus Culhane. "He knew King Cole, Meade Lux Lewis, Jack Teagarden and all

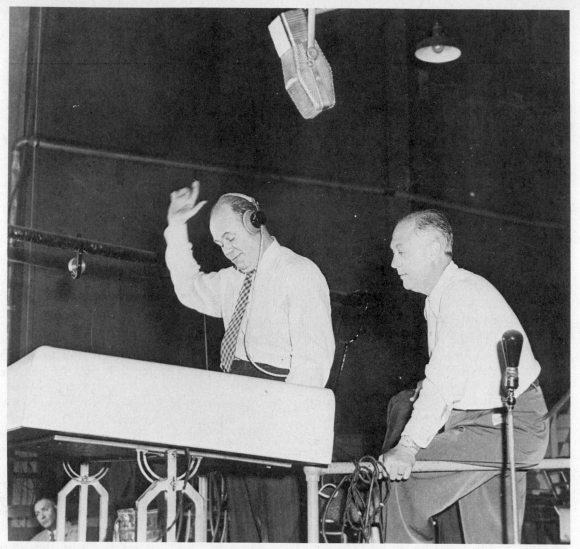

Lantz sits in on one of Darrell Calker's recording sessions in the late 1940s.

these people. Walt had him keep an eye out for when they were a little down and short of money, and then they'd invite them to come and do an evening's work.

"Darrell would say, 'I can get King Cole.' So we'd get some song he would normally play in a nightclub and do that. That would be a presynched thing and we'd animate to that, but the rest would be ad-lib music that Darrell would write."

The most impressive result of the studio's musical efforts came in 1948 when "The Woody Woodpecker Song," introduced in

WET BLANKET POLICY, was nominated for an Academy Award as Best Song of the Year! Although it lost to "Buttons and Bows," it became Woody's popular theme music and remains the only song from a short subject or cartoon to ever receive this nomination.*

Classical music had figured in Lantz cartoons from time to time—most notably in Woody's BARBER OF SEVILLE—but when POET

*Lantz tried to make lightning strike again with The Starlighters singing the title tune for THE WOODY WOODPECKER POLKA and Wee Bonnie Baker rendering an unmemorable theme song for Chilly Willy.

AND PEASANT came out in 1946, it launched a new series, supplanting the SWING SYMPHONIES with the more cultured MUSICAL MINIATURES.

POET AND PEASANT features Andy Panda as the conductor of a barnyard orchestra performing the famous overture of the same name, despite various obstacles—mischievous animals that distract the musicians, and the like. It's a very pleasant cartoon that reaffirms the sure-fire formula of blending gags and classical music themes. The short was extremely successful, and Universal was delighted to discover many big-city theaters holding it over for four to six weeks.

The studio ballyhooed this cartoon with special advertising and publicity, and claimed, "POET AND PEASANT inaugurated an innovation which proved immensely popular. This was the use of classical music by a symphonic orchestra, against which background the cartune [sic] action took place. The "POET AND PEASANT" overture was played by a fifty-piece symphonic orchestra and provided a real thrill for music lovers, as well as offering a comic action story which blended nicely with the fine music. So successful was this production that Lantz is making it the first of a new series to be titled MUSICAL MINIATURES.

"The second release in the MUSICAL MINIATURES series will be CHOPIN'S MUSICAL MOMENTS [sic]. In this picture the score of five Chopin compositions will be played straight with no attempt at comedy distortion. Ted Saidenberg and Ed Rebner, duo pianists, have recorded the music.

"A new-type sound track, double the size now in use, will be used for the first time in connection with the Chopin release. This new method of recording will permit a much wider range of sound than can be obtained from the track now used. Recording engi-

neers believe this new track will revolutionize sound on film."

Well, POET AND PEASANT was in truth neither an innovation in concept nor in execution. Disney's THE BAND CONCERT was just one of many classically inspired cartoons prior to 1946. As to the sound track, it did not leave its mark on the film industry, but it was certainly an ambitious step for Lantz to undertake. This development was the work of William E. Garity, the man who had created such engineering marvels for Walt Disney as the multiplane camera and the famous "Fantasound" stereo system for FANTASIA.

If POET AND PEASANT bore a passing resemblance to THE BAND CONCERT, there was more than coincidence at work. This was the second Lantz cartoon to be directed by Dick Lundy, who joined the studio after fifteen years with Disney.

Lundy explains how a MUSICAL MINIATURE was planned: "Lantz, story men, the musician and myself would meet and make certain suggestions for different gags, both for orchestration and special comedy musical effects. Then it would be prescored and the track would be read so we would know where every beat was, and if necessary, those notes which were important to the animation and/or gags to put the picture over."

This was, of course, a very exacting process, but when done with verve and imagination, it paid off handsomely. Both POET AND PEASANT and MUSICAL MOMENTS FROM CHOPIN were nominated for Academy Awards. Musical selections included the overtures to Zampa and William Tell. "These pieces were all in public domain and we didn't have to pay for them," Lantz explains. He also had access to the Universal studio orchestra, which could record these tried-and-true symphonic pieces in no time at all.

Director Dick Lundy times out a cartoon, with the storyboard for reference, and a metronome for help with setting a rhythm.

Lantz numbers these among his favorite cartoons, and says, "I wish we could have made more of them, but they got to be very expensive. You have to animate to every bar of music."*

Meanwhile, Dick Lundy was getting acquainted with Lantz's other series as he stepped into Shamus Culhane's shoes, becoming sole director of the studio's output by 1946.

To Lundy, "the biggest difference [between Disney's operation and Lantz's] was, of course, the cost—$15,000 to $25,000 at Lantz against Disney's $35,000 plus. At Disney's if your picture turned out well, or very well, nothing was said if you spent $70,000–75,000. Also at Lantz, animators had to turn out twenty-five feet per week. Disney would like to get twenty-five feet per week, but if the animator turned out good, funny personality animation, five feet per week was OK. Animators at Lantz received $125 a week in 1941. Disney, on the other hand, paid animators $75 a week for beginners and up to $250 for more experienced men. It all seemed to hinge on cost.

"When I went to Lantz, I tried to teach the animators some of the Disney ways for better animation. Some of the artists were glad and wanted to learn; others didn't seem to care. I tried to get the animators to put in a little

*The studio returned to a musical format in 1955 for the Woody Woodpecker cartoon CONVICT CONCERTO—with outstanding results. The story was contributed by animation veteran Hugh Harman.

more personality. Naturally, there were some who tried and some who didn't seem to get the idea at all. To get personality in animation cut down on their footage, so it was a compromise to get this and still meet their quota of twenty-five feet per week. I think, as time went on, the quality did raise up just a bit. I think the characters were better liked and more believable because of the better animation."

Lundy is right. BATHING BUDDIES with Woody and Wally Walrus may lack the violent impact of Culhane's cartoons, even though it's basically an action story, but Woody is more likable, and his motivations clearer, in this cartoon than in many earlier entries. The story peg is ideal: A tenant in Wally's apartment house, Woody inserts a dime in his water meter to fill the bathtub, but the dime falls down the drain instead. Naturally, Woody destroys the entire building and drives Wally berserk in order to retrieve his ten-cent piece.

Lundy also worked hard to make Woody a more expressive character, and he succeeded in films like WOODY THE GIANT KILLER. But he achieved even greater success in the Andy Panda cartoons, for here was a truly Disneyesque character. Andy didn't have much personality per se, but he was a friendly figure around whom a solid cartoon could be built. In the hands of the right animator, he was capable of pantomime and expressions befitting any great cartoon star, and the fact that he didn't carry with him a strong voice characterization made it possible to do sight-gag material and keep dialogue to a bare minimum.

In THE BANDMASTER Andy looks and acts for all the world like Mickey Mouse in THE BAND CONCERT, and it isn't hard to understand why—he was drawn in that and other films by Fred Moore, one of Mickey's great-

(Below) Woody Woodpecker in THE MAD HATTER **(1948)**. © Walter Lantz Productions.

(Bottom) Food is Woody's number-one priority in films such as BANQUET BUSTERS **(1948)**, with Andy Panda and unnamed mouse. © Walter Lantz Productions.

Andy Panda in one of his best starring shorts, PLAYFUL
PELICAN (1948). © Walter Lantz Productions.

est animators. Completing the family resemblance, the story for THE BANDMASTER was written by another longtime Disney man, Webb Smith.

PLAYFUL PELICAN is a charming short of Lundy's that relies to a great extent on Andy's winning personality to put it over—and succeeds. The animation here is by Ed Love (lately come from Tex Avery's unit at MGM) and Ken O'Brien (a top Disney feature animator—from BAMBI to SLEEPING BEAUTY—on leave from home base). Their expertise breathes such life into Andy Panda as he tangles with a stubborn pelican—and then plays mother/protector to its wide-eyed offspring—that it becomes doubly difficult to stomach the second-rate animation that was to follow in Lantz cartoons just a few years later.

In fact, PLAYFUL PELICAN was the next-to-last Andy Panda short. Lantz never revived him in the 1950s—a tacit admission that,

with Lundy gone, no one was capable of drawing the necessary personality out of this character to make him workable again.

During World War II, Lantz had accepted government commissions like every other cartoon studio. He is proudest of a Navy medical film called ENEMY BACTERIA, which combined live action and animation, and cost over $100,000 to make. Milburn Stone played the live doctor and Mel Blanc provided the voice of the cartoon "germs." The film was so successful that it played for years after the war in medical schools around the country.

After the war, Lantz continued doing commercial and industrial films to supplement his theatrical income. There were films for power companies, commercials for Coca-Cola, a trailer for Universal's THE EGG AND I, animated sequences for the Gene Autry film SIOUX CITY SUE, and a special segment with Woody Woodpecker for George Pal's DESTINATION MOON.

But the producer faced financial difficulty in the immediate postwar years. In 1947 he squabbled with Universal, which had recently changed management and become Universal-International (U-I). He distributed his cartoons through United Artists (UA) instead for the 1948 season and then ran out of steam. For reasons that are still unclear, Lantz was forced to close his studio for more than a year, while Universal-International reissued older Lantz cartoons to maintain a steady flow of shorts on its release schedule.

Finally, in 1950, Lantz and U-I came to terms. The cartoon studio reopened, and U-I subsequently reissued the UA-Lantz shorts. Both parties prefer to forget that they ever parted company. When Lantz reopened for business, he had to do so with a sharper eye on the budget than ever before. His first

releases utilized storyboards by Ben Hardaway and exposure sheets that Dick Lundy
had prepared at the time of the layoff in 1948.
Rather than hire a director, Lantz piloted
many of these films himself and then had
animator Don Patterson supervise the rest.
There were no writers on staff, so dialogue
was kept to a minimum in these early-1950s
shorts, all of which starred Woody Woodpecker. When dialogue was imperative Lantz
had another foolproof money-saving
scheme: He had his actress-wife Grace Stafford do Woody's voice.

With the skeleton staff on hand, Lantz was
able to deliver only seven cartoons for release
in 1951, and six in 1952, but when the films
were successful and U-I was pleased, Lantz
expanded and doubled his output to thirteen
cartoons a year, a pace he maintained for the
duration of his producing career.

The Lantz crew of the early 1950s consisted of four key animators: Don Patterson,
Ray Abrams, La Verne Harding, and Paul
Smith, most of whom were studio veterans
who stayed with Lantz for many years. (Patterson and Abrams had been with Lantz in
the 1930s and returned after stints with Disney and MGM respectively.) They simplified
Woody's design for the new cartoons, rounding his head and filling out his body to make
him a cuter, less angular character than
before. A thicker ink line was noticeable,
and both character design and backgrounds
were kept to basics.

The gags and situations in many of these
films are quite good, but the draftsmanship
is often downright poor. One has only to
look at contemporary films from the Warner
Brothers and MGM cartoon factories (not to
mention Disney) to appreciate just how
shoddy it was.

This was just one of several erratic qualities in the 1950s Lantz product. Apparently
because of the smaller staff, time pressures,
and lack of inspiration, it was possible for
one key person with a solid idea to effect
sweeping changes in an individual cartoon.
That individual was usually a writer or
director.

Don Patterson was the first of Lantz's animation team to try directing, and he showed
great aptitude for the assignment. His shorts
are among the best of the early-1950s product, showing deft handling of characters and
snappy timing. In 1952 he "supervised" one
of the best Woody Woodpecker cartoons of
all time, TERMITES FROM MARS.

In this ingenious story, Woody learns
about a mysterious Martian invasion from
TV news bulletins, but pays no heed until a
spaceship lands outside his home and a
corps of tiny termites wearing bubble-glass
protectors on their heads and brandishing
ray guns invade the Broken Limbs Apart-
ments. These termites will eat anything and

Wally Walrus and Woody Woodpecker in STAGE HOAX
(1952). © Walter Lantz Productions.

everything, and there's nothing Woody can do to stop them. They demolish the interior and exterior of his home, and one greedy invader even chomps on Woody's beak! Another termite points his ray gun at Woody and freezes him in his tracks—turning Woody a pale pink and obliterating the background of his apartment into a solid gray mass. The insect zaps him again and now Woody is frozen in a more agitated pose, his color a ghastlier shade of gray against a bright red background. One more blast from the gun and Woody is just a white outline of himself, running in place against another colored backdrop. Now the termite grabs one end of his prisoner and unloops Woody's outline like a long strand of spaghetti, twirling him out of frame and enabling him to reform himself before a final zap restores him to normal in his apartment setting.

Just when all seems hopeless, one of the voracious insects tries to bite into some Scotch tape on Woody's desk and finds himself stuck; the more he struggles, the more encased he becomes in the tape. Woody sees his golden opportunity and starts stringing tape around the apartment and then around the entire forest. Within moments he's got hundreds of the tiny termites trapped and in his power.

A dissolve takes us to the imposing forest headquarters of Woody Woodpecker Termite Control. Woody sits in an enormous office beneath a portrait of himself, supervising advertisements for his Little Wonder Termite Tools, which make ingenious use of the captive insects: a bottle opener, a mousetrap, a burglar alarm, and a garbage disposal. It's taken some doing, but Woody finally has the last laugh.

TERMITES FROM MARS is an excellent cartoon by any standards. It is visually impressive, from the opening invasion sequences to the atmospheric red-tinted scenes as the Martians close in on Woody's forest. The ray-gun sequence is about as daring and imaginative an idea as ever appeared in a Walter Lantz cartoon, while the very premise of the short is fresh and funny. (It is interesting to note that this was not the Martian termites' debut, however. These same characters appeared in an incongruous gag during STAGE HOAX earlier that year, when Western outlaw Buzz Buzzard dispatches these creatures with a radar rocket to bite the wooden axle of Wally Walrus's stagecoach in half.)

It is difficult to know who is really responsible for the success of an individual cartoon of this period, especially since in this case there is no credit given for story. But Patterson's cartoons are clearly superior to those directed by others around this time. Moreover, later Woody cartoons with outer-space themes (WOODPECKER FROM MARS, WOODPECKER IN THE MOON) aren't nearly as good, or as innovative. Therefore, it seems fair to assume that Patterson's contributions made TERMITES FROM MARS so successful.

He continued to score bull's eye hits during the next two years he directed for Lantz. SOCKO IN MOROCCO, a pantomime cartoon with a desert theme features some surprisingly good animation, of a sexy princess and then a vicious panther. Its follow-up, ALLEY TO BALI, boasts equally lavish settings and backgrounds, plus the kind of personality animation Dick Lundy used to try for in the late 1940s. Here, Woody and Buzz Buzzard are sailors, fighting pals who dance a sailor's hornpipe punctuated with kicks and double-crossing gags. It's rare that a 1950s Lantz cartoon takes the time to linger over a nondialogue sequence that has nothing to do with the story, drawing its laughs from engaging animation of the characters in a gag situation. Even Woody's appearance, in an oversized sailor suit, is appealing.

Patterson also piloted the studio's only 3-

D cartoon, HYPNOTIC HICK. As usual in these cases, there was nothing all that special in the preparation of the gags and animation for this cartoon; the effects were taken care of for the most part in the technical processing of the film. There was no encore after this one attempt. "It was just a fad," says Lantz. "It wasn't really worthwhile doing." For similar reasons he declined to make his cartoons in CinemaScope.

The year 1953, which saw the release of HYPNOTIC HICK, brought other significant changes to the Lantz studio. This was the year that Lantz expanded to a production schedule of thirteen shorts, necessitating a larger staff and an infusion of new ideas.

First, animator Paul Smith was promoted to director. A veteran of twenty-five years in the business, Smith was with Walt Disney in the late 1920s and then spent most of the 1930s with Warner Brothers before joining Lantz in the 1940s. But like his contemporary Robert McKimson at Warners', Smith's long experience as an animator did not guarantee his qualifications as a director. As it turned out, Smith was a weak director, with no style and little imagination. His earliest films were infused with a certain spirit that must have come from enthusiasm and absorption of ideas from his colleagues. But within a few years his films lost whatever punch they may have had at first and became pale carbon copies of one another.

In 1953, Smith was charged with developing non-Woody Woodpecker cartoons. He worked on FOOLISH FABLES and then launched a mildly amusing series called MAW AND PAW, which took its gags and format directly from Universal's popular MA AND PA KETTLE movies. The following year he introduced another character called Sugarfoot, who, like Maw and Paw, was short lived.

Another addition to the studio roster in 1953 was writer Homer Brightman, a ten-year veteran of the Disney studio who supplied Lantz with stories for more than ten years, interrupted by one brief stint at MGM. Since Brightman was responsible for so many films over such a long period of time, it's practically impossible to judge his style or discern any special characteristics in his work. One must wonder if another writer could have salvaged the Lantz cartoons from creeping mediocrity during this period or if external factors made this decline inevitable.

New animators joined the roster, including Robert Bentley and Gil Turner from MGM, Herman R. Cohen, and Ken Southworth. Cecil Surry, who had been with Lantz twenty years earlier, returned for a brief time.

Then in 1954, two others came to the Lantz studio and gave the finished products rolling off the studio's assembly line an enormous boost. The first was writer Michael Maltese, on a brief sojourn away from Warner Brothers and Chuck Jones. It's easy to spot his distinctively crazy gags in cartoons like HELTER SHELTER and SQUARE SHOOTING SQUARE, and they give a decided lilt to what would otherwise be standard cartoon story lines. But it's equally evident that a director like Paul Smith hasn't the finesse to take a Maltese script and milk it for all it's worth. SQUARE SHOOTING SQUARE is filled with gags reminiscent of earlier Jones cartoons with Bugs and Daffy that just don't come across as they should. Woody keeps getting the best of a hulking Western heavy, with the usual punch line being an explosion in the outlaw's face. In one scene near the end, the heavy grabs what he thinks is his money and runs far off into the hills; we see a distant explosion, and he runs back to tell Woody, "I hate you." Delivered without the resounding frustration of a Daffy Duck, the line just

Chilly Willy in YUKON HAVE IT **(1959).** © **Walter Lantz.**

falls flat. A play on words, with Woody and the outlaw playing tug-of-war with a stick of dynamite and yelling, "It's yours!" "it's mine!" until the heavy insists on *taking* the sizzling TNT, echoes similar moments from Warners' cartoons like RABBIT SEASONING, but without a fraction of the comic impact.*

Fortunately, Maltese was soon joined at Lantz by the one man who could turn the Walter Lantz studio on its heels and revolutionize its reputation: Tex Avery.

Avery, of course, had gotten his first job in animation at the Walter Lantz studio in the early 1930s (as Lantz recalls it, "He came to me with a stack of drawings, and I said,

*It was not much different when Heck Allen, Tex Avery's MGM story man, spent a brief time at Lantz's in 1948 and wrote Western gags for a pair of Woody Woodpecker shorts, WILD AND WOODY and PUNY EXPRESS. Dick Lundy used them much better than Paul Smith did Maltese's material, but it was impossible not to think of Avery doing them even better.

'Can you wash cels?'") and left to make his name at Warner Brothers and MGM, where he directed some of the greatest cartoons ever made. Now he was going to work for Lantz again, and the producer was elated.

For his debut, Avery wrote as well as directed a cartoon called CRAZY MIXED-UP PUP, with a typical Avery gag premise extended to the outer reaches of insanity: A truck runs over a man and his dog, and the hospital attendants inadvertently inject the man with dog plasma and vice versa. The result is a dog with human characteristics and a man with canine tendencies. The gags come one after another, and just when it seems the reversal has reached its peak, Avery tops himself with another turnaround, more outrageous than the one before.

The only discernible difference between this fine cartoon and his MGM efforts is in the technical quality of the film. The fine animation styling just isn't there; the lustrous color and vivid music tracks that made every MGM cartoon look so plush are missing. But the gags are strong, and the timing is superb; it's like nothing else produced at the Lantz studio that decade. The film was nominated for an Academy Award.

Avery followed this with a pair of cartoons featuring a new character named Chilly Willy. Alex Lovy, on a brief return to Lantz in 1953, had initiated the character, but the first film was unsuccessful. Lantz was determined to use this character, however, and Avery went to work, redesigning Chilly to make him cuter. "But the penguin wasn't funny," Avery later told Joe Adamson. "There was nothing to it, no personality, no nothing. So I attempted to get humor—since [Lantz] wanted a penguin so bad—from the dumb dog, or the dumb sea gull, or the dumb polar bear. Shucks, you couldn't do anything with a little fuzzy wuzzy penguin! But the cartoons weren't bad, I worked hard on them."

THE LEGEND OF ROCKABYE POINT reunited Avery with Michael Maltese, who had worked with him many years earlier at Warner Brothers. Together they concocted a wildly funny cartoon in which Chilly and a polar bear compete to steal fish off an Alaskan ship without disturbing the bulldog who's guarding the goods. Avery's mastery of the running gag—knowing how to milk a joke beyond the point of normal endurance with endless variations—serves him well as the bear discovers that the dog will always go to sleep if he sings or plays "Rock-a-bye Baby." Again, Avery's work earned an Academy Award nomination.

Finally, Avery sold Lantz on the idea of making a cartoon from a famous "laughing record" of the 1920s which consisted in its entirety of people slowly erupting into boisterous (and contagious) laughter. Avery's cartoon adaptation, called SH-H-H-H-H, failed to capture the irresistible quality of the old record, partly because it buried the laughing jag in an incompatible story framework about a trip to a sanitarium. But it scored points for Avery, for attempting to try something so radically different, and for Lantz, who backed him up in making the effort.

Sadly, SH-H-H-H-H was Avery's last film for the studio. He left over a salary squabble and in fact made no further theatrical cartoons. But his influence was felt for many years at the Lantz studio. He had brought with him from MGM the idea of a stock deadpan character who reacts to the "star" character's antics in low-key fashion. The Lantz writers and directors saw this character as a prototype with endless possibilities and built around him a formula that was repeated ad nauseam for the next twenty years. The character appeared in virtually every Chilly Willy cartoon (usually in the guise of a bear named Smedley) and many Woody Woodpeckers as well; no matter how his appearance varied from film to film, his

voice, provided by Daws Butler, was always the same.

Character design fell into a similar formula in the mid-1950s, as Lantz's directors and animators found an ideal shortcut in the constant reuse of two or three all-purpose models. From that time on, practically every animal and human in a Lantz cartoon looked alike, by virtue of one-piece construction and single-line caricature of facial features that later became standard operating procedure at Hanna-Barbera.

Music, too, went sadly downhill during this period. Clarence Wheeler was musical director throughout the 1950s and replaced Darrell Calker's brassy jazz of the 1940s with a more sedate, "mickey mouse" brand of scoring. Just as Lantz's 1950s and 1960s cartoons often failed to build in tempo to a big finale, Wheeler's music never bridged the final scene and the end title, leaving audiences stranded even further in midair.*

Alex Lovy returned to Walter Lantz to take the place of Tex Avery and stayed for five years. As the aim of Lantz's cartoons had shifted from characterizations to gag vignettes, Lovy's unaggressive style presented occasional problems. On the Chilly Willy series, Lovy relied mainly on the Tex Avery format and enjoyed considerable success in such early entries as ROOM AND WRATH and SWISS MISS-FIT (which repeated Avery's "Rock-a-bye Baby" gag from THE LEGEND OF ROCKABYE POINT). Lovy also scored with occasional one-shot cartoons like THE PLUMBER OF SEVILLE, which relied mostly on pantomime gags set to music as a plumber tries to fix a leak in Carnegie Hall; and MOUSE TRAPPED, which introduced characters Hickory, Dickory, and Doc—actually

---

*Eugene Poddany filled in for Wheeler in the late 1950s and early 1960s period, and contributed some imaginative scores. Then Darrell Calker returned briefly in the 1960s. Lantz's final music director was Walter Greene.

focusing on Doc, an elegant cat with top hat, starched collar, bow tie, and fine manners. Neither of these cartoons is sensationally funny, but the weaknesses are balanced by pleasing personality delineation.

In 1957 Lantz saw the possibilities of releasing his cartoons to television and put together a half-hour package called THE WOODY WOODPECKER SHOW, which comprised three theatrical cartoons linked by newly animated sequences, and live-action footage featuring Lantz himself. If Walt Disney could host his own television show, why not Lantz? (When Jack Hannah joined the staff, having recently directed some combined live-action and animation sequences for the Disney show, Lantz put him to work doing similar material.) Every week Woody introduced "My boss, Walter Lantz," who spent one segment of the program explaining how animated cartoons are made. This was not the first time the producer had compiled such material—he was featured in a 1936 Universal short called CARTOONLAND MYSTERIES that traced the evolution of an Oswald cartoon, and in the 1940s he prepared a still-photo exhibition illustrating the same elements. These TV sequences were clear-cut and entertaining, putting the accompanying cartoons into a pleasing perspective.

Lantz discovered, however, that in order to pass muster on TV his cartoons would have to undergo strict censorship. In the first fifty-two shorts packaged for television some twenty-five sequences had to be deleted. The producer reviewed some of his problems in a 1957 article for *Hollywood Reporter*:

The first thing that happened was the elimination in one swoop of all my films that contained Negro characters; there were eight such pictures. But we never offended or degraded the colored race and they were all top musical cartoons, too.

The [advertising] agency reasoning was that if there was a question at all on a scene, why leave it in? It might cause some group or other to bring pressure, and if there's one thing the sponsor doesn't want, it's to make enemies.

The next thing we cut out en masse were all drinking scenes. In one cartoon, we showed a horse accidentally drinking cider out of a bucket and then, somewhat pixilated, trying to walk a tightrope. On TV you'll see the tipsy horse on the tightrope but, since we cut out the scene showing his drinking the cider, the TV audience won't understand why he is groggy.

The agency censors also kept a sharp eye out for any material which could be construed as risqué. The entire ABOU BEN BOOGIE film was rejected on the grounds it showed a little harem girl wriggling her hips.

Mental health and physical disabilities weren't overlooked either. In KNOCK KNOCK Woody's activities eventually lead him to a nervous breakdown. When we got through cutting this one, what was left didn't make much sense.

It was a disquieting throwback to the 1930s, when the *Motion Picture Herald* criticized GOLDILOCKS AND THE THREE BEARS by saying, "One very distasteful and objectionable bit, especially in material highly suitable for youngsters, and entirely without justification, is Goldilocks' belching when she tastes of the bears' porridge. It injects a jarring, unpleasant note in what is otherwise entertaining material."

(Lantz had his share of problems with censorship in the 1930s as well. When the famous 1934 Production Code took effect, the first thing to go was outhouse-type humor. "One of our biggest gags used to be someone throwing a chamber pot onto someone's head," he recalls, "but we had to cut that out." Another time in a film set in Mexico, the natives were shown barefoot. The Production office insisted that Lantz put shoes on the Mexicans, so his staff went back to the cels and painted all the feet jet-black. That satisfied the censors.)

Alex Lovy left Walter Lantz in 1959 to become an associate producer at Hanna-Barbera's growing television-cartoon factory. He was replaced by another director of long experience, Jack Hannah, who had spent his entire thirty-year career in animation with Walt Disney. Hannah brought several colleagues to Lantz from his recently curtailed Disney short-subject unit, including animator Al Coe and layout/background man Ray Huffine.

Says Hannah, "Walter Lantz himself is one of the nicest, sweetest guys. He was great to pick up talent already developed. The only trouble is, once you've been at Disney's, it was just a job. The people you worked with were second-rate [compared to Disney's], and no extra effort was expected. I wasn't used to that. So as a result, I just got bored there."

Lantz charged Hannah with finding story ideas, particularly for new series, and Hannah got the word to various veterans and free-lancers in Hollywood. As a result, Lantz cartoon credits carried such names as Tedd Pierce, Bill Danch, Dick Kinney, and Al Bertino over the next few years. Even 1940s story man Milt Schaffer contributed some ideas. Hannah revived two characters from his Disney days: Humphrey the Bear became Fatso Bear (by any name, an early prototype of Hanna-Barbera's Yogi), and the Disney ranger was replaced by Ranger Willoughby, identical to the Lantz studio's newest character, Inspector Willoughby. These cartoons, like HUNGER STRIFE and EGGNAPPER, echoed some of the genial nuttiness of Hannah's bear-and-ranger cartoons of the 1950s, but couldn't match their sustained hilarity. The director also revived his bumblebee, Bootle Beetle, for a handful of cartoons. But his newest star hopeful, Gabby Gator, who menaced Woody Woodpecker in such entries as SOUTHERN FRIED HOSPITALITY and GABBY'S DINER, had nothing to offer in terms of personality or humor. Hannah finished out his stint with Lantz doing Woodpecker, Chilly Willy, Inspector Willoughby, and Doc cartoons.

Inspector Willoughby, who headed the studio's newest series, was a human character reminiscent of Tex Avery's Droopy: a short man with a basset-hound face and low-key character. Dal McKennon even tried to approximate Bill Thompson's Droopy voice, and at the beginning of THE CASE OF THE COLD STORAGE YEGG, the Inspector tells the audience, "That's me, folks!" just as Droopy used to do. Willoughby's cartoons involved the pursuit of notorious criminals like Yeggs Benedict and Vampira Hyde, one wilier than the next, but none tricky enough to outfox the quietly conniving Inspector. The only problem with these cartoons is that they aren't funny. The character survived until 1965.

With Jack Hannah's departure in 1962, a final dose of adrenaline came to the studio in the person of director Sid Marcus. He brought with him an equally talented colleague, animator Art Davis, and the two did their best to pump some life into the Woody Woodpecker and Chilly Willy cartoons. Their efforts met with sporadic success, as the slim budgets and uninspired stories made true innovations difficult to achieve.

Their collaboration was enhanced by the arrival of veteran story man Cal Howard—who'd been with Lantz thirty years earlier—and together they turned out some of the studio's best cartoons of the 1960s. THREE LITTLE WOODPECKERS deals with a determined wolf who tries to break into—or break down—Woody's petrified-tree home. What counts is not so much the gags as the energy behind them.

HALF-BAKED ALASKA, another 1965 entry with Chilly Willy, has *everything* going for it

The early-1960s version of Woody Woodpecker, as seen in ROCKET RACKET (1962). © Walter Lantz Productions.

and represents the Marcus/Howard/Davis team in peak form. The film opens on a long shot of little black dots in a white expanse, moving closer to reveal the dots as a shivering Chilly Willy with his makeshift shoeshine stand in the middle of the Yukon. Longing for food, Chilly notices a nearby snack bar run by Smedley the Bear (the usual drawling character voiced by Daws Butler). Chilly goes inside and orders flapjacks, at ten dollars apiece, while Smedley does his best to please the customer. "Nice?" he asks. "Nice," says Chilly in his cute high-pitched voice. "More syrup?" asks Smedley. "Yes." "More butter?" "Yes." They go on at some length, like an old Senor Wences routine, until Smedley insists that Chilly pay in advance. He can't, so Smedley boots him out, advising him to get a job and earn some money.

Chilly heeds the bear's advice and goes looking for a job. He spots a sign outside a saloon reading "Piano Player Wanted" and goes inside. The tiny penguin spins the stool to reach his height. While an orchestra plays an impressive overture on the sound track, Chilly cracks his knuckles toward the camera, then just manages to reach the edge of the keyboard and plays some kindergarten-level tunes with one finger of each hand. Naturally he's kicked out, but tries his luck in a variety of other jobs (blacksmith, barber, and the like) before returning to Smedley's and obtaining his flapjacks through sleight of hand while the bear tries to serve a paying customer. When the burly patron becomes enraged at the bear, Chilly steps in and helps Smedley dispatch the villain, earning Smedley's gratitude, and a heaping stack of flapjacks.

What's so nice about this cartoon is not just the engaging story line, but the visual emphasis in every scene. Although there is some dialogue, the humor comes mainly from sight gags. Chilly's preparations for playing the saloon piano are hilarious, and the final shot in that sequence, where we see him peering over the edge of the keyboard, barely able to see, let alone reach the keys, is wonderful. Later, when the blacksmith kicks him out of his barnyard shop, the man's foot extends several feet longer than usual to emphasize the strength of the kick. When the angry customer bellows at Smedley, he meets the bear eyeball-to-eyeball and appears to be about four times bigger than the bear, by dint of a hilarious distortion.

HALF-BAKED ALASKA reveals the care and thought that went into its creation. Cal Howard supplied the basic story line, but Sid Marcus knew how to build on that foundation with visual embellishments that would make the gags particularly striking and funny. Art Davis and fellow animator Ray Abrams brought these gags to life. Walter

Greene, Lantz's newest music director, made his contribution in helping to set up the piano-playing gag effectively.

Unfortunately, this cartoon was the exception, and not the rule. When Sid Marcus left the studio, its like was never seen again. From 1966 on, all of Lantz's cartoons were directed by Paul Smith.

Smith was not incompetent by any means, and he still had some capable colleagues in the studio. But he lacked the drive and/or the imagination to overcome the restrictions of budget and the pitfall of monotony that plagued the Lantz series by this time. Even the attractive main-title designs were discontinued, in order to save time and money.

Lantz's cartoons succeeded almost by default in this late-1960s and early-1970s period, when he was one of the few remaining sources for new theatrical cartoon product. Warner Brothers closed its studio in 1969, leaving only DePatie-Freleng and Lantz on the marketplace. Theaters desiring cartoons as extra added attractions, time fillers, or kiddie-show fodder were almost certain to book the Lantz product for simple lack of choice.

Sadly, the distinction between these cartoons and the hack-quality television cartoons that helped to kill off theatrical animation was practically nonexistent. Lantz was quick to point out that animators for TV cartoons had to turn out five times as much footage per week as those on his staff. But unfortunately there was not really an inverse proportion of quality and quantity in this case. Part of the reason was uninspired talent, and the rest of the answer was money: One simply could not spend much money on an animated short and see a profit.

In these final years, Chilly Willy remained a prisoner of his familiar formula. He was joined by a gooney-bird character in several entries and was visited by Woody Wood-pecker in a "cameo appearance" another time.

Chilly and Woody were accompanied on the yearly release schedule by Paul Smith's third thriving series, THE BEARY'S FAMILY ALBUM. Inaugurated in 1962, this series appropriated the TV situation comedy *The Life of Riley* much in the same way Hanna-Barbera used *The Honeymooners* as the blueprint for their FLINTSTONES show. The Beary Family consists of a bungling father named Charlie, his sweet but long-suffering wife, and their knuckle-brained son, named—

Walter and Woody in a 1965 publicity still. © Walter Lantz Productions.

inevitably—Junior. Stories in this series harked back even further than *Riley* to the old Edgar Kennedy two-reelers in which Father tries to put up wallpaper, chase a gopher out of the backyard, kill a turkey for Thanksgiving dinner, or learn to play golf— all resulting in slapstick havoc. Paul Frees and Grace Stafford Lantz provided appropriate voices. The characters' design was pure 1950s sitcom, with Junior even wearing a hat with its rim turned back, like a refugee from an *Archie* comic. The Beary cartoons relied on tried-and-true material that was sure to yield a certain amount of laughs, but the close resemblance to earlier live-action comedies made the animation of this material seem superfluous.

As for Woody, he evolved into a cute, pint-sized mischief maker, the extreme opposite of the brash, noisy upstart who made his debut thirty years earlier. (When a character in THE BARBER OF SEVILLE called Woody impulsive, he replied "Impulsive? I'm *re*pulsive!") In trying to "cuten" the character, various animators and directors made him smaller and smaller, but never with any consistency. In Paul Smith's THE TEE BIRD, for instance, Woody is shorter than villain Dapper Denver Dooley, but he's big enough to hold a golf club; yet in one scene he perches on the hat of a fellow golfer, appearing to be only slightly bigger than a pigeon! Unfortunately, this "cute" Woody simply wasn't funny anymore.

When this writer mentioned to Walter Lantz that he liked the earlier Woody much better, Lantz replied, "I did too, but we got so many complaints from Universal that said he was too raucous that we toned him down." The producer may have also been reacting to the ever-growing demands of TV censors. For Lantz's most recent Saturday morning program on the NBC network, he had to eliminate every sequence in which a character fired a gun or hit someone on the head with a hammer. Repeated questions about violence have made him practically recoil at the mention of the word; he prefers to characterize the content of his films as "slapstick cartoon action."

Is it any wonder that Woody and his cohorts became blander as the years rolled on?

In 1972 Lantz released his usual slate of thirteen cartoons: one Chilly Willy, four Beary Family entries, and eight with Woody Woodpecker. Then he ceased production and laid off his staff.

Why? Lantz explains that it had gotten to the stage where it took ten years to recoup his investment on a cartoon. "If you spent, say, $45,000 on a cartoon today, and you add your print cost and distribution costs to that, you wouldn't get your negative cost back for at least ten years. That's why we all quit. I was the last one to throw in the sponge, because I had full control of the picture myself and I could make them for less of a budget than anyone else. When it got so I couldn't do it anymore, I thought it was time to take a hiatus."

Lantz has made some public-service commercials with Woody since the studio's demise, but doesn't foresee a return to regular production. Universal Pictures is content to reissue thirteen Lantz cartoons a year— which generate the same volume of business that the new ones did—while Lantz busies himself preparing cartoon packages for television, supervising his licensing and business interests, and lecturing at colleges and animation festivals. He is proud of his position as one of animation's elder statesmen, particularly since his films are still so visible (playing, he says, in seventy-two countries around the world).

At the same time, Lantz has few pretensions about himself or the films he made. Perhaps that's why it's impossible to find anyone in animation who has a bad word to say about the man, even if his cartoons don't command the same respect he does. He never said he was out to advance the art. He just wanted to make cartoons, and he did, for more than fifty years. It's difficult to argue with that kind of success.

Ub Iwerks

6

UB IWERKS has been called "animation's forgotten man." He created Mickey Mouse and animated Walt Disney's landmark films STEAMBOAT WILLIE and SKELETON DANCE almost single-handed. For a time there was speculation that Iwerks was the dominant member of the Disney-Iwerks team, but when these longtime colleagues split up, the facts became clear. Iwerks was a prodigious animator, but he had none of Disney's creative spark and imagination. He became a second-echelon cartoon producer while Disney soared ahead and revolutionized the animation business, building an empire in the process.

Ub and Walt were the same age and met as teen-agers in Kansas City. Iwerks's father was a Dutch immigrant who had settled in Missouri and worked as a barber. He named his son Ubbe Ert Iwerks, but even when the young man shortened his name years later, it remained a point of curiosity for moviegoers who noticed it on screen credits.

Iwerks and Disney met toward the end of 1919, when they were both trying to make a living as commercial artists. They were introduced to animation at the same time, while working for the Kansas City Film Ad Company (later known as United Film Ad). When

Walt decided to break away and start his own cartoon studio in 1922, Ub was the first man he hired. This was more than just a friendly gesture; even then, Walt appreciated Iwerks's incredible facility with a pencil. After going broke, Walt moved to Hollywood to start fresh, while Ub went back to work for Kansas City Film Ad. But as soon as Walt contracted to make more cartoons, his first move was to send for Ub. Iwerks moved to California in 1924 and stayed with Walt for six eventful years.

Ub's skill as an animator was awesome to his colleagues during the 1920s. Friz Freleng, who left Kansas City to join the Disney staff in 1927, recalls, "At that time, just making a character move was an accomplishment. He could make characters walk and move; he could move a house in perspective. I thought he was a genius when it came to the mechanics of animation."

Ub was not only accomplished; he was remarkably fast. "We thought of Bill Nolan as the fastest animator that ever lived," says

Grim Natwick, "although Ub Iwerks denied that. He said, 'I think I broke Bill's record: seven hundred drawings a day.'" In fact, Iwerks animated the first Mickey Mouse cartoon, PLANE CRAZY, completely by himself in less than two weeks!

When producer Charles Mintz raided Walt's staff in 1928, Ub remained loyal and stayed with Disney. But the two had their occasional differences, and when Walt's distributor, Pat Powers, offered to finance Ub in a studio of his own in 1930, the animator agreed.

An announcement appeared in the form of an article on March 1, 1930, in *Exhibitors Herald-World:*

A new star of the pen and ink is about to make his hop into public notice. He is "Flip the Frog," and his boss and creator is U.B. [sic] Iwerks, cartoonist of the "Mickey Mouse" and "Silly Symphony" series of animated sound pictures. Iwerks with the "Flip the Frog" group will become a producer in his own right, and the series will be under the auspices of Celebrity Productions, distributors of the Disney cartoons. Releasing arrangements are to be made known soon.

"Flip" is called a character as [sic] will live up to his name in both action and sound. It is pointed out by cartoonist Iwerks that a frog more nearly represents a human being than anything else in all nature. A frog may be the epitome of laziness or lightning-like action as may suit his erratic impulses. . . .

Iwerks at the age of 28 has had fourteen years of experience as an artist and cartoonist. . . . [He] has drawn many animated cartoon characters which are well known to film fans.

Iwerks hired a small staff, mainly from those answering a newspaper want ad, and produced a "pilot" film with Flip the Frog. He did most of the animation himself and designed Flip as a caricature of a real frog, with webbed hands and feet. Flip was humanized by large eyes and a bow tie and buttons on his chest. Flip doesn't speak in FIDDLESTICKS, his first film; he dances on stage for the other forest animals and provides piano accompaniment for a mouse who plays the violin. This mouse bears a definite resemblance to Mickey, particularly with his white shorts and gloves, but the face is less rounded, and the addition of whiskers obscures any direct plagiarism.

Even though it was made in two-color Technicolor (two years before Disney tried his first color short), FIDDLESTICKS and its follow-up, PUDDLE PRANKS, didn't please Iwerks's producer, Pat Powers, who wanted something stronger to sell the series. Apparently, he encouraged Iwerks to modify the design of Flip, and Iwerks obliged by making the character less froglike and more of an anthropomorphized character in the Mickey Mouse vein.

On the strength of the next few films, Powers was able to sell the series to MGM for distribution. This marked Metro-Goldwyn-Mayer's first cartoon venture, and while the company continued to distribute Iwerks's cartoons for four years, their hopes that Flip the Frog would take his place alongside Mickey Mouse in worldwide popularity were

Celebrity Productions PRESENT A FLIP THE FROG SOUND CARTOON Produced and Drawn by UB IWERKS COPYRIGHT MCMXXX. RECORDED ON CINEPHONE SYSTEM

never fulfilled.

Flip had nothing unusual or different to offer movie audiences. He was happy, loose-limbed, and engagingly "cartoony," the chief inhabitant of an animated world that bore little relationship to reality—a world in which even Flip's car was capable of human expressions and emotions. Everything in these films was rounded—buildings, door-ways, telephone poles—giving a stylized stamp to the cartoons that made them completely different from any live-action comedy. A wood block provided beat-by-beat accompaniment every time Flip walked across the screen. If not distinctive or unique, Flip the Frog was, at least, a cartoon creation through and through.

The animation in the Flip films typifies Iwerks's personal approach: They are clean, uncluttered, and smoothly executed, but "soft" in gag impact and meandering in story construction. Ub knew almost all there was to know about animation, but he lacked Disney's story sense and comic know-how.

As soon as the MGM contract was signed, Iwerks augmented his staff. First he lured musical director Carl Stalling (another Kansas Cityite) away from Disney. Then he scoured both coasts for animators and hired Irv Spence and Grim Natwick. Later, other Max Fleischer staffers signed on, including Rudy Zamora, Al Eugster, and Shamus Culhane. Fred Kopietz was one of the first new-comers to be hired by Iwerks, and he recommended a friend from Chouinard Art School named Chuck Jones, who was put to work as a cel washer.

These were just the first of many talented people who came to work at the studio, but their creativity was stifled by Iwerks's laconic attitude. He demanded nothing more of these cartoons than that they meet their monthly schedule, be well animated, and contain as many gags as possible. That the gags were never built on a strong foundation

Flip the Frog registers embarrassment in THE OFFICE BOY (1932).

of story or character didn't concern Iwerks at all. His notion of comedy was limited to what he'd gleaned during his tenure with Disney. Iwerks's comic vocabulary was small, and one animator recalls that his idea of a funny gag was having Flip open the hood of his car and show sixteen cylinders instead of the usual eight.

There are thirty-seven FLIP THE FROG shorts in all, and not one of them rates as an outstanding cartoon. Some of them have clever or unusual ideas, but most are routine and repetitive. Many entries show great potential: In MOVIE MAD Flip crashes a Hollywood studio; in THE CUCKOO MURDER CASE he flirts with Death in an old dark house; and in TECHNO-CRACKED he builds a robot to do his chores. But in all three cases the cartoons fail to capitalize on the natural promise of these ideas. MOVIE MAD is just plain dull. THE CUCKOO MURDER CASE is defeated by slowness. And TECHNO-CRACKED executes a good script in such undramatic fashion that what could have been a robust cartoon in the SOR-

Flip the Frog is ridiculed by Dr. Skinnum's collection of masks in FUNNY FACE **(1933).**

Skinnum ("new faces for old"), where he's taunted by a chorus of singing masks that make fun of his "funny face." Flip chooses the face of a handsome human boy, which the doctor grafts onto his own. Then Flip tries to save his girl from the clutches of an oversized bully. The bully shatters Flip's new face with his punches, but all ends happily when the villain is dispatched and the girl gives her love to Flip, frog face and all.

By the time this series was in full swing, Iwerks was no longer animating. As head of the studio, he supervised every production and participated in the preparation of stories and layouts. But more and more, he busied himself in the studio machine shop. "He was a mechanical genius," says Grim Natwick. "He'd look at a plan for a boat and build it, and it would be perfect in every detail."

"He drew like an engineer," recalls Shamus Culhane. "The first thing I had to do in his place was some FLIP THE FROG cartoon with a stagecoach, and it had these oval wheels. I think he had drawn some layouts of it. Well, hell, I wasn't used to worrying about oval anything. I would just draw wheels and if they came out oblong, it wouldn't matter. It mattered to *him*—he blew his stack, and he sat down and drew them like an engineer. Perfect ovals."

CERER'S APPRENTICE vein turns out to be just another forgettable time filler.

THE BULLY brings some imaginative ideas to a rather ordinary story of Flip being challenged by a burly boxing champ. In one scene, the champ punches Flip so hard that the frog splits in three. During the count, Flip's spirit leaves his body and departs the ring, to walk through a cheering crowd. When Flip regains consciousness, he returns to the fight and is knocked right off the face of the earth—which is accomplished by animating the airborne frog against the backdrop of a live-action globe.

OFFICE BOY is the most outrageous film in the series, with shocking sexual gags involving a shapely secretary. Seldom has any cartoon concentrated so heavily on gags involving a young woman's derriere.

FUNNY FACE, on the other hand, the most clever entry in the series, has Flip trying to make a hit with his girl friend by changing his appearance. He visits the office of Dr.

In 1933 Iwerks developed two new series. The first was designed to take the place of FLIP THE FROG, which had worn out its welcome at MGM. This time Iwerks and his staff developed a human character named Willie Whopper, a little boy who tells tall tales. Willie's face was already somewhat familiar as being the standard little-boy design at the studio—in fact, it was this face that Flip the Frog purchased from Dr. Skinnum in FUNNY FACE.

The first Willie Whopper cartoon, PLAY

BALL, was released at the beginning of the 1933–34 movie season, around the time of the world series. It opens with Willie asking the audience, "Say, did I ever tell you this one?" and proceeds as he spins a yarn about his baseball prowess that includes scenes on the ball field with a caricatured Babe Ruth. At the end of the film, as Flip and Babe are feted with a New York ticker-tape parade, their cartoon car is set against live-action newsreel footage of the real thing.

As with Flip the Frog, Iwerks redesigned this character after just two films, to make him more cartoonlike and endearing. The new Willie made his debut in what may rank as the best film of the series, STRATOS FEAR. The new Willie is a roly-poly youngster with a shock of red hair, freckles on his face, and a ready smile. While having a tooth pulled by Dr. A. King, Willie is given so much gas that he bulges in size and floats through the roof of the dentist's building, soaring upward into space. He lands on a planet where crazy scientists who talk backward are conducting bizarre experiments with a ray gun: One blast and a cow is transformed into slabs of meat, bottles of milk, and a wheel of cheese. Willie tries to escape from their laboratory and lands in an ultramoderne room full of strange beings and wacky inventions—musical instruments that play themselves and other objects that anticipate Bob Clampett's PORKY IN WACKYLAND by five years. A sexy woman lures Willie out of the room, but turns out to be one of the crazy scientists in disguise. Luckily, just when things seem worst, Willie wakes up from his gas-induced slumber, back in the dentist's chair. The picture dissolves to our hero seated at a piano, with his Scottie dog alongside, saying to the audience, "Now *you* tell one."

This and subsequent cartoons in the series have an attractive look to them, and the rea-

son is Iwerks's unusual notion of painting the cels and backgrounds in color even though they would be photographed in black and white. "He said it would give the black-and-white film a different quality, and it was true," says animator Al Eugster. "The grays were a different shade somehow." One Willie Whopper cartoon, DAVY JONES' LOCKER, was actually made in color, but the others in the series boasted unusually rich black-and-white shadings.

Nevertheless, the series made no great impact and lasted only a year. Most of the Willie cartoons were pleasant, and some had striking visual gags and ideas. But like the Flip cartoons, they were built around a character with no real personality, and without that quality, no amount of skillful animation could win mass audience response.

Meanwhile, Iwerks was involved in launching another, more ambitious series called COMICOLOR CARTOONS. Although he had produced a two-color Technicolor cartoon as early as 1930, it wasn't until Walt Disney made FLOWERS AND TREES in the new three-color Technicolor process in 1932 that color became a desirable asset. But Disney had put the squeeze on his competitors by

Master animator Grim Natwick at the Iwerks studio.

securing an exclusive deal with the Technicolor company through the end of 1935. Iwerks's producer, Pat Powers, who had bought the rights to a bootleg sound process in the competitive days of early talkies, now arranged for his cartoon maker to use the Cinecolor process. Cinecolor was a two-color system, but unlike the two-color Technicolor, which utilized only red and green, this one featured red and blue, which offered greater possibilities, particularly for animated films.* Oddly enough, MGM chose not to distribute the ComiColor cartoons, so Pat Powers was forced to release these shorts independently.

To handle the growing work load that two series—both prepared in color—demanded, Iwerks kept expanding his staff. Otto Eng-

lander, George Manuel, and Ben Hardaway comprised the story department. New animators included Berny Wolf, Norm Blackburn, Dick Bickenbach, Lou Zukor, Steve Bosustow, Al Rose, and Frank Tashlin. (Tashlin, Eugster recalls, "would come in and do his animation in the morning and take the rest of the day off. He was a very fast animator. He had a daily one-panel cartoon called 'Van Boring,' and he'd work on that in the afternoon. It always amazed me; he'd just get that work done, and it looked good, too.")

More and more, Iwerks came to rely on Grim Natwick to supervise the actual production of his cartoons. He even offered him a partnership, which Natwick declined in order to take a job with Disney. But during his stay with Iwerks, this animator more than any other influenced the look and character design of the studio product. Unfortunately, in the case of the COMICOLOR CARTOONS, there wasn't much innovation in

*Castle Films released this series for home-movie use in Cinecolor (easily recognizable with its double-emulsion film stock), and surviving prints show off the bright and vivid colors of the films to full advantage.

character design. The character of Jack in JACK AND THE BEANSTALK, the "pilot" film for this series, bore a close family resemblance to the original Willie Whopper and appeared many times again as Tom Thumb, Little Boy Blue, Dick Whittington, and other such heroes.

The one thing these ComiColor cartoons have in common besides recycled character models is that they are uncommonly handsome. The colors are rich, and when the animation is up to par, it's a winning combination. To further enhance the cartoons' appeal, some of them, like ALADDIN AND HIS WONDERFUL LAMP, are strikingly designed as well.

In terms of humor and story values, however, the series is sadly inconsistent. Fancy trimmings cannot overcome the same weaknesses that plagued Iwerks's earlier cartoons. The characters have no depth, and their adventures carry no weight. Even a prime property like THE HEADLESS HORSEMAN yields routine results because of the staff's inability to build vivid dramatic situations.

Surveying the series, one finds that the highlights are aspects of the films and not the films in their entirety. For example, when the miniature hero of TOM THUMB is accidentally swallowed by a goat, it leads to a dazzling sequence inside the goat's mouth; Tom tries to maintain his equilibrium while the goat vigorously chews his mouthful of garbage. There is another dramatic shot in LITTLE BOY BLUE in which Bo Peep falls down a chimney, as seen looking up from the darkened fireplace. Yet neither one of these films—among the best entries in the series—maintains the level of robust imagination indicated by those two scenes.

Some entries that are weak on story feature highly colorful characters and settings. HUMPTY DUMPTY JR. is full of clever ideas: Humpty Jr. takes balancing risks that prompt his mother to scold, "That's how your father got cracked!" The villain of the piece is the Bad Egg, who gives off a pungent odor; when he goes after Humpty's girl friend, she falls off a ledge into a pot of boiling water and comes out hard-boiled—like Mae West! BALLOON LAND (circulated for many years under the title PINCUSHION MAN) creates an entire balloon community, which is threatened by attacks from the pincushion men, who puncture and deflate innocent balloons. Again, the ingenious character design and overall premise give the cartoon its only value; the story itself is trite.

Some of Iwerks's cartoons in this series invite comparison to Disney's SILLY SYMPHONIES—particularly THE LITTLE RED HEN, released the same year as the similar Disney short, THE WISE LITTLE HEN; and LITTLE BOY BLUE, which features a big-bad-wolf character whose voice is provided by the ubiquitous Billy Bletcher. But the most interesting

Typical Iwerks characters in the Comicolor short JACK AND THE BEANSTALK **(1933).**

link between Iwerks and Disney during this period was Iwerks's development of a multiplane camera, several years before Disney unveiled his much-publicized invention. As already mentioned, this device enabled the animation camera to photograph through several layers of artwork, giving the illusion of depth and dimension. Disney's unit cost thousands of dollars to manufacture, and stood about fourteen feet high. Shamus Culhane remembers Iwerks's contraption: "He had bought the rear end of a Chevrolet for seventy-five bucks, taken it apart and used the machinery to make himself a multiplane camera for about three hundred bucks . . . and it worked fine."

The major technological difference between the rival inventions was that Iwerks's was horizontal and the camera could not move, while Disney's more sophisticated model was vertical and permitted the camera to truck back and forth, to move into or out of a scene. This made Disney's camera more versatile, if more troublesome, to operate. However, the most important difference was not the hardware but its application.

Iwerks developed a number of visually striking backdrops to use with his camera— in the Willie Whopper cartoon THE CAVE MAN and in such COMICOLOR episodes as THE KING'S TAILOR and THE HEADLESS HORSEMAN. In THE CAVE MAN, Willie is swinging on a vine à la Tarzan, and we see many layers of jungle foliage behind him. In the other examples, characters are riding along a country road, with several tableaux of scenery behind them, each moving at a different rate—the slightly blurred mountains in the distance remain more stationary than the trees in the foreground, for instance.

But when all was said and done, these moments were throwaways in basically unmemorable cartoons. That fact, coupled with Iwerks's lack of self-promotion, make it easy to understand why he never received much credit or acclaim for his invention while Disney made the history books when he put his machine to work in THE OLD MILL.

The loss of MGM distribution when Willie Whopper expired made it difficult for the Iwerks studio to survive. Pat Powers released the COMICOLOR CARTOONS through his Celebrity Productions, but there was no way to recoup the kind of income that major-studio distribution could provide. By 1935 it was necessary to tighten belts at Iwerks's studio. Some staffers were laid off, while others who saw the handwriting on the wall decided to leave on their own. Grim Natwick, Otto Englander, Al Eugster, and Berny Wolf went to Disney. Shamus Culhane returned to New York and the Van Beuren studio.

The remaining staff worked with Iwerk's to complete a schedule of ten ComiColor Cartoons in 1935 and backlogged a handful more for release in 1936.That year, Iwerks's studio closed, as Pat Powers withdrew his support. The remaining employees dispersed, with music director Carl Stalling following writer Ben Hardaway to the Warner Brothers studio.

It was Warners' producer Leon Schlesinger who helped to bail Iwerks out later that year by subcontracting cartoons from him, but this arrangement was short-lived, and a British-financed series called GRAN' POP never really took root. In 1938 Iwerks moved from his Beverly Hills studio to a new shop on Santa Monica Boulevard and contracted with Charles Mintz to do a series of color cartoons for Columbia release. This kept Iwerks occupied for two years, before he made what must have been a difficult, if ultimately rewarding, move—back to Disney.

Neither Disney nor Iwerks ever commented publicly on their business reunion, but this much is clear: They both benefited

The Ub Iwerks staff, around 1935, in sunny California.

1. Peggy Jones (Chuck's sister) **2**. Frank Tashlin **3**. Art Turkisher **4**. Lee Mackey **5**. Gladys McArthur **6**. Irv Spence **7**. Steve Bosustow **8**. Dick Bickenbach **9**. Charlie Connors **10**. Lou Zukor **11**. Al Eugster **12**. Jimmie (Shamus) Culhane **13**. Ub Iwerks **14**. Grim Natwick **15**. Berny Wolf **16**. Carl Stalling **17**. Ted Dubois **18**. Ralph Somerville **19**. Ed Love **20**. Bob Stokes **21**. Dick Hall **22**. Norm Blackburn **23**. Ed Friedman **24**. Izzy Ellis **25**. Geo. Dane **26**. Mary Tebb **27**. Dorothy Webster (Chuck Jones' future wife) **28**. Jimmie Ciangoli (not sure of spelling) **29**. Al Gould **30**. Ray Farranger **31**. Geo. Manuel **32**. Murray Griffen **Unnumbered**—names not known

from the renewed association. Iwerks was able to drop animation and devote himself completely to technical experimentation; Disney profited from Iwerks's labors. Over the years Ub was honored with two Academy Awards for his achievements. His work with optical printers and matte processes was largely responsible for the effectiveness of Disney's live-action and animation sequences in SONG OF THE SOUTH, THE THREE CABALLEROS, and later, MARY POPPINS. Iwerks remained a valued employee of the Disney organization until his death in 1971. In addition to his film assignments, he worked on several attractions for Disneyland and Walt Disney World.

Examining Iwerks's long and interesting career, one comes to an obvious conclusion: The ten years away from Disney were the least rewarding and productive he spent in the motion picture field. This in no way demeans Iwerks or his talent. It merely underscores the fact that making cartoons was not his goal, but rather a means to an end for him. His ambition—and great love—was to conquer technical challenges. In the 1920s it was mastering the techniques of animation. In the 1940s it was the refinement of optical printing and matte work. In each successive decade Iwerks found new mountains to scale; like Disney, he always looked ahead.

This is why Disney and Iwerks made such a good team. When Disney had creative ideas for entertainment, Iwerks was there to carry them out. When Iwerks perfected new technical processes, Disney was there to provide the perfect vehicles to show them off. Each in his own way possessed a special kind of genius.

Van Beuren Studio

7

THE VAN BEUREN STUDIO is the least-known cartoon company of the 1930s, yet its brief history is dotted with interesting films and major animation talents.

The company was an outgrowth—or, more properly, an extension—of Aesop's Fables Studio, which Paul Terry had started in 1921 with backing from the Keith-Albee vaudeville circuit. Keith-Albee retained controlling interest in the films and in the studio, while Terry owned 10 percent.

In 1928 Keith-Albee sold its interests to Amadee J. Van Beuren, a comparative new-comer to the film business who also produced several live-action short subjects. In November 1928 Van Beuren announced that all of his series would be made in sound from that time onward, and this led to a clash with Paul Terry, who was reluctant to spend the additional money that sound would require. Apparently there were other disputes besides this one, and Terry left Van Beuren in mid-1929. Most of his staff stayed behind.

Van Beuren appointed Fables veteran John Foster as his new animation director, to supervise the work of colleagues Harry Bailey and Mannie Davis. They came to the conclusion that, with the added burden of sound, it would be impossible to maintain Terry's output of fifty-two films a year and cut the quota in half.

During his last months at the studio, Terry had been adding sound tracks to the weekly cartoons, so they could be sold as "talkies," but this was a far cry from actual sound production. There was no marriage of sound and picture in these films.

"We had to have somebody that understood breaking down the timing, because the tempos have to be matched on the sheets that we had to draw the animation on," Mannie Davis explained in a 1970 interview. "We didn't know anything. This was all brand new, and none of us was good [with] music."

At first the studio hired a musician named Carl Edouarde, whose baptism of fire had been the first, disastrous recording session for Walt Disney's STEAMBOAT WILLIE. He was soon dismissed, and two capable men were

195

hired instead: former hoofer Jack Ward and bandleader Gene Rodemich. Their work was described in an article by Douglas Fox in *Exhibitors Herald-World*:

It's the introduction of music which has . . . almost doubled the cost and labor of making animated cartoons. The action now has to fit the music, everything is done in beats and the master mind who can piece together the odds and ends of the jigsaw puzzle becomes a pretty well paid executive. And this fellow is the musical gag man, a chap they wouldn't have had any use for ten or eleven months ago. . . .

The making of an animated cartoon begins with an editorial conference between the animators and the music directors. The general trend of the story is gags and ideas. Then they work out the music to go with it and cut the scenario to fit the music. This is done by Gene Rodemich and Jack Ward, who synchronize the whole business on paper before a line is really drawn. . . .

Ward, who can dance any step that was ever invented and a good many that are just night-

Character design was pretty standard at Van Beuren. Example: GYPPED IN EGYPT **(1930)**

mares, goes from one animator to another, helps him out on the tempo and poses of various routines or invents new ones to fit the action. Characters, of course, along with the trend of the story, have all been determined previously.

Making the transition to sound was a formidable task for the small Van Beuren staff, because it involved more than mere synchronization. It meant developing a whole new approach to the creation of a cartoon. This did not come easily to the silent-film veterans, who continued to practice such obsolete techniques as animating the words "HA HA" alongside a character's mouth when he laughed.

There was another, more basic problem. The Fables staff was still locked into its 1920s approach to animation. None of the lead animators could draw terribly well, much less animate. They had a sense of humor, but they weren't artists by any stretch of the imagination, and it showed in their films.

In CIRCUS CAPERS (1930) the leading characters are a boy mouse and a girl mouse, but by the end of the film their appearance has changed so drastically—through inconsistent drawing—that the male lead looks more like a bear.

Some of the cartoons had funny gags and clever ideas, but just as often the humor was in the crudity of execution and not in the material itself. MAKING 'EM MOVE, a look inside a cartoon studio, is just one example of a high-potential idea carried out in slapdash fashion. The major asset of these early talkies was Gene Rodemich's lively music scores. His original themes and choice of popular songs, played by a peppy little band, buoyed many an ordinary cartoon.

Foster and company maintained the AESOP'S FABLES series, although the morals that ended every film were dropped in 1930. There were no continuing characters per se, but the various animal "stars" were drawn in similar fashion from one film to the next.

Farmer Al Falfa was used for a short time, until Paul Terry claimed the creation as his own. A more interesting claim was made in 1931 by Walt Disney, who accused the studio of plagiarizing Mickey Mouse. In fact, Disney had been influenced by the type of mice used in AESOP'S FABLES during the silent era, but when John Foster singled out a boy and girl mouse in such films as A CLOSE CALL and WESTERN WHOOPEE, the specific resemblance to Mickey and Minnie was too close for comfort. Disney got a temporary court injunction against Van Beuren in April 1931, and a formal decree was issued four months later prohibiting the studio from "employing or using or displaying the pictorial representation of 'Mickey Mouse' or any variation thereof so nearly similar as to be calculated to be mistaken for or confused with said pictorial representation of 'Mickey Mouse.' . . ." Disney did not ask for damages. He simply wanted to establish his right to the character.

That same year staff newcomers George Stallings and George Rufle—both veterans on the New York animation scene—worked with Foster to develop the studio's first original characters: a Mutt-and-Jeff-like duo called Tom and Jerry, one of whom was tall and thin, the other short and round. Their personalities are practically nil, but somehow they project a friendly presence that gives their cartoons a certain likability. Like the AESOP'S FABLES, this series is both primitive and wildly inconsistent, but at its best it shows genuine flair and imagination. Perhaps the best entry of all is the very first, WOT A NITE.

WOT A NITE is bizarre in the best Max Fleischer tradition, with Tom and Jerry as taxi drivers who take two strange Smith-Brothers types to a haunted castle and ven-

(Top) **Mickey and Minnie rip-offs in** A CLOSE CALL **(1929). In some scenes the resemblance was even stronger.**
(Above) **Tom and Jerry in** PIANO TOONERS **(1932).**

Bland but cheerful: Tom and Jerry as HAPPY HOBOES **(1933).**

modicum of personal distinctiveness to an otherwise shallow character.

The studio produced twenty-six Tom and Jerry cartoons over the next few years and ran the gamut from inspired nonsense to dreary time-fillers. The characters never came into sharp focus, but individual gags and story ideas carried them along. There's a cherished moment in PIANO TOONERS when Jerry catches a sour note that emanates from an out-of-tune piano. The note has eyes and a mouth, and struggles to stay alive, forcing Jerry to beat it against a wall and flush it down an off-screen toilet! This film and several others (TIGHT ROPE TRICKS and FARMER-ETTE, from the AESOP'S FABLES series) benefit from a sprightly vocal chorus by a woman who sounds exactly like Betty Boop. Since the Van Beuren cartoons were made in New York—directly across the street from Fleischer's studio, in fact—it's probable that one of the women who did Betty Boop's voice in the early days also worked on recording sessions for this studio.

ture inside. The cartoon is full of unusual sights: a skeleton taking a bath, then screaming at being seen "naked" and disappearing down the bathtub drain; another skeleton painting piano keys on a ledge and pouring the remainder of his paint and bucket into the shape of a piano stool so he can sit down and play; the Smith-Brothers duo materializing from two black dots on the ground, causing Tom to be scared out of his clothes; and, finally, Tom and Jerry discovering nothing but skeletal bones beneath their own shirts!

The characters barely speak and exist mainly as passive figures who react to situations around them. In this film Jerry (the short one) seems to have more personality than usual, because his actions call to mind a mischievous child. For instance, when Tom and Jerry find themselves standing next to a huge bird of prey, Jerry quietly rubs his finger against one of the bird's claws to see how sharp it is. This simple bit of behavior—without dialogue or facial gestures—adds a

But Van Beuren did not enjoy one tenth the success with Tom and Jerry that Fleischer had with Betty Boop. Perhaps the characters were just too low-key; certainly the inconsistency of the series didn't help. By 1933 Van Beuren knew it was time for a change. He fired John Foster, appointed George Stallings director of the studio, and encouraged his staff to come up with new ideas.

Mannie Davis recalled, "Van Beuren called us all over and had dinner with us at the New York Athletic Club. And we didn't know what it was all about. There were about seven or eight of us. Seems that there was a need for a new character. And they wanted to get some new life into the pictures. And we were all told [to bring] our pads with us. . . ."

Mannie Davis sketched a new character

called Cubby Bear, which the boss approved. Someone else suggested buying the rights to Otto Soglow's comic strip character The Little King. Animators Jim Tyer and Steve Muffati were promoted to directorial posts. And everyone got back to work.

Cubby Bear was just another in the long line of Micky Mouse descendants who populated movie screens of the 1930s on the theory that their rounded features and cute characteristics would win some of Mickey's audience. Like most of the others, Cubby failed. Ironically, two Cubby cartoons were produced on the West Coast by Harman and Ising, who had recently parted company with Leon Schlesinger and Warner Brothers. Looking for work, they contracted with Van Beuren to make two shorts featuring an approximation of Cubby that looked, acted, and sounded just like H-I's Bosko. In terms of slick animation, however, CUBBY'S WORLD FLIGHT and THE GAY GAUCHO easily stood out from the rest of Van Beuren's product.

Not that the house staff wasn't trying. Some of the Bear's cartoons were well-made and enjoyable, such as OPENING NIGHT, a spoof of the gargantuan Roxy Theatre, and HOW'S CROPS?, a visually imaginative cartoon in which Cubby and his girl friend operate a farm from underground headquarters, where vegetables are inflated and plugged into the earth for harvesting above.

Cubby's appearance tended to vary from film to film, which didn't do anything to enhance his recognition with audiences. One design gave him realistic eyes with pupils that violated standard cartoon principles and made him look like a manufactured doll—the "dead eyes" effect most animators tried to avoid.

The Little King was an established property that did not present the same kind of problems to the Van Beuren crew. But Otto Soglow's pantomime character was simple and low-keyed—not the best qualities to look for in an animated cartoon star. His panel cartoons brought quiet chuckles because of the incongruity of a childish figure assuming the role of a King. Transferring this genteel brand of humor to the screen was no easy task, and it's amazing that the animators succeeded as well as they did. But even at their best—in such films as PALS and SULTAN PEPPER—these films were pleasant, and nothing more. There was some attempt to retain elements of Soglow's drawing style, and on the whole the series was better animated than most of the studio's other work. In the final analysis, however, the series was not a great success. (Otto Soglow never liked the films, but they must have seemed outstanding compared to Max Fleischer's one-shot endeavor in 1936, in which the King was given a ridiculous speaking voice.)

Van Beuren did not put much promotion behind these shorts, which may have accounted for their modest success as much as any other element within the studio. RKO, which released the cartoons, regarded

Otto Soglow's the Little King in a scene from PALS (1933), also known as CHRISTMAS NIGHT.

them merely as fillers on their annual program.

In 1934, The Little King now a regular part of the studio roster, Van Beuren made another attempt to bolster his cartoons with a presold personality. He contracted with Freeman Gosden and Charles Correll, the stars and creators of radio's *Amos 'n' Andy*, to provide their own voices for a series of animated cartoons. Considering that *Amos 'n' Andy* was the most popular program on the air, this was an auspicious move for the studio, but, unfortunately, the comedians' brand of humor simply wasn't suited to the cartoon medium. There was the added problem of literalizing characters and situations that had captured an audience's imagination through sound alone. Neither THE RASSLIN' MATCH nor THE LION TAMER made the impact everyone thought they would, and the series came to an abrupt halt.

In 1933 and 1934 the studio was brimming with new talent, although it would have been difficult for anyone to predict how far many of these employees would go in the animation field. Their work at the time was ordinary and undistinguished. A gag writer named Frank Tashlin was on the staff, using the name Tish Tash. He later drew a syndicated comic strip called *Van Boring* based on his onetime boss. Another young man got his first animation job at this studio as a story man and then progressed to in-betweener as he sharpened his drawing skills; his name was Joe Barbera. Jack Zander, Alex Lovy, Pete Burness, Larry Silverman, Dan Gordon, Ray Kelly, Phil Klein, Bill Littlejohn, Marty Taras, Carl "Mike" Meyer, and Johnny Gentilella were also there, working in various capacities. They were soon joined by I. Klein and James (Shamus) Culhane.

Still, the studio was not achieving the kind of success Van Beuren wanted so badly, and he decided to make a bold move toward reaching his goal. As Jack Zander tells it, "One day, the boss of the place, Frank Snell, who was just a businessman, came walking through the place with this funny little beady-eyed fellow. Somebody nudged me and said, 'Do you know who that is?' and I said no. 'That's Burt Gillett.' So I said, 'Who's Burt Gillett?' and he said, 'Burt Gillett was the guy who directed THE THREE LITTLE PIGS.'" This was about as important a credential as anyone could have, since Disney's THE THREE LITTLE PIGS was the most successful cartoon short ever released. A short time later Van Beuren announced that Gillett was going to be the new director of his cartoon studio.

No doubt Gillett would have liked to bring some West Coast animators with him, but few, if any, were available. It was tough enough to keep ambitious animators in New York, and it was at this time that Disney began his major talent hunt in preparation for SNOW WHITE. So Gillett was joined only by Tom Palmer, another former Disney man, whose recent stint with Leon Schlesinger had been a fiasco.

Van Beuren also hired animator/director Ted Eshbaugh, whose independently released two-color cartoons had caused some stir in 1933. The producer intended to film most of his new product in color in yet another attempt to capture a bigger share of the market.

Gillett brought sweeping changes to the studio operation. "He worked like Walt did," says Jack Zander. "We'd do pencil tests. Of course, when we were working at Van Beuren, nobody ever heard of a pencil test. We would just animate and they'd ink and paint it and that's all there was to it. He initiated pencil tests and movieolas. We'd have to animate this stuff and look at it; he'd look at it and then he'd make changes. It was a stimulating thing. The only ones who had any trouble were the real old animators, animating for years in a set manner. They found it a little difficult to adjust.''

There was also resentment toward Gillett on the part of studio veterans. ''The people who were there before him felt, 'why the hell did they take this swell-head from Disney?''' I. Klein recalls. ''They often took that attitude, you know; very seldom did they say, 'Gee, that's great—a good man came in.''' But Gillett did not cement relationships through his working attitude. ''He was constantly firing people,'' says Klein. ''There was a swinging door all the time, people coming and going.''

Gillett's first series creation was not geared to winning many friends outside the studio, either. TODDLE TALES combined live-action sequences of nauseatingly ''cute'' children with animated characters enacting stories that taught some sort of moral. Mercifully, only three films were made in this series, which marked Van Beuren's last black-and-white endeavor.

The next Gillett-supervised color series was called RAINBOW PARADE, filmed at first in the two-color process and then in three-strip Technicolor. Musical director Gene Rodemich was replaced by Winston Sharples, who maintained a high standard with his cheerful scores and full orchestration.

The RAINBOW PARADE cartoons alternated between one-shot stories and cartoons with continuing characters. Some of the stories weren't bad, but none of the characters was compelling enough to win major audience interest. In both kinds of cartoons, the results fell far short of the Disney standard for success and popularity—reinforcing the industry belief that the genius behind every Disney cartoon was Disney himself. Gillett may have directed THE THREE LITTLE PIGS, but

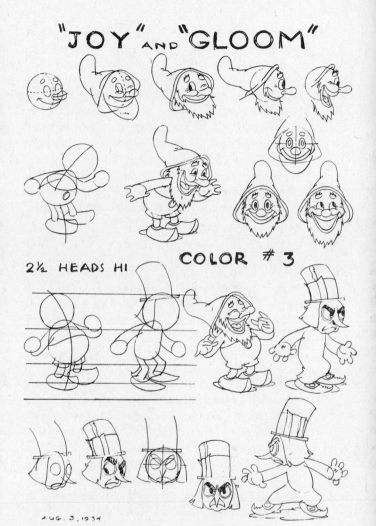

A model sheet of the leading characters from SUNSHINE MAKERS (1935).

he was clearly unable to duplicate the charm, appeal, and originality of that cartoon for Van Beuren, even though he worked hard to drive his staff toward better animation.

Ted Eshbaugh left after directing three cartoons, one of which became a minor classic: SUNSHINE MAKERS. This curious cartoon tells a paper-thin story about happy dwarfs

An animation drawing from SUNSHINE MAKERS.

A model sheet from PARROTVILLE POST OFFICE (1935).

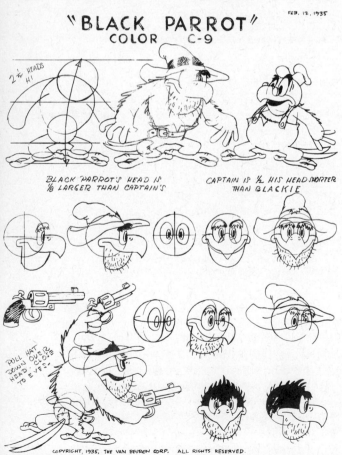

who bottle sunshine, and repel an attack from their gloomy neighbors by catapulting bottles of sunshine into the enemy camp and overtaking the grim-visaged gremlins with happiness. There is something disarming about this jaunty fable that has made SUN-SHINE MAKERS a cult classic for many years. Perhaps it's the elemental conflict of good and evil personified in such a simple and unpretentious manner: When a bottle of sunshine hits one of the gloomies, he glows with happiness and begins dancing a jig. Although one of the last holdouts complains, "I don't want to be happy. I want to be sad!" he too is converted after a dunk in sunshine milk. This is fantasy at its best.

Other Van Beuren efforts included a short-lived series set in Parrotville, a colorful but forgettable series with Molly Moo Cow, and assorted one-shot cartoons with mice, dogs, and kittens as the main characters. The animation was improving under Gillett's supervision, and when the ban was lifted on three-strip Technicolor, these cartoons, with their beautiful rainbow hues, lived up to the name RAINBOW PARADE. Unfortunately, in spite of his enthusiasm Gillett did not understand the proper use of color, and often his films were cluttered. Characters would fail to stand out against the backgrounds, obscuring gags and pieces of action and diminishing their impact.

Off-screen, dissension continued on every level. Several of the in-betweeners tried to form a union, to protect themselves from the financial whims of their boss, and were fired for their activities. Gillett's browbeating approach and inability to make up his mind rankled animators and story men. At one point Van Beuren was obliged to act as peacemaker. Wheelchair-ridden by a recent stroke, he announced to the crew, "I am behind you people one hundred percent, and I am behind Mr. Gillett one hundred and twenty percent." "It was odd mathematics, but we got the general idea," says Shamus Culhane, who decided to quit a short time later.

With budgets already higher than ever before at the studio, Gillett decided to incur one more expense in the hope of insuring greater box-office success: the purchase of two more established properties. The first was Fontaine Fox's *Toonerville Trolley*, a popular comic strip that had inspired a two-reel comedy series in the 1920s, and Felix the Cat, the silent cartoon star who had been off the screen since the beginning of the decade.

These 1936 cartoons were the most elaborate and visually creative films the studio ever produced. Because of the likability of their well-established characters and the lush use of Technicolor, they were the most popular, as well, winning critical plaudits and audience acclaim. Theater owners rated them among the best color cartoons on the market.

Seen today, these cartoons retain their solid assets, but reveal definite liabilities that most viewers were willing to overlook forty years ago. The TOONERVILLE cartoons, featuring the Skipper, the Powerful Katrinka, and the Terrible-tempered Mr. Bang, simply aren't very funny, while the rejuvenated Felix, looking bright and vivid in color, has been transformed into a bland goody two-shoes character. Of the two, the Felix cartoons had greater possibilities, but Gillett and Tom Palmer failed to understand their potential.

In FELIX THE CAT AND THE GOOSE THAT LAID THE GOLDEN EGGS the cartoon star reverts to silent-film days when he detaches his tail to light a cannon fuse, then shapes himself as a cannonball in order to propel himself out to sea. What could have been a rousing turning point in the film, and conferred a mark of individuality on an otherwise Mickey Mouse–like character, becomes instead a

JAN 15-1936

THE TOONERVILLE TROLLEY.

The Toonerville Trolley and its famous Skipper.

throwaway as directed by Gillett and Palmer. The gag is played without fanfare, in long shot, against a highly colored backdrop, and a wonderful opportunity is lost. This film, along with NEPTUNE'S NONSENSE, and especially BOLD KING COLE, have ingenious story elements that could have been wrought into great cartoons, but as they now stand, the parts are greater than the whole, and the least interesting factor is the personality of Felix.

All of this is latter-day criticism, but the greatest blow ironically came at the time these ambitious cartoons were actually in production. One morning the film trade papers announced that Walt Disney, in a sudden, unexpected move, had left United Artists and had made a deal with RKO to distribute his films. RKO had only recently taken full-color advertisements in those same trade papers to boast of its new TOONERVILLE and FELIX cartoons. But Van Beuren staffers knew what the news meant for them: RKO didn't need *two* cartoon series. Van Beuren

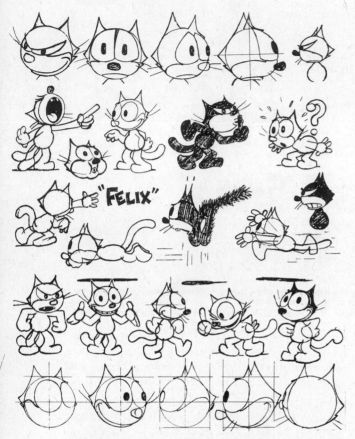

A vivid model sheet captures the essence of Felix the Cat, which the Van Beuren films never managed to do.

would shut down after finally achieving the kind of recognition and popularity it had sought for such a long, long time. Amadee J. Van Beuren died one year later of a heart attack; he was fifty-eight. Burt Gillett's checkered career led him back to the Disney studio for a short time, and then to Walter Lantz.

But the strangest fate was that of the Van Beuren cartoons. In the 1940s they were sold to a company called Official Films, which released them for home-movie sales and rentals on 8mm and 16mm. Official changed many of the films' titles and renamed characters as well: Cubby Bear became Brownie, while Tom and Jerry became Dick and Larry (perhaps to avoid confusion with the MGM cat-and-mouse team). Another company named Commonwealth bought most of the RAINBOW PARADE titles, and along with Official released these cartoons to television in the 1950s, long before packages of major-studio cartoons were widely available. The refilmed titles made it impossible for even an interested viewer to learn that all of these films had been produced by Van Beuren— but the films themselves had a considerable impact on young viewers, many of whom have grown up to be today's cartoon buffs and scholars.

This writer was among the many children whose earliest television experiences included multiple viewings of SUNSHINE MAKERS, TOONERVILLE TROLLEY, and PARROTVILLE POST OFFICE. It's taken many years to track down the unusual story behind these long-neglected cartoons.

had nowhere else to turn for distribution, and, besides, he was old and ill. After delivering ten cartoons to RKO and completing the seasonal 1935–36 contract, the studio closed its doors.

No one could have guessed that the studio

Columbia:
Charles Mintz
and
Screen Gems

It ALL STARTED with Krazy Kat.

Krazy Kat existed long before Columbia Pictures—in fact, George Herriman's creation had been a star of animated cartoons as early as 1916. But like most other comic strip characters who made an early transition to film, Krazy's screen popularity died out within a few years. One possible reason is that the simplified cartoon shorts bore so little resemblance to Herriman's brilliant and graphically complex newspaper panels.

Krazy remained a highly successful comic strip star, however, and when animator Bill Nolan was looking for a proven property to launch an independent cartoon series in 1925, he seemed an ideal candidate. Besides, Nolan had animated the character back in the teens. As before, there was no attempt to emulate the Herriman style, but the name value of Krazy Kat was enough to ensure a certain amount of success.

Nolan was part of an animators' cooperative called Associated Animators, but this well intentioned group didn't last, and soon he was producing his films for distributor M. J. Winkler. No stranger to the animation field, Margaret Winkler had distributed Fleischer's cartoons for several years and was just signing up an unknown from the Midwest named Walt Disney. Her husband, Charles Mintz, was gradually taking over the company and wanted to get out of the independent States' Rights market and into the big time. He was able to secure a contract for Krazy Kat cartoons with F.B.O. (Film Booking Offices) one year, and then a better deal with Paramount the next.

The production of these cartoons was passed from Bill Nolan to the team of Ben Harrison and Manny Gould, both experienced men on the New York animation scene. Neither was a genius or innovator, but that didn't matter. What did matter was

The KRAZY KAT studio staff in New York, circa 1928: Mike Balukas, inker; Al Windley, cameraman; Ira Gould, painter; Al Gould painter; Berny Wolf, inker; Al Rose, animator; Harry Love, assistant animator; Manny Gould, animator-director; Sid Marcus, animator; Ben Harrison, animator-director; Jimmy (later Shamus) Culhane, inker and assistant animator; Art Davis, animator; unknown painter; office boy; Dave Tendlar, inker and assistant animator.

being able to turn out twenty-six cartoons a year to fulfill Mintz's contract. Shamus Culhane, who joined the studio as an inker, recalls, "If you had a gag where somebody was hit by something, you automatically had it happen three times, because you used the drawings over again." Such was the assembly-line life of Krazy Kat.

With the coming of sound, Paramount allied itself with Max Fleischer, and Mintz went shopping for another distributor. He wound up with Columbia Pictures, a hungry young company on the brink of success. In February 1930 he moved his tiny cartoon staff to California, where he hoped they would all prosper. The entourage included Harrison, Gould, Allen Rose, Harry Love, Jack Carr, Art Davis, musician Joe DeNat,

and production manager Jimmy Bronis.

Charles Mintz has earned a niche in film history for his famous encounter with Walt Disney in 1928, when he stole Disney's staff and starring character (Oswald the Lucky Rabbit) in one fell swoop. In so doing, he impelled Disney and his one remaining employee, Ub Iwerks, to create a new character, Mickey Mouse. How ironic that just a few years later Columbia Pictures was distributing both Mintz's and Disney's cartoons—with Disney's coming out the more successful by far.

On the creative level as well, Disney was the competition to beat—and again, Disney came out ahead. Harry Love recalls, "Whenever a Disney cartoon was playing in a theater, we'd go in and pay just to see the cartoon and study it, see what we could steal in ideas and everything."

This keeping-up-with-Disney attitude manifested itself in the kind of films produced at the Mintz shop, and in the films' starring characters as well. Disney's musical formula set the industry standard, and Mintz's music director (former New York pianist Joe DeNat) composed lively scores for a ten-piece orchestra. As for Krazy Kat, he evolved from the simplified version of Herriman's character in the late 1920s into a cuter, rounder, more conventional design; soon he boasted a falsetto voice, look-alike girl friend, and to make the resemblance to Mickey Mouse complete—a pet dog.

Disney parted company with Columbia Pictures in 1932 to make a better financial arrangement with United Artists. Mintz thus became Columbia's sole supplier of cartoons, but he never approached Disney's success, artistically or financially.

This is not to damn the Mintz studio product as worthless. Some of the KRAZY KAT cartoons—like BROADWAY MALADY (1933), a spoof of crowded New York subways, and THE CRYSTAL GAZEBO (1932), in which Krazy plays No-Kan-Du the Magician—are quite enjoyable. The peppy music and rubbery animation create a happy mood that obscures many shortcomings. But the films have no style or personality of their own. Krazy Kat is a nonentity, without any identifiable character traits, so each film relies on its individual gags and ideas. Flashes of imagination keep the series afloat, but in comparison to other contemporary product—particularly Disney's—the films are simply routine. THE MASQUERADE PARTY (1934) is a weak paraphrase of THE WHOOPEE PARTY, made two years earlier with Mickey Mouse. In ideas as well as technique, the Mintz staff was always behind.

The KRAZY KAT series was supervised by Ben Harrison and Manny Gould. "Manny handled the animation and the artwork and Ben did most of the writing," explains Harry Love, who started as an inker at the studio and became an animator by the time he was eighteen. "Ben loved to write in terms of crowd scenes and that used to drive me crazy. If he was talking about laundry, then you'd have a scene with a laundry marching band with all the sheets and pillowcases. No matter what [the story] was, there was a band marching in perspective."

Formulas dictated technique as well as stories. "Everything had to have squash and recoil," says Love, referring to the device of having characters or objects anticipate an action by contracting slightly to emphasize the impact. "But certain things you don't squash and recoil. If a safe fell from a building, to show that it is heavy and weighty, you would not squash it. Ben squashed everything."

By the 1930s, Krazy Kat had fallen under the influence of Mickey Mouse. A scene from THE MASQUERADE PARTY **(1934).**

The Charles Mintz staff in California: Joe DeNat, Manny Gould, Harry Love, Charles B. Mintz, George Winkler, Al Rose, Ben Harrison, Jack Carr.

Mintz was almost completely removed from the production end of his business. He had no concern with the quality of his cartoons so long as they continued to show a profit. His only suggestion to the staff people in the early 1930s was that they limit dialogue as much as possible, so the films would be salable in foreign countries.

Once settled on the West Coast, Mintz tried to expand his operations by selling a separate cartoon series to RKO Radio Pictures. He hired two of Max Fleischer's best animators, Dick Huemer and Sid Marcus, to come to California and head their own unit. Marcus devised the character of Toby the Pup, and RKO bought an initial series of cartoons starring him. Unfortunately, the series was not a success and died after eleven films. So Huemer devised a new character and Mintz persuaded Columbia Pictures to take the series with that character in addition to the one with Krazy Kat. The new "star" was Scrappy, and his "parents" were Huemer,

Marcus, and another Fleischer alumnus, Art Davis.

Scrappy differed from most cartoon stars of the day in that he was supposed to be human: a cute little boy, designed in highly stylized fashion, with an enormous round head, oversized doughlike shoes, and hardly any body in between. Circles dominated his face as well: He had large round eyes, circle-style ears, a button nose, and a face-framing mass of hair that climaxed in a curly forelock. Even Scrappy's dog, Yippy, was designed in an unrealistic manner, with a Scottielike face much too big for his body. Scrappy's juvenile nemesis—at various times called Vonsey and Oopie—was more normally proportioned.

The initial SCRAPPY cartoons used plots and themes associated with childhood— making the series a second cousin to such comic strips as *Skippy* and *Reg'lar Fellers*. The first episode, YELP WANTED, deals with Scrappy's attempt to purchase a bottle of Dr.

Woof's Dog Tonic to save Yippy from what seems to be imminent death (in truth, she is just giving birth to pups). THE LITTLE PEST details Scrappy's annoyance at having little Vonsey tag along on a fishing trip. In SUNDAY CLOTHES Scrappy runs afoul of a tough neighborhood gang determined to push him into a mud puddle while he's wearing his Sunday best.

These early films are miles ahead of KRAZY KAT in terms of characterization; Scrappy, Yippy, and Oopie (or Vonsey) have real, tangible personalities. They also follow the Fleischer school of visual hyperbole, for example using a padlock that extends its "lips" to swallow a key, and a needle that sprouts arms to open its "eye" for a piece of thread. But the occasional gags and pleasing personalities aren't enough to overcome the films' meandering approach. The impact of these cartoons is soft, because they wander so much before getting to the point.

Looking back, this failing comes as no surprise, since the method by which the cartoons were made—before the era of storyboards—didn't encourage story unity, or even conformity. Dick Huemer explains, "Sid, Art, and myself each took a third of the picture, animated and amplified it on our own, with hardly any consultation with each other. We each considered our section our own private affair—gags, interpretation, and all."

Credits on these films are very misleading. For the early SCRAPPY cartoons, Huemer receives story credit, while Marcus and Davis are credited for animation. Says Huemer, "There was no such thing as a director per se at the Mintz studio . . . not like the Disney studio, that is. When I came to the Disney foundry I found a whole new setup prevailing. There, a director was a *director*— and nothing else. He (and I, when I later became one) had an *assistant* director even.

And *two* layout men. *And* a private secretary. What luxury! And, oh yes, a director never touched pencil to animation paper. The stories were concocted by the story department, which never did anything else but that.

"How different at Mintz's. Me and Marcus and Davis were *all of the above*—plus being the head animators. Each of us was our own director, once the story line had been roughly agreed upon. Gags were added as we animated. Only thing we didn't do was paint the backgrounds. It never occurred to any of us to claim the title of Herr Director— at least not in my time there. The same went for Manny Gould and Ben Harrison on KRAZY KAT."

The main responsibility for initiating story ideas rested with Sid Marcus, and after a few years he started to veer away from realistic childhood settings to allow for a broader range of gags and plots. In SCRAPPY'S PARTY (1933) Vonsey suggests that Scrappy throw himself a birthday bash and invite

Oopie and Scrappy in THE GLOOM CHASERS **(1935).**

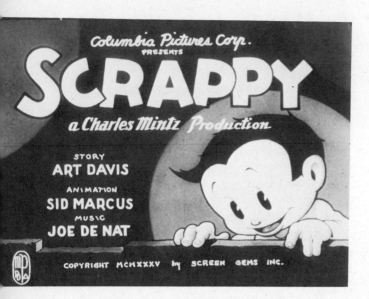

everyone who's anyone. The guests include not only the expected movie stars in caricature (Laurel and Hardy, Greta Garbo, Jimmy Durante), but such diverse world figures as John D. Rockefeller, Albert Einstein, Mahatma Gandhi, Babe Ruth, and Adolf Hitler! Many of these caricatures were reused later that year in THE WORLD'S AFFAIR, in which Scrappy and Vonsey present a successful program at the Chicago World's Fair.

When Dick Huemer left for Disney's in 1933, Marcus and Davis continued the series and decided to redesign Scrappy, to make him a more conventional cartoon boy. This change and the recasting of Scrappy's voice (up to that point an ineffectual, whispery sound) helped to give the films more snap. The gradual improvement of animation and rendering of backgrounds gave another important boost to the series.

Some of this improvement may have been due to an influx of fresh talent. In the early-to-mid-1930s Charles Mintz studios became a way station for many talented animators

who later moved to Disney. One of them, Al Eugster, recalls, "I could name twenty people working there who eventually did quite well; there was a lot of potential at Mintz. They had Preston Blair, Irven Spence, Bob Wickersham, the Patterson brothers (Don and Ray), and Claude Smith."

Much of this potential was untapped, however, because of rigorous schedules and a desire to be only as good as necessary, not as good as possible. One person who feels he benefited from the *laissez-faire* attitude at Mintz's was Emery Hawkins, then just a fledgling animator. "At that studio, if you got excited about something, you did it," he explains. "I tried all sorts of things, and all sorts of special effects there, because I didn't know any better, and nobody like Sid [Marcus] and Art [Davis] said no. They'd just encourage it, and I took advantage of that. Once in a while, Jimmy Bronis would say, 'Look, we want footage, we don't want Rembrandts,' but I always felt that generally speaking I'd had a better break there than I could get anywhere else, because I had that opportunity [to experiment] at a time when it mattered."

Hawkins was one person who turned a possible liability into a personal asset. But others at the studio found frustration. I. Klein, who spent some time at the studio before joining Disney in 1936, recalls showing Mintz a magazine article that decried the fact that Krazy Kat had never been transferred to the screen with Herriman's characters, settings, and humor intact. Mintz was impressed and gave his blessing for such a cartoon to be made.

Klein recalls, "Ben Harrison said to me, 'Gee, this is a great chance for a cheater.' Of all things! Here's the first opportunity to make a real Krazy Kat, and he says, 'chance for a cheater.' Whoever was the background man there really made drawings . . . but it was a senseless story, throwing bricks, and that was the end of it. I was terribly disappointed." The cartoon, LI'L ANJIL, is just as bad as Klein remembers it being. It remained for Gene Deitch to simulate the Herriman style when he supervised production of Krazy Kat cartoons for King Features Television in the 1960s.

Mintz brought another established comic strip to the screen at this time—Billy DeBeck's *Barney Google*—but only four cartoons were made before this project was abandoned.

Meanwhile, Harrison and Gould effected a turnaround by working on a couple of SCRAPPY cartoons—and doing a terrific job of it. Perhaps this is because the characters and format were already set, since few such gems emerged from their KRAZY KAT endeavors. Still, SCRAPPY'S GHOST STORY and, to a lesser degree, GRADUATION EXERCISES, are delightful cartoons by any standards. GHOST STORY—in which playful Vonsey pretends to be a ghost and dances in front of an open fireplace—brims with imagination and charm—as well as fairly sophisticated visual styling. The use of shadows, backlighting, and other effects is particularly impressive, while Joe DeNat's score enhances the juvenile eeriness of the cartoon. Harry Love, who animated on this film under Manny Gould's supervision, has nothing but praise for his longtime colleague. "He never worked for Disney, but I'd match him against any Disney animator. He is more noted as a director, but his timing was superb. He was in demand up until he died [in the 1970s]."

Unfortunately, both Krazy Kat and Scrappy were reassigned to Allen Rose, one of the least inspired men on the Mintz staff, and other various animators. This left Ben Harrison, Manny Gould, Sid Marcus, and Art Davis to concentrate on Mintz's ambitious entry into the color cartoon field. His

COLOR RHAPSODIES series was launched in 1934 with a special Scrappy entry called HOLIDAYLAND, and it went on to emulate Disney's SILLY SYMPHONIES with such titles as The Shoemaker and the Elves, The Make Believe Revue, and A Cat, A Bell, And A Mouse. Like other studios, Mintz had to endure the two-color process for several years while Disney had exclusive rights to three-color Technicolor. But this was not the only resemblance between the RHAPSODIES and color cartoons of rival studios. In trying to duplicate the success of Disney's SILLY SYMPHONIES, all these imitators tried to create warmth, sentiment, and pathos without the *sincerity* that went into Disney's films. Merely drawing cherubic characters is no shortcut to achieving the kind of results Disney did in films like THE FLYING MOUSE or THE GRASSHOPPER AND THE ANT.

Once Mintz *did* get access to full Technicolor, his shorts boasted a delightful rainbow palette, which to moviegoers of the 1930s was often as important as anything else. But the films themselves ran hot and cold—from pale attempts at being cute (GLEE WORMS, for instance) to enjoyable collages of Hollywood caricatures (HOLYWOOD PICNIC, GIFTS FROM THE AIR, and others).

One serious short, NEIGHBORS, attracted attention in *Fortune* magazine, as the cartoon was supposedly based on *Fortune*'s article about improprieties in munitions sales. In the film, a mercenary vulture sows the seeds of suspicion in two rooster friends. First he sells one a gun, then tells the other that he must arm against his friend, escalating the procedure until each rooster has purchased an arsenal. In the end war breaks out and the former friends kill each other, while the vulture profits. *Fortune* praised this striking cartoon subject but, predictably, gave credit to the wrong man, stating, "The Mintz business acumen is curiously marked with a

Penciled animation drawing and finished scene from
Ub Iwerk's Color Rhapsody cartoon MIDNIGHT FROLICS
(1938).

social consciousness that always comes out
in his cartoons." The only social consciousness in NEIGHBORS was that of Sid Marcus,
who devised the story and co-directed it
with Art Davis.

Beginning in 1937 Mintz farmed out half
his quota of COLOR RHAPSODIES to Ub Iwerks,
who produced and directed them at his own
studio. The results were generally undistinguished—and indistinguishable from
Mintz's own product. One entry, SKELETON
FROLIC, was actually a loose remake of the
pioneer talkie SKELETON DANCE, which
Iwerks had animated for Disney in 1929. The
newer version was just a faint reminder of
the first cartoon's originality and charm.

One startling exception to the normal run
of Mintz cartoons was THE LITTLE MATCH
GIRL, released in time for Christmas in 1937.
This outstanding cartoon, supervised by Sid
Marcus and Art Davis, and largely animated
by Emery Hawkins, can hold its own against
any competition—which is quite a statement
to make about any Mintz endeavor. A modern-day retelling of the Hans Christian
Andersen story, it is far from perfect: The
central character, apple-cheeked and as tall
as a basketball, is seriously at odds with the
convincingly realistic settings around her
and the well-animated human beings who
cross her path. But since the story is a fantasy, one is willing to accept this
discrepancy.

The tearful story is told in the setting of a
wintry city, warmed by the glow of festive
lights and holiday-spirited people. Amidst
all this, a little girl dressed in rags tries to sell
her matches, is ignored, stepped upon, even
ridiculed. After making her way "home," to
an isolated spot in the snow along a street of
tenements, she lights a tiny fire with her last
match and imagines herself visiting a heavenly place where luxury abounds and happiness reigns. She sees herself wearing a

lovely dress and holding a beautiful doll in her hands. But soon this reverie is shaken by snow and gusts of wind. Her dress is torn to shreds and the doll split apart. Statues fall, and the world topples around her. All she can do is try to reach the one remaining source of light and warmth—a candle. As she struggles closer and closer, the strength is drained from her tiny body. Just within arm's reach, the flame goes out and she faints in the snow. Now we are back in the city street, where the dream has foretold the truth. The little match girl lies face down in the snow. But a guardian angel comes to take her away, and her happy soul is lifted to a heaven where she will be safe, warm, and welcome at last.

Never before had the Mintz animators tackled something so ambitious. The color styling, handsome backgrounds, use of shadows and modeling—all contribute to the effectiveness of this singular tearjerker. It is by far the finest cartoon this studio ever produced. THE LITTLE MATCH GIRL was rewarded with a play date at the prestigious Roxy Theatre in New York and an Academy Award nomination, but it wasn't promoted nearly as much as it should have been by Columbia Pictures. For once the studio had something to rival Disney, yet the film's potential was barely realized.

Perhaps Columbia was resigned to run-of-the-mill product by this time and that's why it didn't pay attention. The run of the Mintz color cartoons were well received, but failed to make a lasting impression. The black-and-white product—even with the occasional boost that contributions from the "first line" writer-directors gave—was sliding downhill. The KRAZY KAT cartoons were a total waste of time by now, while the SCRAPPY series was getting by with only mildly amusing episodes. One promising short, THE CLOCK GOES ROUND AND ROUND (1937), combined live action with animation, but did so in such a prosaic manner that the results were barely worth the effort. One theater owner wrote *Motion Picture Herald*, "If there is any excuse for these SCRAPPY cartoons, I cannot decide what it is. They are all terrible." KRAZY KAT cartoons were retired in 1939, but the SCRAPPY series survived another year.

Mintz had other problems—among them his health and his financial obligations to Columbia Pictures. "Columbia would advance a certain amount of money for each picture, and he went overboard on the cost of these pictures," Sid Marcus recalls. "He went into debt to Columbia, and they took the company away from him." Mintz continued to run the studio, but then in 1939 his health deteriorated, and Columbia relieved him of his responsibilities. Mintz died on January 4, 1940, at the age of forty-four.

During the next eight years there were seven different regimes at the Screen Gems studio. Jimmy Bronis, who had been production manager, was Mintz's immediate successor; he was followed quickly by George Winkler, Mintz's brother-in-law. Both men tried to retain the status quo, but some changes were inevitable. With the demise of KRAZY KAT and SCRAPPY, there were no starring characters left, only catchall series: the RHAPSODIES in color, and the FABLES and PHANTASIES in black and white. Ben Harrison and Manny Gould departed, going their separate ways, while Sid Marcus, Art Davis, and Allen Rose stayed on.

The most dramatic move occurred in 1941. Frank Tashlin, who had been working for Disney, joined the Screen Gems staff as writer. He was ambitious and full of ideas. When Columbia sent short-subject producer Ben Schwalb to take over as general manager of the studio, Tashlin was installed as production supervisor. The studio closed its doors to prepare for a complete reorganization; most of the remaining Mintz artists left, and Tashlin hired most of his staff off the picket line at Walt Disney studios!

Though Tashlin had an approach rooted in conventional cartoon procedures, he had broken new ground as a director at Warner Brothers, and now he was eager to do that again. He hired ex-Disneyites who were young, creative, and charged with imagination: John Hubley, Zack Schwartz, Dave Hilberman, Bob Wickersham, Howard Swift, Sam Cobean, Phil Klein, Grant Simmons, John MacLeish (a.k.a. Ployardt), Volus Jones, Phil Duncan, Emery Hawkins, Chic Otterstrom, William Shull, Tony Rivera, and such non-Disney talents as Alec Geiss, Jack Cosgriff, and Paul Sommer.

The Fox and Crow.

The result was a new look to Columbia cartoons, which now had better personality animation, more interesting visual stylings, and, in the case of Tashlin's own films, brighter gags. In fact, Tashlin's very first cartoon as writer and director at the studio had tremendous influence throughout the industry. It was called THE FOX AND THE GRAPES, and its style of blackout gags—with a dumb but determined Fox scheming to capture a luscious bunch of grapes dangled from a tree by a wily Crow—was a forerunner of the Road Runner–Coyote antics introduced some years later (a source that Chuck Jones, the creator of Road Runner, has readily acknowledged). In fact, some of the specific gags—such as the Fox hurling a boulder in the air to propel himself off a teeterboard, but having the rock come crashing down on his head, or tying himself to a tree and bending it back for a catapult, but being snapped from side to side instead—became standard jokes in the Coyote repertoire. Oddly enough, when the Screen Gems staff fashioned a series using the Fox and Crow, they did not use this format.

Perhaps Tashlin's greatest contribution was assembling a staff that tried to do something new and different, and encouraging everyone in his wildest pursuits. "He was an inspirational man to work for," says Zack Schwartz. "The staff thought, 'This is it, the ideal studio,'" recalls Phil Klein. And the late John Hubley remarked, "Under Tashlin we tried some very experimental things; none of them quite got off the ground, but there was a lot of ground broken. We were doing crazy things that were anti the classic Disney approach."

As crazy as any was a short-lived series co-directed by Hubley and Paul Sommer and called PROFESSOR SMALL AND MR. TALL. The first film set the pattern for the others that followed: It was about the adventures, largely non-sequiturs, of a quixotic pair (the tall one named Prof. Small and the small one named Mr. Tall) who try to disprove superstitions as they bungle their way through life. The short is painfully unfunny, but for 1942 its graphics are alarmingly modern; there are no backgrounds, just splashes of rich color. The characters are angular and the settings are flat. Several times the characters remain stationary while backgrounds and foregrounds dissolve into place.

"We did cartoons that were really ahead of their time," Hubley boasted in later years. "We did one that was a Horatio Alger spoof called FROM RAGS TO RAGS. Then Milt Gross came around with an idea for an anti-Hitler picture which showed him as a crazy paper-hanger, called HE CAN'T MAKE IT STICK."

It was Tashlin who created the kind of atmosphere in which such cartoons could be made. Unfortunately, a clash with Columbia executives brought his tenure to an untimely end—just one year after he had begun the Great Experiment.

Columbia hired Dave Fleischer to take his place. Having just left the studio he'd run with brother Max for twenty years, Dave seemed an ideal choice to run this shop—except that he immediately clashed with his new employees. After Tashlin he seemed trite and old-fashioned in his views, and by any measurement he was no match for the intellectual, art-school element that filled the studio. It was to the mutual relief of all that the most adventurous staffers left Screen Gems, some for the Army film unit and others for civilian studios.

But Dave Fleischer's stay was just as brief. By 1944 he was replaced with a musician who'd been working on cartoon scores, Paul Worth. His time as general manager was fleeting, for Columbia decided to send an experienced short-subject producer, Hugh McCollum, into the breach.

The Fox and Crow in GRAPE NUTTY (1949).

Throughout this turmoil the key studio directors—Howard Swift and Bob Wickersham—tried to maintain some spirit on-screen, with varying results. Screen Gems cartoons of the 1940s feature some of the least endearing cartoon characters ever created, and suffer from misguided story direction. MASS MOUSE MEETING (1943) reprises the war-horse script about mice placing a bell on the household cat so they'll know when he's coming. But this one's unique approach has the mouse chosen for the job spending four minutes *talking* to the curious cat about his new collar! The cartoon almost literally stands still. GIDDY YAPPING (1944) tries to stretch an entire short out of one "joke"— a delivery horse trying to convince his window-washer boss to give him time off for lunch.

Even the studio's resident stars, the Fox and Crow, display a certain abrasiveness

(*Top*) Li'l Abner and Daisy Mae in one of Columbia's color cartoon versions of the Al Capp comic strip. (*Bottom*) A self-explanatory scene from THE COO-COO BIRD DOG (1949).

that keeps them from creating lasting audience appeal. These characters—the naive, Milquetoast-voiced Fox who just wants to mind his own business, and the brash, Brooklynese-speaking Crow, with cigar and derby hat, whose only pleasure in life is annoying the Fox—have tremendous promise. Some of their outings have moments of high comedy—as in ROOM AND BORED, in which the Crow answers landlord Fox's advertisement for a "quiet, refined tenant" and turns his apartment into a three-ring circus. In WAY DOWN YONDER IN CORN, a long-running chase winds up at an amusement park. The Fox catches the Crow in the car of a roller coaster and is about to strangle him when the Crow pipes up, "Wait a minute! This picture is just about over. Let's stop this quarreling and bickering. I really like you—you're a good straight man. Let's be friends—let's make up." They shake hands, just as the car plummets down a sheer incline and smashes right into the camera lens for an unexpected finale.

The Fox and Crow shorts are among the studio's best, but too often they miss the mark, producing raucousness for its own sake and failing to establish an underlying likability that was essential to this kind of character cartoon.

Another set of problems hampered the studio's attempt to bring Al Capp's *Li'l Abner* comic strip to the screen. Literalizing some of Capp's highly imaginative characters and situations and simplifying others to meet animated-cartoon conventions resulted in a lackluster series with a hit-or-miss track record. Al Capp was not pleased, and neither was anyone else. The project was dropped after five films. One final attempt to launch a new starring character was made in 1946 with the introduction of Flippy, a comic canary, but he was derivative and unmemorable, and he expired after four films.

Screen Gems' last chance to hit the cartoon bull's-eye came in 1946 with its final change of management. Warner Brothers had bought out Leon Schlesinger and deposed his right-hand men Henry Binder and Ray Katz (Schlesinger's brother-in-law). They came to Screen Gems and brought with them some of Warners' top talent, including director Bob Clampett, writers Cal Howard, Dave Monahan, and others who worked on a moonlighting basis, like Michael Maltese and Tedd Pierce. Alex Lovy signed on to direct some cartoons, and another former Lantz staffer, Darrell Calker, composed the music scores. Added to the existing Screen Gems crew, these men comprised a fairly high-powered team.

But in what seemed to be a recurring pattern, the finished products belied the talent that went into them. Clampett's stay was short, and he worked only on stories, not direction, where he might have made a major difference. His colleagues came up with cartoons that were, at best, pale carbons of the Warner Brothers shorts.

Why should there have been such a discrepancy between talent and final results? Perhaps it was the unstable foundation of the studio, an unsettled feeling that made it nearly impossible to establish an esprit de corps. It could have been low budgets. Another possible obstacle might have been the lack of a truly creative producer.

Whatever the reason or reasons, Screen Gems never broke out of the also-ran category, except in isolated films that were few and far between. When in 1948 independent

Willoughby Wren and an ersatz Peter Lorre in COCKA-TOOS FOR TWO (1947); the Warner Brothers influence is clear.

producer Steve Bosustow of UPA approached Columbia about a cartoon contract, the studio agreed to let him try his hand at some Fox and Crow shorts. Satisfied with the results, it contracted for more product from UPA and let its own animation studio die, after trying to keep it alive for so many troubled years.

With the acquisition of UPA product came the prestige, attention, and income that Columbia had never enjoyed before. But there was no feeling that these were Columbia cartoons, except in distribution terms. UPA made its own reputation, and Columbia had to bask in reflected glory.

Warner Brothers

WALT DISNEY was the dominant force in American cartoons during the 1930s. Many emulated him but no one could equal his artistic or financial success during that decade.

The Warner Brothers studio started out by imitating Disney and in fact was peopled with ex-Disney staffers, but in the mid-1930s that group left and a new breed initiated a distinctive style and format that had little in common with Disney's work. The films were bold, brash, and innovative. Most important, they were funny in a way Disney's cartoons had never been.

By 1940 Walt Disney had pioneered the feature-length cartoon, and there was no one to compete with him in that arena. But in the field of short subjects, the young Warners' crew toppled Walt from his throne to dominate the industry for the next twenty years.

Warners' track record during this time was remarkable. It created more lasting star characters than any rival studio. Porky Pig, Daffy Duck, Bugs Bunny, The Road Runner, Wile E. Coyote, Tweety, Sylvester, Elmer Fudd, Yosemite Sam, Pepe LePew, Foghorn Leghorn, and Speedy Gonzales are the leading lights whose names still shine around the world while other contemporary creations are forgotten.

Warner Brothers launched more important cartoon creators than any other studio. Men like Chuck Jones, Bob Clampett, Tex Avery, Friz Freleng, and Frank Tashlin are considered giants in the history of animation; all spent healthy portions of their lives at Warners', and many did their finest work there.

As for the films themselves, critic Manny Farber wrote in 1943, ''The surprising facts about them are that the good ones are masterpieces and the bad ones aren't a total loss.'' It's clear that statement still holds true today, after looking back over nearly one thousand individual cartoons.

What's more, these films have remained fresh twenty to forty years later—no mean achievement, especially when one realizes how much they relied on topical humor and contemporary themes. Considering Warners' unique comic personality, it's ironic to note how close its initial ties were with Disney.

Hugh Harman, Rudolf Ising, and Isadore ''Friz'' Freleng, who inaugurated the studio, had all worked for Walt Disney—Harman and Ising as far back as 1922, in Kansas City.

So had animators Carmen "Max" Maxwell, Norm Blackburn, Paul Smith, and Rollin "Ham" Hamilton. Virtually the entire Warner Brothers cartoon staff had received its baptism of fire with Disney, and been exposed to his ideas, theories, and modus operandi.

Most of these artists left Disney around the same time, in 1928, when producer George Winkler promised greener pastures with his formation of a new studio to produce Oswald the Rabbit cartoons. But when Winkler's distributor, Universal, pulled the rug out from under him and commissioned Walter Lantz to make Oswald shorts at its own cartoon studio, Harman, Ising, Freleng, and others were left without a job.

At this point, in mid-1929, these ambitious and unemployed animators banded together to make their own cartoons. Disney's STEAMBOAT WILLIE had already appeared and proved the commercial value of sound cartoons, so Harman-Ising and company located a small outfit with recording facilities to help produce a "pilot" film, just three minutes long, called BOSKO THE TALK-INK KID. Bosko was a rounded, rubbery character who frolicked in this film with Rudolf Ising on-screen at the drawing board. Animator "Max" Maxwell provided Bosko's voice. There was no plot and little action in this short film, but its creators hoped that the mere novelty of sound and the facility of their animation would intrigue a distributor, especially since Disney's cartoons were doing so well.

Harman and Ising encountered roughly the same difficulty that Disney had in landing a distributor. Two of the "majors," Paramount and Universal, already had cartoons under contract. Others saw no particular value in handling these "fillers."

The first man to express commercial interest in BOSKO was Leon Schlesinger, then the head of Pacific Art and Title, a company that still thrives today preparing main-title cards and artwork for movies. But Schlesinger was no artist. He was a moneyman, an entrepreneur with a good nose for a sound investment. He had helped back the brothers Warner in their risky venture, THE JAZZ SINGER, and when that paid off, Schlesinger remained in their good graces. He saw possibilities in Harman and Ising's product and sold the idea of a cartoon series to Warner Brothers, proposing himself as producer and the studio as his distributor. The only stipulation on Warners' part was that each cartoon should include one full chorus of a song from a Warners' feature film. (The studio owned its own music publishing company and stood to gain in many ways from the continued success of these songs.)

A contract was signed for an initial season of cartoons, and Harman and Ising concocted the name LOONEY TUNES for their series. This blatant (but now cherished) paraphrase of Disney's SILLY SYMPHONIES title gives some indication of the extent of the duo's commitment to originality in these early years—although the coincidence that gave their names a musical connotation (Harman-Ising/harmonizing) was one thing Disney couldn't lay claim to.

SINKING IN THE BATHTUB, the first LOONEY TUNE, was released in May 1930; its title was a play on the popular song title that had been introduced in Warners' feature THE SHOW OF SHOWS.

The film opens with Bosko cheerfully taking a bath (Bosko does *everything* cheerfully), a derby hat perched upon his head. There is no plot to speak of: Bosko leaves the bathtub to call on his girl friend Honey for a day's outing. That is sufficient groundwork for Harman and Ising to fashion a series of musical interludes and occasional gags, many of the barnyard/outhouse variety. (For example, Bosko tears strips of toilet paper in his bathroom and tosses them aloft like flower petals during one number, and later he encounters a haughty cow whose enormous udder swings back and forth when she walks.)

Music is the raison d'être for this cartoon. "A Hot Time in the Old Town Tonight" is played during the main titles, with noisy punctuation. When Bosko dances on the walkway in front of Honey's house, the planks become notes of a xylophone so he can play a tune. Later he devises another ersatz musical instrument when he uses reeds to tap on lily pads. Songs fill the sound track in rapid succession: "Tip Toe Through the Tulips," "Turkey in the Straw," "I'm Forever Blowing Bubbles," and of course "Singing in the Bathtub."

Bosko and Honey are extraordinarily flexible characters, physically speaking. Bosko pulls a hair on top of his head and his lower body lifts into place, while Honey is so caught up in the musical rhythms of the piece that she swings her torso around in wide circular motions.

Physical objects share Bosko's ability to squash, stretch, and bounce at will. Bosko's bathtub gets into the spirit of things by lifting its "forelegs" off the floor and dancing, while his car has a human face and decidedly human characteristics.

The ingredients for SINKING IN THE BATHTUB come together in a most agreeable mixture of snappy music and pleasant comedy. The cartoon is briskly paced and entertaining. But there is no question from where the inspiration for this and subsequent cartoons derived. Bosko was a thinly disguised Mickey Mouse, Honey an obvious Minnie Mouse, and, in later cartoons, a Plutoish dog named Bruno completed the parlay.

"We all came from the same school, and that was with Walt Disney from Kansas City," says Friz Freleng, looking back on this period. "So there was like thinking, and I suppose that's why the characters sometimes looked alike. We were all inspired by the Aesop's Fables type of characters that Paul Terry had been doing . . . later on, of course, that changed."

Some of Harman and Ising's most impressive animation effects were borrowed as well. One of the most striking moments in SINKING IN THE BATHTUB comes when Bosko jumps forward "into" the camera lens, his mouth covering the frame and turning it black; Honey then repeats the action. Another gag has Bosko tripping and, upon hitting the ground, splitting into ten tiny replicas of himself, which scramble about before reconverging into a full-sized figure. Not one but *both* of these animated actions had been done in Walt Disney's Oswald cartoon of 1927, BRIGHT LIGHTS—on which Hugh Harman and Rudolf Ising had labored.

Bosko never caught on the way Mickey Mouse did, but for several years he was the mainstay of the Warners' cartoon studio. One day a porter at the studio said to young animator Jack Zander, "I want to ask you something about that character you've got. I know Mickey Mouse, and Krazy Kat, and Oswald the Rabbit . . . but Bosko the *what*?" What indeed?

If the porter had been able to see a number of the films, he would have realized that Bosko was in fact a cartoonized version of a young black boy. In SINKING IN THE BATHTUB he spoke a Southern Negro dialect, but in subsequent films this characterization was eschewed—or perhaps forgotten. This could be called sloppiness on the part of Harman and Ising, but it also indicates the uncertain nature of the character itself.

One year later when Harman and Ising developed another character, named Foxy, again the inspiration was clear: He was

Foxy makes one of his rare screen appearances in ONE MORE TIME (1932).

Mickey Mouse with pointed ears and a bushy tail. The story line for his initial film, SMILE DARN YA, SMILE, was in turn "borrowed" rather closely from an Oswald the Rabbit film that Harman, Ising, and Freleng had done for Disney in 1928, TROLLEY TROUBLES. Foxy had no distinction whatsoever and disappeared after several appearances. (There was yet a third variation on this funny-animal formula—but Piggy also met an early demise.)

Warner Brothers was so pleased with the success of the LOONEY TUNES that it commissioned a second series of monthly releases from Schlesinger. Harman and Ising put their heads together and came up with the name MERRIE MELODIES. They also decided that it would be wise to divide their duties at this point. Hugh Harman remained the supervisor/director on the Bosko series, while Rudy Ising handled the MERRIE MELODIES, which were one-shot cartoons with titles usually derived from Warner Brothers songs. Although their names were linked in screen credits, Harman and Ising worked independently from that time on.

It is important to note that these cartoons were extremely well-liked at the time of their release, and that individually they remain bright and entertaining today. But the serious fault with the Harman-Ising cartoons was that they did not innovate or improve.

A review of BOSKO'S HOLIDAY in the *Motion Picture Herald*, a publication aimed at theater owners, gave the series its guarded blessing: "The LOONEY TUNE featured player, Bosco [sic] the animated cartoon star, has a great deal of fun himself, and pleases the audience generally with his antics. This number is no exception. Clever drawings, though the story, of course, means little or nothing. Good for a light spot almost anywhere." For comparison, the same issue, dated May 9, 1931, features a review of Disney's MOTHER GOOSE MELODIES that exults: "Walt Disney has done a most unusual piece of work in this SILLY SYMPHONY number. There is indicated a great step forward technically, in animation and synchronization, in addition to excellent subject material, clever animated ideas, and rapidity of action. There is almost the illusion of real life in some of the figures, so fine is the animation. . . . The youngsters will devour this and ask for more, and the elderly children will enjoy it hugely. By all means do not miss it. It is great."

Ising's one-shot musicals offered more opportunities for variety than the Bosko series. At first Warners' trade advertising implied a connection to Max Fleischer's Bouncing Ball cartoons, proclaiming, "Your patrons will join in the songs of MERRIE MELODIES—*compelling* every person in the audience to sing with the screen. Peppy! Novel! Amusing! Synchronized by one of the world's greatest jazz orchestras." Bandleader Abe Lyman was featured on a handful of early cartoons in the series, but the idea of audience participation was strictly a figment of an ad writer's imagination—or a misunderstanding between Warners' and its cartoon studio.

Sadly the MERRIE MELODIES never lived up to their apparent potential. ONE STEP AHEAD OF MY SHADOW (1933) features handsome Oriental settings with cherry blossom trees, pagodas, and the like, but the main boy-girl characters are exactly the same as those in PAGAN MOON or a dozen other titles—except that they have slanted eyes! When the peppy Occidental music begins, the boy and girl bounce up and down in best Bosko fashion. These cartoons seem pleasant and somewhat imaginative—until one watches three in a row.

On the BOSKO brigade, animator Jack Zander recalls, "We were doing something and Hugh Harman said, 'You remember that scene in the Disney picture where Mickey Mouse did so-and-so?' I said, 'You want almost the same thing?' and he said, 'No, I want *exactly* the same thing.' He said that the picture was playing at some theater that night, and he wanted me to go and study the scene, come back and make Bosko do exactly the same thing."

This passionate desire to keep up with Disney, and plagiarize him at the same time, made for a self-defeating process, because Disney was an innovator who insisted that each cartoon be better—and different—than the last one. One can trace the improvement in Disney's cartoons year by year in the 1930s, but there's virtually no progress during Harman and Ising's span of four years at Warners'.

There were no official "gagmen" at this time. As directors, Harman and Ising acted in much the same capacity as Walt Disney, presiding over general staff meetings in which each new picture was roughly mapped out and suggestions were solicited from all those present. (Friz Freleng undertook various functions during this time, actually directing portions of films, although

he received no credit beyond that of animator. The first film he remembers directing on his own was BOSKO IN DUTCH.)

One clever notion made the finale of RIDE HIM, BOSKO! (1933) unusual and different. In this standard outing, Bosko is a Western hero who spends most of his time singing, dancing, and playing the piano at the Red Gulch saloon. Eventually he is called to action when his girl friend Honey is trapped in a runaway stagecoach. Bosko goes riding to the rescue, and in the midst of this chase scene the camera pulls back to reveal a live-action picture of three animators watching him on a tabletop projection screen. Rudy Ising asks his colleagues, "Say, how's Bosko going to save the girl?" One of them replies laconically, "I don't know." "Well, we've got to do *something*," Ising retorts. "Let's go home," says Hugh Harman, and his partners agree. They walk out of the room, leaving Bosko to shrug helplessly on his little screen as the film comes to a close. While this sequence has great novelty value, it still ranks as a kind of cop-out, since it brings the film to such an abrupt ending. One cannot help but wonder whether this might not have represented some of Harman and Ising's true feelings toward the beloved Bosko!

Lacking the drive of Disney, Harman and Ising were content to accept formulas as the easiest way to meet their deadlines and deliver reasonably good cartoons. So formulas became the order of the day, and sometimes it was hard to distinguish one H-I cartoon from another. Certain gags became standard elements—such as Bosko falling and splitting into a dozen miniatures of himself—while other postures and attitudes for characters were soon so uniform that animators could easily reuse sequences from earlier films, or copy them to suit other characters.

Hugh Harman wanted more money to make these films and engaged in a running

Publicity drawing from BUDDY'S GARAGE **(1934).**

battle for higher budgets with Leon Schlesinger, who resolutely refused to cut his profits by spending more on the product. The culmination of these arguments was a split between the producer and his film makers in mid-1933.

Schlesinger was now faced with the dilemma of having a contract to produce cartoons but no one to make them. His first step was by then an obvious one: Raid the Disney studio for talent. He hired Jack King and Tom Palmer to direct, and found animators from other production houses in Hollywood. He even hired people who'd been working for Harman and Ising, including young Bob Clampett and, eventually, Friz Freleng.

When Freleng broke with Harman and Ising to work directly for Schlesinger, he found that Palmer's cartoons had not been accepted by Warners' and required major surgery. He received permission to summon two colleagues from Kansas City, Ben Hardaway and Tubby Millar, to join the staff. Hardaway was soon sharing responsibility for cartoons in the LOONEY TUNES series with Jack King.

Harman and Ising had learned from Walt Disney's earlier misfortune with Oswald the Rabbit and made sure that they owned the character of Bosko. When they left Warners' they took Bosko with them and later revived him at MGM. One might say that Warners' loss was MGM's loss. But Schlesinger was now without a star character for his LOONEY TUNES.

The immediate solution was to devise a character named Buddy, whom Bob Clampett has accurately described as "Bosko in whiteface." More realistically conceived as a human being than Bosko, Buddy has even less personality than the original. Hugh Harman's Bosko cartoons were no classics, but they had a certain style; the Buddy cartoons are generally devoid of style or anything resembling humor. They occasionally featured some imaginative ideas, as in BUDDY'S THEATRE, in which Our Hero becomes part of the movie he's showing in order to save his girl friend Cookie from the clutches of a wild chinchilla; and in BUDDY THE GEE-MAN, he infiltrates Sing Song Prison to expose the inhumane conditions there, turning the jail into a day camp in the process. A young in-betweener at the studio named Chuck Jones graduated to the position of animator on the BUDDY series; looking back, Jones feels he was ill-prepared, but "Fortunately," he says, "nothing in the way of bad animation could make Buddy worse than he was anyway." The character expired after two years and was never missed.

Friz Freleng concentrated on the MERRIE MELODIES series, which remained a fairly routine group of shorts, even with the addition of color. In 1934 Schlesinger, feeling the pinch of competition, decided to spend the additional money to produce a cartoon in the Cinecolor process. As already mentioned, because of Walt Disney's exclusive contract to use the new three-strip Technicolor, rival studios were forced to revert to two-color processes such as Cinecolor, which employed only the red and green portions of the spectrum. The Cinecolor results couldn't compare with the vivid hues of three-strip, but it was a way of easing into color production, and it gave the distributors an edge in promoting their films to theater owners.

HONEYMOON HOTEL and BEAUTY AND THE BEAST were the first color releases in the MERRIE MELODIES series, and the favorable reaction that Warners' received prompted Schlesinger to commission all the films in that series to be made in color, beginning with the 1934–35 season.*

The MERRIE MELODIES remained undistinguished because they were mired in the original Harman-Ising formula: the use of a popular song as a springboard for a thin story line. Without running characters, it was clearly difficult for Freleng and company to devise consistently new approaches to the same kind of material. As a result, cute animals frolicking cute insects cavorting, billboards and shop displays coming to life were repeated ad nauseum. GOIN' TO HEAVEN ON A MULE had the dubious distinction of being far duller than the eye-popping version of the song by the same name in Busby Berkeley's feature film WONDER BAR. If an animated cartoon, with its limitless potential for exaggeration and flights of fancy, couldn't venture beyond the realm of a live-action film, what was the point?

This question expresses precisely the attitude of a young man named Fred "Tex" Avery, who joined the Warners' studio at this time. Avery had risen from animator to director at Walter Lantz's studio, and when he heard of possible job openings at Warners' he presented himself as a director to Leon Schlesinger.

Avery later told Joe Adamson, "Looking back, I don't know why or how Schlesinger gambled on me. Evidently he was quite desperate. He had a fellow by the name of Tom Palmer, I think, and he wasn't satisfied. He said, 'I'll try you. I'll try you on one picture. I've got some boys here—they're not renegades, but they don't get along with the other two crews. They're not satisfied working with the people they're working with.' Evidently there was some rub. And he gave me Chuck Jones, Bob Clampett, and Bob "Bobe" Cannon. Chuck was creative; so was Bob Clampett. Bob Cannon was a terrific draftsman. And they were tickled to death; they wanted to get a 'new group' going, and 'We could do it,' and 'Let's make some funny pictures.' It was very encouraging, and a wonderful thing to step into. . . . [Avery also brought two talented animators with him from Lantz, Virgil Ross and Sid Sutherland.]

"We worked every night—Jones, Clampett, and I were all young and full of ambition. My gosh, nothing stopped us! We encouraged each other, and we really had a good ball rolling. I guess Schlesinger saw the light; he said, 'Well, I'll take you boys away from the main plant.' He put us up in our own little shack over on the [Warner Brothers] Sunset lot, completely separated from the Schlesinger studio, in some old dressing room or toilet or something, a little cottage

---

*LOONEY TUNES were made exclusively in black and white through 1943, but in the early 1970s Warner Brothers had them "remade" in color. The process, executed in Korea, involved tracing over frames of film. (The studio had burned all its original artwork some years earlier in order to make storage space.) These recolored cartoons are now shown on many television stations, creating some confusion as to their origin. At first glimpse, the colors are quite pleasing, but one soon discovers that details have been dropped in the tracing, mechanical errors have been made, and not every frame has been traced. The process of tracing has turned these beautifully executed shorts into simulations of today's cheap-jack television cartoons. One cannot and should not judge the LOONEY TUNES of this period by these color impostors.

Facsimile drawing from I HAVEN'T GOT A HAT (1935), featuring the debut appearance of Porky Pig. © Warner Brothers Inc.

sort of thing. We called it Termite Terrace. And he was smart; he didn't disturb us. We were all alone out there, and he knew nothing of what went on.''

What went on was the development of a new style of cartoon making, built on a foundation of enthusiasm and the desire to do things that were new, wild, and imaginative. Avery, Jones, and Clampett had no interest in making cute six-minute time fillers. And they didn't.

GOLD DIGGERS OF '49, released in January 1936, is a watershed film in the history of Warner Brothers' cartoon studio. It was Avery's first, and it bears his name as well as those of animators Jones and Clampett—a formidable triumvirate in any circumstance.

The inspiration for the title is clear: Busby Berkeley's ongoing GOLD DIGGERS musicals made for the Warners' studio. The inspiration for the short itself is vague, except that it must have tickled Avery's funny bone to take the GOLD DIGGERS title and employ the

term's more traditional meaning just when movie audiences would be expecting a bevy of chorus girls. Therefore, the subject of this cartoon is a gold rush out west.

To find useful characters, Avery screened some of Warners' recent output and singled out a pair of Friz Freleng creations in the 1935 short I HAVEN'T GOT A HAT. This amiable comedy featured a variety of anthropomorphized animals as children in a schoolroom setting. Twin dogs were named Ham and Ex, and a pair of other characters were similarly named Porky and Beans. Porky was a stuttering pig who attempted to recite ''The Midnight Ride of Paul Revere,'' while Beans was a saucy young cat who participated in performing the catchy title song of the cartoon.

Avery adapted these characters for his own purposes in GOLD DIGGERS OF '49. The major change was making them adults. In fact, Beans, who is the film's nominal hero, wants to marry Porky's *daughter*. Porky is an enormous creature who bears virtually no resemblance to the same-named character who would soon make his mark but the fact that no one today manufactures T-shirts or drinking glasses with Beans's picture on them gives some indication of his limited appeal, even though he was the official star of the film.*

GOLD DIGGERS OF '49 represents a kind of bridge from the old to the new Warners' style; it encompassed elements of both. Looking back, one is frustrated by the deliberate pacing, knowing how Avery later refined his use of exaggerated timing for comic effect. There's a sequence in which Beans rides through the Western town shouting the news that he's struck gold in the hills; this leads to a series of sight gags as

*Ham and Ex, incidentally, got star billing in Jack King's cartoon FIRE ALARM (1935), in which they create mischief at a firehouse run by ''Uncle'' Beans.

people drop what they're doing to rush out of town and stake a claim. A quartet is singing barbershop harmony to "Sweet Adeline" when Beans rides by with the news. They break in the middle of a line ("You're the flower of my heart—") and scurry off into the distance, only to rush back a moment later to the exact spot where they were standing to finish ("Sweet Ad-o-line—my Ad-o-line!") before running off once more. It's a funny idea, and fairly typical of Avery's sense of humor, but had he timed the scene a few years later, he would have sped the motion of the men's dash back and forth even faster and made it twice as funny. Still, it was a beginning—the start of a breakthrough in which Warner Brothers cartoons became funny instead of just cute.

This cartoon also has a superbly animated climax involving speed. Most cartoon veterans point to Disney's famous THE TORTOISE AND THE HARE (1934), from the SILLY SYMPHONY series, as the first cartoon that effectively animated speed. If they are right, Avery, Jones, and Clampett learned their lesson well and put it to good use in this cartoon. Beans pours a jug of moonshine into his gas tank, and the jalopy begins to push forward at an incredible rate. Soon we no longer see the car or Beans—just a haze of speed lines with an indication of the figures underneath! The animators extend this dazzling sight when the bad guy is overtaken, pulled by Beans into the backseat—and swallowed into the shooting gray lines. Here again one senses an innovative hand at work, pushing the traditions of Warners' cartoons to new boundary lines.

Shortly thereafter Jones and Clampett endured a brief sojourn away from the lot making cartoons at Ub Iwerks' studio. Iwerks was in financial trouble and Leon Schlesinger decided to farm out some of his product to the veteran cartoon maker, sending his two young animators to work with him. Although Iwerks received "supervision" credit (the term Schlesinger insisted on using instead of "direction"), Jones recalls that he and Clampett actually co-directed the cartoons, much as Iwerks's head animators had done before. Fortunately, the association was short-lived, because the character created for this particular series, Gabby Goat, was an obnoxious and uninteresting one. Iwerks's studio closed for good, and Clampett and Jones returned to the home base.

The next man to promote Warners' cartoon development was Frank Tashlin. Tashlin had been an animator at the studio once before, around the time that Leon Schlesinger broke with Harman and Ising, but he had walked out when the producer wanted a percentage of the income from a comic strip Tashlin was drawing on the side. Now, with Avery and company firmly established, Schlesinger needed someone to replace Jack King (who returned to Disney in 1936) and he called on Tashlin.

Tashlin was a versatile man who had great gifts not only as a cartoonist but as a gagman. He had written his own comic strip, sold panel cartoons to various magazines, and for a brief time was on the payroll of the Hal Roach studio for contributing gags to films with Laurel and Hardy, Our Gang, and Charley Chase. As a director he struck an ideal balance by laying the emphasis equally on the visual appearance and the gag content of his films.

But Tashlin's strongest suit was his interest in the cartoon as *film*. He would carry this concern to its furthest extreme during a later stint at Warners' in the 1940s, but even in this early period he toyed with the possibilities of camera angles, cutting, montage, and other cinematic devices at a time when some of his colleagues were still taking more prosaic approaches to their work.

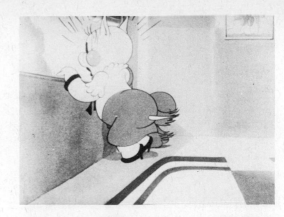

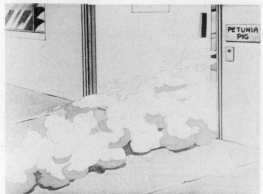

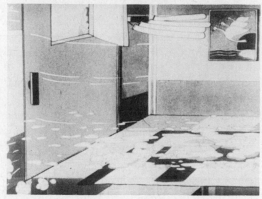

Follows sequence left to right across each page: Porky
has been spurned and walks away, but Petunia spots
his box of candy, runs after and overtakes him, whizzing
him back to her sofa. Innovative cartoon film making
by Frank Tashlin in PORKY'S ROMANCE (1937). © Warner
Brothers Inc.

There's a perfect example in PORKY'S ROMANCE (1937), the fifth cartoon Tashlin directed at Warners'. Here's the setup for a remarkable sequence: Porky has come to call on haughty Petunia Pig to ask her hand in marriage, but she won't even see him. Porky walks away dejectedly, clutching flowers and candy behind his back. Petunia spots the box of candy and has a sudden change of heart. She runs after Porky to bring him—and the candy—back to her house in a flurry of movement that, as measured from the finished film, breaks down like this:

Petunia spins around and exits frame in a cloud of smoke.	29 frames
She runs to door, opens it, and exits.	16 frames
Now just a puff of smoke, she whizzes through the door (exterior shot).	6 frames
The supersonic cloud soars down the front walk.	18 frames
The candy box gets closer and closer, as seen from Petunia's point of view.	12 frames
Petunia overtakes Porky, circles around, and yanks him out of frame, leaving the dust—and the flowers—to settle in her path.	31 frames
Petunia and Porky zoom around the front steps back up to the house.	17 frames
The cloud of smoke whizzes through the front door (exterior shot).	6 frames
Petunia—again visible only as a cloud—enters and slams front door shut before leaving frame.	14 frames
Petunia is suddenly seated casually on her sofa, legs crossed, attentively watching a dazed Porky and ready to devour his candy.	8 frames

The total number of frames is 157—with ten cuts—representing six and a half seconds of screen time! No one had ever tampered with speed this way before, at Warners' or anywhere else. This rapid-fire cutting was new and startling, and it became Tashlin's stock-in-trade during his first year at the studio. There are similar quick-cut sequences in PORKY IN THE NORTH WOODS (1936) and PORKY AT THE CROCADERO (1937), among others.

Tashlin initiated another idea that would soon become standard at Warner Brothers: the kidding self-reference. Again, PORKY'S ROMANCE provides a perfect example. After the Warners, and LOONEY TUNES logos, but before the main titles for this film appear, an announcer's voice is heard declaring, in properly stentorian tones, "Ladies and gentlemen, introducing Leon Schlesinger's new LOONEY TUNE star [fanfare sounds]—Petunia Pig!" A curtain opens to reveal the heavily rouged Petunia, standing nervously at a microphone, script in hand, in front of a gaudy backdrop splashed with the slogans "LOONEY TUNES," "MERRIE MELODIES," "WARNER BROS.," "LEON SCHLESINGER STUDIO," and "HOLLYWOOD, CALIFORNIA." She attempts to read a humble welcome to "her public," but is so nervous and confused that she mangles her words. Finally, the announcer whispers, "Petunia—don't get excited—don't get excited." Petunia turns to the camera (and presumably the announcer) and throws herself into a grotesquely unladylike frenzy, shouting "EXCITED??? WHO'S EXCITED??? I'M NOT EXCITED!!!" At this point the picture fades and the main title appears.

References to Warner Brothers and acknowledgment of the cartoon medium by the characters themselves soon became commonplace in Warners' cartoons—Tex Avery made abundant use of this kind of gag—but Tashlin was the first to take this unorthodox step. He went so far as to have his big-game hunter in THE MAJOR LIED TILL DAWN remark, as he decides to take spinach to increase his strength, "By jove, if it's good enough for that sailor man, it's good enough for me." Years later Tashlin continued this innovative trend as a live-action writer-director.

He accomplished one more coup that probably went unnoticed by everyone except his colleagues: He was the only one allowed to use a pseudonym or nickname in his credits. Many of his early cartoons are signed Frank Tash, or Tish Tash, two variations he favored over his real name. Other directors and writers suffered for years under the pretentious front-office insistence they use their actual names instead of their more familiar monikers. Thus, Tex Avery was billed as Fred, Chuck Jones as Charles M., Friz Freleng as Isadore or just plain I.

Around this time two other people joined the Warner Brothers staff, completing the creative team that soon made the studio's cartoons the best in the business. The first was composer Carl W. Stalling. Like many men who wrote music for films during the 1930s, Stalling had broken into the business accompanying silent movies on the organ and conducting theater orchestras, principally in Kansas City. There he made the acquaintance of Walt Disney, who hired him as his musical director in 1928. Stalling worked for Disney and Ub Iwerks for the next eight years, moving to Warner Brothers when the Iwerks studio closed in 1936.

Unlike the work of his predecessors, Stalling's music was light, graceful, and witty. It complemented the action on-screen instead of smothering it. Both his original themes and his choice of familiar tunes—many of them from Warner Brothers feature films—added substantial humor to the cartoons

Musical director Carl W. Stalling.

without distracting from the animation.

As an accompanist for silent films, Stalling had developed a knack for matching songs to the action on-screen, and since Warner Brothers not only created new songs for feature films but owned several music publishing companies, he had free access to literally hundreds of popular tunes. Chuck Jones recalls, "He developed a memory which related to the titles, so if you had a woman with a red dress on, he always played 'The Lady in Red.' If it was anything to do with food, he played 'A Cup of Coffee, a Sandwich, and You,' because his computer would deliver that song. I did one with a bee one time, so he dug out a song written in 1906 called 'My Funny Little Bumblebee'!" Although some of these reflex actions

Voice expert Mel Blanc.

inger's cartoon factory. Among his first assignments was the task of creating a new voice for Porky Pig. Blanc retained the stutter but made it a humorous one, allowing for wonderful gag lines ("bye-bye . . . so long . . . *auf Wiede—auf Wiede*—toodle-oo!") and enhancing the character's appeal tremendously. He remained the studio's leading voice expert from that time on and won an exclusive contract in the early 1940s. His creation of character voices and his often remarkable performances were certainly as responsible as any other factor for making these cartoons so successful.

Blanc's voice wasn't the only change in Porky Pig at this time, however. Porky had become LOONEY TUNES' starring character and in just a year had been the subject of considerable experimentation. In GOLD DIGGERS OF '49 he was an enormous adult pig, but in Tex Avery's subsequent THE BLOWOUT he was an ingenuous child. Frank Tashlin brought him to courting age, but made his design even more grotesque, giving him apple cheeks and a compressed body.

It remained for animator Bob Clampett to commission a new design for Porky when he was promoted to the director's chair in 1937. Clampett's Porky, combined with Mel Blanc's voice, really revitalized the character and made him funny and appealing. If not always precisely a child, he remained childlike in his innocent manner and wide-eyed appearance for the next few years—and the decision to make Porky the speaker of the studio's immortal "That's all, folks!" sign-off guaranteed him lasting fame.

Although others had worked with Porky and would continue to do so in later years, the series became virtually Clampett's own from 1938 to 1940, and he achieved a wondrous record for consistently inventive and funny cartoons. Like most of his comrades, Clampett was a young man, and when he

became clichés, and, according to Jones, "it didn't mean anything because nobody in the world knew the damn songs even then," this facility was tremendously helpful in maintaining the pace imposed on Stalling. After all, there were three or four directors turning out films, but just one man scoring them all. He often had to compose an entire score in one week's time. Stalling's input became an integral part of these cartoons, along with the creative sound-effects work of Treg Brown.

The other major figure who helped shape the destiny of this studio was Mel Blanc. Blanc was a radio performer who was trying to establish himself in Los Angeles when he was recommended for some work at Schles-

was handed the director's reins he burst forth with new and imaginative ideas. His biggest boon at this juncture was directorial autonomy, something most live-action directors at the time would have given anything to have. "Leon gave us directors almost complete freedom within a set budget and schedule," Clampett later told Mike Barrier. "Short deadlines, short money, but he let us make the pictures without interference." It was this freedom that enabled each director to explore and develop his own individual style.

Clampett's first real gem was the incredible PORKY IN WACKYLAND (1938), in which the intrepid pig pilots his own airplane through "dark—darker—darkest Africa" in search of the elusive Dodo Bird (worth "$4000,000,000,000—P.S. 000,000,000," according to a newspaper headline). He lands at the border of Wackyland and tiptoes in, only to be greeted by a menagerie of strange, silly creatures who cavort against a lopsided, Daliesque backdrop. There's a wild-eyed rabbit suspended on a swing in midair that's anchored to the tips of his ears, a web-footed fellow whose head is a horn that he continually honks, a wide-mouthed duck who sidles through the scene repeating the word "Mammy!" and assorted proponents of Foo, whatever that is.

Finally, Porky meets the Dodo, an aggressive prankster who taunts and teases him unmercifully. Porky gives chase, but the wily Dodo has a magical command over space and its dimensions. He produces a pencil from thin air and draws a solid-looking door, then hoists it up like a curtain to duck underneath and disappear—just in time for the pursuing Porky to slam against it. The Dodo later exits in a two-dimensional elevator that appears on the horizon—without depth or any connection with tangible reality—and rises into the sky. A moment later the bird reappears, resting on the Warner Brothers W-B shield, which springs out of the distance and comes close enough to allow the bird to give Porky a short tweak before retreating. When the Dodo seems cornered in another chase, he merely lifts the "scenery" off the ground to provide himself with more open space, then hurriedly pulls in a brick wall from the side for Porky to crash into. Porky finally outsmarts the bird and jubilantly celebrates his capture of the "last" of the dodos—until a few hundred identical birds give him a hoot to let him know the score!

PORKY IN WACKYLAND is an eye-popping tribute to the unlimited horizons of the animated cartoon, a perfect example of what the medium could do with just some imagination and a lot of talent.

Clampett channeled the same kind of imagination into even more routine cartoons and made them quite special and appealing. PORKY'S FIVE AND TEN has a mischievous

One of the saner moments in PORKY IN WACKYLAND (1938). © Warner Brothers Inc.

(*Bottom*) Some of T. Hee's caricatures for COO-COO NUT GROVE (1936). © Warner Brothers Inc.

gang of fish appropriating the cargo of Porky's ship at sea and playing with the sundry objects and appliances on the ocean floor. The gags are plentiful and ingenious, but it's the happy *spirit* of the cartoon that makes it so endearing. For one thing, the design of the characters is funny in itself; for example, the fish have goofy grins that make them immediately likable. The pacing—as well as the timing—is superb. And Carl Stalling's score makes delightful use of at least a half dozen songs from such recent Warners' features as HOLLYWOOD HOTEL. (There is one amusing change in lyric. When Johnny Mercer wrote the words to "Hooray for Hollywood," he said, "Go out and try your luck/You might be Donald Duck." No one in the Warner's hierarchy gave it a second thought, but when it came time to use the song in this cartoon, Donald's name was changed to Daffy, for obvious reasons.)

While Clampett was making strides in the black-and-white Porky films, other directors were breathing life into the color MERRIE MELODIES cartoons. Friz Freleng began using caricatures of Hollywood stars in many of his subjects, with delightful results. AT YOUR SERVICE, MADAM featured an engaging W. C. Fields character; COO-COO NUT GROVE boasted a gallery of stars, from Clark Gable to Greta Garbo; and CLEAN PASTURES gathered the leading black performers of the day—Louis Armstrong, Fats Waller, Cab Calloway, Bill "Bojangles" Robinson, Stepin Fetchit, and even Al Jolson in blackface! The use of caricatures sometimes improved otherwise routine stories (like A STAR IS HATCHED), and often inspired clever, topical gags keyed to these celebrities' well-known mannerisms or personalities.

"I had a man working for me who was a great caricaturist by the name of T. Hee (later prominent at the Disney studio). He caricatured everybody around the studio so well that I started using that in cartoons," recalls Freleng. "It was difficult for some animators who could not imitate the drawings that closely. A caricature, as you know, would be an exaggeration of a feature, and if that feature moved out of place the character didn't look right. But we had a very good model sheet that showed two or three different angles that the animator was able to follow. If it was a difficult kind of caricature, you were limited in what you could do."

Tex Avery played with the MELODIES format and was responsible for one distinctive if unexciting short, MISS GLORY, which employed highly stylized art-deco designs contributed by Leadora Congdon. But Avery's major contribution to this series came a few years later with a film called THE ISLE OF PINGO PONGO. A spoof of then-popular travelogues, which abounded in spoofable clichés, this cartoon was a great success and introduced a new format to the Warners' studio: the blackout-gag cartoon, strung together by an off-screen narrator. Few follow-ups were as good as PINGO PONGO—in which the inevitable "sun sinking slowly in the west" is made possible by a character machine-gunning Old Sol out of the sky—but Avery and others found this blackout gag formula agreeable for many years to come.

Tex Avery's development of a unique gag style and a free-wheeling approach to the cartoon medium reached its zenith at Warners' in a 1939 entry called THUGS WITH DIRTY MUGS. The film overflows with visual and verbal jokes, many defying cartoon convention, others falling into the general category of "visual puns."

The gags become more startling as the cartoon continues. Racketeer "Killer" and two cohorts sneak into a dimly lit house and soon decide that there are too many people there, so they send their shadows away. Best of all,

during one of Killer's speeches we see the tiny silhouette of a man in the movie "audience" getting up to leave. Killer quickly tells him to sit down, afraid that he'll squeal to the cops, but in the next scene the silhouetted man stands up again to tell the police chief what Killer's next robbery is going to be. He knows because he's seen the film before! (Bob Clampett recalls that this amazingly lifelike illusion was achieved by rotoscoping gagman Tedd Pierce.)

Avery's insistence on wilder and funnier gags every time out led to such amazing results. He was probably his own best gagman, but he inspired the official Warners' writers to stretch their imaginations as far as they would go. The Warners' gag artists are, without a doubt, the unsung heroes of cartoon history. "These kids," said writer Michael Maltese in an interview with Joe Adamson, "these cartoon writers were the backbone of this business. Dave Monahan, Tedd Pierce, Cal Howard, Rich Hogan,

Tex Avery's Egghead in a typical greeting. © Warner Brothers Inc.

Tubby Millar, Jack Miller, and Bugs Harda-way—they're the crazy bunch. They're the ones that came up with the wild humor."

Through most of the 1930s these writers worked in a kind of pool system. Whenever a director was ready to start a new picture, he would see who was free or who had an idea. This way each director worked with most of the staff writers at one time or another. Later, the situation changed as certain writers and directors paired off—Bob Clampett, then Friz Freleng with Warren Foster, Chuck Jones with Michael Maltese.

But even then the longtime studio practice of "jam sessions" continued. Chuck Jones says, "In our place, one of the things that always helped enormously was that we always worked parallel. There was a point when any one of us started a picture and we had a premise that we thought would work. Then the other writers and directors would meet in a room. We would throw gags at that premise, unselfishly. The result was that we were not competing . . . we were helping each other, and it kept us from trying to exceed one another because we were always contributing.

"We had no hesitation in adopting ideas from other people's pictures. If it worked for them, it would work for us. So the result was that unconsciously we were really working as a 'house,' but we were essentially separate also. And then at the end of the picture, when we had the whole thing done on storyboard, before it went into animation, we would have another session for criticism, to see if there were any holes that anybody could recognize."

In this way the Warners' cartoons were produced in a true spirit of collaboration, with creative input by directors, writers, animators, the composer, the voice actors, and the sound effects man going into each film. No one person was ever wholly respon-sible for the finished product—but at the same time each director had the freedom to choose or reject ideas as he pleased and to filter the many suggestions and contributions through his own point of view.

Directors at the studio were not specifically charged with the task of inventing new star characters, but the hope always burned bright that each new cartoon would introduce a personality strong enough to build into a major property. "Stars" were as important to a cartoon studio as they were to a live-action film company: They gave a movie marquee quality and made it easier to sell to theater owners.

After Porky Pig, the next characters to emerge were Daffy Duck and Egghead. Daffy made his debut in PORKY'S DUCK HUNT (1937), directed by Tex Avery. Bob Clampett animated the now-famous scene in which the web-footed loony introduces himself to hunter Porky by declaring, "I'm just a darn-fool duck!" and bouncing off into the horizon, leaping and gesturing madly all the way. Audiences were unaccustomed to such an aggressively screwy character and the Warners' crew realized they had hit on an unusual "find." The duck was officially christened in his second cartoon, DAFFY DUCK AND EGGHEAD, and co-starred with a human character—if that's quite the description—called Egghead, whose bulbous head and nose gave him a certain distinction, and whose voice was patterned after radio comedian Joe Penner.

Daffy's role in life is to act daffy—he sings the LOONEY TUNES theme song, "The Merry-Go-Round Broke Down"—and confound hunter Egghead as much as possible. Just when Egghead thinks he has a chance of snaring the duck, however, two mallards in white suits appear to take their comrade away to the nut house. After saving him from the clutches of Egghead, they abandon their serious pose and join Daffy in a frenzied, hyperactive exit, bouncing merrily and *hoo-hoo*ing all the way. (The "hoo-hoos" were inspired by comedian Hugh Herbert.) It is significant that Ben Hardaway, who wrote this short, also directed PORKY'S HARE HUNT and HARE-UM SCARE-UM, the embryonic Bugs Bunny shorts, and wrote KNOCK KNOCK, the first Woody Woodpecker cartoon for Walter Lantz. The similarities among these cartoons and their respective characters are most intriguing.

Oddly enough, Tex Avery chose to drop Daffy Duck at this time in favor of Egghead, whom he featured in a series of middlingly funny shorts. Egghead was too odd to generate any real charisma, however, and was best used as an incongruous participant in gag situations (as in the delightful HAMATEUR NIGHT), not as a star character. He later evolved into Elmer Fudd.

It remained for Bob Clampett to seize on Daffy as a potential star in 1938 and team him with Porky Pig, making Porky more of a straight man and Daffy the laugh getter. It was difficult to sustain stories or gags at the pace required for Daffy's energetic character, but this challenge perfectly suited Clampett's increasingly frenetic style. Clampett enjoyed playing with the space and dimensions of the cartoon frame and found Daffy an ideal guinea pig for experiments with exaggerated size (as in DAFFY DOC, in which, after iron-lung treatment, various parts of Daffy's body suddenly inflate to blimplike proportions) and relative space (as in A COY DECOY when Daffy runs frantically and plants every step on a different plane in relation to the camera, coming alternately close to and further away from the camera in a dazzling zigzag motion).

Daffy also figured importantly in one of Friz Freleng's most unusual endeavors, YOU OUGHT TO BE IN PICTURES (1940). One of the

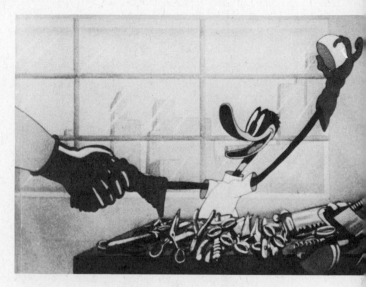

A distinctively Bob Clampett–directed Daffy Duck, in THE DAFFY DOC (1938). © **Warner Brothers Inc.**

few Warners' cartoons ever to make extensive use of live-action film, the short actually takes place at the Leon Schlesinger studio. During a lunch break while all the animators are away, Daffy (in a picture frame on the wall) speaks to Porky (in a drawing on an animator's table) and encourages him to demand a release from his puny contract and try his luck in feature films instead . . . as Bette Davis's leading man, for "three grand a week." Porky allows Daffy to talk him into seeing their boss. "Hello, Mr. Schle—, Mr. Schles—, hello, Leon," says Porky, before explaining that he'd like to get out of his contract. Schlesinger obliges him by tearing up his "cartoon contract" and wishing him luck, but after Porky leaves, he turns to the camera and says knowingly, "He'll be back."

While Porky encounters difficulties just getting admitted to the Warner Brothers lot, Daffy tries to talk Leon into hiring him as his next big cartoon star, knocking his pal Porky in the process. "Why, I'm a better actor than

Porky strikes a bargain with producer Leon Schlesinger in YOU OUGHT TO BE IN PICTURES (1940). © Warner Brothers Inc.

he ever was," Daffy declares. "Porky never did anything; I did all the work." Schlesinger isn't buying Daffy's spiel so fast, and, sure enough, when Porky returns after a harrowing time at the Warners' studio, Leon is ready to welcome him back—leaving Porky to beat the daylights out of Daffy for playing him such a dirty trick.

YOU OUGHT TO BE IN PICTURES capitalizes on the wonderful fantasy of animated cartoons. We know that Porky and Daffy aren't real, yet our eyes tell us to believe in them through this delightful mixture of animation and live action. The film is so charming that we *want* to suspend logic and believe, even if for just a few minutes, that they exist, that they are capable of talking, moving, and having distinct personalities.

The illusion is heightened in this cartoon by the ingenious matte work: Porky shaking hands with Leon Schlesinger; driving his little roadster onto the Warner Brothers lot and finding that he's right in the middle of a Western stampede; being thrown bodily off a sound stage by a member of the crew, and so on. The film ranks as the best of its kind since Fleischer's INKWELL adventures, is considerably more advanced than its predecessors, and would be topped only later in the 1940s by Hanna and Barbera's sequence in ANCHORS AWEIGH with Gene Kelly, and Disney's SONG OF THE SOUTH episodes with Uncle Remus.

How did this unique cartoon come about? "It was just a fun thing to do, and that was the reason for doing it," says Freleng today. When he told Schlesinger what he had in mind, "I don't think he quite understood what I was going to do," Freleng continues, "but he trusted me quite a bit, and he let me do whatever I wanted to do, as long as it didn't cost him a lot of money. You couldn't do that today, because we didn't even use union people. Our cameraman at the time, John Burton, was the live-action cameraman. We just took a black-and-white camera, went out and shot whatever we wanted to, without asking."*

As this cartoon humorously indicates, Schlesinger's cartoon department was considered a stepchild of the Warner Brothers studio, but its facilities came in handy when Warners' needed a short piece of animation for a main title or special sequence (as in Busby Berkeley's FOOTLIGHT PARADE). Schlesinger also accepted free-lance assignments from other companies. In 1937 David Loew commissioned a scene of the zodiac signs coming to life for a Joe E. Brown film, WHEN'S YOUR BIRTHDAY?, and the following year Par-

*Gagman Michael Maltese was pressed into service as an actor for this film to portray a studio cop. But Mel Blanc dubbed his voice (and virtually everyone else's in the live portion) because this footage was shot silent.

amount ordered an illustrated sequence of Shep Fields's Rippling Rhythm band for THE BIG BROADCAST OF 1938. In 1939 Republic Pictures keyed an entire film to a cartoon premise: SHE MARRIED A COP dealt with a singing policeman whose wife uses his voice for the sound track of a cartoon series about a pig! (The same idea was reused some years later by Gene Autry in SIOUX CITY SUE.) Schlesinger even made up animated titles for his own low-budget John Wayne Western, HAUNTED GOLD, but here, as in every other instance, he was the only one to receive screen credit for the special segment.

By the late 1930s there was another director heading his own unit at the Schlesinger studio: Chuck Jones. A skilled animator, he won his director's stripes when Frank Tashlin left the studio and Henry Binder, Schlesinger's assistant, surprised him by suggesting that he take Tashlin's place. Says Jones today, "When I first started animating, it never occurred to me that I'd be a director, I was so delighted to animate. My God, when you were an *assistant* animator in those days. . . . But once I got the feeling of direction and being a director, I never wanted to do anything else and I still don't want to do anything else."

As a director Jones gravitated to subjects that were unusually "cute" for Warner Brothers. His very first cartoon, THE NIGHT WATCHMAN, concerned a kitten who took his father's place as night watchman in a kitchen. Most subsequent cartoons during the next few years dealt with small, quiet characters and their relation to a somewhat forbidding environment: For example, two puppies get caught in a "house of the future" and grapple with all sorts of electronic gadgets (DOG GONE MODERN); a mouse with a cold breaks into a drugstore at night in search of a remedy (NAUGHTY BUT MICE); a dog accidentally throws the switch that acti-

vates an amusement park at night (CURIOUS PUPPY). Following his debut in NAUGHTY BUT MICE, Jones's first original character, Sniffles the Mouse, had a series of similar adventures in the oversized world of humans. Even PORKYS' ANT and PORKY'S MIDNIGHT MATINEE, Jones's initial films with an established character, pitted Porky against tiny creatures.

"I guess," says Jones, "in a way I was exploring a medium to find out what it could do. The miniaturization was one way of doing it."

Jones's most interesting early cartoons include two "miniature" items, TOM THUMB IN TROUBLE and JOE GLOW THE FIREFLY, and one far afield from that premise or, for that matter, anything else in the Warners' bag of tricks: OLD GLORY, commissioned by Warner Brothers to accompany its ongoing series of live-action shorts on patriotic and historical themes. OLD GLORY features Uncle Sam himself, tutoring an impatient Porky Pig on the true meaning of the Pledge of Allegiance. As the studio's first completely serious cartoon,

A publicity pose from Chuck Jones's Disneyesque TOM THUMB IN TROUBLE (1940). © Warner Brothers Inc.

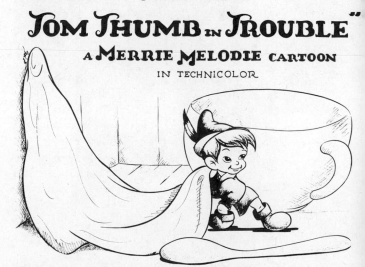

TOM THUMB ᴵɴ TROUBLE"
A MERRIE MELODIE CARTOON
IN TECHNICOLOR

it succeeds remarkably well and makes effective use of rotoscoping, montage, and dramatic camera angles. It remains somewhat jarring to juxtapose such serious matters as the founding of our country with the personality of Porky Pig, but even this character is presented somewhat differently than usual. Jones decided to use modeling on his Porky, here and in other cartoons as well, to make him and other characters more dimensional and realistic. The addition of facial shadows and coloring nuances gave Jones's early cartoons a unique appearance.

TOM THUMB IN TROUBLE is the most Dis-

Chuck Jones (seated) with layout man Earl Klein in the 1940s.

neyesque of all Jones's cartoons. A miniature fairy-tale fantasy, showing young Tom's trials and tribulations when he's left on his own in his father's cabin, it blends elements of music, comedy, personality, and melodramatic action with surprisingly good results. There's even an original song.

JOE GLOW THE FIREFLY is more humorous in intent and dramatic in its exploration of miniature life. The lead character is a firefly who wears a turned-back fireman's hat and inspects a nocturnal campsite with his trusty lantern providing the necessary light. There is no dialogue in this cartoon; Joe wanders in, over, around, and through everything, from a sleeping man's slippery fingernails to a large chunk of Swiss cheese, through which his light is refracted like a tiny aurora borealis. Brimming with clever gags and buoyed by Carl Stalling's fine music score, this is one of Chuck Jones's most satisfying early cartoons.

For the artist himself, one of the most exhilarating experiences during his first days as a director was the opportunity of working with noted comic artist Jimmy Swinnerton, who helped adapt his comic strip *The Canyon Kiddies* for the screen. Intended as the first of a series, MIGHTY HUNTERS turned out to be an especially ambitious project.

Jones, Swinnerton, and several animators went to the Grand Canyon and adjoining Indian villages to take 16mm color footage for future reference. The trip was all personal initiative, however, according to Jones. "Leon didn't put any money into it," he recalls. "We had to pay for our own gas! But it was a great experience. Swinnerton knew the area, spoke Hopi and Navajo." Upon their return, the artist then did a series of oil paintings that were actually used as backgrounds for the short—the first time Warners' deviated from the traditional watercolors. "They were sticky," says Jones. "He used a bit more linseed than most, and it was difficult to deal with because we had to lay cels over them." The effect was quite lovely, even though the cartoon itself was unremarkable. Swinnerton's Indian children were not so far removed from traditionally cute cartoon characters as to make a tremendous impact, and the series idea was dropped. "I wish I'd saved those backgrounds," says Jones in conclusion. "They'd be worth a lot today. His oils are going for fifteen to twenty thousand dollars. He was quite a remarkable guy."

Another remarkable guy was making his debut at Warner Brothers at this time. His name was Bugs Bunny.

Like most characters, Bugs evolved over a period of time, and, because of this, there have been assorted claims on his creation for many years. The following is an attempt to chronicle his early existence and to give credit where credit is due.

In terms of his prehistory, Frank Tashlin told Mike Barrier, "Bugs Bunny is nothing but Max Hare, the Disney character in THE TORTOISE AND THE HARE. We took it—Schlesinger took it, whoever—and used it a thousand times." Opinions differ on this theory of plagiarism, but it is tougher to accept when one studies the earliest versions of Bugs Bunny. Max Hare was a brash, cocky character, it's true, and some of this may have found its way into Bugs Bunny by osmosis, but Warners' rabbit was wilder and wackier than the Disney creation by a country mile.

This is especially true of the first rabbit, who appeared in PORKY'S HARE HUNT, directed by Ben Hardaway in 1938. He bears more than a passing resemblance, personalitywise, to the screw-loose Daffy Duck who debuted a year earlier in Tex Avery's PORKY'S

PORKY'S HARE HUNT (1938) features an enbryonic version of Bugs Bunny—and a now familiar situation. © Warner Brothers Inc.

DUCK HUNT. He has a nutty laugh; he hops around wildly and even flies, spinning his ears like propellers, dispensing wisecracks at every turn ("Here I am, Fat Boy!"). In a remark reminiscent of Daffy's greeting to Porky, the rabbit tells his would-be hunter, "Don't let me worry you, chief—I'm just a trifle pixilated!" Like later incarnations of Bugs, he drops his wise-guy pose at several junctures: first, to turn melodramatic when it seems that Porky has the drop on him ("Don't shoot!" he pleads); then to feign concern and sincerity (when Porky's rifle jams he steps forward to help him examine it, asking, "You're *sure* it won't work?" before taking the opportunity to browbeat Porky even more). Most intriguingly, his laugh bears a strong resemblance to the one later popularized by Woody Woodpecker, which surely is no accident, since Mel Blanc originated Woody's voice and laugh just a few years later. The design of Bugs (yet unnamed) in this short is really that of a conventional white rabbit, somewhat exaggerated and standing on two feet. It was generally agreed at the Warners' studio that this character, unchristened on-screen, was Bugs's Bunny—in other words, Hardaway's creation, although the first model sheet was drawn by Charlie Thorsen.

This same character was revived a year later in HARE-UM SCARE-UM, co-directed by Hardaway and Cal Dalton, and filmed in color. The design was altered somewhat, mostly to accommodate color, but an important feature was added—prominent buck teeth. Again, Bugs was an aggressively nutty character, teasing and torturing an unsuspecting hunter (*not* Elmer Fudd) and singing his own praises in an original ditty ("I'm so goony, looney tuney, touched in the head/ Please pass the ketchup, I think I'll go to bed"). It is significant to note that neither of the Hardaway pictures was popular enough

to warrant immediate adoption of the rabbit as a character with star potential. Joe Adamson has remarked that the reason is that the character "was more annoying to the audience than he was to his antagonist."

In 1940 Chuck Jones used the rabbit in an important transitional cartoon, ELMER'S CANDID CAMERA. The significance of this cartoon lay not in its development of Bugs per se, but in the development of Elmer Fudd, and Bugs's relationship with him. By now Elmer had his distinctive voice (provided by Arthur Q. Bryan, a radio actor best remembered as Doc Gamble on the *Fibber McGee and Molly* show, and as star of a short-lived short-subject series called THE GROUCH CLUB), as well as his name, although in design he still displays lingering signs of Tex Avery's Egghead, such as his derby hat and high starched collar. Elmer goes hunting, not to kill but merely to photograph wild animals, and comes upon "wabbit twacks." This leads him to Bugs, who, as in his earlier appearances, plays merciless and unending tricks on poor Elmer. Finally the amateur shutterbug can't stand it anymore and contorts his face in agonized frustration, shouting, "Wabbits! Wabbits!" and stalking off into the distance. This leaves Bugs to issue a triumphant laugh; and once more he sounds like the later Woody Woodpecker, with a touch of Goofy tossed in for good measure.

Tex Avery then appropriated the rabbit and Elmer Fudd characters for A WILD HARE. Made the same year as ELMER'S CANDID CAMERA, it repeats several of that film's gags verbatim and draws on elements from the other rabbit films, as well as from Avery's own PORKY'S DUCK HUNT. But the essential difference in this cartoon, besides its presenting new designs for both Bugs and Elmer, is a softening of Bugs's character in a successful attempt to remove him from the loony bin and mold him into a more rationally mischievous figure.

Early Bugs Bunny in HARE-UM SCARE-UM (1939). © Warner Brothers Inc.

The film opens on what might be called a classical note: Elmer, in hunter's outfit, turns to the audience and says, "Be vew-wy quiet—I'm hunting wabbits" (echoing Porky's similar statement three years earlier in the duck-hunt cartoon). When Elmer comes upon his first wabbit, the saucy Bugs's opening words are "What's up, Doc?"—a first for that indelible tag line. He quickly ties Elmer's rifle into a bowknot, then kisses him in a typically flamboyant gesture. Hunting gags abound, until Elmer believes he's actually killed Bugs, and the rabbit plays out his death scene with the sort of thespian enthusiasm Sarah Bernhardt would have admired. "I can't hold out much longer," he gasps, "Everything's gettin' dark!" This sends Elmer into a sobbing fit; he's mortified that he's killed a cute wittle bunny wabbit. But naturally it's all a ruse, and Bugs has the last laugh when he sneaks up on Elmer and kicks him soundly in the rear. "Wabbits!" Elmer cries. "Wabbits! Guns! Wabbit twaps!" As in ELMER'S CANDID CAMERA, he wanders off in total defeat, leaving Bugs to retreat to the peace and quiet of his rabbit hole.

Tex Avery is not being immodest when he says, "If anyone views A WILD HARE, they will find the personality that I gave the rabbit has not changed over the years. . . . All characters develop, of course. You take your Woody Woodpecker, your Donald Duck; the first ones were crude, awful-looking things. The same way with the rabbit. He wasn't pleasant, but we kept refining him until we had a good-looking rabbit. But all that came about through one cartoon after another—evolution." Avery is the first to admit that the physical resemblance to Disney's Max Hare is great, but, he adds, "He wasn't Bugs Bunny without the gags that we gave him."

"When we hit on the rabbit," he told Joe Adamson, "we decided he was going to be a smart-aleck rabbit, but casual about it, and I

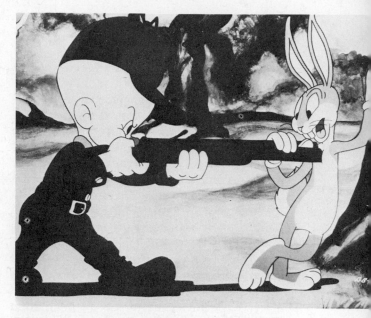

Bugs Bunny and Elmer Fudd in their first great encounter, A WILD HARE (1940). © Warner Brothers Inc.

think the opening line in the very first one [A WILD HARE] was 'Eh, What's up, Doc?' And gee, it floored 'em! They expected the rabbit to scream, or anything but make a casual remark—here's a guy with a gun in his face! It got such a laugh that we said, 'Boy, we'll do that every chance we get.'"

So it was that a great cartoon star was born.

Interestingly enough, Bugs Bunny continued to evolve during the next few years, as other directors worked with him and found what they thought were his particular strengths and attributes. Avery did three more Bugs cartoons before leaving the studio, but within a few years of his official birth, Bugs was also "directed" by Chuck Jones, Friz Freleng, Bob Clampett, and Frank Tashlin. Robert McKimson, who became a director in the late 1940s, was head animator for Clampett and designed a handsome Bugs

Bunny model sheet in 1943 that set the character for a good many years.

While Bugs was being developed, a yearly schedule had to be met, and all the Warners' directors dealt with the ongoing pressure of deadlines with remarkable finesse. During the early 1940s each one offset standard or routine entries with more adventurous endeavors that stretched cartoon boundaries.

Tex Avery directed a deceptively mild-mannered cartoon called PORKY'S PREVIEW in which Porky presented a program of his own hand-drawn animated cartoons. The results are funny and inventive, and the stick-figure animation, meant to simulate childish scrawls, bears a remarkable resemblance to the later animation of UPA. During the next few years, more conscious experimentation in the same area was pursued by Chuck Jones, with the collaboration of layout/background artists John McGrew, Bernyce Polifka, and Eugene Fleury. John Hubley acknowledged the influence of Jones's stylized cartoon THE DOVER BOYS on the later work of UPA (Bob Cannon, a UPA stalwart,

animated on Jones's cartoon); and other entries like FOX POP, BUGS BUNNY AND THE THREE BEARS, and THE ARISTO-CAT had what the director calls "stylized and formalized" backgrounds.

Jones also devised a peculiar and sometimes exasperating minah bird character as the nemesis of a youthful cannibal named Inki in such films as THE LION HUNTER and INKI AND THE MINAH BIRD. Strange, almost surreal, this character thwarted the young hunter's instinctive movements and heroic endeavors by merely appearing at unlikely moments and, with deadpan expression, walking through the scene, to the strains of Mendelssohn's overture to "Fingal's Cave," and hopping on odd beats of the music. Jones later told Mike Barrier, "Those cartoons really baffled Walt Disney. They baffled me, for that matter . . . they were really fourth-dimensional pictures, and I don't understand the fourth dimension."

(Jones has always given credit to Shamus Culhane for his outstanding animation of the lion in INKI AND THE LION. Culhane worked with Bob Cannon on this and other films, but left Warners' after just a few months. Schlesinger had lured him there with the promise that he would be able to direct the studio's war-commissioned films, but Culhane soon discovered that the producer had no such intentions. "So," Culhane says, "I went in and told the old man to perform an impossible sexual act," and he left. It was Warners' loss.)

In 1941 Friz Freleng directed the first of his great musical cartoons, RHAPSODY IN RIVETS, in which a skyscraper is constructed to the strains of Liszt's "Hungarian Rhapsody." There is no dialogue in the film; the construction foreman "conducts" the blueprints like a musical score, and the action gags are timed to, and inspired by, the expressively dramatic music.

"I love music," Freleng explains. "I can't read it, but I can feel it. When I hear it, I see things in my mind. Music inspires my visual thinking. I time my cartoons to music, and I find it helps me. Everything is done rhythmically." Normally, if Freleng had a particular music idea, he would go to see Carl Stalling, and "ask him to put it down for me in black and white on bar sheets so I could follow it, make my actions fit it." In the case of the "Hungarian Rhapsody," however, "I was so familiar with that, I didn't even need a piece of music. I've used that quite a bit. PIGS IN A POLKA was done like a ballet, and I did the story of the Three Little Pigs to the 'Hungarian Dance' by Brahms."

After a story idea or particular gag was established, these musical outings were one-man jobs for Freleng. "You couldn't work with a writer unless he understood the music as well as you did," he says. "The only way to do something [a film] like that was to sit down and plan it yourself."

In 1941 Bob Clampett persuaded Leon Schlesinger to purchase the rights to Dr. Seuss's popular children's book *Horton Hatches the Egg,* but, according to Clampett, "Leon's argument was that if I filmed the book exactly as written, it would cause a big silent smile in the theaters, but wouldn't get any laughs. So, he gave me the go-ahead only on the condition that I would guarantee some theater laughs. By the time all the arrangements had been made, Mike Maltese and I only had about two sessions in which to gag the story. We didn't even have a storyboard on Horton, but sketched the added ideas right on my copy of the book. Then, as of a Friday night, I told my animators, who were all struggling to draw Bugs Bunny alike, 'Guess what, boys? First thing Monday morning I want you all to draw like Dr. Seuss!'" The resulting film is an unusual hybrid that retains the whimsical story and

rhyming dialogue of the book but adds some typical Warners' gags and ideas, including a running joke that has Horton singing "The Hut-Sut Song."

Clampett also hit his stride at this time with some of the finest of all Bugs Bunny cartoons. WABBIT TWOUBLE—in which the credits are spelled out in Elmer Fuddese, including Wobert Cwampett and Cawl W. Stawwing—has the rabbit turning a fattened Elmer Fudd's vacation at Jellostone National Park into a nightmare.

TORTOISE WINS BY A HARE is a screamingly funny follow-up to Avery's TORTOISE BEATS HARE. In the film, Bugs, in a furiously aggressive role, is determined to discover why Cecil Turtle always gets the best of him in a race. The Turtle, a cool and clever fellow, reveals that his secret is streamlined design, so Bugs builds himself a turtle shell for the rematch race. It seems as if he's going to win this time—but members of the rabbit underworld, who've bet heavily on the race, mistake Bugs for the turtle and help the wrong man to the finish line. The movement in this cartoon is frantic, with some gags timed to the split second. Mel Blanc's performance as Bugs nearing the finish line ("I'm gonna win! I'm gonna win! Hooray for the rabbit!") is particularly good.

WHAT'S COOKIN', DOC? features Bugs Bunny as "himself" on Academy Award night, fully expecting to win an Oscar as best actor of the year. The idea is irresistible, and the use of live-action footage and montages makes it a lot of fun. But the most important aspect of this cartoon is the use of Bugs Bunny as a personality—a movie star as real as Jimmy Cagney or Clark Gable. This attitude harks back to Porky and Daffy in YOU OUGHT TO BE IN PICTURES and yields the same delightful result: the persuasive illusion that Bugs Bunny *does* exist.

If Bugs Bunny exists, then he has a life

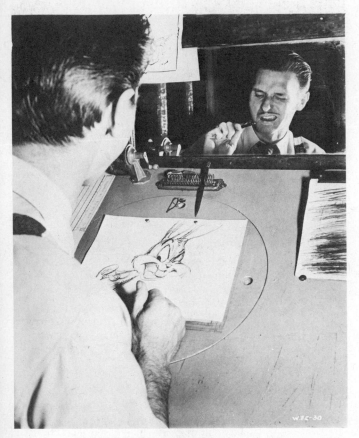

Master animator Ken Harris checks a mirror to capture just the right expression for Bugs Bunny.

history and he will grow old. THE OLD GREY HARE propels a curious Elmer Fudd sixty years into the future, to see if he eventually catches his longtime rival. Now both Elmer and Bugs are old and crotchety, but the hunt continues, and this time, Elmer manages to hit his target. Bugs does a glorious death scene, but before he passes on, he pulls out a scrapbook to recall his and Elmer's first encounter—in infancy!—revealing that nothing has changed in the twosome's long relationship. The flashback over, we return to the dying Bugs, who digs his own grave, as Elmer weeps in sorrow. Somehow though

Elmer winds up *in* the grave and Bugs (who hasn't even been scratched) piles the dirt on top to get another laugh on the thwarted hunter. Elmer rationalizes that at least he's rid of Bugs forever, but the rabbit pops his head in for one last moment and leaves a burning stick of dynamite behind! As the picture ends and the ''That's All, Folks'' title follows, an explosion is heard and the entire picture shakes in reaction.

(Clampett was one of the first to toy with action intruding on the opening and closing titles of a film; many of his cartoons actually feature action—sometimes silhouetted—under the main titles.)

Bob Clampett's output during this period is astounding. During a span of two years he directed a handful of cartoons, any one of which would be enough to cement his reputation as a giant among cartoon creators. A TALE OF TWO KITTIES introduces an embryonic version of Tweety Bird, with two Abbott-and-Costello-like cats trying to catch him for dinner. CORNY CONCERTO is a wacky spoof of Disney's FANTASIA with Elmer Fudd as Deems Taylor, introducing Bugs, Porky, and Daffy in visualizations of such themes as ''Tales from the Vienna Woods.''

Working with writer Warren Foster, Clampett came up with two of his wildest cartoons in 1943. COAL BLACK AND DE SEBBEN DWARFS is a flamboyant wartime spoof of SNOW WHITE with an all-black cast; incredibly rich in gags and in visual ideas, it was originally projected as a two-reeler but curtailed to normal length by the budget-minded Leon Schlesinger. The film's stereotyped characters and 1940s-style enthusiasm for sex leave many modern-day viewers aghast. The dialogue is strictly jive talk, and the pulsating music bounces the action along as the evil queen calls Murder Inc. to ''black out So White'' and keep her from Prince Chawmin', who has sparkling dice for front

Original theatrical poster for one of the Felix silent shorts.

© Columbia Pictures.

© Terrytoons.

© Warner Brothers Inc.

© 1952 Loews Inc. ren. MGM.

A 1936 trade advertisement; Popeye. © King Features Syndicate.

© 1952 Loews Inc. ren. MGM.

© 1949 Loews Inc. ren. MGM.

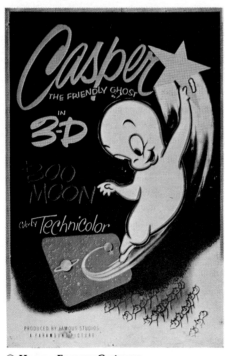

© Harvey Famous Cartoons.

© Walter Lantz Productions.

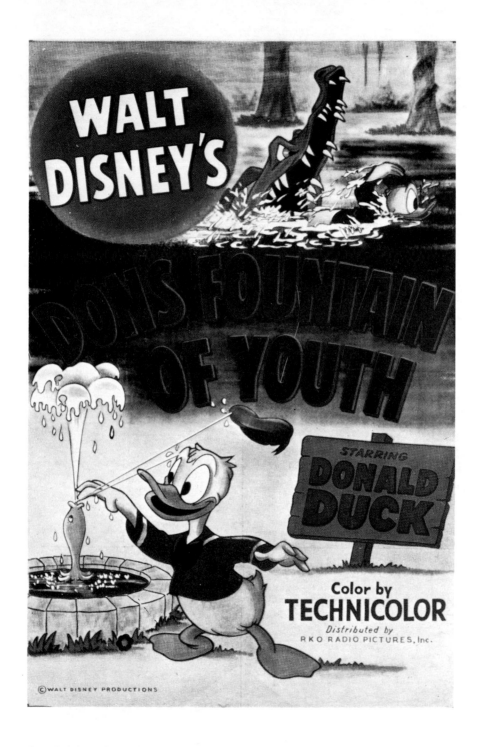

A scene from MICKEY'S GARDEN (1936). © Walt
Disney Productions.

Bugs and his ''Oscar'' from WHAT'S COOKIN,
DOC? (1943). © Warner Brothers Inc.

Woody Woodpecker makes his screen debut
with Andy Panda in KNOCK KNOCK (1940). ©
Walter Lantz Productions.

Hashimoto as he appeared in one of the CinemaScope widescreen Terrytoons of the 1960s. © Terrytoons.

Modern design and Mr. Magoo: ingredients of the UPA feature 1001 ARABIAN NIGHTS (1959). © Columbia Pictures.

teeth. Some scenes are direct parodies of the Disney feature, as when So White sings to her reflection in a washbasin and is joined by the amorous Prince. The Sebben Dwarfs who rescue So White from the frightening forest are in the Army now—and react to the fair damsel's kisses in a way that Disney's dwarfs never thought of. There's even a goofy-looking member of the crew who's an ersatz version of Dopey. The twist comes when little Dopey's kiss awakens the poisoned So White after Prince Chawmin's athletic kisses have failed.

TIN PAN ALLEY CATS offers a different black motif. A saucy Fats Waller character mocks the Salvation Army types outside of Uncle Tomcat's Mission on his way to enjoy the hedonistic pleasures of the Kit Kat Club. Fats thrives on the hot music inside and exhorts the trumpet player to "send me out of this world." With every high note he floats higher and higher until he literally bursts out of this world and into a reincarnation of Porky's Wackyland. Haunted by this apparent hallucination, he pleads for a return to earth and when this happens, he abandons the Kit Kat Club for the straight-and-narrow path of salvation.

It takes one kind of talent to find new paths for established characters, but it's even more impressive to create whole new worlds within the framework of a six- or seven-minute cartoon. Clampett did both. Many independent film makers have labored for years to create a short film as personal and unique as COAL BLACK, which was just one of a dozen shorts Clampett had to put on the assembly line in 1943.

Often it was frustrating for the Warners' directors to work under the severe time and budget restrictions that they did. Once a film was past the actual animation stage and into the finishing processes of inking, painting, and camera work, there was little if any opportunity to alter the creation.

"That was another factor that probably made our directors become very, very fastidious—the animation was fixed," Chuck Jones explains. "When we timed a picture and sent it to the animators, that was it—zero—there was no cutting, no editing at all. So, first some of the pictures were a little lengthy. . . . Then we learned how to time things to precisely the right length. And precisely the right length was 540 feet, six minutes; that's what we were allowed.

"The Disney pictures were edited; that's one of the reasons they're probably a little sloppier in terms of timing, because they knew that if it wasn't right, they could edit it, the way a live-action director edits."

Knowing this makes the achievements of the Warners' directors all the more impressive. As Jones often points out in his lectures on animation, "The difference between humor and nonhumor can be one frame—cutting on one frame or the next."

The man most interested in cinematic

Director Bob Clampett reviews the storyboard for THE GREAT PIGGY BANK ROBBERY **with animator Michael Sasanoff, animator Tom McKimson, and (partially hidden) gag man Hubie Karp. Notice the picture of "So White," from Clampett's** COAL BLACK **cartoon, on the wall.**

techniques for cartoons, Frank Tashlin, returned to Warner Brothers in 1943, after stints at Walt Disney and Columbia studios. Now more than ever, Tashlin was eager to be working in live-action films, and he imbued his cartoons with strange, experimental camera angles and directorial flourishes. BROTHER BRAT probably boasts the most bizarre camera compositions, while SWOONER CROONER is his most conventionally funny effort—a hilarious outing in which Frank Sinatra and Bing Crosby roosters vie for the attention of hens at Porky Pig's farm.

But Tashlin's masterpiece at Warners' this second time around was undoubtedly PORKY PIG'S FEAT (1943). Not only an extremely funny cartoon, it is a directorial tour de force in which every major gag is staged in a flamboyant visual manner. The story involves Porky and Daffy's battle of wits with the officious manager of the Broken Arms Hotel who won't let them leave the premises until they pay their bill. When the manager "insults" Daffy, the dauntless duck responds by shoving his face against the manager's and launching into a breathless tirade. As

Daffy continues, he pushes his head deeper and deeper into the pudgy manager's face, contracting it like a prune before plunging himself free.

Other incidents take place out of camera range or reveal themselves to the audience in unusual ways. When Porky and Daffy send the manager sailing down a long circular staircase, we see him plummet step by step as a reflection in their eyes—first Porky's left pupil, then his right, then Daffy's left and right, until the manager springs out of eyeshot.

But the best gag of all is the finale. Trapped in their hotel room like bonded prisoners, Daffy and Porky bemoan their fate

Elements of a storyboard for A HARE GROWS IN MANHATTAN (1947).

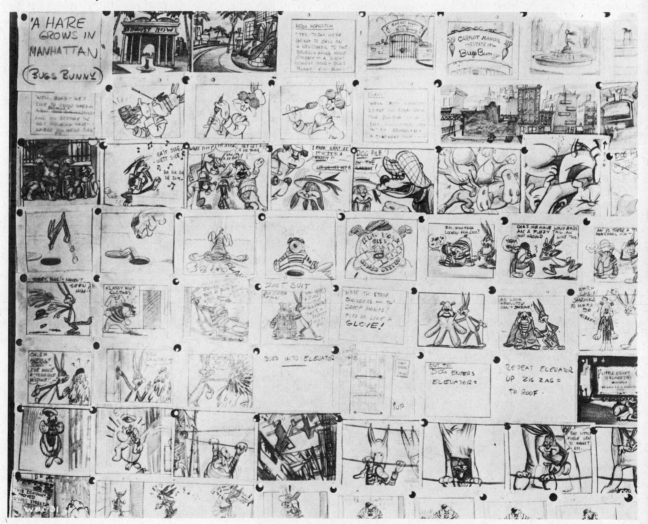

and agree that they'd be free in a moment if only Bugs Bunny were there. "Yeah, Bugs Bunny, my hero—he can get out of any spot!" Daffy exults. "I saw him in a L-L-Leon Schlesinger cartoon once," Porky recalls and he enacts with Daffy Bugs's unfailing triumphs over adversaries. Daffy rolls his ball and chain over to the telephone and calls the rabbit direct. "What's up, Duck?" Bugs replies. "That palooka manager has got us locked up in the Broken Arms Hotel. We thought you could help us get out," Daffy explains.

"Did you try the elevator?" asks Bugs. "Yes!" says Daffy.

"Throw him down the stairs?" "Yes!"

"Use a sheet?" "Yes!"

"Swing across on the rope?" "Yes," says Daffy, "we tried all those ways."

At this point a door opens and we see Bugs in the room next door, talking on a phone and manacled just like Daffy to a ball and chain. "Ahhh," says Bugs cheerfully, "don't work, do they?" Blackout.

Tashlin stayed at Warners' for two years before leaving to pursue a full-time career writing, then directing, live-action films. (While he always favored cartoonish, slapstick sight gags, he particularly dwelled on them in his earliest scripts. Edward Bernds recalls a production conference when he was assigned to film a chase Tashlin had plotted out for KILL THE UMPIRE (1950). Jack Fier, Columbia's production manager, digested Tashlin's elaborate script and snapped, "That son of a bitch has written a cartoon sequence! You gonna get somebody to draw it? We gotta photograph it!")

Before leaving Warners', Tashlin reportedly directed the first PRIVATE SNAFU cartoon. SNAFU was the name for a series of short black-and-white cartoons that were included in wartime issues of THE ARMY-NAVY SCREEN MAGAZINE and shown exclusively to American soldiers. Running three to four minutes, they featured a foul-up named Snafu as a kind of military everyman and dealt with a variety of serious subjects, from learning to use and trust maps to maintaining secrecy in wartime. Becasue it was important to establish an honest rapport with the soldiers, the SNAFU films went beyond traditional Hollywood propriety in the use of four-letter words, broad sexual imagery, and mild scatological humor, and threw in such bonuses as cameo appearances by Bugs Bunny (in THE THREE BROTHERS) or an episode in which the series star appeared as SNAFUPERMAN.

"Storyboards had to be approved by the Pentagon," Chuck Jones recalls, "but it was fairly loose and we did throw in a lot of business. Of course, Geisel was fun to work with—Ted Geisel [Dr. Seuss] and Phil Eastman wrote the series. We did other kinds of training films too, for the Navy. They were usually done on a cost-plus basis."

Aside from these specially commissioned films for the armed forces, Warners' did a fair share of topical cartoons for theatrical audiences as well. Norman McCabe, an animator who served briefly as a director in the early 1940s when Tex Avery left the studio, piloted some undistinguished wartime cartoons like TOKIO JOKIO, CONFUSIONS OF A NUTZY SPY, and THE DUCKTATORS; in the latter, characterizations of Hitler, Mussolini, and Hirohito as web-footed characters prompts a note from "The Management" in the middle of the cartoon reading, "We wish to apologize to the nice ducks and geese who may be in the audience." Similar works by other directors included SCRAP HAPPY DAFFY, FIFTH COLUMN MOUSE, PLANE DAFFY, and HERR MEETS HARE. Subtlety was never the aim of these endeavors: In BUGS BUNNY NIPS THE NIPS, the rabbit sells Japanese soldiers on a Pacific island Good Rumor ice cream bars with hand grenades hidden inside, snapping as he doles out the desserts, "Here y'are, Slant Eyes." Similarly, Bob Clampett's RUSSIAN RHAPSODY features a grotesque caricature of Adolf Hitler and shows him mentally and physically picked clean by a corps of "Gremlins from the Kremlin" who sing of their presence to the strains of "Orchechornya."

War-related gags and slogans found their way into many Warners' cartoons during this time. (Subsequent generations of children have absorbed such timely expressions as "Lights out!", "Is this trip really necessary?", and "food hoarder" through watching these cartoons on television, never understanding their true meaning until more serious confrontation with the history of World War II in school or elsewhere.) In BROTHER BRAT Porky is baby-sitting for a woman who works at the "Blockheed" munitions plant, while SUPER RABBIT ends with Bugs Bunny announcing, "This looks like a job for a *real* Superman"—a U.S. Marine.

One of the best of these "home front" wartime cartoons is Clampett's DRAFTEE DAFFY, in which the loony duck tries to avoid a mousy little man from the draft board who's determined to serve Daffy with his "Greetings" notice. The sheer energy of this cartoon is overpowering. Daffy barricades himself inside his house but can't seem to escape this omnipresent messenger. At one point he soars upstairs and then down a corridor to the isolation of a remote closet. As he streaks up the stairs he produces a furious rocketlike exhaust and creates a suction that pulls all the furnishings in the hall along with him! It's no use, however. Even when Daffy launches himself on a rocket reserved "in case of induction only" and it plummets him through the surface of the earth into hell, he cannot escape the persistent man from the draft board. Like all Clampett characters of the 1940s—particularly those animated by Rod Scribner—Daffy is extremely

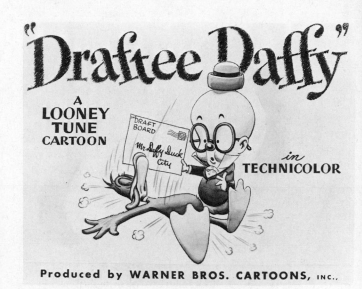

rubbery and tends to poke his face toward the camera during emotional outbursts.

By this time Daffy was the number-two character in the Warners' stable, next only to Bugs Bunny. Porky Pig was still around, but for the most part the writers and directors felt burned out on this character after the flood of films they had made with him in the 1930s and early 1940s. Moreover, the cute stuttering pig simply wasn't as forceful or timely a character as Bugs and Daffy, who were ideally suited to the raucous atmosphere of the war years. When he was featured, Porky now tended to be either a straight man in gag situations or a partner to Daffy.

Daffy, on the other hand, offered the Warners' staff rich opportunities and reached a peak around this time. He shared with Bugs a self-awareness as a cartoon character that was particularly endearing. In DAFFY DOODLES he saves antagonist Porky from falling off a building ledge and comments characteristically, "Mighty sporting of the little black duck!" He was also a flexible enough character to play with in a wide variety of situations—none wilder than Clampett's THE GREAT PIGGY BANK ROBBERY, in which he pictures himself as Detective Duck Twacy, doing battle with such colorful characters as Neon Noodle, Pumpkinhead, and Jukebox Jaw.

In AIN'T THAT DUCKY Daffy meets a most unusual adversary: an Elmer Fudd–like hunter who looks and sounds just like veteran comic actor Victor Moore. That's because it *was* Victor Moore. Friz Freleng recalls, "I approached him and wanted to know if he'd do it. He said he'd love to do it. We did a caricature of him, showed it to him, and he said, 'I love it, if you'd just put more hair on my head.'" Moore did his own voice and wouldn't charge Warners' a cent.

In 1944 what had loosely been referred to as the Warners' studio became that in fact. Leon Schlesinger sold out his interests to Warner Brothers and retired. He was not particularly missed by his employees, but their new boss, a company veteran named Edward

© **Warner Brothers Inc.**

Selzer, proved to be even worse. Like Schlesinger, he had no knowledge of, or fondness for, cartoons, but he tended to interfere more than his predecessor ever did. Chuck Jones recalls the time that Selzer walked into a story session when he and his comrades were laughing over a freshly minted gag and the producer snapped, "What the hell has all this laughter got to do with the making of animated cartoons?" Naturally, it rankled when this man was the one to accept the studio's Academy Awards and take the bows instead of the men who had created the Oscar-worthy films.

There was even greater distance between the cartoon makers and their chief executive Jack L. Warner. Although they frequently dropped his name in their cartoons (Daffy notes a script discrepancy in AIN'T THAT DUCKY and warns the errant animator, "J. L. will hear of this!"), the animators and directors had little, if any, contact with him or his brothers.

"I didn't even see Jack or Harry Warner until fifteen or twenty years after I started working there," says Chuck Jones. "He couldn't even remember my name or Friz's name. When he saw us together, he'd call us Mutt and Jeff because I was tall and Friz was short."

Other changes were taking place at the Warners' studio: Yearly output was now stabilized at twenty-six cartoons a year—thirteen LOONEY TUNES and thirteen MERRIE MELODIES. In fact, distinctions between the series titles disappeared in 1943 when the LOONEY TUNES were graduated to full color: the only difference from that point on was theme music.

Bob Clampett left the studio in 1946 to join the ill-fated Screen Gems group. His head animator, Robert McKimson, was promoted to the director's chair, and cartoon veteran Art Davis was recruited to share the responsibility of maintaining the yearly output. Davis's reign was short, but he turned out some excellent cartoons, and in films like WHAT MAKES DAFFY DUCK? he tried to carry on the frantic Clampett style. He was reportedly the one who recolored Clampett's PORKY IN WACKYLAND for its 1949 release as DOUGH FOR THE DO-DO. (Davis subsequently returned to the studio to become one of Freleng's top animators.) Some of the distinctive humor in Davis's cartoons can also be credited to a young staff writer named Bill Scott, who left around the same time Davis did, to join UPA. Scott later wrote and co-produced the memorable Bullwinkle television cartoons with Jay Ward. Another short-lived staffer was Pete Burness, who animated for McKimson in the late 1940s before joining UPA as director of the MR. MAGOO series.

It is worth noting that some of the cartoons in this period were filmed and released in the two-color process Cinecolor, for the presumed purpose of saving money. Fortunately this decision was soon reversed and the studio reverted to the brilliant hues of Technicolor.

Besides staff and procedural changes, the mid-to-late 1940s saw the development of several new cartoon stars as well.

Bob Clampett had featured a tiny canary who uttered the famous phrase "I tawt I taw a putty tat" in several films, including A TALE OF TWO KITTIES. But the character was dormant until Friz Freleng resurrected him, changed his design, and paired him with another recent creation, Sylvester the Cat. The resulting cartoon. TWEETIE PIE, won an Academy Award at the 1947 Oscar ceremonies. Thereafter, Tweety was used by Freleng exclusively (with occasional exceptions, such as his "cameo" appearance in Jones's NO BARKING), but Freleng and other directors

Tweety as he first appeared in Bob Clampett's cartoons. © Warner Brothers Inc.

found that Sylvester was a flexible enough character to fit into a variety of situations. Freleng cast him with delightful results in such films as BACK ALLEY OPROAR (in which his nocturnal vocalizing keeps Elmer Fudd awake) and DR. JERKYL'S HIDE (in which Sylvester turns into a monster after drinking a scientist's potion), while Robert McKimson gave him a pint-sized son named Junior for a series of shorts that ran for many years, ranging from POP 'IM POP (1950) and TOO HOP TO HANDLE (1956) up through CLAWS IN THE LEASE (1963). (Sylvester's sibilant voice, incidentally, was originally the same as Daffy Duck's but recorded at normal speed. Later, Mel Blanc evolved separate voice personalities for the two characters.)

Freleng counts Sylvester as one of his favorite characters and points out, "When he was after Tweety, what happened to *him* was the fun of the show. People would say, 'Oh, Tweety was so good.' Well, Tweety didn't do anything, really, it was all Sylvester."

While this is basically true, Tweety scored his points as the funniest straight man in a cartoon team. His wide-eyed, babyish delivery and sentiments mask a character as wily and resourceful as Bugs or Daffy, and his "innocent" remarks while he pummels the hapless Sylvester ("You know, I lose more putty tats that way!") are often the delight of the films. The addition of a permanent owner for Tweety, a kindly old woman named Granny, provided Sylvester with just one more obstacle to his goal of devouring the little bird.

In point of fact, Sylvester does swallow Tweety on many occasions, but, because of cartoon license, he never gets to the point of digestion. In BAD OL' PUTTY TAT, when Sylvester pops the bird in his mouth, Tweety becomes visible in the whites of Sylvester's eyes and then appears in one of Sylvester's ears and decides to "engineer" the cat like a locomotive. One of the funniest cartoons in the series is built around Sylvester's profound sense of guilt when he thinks he *has* eaten the bird. THE LAST HUNGRY CAT paints a melodramatic picture of Sylvester's anguish, framed by an Alfred Hitchcock–

© Warner Brothers Inc.

type narrator. Of course, there's a happy ending and the promise of further scraps between the two, Sylvester's remorse notwithstanding. Needless to say, Tweety always survives.

Hinged on a one-note relationship, the Tweety and Sylvester films were seldom innovative, but usually enjoyable; some, like I TAW A PUTTY TAT and BAD OL' PUTTY TAT, are excellent by any standards.

Chuck Jones's concurrent creation, Pepe LePew, introduced in THE ODOR-ABLE KITTY, suffered from an even more restrictive formula and never escaped the sameness of story lines, which Tweety and Sylvester avoided. As a one-shot idea, the formula was superb, and the impact of Pepe's third appearance, in FOR SCENT-IMENTAL REASONS, was strong enough to win the film an Academy Award. The premise is simple: Somehow, white paint is poured on the back of a female cat, making her appear to be a skunk. Pepe LePew, an aggressively amorous French skunk, falls madly in love with the cat and pursues her, blind to the fact that she is repelled by him.

Since the story is essentially the same in most Pepe cartoons, the fun derives from bogus French dialogue ("Un skunk de pew!") and signposts ("Le Village de N'est-ce Pas" or, in translation, "The Village of Nasty Pass"), and Pepe's overripe remarks about his sexual prowess ("Not every man would put up with thees—lucky for her, I am not any man!"). If nothing else, these cartoons gave Mel Blanc ample opportunity to test his Gallic dialect and Jones's designers a chance to fill the screen with ornate French furniture.

Another character emerged from the newly formed Robert McKimson unit. WALKY TALKY HAWKY (1946) officially starred Henery Hawk, whom Chuck Jones had introduced four years earlier in SQUAWKIN' HAWK, but a

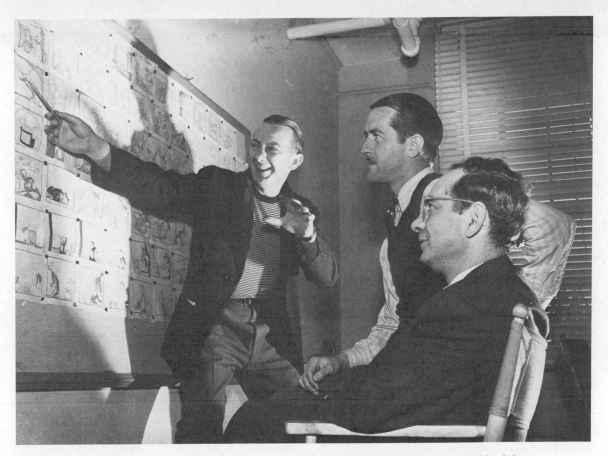

Story man Warren Foster acts out a storyboard for director Robert McKimson and producer Eddie Selzer.

new character stole the show: Foghorn Leghorn, a garrulous rooster. While most people thought he was based on Kenny Delmar's Senator Claghorn, from the Fred Allen radio show, McKimson traced his ancestry to the sheriff character on an earlier program, *Blue Monday Jamboree*. Whatever the case, this loud-mouthed southern rooster made such an impression that he, and not Henery, became the star of a long-running series, with the little chicken hawk in a supporting role and a grumpy barnyard dog as his chief nemesis.

Much of the fun in these cartoons derives from Foghorn's movements, which are broad and overstated, just like his nonstop chatter ("Pay attention, boy . . . Now listen here—I say, listen here. . . ."). Perhaps because it was his creation, McKimson was able to spark this series with enthusiasm and imag-

ination—qualities sorely missing in his other cartoons.

A fine animator, McKimson turned out to be an uninspired director. Working alongside Jones and Freleng, with the same characters and access to the same talent pool, he missed the mark with alarming frequency. It may have been his practice of starting with a written script and then preparing his production sketches that gave his films such an earthbound feeling. He was capable of making good cartoons, and sometimes did—but there is no question that his were the weakest entries in the Warners' output.

Aside from Foghorn Leghorn, McKimson introduced several other characters: Sylvester's sharp-tongued son; Hippety Hopper, a nondescript kangaroo; and the Tasmanian Devil, a pint-sized, growling monster who was cast opposite Bugs Bunny.

Director Friz Freleng (seated) goes over plans for a Daffy Duck cartoon with his layout man Hawley Pratt.

"I developed him because we were looking for a new character," McKimson told Roger Bullis in 1970 with regard to the monster. "I made two of them, I think, and my boss [Edward Selzer] told me not to make any more because he was too obnoxious. Actually he was just a stupid foil. He could tear things apart, but a guy like Bugs Bunny could frustrate him. Shortly after that, Jack Warner asked Eddie Selzer, 'What's happened to the Tasmanian Devil?' And Eddie said that he'd stopped making them. 'Get back and make some more of those,' [said Warner] 'He's a funny character.'" And

that's how one character survived.

Bugs's most *durable* antagonist was created in the mid-1940s. Yosemite Sam, that sawed-off cowboy, made his debut in HARE TRIGGER (1944) and came into his own in subsequent appearances throughout the 1940s and 1950s. Writer Michael Maltese says he actually patterned Sam after the volatile Friz Freleng! A rip-roaring outlaw type whose pint size matches his brain capacity, Sam is Bugs Bunny's ultimate patsy, and this was what made him so appealing to his director. "You couldn't do anything with Bugs unless you had a very strong adversary," Freleng contends. "Yosemite Sam was the power character," and, echoing his feelings about Tweety and Sylvester, he explains, "The things that happened to Yosemite Sam were the fun of the picture, not what happened to Bugs, 'cause nothing could happen to Bugs—he caused it all."

The "unreality" of Sam's appearance—his height, his oversized cowboy hat, enormous eyebrows and moustache, his uncontrollable temper—enabled Freleng to use him in a variety of incongruous settings with amusing results; the runt-sized villain turned up in various films as a desert sheik, a pirate captain, a medieval knight, and a Roman gladiator.

In BUGS BUNNY RIDES AGAIN Sam orders the rabbit to "dance" when he fires his gun, prompting Bugs to perform a vaudeville buck-and-wing. After one chorus Bugs hollers, "Take it, Sam!" and the outlaw goes into his time step right on cue. In BUCCANEER BUNNY Sam tries to outbluff Bugs after the rabbit threatens to explode his ship—even turning to a game of jacks in a futile attempt at nonchalance. And in the Academy Award–winning KNIGHTY KNIGHT BUGS, Sam's agitated demand that Bugs lower a drawbridge brings the heavy plank right down on his head—and leaves him pancake-shaped underneath. Yosemite Sam seemed to inspire the best in Freleng and his able gag writers.

Aside from his usual quota of short subjects, Friz Freleng directed two cartoon sequences for Warner Brothers features in the late 1940s. His first assignment was TWO GUYS FROM TEXAS (1948), in which Jack Carson and Dennis Morgan play friendly rivals. Carson describes a recurring [animated] dream to his psychiatrist in which he's a shepherd whose sheep are constantly lured away by Morgan, who makes them swoon with his rendition of "Every Day I Love You Just a Little Bit More." Bugs Bunny emerges from his rabbit hole to give Jack some advice, but it's to no avail, and "when I wake up I'm all covered with wool," says Carson. The sequence is very entertaining, and the caricatures of Morgan and Carson are first-rate.

Carson figures in the second feature-spot as well. In MY DREAM IS YOURS (1949), he's reading a Bugs Bunny bedtime story to Doris Day's son "Freddie." The youngster falls asleep and dreams of Bugs coming to life. He steps out of his book and sings a song called "Freddie Get Ready," based on—guess what?—the "Hungarian Rhapsody." Soon Doris Day and Jack Carson join Bugs in a song-and-dance number in which the live-action humans are dressed as rabbits, but Bugs Bunny, the make-believe rabbit, is wearing a dress suit. Built around an Easter motif, the number gives Freleng the chance to include a cameo appearance by Tweety Pie, who turns up inside one of the Easter eggs. Having worked with a combination of live action and animation before, on YOU OUGHT TO BE IN PICTURES, Freleng found no difficulty in plotting this musical number. The unpretentious handling of these unexpected cartoon interludes accounts for much of their effectiveness.

The Warners' cartoon department did no further feature-film work for fifteen years, although it did accept some government assignments for special short subjects during the 1950s.

The period from 1946 to 1956 saw the flowering of Chuck Jones's career at Warner Brothers, and the establishment of his own working team. As the studio solidified its three cartoon units—under Jones, Freleng, and McKimson—key creative people gravitated toward one of the three and remained somewhat constant for many years. Jones's collaborators became writer Michael Maltese; animators Ken Harris, Ben Washam, Phil Monroe, and Lloyd Vaughn (Abe Levitow and Richard Thompson joining later); layout men Robert Gribbroek and Maurice Noble; and background artist Philip De Guard.

Jones is perhaps the most articulate member of the Warners' unit, but he is hard pressed to discuss his cartoon style or personality. In terms of his approach to already-established characters, he says, "It wasn't an intellectual process, an *overt* intellectual process; it was more of a subconscious intellectual process, and things happened. I suppose it's how you change your own life-style or you change your way of dress. Unless you're an actor or a dress model, I don't suppose you do that consciously. But you gradually evolve a kind of dress style that agrees with you."

Jones's attitude towards Bugs Bunny was formulated as early as 1940, in ELMER'S PET RABBIT when Bugs declares, "Of course you realize, this means war!"* after one of Elmer's provocations. This became the slogan of Jones's Bugs Bunny. The director felt that Bugs was not insanely aggressive or antagonistic, and demanded that there always be a reason for his mischief. A quin-

*Even though the phrase had been used by the Bugs prototype in PORKY'S HARE HUNT two years earlier.

tessential example of this pattern is HOMELESS HARE (1949), in which a construction worker digs up Bugs's rabbit hole and surrounding turf to make way for a superskyscraper. Naturally, the rabbit doesn't take this lying down and engages in a series of skirmishes with the construction man that ends with the hapless worker waving a white flag. In the final shot Bugs is lounging in his rabbit hole, preserved intact right in between two enormous buildings. "After all," says our hero, "a man's home *is* his castle!"

Jones loved to explore his characters—"to find out how much you could do with them." He refined his grasp of comic nuance to the point where he could get a laugh just by having a character wriggle his eyebrow.

He and writer Michael Maltese had particular fun casting Daffy Duck as a frustrated fall guy and pitting him against super-cool Bugs Bunny in films like RABBIT FIRE, RABBIT SEASONING, and DUCK! RABBIT! DUCK! Maltese provided brilliant comic dialogue for these cartoons, and Jones used that dialogue to key

his characters' expressions. The visual and verbal humor is brilliantly unified in films that might have been static talkfests in another director's hands. One could watch RABBIT SEASONING silent and still be entertained; Daffy's facial contortions and body language explain as much as the dialogue.

In 1953 Jones and Maltese created a miniature masterpiece called DUCK AMUCK, in which Daffy's angst reaches its zenith. It opens with Daffy in a D'Artagnanlike role, brandishing his sword and lunging toward the left of the screen. Eventually he moves past the painted backdrop and finds himself against a blank white space. At this point he addresses the unseen animator: "Hey, *psst* . . . whoever's in charge here . . . the scenery! Where's the scenery?" A series of confrontations with the animator follows in which the scenery repeatedly changes behind Daffy's back, just as he's adapted his costume and manner to the previous setting. Daffy's all-powerful "master" changes the duck's looks, replaces his voice with a rash of sound effects, and plays with the film frame. When Daffy yells for a close-up, the camera moves in so far that the screen is filled with Daffy's bloodshot eyes.

These outrageous tricks continue until Daffy can take no more. Exhausted, defeated, he pleads, "All right, enough is enough. This is . . . the very last straw. Who is responsible for this? I *demand* that you show yourself!" The camera pulls back to reveal the unseen figure at the drawing board as Bugs Bunny, who turns to the audience and says with an impish smile, "Ain't I a stinker?"

DUCK AMUCK has its roots in the silent-film antics of Koko the Clown and Max Fleischer, but, in its battle between character and creator, goes beyond mere novelty to reach a plateau of high comedy.

Film buffs love DUCK AMUCK because it offers several levels of interpretation. Louis

Black has written, "The cartoon stands as an almost clinical study of deconstruction of a text, in the way it presents a whole at the beginning and then dismembers every facet of the cartoon, only to put them together at the end."

To Jones, the purpose of the film was simpler, but no less admirable: "To say that Daffy can live and struggle on an empty screen, without setting and without sound, just as well as with a lot of arbitrary props. He remains Daffy Duck."

Proof that this cartoon is based as much on character motivation as it is on comic technique is provided by a look at Jones's remake, RABBIT RAMPAGE. This time Bugs Bunny is the animated victim and Elmer Fudd is at the drawing board. Although some of the visual gimmicks are fun to watch, the concept of the film is all wrong. We don't enjoy Bugs's frustration as we do Daffy's; it's an unlikely defeat for a normally indefatigable character.

Although DUCK AMUCK represents a high point in the treatment of Daffy Duck, Jones continued to have fun with the character in a number of other situations. And he found a new use for Porky Pig—as a Greek-chorus sidekick to balance Daffy's bombastic blunders. In DUCK DODGERS IN THE 24½TH CENTURY Daffy is a futuristic hero who's more concerned with his ego than anything else, and Porky is a space cadet; in DRIPALONG DAFFY and MY LITTLE DUCKAROO he's the Masked Avenger, and Porky (with stubble on his face!) is called Comedy Relief; in DEDUCE YOU SAY, Daffy is Dorlock Homes and Porky is his Dr. Watson; and in ROBIN HOOD DAFFY the duck tries to prove his identity to a doubting Friar Tuck, played by Porky.

Challenging and satisfying as his cartoons with Daffy, Bugs, Porky, and other characters were during this time, Jones did some of

his finest, most personal work in the assorted "one-shot" cartoons that appeared every year. Occasionally, running characters emerged from these cartoons—Hubie and Bertie, Claude Cat, Charlie Dog—but most of them were limited and short-lived.

Among these one-shot films are some hilarious Three Bears cartoons featuring a diminutive, hot-tempered Papa Bear, voiced by veteran Billy Bletcher (best remembered as the Big Bad Wolf); a sweet but stupid Mama Bear (who in recent years Jones has compared to ALL IN THE FAMILY's Edith Bunker), voiced by Bea Benadaret; and a delightfully dimwitted, overgrown baby bear named Junior, blessed with a memorably dumb voice by Stan Freberg. In WHAT'S BREWIN', BRUIN? the fairly simple premise has the bears trying to get to sleep for winter hibernation, but being disturbed by all manner of annoying sounds. In A BEAR FOR PUN-

"Marvin Martian" has just met his interplanetary match in DUCK DODGERS IN THE 24½TH CENTURY (1953). © Warner Brothers Inc.

ISHMENT the traditional series formula goes haywire as Mama and Junior present the unwilling Papa with an extravagant Father's Day pageant of songs, dances, and readings. Among the highlights is a preposterous tap dance performed with an utter deadpan expression by Mama. Jones considers that dance, executed by Ken Harris, "one of the finest pieces of animation ever done any place." It was inspired by Mike Maltese, "who could really dance that way," adds Jones.

Many of Jones's one-shots involve cute animal characters, while others are disturbingly wicked or violent (SCAREDY CAT, CHOW HOUND, FELINE FRAME-UP). PUNCH TRUNK doesn't really have a point, or a punch line, but presents a disarming situation in which an elephant five inches tall sends a big city into an uproar. FROM A TO Z-Z-Z takes an unusual turn in featuring a little-boy character who daydreams. But one of the most successful of these one-shots, which manages to be endearing but never cloying, is FEED THE KITTY (1952), in which the enormous bulldog Marc Anthony jeopardizes his relationship with his mistress in order to protect an adorable little kitten whom he's adopted. Again, it's character expressions and attitudes that "make" this cartoon as much as the actual story line—and no one could beat Jones for designing and then "posing" expressive characters.

Jones's were also the best-*looking* cartoons at Warners', not only because of his talented staff of animators, but because of his close collaboration with layout man Maurice Noble, who replaced the talented Robert Gribbroek about 1953. To help clarify this misunderstood term "layout", Friz Freleng explains, "Every director works with their layout man a little differently. I made my rough sketches and poses, and used Hawley Pratt to work over the characters and clean

them up for the animators. Other directors used a layout man to do the backgrounds only. Hawley did the backgrounds *and* cleaned up my poses. Jones would pose all his own characters and his layout man would just do backgrounds, he couldn't draw characters. Bob McKimson was the same; he'd draw all his poses, and his layout man was just a background artist."

Explaining the distinction between layout man Noble and officially credited background-artist Philip de Guard, Jones has said, "Phil was an excellent follow-up man, certainly, and he's a fine painter, but he bears the same relationship to the layout man, in preparing a picture, that a contractor does to an architect in constructing a building." Again, the importance of collaboration comes through as one examines these cartoons.

Noble explained to Joe Adamson in a 1971 interview: "We always tried to find a solution which seemed appropriate to a story, whether from the directorial standpoint or the graphic standpoint. The style came out of the cartoon, instead of vice versa. I think one of the strengths in Chuck's cartoons has always been just that: approaching each one as a fresh start. . . . Chuck was the kind of person that *wanted* fresh ideas.

"Many times Chuck would have an idea for a cartoon, and it would be either a rough storyboard or just a rough outline of a story. And he'd call me in and give me a general idea of what we were going after. He might say, 'I need material there and here.' So I would take his sketches and start weaving them into a continuity of graphics. And out of the graphics, sometimes, would come another facet of the cartoon: a gag, or staging, or even a complete dramatic switch in the middle of the cartoon. Then he would go back and introduce it into the story as he developed it and laid out the animation."

Noble's contributions are most apparent in Jones's spectacular cartoons—DUCK DODGERS IN THE 24½TH CENTURY and the later WHAT'S OPERA, DOC?—but his talents enhanced even unspectacular cartoons with appealing and often striking graphic designs. (In TO HARE IS HUMAN he put modern art on the walls of Bugs Bunny's rabbit-hole home.)

Graphic design was just one of many factors that contributed to the success of the ROAD RUNNER series, Jones's most popular and successful creation at Warner Brothers. Launched in 1948 with FAST AND FURRY-OUS, this series satisfied Jones's fondness for working within a disciplined structure and challenged his ability to formulate new ideas within that framework. The stories pit the Coyote, a scraggly character with eyes that can be alternately shifty and pitiful, against the lightning-quick and ever-smiling Road Runner, who escapes the Coyote's various traps unharmed, while the hapless creature suffers the consequences of each backfired contraption. In the history of Hollywood cartoons there has never been another series with so many consciously applied ground rules, most of which appeared in the very first film featuring The Road Runner (*Accelerati Incredibus*) and Wile E. Coyote (*Carnivorous Vulgaris*).

Among the rules that Jones adhered to are the following: The cartoons always take place in the same desert setting. The Road Runner and Coyote never speak.* The Road Runner never leaves the road. The Coyote's injuries are always self-inflicted. No matter what misfortune the Coyote suffers, he always appears intact after the fade-out, ready to try again. His mail-order machines and appli-

*Several attempts to give the coyote a voice were unsuccessful.

Wile E. Coyote and The Road Runner. © Warner Brothers Inc.

ances are almost always from the Acme Corporation. He and the Road Runner are always introduced by bogus Latin names. And, finally, the Coyote never catches the Road Runner.

Jones has admitted that a primary influence on his series was Frank Tashlin's 1941 Columbia cartoon THE FOX AND THE GRAPES, and similarities between this Fox and Crow "blackout" cartoon and the ROAD RUNNER series are remarkable. But Tashlin didn't pursue his idea and rejected the notion of the formula as a self-imposed discipline. Jones developed an almost classic format based on the age-old idea of blackout jokes, and enhanced it with intriguing characters.

Those who feel that the ROAD RUNNER cartoons are senselessly violent are missing the point. The ROAD RUNNER format has been copied in television and theatrical cartoons since the mid-1950s, but in none of the imitations have the characters been imbued with the qualities that set Jones's work apart. The Coyote is a tangible and completely sympathetic character, even though he appears in the guise of a "villain" stalking his innocent prey. (The Road Runner's perpetual smile may not be so innocent, but he never actually causes the Coyote any harm, except by sneaking up on him and uttering his "Beep Beep" call). The Coyote, says Jones, "represented me and my failure with tools," and won the hearts of audiences through his incredible determination in the face of total ineptitude.

The Coyote's facial expressions are as important to the films' success as any of the elaborate gags Jones and Michael Maltese devised. When the Coyote propels a huge rock from a teeterboard and it crashes down on his own instead of the Road Runner's head, the laugh comes not only from the backfired scheme, but from the look of utter futility on the Coyote's face as the shadow of the boulder looms overhead.

Jones has said that speed and gravity are the major forces at work in the ROAD RUNNER cartoons, and certainly they account for a large number of the Coyote's problems in catching his would-be victim. It follows that if the Coyote manages to get his rocket-propelled roller skates to work, he will not only catch up to the Road Runner but pass him, out of control, and soar off the edge of a cliff. In ZIPPING ALONG, the Coyote (*Road Runnerus Digestus* this time) chops a tree in order to set a trap. But the tree turns out to be a telephone pole, and when it falls the wires pull down a row of poles, one of which batters the Coyote into the ground. In READY, SET, ZOOM, the Coyote (*Famishus-Famishus*) spreads glue on the road; the Road Runner races through and splashes the gook on his adversary, who finds himself welded to a burning stick of TNT. In THERE THEY GO-GO-GO, Wile E. (*Famishus Fantasticus*) mounts eight sticks of dynamite on the spokes of a wheel which he pushes into the path of the Road Runner as he whizzes by—but as the wheel rolls away, the sticks of dynamite remain resolutely in place, to explode in the Coyote's face.

Jones soon discovered that it took an average of eleven such gags to fill a ROAD RUNNER cartoon; some were extended, some unexpectedly brief, and some bounced off each other for a cumulative effect. He also called on special talents from some of his collaborators, including meticulous effects-animation by men like A. C. Gamer and Harry Love, and the unique sound effects of Treg Brown.

"Treg Brown was a fabulous character," says Jones. "He'd once been a guitarist and vocalist for Red Nichols and his Five Pennies. He was one of the few great comic sound cutters; I told him to look for incongruities, and he did. Once we had a coyote and sheep-dog film and we showed boulders rolling towards the wolf. Instead of using the regular sound effect, he used the sound of a locomotive—and it worked. In ZOOM AND BOARD, the Coyote uses a Captain Ahab harpoon gun, and of course his foot gets caught up in the rope. Well, Treg used every sound effect except the proper ones for this scene— he had horns, and oinks, and all kinds of things—and I'll tell you something, people have looked at that thing, people who know about film, and they don't notice it . . . which is wonderful, of course. His sound effects gave the cartoons a great deal of subconscious humor." In keeping with the idiosyncratic way of giving credits at Warner Brothers, this innovative sound-man was listed as "film editor" throughout his career at the studio.

Discussing the phenomenal worldwide popularity of the ROAD RUNNER series, Jones says, "The coyote is only trying to get the Road Runner to eat. Now, I think that can be understood anyplace. And yet, if you want to make it philosophical, it comes back to a quotation by Santayana: 'A fanatic is someone who redoubles his effort when he's forgotten his aim.' Obviously, he doesn't even want the Road Runner anymore. He's now become compelled to follow something he doesn't even want! It seems to me my life is composed of things like that. If there's a universal thing, it is our attempt to accomplish things that are very small, but become big because we can't do them."

The Coyote was such a wonderful comic character that Jones decided to try him outside of the ROAD RUNNER series. He turned up in occasional films with Bugs Bunny, including TO HARE IS HUMAN, but he was used more effectively in another formula series featuring a taciturn sheep dog. These pun-ny titles (SHEEP AHOY; DOUBLE OR MUTTON; READY, WOOLEN AND ABLE; A SHEEP IN THE DEEP) featured Road Runnerish blackouts of the Coyote, now supposedly a wolf, trying to evade an omniscient sheep dog and to abduct some of his flock. The key difference between these films (all of them extremely funny) and the ROAD RUNNERS was a cunning concept: At the beginning and end of each story, the coyote and sheep dog are replaced by look-alikes, who, as they matter-of-factly punch a time clock and set their lunch pails aside before going to "work," mutter a tired "Hello, Sam," "Hello, Ralph" to their colleagues!

There was a definite advantage to doing a formula-gag series like the ROAD RUNNER, as Jones explains: "We made ten pictures a year and they had to average 540 feet. Of course, we cheated. We never saw budgets, we never dealt with money at all. But they [the administrators] knew that there was a director, a writer, a layout man, a background

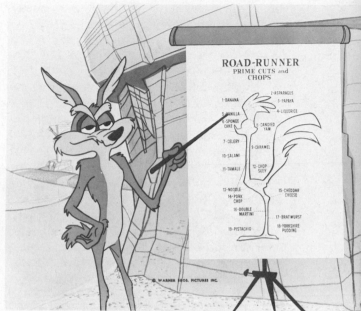

© **Warner Brothers Inc.**

man, four animators and four assistants, a week of a musician, a week of a cutter, and they knew what the ink and paint cost generally because we all used the same ink and paint. If we turned out a picture every five weeks, we didn't have to have a budget—but we had to finish the picture. The way we cheated was, if I got an idea like WHAT'S OPERA, DOC?, which actually ran more than 540 feet and took maybe seven weeks to do, I knew the ROAD RUNNER so well that I could do a ROAD RUNNER in *three* weeks. So the two pictures together would come out at ten weeks. And the front office never knew the difference, because I had everybody cheat on their time cards. So they thought we were working on the ROAD RUNNER for two weeks before we actually were.

"They were always a little surprised when it went to ink and paint; the cost of ink and paint would drive up, and then they'd raise hell . . . because there were more drawings and they were more intricate. Fortunately, the producers were not very bright and they sure didn't understand animation. So as long as it came out even over a period of a year you could get away with it.''

The kind of special projects Jones refers to include two of his finest and most celebrated cartoons: WHAT'S OPERA, DOC? and ONE FROGGY EVENING. WHAT'S OPERA, DOC? is the film in which ''we took the entire fourteen-hour *Ring of the Nibelungen* music and crushed it down to six minutes.'' Elmer Fudd and Bugs Bunny star in this Wagnerian opera, performing against awesome rock-formation settings, with Elmer as a helmeted warrior and Bugs eluding the hunter by disguising himself as a golden-tressed Brunhild. Their dialogue is sung, not spoken, and opens appropriately enough with Elmer singing, ''Be vew-wy quiet/I'm hunting wabbits.'' Later he vows to ''kill the wabbit,'' to the strains of the Valkyries' theme, and in the film's major set-piece, he and Bugs sing a duet entitled ''Return, My Love,'' penned by that well-known librettist Michael Maltese. Elmer finally *does* kill the wabbit, and then mourns his loss, carrying him off into a blazing sunset as the orchestra swells on the sound track. But then Bugs suddenly lifts his head and says to the audience, ''Well, what did you expect in an opera—a *happy* ending?''

It isn't difficult to see why this short took so long to make. While there are normally 60 backgrounds in a six-minute short, this one has 104—and each shot in WHAT'S OPERA, DOC? is a complicated affair. The designs are bold and forceful, with vibrant colors and shadows. (''They thought I was bats when I put that bright red on Elmer with those purple skies,'' Maurice Noble recalled. ''I had the Ink and Paint Department come in and say, 'You *really mean* you want that magenta red on that?''')

The musical aspects of the film are equally impressive. The full Warner Brothers orchestra rises to the occasion, as do Mel Blanc and Arthur Q. Bryan in their singing roles. Blanc always sang well, but Jones was delighted to discover that Bryan had a fine, legitimate singing voice that came through even in his Elmer Fuddese rendition. For the serious ballet sequence, Jones and his animators studied Titania Riavachinska and David Lichine of the Ballet Russe. Tremendous effort was expended to make this an exceptional film, which it remains today.

Not that WHAT'S OPERA, DOC? was noticed any more by Warner Brothers executives, film critics, or journalists than other assembly-line cartoons of the period. (It wasn't even nominated for an Academy Award.) But as Jones is quick to point out when he introduces programs of his work, ''These cartoons were never made for children. Nor were they made for adults. They were made for *me*.''

Of all the characters Jones created, the one that means more to him than any other is the main character in ONE FROGGY EVENING, unofficially known as Michigan J. Frog. ''I think he's my favorite because I don't understand him,'' Jones contends. The centerpiece of an offbeat allegory, the frog is discovered by a construction worker in the cornerstone of a demolished 1892 building. Without warning, the frog produces a top hat and cane and performs a cakewalk as he loudly sings, ''Hello, My Baby.'' The worker is mesmerized, and fancies himself a millionaire when he thinks of how he can exploit his ''discovery.'' This happiness is fleeting, however, because the frog resolutely refuses to perform for anyone—be it a booking agent, a theater audience, or a cop on the beat. In the man's presence he launches into exuberant performances of ''Please Don't Talk About Me When I'm Gone'' and ''Come

Back to Erin," but he manages to finish just as outsiders appear, whereupon he drops his professional pose and reverts to the limp posture and sullen expression of an ordinary frog. Defeated, broke, and having been committed to a mental institution, the former construction worker finally seizes an opportunity to dump the frog in the cornerstone of a new building. The picture dissolves to the year 2056; in this future society, the Tregoweth Brown Building is being demolished by a man with an Acme disintegrator gun. When he comes to the cornerstone, out jumps the very same frog to sing "Hello, My Baby" and inspire mercenary thoughts in his newest discoverer, who carries him off to start the cycle all over again.

Critic Jay Cocks has called ONE FROGGY EVENING "a morality play in cameo that comes as close as any cartoon ever has to perfection." Neither Jones nor Maltese set out to preach a lesson or create a meaningful parable. But somehow their film possesses a hypnotic fascination that offers renewed pleasures with each successive screening.

"The frog took a lot of study to make it work," says Jones. The key to the film's success was the creation of a character who alternated between complete believability as a garden-variety frog and credible exaggeration as a high-stepping entertainer; moreover, the transition had to be plausible. Jones and his animators took the time to study real-life frogs in order to reach this happy result. And, for collectors of such trivia, it might be noted that Jones and Michael Maltese made one other contribution to the film: an original song called "The Michigan Rag," which masqueraded as an authentic 1890s tune.

Jones also presided over two different kinds of milestones during the 1950s: the only cartoon ever to win an Academy Award as best documentary of the year, and the stu-dio's one-and-only 3-D cartoon. The documentary was called SO MUCH FOR SO LITTLE, and it was commissioned by the Public Health Service. Jones and Friz Freleng met with representatives in Washington, who Freleng recalls, "felt that this [a cartoon] was a way of reaching a lot of people" with their message on the importance of health services and sanitation. Jones and Freleng wrote the script on their train ride back to California, and then Jones directed the eleven-minute film. No one was more surprised than they when, a year later, at the 1950 Academy Award ceremonies, it was awarded an Oscar.

The 3-D cartoon was commissioned by Jack Warner in 1953, at the height of popularity for the 3-D theatrical gimmick. LUMBER JACK RABBIT was heavily promoted and presumably intended to be shown with such 3-D Warners' features as HONDO and HOUSE OF WAX, but it failed to generate much excite-

Bugs Bunny in his only 3-D cartoon, LUMBER JACK RABBIT **(1954).** © **Warner Brothers Inc.**

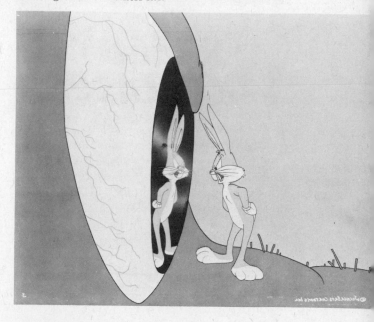

ment. The *Motion Picture Exhibitor* commented, "This cartoon does not seem to take full advantage of the 3-D medium. The humor is not as sharp as in most Bugs Bunny cartoons, and gimmicks in 3-D are conspicuous by their absence." In fact, the film's major bow to the process comes directly at the beginning, when the Warner Brothers shield springs much closer to the camera than usual—as if to pop out of the screen—before retreating to its usual position amid the familiar concentric circles.

In making this cartoon, the actual simulation of 3-D was engineered by the studio's veteran cameraman/handyman John Burton, but director Jones could not completely disguise his boredom with the gimmick itself.

At this point Jack Warner decided to close the department, concluding that the industry would soon be shifting to 3-D on a permanent basis and that it would be too expensive to produce all his animated cartoons in this process. Most of the staff was laid off, and Chuck Jones spent four months working for Walt Disney before studio chief Warner changed his mind and reactivated the cartoon unit. The 3-D craze died out almost as quickly as it had flared up.

The cartoon department did make other transitions at this time, however. One was the adoption of stylized, less literal backgrounds, in the wake of the UPA design revolution. "I thought it was the trend," says Friz Freleng. "And we wanted to be contemporary, so we stylized them a little, but I didn't know if they fit our characters as well. Our characters weren't stylized the same way the backgrounds were, so we tried to hit a happy medium and didn't go to extremes the way UPA did. UPA did highly stylized backgrounds, but the characters *fit* the backgrounds. Our characters were set, so it was pretty hard to do. Bugs Bunny was a dimensional character, so we didn't want to use flat backgrounds."

But Freleng, Jones, and McKimson did find an inspiration in this revisionist approach that certainly fit some of their one-shot endeavors. Freleng's PIZZICATO PUSSYCAT bears at least passing resemblance to UPA's GERALD MCBOING BOING and CHRISTOPHER CRUMPET in telling the story—with narration—of an ordinary human couple, their cat, and an extraordinary mouse, who wears oversized eyeglasses and plays jazz on their toy piano.

Freleng's latest discovery was another starring character, the last to join the Warners' roster and the latest to win an Academy Award: Speedy Gonzales. The idea for Speedy was hatched in a McKimson cartoon of 1953 called CAT TAILS FOR TWO, in which a dumb cat-and-dog team (reminiscent of Tex Avery's Steinbeck-inspired characters,

One of Friz Freleng's Academy Award winners. © Warner Brothers Inc.

"SPEEDY GONZALES"

a Merrie Melodie ~ CARTOON ~ COLOR BY TECHNICOLOR

© WARNER BROS. CARTOONS INC.

A WARNER BROS. CARTOON

George and Lenny) sneak onto a Mexican ship in search of mice, but find that the Latin rodents are too fast and too smart to be caught. The leading mouse is unnamed in this cartoon and bears little resemblance to the later Speedy: He is scrawnier and much toothier, a caricature of a Mexican peon.

McKimson let the character go after this one film, but Freleng remembered him two years later, redesigned him, established a working formula, and decided to use Sylvester as his adversary. The resulting cartoon, SPEEDY GONZALES (1955), won an Academy Award and launched yet another Warners' series. Speedy, like the Road Runner, is an ever-smiling, ever-confident character who always comes out on top of a situation. His primary asset is his speed; neither Sylvester nor anyone else can catch or even come near him when he zips along in search of cheese. Speedy earns his title as "the fastest mouse in all Mexico," but has little else going for him. He is a one-note personality, and the success of his films depends entirely on strong gags. When they're good, as in SPEEDY GONZALES, the results are excellent. Later entries tend to be repetitious, however.

Freleng added more feathers to his cap by directing two more Academy Award-winning cartoons at this time: BIRDS ANONYMOUS (1957) and KNIGHTY KNIGHT BUGS (1958). These are neither Warners' nor Freleng's best, but there is even less logic in the short-subject awards than in the feature-film category, so one must appreciate any recognition of the Warners' cartoon studio, which for years saw its best product bypassed at Oscar time in favor of Disney, MGM, and UPA cartoons.

BIRDS ANONYMOUS is an ingenious parody by Warren Foster in which Sylvester is persuaded to attend a "B.A. meeting." The persuading is done by a mild-mannered cat who sees Sylvester about to devour Tweety and

The ultimate in role reversal. © Warner Brothers Inc.

warns, "I wouldn't do that if I were you." At the meeting reformed felines get up to speak. "I was a three-bird-a-day pussycat," says one. "Being on a bird kick cost me five homes," another declares. Sylvester is inspired by their dedication and vows to give up birds. Back home, his willpower is tested by constant reminders of birds: a cooking show on TV that features a luscious turkey, a radio medley of such songs as "Bye, Bye, Blackbird," and the like. His B.A. friend stops him from weakening on several occasions, but Sylvester finally breaks down, throws a tantrum, and wails, "I'm weak! I can't help it! After all, I *am* a pussycat!" He's especially game to return to his former ways when his even-tempered B.A. counselor suddenly reverts to native instinct and takes after Tweety. In the end the canary concludes, "Once a bad ol' putty tat, always a bad ol' putty tat!"

KNIGHTY KNIGHT BUGS is an amusing, if unexceptional, contretemps between Bugs

"The HONEY-MOUSERS"

A LOONEY TUNE CARTOON TECHNICOLOR®

A WARNER BROS. CARTOON

One of Robert McKimson's many television spoofs in the 1950s. © Warner Brothers Inc.

and a Black Knight who bears an uncanny resemblance to Yosemite Sam.

Freleng and Warren Foster worked as closely together as Jones and Michael Maltese, and turned out some excellent cartoons in the 1950s. Among the most unusual is a Bugs Bunny called HARE BRUSH, which takes the relationship of Bugs and Elmer Fudd to its most outrageous extremes: Millionaire industrialist Elmer J. Fudd is committed to the Fruit Cake Sanitarium because he thinks he's a bunny rabbit! One day Bugs goes strolling by, and Elmer convinces him to switch places in return for an unlimited supply of carrots. Elmer hops away and Bugs is left to be treated by the resident psychiatrist, who gives him a special pill and makes him repeat the words, "I am Elmer J. Fudd, millionaire. I own a mansion and a yacht," until he is completely brainwashed. Now Bugs takes the place of Elmer, donning his hunting clothes and telling us, "Be vew-wy quiet, I'm hunting wabbits!" Elmer pops out

of his rabbit hole and asks, "What's up, Doc?"

At this point the film sadly falters and becomes a standard Bugs-Elmer hunting encounter. The novelty of role reversal quickly wears thin, and the idea of Bugs being placed in the position of fall guy is predictably uncomfortable. The story ends when an IRS official comes to take Bugs (as Elmer) away to jail for nonpayment of back taxes. Elmer turns to the camera and says, "I may be a screwy wabbit, but I ain't going to Alcatraz!"

It's a shame that such an intriguing premise couldn't have been followed through in wackier fashion, by turning other cartoon conventions topsy-turvy instead of remaining grounded to them. One can only imagine what Tex Avery might have done with such an idea!*

Through the years Freleng's brightest inspirations continued to come from musical sources. From A HARE GROWS IN MANHATTAN (1947), which is keyed to Bugs's jaunty rendition of "The Daughter of Rosie O'Grady," to SHOW BIZ BUGS (1957), in which rival Daffy plants a bomb to go off if and when Bugs hits the proper note in a xylophone rendition of "Those Endearing Young Charms," Freleng never missed with this kind of material. One of his favorite routines involved a particular piece of old-fashioned music summoned forth whenever Bugs Bunny found himself in a tap-dancing situation—in such films as STAGE DOOR CARTOON and BUGS BUNNY RIDES AGAIN—and always with delightful results.

*This example lends further support to the notion that Warners' cartoons are properly identified by their director's stamp. When he was writing for Bob Clampett in the 1940s, Warren Foster was wild and uninhibited. His cartoons for Friz Freleng in the 1950s are still very amusing, but much more even-tempered. The change is in the collaboration, and the dominant factor is the director's personality and point of view.

His most bizarre musical cartoon is MOUSE MAZURKA, in which a mouse explodes himself into the hereafter by drinking liquid TNT and performing a Russian dance with a bit too much gusto. But his last innovative musical cartoon was THE THREE LITTLE BOPS, in which the story of the Three Little Pigs was transposed to a tale of three jazz musicians and a wolf whose trumpet playing is strictly square. With music by Shorty Rogers ("Carl Stalling didn't know that kind of music at all," says Freleng), rhyming narration by Warren Foster, and sung in jazzy fashion by Stan Freberg, THE THREE LITTLE BOPS is a charming and unique cartoon.

Few such gems emerged from the Robert McKimson unit during the 1950s. The director's favorite, and justifiably so, was THE HOLE IDEA (1955), a clever short about a man who invents portable holes. But this was more a triumph of concept than of execution. McKimson worked first with Warren Foster, and then with Tedd Pierce on stories. From the late 1940s to the mid-50s, his animators included Rod Scribner, Phil DeLara, John Carey, J. C. Melendez, and Charles McKimson; then from that point on he worked steadily with Warren Batchelder, Tom Ray, George Grandpre, and Ted Bonnicksen. McKimson occasionally did some animation himself.

His most distinctive cartoons were a series of television-show parodies. Some of them, like THE HONEYMOUSERS and its sequel, CHEESE IT, THE CAT, are amusing in their portrayals of still-familiar performers (Jackie Gleason and Art Carney)—even though the humor derives mostly from the imitations, and not original gag or story ideas. But other TV-inspired efforts like CHINA JONES, PEOPLE ARE BUNNY, and WILD WILD WORLD have lost whatever topical impact they may once have had and cannot boast the period charm that distinguishes the cartoons of the 1930s or the war years. The most interesting aspect of WILD WILD WORLD is its Stone Age sequence, with gags that predate THE FLINTSTONES by several years.

A notable curio among McKimson's films in this category is THE MOUSE THAT JACK BUILT. Again, the cartoon is only mildly funny, the gags and story heavily dependent on its parody source, *The Jack Benny Show*. As in THE HONEYMOUSERS, the entire cast is portrayed as mice. But the difference here is that Jack Benny, Mary Livingstone, Don Wilson, and Eddie "Rochester" Anderson provided their own voices. The story involves defeating a cat who wants to get into Jack's notorious cheese vault. At the end of the film Jack Benny appears in live action, sitting in a living room chair and saying to the audience, "Gosh, what a crazy dream!" At that point the cartoon mice parade in front of him, evoking a typical Benny reaction.

It's too bad that after caricaturing Benny for years—in such films as DAFFY DUCK AND THE DINOSAUR, MALIBU BEACH PARTY, and HOLLYWOOD DAFFY—that the Warners' crew couldn't have made better use of the real Benny when they had the chance. Benny and Mary Livingstone enjoyed the novelty of doing this cartoon, however, and asked only for a print of the film as payment for their services.

One of McKimson's best cartoons was a Foghorn Leghorn that incorporated the character of Daffy Duck. THE HIGH AND THE FLIGHTY anticipates the later teamings of Warners' star characters, but does so with considerably more finesse. Tedd Pierce's inventive story has Daffy Duck coming upon Foghorn Leghorn and the barnyard dog in the midst of a typical tit-for-tat feud. "Brother!" says Daffy. "What a golden opportunity for a go-getting salesman in my line of merchandise. A traveling salesman for the Ace Novelty Company of Walla Walla,

Washington, Daffy sells Foghorn and the dog (one by one and unbeknownst to each other) elaborate practical jokes. The gags themselves are quite funny, but Daffy pushes his luck when he sells the Pipe Full o' Fun Kit #7 to the rooster and the dog at the same time. "We have been flimflammed," says Foghorn. "Yeah," answers the dog, "Hoodwinked!" Together they conspire to trap Daffy in his own novelty device, shooting him through a series of pipes and into a tiny bottle. Foghorn holds up the contorted character and says, "You know, there might—I say, there just *might* be a market for bottled duck!"

Unfortunately, later pairings of established characters failed to find as suitable a situation as this one, recklessly abandoning well-known personality traits in order to shoehorn certain characters into a ready-made story line.

The turn of the decade from the 1950s to the 1960s saw a definite decline in the quality of Warners' cartoons. It may have had something to do with a gradual breakup of the longtime studio team, or it may have been the natural winding-down after tremendous productivity for so many years.

Carl Stalling retired as music director in 1958. He was replaced by the man who had been his arranger, Milt Franklyn. Because Franklyn was so familiar with the music, it was a very natural transition. (Franklyn had filled in for Stalling before, as had Stalling's music copyist Eugene Poddany, who went on to score many cartoons for Chuck Jones at MGM.) During a musicians' strike in 1958, a man named John Seely received music credit for merely compiling stock-music themes together, for use in cartoons like GOPHER BROKE.

A major blow to the studio was the loss of writers Warren Foster and Michael Maltese, both of whom went to work for Hanna-Barbera. ("Soon all our story ideas turned up at Hanna-Barbera," says Jones. "But the difference was that they only had to do a dozen a year for us, and there they had to do one a week, so they used up the material pretty fast.")

These ingenious idea men were not easily replaced. Ward Kimball recommended a man named John Dunn from the Disney story department, and he was hired. Dunn soon did double-and triple-duty, fashioning stories for all three Warners' directors, but somehow much of the old spirit was missing.

In the early 1960s both Jones and Freleng decided to bestow "co-director" credit on their longtime layout men Maurice Noble and Hawley Pratt. "Friz and I felt the same way," Jones relates. "It seemed logical and proper; graphics had come to mean more in the cartoons. Besides, that was after Eddie Selzer had left, and we could do pretty much as we wanted. We tried to be fairer to a lot of those guys." For the first time others besides Mel Blanc were credited for doing incidental voices.

But by this time graphics were virtually the brightest thing about these cartoons; in some cases the characters seemed lost amid the bold styling and colors. Milt Franklyn died in 1962 and was replaced as music director by William Lava, a talented veteran who lacked the insouciance and song-interpolating agility that gave the earlier cartoons so much pep. Gone too was the mammoth Warners' studio orchestra, a victim of "new Hollywood" economy.

Even Arthur Q. Bryan, the voice of Elmer Fudd, was gone, having died in 1959. His absence was first noticed when Mel Blanc attempted to imitate the voice in segments of the ABC television network BUGS BUNNY

SHOW in 1960; for all his enormous talent, Blanc was never able to duplicate precisely Bryan's vocal qualities.

THE BUGS BUNNY SHOW represented the studio's last ambitious creative project. For the first time Chuck Jones and Friz Freleng worked together, assembling existing six-minute cartoons into unified half-hour programs through the use of new animation and clever linking devices. The extension of SHOW BIZ BUGS into a half-hour running gag, for instance, was inspired. But the effort that went into creating this successful television show seems to have taken its toll on the studio's continuing theatrical commitments.

The last years of production were marked by a weariness one never associated with Warners' cartoons. Fresh ideas and truly funny gags were almost nonexistent, and while Chuck Jones devised some offbeat one-shot cartoons (HIGH NOTE, NELLY'S FOLLY, I WAS A TEENAGED THUMB), these were more "interesting" than successful. Long-running series reached low points in 1963 with films like AQUA DUCK (with Daffy) and TRANSYLVANIA 6-5000 (with Bugs). Animators Gerry Chiniquy and Phil Monroe tried their hand at directing, but lacked the drive or experience to overcome weak story material.

By the time Warner Brothers decided to close its cartoon studio, the last vestige of its once-striking personality had been stripped away: The W-B shield and closing, "That's all, Folks!" were replaced by unappealing lettering and a "modern" rendition of "The Merry-Go-Round Broke Down." It was almost a symbolic break with tradition that was reflected in the quality of the cartoons themselves.

However, this was not the end of Warner Brothers cartoons. When the studio closed its doors in 1963, Friz Freleng and Warners' executive David H. DePatie arranged to lease

(*Top*) A typical example of inappropriate character match-ups from the waning days of Warner Brothers cartoons. © Warner Brothers Inc.
(*Bottom*) Merlin the Magic Mouse in action; character design in all four characters seen here is clearly influenced by Hanna-Barbera television output. © Warner Brothers Inc.

the animation plant, to start their own business. Within one year, however, someone in the Warners' hierarchy decided that it would be worthwhile to release new theatrical cartoons after all. Warners' was then in the odd position of having to contract with DePatie-Freleng Enterprises—housed right on the Warner lot—to make cartoons to be released under the Warners' banner!

Reportedly, the budgets for these cartoons were less than half the latest figure of $35,000 apiece—and the economy shows on-screen. DePatie-Freleng produced more than sixty "Warner Brothers" cartoons during the next five years, and on the whole they are abysmal.

For some reason, Bugs Bunny was never featured in these shorts. Instead, the studio relied on the most formularized of characters—the Road Runner and Speedy Gonzales—to fill out the release schedule. Woefully dry on ideas, they paired other characters together in the hope of striking comic sparks. One cartoon, THE WILD CHASE, actually starred The Road Runner, the Coyote, Sylvester, and Speedy Gonzales—with

footage rotoscoped from earlier cartoons! Daffy Duck was transformed into a humorless villain on the prowl for Speedy, and made enough appearances of this kind for one film (MUCHOS LOCOS) to be fashioned entirely from Daffy-Speedy stock footage.

The Road Runner cartoons are even worse. Directed in most cases by former animator Rudy Larriva, they destroy the mythology and *modus operandi* that Chuck Jones worked so long to establish. These cartoons are witless in every sense of the word.

Despite this decline in quality, the cartoons were still successful, and in 1967 Jack Warner decided to reorganize his own animation department. DePatie-Freleng moved off the Warner lot, and Bill Hendricks became the newest producer of Warner Brothers cartoons. Veteran Alex Lovy was hired away from Hanna-Barbera to direct a new series of Speedy and Daffy cartoons and, more importantly, to create some new characters. The results were Cool Cat, a hip kind of tiger, and Merlin the Magic Mouse, a globe-trotting adventurer with a W. C. Fields voice. While neither of these characters made a lasting impression, they were at least on a par with contemporary creations for TV.

In 1968 Lovy was replaced by Warners' veteran Robert McKimson, who introduced still more characters: Rapid Rabbit (and his nemesis Quick Brown Fox) and another pair of rabbits whose topical debut brought the studio some short-term notoriety—Bunny and Claude. Unfortunately, the aborted series was based on just one joke, a takeoff on Warren Beatty's proclamation in the Warners' feature BONNIE AND CLYDE: "We're Bunny and Claude. We steal carrots." The balance of these cartoons consisted of a redneck-sheriff chasing the rabbit couple through the countryside.

In 1969 Warner Brothers decided to stop

distributing short subjects, and that included cartoons. Bill Hendricks says today, "Although production costs had risen, the cartoons were still paying their way in theaters, with later television use still a potential. Personally, I feel that a mistake was made when the decision was made to stop producing cartoons."

Maybe so, but from the look of Warners' latest efforts, the studio had nothing much of value to offer. Without the money, or critical prestige, to draw new talent with fresh ideas, the theatrical cartoon studios were digging their own grave in the 1960s. Perhaps their demise was justified.

Warner Brothers' final shutdown also meant that the established studio stars— Bugs Bunny, Daffy Duck, Porky Pig, and the rest—would not have to be cheapened in further examples of low-budget production, and this was certainly a good thing. These characters, like their talented creators, served audiences long and well and had no need to prove themselves any further. Their heritage is among the proudest in cartoon history.

One happy postscript: Chuck Jones has in the late 1970s brought the Warner Brothers' cartoon stars back to life, in a series of new television specials, a feature-length film (THE BUGS BUNNY—ROAD RUNNER MOVIE, which incorporates new footage with old cartoons), and, best of all, a new theatrical short-subject: a sequel to DUCK DODGERS IN THE 24 1/2TH CENTURY. Ironically, interest in the latter was sparked by director George Lucas, who asked that a 70mm print of the original cartoon be shown along with his mega-hit STAR WARS in his hometown of San Francisco. (Clips from this short were also featured in Steven Spielberg's science-fiction hit CLOSE ENCOUNTERS OF THE THIRD KIND). Reaction was so strong that Warner Brothers was persuaded to finance a fully animated sequel to the twenty-five-year-old cartoon (the first of a projected series of new short subjects), and Jones succeeded in luring writer Michael Maltese out of retirement for the occasion. The film may have been completed and shown by the time this book is published. Reportedly, Friz Freleng will also undertake some of these assignments.

If some of these new projects lack the snap and sparkle of the old Warners' shorts, they nonetheless maintain Jones' high standard of animation excellence and, best of all, they keep these beloved characters alive and "working."

10

MGM

METRO-GOLDWYN-MAYER—known to all as MGM—was the Tiffany's of motion picture studios. At one time it boasted "more stars than there are in heaven," and these luminaries were showcased by the top directors, writers, cameramen, art directors, costume designers, and technicians in Hollywood. Even MGM's grade-B pictures were slick and good-looking.

There was no question that MGM would demand commensurate quality from its cartoon department. But it quickly discovered that there are some things money cannot buy.

MGM had no cartoon releases in the silent era and seemed disinterested in animation until the great success of Walt Disney. Metro reportedly wanted to sign a contract with Disney in 1929, but recoiled at the thought of a battle with Walt's financier-distributor Pat Powers. Some months later the studio dealt with Powers on behalf of his new client, Ub Iwerks, and agreed to distribute a series of FLIP THE FROG cartoons. The relationship with Iwerks lasted four years, through a second series called WILLIE WHOPPER.

Then in 1934 the studio signed a contract with two of Iwerks's contemporaries—and former Disney colleagues—Hugh Harman and Rudolf Ising. Harman and Ising had been producing cartoons for Leon Schlesinger and Warner Brothers since 1930, but left in 1933 after a financial dispute with Schlesinger. With them went the animators who had created the first Warner Brothers' cartoons, including Carmen "Max" Maxwell, Rollin "Ham" Hamilton, Norm Blackburn, Larry Martin, Robert Stokes, Robert and Tom McKimson. MGM offered the team double their Warner's budget to produce a new series of color cartoons, to be called HAPPY HARMONIES. Harman and Ising readily agreed and proceeded to turn out from eight to twelve short subjects a year for MGM release.

The HAPPY HARMONIES were just the latest in a series of titular rip-offs of Disney's SILLY SYMPHONIES—but the paraphrasing didn't stop there. Though Harman and Ising worked separately, directing their own cartoons, they shared a common goal: to rival Disney's award-winning series, with its appealing characters, imaginative stories, and elaborate trappings.

To this end an original decision to retain

275

THIS YEAR *it's* HARMAN-ISING!

Discontented Canary   Hey, Hey, Fever   When the Cat's Away   Toyland Broadcast   Lost Chick   Calico Dragon

CARTOON CHAMPS HARMAN-ISING

EXTRA!
Just Previewed
"GOOD LITTLE MONKEYS"
The Best Yet!

Look who's copped the Top Spot of the Cartoon field!

There's a New Deal in Cartoons.   It's M-G-M's Happy Harmonies Cartoons in Technicolor. When audiences began to yawn at the same old stuff, along came the Young Bloods of the Cartoon field and with a splash of color and ideas—

A 1935 trade advertisement.

the character of Bosko, from the Warner days, was reversed after two cartoons (later, Bosko was revived, but completely redesigned as a caricatured Negro boy). Instead, Harman and Ising concentrated on one-shot stories concerning cute, cherubic animals (Ising's specialty) and stylized characters personifying a particular setting or theme (Harman's forte). Typical early examples were POOR LITTLE ME, about a baby skunk who is shunned by the forest animals, and THE CALICO DRAGON, in which a rag doll and a toy horse ride for adventure in a land of calico.

The series was an immediate success. One exhibitor wrote to *Motion Picture Herald*, "Oh, how happy are we to be able to offer our patrons Metro's HAPPY HARMONIES cartoons, thus enabling us to rid our theater of the atmosphere created, in the last two years, by Willie Whopper and Flip the Frog." MGM was just as pleased, giving special promotion to the Christmastime release TOYLAND BROADCAST. Exuberant advertising copy read, "Gosh, it's a honey! Just a single reel but one of those things that steals the show!"

Personality animation, the major goal of Walt Disney, became increasingly sophisticated at the studio of Harman and Ising, and some of their work seriously rivaled the Disney artists'. A series of films about a pair of playful puppies (TWO LITTLE PUPS, PUPS' PICNIC, and the like) brought two adorable characters to life, while Rudy Ising's Little Cheezer introduced a cute mouse with a curious nature—and an irresistible voice by Bernice Hansen.

Seeing any one of the Harman-Ising cartoons of this period, one cannot fail to be impressed. They are a feast for the eye, filled with rich colors, clever designs, expressive animation. But when one examines the *body* of Harman-Ising's work, the sameness is stultifying, and the cartoons' virtues diminish in importance.

Engaging visual designs cannot take the place of stories and characterization. Personality animation is a notable achievement, but not when every personality is the same. Hugh Harman was more adventurous than his partner, but even he seemed content with hackneyed story situations once the basic concept of a cartoon was established. What's more, as their own producer-directors, Harman and Ising could indulge themselves and devote as much as eleven minutes to a single cartoon—when the story lines weren't strong enough to sustain half that length.

MGM was not happy about the cost over-runs on Harman and Ising's cartoons, and in 1937 decided that it was time to develop its own cartoon studio instead of relying on outside contractors. In a move typical of its corporate thinking, MGM installed as head of the new animation department a man with no previous experience in the field. His name was Fred Quimby, and it is popularly believed that he received this position as a reward for his long years of service as a top film salesman and executive. The most notable aspect of Quimby's personality, with regard to his new job, is that he had no sense of humor.

It was now Quimby's job to organize an in-house animation staff. But the way he went about it caused the new department several years of internal strife. First, he hired away most of Harman and Ising's staff and made Max Maxwell production manager, and Bill Hanna and Bob Allen directors. Other animators like Bill Littlejohn and Emery Hawkins were signed. Then Maxwell called his former colleague Jack Zander, who was working for Terrytoons in New York, and told him to round up as many talented animators and story men as possible. Zander, Joe Barbera, Dan Gordon, Carl "Mike" Mayer, Ray Kelly, and Paul Sommer answered the call; George Gordon followed later. A schism soon developed between East Coast and West Coast factions in the studio.

Then Quimby called Friz Freleng. "I was tempted by Fred Quimby through flattery of my work at Warner's, and an increase to almost double of what I was earning at Warner Brothers," Freleng later told Mark Mayerson. "Of course, after I had committed myself to MGM, Leon Schlesinger offered me more to stay at Warner's, but he was too late with his offer. I was committed to MGM in August, but my contract with Schlesinger expired in October 1937.

"During the period from August to October, MGM's top brass bought the rights to [the comic strip] *The Captain and the Kids*. I balked at making these characters into an animated series and expressed myself thusly, but to no avail. MGM said they were dedicated to making good cartoons, and they thought that this being printed in so many papers would make it a popular cartoon. I was forced to prove them wrong."

Theatrical poster for this unsuccessful series.

THE CAPTAIN AND THE KIDS series turned out to be something of a disaster, even though the cartoons were beautifully animated. MGM had spent a lot building animation facilities and hiring a staff; now it decided to save some money by filming this series in black and white (releasing the films in sepia tone). Even so, the money flowed more freely than it did at most other studios.

"The budgets there were much larger than the Warner's budget," confirms Freleng, "but it didn't help the pictures any because they had wrong concepts to start with. The animation might have been better, but the audience didn't recognize that. If you had more money and more time, you could get better people working on them, and you can make the characters act a little more, but if the concept was wrong it didn't matter at all." It was generally agreed that Freleng's comic expertise accounted for the best entries in this unmemorable series, with MAMA'S NEW HAT a standout among them.

Now Quimby and the MGM brass floundered. THE CAPTAIN AND THE KIDS was a flop, and something had to be done. First they hired an established comic artist, Milt Gross, whose zany ideas, zanier drawing style, and dialect humor had made him nationally famous. He started by working on some CAPTAIN AND THE KIDS cartoons, then prepared stories for two of his established characters, Count Screwloose from Toulousse and J. R. the Wonder Dog. Some of the animators balked at trying to animate Gross's intricate, highly individual drawings, and Bill Littlejohn recalls, "I got tired of hearing this, so one night I just stayed overnight and animated about twenty feet of the dog, J. R.— just slashed it out. Milt grabbed it, had it shot, and it was then proved that the things could animate."

Quimby was shocked at the finished product, however. "He didn't want to release them," says Littlejohn, "because he said they were 'below the dignity of films that MGM would want to have.' And they were *so* funny. I've never seen a bunch of animators laugh so hard. It was like Mel Brooks's kind of humor. The vitality of [Gross's] comic strips was right in the picture."

To anyone mildly familiar with Gross's work, a mere description of JITTERBUG FOLLIES, from a *Motion Picture Herald* review, is enough to bring a smile to the lips:

Count Screwloose and his Wonder Dog, pen portraits from the screwball imagination of Milt Gross, exploit a dance contest. A sour note in this musical program is the entrance of two touchy characters from the Citizen's Fair Play Committee to see that the exhibition is run on the "up and up." The contestants include Lizzy Swish, bovine swing songstress, a vocal harmony team of two penguins, and several characters from nursery rhyme fiction. An ostrich doing a fan dance wins the house's applause. The contest holders, who have been planning to take it on the "lam" with the box-office receipts, do an exit without the money bags.

Sadly, JITTERBUG FOLLIES and WANTED: NO MASTER were Gross's first and last endeavors for MGM. He was replaced by another newspaper cartoonist, Harry Hershfield, but Hershfield's indifference made his stay a total fiasco.

Finally, Quimby was obliged to turn to Hugh Harman and Rudolf Ising in a desperate attempt to save the MGM cartoon department from collapse. The two joined many of their former employees on the Culver City lot and continued making cartoons for several years until new production teams were established. Friz Freleng was delighted to receive an offer to return to Schlesinger's around this time and departed MGM with no regrets. He left behind an echo of his comedy

Model sheet for Rudolf Ising's original version of Barney Bear, as he appeared in THE BEAR THAT COULDN'T SLEEP (1939). © **Metro-Goldwyn-Mayer Inc.**

expertise, however, and studio animators acknowledge their debt to him.

The new Harman and Ising cartoons were hardly different from the old ones, except for certain improvements in animation. But among their first releases, in 1939, were two particularly significant cartoons.

Rudy Ising was kidded for years about his sleepy personality, and many of his colleagues felt he was the inspiration for THE BEAR THAT COULDN'T SLEEP. This fairly conventional cartoon introduced the character of Barney Bear—a likable, lumbering animal who in the cartoon is trying to hibernate for the winter, amid an endless series of disturbances. Barney was designed with so much detail—six eyebrows and piles of shaggy fur—that animating him seemed quite a feat. But Carl Urbano went beyond mere rudiments and gave the bear terrific feeling and personality. Says Jack Zander, "I recall scenes that Carl would animate of Barney Bear lying down in bed, snuggling down, pulling the covers up over himself, up with one eye looking around—beautiful animation. This tickled Rudy like crazy, because it was the sort of thing he just loved."

When THE BEAR THAT COULDN'T SLEEP was deemed a success, Ising directed a series of Barney Bear cartoons through the early 1940s. All of them boasted fine character animation and scored points in the development of this utterly likable character, but there was never the kind of gag and story support that would have helped to make Barney a major cartoon star.

THE BEAR AND THE BEAVERS, for instance, has a surefire situation at its core: Barney runs out of firewood and "borrows" some from a nearby beaver village. When the beavers find out, they march on Barney's house and chop it to bits, in order to retrieve their wood.

In the hands of a gag-oriented director, this could have been a very funny cartoon. But Ising does everything imaginable to *avoid* getting laughs. The film opens with a superfluous (and misplaced) storybook introduction, and the beavers are designed in the cuddly-cute manner associated with Ising's fairy tales. Everything happens at the same measured tempo, with no acceleration or exaggeration of timing. When the beavers disassemble Barney's house, they do it in regimented fashion; Ising even cuts to shots of beavers sawing, knocking away, and so forth. By making this climax so realistic in timing and treatment, he eliminates what should have been the comic highpoint of the film.

Hugh Harman's finest hour came in 1939 with the release of PEACE ON EARTH. Shown in theaters at Christmas time, when war had broken out in Europe, the film has a pacifist theme that was especially timely and a unique approach that's disarming. When yuletide carolers sing of "peace on earth, good will to men," two infant squirrels ask their grandfather what "men" are. Grandpa explains that there are no men anymore; he remembers them as "uniformed monsters"

who continually fought each other. No sooner did they finish fighting about one thing than they'd start over something else. His memories are illustrated with grim, dark, realistic scenes of men in battle, in trenches and mud fields under gloomy, clouded skies. The wars, Grandpa continues, came to a climax when the meat eaters attacked the vegetarians. Finally it boiled down to two men; when they killed each other, the world was in ruins and mankind was wiped from the face of the earth. Then the animals found, amid the debris of a bombed-out church, a Book, which laid down a series of laws that seemed to make sense. Among its admonitions was one to "rebuild the old wastes." The animals did and forged a new and happy life for themselves—which brought them to this joyous holiday season. The carolers continue their singing and proclaim once more, "Peace on earth, good will to men."

PEACE ON EARTH is a considerable achievement, of which Hugh Harman was justifiably proud. If the juxtaposition of a serious theme with "cute" animal characters is a bit jarring today, one must still applaud the film's intentions, and its overall success. MGM recognized its value and gave the short special promotional treatment, resulting in widespread publicity and several honors, including a *Parents' Magazine* medal, never before given to a short subject. It was also nominated for an Academy Award. But perhaps the greatest tribute to Harman's film was that Hanna and Barbera were able to remake it, scene for scene, in CinemaScope sixteen years later and find that it retained its original effectiveness. The 1955 version was called GOOD WILL TO MEN.

Harman never tackled anything quite like this film again, but he did achieve a potent sense of melodrama in some of his subsequent cartoons. THE FIELD MOUSE, for instance, has some harrowing scenes as the

The forest animals frolic with remnants of mankind's final war in PEACE ON EARTH (1939). © Metro-Goldwyn-Mayer Inc.

"hero" mouse is almost swallowed by a thrashing machine. THE LITTLE MOLE features similar turmoil, as a nearsighted mole, crying for its mother, is carried by the sweeping currents of a river and caught in the rapids and a whirlpool. The superlative "acting" of Harman's animators helped to make these scenes emotionally effective and to give substance to the otherwise predictable stories.

Great animation highlighted another Hugh Harman cartoon, which MGM staffers still remember with awe. A RAINY DAY features three bears, and while it isn't particularly funny (a major gag is the Papa Bear walking into a door), there is one incredible sequence in which Papa tries to repair his leaky roof during a heavy rainfall. Wind buffets the roof and turns the shingles into an ocean that sweeps about and attacks the bear, like a wave breaking against the shore! That scene was animated by Bill Littlejohn, who remembers, "I'd gotten excited about it and said, 'That's one of the ones I want to do,' and oh God, I was an idiot for volunteering. It was a staggering amount of work. There were a lot of shingles there!''

Ising concentrated on Barney Bear cartoons during his last few years at MGM, but he continued to make one-shot films as well. One of them, THE MILKY WAY, wrested the Academy Award from Disney hands after seven consecutive years. In truth, this entertaining film was no more outstanding than Ising's LITTLE BUCK CHEEZER of 1938, which, like this one, took cute animal stars on a trip to outer space.

But Ising's unit spawned something very new and special in the early part of 1940 that was to change the course of MGM cartoon production. The film was PUSS GETS THE BOOT, and while it carried only Ising's name on the credits, it was actually directed by Bill Hanna and Joe Barbera. It introduced two characters, who, as Tom and Jerry, would become the studio's leading cartoon stars.

William Hanna had had no formal training in art when he went to work for Harman and Ising in 1931. He'd studied journalism and engineering in college and worked for a short time as a structural engineer. But like so many others, he was bitten by the cartoon bug and happily accepted a low-paying job in the industry; he later described his responsibilities as having ''to run for coffee, to wipe cels, to sweep up, and to drown my bosses with story ideas.'' He stayed with Harman and Ising until 1937, when many H-I staffers moved to MGM. With his experience as story man and sometimes animator, he volunteered his services as director to Fred Quimby and was given a trial run. No one was terribly impressed, and he returned to story work. ''I was never a good artist,'' Hanna freely admitted in later years.

Joseph Barbera was a New Yorker who'd also gone to college, and had prepared for a career in banking. However, he devoted more energy to selling magazine cartoons on the side than he did to his paying job at the Irving Trust Company, and finally he decided to find full-time work in his chosen field. He landed a job at the Van Beuren studio as an in-betweener, but his enthusiasm and knack for comedy ideas led him to the story department. When Van Beuren closed, he moved to Paul Terry's studio in New Rochelle. Then he joined Jack Zander and other colleagues in a mass migration to the new MGM studio in 1937, where again he settled in the story department. His ability to sketch ideas was the envy of all his colleagues. Said Hanna, ''He has the ability to capture mood and expression in a quick sketch better than anyone I've ever known.''

Hanna and Barbera saw something in each other and fused into a tremendous working team. Hanna's background was Harman and Ising: cuteness, warmth, and the like. Barbera's forte was gag comedy. Hanna aspired to be a director and possessed a keen sense of timing. Barbera found his creative outlet in writing. They complemented each other perfectly.

PUSS GETS THE BOOT was an auspicious debut for the twosome. In addition to introducing the cat-and-mouse team that would soon achieve cartoon stardom, it drew on both directors' skills to produce comedy through situation *and* characterization. In the first place, the story is ideal: House cat Jasper is warned by his ''mammy'' housekeeper that if he breaks one more thing he'll be kicked out on his ear. A mouse (unnamed in the cartoon) sees his opportunity to get back at the bullying feline by leading him on, then threatening to break a glass, forcing Jasper to retreat. Naturally, there are twists and developments that seesaw the ''balance of power,'' but at the end the cat is ejected, while the mouse places a "Home Sweet Home" sampler above his little mouse hole.

The situations—funny enough in themselves—are enhanced by the persuasive animation of the leading characters. Tom (or Jasper, as he's called here) is mangy, moon-faced, and designed with a plethora of drawing details (no less than three eyebrows, for instance). He's convincingly real as he chases after the mouse, harassing his prey with undisguised delight—and equally credible when he cowers in fear, certain that the smashing of a vase or dish is going to get him kicked outside. The mouse bears a strong resemblance to the later Jerry, although this one is skinnier and more angular than the cuter version that evolved. However, he already possesses the range of expression—registering everything from mischievous glee to cocky pride—that made him so endearing. There is no dialogue between the cat and mouse, and none is necessary. The situations establish their adversary relationship, and the animation pinpoints their character traits.

The story is told that Fred Quimby saw nothing special in the cat and mouse and had his new directing team doing one-shots, until PUSS GETS THE BOOT was released and became an enormous hit. It was held over at many theaters and nominated for an Academy Award. At this point Bill and Joe returned to their cat and mouse, christened them Tom and Jerry, and devoted themselves to nothing else for the next fifteen years!

THE MIDNIGHT SNACK, their second film, reworked the basic premise of PUSS GETS THE BOOT with even better gag material. THE NIGHT BEFORE CHRISTMAS, released at the end of 1941, fleshed out the characters' relationship with a seasonal message of peace, as Tom befriended Jerry at the fade-out. This cartoon won Hanna and Barbera their second Academy Award nomination.

Early version of Tom and Jerry, as they appeared in PUSS 'N' TOOTS (1942). © Loews Inc. Ren. 1967 MGM.

If Quimby had any doubts about Hanna and Barbera working out as a team, they were quickly dispelled. The two clicked, and their films proved the success of the collaboration. Their working methods, in the early days, were simple, according to Jack Zander: "Joe wrote all the stories, made all the sketches, made all the layouts, and Bill Hanna wrote the exposure sheets. Joe could sit with a pencil, and ideas would come off the end of his pencil just as fast as he could move it. He could draw a storyboard so fast that it would take two people to pin the drawings up on the board while he was making them."

Although both Hanna and Barbera made use of other talents at the studio to do sketches and "pose reels" from time to time (including a highly regarded assistant animator named Harvey Eisenberg), there was no question about the creative force behind Tom and Jerry. "Bill and Joe had it all planned out, with Joe's thumbnail sketches

One of Jack Zander's expressive drawings of Jerry Mouse. © 1940 Loews Inc. Ren. 1967 MGM.

and Bill's timing, before the animators ever got it," says Irven Spence, who worked on these cartoons from the beginning to the very end of their run. "When they would hand out the work to the animators, there was a discussion, and they would act out the entire picture, in a very hammy fashion, which seemed exaggerated when they would do it, but it was just right for animation."

Bill Littlejohn concurs and says, "The storyboards looked like animators' extremes. It moved for you right there."

Because the directors planned out each short so carefully, they knew exactly the results they wanted to achieve; the animators had to work hard to measure up to those standards. Pencil tests were the route to perfection for Hanna and Barbera. Animators had to redo certain scenes as many as three and four times to catch an expression just right or sharpen the timing of a gag.

One of the best early pictures in the series is BOWLING ALLEY CAT. Just a series of gags set in a deserted bowling alley, it manipulates the attitudes and expressions of Tom and Jerry to make a funny script into a gem of a film. The stylized, slightly diffuse backgrounds that are intended to focus attention on the characters and the meticulous detail—as in the reflection of Tom and Jerry on the highly polished bowling alley floor—make this an outstanding animated film as well as a crackerjack comedy.

The frosting on the cake came from musical director Scott Bradley, who went to work for Harman and Ising in 1934 and adapted his music to suit the changing style of story and animation in the MGM cartoons. Like Carl Stalling at Warner Brothers, he had free access to the studio music library and used songs from MGM features as often as he did classical themes like the "William Tell Overture." "The Trolley Song" from MEET ME IN ST. LOUIS became a Bradley standard, and virtually every time Tom or Jerry strolled into a kitchen for food, he played "Sing Before Breakfast," from THE BROADWAY MELODY OF 1936. As the cartoons became faster-paced and more violent, Bradley's scores assimilated these qualities and complemented the action with verve and wit, not to mention superb musicianship. It is easy to take cartoon scores for granted, but Bradley devoted as much thought to his work as any feature-film composer, and utilized a broad range of musical ideas, from twelve-tone progressions to selective instrumentation. This virtuosity was not lost on the musicians in MGM's staff orchestra, to be sure. "Scott writes the most blank-blank-blank difficult fiddle music in Hollywood," concertmaster Lou Raderman complained good-naturedly to John Winge of *Sight and Sound*. "He is going to break my fingers."

Since there was seldom any dialogue in the Tom and Jerry cartoons, Bradley's contributions were particularly important—and he provided original scores for virtually *every* MGM cartoon for more than twenty years. His work remains rich and impressive today.

In 1943 Hanna and Barbera won an Academy Award for YANKEE DOODLE MOUSE. It was the first of seven Oscars their Tom and Jerry cartoons would gather during the next nine years—a record that knocked Disney out of the running for a decade and established Bill and Joe as animation's newest wonder boys.

Looking back, however, one can see that it took time for the series to really hit its stride. Some of the early cartoons are overladen with detail, particularly in the design of Tom, and many of them pace their action scenes too slowly. The directors remained somewhat earthbound, a final vestige of Harman-Ising influence.

This approach changed with the final departure of Hugh Harman and Rudolf Ising in the early 1940s and the arrival of Tex Avery, who had made his name at Leon Schlesinger's studio. "When Tex moved in, it was like an avalanche hit," recalls his long-time colleague Michael Lah.

Tex Avery, perhaps more than any other single person in animation, perfected the art of the gag cartoon. While his work at Schlesinger's was fresh and innovative, he really blossomed at MGM, where he developed his ideas to their outlandish extremes.

Avery knew how to make the most of the cartoon medium. He had no interest in duplicating or imitating reality. In his mind, the broader, the more unreal, the better. At worst, his films are strident and silly. At best, they are shatteringly funny. In either case, they are unlike anyone else's cartoons,

Tex Avery shows his boss, Fred Quimby (peering over Avery's shoulder), and some guests the artwork for his hit cartoon RED HOT RIDING HOOD (1943).

Avery at work: LUCKY DUCKY (1948). © Metro-Goldwyn-Mayer Inc.

before or since.

Within one year of his arrival at MGM, Avery had originated most of the characters and themes that would carry him through the mid-1950s. One trademark of his was the visual pun. When a character says, "I was down in the dumps," this is a signal for the camera to shoot back fifty feet from its close-up position to show the fellow pacing amid a sea of garbage. Other expressions such as "The drinks are on the house" and "I didn't know if I was coming or going" receive literal and hilarious treatment in Avery cartoons.

Another favorite device Avery had was playing with the conventions of animated cartoons. An Avery character may skid off the edge of the film frame or go to the movies and find the character he just left in another scene saying hello to him from the screen. In one film two characters are informed that they're in the wrong picture, and in another the story is well underway when the leading player realizes that there have been no main titles and says, "Who's directing this picture? Where's the MGM lion?" In LUCKY DUCKY the characters run past a signpost without stopping to read its slogan, only to find that they and the backgrounds have turned various shades of black and white. A stroll back to the sign reveals its message: "TECHNICOLOR ENDS HERE."

If some of these jokes sound obvious on the printed page, it should be emphasized that Avery presents them with a delicious double edge. It's not just the joke that matters, but the sheer outrageousness of performing it. This self-conscious attitude became an Avery trademark and was frequently expressed by such signs and declarations as "Monotonous, isn't it?" or "Pretty darn long, eh?"

Avery's attempts to create cartoon "stars" at MGM were halfhearted at best. His characters were strange and anarchic, merely vehicles for his crazy gags. The first and most durable was Droopy, a tiny basset hound inspired by Bill Thompson's voice as Mr. Whipple on the *Fibber McGee and Molly* radio show. Thompson's hilarious voice was fitted to a quiet, low-key, barely mobile character whose principal raison d'être was to frustrate overconfident adversaries. In some cases it was brains that put Droopy on top, but more often it was a form of white magic. His most frequent enemy, the Wolf, seemed to have everything going for him, except luck—while Droopy drew on luck plus a certain amount of gumption. "You know what?" he'd say in his meek, marble-mouthed way after five minutes of constant assault. "That makes me mad!" Then he'd spring into action, leaving the Wolf completely destroyed.

The Wolf also figures in a series of films in which his libido is stimulated by a sexy show girl. The first of these was RED HOT

RIDING HOOD, and it seemed that each successive film—WILD AND WOLFY, SWING SHIFT CINDERELLA, UNCLE TOM'S CABANA, LITTLE RURAL RIDING HOOD—went to extremes trying to top its predecessor with explosive gag variations on the same funny theme. The Wolf is so aroused by the Girl's sexy performance that he cannot contain himself. Seated at a nightclub table, he distractedly eats his hands, pounds himself on the head with a sledgehammer, lights his nose instead of his cigarette, devours part of the table, etc., etc., etc. Every time one thinks he has gone as far as he can go, Avery tops the gag with another, more outrageous one, still.

The Wolf's original reaction—springing into a stiffened-board pose in midair—was too phallic for the Hollywood censors, who ordered Avery to tone things down. But the Red Riding Hood films went on to become something of a cause célèbre. They were tremendously popular with military audiences during World War II and caused quite a stir back home as well. MGM claimed that they were the most successful short subjects in the company's history. That people could find any pen-and-ink creation like Red Riding Hood so believably sexy was a tribute to Avery, his model designer Claude Smith, and the animator who brought her to life, Preston Blair.

Blair recalls: "The Girl just 'happened' in the Avery MGM epics. The first of the Girl pictures was planned strictly around the Wolf and the 'Peter Arno' grandmother [who was] crazy about wolves. I animated the first Girl scene, and we looked at it with the crazy wild wolf reaction. Avery, ever on his mental toes, was quick to reinforce the Girl charac-

Typical wolfish reactions, from LITTLE RURAL RIDING HOOD (1949). © Metro-Goldwyn-Mayer Inc.

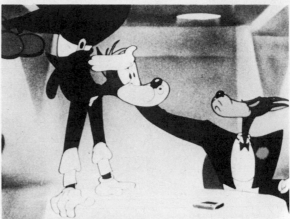

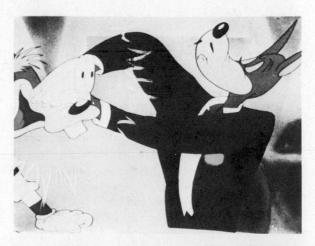

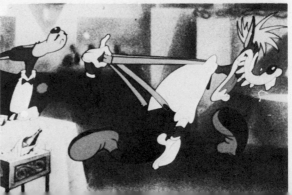

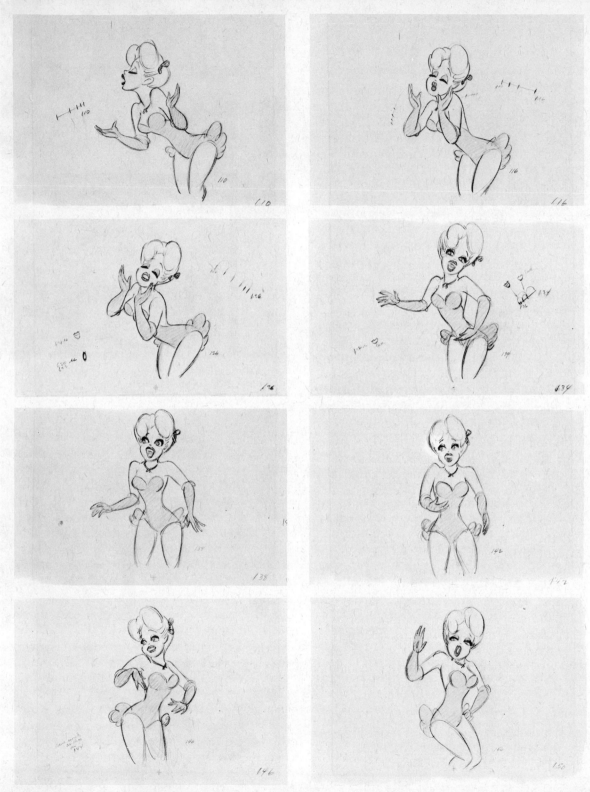

ter, even in the first picture. The reaction was instantaneous, even on the main lot. Cutters were calling in studio friends to see it. It created such an uproar in some theaters that the management was forced to stop the feature and rerun the cartoon.

"One of the greatest compliments I have ever received in my life happened on the second or third 'Red' picture. Somebody, at night, stole several of the 'Red' cels right off the camera stand before the cameraman had a chance to photograph them. We were all in a panic the next day. Fortunately, I had saved my original roughs, and it was simple to clean up, re-ink, and paint these cels. 'Red' was worth stealing . . . wow!"

Blair is quick to point out that contrary to some reports, the Girl—so sexy, so real—was *not* rotoscoped, but created entirely from his own artistic imagination. As a former illustrator, he was accustomed to creating the illusion of reality, even when, as in this case, it was achieved by breaking anatomical rules and using cartoon license.

Avery's most concentrated effort to build a starring character in conventional 1940s fashion came with the debut of Screwball (or Screwy) Squirrel in 1944. Screwy had all the brashness associated with such recent stars as Bugs Bunny and Woody Woodpecker. But Avery took his character further and made him so aggressive, so completely obnoxious, that there was no room left for "lovability." Screwy died after four films, but not without leaving some pleasant memories behind. It's hard to completely dislike a character who can lead a pursuing dog into a darkened cave—where all light is cut off, even to us—and after an enormous crash light a match

Screwball Squirrel in a completely typical pose, from LONESOME LENNY (1946). © Metro-Goldwyn-Mayer Inc.

and say, "Sure was a funny gag—too bad you couldn't see it!"

In many of Avery's films the parts are greater than the whole. Rare is the film without at least a handful of stunning gags. But his finest films—like LITTLE TINKER, BAD LUCK BLACKIE, WHO KILLED WHO?, and KING-SIZE CANARY—have a story or theme that builds to a climax and dispenses gags along the way. The best gags, like the best of his films, rely on *visual impact* to succeed as they do. Music, dialogue, jokes, and sound effects are all important, but Avery thinks in strictly cartoon terms. He is not content to stretch reality for comic effect; he turns it inside out, upside down, and into a fourth dimension that leaves one breathless.

KING SIZE CANARY deals with a bird, a cat, and a mouse who compete for power with the help of a plant food called Jumbo-Gro, which when swallowed turns the drinker

What all the shouting was about: some of Preston Blair's original animation drawings of "Red." This is animation at its best. © Metro-Goldwyn-Mayer Inc.

Tom and Jerry in the classic CAT CONCERTO (1947), which won an Academy Award. © 1940 Loews Inc. Ren. 1967 MGM.

into a gargantuan blowup of himself. As Joe Adamson relates: "The stray bottle of Jumbo-Gro . . . enjoy[s] a lengthy career of being tested out by a random sampling of neighborhood pets, each of whom suddenly discovers in himself an unmanageable potential for turning into a monster. There is a double take every instant, as one of the animals stops and comprehends that some new giant is here to be contended with. A bird the size of an elephant is chased by a cat the size of a truck, until they both stop and meet a woolly mammoth dog the size of a house. (And this is all from one bottle of the stuff. Which was half-used to begin with.) The stodgiest kind of representational drawing is used to good effect in the backgrounds: Here, over houses and garages from a 1940s textbook in accounting, are clambering outlandish creatures out of some dietician's nightmare. The sun has come up by this time, and the chases extend downtown, where the four-story dog is hot on the trail of the two-story cat. Until they get to the corner and meet a seven-story mouse." The animals just grow bigger and bigger—in a constant game of one-upmanship—until the bottle is emptied. With that, the mouse announces that they'll have to end the film, since they've just run out of the "stuff." The outsized animals, now seated on top of the earth itself, wave an inane goodbye as the camera pulls back into the stratosphere!

Few, if any, cartoon directors could approach Avery's sense of the absurd, which flourished in a world of self-contained logic. Even his craziest gags made sense—on their own terms—and this was the wonder of an Avery film.

Perhaps more than anything else, Avery understood comedy timing. "I found out the eye can register an action in five frames of film," he told Joe Adamson. "Five frames of film at twenty-four a second, so it's roughly a fifth of a second to register something, from the screen to your eye to the brain. I found out, if I wanted something to barely be seen, five frames was all it needed. . . . Say we had an anvil falling, we would bring it in perhaps four or five frames before the hit, that's all you need—djuuuuuu . . . *Bam!* it's there, and you don't know where in the hell it came from. It makes that gag that much funnier. If you saw this thing coming down, and you panned down with it, and it hits—uh uh."

The example Avery uses of an anvil falling was put to work in BAD LUCK BLACKIE and formed the foundation of the entire film. Its premise—a good-Samaritan black cat causing catastrophes to befall a bullying dog—depended completely on the surprise element of objects falling onto the hapless dog's head.

Avery's accelerated pacing had its effect on many cartoon directors in Hollywood, including Hanna and Barbera. "Tex had a crazy way of pacing things, and it started to wipe off on Bill and Joe," says Michael Lah. "Then it became a race. Each picture that would come out, from one unit or the other, was faster. Pretty soon you got to the point where the only guys who could understand it were the guys who had worked on it. In fact, one day when Quimby saw a picture, he said, 'That's so damn fast, you're going to have to run it again for me to understand it.' Well, we had to run it over about three times before he understood it."

This in-house influence worked wonders for the Tom and Jerry films. Faster pacing—coupled with more aggressive gags—added the final ingredients to an already satisfying formula. Hanna and Barbera hit their stride in the mid-1940s and produced a series of outstanding shorts that exemplify the Hollywood cartoon at its best.

This writing-directing team may hold a record for producing consistently superior cartoons using the same characters year after year—without a break or change in routine. Naturally, not every Tom and Jerry outing is a gem; some, like CUEBALL CAT, substitute violence for imagination, while others, like TOM AND JERRY IN THE HOLLYWOOD BOWL, promise more than they deliver. But Hanna and Barbera's batting average was tremendous.

THE CAT CONCERTO—an Academy Award winner for 1947—features Tom as a concert pianist who approaches the keyboard with a virtual panoply of pompous expressions and gestures. His equilibrium is shattered, however, when Liszt's "Hungarian Rhapsody" awakens Jerry, who's asleep inside the piano. A battle of wits ensues, with Tom never losing a beat despite tremendous

odds. Superbly funny and eminently musical (the animators studied Scott Bradley at the keyboard to achieve correct fingering for the piece), THE CAT CONCERTO is a gem in every respect.

Another classic is MOUSE CLEANING, which typifies the development of this series by taking the same story idea as PUSS GETS THE BOOT and playing it in modern Tom-and-Jerry fashion, with hilarious gags, razor-sharp timing, and riveting "takes," or reactions. For sheer belly laughs, this cartoon is difficult to top. The story has Mammy Two-Shoes threatening to eject Tom from the house if there's a mess when she returns from shopping, so naturally, Jerry tries to make the biggest mess he can. Tom's frantic attempts to clean up after the mouse account for most of the comedy, but there are specific moments that linger in the memory. At one point Tom tries to stop Jerry by hurling a

The Tex Avery influence: Tom reacts to Jerry's household mess in the Oscar-winning MOUSE CLEANING **(1948). © 1940 Loews Inc. Ren. 1967 MGM.**

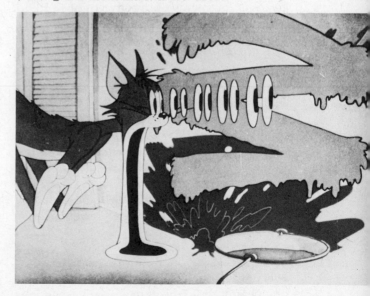

tomato at his head. Jerry ducks and the tomato hits the wall instead, leaving not just a stain, but a *funny* stain, which grows in a delayed reaction after the audience has its first chance to laugh. Tom's jaw drops and his eyes bulge in a sidesplitting array of comic techniques.

The long-running success of Tom and Jerry was due to superb coordination of three key elements: great personality animation, great story ideas, and great gags. All three were vital to the series.

Personality animation is a dying art, but it flourished in the hands of Hanna and Barbera's animators. Jack Zander, who first animated Jerry in PUSS GETS THE BOOT, says, "Making the mouse do certain things and making him react—giving him a personality—only became possible because I threw out about three times as many drawings as I used. It's very subtle to get that movement and the expression on the face, whether the eyes looked at you and whether there was a proper reaction every time. If a character just moves from here to here, it's wrong. I think in those days we were pretty young, and we were all trying very hard. We were *thinking* as we drew."

Ray Patterson agrees that this is the key to personality animation. "Give the character a mind and the personality comes out. It's like Pluto—he'd stop and *think*." Irv Spence says, "When I'd animate Tom, I'd get inside the character . . . I really felt him."

Spence, Patterson, Ken Muse, and Ed Barge were the four main animators of Tom and Jerry from the mid-1940s to the mid-1950s. Their talents, expertly orchestrated by Bill Hanna and Joe Barbera, brought these cartoons to life.

The stories were almost entirely the work of Barbera, one of the most creative minds ever to function in the animation field. That one person could develop so many variations on a basic theme is astounding. In addition to comedy, Barbera worked with characterization, which added fuel to his story repertoire. Thanks to his animators' skills, Tom and Jerry developed into full-bodied characters, with thoughts and feelings. Barbera learned to channel these nuances into effective story ideas. Tom chasing Jerry is the ritual of the series. But somehow the audience realizes that when all is said and done, the cat doesn't *want* to eat the mouse; it's the thrill of the chase that counts. There is an underlying bond between Tom and Jerry that gives these cartoons tremendous strength and likability. On occasion they will team up to dispatch an intruder who muscles into their domain (as in OLD ROCKIN' CHAIR TOM and DOG TROUBLE). In other instances Tom or Jerry will put his love-hate relationship on the line. In NIT WITTY KITTY, Tom contracts amnesia and acts like a mouse; Jerry regards it as his duty to shock him back to normalcy. In FLIRTY BIRDY a hawk competes with Tom for Jerry's hide, and Tom must assert his supremacy. Sometimes these twists on the normal routine would fail—none so miserably as the late entry BLUE CAT BLUES, in which Tom and then Jerry plans to commit suicide.

Best of all is HEAVENLY PUSS, a brilliant cartoon that only could have worked with characters as likable and well-defined as these. Tom dies and approaches the pearly gates, where he's told that his record is not good at all. His torturing of the mouse has all but eliminated any chance of his going to heaven. This is just fine with the Devil, who's pictured as a bulldog standing next to a pot of boiling water in a fiery hell, shouting, "Let me have him! Send him down!" The gatekeeper "upstairs" tells Tom that he has one hour to catch the Heavenly Express. If he can return to earth and get Jerry to sign a Certificate of Forgiveness he'll be able to climb on board. Tom's machinations—and

The Tom and Jerry team with its seven Academy Awards: animators Ed Barge and Irv Spence, layout man Dick Bickenbach, directors Joe Barbera and Bill Hanna, and animator Ken Muse.

frustrations—trying to meet this deadline and win Jerry's sympathy are both hilarious and hair raising, as the prospect of failure is vividly recounted with each passing minute. The fantasy element of this cartoon is wonderfully realized, enhancing both the drama and comedy the story has to offer. Finally, when all seems lost, Tom wakes up from his nightmare. He's so relieved to be alive and well that he runs to Jerry and smothers him with hugs and kisses. The film ends with Jerry shrugging at us, the audience, in complete bewilderment.

Hanna and Barbera enjoyed tremendous success with the Tom and Jerry series, winning seven Academy Awards and making a lot of money for MGM. Yet in 1944, when Gene Kelly had the idea of doing a dance with a cartoon character, his first thought was to contact Walt Disney—even though his film was being made at MGM! Disney turned down the assignment, but told Kelly that his idea was certainly feasible; only then did the dancer and his associates come to Bill and Joe. The resulting sequence, in ANCHORS AWEIGH, is one of the most famous and unusual in the history of movie musicals—a delightful number with Jerry Mouse matching Kelly's movements every step of the way through an intricate dance routine.

The work involved in planning and executing this sequence was considerable. First, everything was noted on a storyboard. Then Kelly's live-action dance was filmed, with both the star and the cameraman acting as if the mouse character was in the scene. Now

Tom and Jerry with Esther Williams in DANGEROUS WHEN WET (1953). © Metro-Goldwyn-Mayer Inc.

A frame blowup of the pencil-test reel prepared by animator Michael Lah for Gene Kelly's INVITATION TO THE DANCE in the 1950s. © Metro-Goldwyn-Mayer Inc.

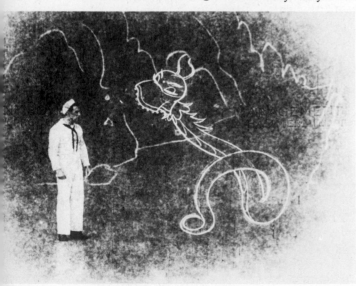

the entire sequence was rotoscoped—Kelly traced onto animation paper—so the frame-by-frame animation of Jerry could be matched precisely to Kelly's movements. The result is technically superb—and irresistibly entertaining.

After the success of ANCHORS AWEIGH, the film's director, George Sidney, called on Hanna and Barbera to provide an animated opening for his musical feature HOLIDAY IN MEXICO. Several years later Tom and Jerry were recruited to swim with Esther Williams in another MGM feature, DANGEROUS WHEN WET. But it was Gene Kelly who returned to Bill and Joe in 1953 with the most ambitious project of all: An entire segment of his feature film INVITATION TO THE DANCE, which would be called "Sinbad the Sailor," was to be set against cartoon backgrounds.

Michael Lah, who worked on this sequence, says, "Animating Jerry with his legs and arms [in ANCHORS AWEIGH] was just a matter of imitating Kelly, but to do the same thing with the character of the serpent in INVITATION TO THE DANCE was a different challenge. I figure that was the greatest animation problem I ever had, to create that dance with a serpent who had no legs or arms."

For this part of the sequence, Kelly filmed the dance with Carol Haney imitating the serpent. Then he performed the dance again without her. "We had to rotoscope Kelly, to make it all work," Lah explains, "but we had the dance of Haney as a separate film to use as a reference, to run over and over on a movieola." The serpent *wasn't* traced from Haney's movements. She was created by the animators, "and that's where the creativity comes in," says Lah. Critics agreed that "Sinbad the Sailor" was the most successful and entertaining segment of INVITATION TO THE DANCE.

Not to be completely outdone, Tex Avery

used live-action footage with Dave O'Brien, star of MGM's PETE SMITH SPECIALTIES comedy series, in his inventive gag cartoon TV OF TOMORROW. The short showed, for instance, how a television in the bathroom could be maintained with utmost discretion, since turning the set around caused O'Brien to turn around inside the set, so that his eyes were away from the naked bather.

A gag appearance like this—or the participation of Latin beauty Lina Romay in the punch line of Avery's SENOR DROOPY—came about because of the general camaraderie on the MGM lot. Preston Blair told Mark Mayerson: "Any article about the Metro cartoon studio should describe the actual setting of the place. It was on Lot 2, which is an integral part of the Main Lot at Culver City (or used to be). The whole setup should be of great interest to the nostalgic film buff of today. [It] was like a film buff's dream of heaven . . . right inside the fabulous Louis B. Mayer star-studded era at MGM. The cartoonists had the run of the place. We saw everybody—saw many productions being made—ate at our table in the legendary MGM commissary. The environment was an experience for any film maker. The work on the sets, etc., was fantastic and I'll never forget the whole experience. This is notable because other studios like Warner's were outside the mainstream of that glamorous live-action era."

Another less physical link with the MGM studio was the feeling of perfectionism that pervaded the cartoon department. This was something that Hanna-Barbera and Tex Avery had in common. Bill and Joe used pencil-test reels to perfect the timing and animation in their films; Avery often went further. "He flipped over every one of your scenes, and he would take your extremes and go over them a little bit," Irven Spence recalls. "At the time, you felt like you were

Gags and gadgetry: a scene from Tex Avery's TV OF TOMORROW (1953). © Metro-Goldwyn-Mayer Inc.

Only Avery would try it; only Avery could get away with it. A reaction shot from LITTLE RURAL RIDING HOOD (1949). © Metro-Goldwyn-Mayer Inc.

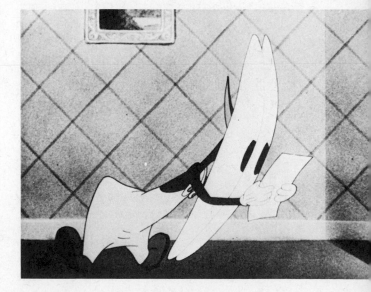

animating something that was really exaggerated, but then Tex would take it and *double* it! Wow!!!''

Avery was something of a one-man band at MGM. "I think that's what tired him out," says Spence. "He was doing his own stories, almost; he had one story man, but he was the one who came up with ideas. Then he was doing rough layouts for the animators. Then when the tests were finished he would want a lot of changes. And my gosh, even when the animation was on cels, he would cut frames on the movieola, to get the effect he wanted!"

Michael Lah elaborates: "When Tex's pictures came back in animation, we found that instead of having to add drawings, we had to throw drawings out. Drawings were made that weren't necessary.

"It comes back to this: We'd make pose reels, and they'd be funny as hell. Then when we'd get 'em back, and they'd be animated, they'd be mushy and soft, and they'd lost a lot of guts. The reason for it was, there wasn't enough time to 'read' the poses.

"Posing and reading poses was a technique that sort of developed there. It was sort of a storyboard on film, with a few more poses here and there. The pose reels got to be pretty doggone complete, and they began to be entertaining by themselves, without the addition of legs moving and such. But some of that pacing was so fast that you didn't need any in-betweens or drawings to carry out the action."

So it was that year by year, Avery—and Lah, who became his co-director for a while and then succeeded him at the studio—came to soft-pedal the full, flowing Disney-style animation in favor of animation that strove primarily for gag effect.

Lah had his first taste of directing in the late 1940s, when producer Quimby teamed him with Preston Blair in the hopes that another Hanna-and-Barbera would result. "That was far from inevitable," says Lah today. "It just didn't work out, and about that time Quimby got orders from upstairs not to expand, but to cut down, and Preston and I were the first victims of that." Lah and Blair were assigned to Barney Bear, who had been handled for a while by George Gordon in the mid-1940s, then abandoned.

Says Blair, "We used to discuss story situations for hours, trying to improve. We should have been more aware of the budget. We didn't overcost, but we were not cheap enough for Quimby, and the unit was discontinued."

Too bad, because the Barney Bear cartoons that came out of this unit were quite good. THE BEAR AND THE BEAN and THE BEAR AND THE HARE are top-notch in every way. Barney has less anatomical detail than he did during the Ising days, but he remains lumbering and likable. The gags, clean and well-paced, are punched across with echoes of both Avery and Hanna-Barbera.

In 1950 Tex Avery left MGM for a hiatus; just plain overwork is the reason commonly cited. To replace him Quimby hired veteran animator-director Dick Lundy. Lundy did one Droopy cartoon, but his main assignment was to revive (for yet another go-round) Barney Bear.

"I felt the Wally Beery–type character was a lovable and sympathetic personality," says Lundy today. "Tex's pictures were mostly gag-type pictures with good timing and a little personality thrown in. The Cat and Mouse had personality with slapstick gags. Both of these series were set at a very fast pace. I wanted Barney to have a slower pace and likable appeal to the audiences. Disney had this type of action in the SILLY SYMPHONIES. That is what I was striving for in Barney. Sometimes I achieved this and sometimes I failed."

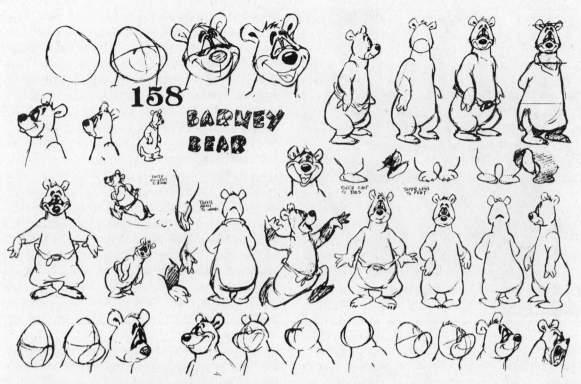

158 BARNEY BEAR

Barney Bear, as redesigned by Preston Blair and Michael Lah in the late 1940s; compare this streamlined version with the Ising original. © Metro-Goldwyn-Mayer Inc.

Lundy's failures were not abysmal by any means—but Barney was no Pluto, and the gag structure of his cartoons didn't seem to suit the softer, personality-conscious approach the director had in mind. When he took a harder line with gags, as in SLEEPY-TIME SQUIRREL, he hit the bull's-eye. BUSY BODY BEAR, THE IMPOSSIBLE POSSUM, and other cartoons are enjoyable but uninvolving, because they're trapped somewhere between Ising's and Avery's styles.

Lundy left when Tex Avery returned to MGM in October 1951. The discrepancy between this date and 1954, through which films with Lundy's name on them continued to be released offers some idea of: a) how much the studio stockpiled its cartoons before releasing them; and b) how long it took to complete a cartoon. The average Hanna-Barbera Tom and Jerry short took *a year and a half* from initial story work to finished film.

In the 1950s Hanna and Barbera tried to develop some new supporting characters, in order to keep the Tom and Jerry series fresh. From THE MILKY WAIF came Little Nibbles (sometimes called Tuffy), Jerry's infant counterpart and tag-along, who figured in such later films as TWO MOUSEKETEERS, TWO LITTLE INDIANS, and TOUCHÉ PUSSY CAT. Later on there was a duck (in SOUTHBOUND DUCKLING and others) with a cute, squawky voice who

A handsome layout sketch for the elaborate Tom and Jerry cartoon TWO MOUSEKETEERS **(1952). © Metro-Goldwyn-Mayer Inc.**

resurfaced on Hanna and Barbera's TV programs under the name of Yakky Doodle. Finally, Hanna and Barbera introduced a bulldog and his son, named Spike and Tyke. From their debut as neighbors of Tom and Jerry in BARBECUE BRAWL they went on to star in their own short-lived, forgettable series. (In manner, if not in appearance, they too formed the basis for later H-B television characters—Augie Doggy and Doggy Daddy.)

The 1950s were bringing changes to the cartoon industry, and MGM was affected as much as any other studio. Costs were rising, and Quimby tried to keep his budgets under control. Perhaps to compensate for the fact that their cartoons were budgeted higher than Tex Avery's, Hanna and Barbera did their bit by producing a "cheater" cartoon about once a year. This would be a film in which the bulk of footage was lifted from earlier cartoons and framed by the device of a scrapbook or series of reminiscences

(among the examples are LIFE WITH TOM, and THE SMITTEN KITTEN). Quimby became stricter about running time, as well. Whereas eight minutes had been acceptable in the 1940s, seven minutes became the upper limit and six minutes was preferable. Saving one minute reduced costs considerably—fewer drawings made, less time spent on production, less Technicolor footage developed for every print processed.

One new expense was necessary to stay in business, however, and this was the adoption of CinemaScope. MGM released its first wide-screen cartoon in late 1954, and by 1956 every cartoon was filmed that way. The staff adapted to this new technique with relative ease, but Irven Spence remembers, "The in-betweens had to be more accurate, because the screen was so large, you'd see any little wiggle or jump in the line; even the inking had to be better."

To compensate for this problem, a heavier ink line was used in some of the later cartoons, and this completed a streamlining process that had changed the design of Tom and Jerry in recent years. Tom, whose ruffled hair gave way to a smooth body line suffered the most from the change.

Simpler character design and backgrounds were part of an evolutionary process that affected every cartoon studio. Tex Avery told Joe Adamson: "Well, actually, it was a matter of cost. UPA started the new trend in their backgrounds. I liked them; they were so simple and your characters read better. Then Warner's came into it, and we came into it last of the three big majors. We tried to get away from the blue sky and the green grass, and just do anything that made for pleasant color combinations. But it was a matter of time saving. If you had a prairie, or a desert—in the old days we'd put sagebrush and plateaus and shading and all this. Now, poom! A flat color along here, and this and that, and a couple of plateaus and that's it!

And then your character had to read, no matter where he was! Anywhere in the frame, he'd read."

Ed Benedict was influential in creating fresh designs for Avery, and Richard Bickenbach worked on layout design for Hanna and Barbera at this time.

Tex Avery left MGM in 1954 and Michael Lah was named his successor. He had received co-director credit on some of Avery's last films and had worked with him so long that the changeover seemed natural. Lah directed five cartoons with Avery's Droopy character; ONE DROOPY KNIGHT, released in 1957, was nominated for an Academy Award. But the vastness of CinemaScope did not really suit little Droopy, and even the best Avery-type gags registered much weaker than they did in earlier, more conventional surroundings.

Lah did retain a wolf character that he had developed with Avery in such films as THREE LITTLE PUPS and BILLY BOY. Like so many other characters, this one was based on a voice, by Daws Butler—a drawling, low-key kind of voice. "This wolf would never get excited," Avery explained. "But he'd get the hell beat out of him. We'd use him in very violent action; then we'd freeze him and he'd make his crack: 'Pretty smart li'l ol' dogs in there.' . . . Even Quimby was enthused. He said, 'Yes sir, them things are funny. Every time he opens his mouth, he gets a laugh.'"

When the MGM cartoon department closed, Daws Butler made a healthy career out of doing that voice for other studios. Walter Lantz turned him into a bear named Smedley, and, more importantly, Hanna and Barbera made his voice the basis of their first television cartoon star, Huckleberry Hound.

Fred Quimby retired in 1955. In recognition of their organizational skills—and valued contributions to the MGM coffers—

Hanna and Barbera were appointed his successors. Hal Elias stayed on as production manager.

Hanna and Barbera did their last group of Tom and Jerry cartoons in 1955 and 1956. Some of these rank alongside the best this series had to offer. DESIGNS ON JERRY is a highly imaginative short in which Tom's blueprints for a Rube Goldberg mousetrap come to life during a dream in which Tom and Jerry are represented as chalk-white stick figures. MUSCLE BEACH TOM, in CinemaScope, is a violent, funny outing at the beach and has some wonderful sight gags. (For example, Tom stuffs helium balloons inside his one-piece bathing suit to make him look more muscular—with disastrous results.)

At the other end of the spectrum are cartoons so bad that it's hard to believe the

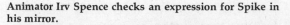

Animator Irv Spence checks an expression for Spike in his mirror.

same people made them. There *were* new additions to the staff—animators like Lewis Marshall and Ken Southworth, and writer Homer Brightman, the first man to get story credit on a Tom and Jerry cartoon—but Hanna and Barbera were still firmly in charge, and most of their colleagues were studio veterans.

There is no way to understand how the characterizations could go so far astray. In such entries as BUSY BUDDIES and TOT WATCHERS, Tom and Jerry are nonviolent pals who team up to keep an eye on a mischievous infant. In the aforementioned BLUE CAT BLUES they plan to commit double suicide!

The look of these late-release films is also distressing. ROYAL CAT NAP returns to the milieu of such films as THE TWO MOUSEKETEERS, but doesn't begin to recapture the sumptuousness of the original settings. Worse yet, Tom and Jerry begin to look strange. In HAPPY GO DUCKY Jerry's ears are far too big, and Tom—already suffering from the thickened ink line around his body—has features that, instead of retaining their anatomical dimension, are squashed onto his face. He has become a cardboard caricature of his former "self."

Considering all this, perhaps it wasn't so tragic that MGM decided to close its cartoon studio in the spring of 1957. Hanna and Barbera are happy to declare that despite the initial shock, this was the luckiest break they ever had. It forced them to open their own studio, which has grown to be the largest and most successful in the world. Ironically, Bill and Joe first offered their idea to make low-cost cartoons for television to MGM and were turned down. One story goes that Metro production executive Eddie Mannix said there was no future for TV cartoons. Michael Lah remembers someone accusing Hanna and Barbera of simply wanting to keep their jobs, and remarking, "Why didn't you make them that cheap before?"

Whatever the case, the studio closing brought to an end over twenty years of quality cartoon production and retired two of the country's biggest cartoon stars, Tom and Jerry.

But not for long.

Due in part to Hanna-Barbera's tremendous success in television, several major studios felt there was a renaissance of interest in cartoons during the early 1960s. MGM decided that it would be worthwhile to release new cartoons to theaters—if the price was right.

An appropriate bid came from producer William Snyder, who represented American émigré Gene Deitch, a talented cartoon director who lives and works in Prague. In 1961 and 1962 Deitch turned out thirteen brand-new Tom and Jerry shorts. His Czech animators were able to view just six Hanna-Barbera cartoons in order to get to know their characters. Despite low budgets, some of the animation is quite good, but these films are pale imitations of vintage Tom and Jerry cartoons. There is movement, but no comedy; there is animation, but no characterization. The music, which seems to have been recorded in a lavatory, weighs down the cartoons instead of enhancing them as Scott Bradley's scores always did. Deitch had no illusions about this assignment. He later told David Rider of *Films and Filming* magazine, "The reason Metro did them had nothing to do with bringing Tom and Jerry to life. They simply wanted to cash in on their popularity as cheaply as possible. Any qualities the finished pictures have is strictly the result of the personal craftsmanship of the artists."

Whatever their faults, these shorts did prove to MGM that theatrical cartoons were

Variations on Tom and Jerry: at left, Gene Deitch's version; center and right, Chuck Jones' designs. © 1940 Loews Inc. ren. 1967 MGM.

still a viable commodity—and that Tom and Jerry were still major "stars." (In 1962 the company even released an ersatz feature called THE TOM AND JERRY FESTIVAL OF FUN, which consisted of eighteen vintage cartoons.)

When Warner Brothers shut down its cartoon studio, Chuck Jones and producer Les Goldman formed a company called Tower 12 Productions. After working on some projects of their own, they were approached by MGM to do yet another Tom and Jerry series. "I accepted solely because the budgets I submitted would allow me to continue with full animation," Jones says today. At $42,000, they were $12,000 higher than the last Warner Brothers budgets.

Jones had the services of his excellent Warner's colleagues: writer Michael Maltese, co-director and layout man Maurice Noble, background artist Philip De Guard, and such animators as Ben Washam, Richard Thompson, and Tom Ray.

The results were, without question, the handsomest cartoons of the 1960s—and among the most strikingly designed cartoon shorts ever made. The only problem was that they weren't funny.

Jones redesigned Tom and Jerry to conform to his style, which meant enlarging Jerry's eyes (for cuteness) and restructuring Tom's face (for expressions of frustration). Jones had no interest in perpetuating Hanna and Barbera's chase-and-violence formula; he was more interested in using Tom and Jerry as characters, with the kind of facial gestures and nuances of personality that made his work at Warner's so distinctive. But far too often this goal was unsupported by gag and story elements, and the cartoons became just one pose or gesture after another.

The notable exceptions are those cartoons with stories by gagster Michael Maltese, particularly THE CAT ABOVE AND THE MOUSE BELOW, which shows Maltese *and* Jones in top form, working within a musical format. Tom is baritone Thomassino Catti-Cazzaza, singing "Largo el Factotum" from *The Barber of Seville* while Jerry tries to sleep in his home beneath the concert-hall stage. Their resulting battle is reminiscent of such fine cartoons as CAT CONCERTO with Tom and Jerry and Jones's earlier LONG-HAIRED HARE.

Jones, philosophical about his work on this series, says, "Any calisthenics will keep the muscles loose, but nobody is ever going to work with another man's characters as well as the originators. Joe and Bill would have had the same problems with the Road Runner and the Coyote that I had with Tom and Jerry."

After production was well under way with this series, Tower 12 Productions was absorbed by MGM and renamed MGM Animation/Visual Arts. Jones's agreement with the studio brass enabled him to launch other projects for theaters and television. He handed directing assignments on Tom and Jerry to Abe Levitow, Ben Washam, Jim Pabian, and Tom Ray, freeing himself to work on two unusual shorts—THE DOT AND THE LINE and THE BEAR THAT WASN'T.

THE DOT AND THE LINE (A ROMANCE IN LOWER MATHEMATICS) is a charming and imaginative film based on Norton Juster's book about a straight line that vies with a squiggle for the affections of a dot. The script, closely following Juster's book, is beautifully read by Robert Morley. But giving expression to geometric shapes, and placing them in an attractive setting, was Jones's major challenge. At one point a hairy line was needed, and this led to a variety of experiments. Finally Jones inked his line on Japanese rice paper, let it bleed, and photo-copied the result onto cels. THE DOT AND THE LINE won a well-deserved Academy Award as Best Animated Short Subject and provided a pleasant cap to MGM's long involvement with cartoons.

Jones's second "special" short, based on Frank Tashlin's book THE BEAR THAT WASN'T, was neither as compelling or successful, and his feature film THE PHANTOM TOLLBOOTH, from another Norton Juster book, got caught up in studio politics and barely received theatrical release. MGM also decided to end the Tom and Jerry series.

Jones continued producing television specials for MGM, including the first animated treatment of Walt Kelly's *Pogo,* and several Dr. Seuss stories. Despite their success, the studio—then in the midst of executive upheaval—lost interest in animation altogether. Says Jones, "[They] saw no future in $100,000 a year net from every TV special, so that was that."

This time there was no reprieve. Like other major studios with major cartoon properties, MGM failed to see how continued production—for television or theaters— could stack up against the millions one could derive from live-action features and TV series.

The Tom and Jerry cartoons were first played on television as a Saturday-morning network show; at that time the character of Mammy Two-Shoes, a black stereotype who figured in many of the best episodes, was reanimated and dubbed by June Foray as an Irish housemaid. But the ultimate irony came in 1975 when Hanna and Barbera proposed a *new* series of Tom and Jerrys especially for television. Barbera screened some of the old shorts for ABC network executives, who laughed heartily but told him that the violence would never be acceptable today. Thus, when the new series was produced, Tom and Jerry were completely re-created—

walking on twos instead of fours, united as pals instead of enemies, and engaging in insipid and colorless adventures. Jerry sported a curious bow tie, and the characters' faces were devoid of expression. It was a long way from PUSS GETS THE BOOT. Predictably, this new series failed to score a hit with the new kiddie generation.

MGM's history in the cartoon field was checkered and unusual. It sponsored independent producers and ran its own studio as well. It committed itself to quality for twenty years, and then destroyed that image in the following years. But when the MGM cartoon department was humming, with Tex Avery, Bill Hanna, and Joe Barbera at the reins, and a talented staff in tow, it turned out some of the finest animated shorts ever made—and set quality standards that have never been recaptured.

Paramount/Famous Studios

11

WHEN PARAMOUNT PICTURES removed Max and Dave Fleischer from control of its studio in January 1942, the key personnel were assured that there would be "business as usual" without interruption.

It was not really as simple as that.

The inflated staff that had been required to work on the feature film MR. BUG GOES TO TOWN was immediately cut back, leaving only the key Fleischer animators and technicians, who were signed to new contracts. In May 1942 the company was placed in the hands of Sam Buchwald, who had been production manager; Seymour Kneitel, a head animator who also happened to be Max Fleischer's son-in-law; and Izzy Sparber, who had worked his way up from office boy to story man. The name of the company was changed to Famous Studios (derived from Paramount's original corporate name, Famous Players), and within a year the operation was moved from Miami Beach back to New York, where it took up residence on West Forty-fifth Street, not far from the original Fleischer shop.

Because the entire Famous crew was held over from Fleischer's regime, Paramount clearly expected no change in the quality of its films. Considering the lackluster efforts Fleischer had produced in the early 1940s, there was even hope for improvement.

From a business point of view, Famous Studios fulfilled all of Paramount's requirements. The shorts it turned out were well-received in the marketplace and financially successful. "Critical reaction" was never a corporate barometer of success, so it didn't seem to matter that in twenty-five years Famous-Paramount never received an Academy Award nomination, let alone the coveted Oscar. In the 1940s, when they might have had a chance, Paramount backed its more prestigious PUPPETOONS series, produced by George Pal on the West Coast. By the 1950s, the Famous product had sunk into such a rut that any discussion of awards was rendered unlikely.

That the studio survived until 1967 is positively miraculous and offers some indication of how little anyone cared about the quality of theatrical cartoons, so long as six minutes of screen time were filled.

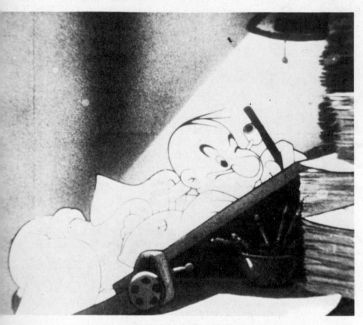

Popeye turns animator in CARTOONS AIN'T HUMAN **(1943).**
© **King Features Syndicate.**

It was not always so.

Everyone seemed to care a lot more in the 1940s—theater owners, moviegoers, and the people who made the films. One of Famous's first jobs was to spruce up its image and stimulate new interest in its product. POPEYE was still the company's major breadwinner, but exhibitors were complaining that the novelty of the SUPERMAN shorts had worn off.

So Paramount announced a major overhaul for the 1943–44 movie season. Henceforth all Famous Studios cartoons would be made in Technicolor, including POPEYE. SUPERMAN was dropped, and a new star was introduced: Little Lulu, already a great favorite in *Saturday Evening Post* panel cartoons by Marge (Marjorie Henderson Buell).

Lulu's deadpan approach to childish mischief made her an engaging character to work with, and the series turned out to be one of Famous's best. Going for smiles instead of belly laughs, these cartoons had considerable charm and benefited from a delightful theme song written by Fred Wise, Sidney Lippman, and Buddy Kaye. At their best, they managed to be cute, but not cloying—a feat the Famous staff was unable to duplicate in later years.

LULU IN HOLLYWOOD, one of the first series entries, plays on the incongruity of Lulu getting the "star treatment" in Hollywood while preferring her lollipops to more obvious movie-star trappings. In her screen test she elicits cries of "Marvelous!" from a *mittel-*European director for expressing a "range" of emotions with the same stoic face. Other, more typical outings portray Lulu as a curious young girl with a penchant for mischief, who is bedeviled by a stern but loving housemaid name Mandy. Original songs and dream sequences figure in some of the better shorts, such as LULU'S BIRTHDAY PARTY and THE BABY SITTER.

LITTLE LULU ran for five years and seemed to be a great success. Whether it was that negotiations with Marge forced the issue or that Famous was simply looking for a way to save money, in any case the series was dropped in 1948 and a "new" character named Little Audrey was introduced. Audrey looked, sounded, and acted differently than Lulu, but the inspiration was clear—and now Famous didn't have to pay royalties to anyone for a copyrighted character.

At the same time that LULU debuted, Famous launched a series called NOVELTOONS. "The public wants NOVELTY and COLOR," proclaimed a trade advertisement. "This NEW series gives them both . . . with different characters in each short!" While Famous produced a fair amount of "one-shot" cartoons in this series, it also used the NOVELTOONS name as an umbrella for miniseries starring various running characters who didn't warrant separate billing.

One of the studio's intentions was to create a new format for Johnny Gruelle's Raggedy Ann and Andy, who had appeared in an earlier Max Fleischer "special." Raggedy Ann returned in a 1944 NOVELTOON called SUDDENLY IT'S SPRING, which boasted some of Famous's most impressive artwork. But the elaborate settings and highly sentimental story (about a little girl who will die unless the sun, with its healing powers, shines through the winter clouds) did nothing to develop or showcase Raggedy Ann's personality, and no series ensued. There was just one sequel, THE ENCHANTED SQUARE, three years later.

Another sentimental cartoon, produced in 1945, had considerably greater repercussions. Animator Joe Oriolo brought a ready-made children's story to the studio, where it was put into production as THE FRIENDLY GHOST. No one regarded it as anything more than a one-shot premise about a ghostly little boy who wants to make friends with people, not scare them. But Famous president Sam Buchwald liked the idea and suggested another go-round two and a half years later. THERE'S GOOD BOOS TONIGHT was released in April 1948, and a follow-up (with practically the same plot) called A HAUNTING WE WILL GO came out in May 1949.

Finally in 1950 Buchwald gave his approval to make CASPER, THE FRIENDLY GHOST a regular series. It was the most profitable decision he ever made, for unlike Popeye, Casper was wholly owned by Paramount, and the licensing rights—for comic books, records, toys, and novelties—reaped a small fortune from that time onward. This belied the fact that Casper was the most monotonous character to invade cartoonland since Mighty Mouse. It seemed as if every Casper cartoon followed the same story line, with only minor variations.

Animator Myron Waldman, who worked on the series from its inception, says, "The boys at the studio used to kid me when we were doing the CASPERS; they'd call them the 'ooh-ahh' pictures, but I always felt those pictures would last much longer than a picture that was just based on gags, because nobody can remember the gags. When they go to see it again, or talk about it, I think they like a story—kids especially."

Waldman is right. Children like stories, and they also crave repetition. Casper, like a

A theatrical poster for LITTLE LULU.

Early model sheet by Bill Hudson for Herman the mouse.

growing number of Famous cartoons, was aimed strictly at children—which limited its appeal in theaters, but made it doubly marketable in other ways. Later, the Casper cartoons scored an even bigger hit on TV, to such a degree that a new series of shorts was commissioned especially for television in the 1960s.

Myron Waldman was one of five head animators who put in long tenures at Famous. He, Al Eugster, Tom Johnson, Steve Muffati, and Dave Tendlar were Fleischer veterans who worked in the same manner that Max and Dave had established years before. The official directors acted more as supervisors, while the head animators did all the timing and layouts on the cartoons and handed out the work to their staff of three animators. The head animator was also responsible for designing incidental characters who appeared in each cartoon; most

other studios had people who did nothing but that.

"While each group was animating, the head animator would have a chance to do a little animating on his own," Al Eugster explains. "Then we would have the scenes photographed and have a 'sweatbox' session. It would just consist of a movieola in a small room; the head animator would go over the rough reel with the director. The head animator would write down changes and so forth, and then he would go into the sweatbox with his animators. So the head animator was kind of a go-between. Sometimes there would be a retake, and other times changes would be made without shooting it again."

Animators at Famous included George Cannata, Orestes Calpini, George Germanetti, Johnny Gentilella, Jim Tyer, Bill Hudson, Chuck Harriton, Tom Johnson, Phil Klein, Russ Dyson, Bill Pattengill, George Rufle, Allen Rose, Morey Reden, Marty Taras, Nick Tafuri, Gordon Whittier, Dante Barbetta, and Sal Maimone. Many of the assistants and in-betweeners went on to illustrious careers in animation, some of them running their own studios: Phil Kimmelman, Howard Post, Lee Mishkin, Howard Beckerman, Cliff Augustson, Jack Dazzo, Ben Farrish, Dan Hunn, Jon Swojak, George Bakes, Sal Fallaice, and Milt Stein.

The Famous artists averaged twenty-four feet of animation a week, which meant that each short would be in animation for five to six weeks, all told. It took about the same amount of time to develop a story.

There were usually four story men on staff, working alone or in teams to keep pace with the studio's deadlines. Writers in the 1940s included Fleischer veterans Jack Ward, Bill Turner, Joe Stultz, Larry Riley, and Jack Mercer, who doubled as voice man. Joining them briefly was Otto Messmer, who was unemployed when the electric signs he designed for Times Square were dimmed by World War II blackout requirements. By the end of the decade the story crew boiled down to four main people, however, who carried the production load well into the 1950s: I. Klein, Carl "Mike" Meyer, Larz Bourne, and Jack Mercer. Later in the 1950s animator Irv Spector also contributed cartoon stories.

The story men worked on their own until a storyboard was ready for presentation. Then the director would be called in for a conference, and eventually others, such as Sam Buchwald and the particular cartoon's head animator, would join in. Once changes were hammered out and a finished "board" was prepared, the director would hold a recording session.

A handful of voice experts provided the sound tracks for almost every character appearing in Famous cartoons, from the mid-1940s to the early 1960s. Mae Questel did most of the female and children's voices, including Olive Oyl and Little Audrey. Arnold Stang was the voice of Herman the mouse. Comedian Sid Raymond did "dumb" voices for Katnip and Baby Huey. Jackson Beck was Bluto in the Popeye series, and Buzzy the crow. And Jack Mercer, whom Beck calls "the most versatile voice man I've ever met," played Popeye and a variety of other characters. (During World War II, when Mercer was in the service, the studio backlogged scripts, hoping to arrange recording sessions when he was on furlough. When he wasn't available, Mae Questel did the voice of Popeye!)

With so many former Fleischer people on the payroll, it isn't surprising that the search for "new" ideas often led into the past. Famous did a fair number of remakes and found ways of incorporating old footage as well. But the major throwback to earlier times was in the return of the Bouncing Ball,

for a new SCREEN SONG series. Each cartoon was based on a theme—such as gold rush days, Mississippi River showboats, and the like—with blackout gags that eventually led to an appropriate song. Unlike the earlier cartoons, this series had no big-name guest stars, no live-action footage, and the bouncing ball itself was animated instead of a live-action pointer as it had been in Fleischer days.

Puns and violence were the strange bedfellows in Famous Studios' humor. Every cartoon studio relied on visual puns from time to time, but Famous cartoons were riddled with them. At times it seemed the only kind of gag Famous knew. Whole cartoons were built around them—VEGETABLE VAUDEVILLE, with its "stewed" tomato doing a tipsy walk and alligator pears that have long, scaly snouts is just one example—and studio employees were offered five dollars for pun-ny cartoon titles.

The cartoons that relied more on story and character indulged in endless—and often mindless—violence with a nonchalance that made Tom and Jerry look refined by comparison. The finale of MICE MEETING YOU has Herman the mouse decorating Katnip the cat like a Christmas tree and plugging his tail into an electric socket to light the ornaments while singing "Merry Christmas to you"!

The most discouraging aspect of Famous cartoons, however, was their utter reliance on formulas. This trend evolved during the late 1940s and early 1950s and represented a final break from the Fleischer tradition. As new series developed (CASPER THE FRIENDLY GHOST, LITTLE AUDREY, BABY HUEY, HERMAN AND KATNIP, BUZZY THE CROW), the writers and directors so standardized story formats that they made the continuation of these series a mere matter of filling in the blanks.

Casper is forever in search of a friend, but wherever he goes, the people he meets take

© HARVEY FAMOUS CARTOONS

Casper plays with Famous characters Little Audrey, Baby Huey, Herman, and Katnip in this publicity drawing.

one look and shriek (their eyes bulging), "A *g-g-ghost!*"Generally, it's children or young animals who welcome his friendship. Little Audrey is forever visiting fantasy lands and learning a lesson about tolerance. Herman the mouse saves his little cousins from the clutches of menacing Katnip. Buzzy the Crow is pursued by a stupid cat who needs crow meat to cure some malady. Baby Huey either wants to play with his uninterested duck friends and saves them from the clutches of a fox, or he drives his mother and father crazy in his clumsy attempts at being helpful.

Most of these scripts are so repetitive that one wonders why the animators had to bother redoing their work from one film to the next. Even Winston Sharples's music scores sound alike. The shame of it is that through the early 1950s the Famous cartoons maintained a decent standard of quality. The animation was usually good; the backgrounds were often superior, particularly when seen in Technicolor.

But standard fare at Famous was just that—standard—and it was rare that the pattern was broken. Unsurprisingly, it's the nonformula cartoons that stand out in most of the long-running series. One of the story men's favorite standbys was setting a film inside the cartoon studio itself, which always provided a pleasant break from the routine. HERMAN THE CATOONIST, which harks back to OUT OF THE INKWELL, has Herman and Katnip coming to life on an artist's drawing board, while GHOST OF HONOR has Casper relating the story of his movie career and recalling the time he scared everyone except for his fellow cartoon stars away from the studio.

One brief experiment occurred in 1953–54 when Famous produced two cartoons in the new 3-D process. The Popeye entry, THE ACE OF SPACE, was a fairly standard outing, but the Casper cartoon, BOO MOON, took the opportunity to try an offbeat, science fiction–type of story and to resurrect an old Fleischer character, King Bombo from GULLIVER'S TRAVELS. Of course, 3-D proved to be a passing fad, and no further attempts were made to capitalize on the process.

By this time supervision of the Famous product was almost entirely in the hands of two men, Seymour Kneitel and Izzy Sparber. Sam Buchwald died in 1951, and with him, some feel, died an important guiding spirit. It may not be coincidental that the studio fell into a rut just around this time. "Kneitel and Sparber were only so-so creative men," Dave Tendlar told Fleischer chronicler Leslie Cabarga. "They stuck to clichés of the past and the studio didn't advance." Tendlar followed their lead when he was promoted from animator to director in the early 1950s.

For a short time it seemed as if there might be hope when Famous hired the formidable Bill Tytla as director in the mid-1940s. He stayed six years, but his talents were wasted on trite material and his ability as an animator was barely used. "He helped carry the films with his drawings, and also his criticism," says colleague I. Klein. "He had ways of telling the animators how to improve their work. In that way he was more of a benefit to the fellows he worked with than they were to him. The studio contributed nothing to his reputation."

In the mid-1950s, Famous, affected somewhat by the enormous impact of UPA, started to experiment with different kinds of films. But the studio's attempts at fanciful stories and stylized settings and characters were hampered by heavy-handedness and insincerity. It was trying to duplicate in 1958 what UPA had done to perfection six or seven years earlier. A film like DANTE DREAMER (about a little boy with a big imagination) is nothing more than a mild imitation of CHRISTOPHER CRUMPET, with by-then conventional graphics.

In 1956 Famous Studios was dissolved and its name changed to Paramount Cartoon Studios. Reassurances of retaining the status quo went up in smoke when both staff and budget were severely curtailed just a few months later. The result shows up on-screen: From 1956 on Famous cartoons have thicker lines around their characters, and less movement. Some shorts look as if the characters have been animated with no in-betweens whatsoever.

For some studios this sudden change would have spelled the end. In the case of Paramount, it was just the beginning of the end.

A major turning point was Popeye's retirement as a theatrical cartoon subject in 1957, which was brought about not by any decline in popularity but by the sale of the entire POPEYE cartoon backlog to television that year.

Popeye had fared somewhat better than most series at Famous, because it was built on such a strong foundation. The transition from Fleischer to Famous was least apparent in this series during the 1940s, and late black-and-white entries like SCRAP THE JAPS and CARTOONS AIN'T HUMAN matched anything done under Dave Fleischer's supervision. Early color shorts like WE'RE ON OUR WAY TO RIO got the "new" series off to a flying start, and later travels off the beaten path in films like ROCKET TO MARS (an impressive postwar sci-fi short) maintained a high level of quality.

But in the early 1950s the POPEYE shorts fell into a treadmill pattern just like the other Famous series and repeated the same worn-out stories ad nauseam. Some of the most promising-sounding titles—POPEYE FOR PRESIDENT, released in the election year of

Promotion for BOO MOON. © **Harvey Famous Cartoons.**

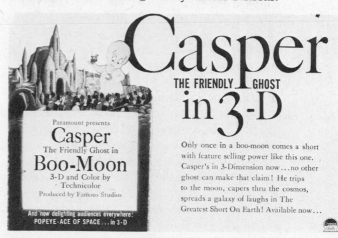

Sound mixer Maurice Manne screens a Popeye sequence on his movieola for Seymour Kneitel, Izzy Sparber, and business manager Seymour Schultz in the 1950s.

1956, and POPEYE'S 20TH ANNIVERSARY— offered the biggest disappointments when they reverted to formula; particularly the latter title, which turned out to be a "cheater" full of footage from older cartoons, was dismaying.

The best POPEYES of the 1950s were remakes of earlier cartoons—without much of their predecessors' spontaneity and minus the freewheeling mumbles of Jack Mercer, who in later years toned down this charming trait. SPREE LUNCH has restaurateurs Popeye and Bluto vying for Wimpy's patronage, as they did in WHAT! NO SPINACH? and WE AIM

TO PLEASE. BABY WANTS SPINACH and THRILL OF FAIR repeat the premise of LITTLE SWEE' PEA, with the innocent infant crawling in and out of trouble as Popeye follows in hot pursuit. A HAUL IN ONE echoes the rivalry of LET'S GET MOVIN, made some twenty years before. The examples could go on and on.

The missing ingredient in these later POPEYES was *fun*—the kind of lighthearted attitude that made the 1930s shorts so entertaining. The Famous cartoons took themselves much too seriously and lost the vitality that distinguished the earlier films.

Shortly after the POPEYE series expired, Paramount sold its backlog of remaining post-1950 cartoons to the Harvey Company, a publishing firm that had turned all the Famous Studios characters into comic book stars. With this major transaction, Harvey acquired not only the films but the rights to the characters, in perpetuity. The company refilmed the main titles of every short, replacing the Paramount emblem with a Harveytoons logo, and prospered from the television sales of this all-color package.

Paramount not only lost all its starring characters at this time, but also one of its principals. Izzy Sparber died in the late 1950s, leaving Seymour Kneitel in sole command. Attempts to generate interest in new characters like the Cat and Jeepers and Creepers during 1960 produced nothing but yawns, and for the balance of his cartoon output Kneitel relied on story men to come up with a steady supply of "one-shot" ideas. The Paramount crew tried to keep up to date with stories about outer space, but quickly drove that theme into the ground through endless repetition.

In 1961 Paramount acquired a cartoon short for theatrical distribution from an outside producer, William Snyder; the cartoon, MUNRO, won an Academy Award, and Paramount subsequently distributed other shorts obtained from Snyder and the director Gene Deitch. Later in the 1960s Paramount purchased a whole series called NUDNICK, which Deitch directed at his studio in Czechoslovakia.

Meanwhile, Kneitel and the Paramount studio were hired by King Features as one of the suppliers for its new package of television cartoons. Executive producer Al Brodax wanted to make 212 new POPEYES, 50 BEETLE BAILEYS, 50 KRAZY KATS, and 50 SNUFFY SMITH cartoons—all in the space of two or three years. The logistics were staggering, and no one animation house could handle it all. Instead, the work was farmed out all over the world, with most of the storyboards and sound tracks divided between New York and California production companies. To say that the results were inconsistent would be a mild understatement.

While Kneitel and his staff had already been cutting back on animation to keep within theatrical budgets, the exigencies of TV production made the operation tighter still. Whereas storyboards had once taken six weeks to develop, they were now turned out in one week. Animation was reduced to an absolute minimum, and whole scenes were indexed for reuse. No one at Paramount had ever heard of such a thing before—although the repetitious nature of its cartoons would seem to have suggested it. When Kneitel learned that reuse of animation was a staple of TV mass production, he exclaimed, "We should have thought of this years ago!" As part of the production arrangement, Paramount released some of the King Features TV cartoons to theaters, where they must have looked particularly poor.

With the completion of these television cartoons, Paramount returned to its theatrical schedule. Then on July 30, 1964, Seymour

Kneitel suffered a heart attack and died.

He was replaced by Howard Post, a young man who had been an in-betweener at the studio ten years earlier and had left for the greener pastures of comic books. He worked with Kneitel on stories for the King Features cartoons, and it was this association that led to his recruitment by Paramount.

There was some resentment that a younger man had been brought in from "outside" to take over the reins of this department, but Post did his best to live up to the job. "At that time," he recalls, "animation was not as limited as it is now. My feeling was that if you got to the key positions that told the story, you could get there without innumerable drawings. At the time I was producing theatrical shorts in a range from $12,000 to $17,000. I had reasonably good crews, not really up to the talent pool

Paramount stars Jerry Lewis, Dean Martin, Bob Hope, and Bing Crosby salute Popeye on his anniversary in a publicity drawing from POPEYE'S 20TH ANNIVERSARY **(1954). © King Features Syndicate.**

Honey Halfwitch and her friend Silent Knight in BAG-GIN' THE DRAGON (1966).

on the West Coast, but I had a couple of guys who could draw well, and a couple of guys who could animate well, and between them we were capable, I felt, of putting out some nice pictures.

"The idea at that point was to come up with something different. I felt that one of the strengths of Disney was music, and I thought that instead of just writing musical effects, we should make a conversion to writing songs. If a song took off, you had a hit show, and a hit song. Even though we had a five- or six-minute format, there was still time to get something in."

Post composed several songs himself and encouraged music director Winston Sharples to think in terms of melodies and themes, but the idea didn't cause any particular stir. Certainly Post's syrupy theme song for the HONEY HALFWITCH series didn't help to sell the doggedly cute apprentice witch to audiences—nor did the stories that revolved around this character.

The director/producer also inherited Seymour Kneitel's SWIFTY AND SHORTY series,

which was nothing to shout about. Comedian Eddie Lawrence ("the old philospher") provided the voices for these stories about a tall, chain-smoking con man and a short, bulbous patsy—as unappealing a cartoon team as ever created.

Post fared much better with one-shot gag cartoons—but the abbreviated production schedules imposed on him sometimes inspired a certain inventiveness even in series entries. For one SWIFTY AND SHORTY cartoon he instructed his staff to paint the two characters solid white, with no delineations within those outlines; this procedure not only saved time but enabled his background artist to render more colorful and elaborate paintings, since the characters couldn't possibly clash with them.

One of the studio's brightest moments came when newspaper cartoonist Jack Mendelsohn tried his hand at writing and directing. He did two cartoons based on a kid's eye view of the world. One of them, THE STORY OF GEORGE WASHINGTON, is a delightful film that deserves revival and wider exposure. In it, a schoolboy narrates the story of Washington as childish crayon-type drawings illustrate his words, making visual puns based on a misunderstanding of phrases and meanings (the King of England putting too many "tacks" on America, and the like). Animator Al Eugster followed Mendelsohn's storyboard drawings as closely as possible, to retain the deliberately unspoiled, childlike appearance.

At this time only one animator worked on a film. Given the simplified methods of limited animation, the footage quota was somewhere between seventy-five to a hundred feet a week, which meant that one man could do the job previously tackled by four. Eugster, Marty Taras, Morey Reden, Bill Pattengill, and Nick Tafuri were the mainstays of the department during this period.

But Howard Post's days were numbered.

Long-standing difficulties between him and his supervisor at Paramount came to a head toward the end of 1965. There were problems regarding the completion of a television pilot featuring Bill Dana (as José Jiménez), and an embarrassing moment when TWO BY TWO— one of Post's favorite cartoons, about a duck reluctant to find a mate for Noah's Ark—was rejected as "blasphemous" by a sensitive member of Paramount's board of directors.

Shamus Culhane replaced Howard Post in November 1965; he was determined to revamp and reorganize the studio and felt that there was much room for improvement. One of his first moves was to double the sum paid out to free-lance story men, in the hope of attracting better material. "You can't hang good animation on a bad story and expect to do anything with it," he explains. Among his contributors were Eli Bauer, Joe Sabo, and Howard Beckerman.

He also wanted to avoid possible ruts and, interestingly enough, scored his greatest success in much the same way that Post had before him, with a child-oriented film called MY DADDY, THE ASTRONAUT; like its predecessor, the film is drawn in juvenile scrawl. It tells the story of a father who has gone to the moon, but doesn't survive a day at the amusement park nearly as well. The short was quite successful and marked the first Paramount film ever shown at the International Animation Festival in Annecy, France.

Trying new ideas was not in line with corporate policy for cartoons, however. Culhane recalls: "The sales department at Paramount was a bunch of fat, cigar-chewing gentlemen who looked at these new things I was attempting in horror. They got more and more hostile. They said, 'Why can't you figure out something like Bugs Bunny?' and I tried to explain to them that Bugs Bunny didn't come about because somebody said, 'Let's make Bugs Bunny.' It had to be done almost by accident, to find a character who was a good 'actor.' It just happened, you couldn't order one. But they didn't believe it. They thought I was lying down on the job. They were old, tired guys who symbolized some of the antique attitudes in the business."

The studio's apparent salvation came with a contract to make television segments of THE MIGHTY THOR for producer Steve Krantz. Culhane took the assignment and augmented his staff with youngsters from art school. He says today that the challenge of doing a new type of cartoon, using a staff of old-timers and newcomers learning together, created a wonderful esprit de corps. Among the animators on staff were Doug Crane, Jack Schnerk, and Chuck Harriton, who also directed some shorts. Culhane hoped to expand even further, into production of television commercials and industrial films, and he felt that the prestige of the Paramount name would be a tremendous asset in getting started.

Unfortunately, production problems on THE MIGHTY THOR resulting from inexperience reduced the studio's profit on this job to a very small amount. When Krantz returned to Paramount with a large order for episodes of SPIDERMAN, the studio hierarchy turned him down. The studio had recently been purchased by the Gulf and Western conglomerate, and ledger sheets were being scrutinized. "What was unseen was that we had trained a whole group of people to do the new thing, and they were ready and willing to go on," says Culhane. "Also, prior to my arrival, Paramount had had a bad year, and took all the cartoons they owned and sold them off, which boosted their income— that was sheer profit. But they cleaned the place out . . . and here we were with no income except for what we were turning out."

The rejection of Krantz's lucrative offer sent Culhane packing, and the animation crew had to adust to yet another change of leadership. This time, the new producer-director was Ralph Bakshi, the twenty-nine-year-old "wonder boy" of Terrytoons. Bakshi arrived in May 1967 and before long had six cartoons in production—each of them unusual in terms of story or design. He worked closely with his talented designer/layout man Cosmo Anzilotti, and with such story men as Eli Bauer, whom he had known at Terrytoons.

Some of the Bakshi cartoons are worthy efforts at trying something new and different. MINI-SQUIRTS is about a shrimp-sized boy and girl who "play" at marriage with uncompromising seriousness, while MARVIN DIGS is about a hippie (depicted as a ball of hair with big eyes and a friendly smile) who paints his parents' house in psychedelic patterns. While visually pleasing, these cartoons score points for good intentions, not for results. Both premises are sabotaged by heavy-handed treatment—a common fault in Bakshi's early work. It wasn't until the young director made his first feature film, FRITZ THE CAT, that he was able to break loose from traditional commercial considerations and express himself openly and honestly.

Shortly after Election Day in 1967, animator Al Eugster went to Bakshi for advice on a scene. "Here I was, concerned with the inner workings of my scene," he recalls, "and Ralph said, 'Forget it, Al, we're closing.' That took care of *that* problem!"

Bakshi was able to complete a few works in progress before Gulf and Western closed the doors of Paramount's cartoon studio for good in December. Some of the people who were put out of work had been with the studio for more than thirty years.

But unemployment was the only tangible loss involved in Paramount's shutdown. No one seemed to miss the cartoons. They had made no impact on audiences, and they didn't mean very much to their creators either.

No one mourned the death of Paramount's cartoon studio for what it was—a small outfit turning out uninspired shorts. But there were sad feelings in the animation business for what *might* have been—and what *had* been many years ago.

After all, the same animators had brought Popeye and Betty Boop to life.

12

UPA

I n 1952 the distinguished critic Gilbert Seldes wrote in *Saturday Review*, "The best way to identify United Productions of America is to say: 'They're the people who made GERALD MCBOING BOING.' And the best way to identify the quality of the product is to say that every time you see one of their animated cartoons, you are likely to recapture the sensation you had when you first saw STEAMBOAT WILLIE, the early SILLY SYMPHONIES, THE BAND CONCERT—the feeling that something new and wonderful has happened, something almost too good to be true."

Other critics shared Seldes's enthusiasm and accorded the UPA cartoons a response unheard of in animation since those early days of Disney triumphs.

Yet UPA was no overnight success. Although its breakthrough with audiences and critics came in the early 1950s, the company had been hard at work since the mid-1940s. And while its reputation was based on its films' radical departures from the Disney style, virtually all of UPA's staff had received its animation training at the Walt Disney studio.

In the late 1930s Disney was hungry for talent. His company offered gainful employment—and considerable challenge—to young men fresh out of art school, and they responded by the score. This "new breed," recruited during the SNOW WHITE period of studio expansion, tended to be more progressive and artistically aware than the earlier wave of Disney animators. This difference eventually caused a schism, the younger men feeling they had to take the brunt of an anti-art bias among senior staffers who had little or no fine arts background.

Bill Hurtz says, "The younger people were also suffficiently independent and didn't have stars in their eyes about Walt, so that when the strike came at Disney's [in 1941] they were the leaders. They had knocked about during the Depression, and they had some kind of social consciousness. Whereas the typical young kid who was president of his high school cartoon club and got his art education at Disney—and a very good one it was—tended to say, 'If it weren't for Walt I wouldn't be where I am.'"

The Disney strikers, who were active in the recently formed Screen Cartoonists

317

Guild, encouraged their colleagues to think about change and progress in the cartoon medium. A March 1942 issue of *The Animator*, prepared by such members as Phil Eastman, John Hubley, and Eugene Fleury, featured one articulate plea:

When the title to an animated cartoon flashes on the screen, there is invariably a feeling of joyous anticipation on the part of the audience. "This is going to be good!" they seem to be saying. The public is automatically sympathetic and is more willing to accept innovation and originality in the animated cartoon than in any other motion picture medium. And yet, in most of the pictures we turn out there is a tendency to rely on something that has always worked in the past. (While story is admitted to be a major weakness in cartoons, it is not our purpose to discuss that department now.)

A progressive, intelligent approach to animation, and realization that it is an expressive and not a mechanical medium, is imperative if we want to keep animated cartoons from stagnating. Development and growth of animation is dependent upon varied, significant subject matter presented in an organized form, evolved from elements inherent in the medium. Among the least understood of these elements are the graphic ones, in spite of the fact that animation is almost entirely concerned with drawings, drawings which must function in both time and space.

This was the voice of Art, trying desperately to break through the barriers of apathy and the assembly line in a very tight-knit industry. The first break came when ex-Disneyite Frank Tashlin was given creative control of the Screen Gems studio and hired virtually his entire staff off the Disney picket line.

As creative head, Tashlin encouraged his men to experiment—in style as well as with content. The films were still gag-oriented, but Tashlin's particular brand of manic comedy, plus the graphic innovations of design-

ers like Zack Schwartz, John Hubley, John McLeish, and Ted Parmelee, made the Screen Gems product decidedly different.

This attitude was the embryo of UPA.

Many of these Screen Gems artists reconverged in the Army's First Motion Picture Unit, stationed at Fort Roach in Culver City, California, during World War II. Here they joined animators and artists from other studios, to tackle the considerable demand of Uncle Sam for war-related films. The atmosphere was surprisingly creative. The armed forces' concern with film was functional, not artistic; they didn't care about graphic style as long as it didn't interfere with the point being made. Some adventurous artists took advantage of this situation and tried out new ideas that wouldn't have survived at a commercial studio.

Again, the ideas that were to solidify at UPA received an important trial run.

Meanwhile the company that actually became UPA was born, under modest circumstances. Two friends who had both worked at Disney's decided to rent some space in a Los Angeles office building, in order to have a studio where they could paint in their spare time. Zachary Schwartz was then working at Screen Gems, and Dave Hilberman was with Graphic Films (although he soon left to join the Frank Capra Army First Motion Picture Unit).

Another Disney alumnus, Stephen Bosustow, had convinced his superiors at Hughes Aircraft to do a filmstrip on safety, and he brought the idea to Graphic Films. When Graphic's Lester Novros turned it down, Hilberman suggested that he and Schwartz give it a try. When this job was completed, the three moonlighting artists looked around for other work.

Just at this time the United Auto Workers union became interested in sponsoring a pro-Roosevelt campaign film for the upcom-

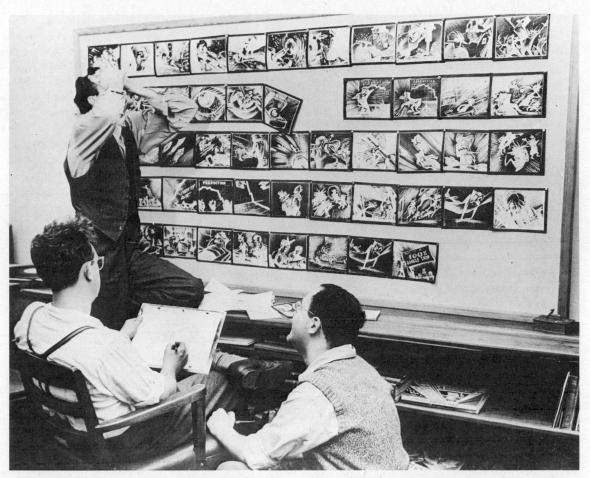

Steve Bosustow strikes a histrionic pose while discussing a storyboard with Zack Schwartz and Dave Hilberman in the early 1940s.

ing 1944 presidential election, and Screen Cartoonists Guild business agent Bill Pomerance was approached to help get it made. He contacted John Hubley, who was then stationed at Fort Roach, and Hubley prepared a storyboard with Phil Eastman and Bill Hurtz.

Dave Hilberman remembers, "When the board was ready for production, it first went to Leon Schlesinger at Warner's, because Chuck Jones had directed—and I had

designed—a film on point rationing, as a union contribution to the war effort. Schlesinger had made studio facilities available evenings as his contribution for that film . . . but this new one was too political, and he turned it down. Only then did the UAW people come to our little one-room painting studio at the Otto K. Olsen Building to see if we could handle it."

Adrian Woolery recalls, "They bid on the film, and in January were awarded the contract. The film was to be completed before the convention in August, which meant that starting from scratch, the completed film had to be done in six months' time. Zach, Steve, and Dave formed a company, called it Industrial Films and Poster Service, and I was the first employee.''

The film was named HELL BENT FOR ELECTION, and its production was a communal effort. Zack Schwartz recalls, "Overnight, the little studio room that was supposed to have been a hideaway for Dave and myself was crammed to the walls with people. All our friends, from Screen Gems and Warner Brothers mainly, were up to their necks with us to get that film out. We rented more space in the same building. During the day it was a ghost town, but at night the whole crew arrived and the joint was jumping. All those wonderful people, after working in their regular jobs all day, were working almost to sun-up on HELL BENT.

"It was one of the most exciting and fulfilling experiences of my life and I could probably say the same for everyone else who knocked himself out to deliver that picture on time."

Why did everyone pitch in this way? "Because the election was so important, we wanted F.D.R. to win," says Schwartz. "And I think because there was great excitement in doing an animated film for this purpose." The commitment was real; many of these people worked for free, including director Chuck Jones. Music was written by Earl Robinson, with lyrics by E. Y. "Yip" Harburg (of THE WIZARD OF OZ fame).

The film symbolized the upcoming election with a pair of trains: the Win the War Special (a sleek super-chief with FDR's face on the locomotive) versus the Defeatist Limited (dated 1929, its second car labeled Hot Air and floating above the track). Some of the other cars were the Business as Usual Sleeper and the Jim Crow Special (a caboose). The "enemy" tries to sidetrack Joe Worker from voting by lulling him to sleep. During a dream sequence we see Joe in white outline, moving in a trance against dark blue backgrounds as he tries to regain his grasp on the election realities and what they will mean to America.

HELL BENT FOR ELECTION is handsome, stylish, and persuasive. It has a lean graphic style that is vibrant, modern, and reminiscent of some contemporary Jones cartoons like THE ARISTO-CAT and THE DOVER BOYS, which had many of the same artists. The film is not as advanced as the later UPA product, but it's a giant step away from Disney styling.

Most importantly, it was a major success. The Industrial team had produced its first film, and the UAW was pleased. But during production, Schwartz, Bosustow, and business manager Ed Gershman had quit their day jobs to devote themselves to this all-important project. Now they needed work, and, aside from some slide films commissioned by the Auto Workers, there was nothing in the wind.

Says Adrian Woolery, "Just about the time it looked as though we were out of business, a job that we had bid on for the Signal Corps came through. From this point on we always seemed to have work coming in, both in industrial-type films, government films, slides, and so forth. We were able to build a pretty sizable full-time staff and move to new and larger quarters. It was also decided that the name of the company should be changed, and it was then that United Productions of America came into existence, shortened thereafter to UPA. It was a three-way partnership, with Zack Schwartz, Dave Hilberman, and Steve Bosustow owning equal parts."

After HELL BENT FOR ELECTION, the next

important UPA film was FLAT HATTING. Made for the Navy as part of the FLIGHT SAFETY SERIES, it was remarkable for its use of cunning satire to warn pilots about the perils of flying low. But it achieved equal notoriety within the animation industry for its modern graphic style. The designer was *New Yorker* cartoonist Robert Osborne. "HELL BENT was good," says Jules Engel, "but it was still a touch of yesterday. FLAT HATTING was the beginning of something very special, in the artwork, and in the way the picture was put together."

This achievement was followed by another "milestone" film, BROTHERHOOD OF MAN, which John Hubley feels was the artistic turning point for the studio. "We went for very flat stylized characters instead of the global three-dimensional Disney characters," he explained in a 1973 interview with John D. Ford of the Mid-America Film Center. "It was greatly influenced by Saul Steinberg and that sharp-nosed character he was doing at that time. . . . Paul Julian did all the backgrounds very flat; he used areas of color that would be elided from the line. Very advanced graphics for that period. Up until this time the Disney tradition hadn't been broken very much, although there had been a few attempts. None of them were as 'pure' or all-out as this one."

"That was Bobe Cannon's great film," adds Dave Hilberman, "because he conceived the little negative person in all of us, and visualized him as this little green man. Bobe was the first animator who developed a style that organically grew out of the new kind of characters we were designing."

BROTHERHOOD OF MAN was equally significant for what it set out to do. Like HELL BENT FOR ELECTION, it was sponsored by the United Auto Workers. "That was a case of the union organizing in the South, and having problems getting blacks and whites to join the same local," Hilberman explains. "So the film was made not for any altruistic purpose, but to help the organizing in the South." Later the film received wide distribution and spread its message far beyond the confines of union membership.

The script, by Ring Lardner, Jr., Maurice Rapf, Hubley, and Phil Eastman, was based on a pamphlet written by two anthropologists from Columbia University. It presented a simple case for tolerance and understanding, and scored points for UPA as a studio that was capable of tackling meaty subject matter in a new and dynamic format.

This helped the company win other nontheatrical assignments in the aftermath of World War II. Slowly, a full-time staff was built, including Hubley; director-animator Robert (Bobe) Cannon; writer Phil Eastman; designers William (Bill) Hurtz, Paul Julian, Jules Engel, and Herb Klynn, and animator Joyce Weir.

In 1946 differences arose between Schwartz and Hilberman on one side and their partner Bosustow on the other. Although each principal has his own version of how the split came about, the result is a matter of fact: that year Zack Schwartz and Dave Hilberman reluctantly sold out their interest in the company. (Subsequently they opened another studio in New York called Tempo Productions.)

"And then we made a very serious mistake," says Hilberman. "Instead of offering our stock to Hub [John Hubley], Bill Hurtz, and the others, principally Bobe Cannon, in attempting to keep it quiet we offered it to Steve Bosustow, and that's how he got control of the studio. That was a very serious blunder which I regretted years later, because the artists could have been running the studio, and it would have been quite a different story."

As it happens, Bosustow did sell shares of

One of UPA's stylized renditions of the Fox and Crow:
THE MAGIC FLUKE (1949).

his stock to most of the key staff members—
an important move since the company's fluc-
tuating fortunes made it impossible for it to
issue a regular weekly paycheck during the
next few years. But Bosustow retained controlling interest of UPA, naming himself
executive producer and appointing John
Hubley his supervising director. Adrian
Woolery stayed on as production manager,
and Ed Gershman remained the company's
business manager.

Looking back, Woolery comments,
"Though this period of Industrial Films and
UPA were exciting years, at no time were we
able to make a profit big enough to get out
from under the burden of bank loans, and
the resulting interest payments. By hook and
crook, however, we managed to buy some
property in Burbank and arranged for the
construction of a building."

Around this same time Bosustow effected

his first coup by interesting Columbia Pictures in the distribution of UPA cartoons.
Columbia was dissatisfied with the product
of its Screen Gems studio and offered UPA a
trial run if they agreed to use the company's
established characters, the Fox and Crow.
Bosustow said yes, and his staff went to
work.

"The first one with the Fox and the Crow
was ROBIN HOODLUM," John Hubley recalled
years later. "The Fox as Robin Hood, the
Crow as the Sheriff of Nottingham. The
Merry Men were a sanguine bunch of tea-
drinking Englishmen. It was funny and very
sophisticated. Columbia didn't like it—it
wasn't a standard audience film. We made
another one called THE MAGIC FLUKE, which
was a more popular story using the same
characters, the Fox and Crow. It was more
successful. We were using very modern techniques even though we had to use the conventional characters. . . . We were doing
very modern backgrounds with flat patterns,
opaque paint, and other things that weren't
particularly 'classical.'"

Classical or not, both ROBIN HOODLUM and
THE MAGIC FLUKE were nominated for Academy Awards, and Columbia realized that
UPA could handle its cartoon requirements
from that time on.

There was one final barrier to break down,
however—that of getting Columbia to let the
studio create its own characters. Hubley and
the others wanted to get away from funny
animals and try something different, something with a *human* character. They proposed a story that Columbia reluctantly
accepted, only because it had an animal as
well as a human and bore the title RAGTIME
BEAR. The real star of the film was the nearsighted Mister Magoo.

Magoo was presented in this film as a

crotchety old man who goes on vacation with his lunkheaded nephew Waldo. The youngster wears a raccoon coat and plays a banjo; when he's lost en route and a grizzly bear goes after the banjo, Magoo mistakes the animal for his nephew, with hilarious consequences.

It was a funny idea, and the rendering of the main character was dynamic and different. A key element was the selection of Jim Backus to do the voice. Jerry Hausner, who recommended Backus and played the part of Waldo, told Magoo chronicler Howard Rieder that on RAGTIME BEAR, "We went into the studio with two pages of dialogue. We read all of the speeches that had been written down. Then Hubley did something that no other animated cartoon director has ever done in my presence. He said, 'Let's do it again and ad-lib around the subject. Throw in any wild thoughts you might have.' We did another version of it. Backus began to go crazy and have a good time. . . . He invented a lot of things and brought to the cartoons a fresh, wonderful approach."

Though the character was fictitious, and a perfect candidate for visually oriented cartoon gags, he was derived from several real-life figures. Hubley patterned his concept of Magoo after a bullheaded uncle. Backus drew on observations of his businessman father. And others who worked on the early films looked to W. C. Fields's screen character as a source of inspiration.

Eventually, several people claimed credit for the creation of Mister Magoo. The one man hardly mentioned was Millard Kaufman, who wrote the story for RAGTIME BEAR. But Bill Hurtz sums up a general feeling among UPA veterans when he says, "There may have been four or five people really responsible for evolving Magoo, but you could easily say that Hub's stamp was by far the strongest."

John Hubley loved "the old coot," and even though he disliked the idea of a continuing series, he made a second short, SPELLBOUND HOUND, and then returned to the series a year later for one of the very best entries, FUDDY DUDDY BUDDY. Animator Pete Burness took over the direction of this series from Hubley and made some fine cartoons in the early 1950s, but Hubley's FUDDY DUDDY BUDDY was hard to top. It presented one of the rare moments of character insight in the series' long history—when Magoo, confronted with the fact that he has mistaken a walrus for his tennis-playing chum, hangs his head, momentarily defeated by his nearsightedness and unable to deny it, even to himself. Then he pulls himself together, bucks up his spirit, and declares that, walrus or not, "I *like* him!" and he determines to rekindle his relationship with the amiable creature. Such character nuances were rare in later Magoo cartoons.

Magoo gave UPA its first popular success, but it was another film that solidified the studio's reputation: GERALD MCBOING BOING,

Early sketches of Mister Magoo.

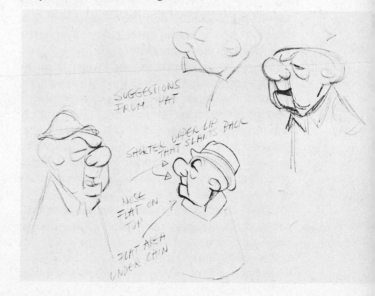

GERALD McBOING BOING (1951), UPA's first great success. © **Columbia Pictures.**

completed in 1950 and released in January 1951.

On February 5, 1951, *Time* magazine reported, "For five years Bosustow's UPA has been trying to break away from such familiar Disneyisms as animal slapstick for its own sake, careful airbrushing to give figures the illusion of three dimensions, painstaking imitation of live movement. In their latest short, already delighting moviegoers at Manhattan's Paris Theater, the UPA craftsmen make a clean break.

"GERALD MCBOING BOING tells a funny story about a small boy whose efforts to talk produce only such sound effects as 'Boing! Boing!' Everything about the film is simple but highly stylized: bold line drawings, understated motion, striking color and airy design in the spirit of modern poster art, caricatured movements and backgrounds as well as figures."

Time concluded, "Little Gerald's talents are too specialized for many other stories, but in its own way, his 'Boing!' may prove as resounding as the first peep out of Mickey Mouse."

The magazine's prophecy was right on target. This film—one of the finest animated cartoons ever made—had an impact that was both immediate and long-lasting. On a short-term basis, it established UPA as the predominant force in animation. Gerald won raves from highbrow critics, newspaper reviewers, and the toughest audience of all: the motion picture trade reporters, who recognized how superior it was to the assembly-line output of most other studios.

In the spring of 1951 GERALD MCBOING BOING was voted an Academy Award as best animated short subject. (The competition was an MGM Tom and Jerry cartoon, JERRY'S COUSIN, and another UPA entry, TROUBLE INDEMNITY, with Mister Magoo.) It was a moment of triumph for UPA—formal recognition of their groundbreaking efforts in a year when no Disney short was even nominated.

What was all the shouting about?

Gilbert Seldes explained in *Saturday Review:*

In a sense, the UPA product is not so much new as it is a return to the principles of the animated cartoon, those fundamentals which Disney understood and exploited more fully than anyone before him, and which he has abandoned. . . . As Disney has come closer and closer to photographic realism, he has subtly violated the character of the cartoon (which is a drawing on a flat surface) by giving it depth and, in a brilliant combination of artwork and machinery, has substituted movement—remarkably lifelike—for animation.

The UPA cartoons are flat; whatever sense of depth you get comes from perspective. . . . And because they use one drawing for every two or three frames of the film, instead of Disney's one for each frame, the figures move less smoothly, they have a galvanic animation.

The delight which these pictures gives is, however, not merely pleasure taken in any return to the primitive. The positive virtues of UPA are their impudent and intelligent approach to subject matter and a gay palette, a cascading of light colors, the use of color and line always to suggest, never to render completely, a great deal of warmth, and an unfailing wit. Some of the cartoons recall stock episodes—tubas grunt and Mr. Magoo steps off a girder into thin air—but the best of them are as fresh in concept as in execution.

In the case of GERALD, the concept came from a particularly fruitful source: popular author/humorist Dr. Seuss, who, as Theodore Geisel, had worked with many of the UPA staff on Army films during the war. His story was adapted for animation by Phil Eastman and Bill Scott; elements in Geisel's rhyming dialogue that would be redundant with a visual context were dropped or consolidated. Other elements, like the "sound effects script" that Gerald performs on radio, were purely Eastman and Scott's invention.

When they were through with the storyboards, the film was passed on to director Bobe Cannon and designer Bill Hurtz. Says Hurtz today, "We had a concept that the style really came out of the story, or out of the material. In GERALD MCBOING BOING, we were trying for absolute simplicity—how few lines could be in this picture? How elemental could it get? That was a challenge.

"We also had a concept that the path of action should look continuous: When the character is walking down the street and he turns and runs into his house, the next cut, he comes upstairs; next cut, he goes through his bedroom. This was a continuous path of action that the eye can trace, with a dissolve to the next place and he is there." The collaborators also developed an innovative method of holding a character in place while the background dissolves behind him. "We used a lot of those camera tricks in lieu of animation," Hurtz explains. "We were very sensitive to the means the camera afforded us.

"Also, we thought of this as a picture without walls. There are no lines defining the difference between the ceiling and a wall. A picture is on a space, and then there's a rug. So 'rug' means that's the floor and 'picture' means that's the wall. Then the props were placed relative to the action; we thought of them as standing characters. Every line in that picture was carefully conceived.

"Then the action was charted and the music was written to that action before it was ever animated. They recorded it and animated to that music. Bobe did a masterful job of timing the action." Animation was in the extremely capable hands of Bill Melendez, Rudy Larriva, Pat Matthews, Willis Pyle, and Frank Smith.

The final touch was the use of color, supervised by Jules Engel and Herb Klynn. Bright, flat colors predominated—with color often representing a background in itself,

The scene inspired by THE FALLEN IDOL. © **Columbia Pictures.**

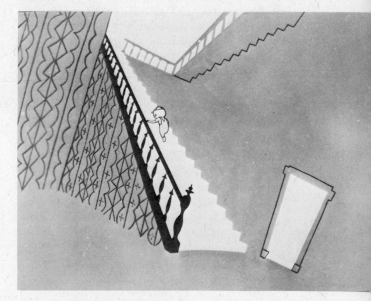

broken only by the sparest use of "props."

GERALD also impressed audiences with its simple, psychological use of color to convey moods. During the first part of the film, when Gerald is happy, the major colors are yellow/ocher and green. At the first sign of rejection, however, the colors darken, and when Gerald runs away from home it is nighttime. The moment a radio executive finds the boy and offers him a job, the colors begin to brighten, and the film ends on the same happy note with which it began. (The highly dramatic, abstract composition of Gerald sadly walking upstairs after being rejected by his schoolmates was inspired by the British film THE FALLEN IDOL, which some of the UPA staffers had recently seen.)

The accolades that greeted GERALD MCBOING BOING on its New York debut resounded for several years and prepared a growing audience for other UPA endeavors.

Some critics less perceptive than Gilbert Seldes seized on UPA's visual style as the cartoon's primary asset, minimizing the importance of story selection and treatment. Nothing proved their point more eloquently than the studio's eventual follow-ups to GER-ALD MCBOING BOING, all directed by Bobe Cannon. GERALD MCBOING BOING'S SYM-PHONY (1953), HOW NOW MCBOING BOING (1954), and GERALD MCBOING BOING ON THE PLANET MOO (1955) emulated, and in some ways duplicated, the visual appeal of the original cartoon. The character of Gerald was presented in the same winning fashion. But the cartoons themselves were mediocre, for the simple reason that the stories were contrived and unconvincing. Even Bobe Cannon could not imbue these hollow scripts with charm.

The triumph of UPA was not in its artwork, but in its marriage of form *and* con-

tent. When these elements were perfectly matched, the results were unbeatable.

For the staff, UPA's "vision" of animated cartoons offered a welcome change—and a host of challenges. Artists at other studios might have rebelled at having to animate angular or boxy characters like the original Magoo, but the UPA staff didn't mind. Since most of them had animated training films during the war, the notion of drawing and moving oddly shaped objects was already familiar.

As a break from the repetition and the formula procedures at other studios, UPA was unique. "I was working at Warner Brothers before I went to UPA, and boy, it was just like a breath of fresh air," says animator Bill Melendez. "It was really a great adventure."

But this great adventure had its problems. First, there were constant financial pressures. UPA's initial contract with Columbia provided a budget of approximately $27,000 for each seven-minute short, with UPA retaining 25 percent ownership of the film. But every film came in over budget, and the studio was forced to sell back shares of its ownership to Columbia in order to make up the difference.

The only reason the studio got itself into such a predicament was its artists' total commitment to quality. Men like Hubley were not budget-oriented; they were film-oriented. In later years UPA's stylized formats were misinterpreted as attempts at *limited* animation. This simply isn't true. "We talked of *good* animation," says Bill Melendez. "It's like accusing Chaplin of walking with his funny little walk so he could get across the screen faster and save film."

Jules Engel concurs. "Even if we had more money . . . let's say, even if we had another $20,000, we would have refined a picture more, but the character of the picture would have been the same. We would have taken

Steve Bosustow (left) and Walt Disney accept British achievement awards—Bosustow for GERALD McBOING BOING and Disney, ironically enough, for a live-action short, BEAVER VALLEY.

back scenes and done them again and improved things. In that respect, the money would have helped, but not in ideas and graphic presence."

Still, the pressures existed and caused various reverberations throughout the studio—from payroll inconsistencies to periodic lay-offs. No one wanted to compromise on the production of a film just for the sake of budget. "For the studio to have survived, with this attitude prevailing, was a sheer miracle," contends Adrian Woolery. "We were going broke fast. Had it not been that television was creating a new market, with TV commercials, UPA could *not* have survived.

"We contracted with J. Walter Thompson to do a series of eight 60-second commercials for Ford Motors with Dr. Seuss. I worked out

a good budget, which if we could hold to, would provide a substantial profit, perhaps the first realized by UPA in all its existence. Out of desperation, and I sat on top of the entire production like a mother hen, lo and behold we made a dandy profit. It did wonders for morale. At last it seemed there was a feeling of job security—a paycheck every week, and some raises were handed out."

Meanwhile, the returns on GERALD McBOING BOING and the first MR. MAGOO cartoons enabled Bosustow to get a budget increase from Columbia to nearly $35,000 per short. Things were looking up.

The early 1950s saw a remarkable output of dazzling, creative cartoons. Bobe Cannon was especially productive, and directed a series of shorts that emphasized charm and imagination over gags and stories. GEORGIE

Ludwig Bemelman's MADELINE (1952), brought to the screen by Bobe Cannon. © Columbia Pictures.

John Hubley's ROOTY TOOT TOOT (1952). © Columbia Pictures.

AND THE DRAGON was a delightful comedy about a Scottish lad and his fast-growing, fire-breathing pet; THE OOMPAHS concerned a family of musical instruments; CHRISTOPHER CRUMPET was about a boy who vented his frustrations by turning himself into a chicken; and MADELINE was a delicate rendition of Ludwig Bemelmans's popular children's story.

John Hubley found himself too busy with supervisory duties to spend much time on his own films. Finally he created ROOTY TOOT TOOT, one of the best-known UPA films, "and nearly broke the studio making it," according to one colleague. The effort was worthwhile, for this stylized rendition of the Frankie and Johnny story proved to be a classic of modern animation. Hubley worked with Bill Scott on the adaptation, and with Paul Julian on color and design. Hubley and Julian were kindred spirits, with similar tastes and backgrounds; they were influenced and inspired by many modern artists and designers and weren't afraid to incorporate their ideas into a seven-minute entertainment cartoon. Hubley also gave what he believed to be the first screen credit to a black composer for a film score, to Phil Moore for the jazz score of ROOTY TOOT TOOT.

The same year that ROOTY TOOT TOOT was released (1952), Hubley and Julian collaborated on another piece of animation that won UPA wide acclaim: the main titles and linking segments of Stanley Kramer's live-action feature THE FOURPOSTER.

THE FOURPOSTER is a charming, intelligent adaptation of Jan de Hartog's two-character play, starring Lilli Palmer and Rex Harrison, which traces the relationship of a married couple over some thirty-five years. UPA contributed seven "intrascenes" that were not so much counterparts as integrated parts of the story—telling in a few moments of cartoon images about the passage of time or change in character between one live segment and the next. The film opens with imaginative main titles. The first intrascene shows Harrison's school years at the turn of the century, while the next depicts his success as an author—and his growing ego. Then comes a passage of years and "progress" in the civilized world. This is followed by World War I, in which the couple's son is killed. A fifth segment establishes the setting as the roaring twenties, the sixth introduces the couple's second honeymoon, and the final segment reveals the wife's death.

These witty, quietly expressive sequences represent some of UPA's finest work, achieving that all-important goal of superbly intertwining form and content.

(The distribution of THE FOURPOSTER had one unexpected result. It was the first UPA "cartoon" to be shown in Yugoslavia, where its stylistic innovations inspired a group of young artists. Fired with enthusiasm, and suddenly freed from the idea that animation had to be full-blown and literal, they started making films and eventually became the Zagreb Animation Studio, one of the finest studios in the world today.)

As Hubley moved on to projects such as this, two former designers were promoted to directorial status on the theatrical shorts. Bill Hurtz, who had been directing industrial and commercial films for the company, scored a personal triumph in adapting James Thurber's A UNICORN IN THE GARDEN for the screen. In later years the animation of highly individual artists' drawings became more familiar, but in 1953 the faithful reproduction of Thurber's characters and settings was particularly impressive. Hurtz recalls that he deliberately assigned the cleanup work on this film to "some of the poorest draftsmen in the studio, [to get] that nice lumpy look." He also captured the low-key charm of Thurber's fable, which, possibly, was more diffi-

Bill Hurtz's adaptation of A UNICORN IN THE GARDEN (1953). © Columbia Pictures.

cult than reproducing the visual style.

(One person who was not impressed with the finished product was producer Bosustow, who refused to enter UNICORN in competition for the Academy Award.)

Ted Parmelee had been a designer, like Hurtz, but moved on to directing and made his mark with an outstanding rendition of THE TELL-TALE HEART. Bill Scott and Fred Gable adapted the Edgar Allan Poe story, and James Mason was hired to narrate the film. The *Motion Picture Exhibitor*, a publication aimed at theater owners, wrote:

This much-discussed cartoon should have a wide appeal because of its highly imaginative art style. It tells the famous Edgar Allan Poe story of the maniac who had to kill an old man, not for greed, but because he possessed an "evil eye." The technique involved in spinning the eerie yarn is original, daring, and expressive. The whole thing is done in sketches, with the maniac never actually

One of UPA's most striking creations, THE TELL-TALE HEART **(1953).** © **Columbia Pictures.**

appearing. However, his presence is doubly felt by the use of light and shadow to give the effect of impending disaster. The art style is derived from Eugene Berman, scenic designer and ballet designer of the Metropolitan Opera. This is on the same high level as other UPA offerings. James Mason narrates, and the film was produced by Stephen Bosustow and directed by Ted Parmelee. Paul Julian was art designer.

For the blasé reviewer of this trade publication to single out director and designer for crediting in a cartoon was no small triumph. It was just another indication of the respect and admiration that UPA cartoons commanded, even in the strictly-business world of film distribution. THE TELL-TALE HEART was not just another cartoon, to be treated the same way as the new HECKLE AND JECKLE release. It generated feature-caliber reviews and publicity—and had independent marquee value. James Mason's name on the film also gave it an extra boost.

Seen today, THE TELL-TALE HEART remains stylistically impressive, although as an adaptation of Poe it has been eclipsed by the Zagreb Studio's stunning and somber MASQUE OF THE RED DEATH. THE TELL-TALE HEART's biggest problem is pacing; it moves just a bit too quickly to realize the full potential of its eerie narrative. It is one instance in which seven minutes was too short a time to do the job. Steve Bosustow remembers, with some pain, that audiences laughed when they first saw this film. The problem was not just preconditioning, but the cartoon's inability to draw viewers into its dramatic world in such a fast-paced manner.

(This short was specially photographed to achieve a 3-D effect. This was at the height of the 3-D craze, when Bosustow, like many other cartoon producers, thought the new gimmick would revolutionize motion pictures. Needless to say, it did not, and THE TELL-TALE HEART was never released in that format.)

The magic of UPA was to be found in the variety of its films, each one based on a new idea, with a new concept in design and color. (Some of the company's industrial and sponsored films were so enjoyable to watch that they received theatrical bookings.) Instead of having a musical director on staff, UPA hired well-known writers like David Raksin and Ernest Gold, as well as journeymen composers, to do their scores, feeling that it was just as important to have a fresh sound track as to have an individual graphic style for every film. The results were consistently rewarding.

While the founders of UPA reached for a common goal of stylization in the 1940s, their artistic approaches began to differ as the yearly output increased and separate working units were established.

In the early days of the theatrical shorts,

master animator Art Babbitt was hired to direct at UPA, and hewed to a much more conventional approach than the rest of the staff. Such films as GIDDYAP, THE POPCORN STORY, and THE FAMILY CIRCUS were barely recognizable as UPA creations. Babbitt eventually returned to animating, where his talent was put to much better use.

At first the main UPA directors paired off with designers—Hubley with Paul Julian, Cannon with Bill Hurtz. But as the studio grew, assignments were spread out, and new designers came on staff to add even greater variety to the company products. Among the talented art directors were Robert Dranko, Sterling Sturtevant, Lew Keller (later a director), Art Heinemann (who designed MADE-LINE), and the distinctive T. Hee, who doubled as a story man.

As for the MAGOO series, although it bore definite markings of UPA, it followed a more conventional path than any of the contemporary one-shot cartoons. "Naturally, you didn't want to put him into the kind of terrain you put GERALD MCBOING BOING," says Jules Engel, "but the graphic art was still far superior to anything in the indsutry." Many of the early films were designed by Abe Liss.

Pete Burness, who directed most of the MAGOOS, told Howard Rieder, "We got as much design value or high styling as we could into the backgrounds. . . . If you wanted a stone wall or stucco wall, or even the ground, you would never paint it as such. The artist would take a sponge and simulate a texture. He would never take his brush and carefully render a three-dimensional, representational image. Many times on interiors we used colored papers, textured and patterned papers, even wallpaper samples."

These shorts were considered UPA's bread-and-butter product and seldom received artistic accolades, but, looking back at them today, one is startled at the richness of color and design, particularly in the early 1950s titles (which are also the funniest).

The problem with MAGOO was the same one faced by every cartoon series: how to avoid going stale. It wasn't easy. John Hubley felt that the character was somewhat diluted as he became a series star: "They just took very limited aspects of the character—mostly his nearsightedness—and hung on to it. A great deal in the original character, the strength of him, was the fact that he was so damn bullheaded. It wasn't just that he couldn't see very well; even if he had been able to see, he still would have made dumb mistakes, 'cause he was such a bullheaded, opinionated old guy."

Burness conceded the point to Howard Rieder, who wrote a Master's thesis on Magoo, and adapted his paper for publication in *Cinema Journal.* Burness explained that he and others went against Hubley in softening Magoo's personality, in order to

One of Mister Magoo's funnier vehicles, CAPTAINS OUT-RAGEOUS **(1952). © Columbia Pictures.**

make him more appealing. Later Burness revised his thinking somewhat: "I wondered if I was right. I have wondered because he got progressively warmer until he was weakened. It should have been used with discrimination. He might break out from time to time in a sentimental mood, but I believe that his basic character would have been stronger if he had continued crotchety, even somewhat nasty."

Such considerations were a benefit of hindsight, as Magoo maintained his status as a popular, money-making character in theatrical cartoons right through the 1950s. In fact, two of Burness's cartoons—WHEN MAGOO FLEW (1954) and MAGOO'S PUDDLE JUMPER (1956)—won Academy Awards. The first, UPA's initial CinemaScope cartoon, has an amusing mistaken-identity premise, with Magoo boarding an airplane thinking he's going to a movie theater. When the "Fasten Seat Belt" sign lights up, he's all prepared for a HIGH AND THE MIGHTY kind of epic, but instead he's witness to a real-life adventure involving a thief on the lam. As he leaves the plane, he remarks to the stewardess that his only regret is that they didn't show a cartoon—particularly one with that delightful nearsighted fellow. Story credit for this short was shared by Barbara Hammer and veteran cartoon gagman Tedd Pierce, who had recently joined the staff.

MAGOO'S PUDDLE JUMPER deals with Magoo's purchase of an electric car, and an eventful ride underwater for Magoo and his nephew Waldo, with a motorcycle cop in pursuit. The cartoon's chief distinction—aside from good gags by Dick Shaw—is that it won the Academy Award in a year when both of the rival shorts being considered were also UPA cartoons: THE JAYWALKER and GERALD MCBOING BOING ON THE PLANET MOO.

By this time, however, theatrical shorts were the least of UPA's activities. In 1956 CBS commissioned a half-hour series called THE GERALD MCBOING BOING SHOW, which was the first animated program made especially for network television. It required more film material than UPA had ever turned out on a regular basis and necessitated an immediate talent hunt. Many of the studio mainstays (Hubley, Eastman, Scott, Hurtz, Parmelee, and Melendez, among others) were gone, which opened the door for newcomers, who were given immediate creative responsibility. Among the veterans who signed on were Canadian animator-director George Dunning; story man Leo Salkin; and artists Aurie Battaglia, Dun Roman, and Bob McIntosh. Heading the crop of young talent were Ernie Pintoff, Fred Crippen, Jimmy Murikami, Jim Hiltz, and Mordi Gerstein.

Pintoff, whose background was graphic design and who had no animation experience prior to joining UPA, was given the freedom to write, direct, and design three-minute segments for the CBS show—an unparalleled opportunity that launched a bright career. Pintoff's mini-projects for the show ranged from the pictorialization of a satirical Stan Freberg song (FIGHT ON FOR OLD) to a collaboration with experimental film maker John Whitney (LION HUNT).

The only problem with THE GERALD MCBOING BOING SHOW was that it had no punch. Its many components (including old UPA cartoons) were prepared separately, and when series producer Bobe Cannon saw the results, he realized that the overall effect was somewhat "precious." He immediately called in writer Bill Scott to punch up the comedy aspects of the show, but it was a bit late for a satisfactory overhaul.

The show had definite merit, but the parts were greater than the whole and the program's gentle spirit endeared it more to PTA groups and television critics than to children. It survived as a token of good taste on CBS from December 16, 1956, to October 3, 1958.

Meanwhile UPA was thriving in a separate, semiautonomous studio established in New York to handle commercial and nontheatrical work exclusively. Columbia Pictures financed the operation, which opened in the early 1950s with Abe Liss as creative director and Don McCormack as production manager. Ed Cullen, who was then executive vice-president of UPA, points out that it was not only important to be in New York because it was the center of television production and ad agencies, but because it was also the home of Columbia Pictures, which as financial backer and distributor of UPA held a fairly tight rein on the company's activities.

The New York studio had great success in the commercial field, because of the artistic quality of its work, and also because of its reputation. "Agencies liked the idea of working with an Academy Award–winning studio," Cullen recalls. The biggest success the studio ever had was the original Bert and Harry Piel campaign, created by Ed Graham of Young and Rubicam. These personality-oriented beer commercials, with the voices of Bob Elliott and Ray Goulding, took the New York area by storm and were tantamount to a theatrical "hit."

One important talent who made a niche for himself at UPA/New York was Gene Deitch. Deitch had joined the California studio in the late 1940s as an assistant to Bill Hurtz and later claimed that he was the first person to receive all his animation training at UPA—the only one who didn't have the "classical" Disney background. Because he was an assistant, however, Deitch was among the first to be laid off during the company's periodic lulls. Eventually he joined Jam Handy, a major nontheatrical film company in Detroit. When the New York studio was looking for talent, it called on Deitch and he became a principal director at the prestigious commercial house. He was involved in

The last theatrical MAGOO cartoon, made in New York: TERROR FACES MAGOO (1959). © Columbia Pictures.

the success of the Bert and Harry commercials, and that gave him a springboard, first to John Hubley's studio and then to Terrytoons, where he became creative director in 1956—and to which he lured away the Piel campaign. (See Chapter 4.)

After Deitch and Liss left UPA, art director Chris Ishii and animator Jack Goodford assumed the roles of artistic supervisors. The New York staff included such veteran animators as Grim Natwick, Lu Guarnier, and Irv Spector, and promising newcomers like Tissa David and Howard Beckerman. Contact with the West Coast office was provided by a teletype machine, and Beckerman recalls that the day after WHEN MAGOO FLEW won an Academy Award, a message on the machine read, "We are all celebrating. Why don't you do the same?" The New York staff also tackled one theatrical short when commercial work was slow, TERROR FACES MAGOO. Chris Ishii directed this film, which had the dubious distinction of being the last theatrical short the studio ever released.

By this time UPA was more than just the name of a company. The term "UPA animation" was a shorthand way of describing modern animation in general, as the break from Disney-type literalism was followed by studios and independent film makers around the world. In America, UPA-inspired graphics were adopted by many producers of television commercials, and even the major theatrical studios (Warner's, MGM, and the rest) changed their formal approach to design and backgrounds to keep pace with UPA. Perhaps the highest compliment was Disney's use of UPA-type stylization in such shorts as TOOT, WHISTLE, PLUNK AND BOOM and PIGS IS PIGS.

Unfortunately, the studio that had revolutionized animated film suffered incurable growing pains and soon found itself eclipsed by other companies (many run by UPA alumni) that carried the torch UPA had lit.

The man usually blamed for UPA's demise is Steve Bosustow, whose apparent opportunism, and willingness to take credit for the studio's many achievements, made him both disliked and a center of controversy. No one disputed his determination—it was Bosustow who acquired the camera that shot Industrial Films' first motion picture—but when he presented himself as the creator of Mister Magoo in later years, it rankled many of his creative colleagues.

One longtime employee recalls, "It was said of Bosustow that of every ten decisions that he made as president, nine were disastrous and the tenth saved the company."

But Adrian Woolery, who resigned from UPA after a dispute with Bosustow, maintains, "I feel certain that UPA would never have come into existence had it not been for Steve. . . . He was ambitious, aggressive, and sometimes ruthless. As president, he was of course front and center at awards time. But he did know and recognize good talent and provided every opportunity within his domain for an unimpaired expression of creativity."

There are other points to think about. Considering the company's track record, it seems unlikely that UPA could have survived if it had been run solely by artists. Someone had to make the decisions that would keep the company alive and maintain its artistic independence. For better or worse, that man was Bosustow. Somehow, he was able to keep the studio afloat.

Growing pains can do terrible damage to any enterprise. UPA worked best when it was small and everyone was dedicated to a common goal. Expansion was a natural enemy, and success created personality conflicts that had nothing to do with the man in charge. The atmosphere was far from Utopian later on.

Certainly Bosustow wanted no part of the notorious motion picture blacklist that circulated in the early 1950s, at the height of America's Communist witch-hunt. Pressure was brought to bear on every film studio to remove employees who were "branded" by supposed affiliations with left-wing causes. The loss of John Hubley and Phil Eastman, who resigned rather than cause UPA undue hardship, was a terrible blow to the studio's artistic growth.

This and other factors muted the impact of UPA's later work, which continued in a fine tradition but lacked the groundbreaking excitement of the early hits. Columbia Pictures pressured Bosustow to drop the one-shot cartoons and concentrate on Magoo, which he did, except for one final, offbeat series called HAM AND HATTIE. Each episode of this series paired 2 three-and-a-half-minute cartoons, the first starring a little girl named Hattie, the second following a musical theme with Hamilton Ham. These bright and enjoyable cartoons, many of them directed by Lew Keller, brought some distinction to UPA in the waning days of its short-subject period. The first HAM AND HATTIE cartoon, TREES AND JAMAICA DADDY, gave UPA its final Academy Award nomination.

In 1958 three staff animators (Rudy Larriva, Tom McDonald, and Gil Turner) were chosen to direct MAGOO cartoons, so that Pete Burness could begin working on the studio's first full-length feature, 1001 ARABIAN NIGHTS.

Since the days of UPA's initial success there had been talk of an animated feature. Ben Jonson's *Volpone*, a Gilbert and Sullivan operetta, and James Thurber stories were mentioned as likely subjects. The Thurber material was even optioned for possible use, but nothing came of it.

"We wanted to do *Don Quixote* with Magoo as Don Quixote," recalls Jules Engel. "We had Aldous Huxley in to write a script for that. He did about a thirty-page skeleton script, but the bank wouldn't buy it. They had never heard of Don Quixote, but they had heard of the *Arabian Nights*, so we got the money for *Arabian Nights*."

The production did not go smoothly. Pete Burness quarreled with Bosustow and left the studio. A search for someone with good comedy credentials to direct the film led Bosustow to Disney veteran Jack Kinney, whose brother Dick was also hired to work on story. Overall production design was supervised by Robert Dranko.

The finished film is attractive and well-made, but it suffers from one cardinal fault: dullness. While every effort is made to give Mister Magoo some relevance to the story, he remains tangential, a contrived representative of comedy relief in the tale of Aladdin, a beautiful princess, and a wicked Wazir who tries to use a magic lamp to gain control of a kingdom.

1001 ARABIAN NIIGHTS is a pleasant film that boasted sophisticated design and color,

UPA's last theatrical series, HAM AND HATTIE, was launched with TREES AND JAMAICA DADDY, the latter part of which is illustrated here. © Columbia Pictures.

but little else. It added no distinction to UPA's credits and failed to generate the kind of box-office response Columbia Pictures had hoped for. There was no sequel.

This was UPA's third major setback within two years. The New York office closed in 1958, when competition for commercial work made survival impossible. The same year saw the collapse of an ambitious London branch, which was perhaps the company's biggest fiasco.

In 1959 Herb Klynn and Jules Engel left what they felt was a sinking ship and took with them several dozen talented people, to create Format Films. Other UPA veterans like Bill Scott, Bill Hurtz, Pete Burness, Ted Parmelee, and Lew Keller were making waves with their hilarious ROCKY AND BULLWINKLE TV cartoons for Jay Ward Productions. This left none of the original UPA team on staff except Steve Bosustow, and he sold out shortly thereafter to producer Henry G. Saperstein.

A scene from UPA's second and last theatrical feature, GAY PURR-EE (1962), released by Warner Brothers.

Under Saperstein, UPA actively entered the field of television cartoons and discarded its reputation for quality in one fell swoop. The 130 MAGOO cartoons produced between 1960 and 1962 (and an equal number of DICK TRACY episodes done at the same time) made the contemporary Hanna-Barbera product look elaborate by comparison. The TRACY cartoons had strong comic characters, but like the MAGOOS, they depended on formulas, repetition, and settings that were not so much sparse as nonexistent.

Later the company tackled more ambitious projects, including some one-hour specials directed by veteran animator Abe Levitow (the best being the first, MAGOO'S CHRISTMAS CAROL), and a handsome but decidedly offbeat prime-time series called THE FAMOUS ADVENTURES OF MR. MAGOO, in which the character starred in serious adaptations of classic stories, from *Don Quixote* to *Moby Dick!*

In 1962 Levitow directed UPA's second feature-length cartoon, GAY PURR-EE. This unusual film boasted handsome Technicolor settings (with art direction by Victor Haboush), the voices of Judy Garland and Robert Goulet, and an original score by Harold Arlen and E. Y. "Yip" Harburg. But the story, by Chuck Jones and his wife Dorothy, was too labored—and too coy—to warrant such trappings. *Newsweek* commented, "There seems to be an effort to reach a hitherto undiscovered audience—the fey four-year-old of recherché taste."

GAY PURR-EE marked the end of the line for UPA. The post-1960 films had nothing to do with UPA as it had existed for so many years, but traded on its reputation. As years went by and the original UPA cartoons drifted into obscurity, even that reputation diminished (outside of the animation industry). To anyone weaned on UPA's made-for-TV product, it is impossible to believe that the nearsighted Mister Magoo was once a truly funny character.* And to anyone dismayed by the artlessness of television's "limited animation," it is difficult to realize that the trend began on the highest note of artistic endeavor.

But UPA's influence on the world of animation can never be forgotten. Young animators who have never seen a UPA cartoon still owe a debt of thanks to the men who pioneered this studio some thirty years ago. They expanded the horizons of animation—within a commercial context—and paved the way for new ideas that might otherwise have lain dormant.

If there hadn't been a UPA, someone would have had to invent it. Luckily, someone did.

*In 1977 UPA licensed DePatie-Freleng studios to do sixteen half-hour Saturday morning TV shows bearing the title WHAT'S NEW, MR. MAGOO? The quality may have been a notch above the 1960 efforts.

The Rest of the Story

W HAT CAUSED THE DEATH of the theatrical cartoon short? Paul Terry had a candid and comprehensive answer, when asked this question in 1969. "Well, the cartoon never demanded a price," he told Harvey Deneroff, "and it got too expensive to make them. Production costs continued to rise and you could never get any more money from the exhibitor for your product.

"The cartoon has no drawing power in a theater," he continued. "You go to a theater and you *enjoy* the cartoon, to be sure, but you'd pay the same amount of money to see the show if they didn't have a cartoon. It's sort of an added something that doesn't make any difference to a show whether it is there or not."

Walt Disney was one of the first to curtail short-subject production in the 1950s, because he refused to trim his generous budgets. "I'll make an occasional short now to go with one of my features," he said in 1961, "just to keep the theater owners from booking some horrible short subject with my own picture, but it costs $100,000 to make a seven-minute cartoon, and you can't get your money back."

Disney, of course, had alternatives—animated features, live-action films, television, and amusement parks—to keep his company running. Other studios had nowhere to turn except television, and many of the old-line companies would not (or could not) adapt to the rigors of mass production.

Television, which might have been a spawning ground for great new animated films, became the cartoon's graveyard instead.

After leaving MGM in 1957, Bill Hanna and Joe Barbera interested Columbia Pictures in made-for-TV cartoons and guaranteed that they could deliver fresh, appealing programs on television's time-and-money terms. The first shows were so successful that the company quickly expanded. Soon Hanna and Barbera were producing more animation in one week than they used to turn out in a year.

How did they do it? Bill Hanna explained,

One of Hanna-Barbera's limited-animation theatrical cartoons, CHILD SOCK-OLOGY (1961), starring Loopy de Loop. © Columbia Pictures.

"Disney-type animation is economically unfeasible for television, and we discovered that we could get away with less."

Limited animation, as it came to be known, paved the way for a systematic destruction of the cartoon art form. By reducing movement to a bare minimum, eliminating personality animation and nuance, and emphasizing slickly made sound tracks, this form of production earned the nickname "illustrated radio."

At first Hanna-Barbera cartoons compensated for their visual shortcomings with excellent comedy scripts, but before long all the good intentions were defeated by the sheer volume of work. Repetition—of character design and development as well as of stories—became stultifying in the studio's enormous output. However, kids didn't seem to mind, so advertisers and television executives had no cause for complaint. Other studios followed Hanna-Barbera's lead, and soon this kind of assembly-line product was considered the norm.

(Some people resisted this cookie-cutter method: Jay Ward Productions, with its hilarious BULLWINKLE and GEORGE OF THE JUNGLE scripts; Bob Clampett, in his clever animated version of BEANY AND CECIL; Chuck Jones, in his ongoing series of fully animated half-hour specials; Gene Deitch, with his ingenious though ultra-low-budget TOM TERRIFIC series; and Bill Melendez, in his thoughtful adaptations of Charles M. Schulz's *Peanuts* comic strip.)

Meanwhile, the shrinking theatrical cartoon business was having troubles of its own. Most studios had to cut their budgets in order to stay alive, with the unhappy result that these theatrical shorts began to resemble their TV counterparts. The ultimate blurring of definition came when Hanna-Barbera produced a new series for theaters called LOOPY DE LOOP; it was indistinguishable from an episode of their TV series.*

There was another serious problem in the theatrical field: stagnation. Most of the people making cartoons in the 1960s were twenty- to fifty-year veterans in the business. They had started as youngsters, full of ambition and energy, when the medium was new and the competitive spirit was strong. Now there were fewer incentives than ever before, as well as low budgets, lack of competition, and widespread disinterest in the product. What's more, the studios did not seek out or attract young people, who might have contributed valuable new ideas.

Small wonder that independently made animated shorts, from America and other countries around the world, began to receive the acclaim (and bookings) once given studio cartoons.

A notable exception to this trend was

*Hanna-Barbera produced two theatrical features based on the hit TV shows: HEY THERE, IT'S YOGI BEAR (1964) and THE MAN CALLED FLINTSTONE (1966).

DePatie-Freleng Enterprises, formed in 1963. When Warner Brothers closed its cartoon studio, Friz Freleng and David H. DePatie leased the physical plant, to produce their own animated films. They survived by doing TV commercials until director Blake Edwards approached them about creating animated titles for his feature film THE PINK PANTHER.

More than one critic remarked that the film's title sequence, with its saucy character and Henry Mancini theme music, was better than the film that followed. United Artists took the hint and contracted with DePatie-Freleng for a series of theatrical shorts to star the Pink Panther. THE PINK PHINK launched the series in fine fashion, with excellent pantomime comedy (directed by Freleng and written by John Dunn), stylish color and design. It not only won an Academy Award, but got more bookings for the series than UA ever envisioned.

DePatie-Freleng turned out one PINK PANTHER a month from that time on, Freleng leaving the direction to longtime assistant Hawley Pratt after the first handful. Other series followed: THE INSPECTOR, based on Peter Sellers's character Inspector Clouseau; and THE ANT AND THE AARDVARK, ROLAND RATFINK, THE TIJUANA TOADS, BLUE RACER, and HOOT KLOOT. Unfortunately, the quality of these shorts went straight downhill after the first year, and their always-pleasing graphic design could barely make up for the labored attempts at comedy. Their financial success was due to the fact that by the 1970s they were the only new studio cartoons on the market.

Eventually DePatie-Freleng redirected its efforts toward television and joined Hanna-Barbera and Filmation as leading suppliers of Saturday-morning kiddie fodder. Friz Freleng has no illusions about this work and finds definite points of comparison with the bygone era of theatrical cartoons:

"We've all done flops in our lives or we wouldn't be human. But I look back on some I thought were terrible in the Warner's days, and they look good compared to today's stuff.

"In those days, if you made a real good

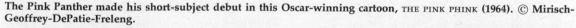

The Pink Panther made his short-subject debut in this Oscar-winning cartoon, THE PINK PHINK **(1964). © Mirisch-Geoffrey-DePatie-Freleng.**

All you need is love—and imagination. A scene from
YELLOW SUBMARINE (1968). © King Features–Subafilms
Ltd.

one, you had a chance to have it in a lot of theaters, you got an audience reaction, and it stayed in the theaters a year or two. We'd take these pictures out, run them in a theater, and if people laughed where you planned the laugh, there was great satisfaction. Today [in television] you don't know what the result is. You can only go by the ratings, and you don't know whether people really enjoyed it.

"I think that's why people don't care as much, and don't work as hard making good pictures, because they don't get any self-satisfaction out of it. That's the trouble with the whole cartoon business. The people are not dedicated to it anymore. Some of the people we've got working here next year will be working for Hanna-Barbera or Filmation, or somewhere else. They're not like we were at Warner Brothers. We had a team, and we were trying to beat Disney. Today nobody cares."

It seems that all the care and creativity go into the making of television commercials, not television shows. Innovations in design, animation, and humor can more often be found in commercials than in the shows they interrupt. Some of America's leading animation talents—young and old—are working in this field, along with top magazine cartoonists, illustrators, and designers.

There are many other talented people making animated films, of course, but not in the old-line studio tradition. The "festival circuit" is alive and well, serving the needs of independent film makers and acting as a showcase for high-school and college-age animators.

The most surprising development of recent years, however, is the emergence of animated feature films. For years this format was considered a high-risk area where only Disney dared to tread. Now that situation has undergone a dramatic change.

It all began with YELLOW SUBMARINE in 1968. For the first time since Disney's earliest hits, grown-ups and young adults paid admission to see a cartoon feature in theaters. Naturally, it was the Beatles' name that brought most people in, but it was the film makers' imagination that made them stay—and return to see it again. Directed by

George Dunning and designed by Heinz Edelman, this groundbreaking film, with its psychedelic images and stylized movement, influenced commercial design for many years. But YELLOW SUBMARINE had a witty script and irresistible music to complement its visual innovations.

Ironically, the first company to benefit from YELLOW SUBMARINE's success was Disney, which promoted a reissue of FANTASIA as the "ultimate visual experience" and now reached the all-important youth audience. (Animator Art Babbitt was asked by some young people who saw the film for the first time if he and his colleagues had used drugs when they made the film thirty years before. "Yes, I was on drugs," Babbitt replied, "Ex-Lax and Pepto Bismol!")

Now that there was a growing audience receptive to theatrical animation, producer Steve Krantz and director Ralph Bakshi took another step forward with FRITZ THE CAT (1971). Based on Robert Crumb's underground comic strip, the film achieved instant notoriety as the screen's first X-rated cartoon feature. But Bakshi gave his audience much more: a vibrant, personal statement about life in the 1960s, the sexual and political revolution, and hypocritical attitudes regarding "good taste." The film maker was elated with the audience reaction to his film. "Everyone makes the turn," he told Mike Barrier. "They forget it's animation. They treat it like film."

Bakshi sharpened his focus in a second film that many consider his best, HEAVY TRAFFIC. Again, he earned his X-rating, through a seamy depiction of New York low life, but he fashioned his images in a vehicle of almost electrifying intensity. HEAVY TRAFFIC was like no previous animated film—and it seemed as if Ralph Bakshi was redefining the medium.

His work has remained unusual and pro-

A dramatic scene from FRITZ THE CAT (1972). © Steve Krantz Productions.

Animation comes of age, in a manner of speaking: Ralph Bakshi's HEAVY TRAFFIC (1973). © Steve Krantz Productions.

vocative. COONSKIN, HEY GOOD LOOKIN', WIZ-ARDS, and THE LORD OF THE RINGS don't fit into any convenient categories, and that's just the way Bakshi wants it.

There is no question about the impact his early films had on the animation business, however; FRITZ THE CAT and HEAVY TRAFFIC opened the door for new and different kinds of animated features. The 1970s saw a remarkable proliferation of feature cartoons, from here and abroad, for every possible type of audience: A BOY NAMED CHARLIE BROWN and the PEANUTS films, THE NINE LIVES OF FRITZ THE CAT, CHARLOTTE'S WEB, DIRTY DUCK, HUGO THE HIPPO, FANTASTIC PLANET, RAGGEDY ANN AND ANDY, ALLEGRO NON TROPPO, TUBBY THE TUBA, THE MOUSE AND HIS CHILD, WATERSHIP DOWN, and such short-subject compilations as BUGS BUNNY SUPERSTAR and FANTASTIC ANIMATION FESTIVAL.

Is this a cartoon renaissance? Possibly. It certainly marks a new burst of activity and acceptance. And if we never see a level of productivity and imagination which matches that of the 1930s and 1940s, there may be other exciting prospects around the corner. Animation is a limitless medium and anything is possible with time, tools, and thought.

Filmographies by Studios

The Walt Disney Cartoons

Following is a complete list of animated short subjects produced by Walt Disney for theatrical release; it does not include his many industrial, sponsored, and war-related cartoons.

Except for the Oswald series (which was distributed by Universal), Disney's shorts were released on a states' rights basis until 1929. The balance of Disney's films were distributed by Columbia Pictures (1929–1932), United Artists (1932–1937), RKO Radio Pictures (1937–1956), and Buena Vista (1956 to date), Disney's own distribution firm.

Silent films are grouped under year of release. There were no release dates for Disney's talkie cartoons until mid-1932; the dates listed here are delivery dates recorded in studio files. The remaining release dates were supplied by Walt Disney Archives and do not always conform with those listed in trade magazines, normally our source for such information. The Archives also supplied director credits for Disney shorts, which did not appear on screen until 1944.

Short subjects are identified by series title. In the late 1930s, however, "Mickey Mouse" cartoons often starred Donald Duck, Pluto, or a combination of characters. Therefore, we have retained the series label but listed all the starring characters in parentheses. For simplicity's sake, we have used this key: MM = Mickey Mouse. DD = Donald Duck. G = Goofy. P = Pluto. CD = Chip 'n' Dale. HB = Humphrey Bear.

FLOWERS AND TREES was the first Disney short in color. From that point on, all but one of the SILLY SYMPHONIES were produced in color, but the MICKEY MOUSE shorts remained in black and white until THE BAND CONCERT. After two final black-and-white shorts, MICKEY'S SERVICE STATION (1935), and MICKEY'S KANGAROO (1935), every Disney release was filmed in Technicolor.

One dagger (†) next to a film's title indicates an Academy Award nominee; a double dagger (‡) indicates an Academy Award winner.

1922–1923

THE FOUR MUSICIANS OF BREMEN—Laugh-O-Gram

LITTLE RED RIDING HOOD—Laugh-O-Gram

PUSS IN BOOTS—Laugh-O-Gram

JACK AND THE BEANSTALK—Laugh-O-Gram

GOLDIE LOCKS AND THE THREE BEARS—Laugh-O-Gram

CINDERELLA—Laugh-O-Gram

MARTHA—Song-O-Reel

ALICE'S WONDERLAND—Alice Comedy

1924 ALICE COMEDIES SERIES (*Arranged in production order; release dates given when known.*)

ALICE'S DAY AT SEA—March 1

ALICE HUNTING IN AFRICA—November 15

ALICE'S SPOOKY ADVENTURE—April 1

ALICE'S WILD WEST SHOW—May 1

ALICE'S FISHY STORY—June 1

ALICE AND THE DOG CATCHER—July 1

ALICE THE PEACEMAKER—August 1

ALICE GETS IN DUTCH—November 1

ALICE AND THE THREE BEARS—December 1

ALICE THE PIPER—December 15

1925   ALICE IN CARTOONLAND SERIES (*Arranged in production order; release dates given when known.*)

ALICE CANS THE CANNIBALS—January 1, 1925

ALICE THE TOREADOR—January 15, 1925

ALICE GETS STUNG—February 1

ALICE SOLVES THE PUZZLE—February 15

ALICE'S EGG PLANT

ALICE LOSES OUT

ALICE STAGE STRUCK

ALICE WINS THE DERBY

ALICE PICKS THE CHAMP

ALICE'S TIN PONY

ALICE CHOPS THE SUEY

ALICE THE JAIL BIRD—September 15

ALICE PLAYS CUPID—October 15

ALICE RATTLED BY RATS—November 15

ALICE IN THE JUNGLE—December 15

ALICE ON THE FARM—January 1, 1926

ALICE'S BALLOON RACE—January 15, 1926

ALICE'S ORNERY ORPHAN

ALICE'S LITTLE PARADE—February 1, 1926

ALICE'S MYSTERIOUS MYSTERY—February 15, 1926

1926   ALICE IN CARTOONLAND SERIES (Arranged in production order; release dates given when known.)

ALICE IN THE WOOLY WEST—October 4

ALICE'S MONKEY BUSINESS—September 20

ALICE CHARMS THE FISH—September 6

ALICE THE FIRE FIGHTER—October 18

ALICE CUTS THE ICE—November 1

ALICE HELPS THE ROMANCE—November 15

ALICE'S SPANISH GUITAR—November 29

ALICE'S BROWN DERBY—December 13

ALICE THE LUMBER JACK—December 27

1927   ALICE IN CARTOONLAND SERIES (*Arranged in production order; release dates given when known.*)

ALICE THE GOLF BUG—January 10

ALICE FOILS THE PIRATES

ALICE AT THE CARNIVAL—February 7

ALICE'S RODEO, a.k.a. ALICE AT THE RODEO—February 21

ALICE THE COLLEGIATE—March 7

ALICE IN THE ALPS—March 21

ALICE'S AUTO RACE—April 4

ALICE'S CIRCUS DAZE—April 18

ALICE'S KNAUGHTY KNIGHT—May 2

ALICE'S THREE BAD EGGS—May 16

ALICE IN THE KLONDIKE—June 27

ALICE'S PICNIC—May 30

ALICE'S CHANNEL SWIM—June 13

ALICE'S MEDICINE SHOW—July 11

ALICE THE WHALER—July 25

ALICE IN THE BIG LEAGUE—August 22

ALICE THE BEACH NUT—August 8

1927   OSWALD THE LUCKY RABBIT SERIES (*Arranged in production order; release dates given when known.*)

POOR PAPA—June 11

TROLLEY TROUBLES—September 5

OH, TEACHER—September 19

GREAT GUNS—October 17

THE MECHANICAL COW—October 3

ALL WET—October 31

THE OCEAN HOP—November 14

THE BANKER'S DAUGHTER—November 28

HAREM SCAREM—January 9

RICKETY GIN—December 26

1928 OSWALD THE LUCKY RABBIT SERIES

(Arranged in production order; release dates given when known.)

NECK 'N' NECK—January 23

EMPTY SOCKS—December 12

THE OL' SWIMMIN' 'OLE—February 6

AFRICA BEFORE DARK—February 20

RIVAL ROMEOS—March 5

BRIGHT LIGHTS—March 19

SAGEBRUSH SADIE—April 2

RIDE 'EM PLOWBOY—April 16

OZZIE OF THE MOUNTED—April 30

HUNGRY HOBOES—May 14

OH, WHAT A KNIGHT

SKY SCRAPPERS

THE FOX CHASE—June 25

TALL TIMBER—July 9

SLEIGH BELLS—July 23

HOT DOG—August 20

1928

PLANE CRAZY—May 15—Mickey Mouse—Walt Disney

STEAMBOAT WILLIE—July 29—Mickey Mouse—Walt Disney

GALLOPIN' GAUCHO—August 7—Mickey Mouse—Walt Disney

THE BARN DANCE—November 15—Mickey Mouse—Walt Disney

THE OPRY HOUSE—March 20—Mickey Mouse—Walt Disney

WHEN THE CAT'S AWAY—May 3—Mickey Mouse—Walt Disney

THE SKELETON DANCE—May 10—Silly Symphonies—Walt Disney

THE PLOW BOY—June 28—Mickey Mouse—Walt Disney

THE BARNYARD BATTLE—July 2—Mickey Mouse—Walt Disney

THE KARNIVAL KID—July 31—Mickey Mouse—Walt Disney

MICKEY'S FOLLIES—August 28—Mickey Mouse—Wilfred Jackson

EL TERRIBLE TOREADOR—September 7—Silly Symphonies—Walt Disney

MICKEY'S CHOO-CHOO—October 1—Mickey Mouse—Walt Disney

SPRINGTIME—October 4—Silly Symphonies—Ub Iwerks

THE JAZZ FOOL—October 15—Mickey Mouse—Walt Disney

HELL'S BELLS—November 11—Silly Symphonies—Ub Iwerks

JUNGLE RHYTHM—November 15—Mickey Mouse—Walt Disney

THE MERRY DWARFS—December 1—Silly Symphonies—Walt Disney

THE HAUNTED HOUSE—December 2—Mickey Mouse—Walt Disney

WILD WAVES—December 21—Mickey Mouse—Burt Gillett

1930

SUMMER—January 4—Silly Symphonies—Ub Iwerks

AUTUMN—February 15—Silly Symphonies—Ub Iwerks

JUST MICKEY (copyrighted as FIDDLIN' AROUND)—March 6—Mickey Mouse—Walt Disney

CANNIBAL CAPERS—March 15—Silly Symphonies—Burt Gillett

THE BARNYARD CONCERT—April 5—Mickey Mouse—Walt Disney

NIGHT—April 18—Silly Symphonies—Walt Disney

THE CACTUS KID—May 10—Mickey Mouse—Walt Disney

FROLICKING FISH—May 23—Silly Symphonies—Burt Gillett

THE FIRE FIGHTERS—June 20—Mickey Mouse—Burt Gillett

ARCTIC ANTICS—June 26—Silly Symphonies—Ub Iwerks

THE SHINDIG—July 11—Mickey Mouse—Burt Gillett

MIDNITE IN A TOY SHOP (copyrighted as MIDNIGHT IN A TOY SHOP)—July 28—Silly Symphonies—Wilfred Jackson

THE CHAIN GANG—August 18—Mickey Mouse (MM, P)—Burt Gillett

MONKEY MELODIES—September 2—Silly Symphonies—Burt Gillett

THE GORILLA MYSTERY—September 22—Mickey Mouse—Burt Gillett

THE PICNIC—October 9—Mickey Mouse (MM, P)—Burt Gillett

WINTER—October 22—Silly Symphonies—Burt Gillett

PIONEER DAYS—November 20—Mickey Mouse (MM) Burt Gillett

PLAYFUL PAN—December 16—Silly Symphonies—Burt Gillett

1931

THE BIRTHDAY PARTY—January 2—Mickey Mouse—Burt Gillett

BIRDS OF A FEATHER—January 23—Silly Symphonies—Burt Gillett

TRAFFIC TROUBLES—March 7—Mickey Mouse—Burt Gillett

THE CASTAWAY—March 27—Mickey Mouse—Wilfred Jackson

MOTHER GOOSE MELODIES—April 11—Silly Symphonies—Burt Gillett

THE MOOSE HUNT—April 30—Mickey Mouse (MM, P)—Burt Gillett

THE CHINA PLATE—May 16—Silly Symphonies—Wilfred Jackson

THE DELIVERY BOY—June 6—Mickey Mouse—Burt Gillett

THE BUSY BEAVERS—June 22—Silly Symphonies—Wilfred Jackson

MICKEY STEPS OUT—July 10—Mickey Mouse (MM, P)—Burt Gillett

THE CAT'S OUT (copyrighted as THE CAT'S NIGHTMARE)—July 20—Silly Symphonies—Wilfred Jackson

BLUE RHYTHM—August 7—Mickey Mouse—Burt Gillett

EGYPTIAN MELODIES—August 19—Silly Symphonies—Wilfred Jackson

FISHIN' AROUND—September 1—Mickey Mouse (MM, P)—Burt Gillett

THE CLOCK STORE (copyrighted as IN A CLOCK STORE)—September 16—Silly Symphonies—Wilfred Jackson

THE BARNYARD BROADCAST—September 30—Mickey Mouse—Burt Gillett

THE SPIDER AND THE FLY—October 13—Silly Symphonies—Wilfred Jackson

THE BEACH PARTY—October 28—Mickey Mouse (MM, P)—Burt Gillett

THE FOX HUNT—November 10—Silly Symphonies—Wilfred Jackson

MICKEY CUTS UP—November 25—Mickey Mouse (MM, P)—Burt Gillett

MICKEY'S ORPHANS—December 5—Mickey Mouse (MM, P)—Burt Gillett

THE UGLY DUCKLING—December 12—Silly Symphonies—Wilfred Jackson

1932

THE BIRD STORE—January 5—Silly Symphonies—Wilfred Jackson

THE DUCK HUNT—January 21—Mickey Mouse (MM, P)—Burt Gillett

THE GROCERY BOY—February 8—Mickey Mouse (MM, P)—Wilfred Jackson

THE MAD DOG—February 27—Mickey Mouse (MM, P)—Burt Gillett

BARNYARD OLYMPICS—April 13—Mickey Mouse (MM, P)—Wilfred Jackson

MICKEY'S REVUE—May 12—Mickey Mouse (MM, P, G)—Wilfred Jackson

MUSICAL FARMER—June 8—Mickey Mouse—Wilfred Jackson

THE BEARS AND THE BEES—July 9—Silly Symphonies—Wilfred Jackson

MICKEY IN ARABIA—July 11—Mickey Mouse—Wilfred Jackson

JUST DOGS—July 30—Silly Symphonies (P)—Burt Gillett

‡ FLOWERS AND TREES—July 30—Silly Symphonies—Burt Gillett (first color Silly Symphony)

MICKEY'S NIGHTMARE—August 13—Mickey Mouse (MM, P)—Burt Gillett

TRADER MICKEY—August 20—Mickey Mouse (MM, P)—David Hand

KING NEPTUNE—September 10—Silly Symphonies—Burt Gillett (in color)

THE WHOOPEE PARTY—September 17—Mickey Mouse (MM, G)—Wilfred Jackson

BUGS IN LOVE—October 1—Silly Symphonies—Burt Gillett

TOUCHDOWN MICKEY—October 15—Mickey Mouse—Wilfred Jackson

THE WAYWARD CANARY—November 12—Mickey Mouse (MM, P)—Burt Gillett

THE KLONDIKE KID—November 12—Mickey Mouse (MM, P)—Wilfred Jackson

BABES IN THE WOODS—November 19—Silly Symphonies—Burt Gillett (all Silly Symphonics in color from this point on)

SANTA'S WORKSHOP—December 10—Silly Symphonies—Wilfred Jackson

MICKEY'S GOOD DEED—December 17—Mickey Mouse (MM, P)—Burt Gillett

1933

† BUILDING A BUILDING—January 7—Mickey Mouse—David Hand

THE MAD DOCTOR—January 21—Mickey Mouse (MM, P)—David Hand

MICKEY'S PAL PLUTO—February 18—Mickey Mouse (MM, P)—Burt Gillett

BIRDS IN THE SPRING—March 11—Silly Symphonies—David Hand

MICKEY'S MELLERDRAMMER—March 18—Mickey Mouse (MN, G)—Wilfred Jackson

YE OLDEN DAYS—April 8—Mickey Mouse (MN, G)—Burt Gillett

FATHER NOAH'S ARK—April 8—Silly Symphonies—Wilfred Jackson

THE MAIL PILOT—May 13—Mickey Mouse—David Hand

‡ THREE LITTLE PIGS—May 27—Silly Symphonies—Burt Gillett

MICKEY'S MECHANICAL MAN—June 17—Mickey Mouse—Wilfred Jackson

MICKEY'S GALA PREMIERE—July 1—Mickey Mouse (MM, P)—Burt Gillett

OLD KING COLE—July 29—Silly Symphonies—David Hand

LULLABY LAND—August 19—Silly Symphonies—Wilfred Jackson

PUPPY LOVE—September 2—Mickey Mouse (MM, P)—Wilfred Jackson

THE PIED PIPER—September 16—Silly Symphonies—Wilfred Jackson

THE STEEPLE-CHASE—September 30—Mickey Mouse—Burt Gillett

THE PET STORE—October 28—Mickey Mouse—Wilfred Jackson

GIANT LAND—November 25—Mickey Mouse—Burt Gillett

THE NIGHT BEFORE CHRISTMAS—December 9—Silly Symphonies—Wilfred Jackson

1934

THE CHINA SHOP—January 13—Silly Symphonies—Wilfred Jackson

SHANGHAIED—January 13—Mickey Mouse—Burt Gillett

THE GRASSHOPPER AND THE ANTS—February 10—Silly Symphonies—Wilfred Jackson

CAMPING OUT—February 17—Mickey Mouse—David Hand

PLAYFUL PLUTO—March 3—Mickey Mouse (MM, P)—Burt Gillett

FUNNY LITTLE BUNNIES—March 24—Silly Symphonies—Wilfred Jackson

THE BIG BAD WOLF—April 14—Silly Symphonies—Burt Gillett

GULLIVER MICKEY—May 19—Mickey Mouse—Burt Gillett

THE WISE LITTLE HEN—June 9—Silly Symphonies (DD)—Wilfred Jackson

MICKEY'S STEAMROLLER—June 16—Mickey Mouse—David Hand

THE FLYING MOUSE—July 14—Silly Symphonies—David Hand

ORPHANS' BENEFIT—August 11—Mickey Mouse (MM, DD)—Burt Gillett

PECULIAR PENGUINS—September 1—Silly Symphonies—Wilfred Jackson

MICKEY PLAYS PAPA—September 29—Mickey Mouse (MM, P)—Burt Gillett

THE GODDESS OF SPRING—November 3—Silly Symphonies—Wilfred Jackson

THE DOG NAPPER—November 17—Mickey Mouse (MM, DD)—David Hand

TWO-GUN MICKEY—December 15—Mickey Mouse—Ben Sharpsteen

1935

‡ THE TORTOISE AND THE HARE—January 5—Silly Symphonies—Wilfred Jackson

MICKEY'S MAN FRIDAY—January 19—Mickey Mouse—David Hand

THE BAND CONCERT—February 23—Mickey Mouse (MM, DD)—Wilfred Jackson (first color Mickey Mouse)

MICKEY'S SERVICE STATION—March 16—Mickey Mouse (MM, DD, G)—Ben Sharpsteen

THE GOLDEN TOUCH—March 22—Silly Symphonies—Walt Disney

MICKEY'S KANGAROO—April 13—Mickey Mouse (MM, P)—David Hand (last black-and-white Disney cartoon)

THE ROBBER KITTEN—April 20—Silly Symphonies—David Hand

WATER BABIES—May 11—Silly Symphonies—Wilfred Jackson

THE COOKIE CARNIVAL—May 25—Silly Symphonies—Ben Sharpsteen

†WHO KILLED COCK ROBIN?—June 29—Silly Symphonies—David Hand

MICKEY'S GARDEN—July 13—Mickey Mouse (MM, P)—Wilfred Jackson

MICKEY'S FIRE BRIGADE—August 3—Mickey Mouse (MM, DD, G)—Ben Sharpsteen

PLUTO'S JUDGMENT DAY—August 31—Mickey Mouse (MM, P)—David Hand

ON ICE—September 28—Mickey Mouse (MM, DD, G, P)—Ben Sharpsteen

MUSIC LAND—October 5—Silly Symphonies—Wilfred Jackson

‡THREE ORPHAN KITTENS—October 26—Silly Symphonies—David Hand

COCK O' THE WALK—November 30—Silly Symphonies—Ben Sharpsteen

BROKEN TOYS—December 14—Silly Symphonies—Ben Sharpsteen

1936

MICKEY'S POLO TEAM—January 4—Mickey Mouse (MM, DD, G)—David Hand

ORPHANS' PICNIC—February 15—Mickey Mouse (MM, DD)—Ben Sharpsteen

MICKEY'S GRAND OPERA—March 7—Mickey Mouse (MM, P)—Wilfred Jackson

ELMER ELEPHANT—March 28—Silly Symphonies—Wilfred Jackson

THREE LITTLE WOLVES—April 18—Silly Symphonies—David Hand

THRU THE MIRROR—May 30—Mickey Mouse—David Hand

MICKEY'S RIVAL—June 20—Mickey Mouse—Wilfred Jackson

MOVING DAY—June 20—Mickey Mouse (MM, DD, G)—Ben Sharpsteen

ALPINE CLIMBERS—July 25—Mickey Mouse (MM, DD, G)—David Hand

MICKEY'S CIRCUS—August 1—Mickey Mouse (MM, DD)—Ben Sharpsteen

TOBY TORTOISE RETURNS—August 22—Silly Symphonies—Wilfred Jackson

DONALD AND PLUTO—September 12—Mickey Mouse (DD, P)—Ben Sharpsteen

THREE BLIND MOUSKETEERS—September 26—Silly Symphonies—David Hand

MICKEY'S ELEPHANT—October 10—Mickey Mouse (MM, P)—Hamilton Luske

‡THE COUNTRY COUSIN—October 31—Silly Symphonies—David Hand

MOTHER PLUTO—November 14—Mickey Mouse (P)—David Hand

MORE KITTENS—December 19—Silly Symphonies—Wilfred Jackson

1937

THE WORM TURNS—January 2—Mickey Mouse (MM)—Ben Sharpsteen

DON DONALD—January 9—Mickey Mouse (DD)—Ben Sharpsteen

MAGICIAN MICKEY—February 6—Mickey Mouse (MM, DD)—David Hand

MOOSE HUNTERS—February 20—Mickey Mouse (MM, DD, G)—Ben Sharpsteen

WOODLAND CAFE—March 13—Silly Symphonies—Wilfred Jackson*

MICKEY'S AMATEURS—April 17—Mickey Mouse (MM, DD, G)—Pinto Colvig, Walt Pfeiffer, Ed Penner

LITTLE HIAWATHA—May 15—Silly Symphonies—David Hand

MODERN INVENTIONS—May 29—Mickey Mouse (DD)—Jack King

HAWAIIAN HOLIDAY—September 24—Mickey Mouse (MM, DD, G, P)—Ben Sharpsteen

CLOCK CLEANERS—October 15—Mickey Mouse (MM, DD, G)—Ben Sharpsteen

‡THE OLD MILL—November 5—Silly Symphonies—Wilfred Jackson

PLUTO'S QUIN-PUPLETS—November 26—Mickey Mouse (P)—Ben Sharpsteen

DONALD'S OSTRICH—December 10—Donald Duck—Jack King

LONESOME GHOSTS—December 24—Mickey Mouse (MM, DD, G)—Burt Gillett

1938

SELF CONTROL—February 11—Donald Duck—Jack King

BOAT BUILDERS—February 25—Mickey Mouse (MM, DD, G)—Ben Sharpsteen

DONALD'S BETTER SELF—March 11—Donald Duck—Jack King

THE MOTH AND THE FLAME—April 1—Silly Symphonies—Burt Gillett

*erroneously credited to Dick Lundy in earlier indexes.

DONALD'S NEPHEWS—April 15—Donald Duck—Jack King

MICKEY'S TRAILER—May 6—Mickey Mouse (MM, DD, G)—Ben Sharpsteen

WYNKEN, BLYNKEN AND NOD—May 27—Silly Symphonies—Graham Heid

POLAR TRAPPERS—June 17—Donald Duck (DD, P)—Ben Sharpsteen

† GOOD SCOUTS—July 8—Donald Duck—Jack King

THE FOX HUNT—July 29—Donald Duck (DD, G)—Ben Sharpsteen

THE WHALERS—August 19—Mickey Mouse (MM, DD, G)—Dick Huemer

MICKEY'S PARROT—September 9—Mickey Mouse (MM, P)—Bill Roberts

† THE BRAVE LITTLE TAILOR—September 23—Mickey Mouse—Burt Gillett

FARMYARD SYMPHONY—October 14—Silly Symphonies—Jack Cutting

DONALD'S GOLF GAME—November 4—Donald Duck—Jack King

†FERDINAND THE BULL—November 25—Special—Dick Rickard

MERBABIES—December 9—Silly Symphonies—George Stallings

† MOTHER GOOSE GOES HOLLYWOOD—December 23—Silly Symphonies—Wilfred Jackson

1939

DONALD'S LUCKY DAY—January 13—Donald Duck—Jack King

SOCIETY DOG SHOW—February 3—Mickey Mouse (MM, P)—Bill Roberts

THE PRACTICAL PIG—February 24—Special—Dick Rickard

GOOFY AND WILBUR—March 17—Goofy—Dick Huemer

‡ THE UGLY DUCKLING—April 7—Silly Symphonies—Jack Cutting

THE HOCKEY CHAMP—April 28—Donald Duck—Jack King

DONALD'S COUSIN GUS—May 19—Donald Duck—Jack King

BEACH PICNIC—June 9—Donald Duck (DD, P)—Clyde Geronimi

SEA SCOUTS—June 30—Donald Duck—Dick Lundy

† THE POINTER—July 21—Mickey Mouse (MM, P)—Clyde Geronimi

DONALD'S PENGUIN—August 11—Donald Duck—Jack King

THE AUTOGRAPH HOUND—September 1—Donald Duck—Jack King

OFFICER DUCK—October 10—Donald Duck—Clyde Geronimi

1940

THE RIVETER—March 15—Donald Duck—Dick Lundy

DONALD'S DOG LAUNDRY—April 5—Donald Duck (DD, P)—Jack King

TUGBOAT MICKEY—April 26—Mickey Mouse (MM, DD, G)—Clyde Geronimi

BILL POSTERS—May 17—Donald Duck (DD, G)—Clyde Geronimi

MR. DUCK STEPS OUT—June 7—Donald Duck—Jack King

BONE TROUBLE—June 28—Pluto—Jack Kinney

PUT-PUT TROUBLES—July 19—Donald Duck (DD, P)—Riley Thomson

DONALD'S VACATION—August 9—Donald Duck—Jack King

PLUTO'S DREAM HOUSE—August 30—Pluto (P, MM)—Clyde Geronimi

WINDOW CLEANERS—September 20—Donald Duck (DD, P)—Jack King

MR. MOUSE TAKES A TRIP—November 1—Mickey Mouse (MM, P)—Clyde Geronimi

GOOFY'S GLIDER—November 22—Goofy—Jack Kinney

FIRE CHIEF—December 13—Donald Duck—Jack King

PANTRY PIRATE—December 27—Pluto—Clyde Geronimi

1941

TIMBER—January 10—Donald Duck—Jack King

PLUTO'S PLAYMATE—January 24—Pluto—Norman Ferguson

THE LITTLE WHIRLWIND—February 14—Mickey Mouse—Riley Thomson

THE GOLDEN EGGS—March 7—Donald Duck—Wilfred Jackson

A GENTLEMAN'S GENTLEMAN—March 28—Pluto (P, MM)—Clyde Geronimi

BAGGAGE BUSTER—April 18—Goofy—Jack Kinney

A GOOD TIME FOR A DIME—May 9—Donald Duck—Dick Lundy

CANINE CADDY—May 30—Pluto—Clyde Geronimi

THE NIFTY NINETIES—June 20—Mickey Mouse (MM, DD, G)—Riley Thomson

EARLY TO BED—July 11—Donald Duck—Jack King

† TRUANT OFFICER DONALD—August 1—Donald Duck—Jack King

ORPHANS' BENEFIT—August 22—Mickey Mouse (MM, DD, G)—Riley Thomson

OLD MACDONALD DUCK—September 12—Donald Duck—Jack King

† LEND A PAW—October 3—Pluto (P, MM)—Clyde Geronimi

DONALD'S CAMERA—October 24—Donald Duck—Dick Lundy

THE ART OF SKIING—November 14—Goofy—Jack Kinney

CHEF DONALD—December 5—Donald Duck—Jack King

THE ART OF SELF DEFENSE—December 26—Goofy—Jack Kinney

1942

THE VILLAGE SMITHY—January 16—Donald Duck—Dick Lundy

MICKEY'S BIRTHDAY PARTY—February 7—Mickey Mouse (MM, DD, G)—Riley Thomson

PLUTO, JUNIOR—February 28—Pluto—Clyde Geronimi

SYMPHONY HOUR—March 20—Mickey Mouse (MM, DD, G)—Riley Thomson

DONALD'S SNOW FIGHT—April 10—Donald Duck—Jack King

DONALD GETS DRAFTED—May 1—Donald Duck—Jack King

THE ARMY MASCOT—May 22—Pluto—Clyde Geronimi

DONALD'S GARDEN—June 12—Donald Duck—Dick Lundy

THE SLEEPWALKER—July 3—Pluto—Clyde Geronimi

DONALD'S GOLD MINE—July 24—Donald Duck—Dick Lundy

T-BONE FOR TWO—August 14—Pluto—Clyde Geronimi

HOW TO PLAY BASEBALL—September 4—Goofy—Jack Kinney

THE VANISHING PRIVATE—September 25—Donald Duck—Jack King

THE OLYMPIC CHAMP—October 9—Goofy—Jack Kinney

HOW TO SWIM—October 23—Goofy—Jack Kinney

SKY TROOPER—November 6—Donald Duck—Jack King

PLUTO AT THE ZOO—November 20—Pluto—Clyde Geronimi

HOW TO FISH—December 4—Goofy—Jack Kinney

BELLBOY DONALD—December 18—Donald Duck—Jack King

1943

‡ DER FUEHRER'S FACE—January 1—Donald Duck—Jack Kinney

EDUCATION FOR DEATH—January 15—Special—Clyde Geronimi

DONALD'S TIRE TROUBLE—January 29—Donald Duck—Dick Lundy

PLUTO AND THE ARMADILLO—February 19—Pluto—Clyde Geronimi

FLYING JALOPY—March 12—Donald Duck—Dick Lundy

PRIVATE PLUTO—April 2—Pluto—Clyde Geronimi

FALL OUT—FALL IN—April 23—Donald Duck—Jack King

VICTORY VEHICLES—July 30—Goofy (G, P)—Jack Kinney

† REASON AND EMOTION—August 27—Special—Bill Roberts

FIGARO AND CLEO—October 15—Figaro—Jack Kinney

THE OLD ARMY GAME—November 5—Donald Duck—Jack King

HOME DEFENSE—November 26—Donald Duck—Jack King

CHICKEN LITTLE—December 17—Special—Clyde Geronimi

1944

THE PELICAN AND THE SNIPE—January 7—Special—Hamilton Luske

HOW TO BE A SAILOR—January 28—Goofy—Jack Kinney

TROMBONE TROUBLE—February 18—Donald Duck—Jack King

HOW TO PLAY GOLF—March 10—Goofy—Jack Kinney

DONALD DUCK AND THE GORILLA—March 31—Donald Duck—Jack King

CONTRARY CONDOR—April 21—Donald Duck—Jack King

COMMANDO DUCK—June 2—Donald Duck—Jack King

SPRINGTIME FOR PLUTO—June 23—Pluto—Charles Nichols

THE PLASTICS INVENTOR—September 1—Donald Duck—Jack King

† HOW TO PLAY FOOTBALL—September 15—Goofy—Jack Kinney

FIRST AIDERS—September 22—Pluto—Charles Nichols

DONALD'S OFF DAY—December 8—Donald Duck—Jack Hannah

1945

TIGER TROUBLE—January 5—Goofy—Jack Kinney

THE CLOCK WATCHER—January 26—Donald Duck—Jack King

DOG WATCH—March 16—Pluto—Charles Nichols

THE EYES HAVE IT—March 30—Donald Duck (DD, P)—Jack Hannah

AFRICAN DIARY—April 20—Goofy—Jack Kinney

†DONALD'S CRIME—June 29—Donald Duck—Jack King

CALIFORNY 'ER BUST—July 13—Goofy—Jack Kinney

CANINE CASANOVA—July 27—Pluto—Charles Nichols

DUCK PIMPLES—August 10—Donald Duck—Jack Kinney

THE LEGEND OF COYOTE ROCK—August 24—Pluto—Charles Nichols

NO SAIL—September 7—Donald Duck (DD, G)—Jack Hannah

HOCKEY HOMICIDE—September 21—Goofy—Jack Kinney

CURED DUCK—October 26—Donald Duck—Jack King

CANINE PATROL—December 7—Pluto—Charles Nichols

OLD SEQUOIA—December 21—Donald Duck—Jack King

1946

A KNIGHT FOR A DAY—March 8—Goofy—Jack Hannah

PLUTO'S KID BROTHER—April 12—Pluto—Charles Nichols

IN DUTCH—May 10—Pluto—Charles Nichols

SQUATTER'S RIGHTS—June 7—Pluto (P, MM, CD)—Jack Hannah

DONALD'S DOUBLE TROUBLE—June 28—Donald Duck—Jack King

THE PURLOINED PUP—July 19—Pluto—Charles Nichols

WET PAINT—August 9—Donald Duck—Jack King

DUMBBELL OF THE YUKON—August 30—Donald Duck—Jack King

LIGHTHOUSE KEEPING—September 20—Donald Duck—Jack Hannah

BATH DAY—October 11—Figaro—Charles Nichols

FRANK DUCK BRINGS 'EM BACK ALIVE—November 1—Donald Duck (DD, G)—Jack Hannah

DOUBLE DRIBBLE—December 20—Goofy—Jack Hannah

1947

PLUTO'S HOUSE WARMING—February 21—Pluto—Charles Nichols

RESCUE DOG—March 21—Pluto—Charles Nichols

STRAIGHT SHOOTERS—April 18—Donald Duck—Jack Hannah

SLEEPY TIME DONALD—May 9—Donald Duck—Jack King

FIGARO AND FRANKIE—May 30—Figaro—Charles Nichols

CLOWN OF THE JUNGLE—June 20—Donald Duck—Jack Hannah

DONALD'S DILEMMA—July 11—Donald Duck—Jack King

CRAZY WITH THE HEAT—August 1—Donald Duck (G)—Bob Carlson

BOOTLE BEETLE—August 22—Donald Duck—Jack Hannah

WIDE OPEN SPACES—September 12—Donald Duck—Jack King

MICKEY'S DELAYED DATE—October 3—Mickey Mouse (MM, P)—Charles Nichols

FOUL HUNTING—October 31—Goofy—Jack Hannah

MAIL DOG—November 14—Pluto—Charles Nichols

†CHIP 'N' DALE—November 28—Donald Duck (DD, CD)—Jack Hannah

†PLUTO'S BLUE NOTE—December 26—Pluto—Charles Nichols

1948

THEY'RE OFF—January 23—Goofy—Jack Hannah

THE BIG WASH—February 6—Goofy—Clyde Geronimi

DRIP DIPPY DONALD—March 5—Donald Duck—Jack King

MICKEY DOWN UNDER—March 19—Mickey Mouse (MM, P)—Charles Nichols

DADDY DUCK—April 16—Donald Duck—Jack Hannah

BONE BANDIT—April 30—Pluto—Charles Nichols

DONALD'S DREAM VOICE—May 21—Donald Duck—Jack King

PLUTO'S PURCHASE—July 9—Pluto (P, MM)—Charles Nichols

THE TRIAL OF DONALD DUCK—July 30—Donald Duck—Jack King

CAT NAP PLUTO—August 13—Pluto—Charles Nichols

INFERIOR DECORATOR—August 27—Donald Duck—Jack Hannah

PLUTO'S FLEDGLING—September 10—Pluto—Charles Nichols

SOUP'S ON—October 15—Donald Duck—Jack Hannah

THREE FOR BREAKFAST—November 5—Donald Duck (DD, CD)—Jack Hannah

†MICKEY AND THE SEAL—December 3—Mickey Mouse (MM, P)—Charles Nichols

†TEA FOR TWO HUNDRED—December 24—Donald Duck—Jack Hannah

1949

PUEBLO PLUTO—January 14—Pluto (P, MM)—Charles Nichols

DONALD'S HAPPY BIRTHDAY—February 11—Donald Duck—Jack Hannah

PLUTO'S SURPRISE PACKAGE—March 4—Pluto—Charles Nichols

SEA SALTS—April 8—Donald Duck—Jack Hannah

PLUTO'S SWEATER—April 29—Pluto—Charles Nichols

WINTER STORAGE—June 3—Donald Duck (DD, CD)—Jack Hannah

BUBBLE BEE—June 24—Pluto—Charles Nichols

HONEY HARVESTER—August 5—Donald Duck—Jack Hannah

TENNIS RACQUET—August 26—Goofy—Jack Kinney

ALL IN A NUTSHELL—September 2—Donald Duck (DD, CD)—Jack Hannah

GOOFY GYMNASTICS—September 23—Goofy—Jack Kinney

THE GREENER YARD—October 14—Donald Duck—Jack Hannah

SHEEP DOG—November 4—Pluto—Charles Nichols

SLIDE DONALD SLIDE—November 25—Donald Duck—Jack Hannah

†TOY TINKERS—December 16—Donald Duck (DD, CD)—Jack Hannah

1950

PLUTO'S HEART THROB—January 6—Pluto—Charles Nichols

LION AROUND—January 20—Donald Duck—Jack Hannah

THE WONDER DOG—April 7—Pluto—Charles Nichols

TRAILER HORN—April 28—Donald Duck (DD, CD)—Jack Hannah

PRIMITIVE PLUTO—May 19—Pluto—Charles Nichols

PUSS-CAFE—June 9—Pluto—Charles Nichols

MOTOR MANIA—June 30—Goofy—Jack Kinney

PESTS OF THE WEST—July 21—Pluto—Charles Nichols

FOOD FOR FEUDIN'—August 11—Pluto (P, CD)—Charles Nichols

HOOK LION AND SINKER—September 1—Donald Duck—Jack Hannah

CAMP DOG—September 22—Pluto—Charles Nichols

BEE AT THE BEACH—October 13—Donald Duck—Jack Hannah

HOLD THAT POSE—November 3—Goofy—Jack Kinney

MORRIS, THE MIDGET MOOSE—November 24—Special—Jack Hannah

OUT ON A LIMB—December 15—Donald Duck (DD, CD)—Jack Hannah

1951

LION DOWN—January 5—Goofy—Jack Kinney

CHICKEN IN THE ROUGH—January 19—Chip 'n Dale—Jack Hannah

COLD STORAGE—February 9—Pluto—Jack Kinney

DUDE DUCK—March 2—Donald Duck—Jack Hannah

HOME MADE HOME—March 23—Goofy—Jack Kinney

CORN CHIPS—March 23—Donald Duck (DD, CD)—Jack Hannah

COLD WAR—April 27—Goofy—Jack Kinney

PLUTOPIA—May 18—Pluto (P, MM)—Charles Nichols

TEST PILOT DONALD—June 8—Donald Duck (DD, CD)—Jack Hannah

TOMORROW WE DIET—June 29—Goofy—Jack Kinney

LUCKY NUMBER—July 20—Donald Duck—Jack Hannah

R'COON DAWG—August 10—Mickey Mouse (MM, P)—Charles Nichols

GET RICH QUICK—August 31—Goofy—Jack Kinney

COLD TURKEY—September 21—Pluto—Charles Nichols

FATHERS ARE PEOPLE—October 21—Goofy—Jack Kinney

OUT OF SCALE—November 2—Donald Duck (DD, CD)—Jack Hannah

NO SMOKING—November 23—Goofy—Jack Kinney

BEE ON GUARD—December 14—Donald Duck—Jack Hannah

1952

FATHER'S LION—January 4—Goofy—Jack Kinney

DONALD APPLECORE—January 18—Donald Duck (DD, CD)—Jack Hannah

†LAMBERT THE SHEEPISH LION—February 8—Special—Jack Hannah

HELLO ALOHA—February 29—Goofy—Jack Kinney

TWO CHIPS AND A MISS—March 21—Chip 'n' Dale—Jack Hannah

MAN'S BEST FRIEND—April 4—Goofy—Jack Kinney

LET'S STICK TOGETHER—April 25—Donald Duck—Jack Hannah

TWO GUN GOOFY—May 16—Goofy—Jack Kinney

SUSIE, THE LITTLE BLUE COUPE—June 6—Special—Clyde Geronimi

TEACHERS ARE PEOPLE—June 27—Goofy—Jack Kinney

UNCLE DONALD'S ANTS—July 18—Donald Duck—Jack Hannah

THE LITTLE HOUSE—August 8—Special—Wilfred Jackson

PLUTO'S PARTY—September 19—Pluto (P, MM)—Milt Schaffer

TRICK OR TREAT—October 10—Donald Duck—Jack Hannah

TWO WEEKS' VACATION—October 31—Goofy—Jack Kinney

PLUTO'S CHRISTMAS TREE—November 21—Mickey Mouse (MM, DD, P, G, CD)—Jack Hannah

HOW TO BE A DETECTIVE—December 12—Goofy—Jack Kinney

1953

FATHER'S DAY OFF—March 28—Goofy—Jack Kinney

THE SIMPLE THINGS—April 18—Mickey Mouse (MM, P)—Charles Nichols

FOR WHOM THE BULLS TOIL—May 9—Goofy—Jack Kinney

MELODY—May 28—Special—Ward Kimball & Charles Nichols (in 3-D)

DON'S FOUNTAIN OF YOUTH—May 30—Donald Duck—Jack Hannah

FATHER'S WEEKEND—June 20—Goofy—Jack Kinney

HOW TO DANCE—July 11—Goofy—Jack Kinney

THE NEW NEIGHBOR—August 1—Donald Duck—Jack Hannah

FOOTBALL (NOW AND THEN)—October 2—Special—Jack Kinney

†RUGGED BEAR—October 23—Donald Duck (DD, HB)—Jack Hannah

‡TOOT, WHISTLE, PLUNK, AND BOOM—November 10—Special—Ward Kimball & Charles Nichols*

†BEN AND ME—November 11—Special—Hamilton Luske

WORKING FOR PEANUTS—November 11—Donald Duck (DD, CD)—Jack Hannah (in 3-D)

HOW TO SLEEP—December 25—Goofy—Jack Kinney

CANVASBACK DUCK—December 25—Donald Duck—Jack Hannah

1954

SPARE THE ROD—January 15—Donald Duck—Jack Hannah

DONALD'S DIARY—March 5—Donald Duck—Jack Kinney

THE LONE CHIPMUNKS—April 7—Chip 'n Dale—Jack Kinney

†PIGS IS PIGS—May 21—Special—Jack Kinney

CASEY BATS AGAIN—June 18—Special—Jack Kinney

DRAGON AROUND—July 16—Donald Duck (DD, CD)—Jack Hannah

GRIN AND BEAR IT—August 13—Donald Duck—Jack Hannah

SOCIAL LION—October 15—Special—Jack Kinney

THE FLYING SQUIRREL—November 12—Donald Duck—Jack Hannah

*GRAND CANYONSCOPE—December 23—Donald Duck—Charles Nichols

1955

†NO HUNTING—January 14—Donald Duck—Jack Hannah

*BEARLY ASLEEP—August 19—Donald Duck (DD, HB)—Jack Hannah

*BEEZY BEAR—September 2—Donald Duck (DD, HB)—Jack Hannah

UP A TREE—September 23—Donald Duck (DD, CD)—Jack Hannah

1956

*CHIPS AHOY—February 24—Donald Duck (DD, CD)—Jack Kinney

*HOOKED BEAR—April 27—Humphrey Bear—Jack Hannah

*HOW TO HAVE AN ACCIDENT IN THE HOME—July 8—Donald Duck—Charles Nichols

JACK AND OLD MAC—July 18—Special—Bill Justice

*IN THE BAG—July 27—Humphrey Bear—Jack Hannah

A COWBOY NEEDS A HORSE—November 6—Special—Bill Justice

*In CinemaScope.

1957

THE STORY OF ANYBURG U.S.A.—June 19—Special—Clyde Geronimi

†THE TRUTH ABOUT MOTHER GOOSE—August 28—Special—Wolfgang Reitherman and Bill Justice

1958

†PAUL BUNYAN—August 1—Special—Les Clark

1959

DONALD IN MATHMAGIC LAND—June 26—Donald Duck—Hamilton Luske

HOW TO HAVE AN ACCIDENT AT WORK—July 1—Donald Duck—Charles Nichols

†NOAH'S ARK—November 10—Special—Bill Justice

1960

†GOLIATH II—January 21—Special—Wolfgang Reitherman

1961

†AQUAMANIA—February 20—Goofy—Wolfgang Reitherman

THE SAGA OF WINDWAGON SMITH—March 16—Special—Charles Nichols

DONALD AND THE WHEEL—June 21—Donald Duck—Hamilton Luske

THE LITTERBUG—June 21—Donald Duck—Hamilton Luske

1962

†A SYMPOSIUM ON POPULAR SONGS—December—Special—Bill Justice

1965

FREEWAYPHOBIA NO. 1—February 13—Special—Les Clark

GOOFY'S FREEWAY TROUBLE (FREEWAYPHOBIA NO. 2)—September 22—Goofy—Les Clark

1966

WINNIE THE POOH AND THE HONEY TREE—February 4—Special—Wolfgang Reitherman

1967

SCROOGE MCDUCK AND MONEY—Uncle Scrooge, Hewey Dewey and Louie—Hamilton Luske

1968

‡WINNIE THE POOH AND THE BLUSTERY DAY—Special—Wolfgang Reitherman

1969

‡IT'S TOUGH TO BE A BIRD—December 10—Special—Ward Kimball

1974

†WINNIE THE POOH AND TIGGER TOO—December 20—Special—John Lounsbery

1978

THE SMALL ONE—Special—Don Bluth

Walt Disney Features

Following is a complete list of animated feature films produced by the Walt Disney studio. RKO Radio Pictures released all titles up through PETER PAN (with the exception of VICTORY THROUGH AIR POWER, which was distributed by United Artists). Subsequent films—and all reissues—have been distributed by Buena Vista.

SNOW WHITE AND THE SEVEN DWARFS—February 4, 1938 (world premiere, December 21, 1937)—Supervising director: David Hand—Sequence directors: Perce Pearce, Larry Morey, William Cottrell, Wilfred Jackson, Ben Sharpsteen.

PINOCCHIO—February 23, 1940 (world premiere, February 7, 1940)—Supervising directors: Ben Sharpsteen, Hamilton Luske—Sequence directors: Bill Roberts, Norman Ferguson, Jack Kinney, Wilfred Jackson, T. Hee.

FANTASIA—World premiere, November 13, 1940—Production supervisor: Ben Sharpsteen; directors of individual sequences:
Samuel Armstrong ("Toccata and Fugue in D Minor ")
Samuel Armstrong ("The Nutcracker Suite")
James Algar ("The Sorcerer's Apprentice")
Bill Roberts, Paul Satterfield ("The Rite of Spring")
Hamilton Luske, Jim Handley, Ford Beebe ("Pastoral Symphony")
T. Hee, Norman Ferguson ("Dance of the Hours")
Wilfred Jackson ("Night on Bald Mountain," "Ave Maria")

THE RELUCTANT DRAGON—June 20, 1941—Cartoon directors: Hamilton Luske, Jim Handley, Ford Beebe, Erwin Verity, Jasper Blystone—Live-action director: Alfred L. Werker—"How to Ride a Horse" sequence directed by Jack Kinney. Later excerpted as "Behind the Scenes of Walt Disney Studios."

DUMBO—October 23, 1941—Supervising director: Ben Sharpsteen—Sequence directors: Norman Ferguson, Wilfred Jackson, Bill Roberts, Jack Kinney, Samuel Armstrong.

BAMBI—August 13, 1942—Supervising director: David Hand—Sequence directors: James Algar, Bill Roberts, Norman Wright, Samuel Armstrong, Paul Satterfield, Graham Heid.

SALUDOS AMIGOS—February 6, 1943—Production supervisor: Norman Ferguson—directors of individual sequences (later released separately):
Bill Roberts ("Lake Titicaca")
Hamilton Luske ("Pedro")
Jack Kinney ("El Gaucho Goofy")
Wilfred Jackson ("Aquarela do Brasil")

VICTORY THROUGH AIR POWER—July 17, 1943—Supervising director: David Hand—Sequence directors: Clyde Geronimi, Jack Kinney, James Algar; Live-action director: H. C. Potter—Later excerpted as HISTORY OF AVIATION.

THE THREE CABALLEROS—February 3, 1945—Supervising director: Norman Ferguson—Sequence directors: Clyde Geronimi, Jack Kinney, Bill Roberts; Live-action director Harold Young—"The Flying Gauchito" sequence directed by Jack Kinney was later released separately.

MAKE MINE MUSIC—August 15, 1946—Production supervisor: Joe Grant; directors of individual sequences:
Jack Kinney ("The Martins and the Coys," later released separately)
Samuel Armstrong ("Blue Bayou")
Jack Kinney ("All the Cats Join in")
Clyde Geronimi ("Casey at the Bat," later released separately)
Robert Cormack ("Without You")
Jack Kinney ("After You've Gone")
Clyde Geronimi; Introduction director: Joshua Meador ("Peter and the Wolf," later released separately)
Jack Kinney ("Johnny Fedora and Alice Blue Bonnet," later released separately)
Robert Cormack ("Two Silhouettes")
Clyde Geronimi, Hamilton Luske ("The Whale Who Wanted to Sing at the Met," later released separately as "Willie the Operatic Whale")
Titles and inserts by Hamilton Luske

SONG OF THE SOUTH—November 12, 1946—Cartoon director: Wilfred Jackson; Live-action director: Harve Foster.

FUN AND FANCY FREE—September 27, 1947—Production supervisor: Ben Sharpsteen; directors of individual sequences:
Jack Kinney ("Bongo," later released separately)
Bill Roberts, Hamilton Luske ("Mickey and the Beanstalk")
Live-action director: William Morgan

MELODY TIME—May 27, 1948—Production supervisor: Ben Sharpsteen; directors of individual sequences:
Hamilton Luske ("Once upon a Wintertime")
Jack Kinney ("Bumble Boogie," later released with "Trees" as "Contrasts in Rhythm")
Wilfred Jackson ("Johnny Appleseed," later released separately)
Clyde Geronimi ("Little Toot," later released separately)
Hamilton Luske ("Trees")
Clyde Geronimi ("Blame It on the Samba," later released separately)
Clyde Geronimi ("Pecos Bill")

SO DEAR TO MY HEART—January 19, 1949—Cartoon director: Hamilton Luske; Live-action director: Harold Schuster.

ICHABOD AND MR. TOAD (a.k.a. THE ADVENTURES OF ICHABOD AND MR. TOAD)—October 5, 1949—Production supervisor: Ben Sharpsteen; directors of individual sequences:

> Jack Kinney, James Algar ("The Adventures of Mr. Toad" / "Wind in the Willows," later released separately)
>
> Clyde Geronimi ("Ichabod Crane or The Legend of Sleepy Hollow," later released separately)

CINDERELLA—February 15, 1950—Production supervisor: Ben Sharpsteen—Directors: Wilfred Jackson, Hamilton Luske, Clyde Geronimi.

ALICE IN WONDERLAND—July 28, 1951—Production supervisor: Ben Sharpsteen—Directors: Clyde Geronimi, Hamilton Luske, Wilfred Jackson.

PETER PAN—February 5, 1953—Directors: Hamilton Luske, Clyde Geronimi, Wilfred Jackson.

LADY AND THE TRAMP—June 16, 1955—Directors: Hamilton Luske, Clyde Geronimi, Wilfred Jackson.

SLEEPING BEAUTY—January 29, 1959—Supervising director: Clyde Geronimi—Sequence directors: Eric Larson, Wolfgang Reitherman, Les Clark.

ONE HUNDRED AND ONE DALMATIONS—January 25, 1961—Directors: Wolfgang Reitherman, Hamilton Luske, Clyde Geronimi.

THE SWORD IN THE STONE—December 25, 1963—Director: Wolfgang Reitherman.

THE JUNGLE BOOK—October 18, 1967—Director: Wolfgang Reitherman.

THE ARISTOCATS—December 24, 1970—Director: Wolfgang Reitherman.

ROBIN HOOD—November 8, 1973—Director: Wolfgang Reitherman.

THE RESCUERS—June 22, 1977—Directors: Wolfgang Reitherman, John Lounsbery, Art Stevens.

The Max Fleischer Cartoons

Following is the most complete list of Max Fleischer's cartoons assembled to date. It includes only his theatrical releases and does not encompass technical, scientific, or commercial films, many of which are referred to by name in the preceding chapter.

Fleischer's first shorts were produced by John R. Bray and released in his PARAMOUNT (then Goldwyn) SCREEN MAGAZINES. When Fleischer formed his own studio in 1921, he sold his films on a states' rights basis and then operated a short-lived distribution firm, Red Seal Pictures. In 1927 Paramount acquired distribution rights to his cartoons and continued to release them through 1942.

Short subjects are identified by series title, where applicable. Copyright dates are listed when it was impossible to ascertain release dates. However, many silent shorts were not copyrighted, making it difficult to authenticate this part of the filmography, or determine accurate chronological order.

Dave Fleischer received director credit on every cartoon released by this studio.

All Fleischer cartoons were made in black and white, except the COLOR CLASSICS and POPEYE SPECIALS in the 1930s, and these post-1940 series: ANIMATED ANTICS, GABBY, TWO-REEL SPECIALS, and SUPERMAN.

In the early 1940s several non-Fleischer shorts were released under Fleischer's name by Paramount: a stop-motion animated short, POP AND MOM IN WILD OYSTERS, and the first SPEAKING OF ANIMALS episode.

One dagger (†) next to a film title indicates an Academy Award nominee.

1915–1920 *(Produced by John R. Bray)*

EXPERIMENT NO. 1

EXPERIMENT NO. 2

EXPERIMENT NO. 3

THE CLOWN'S PUP—Out of the Inkwell

TANTALIZING FLY—Out of the Inkwell

SLIDES—Out of the Inkwell

KANGAROO—Out of the Inkwell

THE CHINAMAN—Out of the Inkwell

THE CIRCUS—Out of the Inkwell

THE OUIJA BOARD—Out of the Inkwell

THE CLOWN'S LITTLE BROTHER—Out of the Inkwell

THE CARD GAME—Out of the Inkwell

PERPETUAL MOTION—Out of the Inkwell

THE RESTAURANT—Out of the Inkwell

CARTOONLAND—Out of the Inkwell

THE AUTOMOBILE RIDE—Out of the Inkwell

CIRCUS—Out of the Inkwell

1921

THE FIRST MAN TO THE MOON—Out of the Inkwell

MODELING—Out of the Inkwell

FISHING—November—Out of the Inkwell

NOVEMBER (unconfirmed title)—Out of the Inkwell

INVISIBLE INK—December—Out of the Inkwell

THE HYPNOTIST—Out of the Inkwell

1922

THE DANCING DOLL (listed in some sources as DRESDEN DOLL)—January—Out of the Inkwell

MOSQUITO—March—Out of the Inkwell

BUBBLES—April—Out of the Inkwell

THE CHALLENGE—Out of the Inkwell

PAY DAY—July—Out of the Inkwell

THE SHOW—September—Out of the Inkwell

REUNION—October—Out of the Inkwell

BIRTHDAY—November—Out of the Inkwell

JUMPING BEANS—December—Out of the Inkwell

1923

FLIES—January—Out of the Inkwell

SURPRISE—March—Out of the Inkwell

PUZZLE—April—Out of the Inkwell

TRAPPED—May—Out of the Inkwell

THE BATTLE—July—Out of the Inkwell

FALSE ALARM—August—Out of the Inkwell

BEDTIME—Out of the Inkwell

THE CONTEST—Out of the Inkwell

BALLOONS—Out of the Inkwell

THE FORTUNE TELLER—Out of the Inkwell

LAUNDRY—Out of the Inkwell

SHADOWS—Out of the Inkwell

1924

GOODBYE MY LADY LOVE (released with sound)—June—Song Cartune

MOTHER, MOTHER, MOTHER PIN A ROSE ON ME (released with sound)—June—Song Cartune

COME TAKE A TRIP IN MY AIRSHIP (released with sound)—June—Song Cartune

VAUDEVILLE—November—Out of the Inkwell

VACATION—November—Out of the Inkwell

LEAGUE OF NATIONS—November—Out of the Inkwell

THE CURE—December—Out of the Inkwell

A TRIP TO MARS—Out of the Inkwell

SPARRING PARTNER—Out of the Inkwell

OH MABEL—Song Cartune

THE RUNAWAY—Out of the Inkwell

THE MASQUERADE—Out of the Inkwell

KO-KO IN 1999—Out of the Inkwell

KO-KO THE HOT SHOT—Out of the Inkwell

1925

CARTOON FACTORY—Out of the Inkwell

MOTHER GOOSE LAND—Out of the Inkwell

BIG CHIEF KO-KO—Out of the Inkwell

KO-KO IN TOYLAND—Out of the Inkwell

I LOVE LASSIE—Song Cartune

THE STORM—Out of the Inkwell

KO-KO THE BARBER—Out of the Inkwell

SUWANEE RIVER—Song Cartune

KO-KO TRAINS 'EM—Out of the Inkwell

DAISY BELL—Song Cartune

KO-KO CELEBRATES THE FOURTH—Out of the Inkwell

KO-KO SEES SPOOKS—Out of the Inkwell

OLD FOLKS AT HOME—Song Cartune

KO-KO NUTS—September 5—Out of the Inkwell

MY BONNIE—September 12—Song Cartune

KO-KO ON THE RUN—September 26—Out of the Inkwell

NUTCRACKER SUITE (unconfirmed title)—September—Song Cartune

TA-RA-RA-BOOM-DEE-AYE—Song Cartune

KO-KO EATS—Out of the Inkwell

DIXIE—Song Cartune

KO-KO PACKS UP—October 17—Out of the Inkwell

KO-KO'S THANKSGIVING—Out of the Inkwell

SAILING SAILING—Song Cartune

1926

MY OLD KENTUCKY HOME (released with sound)—January—Song Cartune

KO-KO STEPS OUT—January—Out of the Inkwell

DARLING NELLIE GRAY (released with sound)—February—Song Cartune

KO-KO'S PARADISE—February—Out of the Inkwell

KO-KO BAFFLES THE BULLS—March—Out of the Inkwell

HAS ANYBODY HERE SEEN KELLY (released with sound)—March—Song Cartune (hand-colored)

IT'S THE CATS—May—Out of the Inkwell

TRAMP, TRAMP, TRAMP THE BOYS ARE MARCHING—May—Song Cartune

SWEET ADELINE (released with sound)—June—Song Cartune

TOOT! TOOT!—July—Out of the Inkwell

OLD BLACK JOE (released with sound)—July—Song Cartune

BY THE LIGHT OF THE SILVERY MOON (released with sound)—August—Song Cartune

KO-KO IN THE FADE-AWAY—September—Out of the Inkwell

IN THE GOOD OLD SUMMERTIME—Song Cartune

OH YOU BEAUTIFUL DOLL—Song Cartune

KO-KO AT THE CIRCUS—Out of the Inkwell

KO-KO GETS EGG-CITED—Out of the Inkwell

KO-KO HOT AFTER IT—Out of the Inkwell

KO-KO KIDNAPPED—Out of the Inkwell

KO-KO THE CONVICT—Out of the Inkwell

KO-KO'S QUEEN—December—Out of the Inkwell

1924–1926 (*Undated Song Cartunes*)

DEAR OLD PAL

WHEN THE MIDNIGHT CHOO-CHOO COMES TO ALABAM

COMING THROUGH THE RYE

YAKA-HULA-HICKA-OOOLA

WHEN I LOST YOU

OH, SUZANNA

MY WIFE'S GONE TO THE COUNTRY

TRAIL OF THE LONESOME PINE

MARGIE

ANNIE LAURIE

PACK UP YOUR TROUBLES

OH, HOW I HATE TO GET UP IN THE MORNING

EAST SIDE, WEST SIDE

1927 (*Copyright dates listed*)

KO-KO MAKES 'EM LAUGH—Inkwell Imps

KO-KO PLAYS POOL—August 6—Inkwell Imps

KO-KO'S KANE—August 20—Inkwell Imps

KO-KO THE KNIGHT—September 3—Inkwell Imps

KO-KO HOPS OFF—September 17—Inkwell Imps

KO-KO THE KOP—October 1—Inkwell Imps

KO-KO EXPLORES—October 15—Inkwell Imps

KO-KO CHOPS SUEY—October 29—Inkwell Imps

KO-KO'S KLOCK—November 12—Inkwell Imps

KO-KO KICKS—November 26—Inkwell Imps

KO-KO'S QUEST—December 10—Inkwell Imps

KO-KO THE KID—December 24—Inkwell Imps

KO-KO BACK TRACKS—Inkwell Imps

KO-KO NEEDLES THE BOSS—Inkwell Imps

1928 (*Silent releases; copyright dates listed*)

KO-KO'S KINK—January 7—Inkwell Imps

KO-KO'S KOZY KORNER—January 21—Inkwell Imps

KO-KO'S GERM JAM—February 4—Inkwell Imps

KO-KO'S BAWTH—February 18—Inkwell Imps

KO-KO SMOKES—March 3—Inkwell Imps

KO-KO'S TATTOO—March 17—Inkwell Imps

KO-KO'S EARTH CONTROL—March 31—Inkwell Imps

KO-KO'S HOT DOG—April 14—Inkwell Imps

KO-KO'S HAUNTED HOUSE—April 28—Inkwell Imps

KO-KO LAMPS ALADDIN—May 12—Inkwell Imps

KO-KO SQUEALS—May 26—Inkwell Imps

KO-KO'S FIELD DAZE—June 9—Inkwell Imps

KO-KO GOES OVER—June 23—Inkwell Imps

KO-KO'S CATCH—July 7—Inkwell Imps

KO-KO'S WAR DOGS—July 21—Inkwell Imps

KO-KO'S CHASE—August 11—Inkwell Imps

KO-KO HEAVES HO—August 25—Inkwell Imps

KO-KO'S BIG PULL—September 7—Inkwell Imps

KO-KO CLEANS UP—September 21—Inkwell Imps

KO-KO'S PARADE—October 8—Inkwell Imps

KO-KO'S DOG GONE—October 22—Inkwell Imps

KO-KO IN THE ROUGH—November 3—Inkwell Imps

KO-KO'S MAGIC—November 16—Inkwell Imps

KO-KO ON THE TRACK—December 4—Inkwell Imps

KO-KO'S ACT—December 17—Inkwell Imps

KO-KO'S COURTSHIP—December 28—Inkwell Imps

1929 *(Silent releases; copyright dates listed)*

NO EYES TODAY—January 11—Inkwell Imps

NOISE ANNOYS KO-KO—January 25—Inkwell Imps

KO-KO BEATS TIME—February 8—Inkwell Imps

KO-KO'S REWARD—February 23—Inkwell Imps

KO-KO'S HOT INK—March 8—Inkwell Imps

KO-KO'S CRIB—March 23—Inkwell Imps

KO-KO'S SAXAPHONIES—April 5—Inkwell Imps

KO-KO'S KNOCK-DOWN—April 19—Inkwell Imps

KO-KO'S SIGNALS—May 3—Inkwell Imps

KO-KO'S CONQUEST—May 31—Inkwell Imps

KO-KO'S FOCUS—May 17—Inkwell Imps

KO-KO'S HAREM SCAREM—June 14—Inkwell Imps

KO-KO'S BIG SALE—June 28—Inkwell Imps

KO-KO'S HYPNOTISM—July 12—Inkwell Imps

CHEMICAL KO-KO—July 26—Inkwell Imps

1929 *(Talkies; copyright dates marked by ©)*

THE SIDEWALKS OF NEW YORK—February 5—Screen Song

OLD BLACK JOE—April 5—Screen Song

YANKEE DOODLE BOY—March 1—Screen Song

YE OLDE MELODIES—© May 3—Screen Song

DAISY BELL—May 31—Screen Song

MOTHER PIN A ROSE ON ME—© July 6—Screen Song

DIXIE—August 17—Screen Song

GOODBYE MY LADY LOVE—© August 31—Screen Song

CHINATOWN MY CHINATOWN—August 29—Screen Song

MY PONY BOY—© September 13—Screen Song

SMILES—September 27—Screen Song

OH, YOU BEAUTIFUL DOLL—October 14—Screen Song

NOAH'S LARK—© October 25—Talkartoon

AFTER THE BALL—November 8—Screen Song

PUT ON YOUR OLD GRAY BONNET—November 22—Screen Song

ACCORDION JOE—© December 12—Talkartoon

I'VE GOT RINGS ON MY FINGERS—December 17—Screen Song

1930 *(Copyright date marked by ©)*

BEDELIA—January 3—Screen Song

MARRIAGE WOWS—© January 8—Talkartoon

IN THE SHADE OF THE OLD APPLE TREE—January 16—Screen Song

I'M AFRAID TO COME HOME IN THE DARK—January 30—Screen Song

RADIO RIOT—February 13—Talkartoon

PRISONER'S SONG—March 1—Screen Song

LA PALOMA—March 20—Screen Song

HOT DOG—March 29—Talkartoon

I'M FOREVER BLOWING BUBBLES—March 30—Screen Song

YES! WE HAVE NO BANANAS—April 25—Screen Song

FIRE BUGS—May 9—Talkartoon

COME TAKE A TRIP IN MY AIRSHIP—May 23—Screen Song

IN THE GOOD OLD SUMMER TIME—June 6—Screen Song

WISE FLIES—July 18—Talkartoon

A HOT TIME IN THE OLD TOWN TONIGHT—August 1—Screen Song

DIZZY DISHES—August 9—Talkartoon

THE GLOW WORM—August 18—Screen Song

BARNACLE BILL—August 31—Talkartoon

THE STEIN SONG—September 5—Screen Song (with Rudy Vallee)

SWING, YOU SINNERS—September 24—Talkartoon

STRIKE UP THE BAND—September 26—Screen Song

THE GRAND UPROAR—October 3—Talkartoon

MY GAL SAL—October 18—Screen Song

SKY SCRAPING—November 1—Talkartoon

MARIUTCH—November 15—Screen Song

UP TO MARS—November 20—Talkartoon

ON A SUNDAY AFTERNOON—November 25—Screen Song

ROW, ROW, ROW—December 19—Screen Song

MYSTERIOUS MOSE—December 26—Talkartoon

1931 (Copyright dates marked by ©)

PLEASE GO 'WAY AND LET ME SLEEP—January 9—Screen Song

THE ACE OF SPADES—January 16—Talkartoon

BY THE BEAUTIFUL SEA—January 23—Screen Song

TREE SAPS—February 3—Talkartoon

TEACHER'S PEST—February 7—Talkartoon

I WONDER WHO'S KISSING HER NOW—February 13—Screen Song

I'D CLIMB THE HIGHEST MOUNTAIN—March 6—Screen Song

THE COW'S HUSBAND—March 13—Talkartoon

SOMEBODY STOLE MY GAL—© March 20—Screen Song

THE BUM BANDIT—April 3—Talkartoon

ANY LITTLE GIRL THAT'S A NICE LITTLE GIRL—April 16—Screen Song

THE MALE MAN—April 24—Talkartoon

TWENTY LEGS UNDER THE SEA—© May 5—Talkartoon

ALEXANDER'S RAGTIME BAND—May 9—Screen Song

SILLY SCANDALS—May 23—Talkartoon (Betty Boop)

AND THE GREEN GRASS GREW ALL AROUND—June 1—Screen Song

MY WIFE'S GONE TO THE COUNTRY—© June 12—Screen Song

THE HERRING MURDER CASE—June 26—Talkartoon

THAT OLD GANG OF MINE—© July 9—Screen Song

BIMBO'S INITIATION—July 24—Talkartoon (Betty Boop)

BETTY CO-ED—August 1—Screen Song (with Rudy Vallee)

BIMBO'S EXPRESS—August 22—Talkartoon (Betty Boop)

MR. GALLAGHER AND MR. SHEAN—August 29—Screen Song

YOU'RE DRIVING ME CRAZY—September 19—Screen Song

MINDING THE BABY—September 26—Talkartoon (Betty Boop)

LITTLE ANNIE ROONEY—October 10—Screen Song

IN THE SHADE OF THE OLD APPLE SAUCE—October 16—Talkartoon

KITTY FROM KANSAS CITY—November 1—Screen Song (with Rudy Vallee)

MASK-A-RAID—November 7—Talkartoon (Betty Boop)

BY THE LIGHT OF THE SILVERY MOON—November 14—Screen Song

JACK AND THE BEANSTALK—November 21—Talkartoon (Betty Boop)

MY BABY CARES FOR ME—December 5—Screen Song

DIZZY RED RIDING HOOD—December 12—Talkartoon (Betty Boop)

RUSSIAN LULLABY—December 26—Screen Song (with Arthur Tracy)

1932

ANY RAGS—January 2—Talkartoon (Betty Boop)

SWEET JENNY LEE—January 9—Screen Song

BOOP-OOP-A-DOOP—January 16—Talkartoon (Betty Boop)

SHOW ME THE WAY TO GO HOME—January 30—Screen Song

THE ROBOT—February 5—Talkartoon

WHEN THE RED RED ROBIN COMES BOB BOB BOBBIN' ALONG—February 19—Screen Song

WAIT TILL THE SUN SHINES, NELLIE—March 4—Screen Song

MINNIE THE MOOCHER—© March 11—Talkartoon (Betty Boop with Cab Calloway and his orchestra)

SWIM OR SINK—March 11—Talkartoon (Betty Boop)

CRAZY TOWN—March 25—Talkartoon (Betty Boop)

JUST ONE MORE CHANCE—April 1—Screen Song

THE DANCING FOOL—April 8—Talkartoon (Betty Boop)

OH! HOW I HATE TO GET UP IN THE MORNING—April 22—Screen Song

CHESS NUTS—April 13—Talkartoon

A HUNTING WE WILL GO—April 29—Talkartoon (Betty Boop)

SHINE ON HARVEST MOON—May 6—Screen Song

LET ME CALL YOU SWEETHEART—May 20—Screen Song (with Ethel Merman)

HIDE AND SEEK—May 26—Talkartoon

ADMISSION FREE—June 10—Talkartoon (Betty Boop)

I AIN'T GOT NOBODY—June 17—Screen Song (with the Mills Brothers)

THE BETTY BOOP LIMITED—July 1—Talkartoon (Betty Boop)

YOU TRY SOMEBODY ELSE—July 29—Screen Song (with Ethel Merman)

RUDY VALLEE MELODIES—August 5—Screen Song (Betty Boop)

STOPPING THE SHOW—August 12—Betty Boop

BETTY BOOP BIZZY BEE—August 19—Betty Boop

DOWN AMONG THE SUGAR CANE—August 26—Screen Song (with Lillian Roth)

BETTY BOOP, M.D.—September 2—Betty Boop

JUST A GIGOLO—September 9—Screen Song (with Irene Bordini)

BETTY BOOP'S BAMBOO ISLE—September 23—Betty Boop (with the Royal Samoans and Miri)

SCHOOL DAYS—September 30—Screen Song (with Gus Edwards)

BETTY BOOP'S UPS AND DOWNS—October 14—Betty Boop

ROMANTIC MELODIES—October 21—Screen Song (with Arthur Tracy)

BETTY BOOP FOR PRESIDENT—November 4—Betty Boop

WHEN IT'S SLEEPY TIME DOWN SOUTH—November 11—Screen Song (with the Boswell Sisters)

I'LL BE GLAD WHEN YOU'RE DEAD YOU RASCAL YOU—November 25—Betty Boop (with Louis Armstrong)

SING A SONG—December 2—Screen Song (with James Melton)

BETTY BOOP'S MUSEUM—December 16—Betty Boop

TIME ON MY HANDS—December 23—Screen Song (with Ethel Merman)

1933

BETTY BOOP'S KER-CHOO—January 6—Betty Boop

DINAH—January 13—Screen Song (with the Mills Brothers)

BETTY BOOP'S CRAZY INVENTIONS—January 27—Betty Boop

AIN'T SHE SWEET—February 3—Screen Song (with Lillian Roth)

IS MY PALM RED—February 17—Betty Boop

REACHING FOR THE MOON—February 24—Screen Song (with Arthur Tracy)

BETTY BOOP'S PENTHOUSE—March 10—Betty Boop

ALOHA OE—March 17—Screen Song (with the Royal Samoans)

SNOW WHITE—March 31—Betty Boop (with Cab Calloway)

POPULAR MELODIES—April 7—Screen Song (with Arthur Jarrett)

BETTY BOOP'S BIRTHDAY PARTY—April 21—Betty Boop

THE PEANUT VENDOR—April 28—Screen Song (with Armida)

BETTY BOOP'S MAY PARTY—May 12—Betty Boop

SONG SHOPPING—May 19—Screen Song (with Ethel Merman and Johnny Green)

BETTY BOOP'S BIG BOSS—June 2—Betty Boop

BOILESK—June 9—Screen Song (with The Watson Sisters)

MOTHER GOOSE LAND—June 23—Betty Boop

SING, SISTERS, SING!—June 30—Screen Song (with the Three X Sisters)

POPEYE THE SAILOR—July 14—Betty Boop

DOWN BY THE OLD MILL STREAM—July 21—Screen Song (with the Funny Boners)

THE OLD MAN OF THE MOUNTAIN—August 4—Betty Boop (with Cab Calloway)

STOOPNOCRACY—August 18—Screen Song (with Colonel Stoopnagle and Budd)

I HEARD—September 1—Betty Boop (with Don Redman)

WHEN YUBA PLAYS THE RUMBA ON THE TUBA—September 15—Screen Song (with the Mills Brothers)

I YAM WHAT I YAM—September 29—Popeye

BOO, BOO, THEME SONG—October 3—Screen Song (with the Funny Boners)

MORNING NOON AND NIGHT—October 6—Betty Boop—(with Rubinoff)

BLOW ME DOWN—October 27—Popeye

BETTY BOOP'S HALLOWEEN PARTY—November 3—Betty Boop

I LIKE MOUNTAIN MUSIC—November 10—Screen Song (with the Eton Boys)

I EATS MY SPINACH—November 17—Popeye

PARADE OF THE WOODEN SOLDIERS—December 1—Betty Boop (with Rubinoff)

SEASON'S GREETINKS—December 17—Popeye

SING, BABIES, SING—December 15—Screen Song (with Baby Rose Marie)

WILD ELEPHINKS—December 29—Popeye

1934 *(Copyright date marked by ©)*

SHE WRONGED HIM RIGHT—January 5—Betty Boop

KEEPS RAININ' ALL THE TIME—January 12—Screen Song (with Gertrude Niesen)

SOCK-A-BYE BABY—January 19—Popeye

RED HOT MAMA—February 2—Betty Boop

LET'S ALL SING LIKE THE BIRDIES SING—February 9—Screen Song (with Reis and Dunn)

LET'S YOU AND HIM FIGHT—February 16—Popeye

HA! HA! HA!—March 2—Betty Boop

TUNE UP AND SING—March 9—Screen Song (with Lanny Ross)

THE MAN ON THE FLYING TRAPEZE—March 16—Popeye

BETTY IN BLUNDERLAND—April 6—Betty Boop

LAZY BONES—April 13—Screen Song (with Borrah Minnevitch and his Harmonica Rascals)

CAN YOU TAKE IT—April 27—Popeye

BETTY BOOP'S RISE TO FAME—May 18—Betty Boop

THIS LITTLE PIGGIE WENT TO MARKET—May 25—Screen Song (with Singin' Sam)

SHOEIN' HOSSES—June 1—Popeye

BETTY BOOP'S TRIAL—June 15—Betty Boop

SHE REMINDS ME OF YOU—June 22—Screen Song (with the Eton Boys)

STRONG TO THE FINICH—June 29—Popeye

BETTY BOOP'S LIFEGUARD—July 13—Betty Boop

LOVE THY NEIGHBOR—July 20—Screen Song (with Mary Small)

SHIVER ME TIMBERS—July 27—Popeye

POOR CINDERELLA—August 3—Color Classic (first short in color)

THERE'S SOMETHING ABOUT A SOLDIER—August 17—Betty Boop

AXE ME ANOTHER—August 30—Popeye

BETTY BOOP'S LITTLE PAL—September 21—Betty Boop

A DREAM WALKING—© September 26—Popeye

BETTY BOOP'S PRIZE SHOW—October 19—Betty Boop

THE TWO-ALARM FIRE—October 26—Popeye

LITTLE DUTCH MILL—October 26—Color Classic

KEEP IN STYLE—November 16—Betty Boop

THE DANCE CONTEST—November 23—Popeye

WHEN MY SHIP COMES IN—December 21—Betty Boop

WE AIM TO PLEASE—December 28—Popeye

1935 *(Copyright dates marked by ©)*

AN ELEPHANT NEVER FORGETS—© January 2—Color Classic

BABY BE GOOD—January 18—Betty Boop

BEWARE OF BARNACLE BILL—January 25—Popeye

TAKING THE BLAME—February 15—Betty Boop

BE KIND TO ANIMALS—February 22—Popeye

THE SONG OF THE BIRDS—© February 27—Color Classic

STOP THAT NOISE—March 15—Betty Boop

PLEASED TO MEET CHA!—March 22—Popeye

SWAT THE FLY—April 19—Betty Boop

THE HYP-NUT-TIST—April 26—Popeye

THE KIDS IN THE SHOE—May 19—Color Classic

NO! NO! A THOUSAND TIMES NO!!—May 24—Betty Boop

CHOOSE YOUR WEPPINS—May 31—Popeye

A LITTLE SOAP AND WATER—June 21—Betty Boop

FOR BETTER OR WORSER—June 28—Popeye

DANCING ON THE MOON—July 12—Color Classic

A LANGUAGE ALL MY OWN—July 19—Betty Boop

DIZZY DIVERS—July 26—Popeye

BETTY BOOP AND GRAMPY—August 16—Betty Boop

YOU GOTTA BE A FOOTBALL HERO—August 30—Popeye

TIME FOR LOVE—September 6—Color Classic

I WISHED ON THE MOON—September 20—Screen Song (with Abe Lyman and orchestra)

JUDGE FOR A DAY—September 20—Betty Boop

KING OF THE MARDI GRAS—September 27—Popeye

MAKING STARS—October 18—Betty Boop

ADVENTURES OF POPEYE—October 25—Popeye

MUSICAL MEMORIES—November 8—Color Classic

THE SPINACH OVERTURE—December 7—Popeye

BETTY BOOP, WITH HENRY, THE FUNNIEST LIVING AMERICAN—December 22—Betty Boop

IT'S EASY TO REMEMBER—December 29—Screen Song (with Richard Himber and orchestra)

1936

VIM, VIGOR AND VITALIKY—January 3—Popeye

SOMEWHERE IN DREAMLAND—January 17—Color Classic

NO OTHER ONE—January 24—Screen Song (with Hal Kemp and orchestra)

LITTLE NOBODY—January 27—Betty Boop

BETTY BOOP AND THE LITTLE KING—January 31—Betty Boop

A CLEAN SHAVEN MAN—February 7—Popeye

NOT NOW—February 28—Betty Boop

BROTHERLY LOVE—March 6—Popeye

THE LITTLE STRANGER—March 13—Color Classic

BETTY BOOP AND LITTLE JIMMY—March 27—Betty Boop

I FEEL LIKE A FEATHER IN THE BREEZE—March 27—Screen Song (with Jack Denny and orchestra)

I-SKI LOVE-SKI YOU-SKI—April 3—Popeye

WE DID IT—April 24—Betty Boop

BRIDGE AHOY—May 1—Popeye

WHAT, NO SPINACH?—May 7—Popeye

THE COBWEB HOTEL—May 15—Color Classic

A SONG A DAY—May 22—Betty Boop

I DON'T WANT TO MAKE HISTORY—May 22—Screen Song (with Vincent Lopez and orchestra)

MORE PEP—June 19—Betty Boop

I WANNA BE A LIFEGUARD—June 26—Popeye

GREEDY HUMPTY DUMPTY—July 10—Color Classic

YOU'RE NOT BUILT THAT WAY—July 17—Betty Boop

LET'S GET MOVIN'—July 24—Popeye

THE HILLS OF WYOMIN'—July 31—Screen Song (with the Westerners)

HAPPY YOU AND MERRY ME—August 21—Betty Boop

NEVER KICK A WOMAN—August 28—Popeye

HAWAIIAN BIRDS—August 28—Color Classic

TRAINING PIGEONS—September 18—Betty Boop

I CAN'T ESCAPE FROM YOU—September 25—Screen Song (with Joe Reichman and orchestra)

LITTLE SWEE' PEA—September 25—Popeye

PLAY SAFE—October 16—Color Classic

GRAMPY'S INDOOR OUTING—October 16—Betty Boop

HOLD THE WIRE—October 23—Popeye

BE HUMAN—November 20—Betty Boop

THE SPINACH ROADSTER—November 26—Popeye

TALKING THROUGH MY HEART—November 27—Screen Song (with Dick Stabile and orchestra)

†POPEYE THE SAILOR MEETS SINDBAD THE SAILOR—November 27—Popeye special (in color)

CHRISTMAS COMES BUT ONCE A YEAR—December 4—Color Classic

MAKING FRIENDS—December 18—Betty Boop

I'M IN THE ARMY NOW—December 25—Popeye

1937

HOUSE CLEANING BLUES—January 15—Betty Boop

THE PANELESS WINDOW WASHER—January 22—Popeye

NEVER SHOULD HAVE TOLD YOU—January 29—Screen Song (with Nat Brandywine and orchestra)

WHOOPS! I'M A COWBOY—February 12—Betty Boop

BUNNY MOONING—February 12—Color Classic

ORGAN GRINDER'S SWING—February 19—Popeye

THE HOT AIR SALESMAN—March 12—Betty Boop

MY ARTISTICAL TEMPERATURE—March 19—Popeye

TWILIGHT ON THE TRAIL—March 26—Screen Song (with the Westerners)

PUDGY TAKES A BOW-WOW—April 9—Betty Boop

HOSPITALIKY—April 16—Popeye

CHICKEN A LA KING—April 16—Color Classic

PUDGY PICKS A FIGHT—May 14—Betty Boop

THE TWISKER PITCHER—May 21—Popeye

PLEASE KEEP ME IN YOUR DREAMS—May 28—Screen Song (with Henry King and orchestra)

THE IMPRACTICAL JOKER—June 18—Betty Boop

MORNING, NOON AND NIGHTCLUB—June 18—Popeye

A CAR-TUNE PORTRAIT—June 26—Color Classic

LOST AND FOUNDRY—July 16—Popeye

DING DONG DOGGIE—July 23—Betty Boop

YOU CAME TO MY RESCUE—July 30—Screen Song (with Shep Fields and orchestra)

I NEVER CHANGES MY ALTITUDE—August 20—Popeye

PEEPING PENGUINS—August 26—Color Classic

THE CANDID CANDIDATE—August 27—Betty Boop

I LIKE BABIES AND INFINKS—September 18—Popeye

SERVICE WITH A SMILE—September 23—Betty Boop

WHISPERS IN THE DARK—September 24—Screen Song (with Gus Arnheim and orchestra)

THE FOOTBALL TOUCHER DOWNER—October 15—Popeye

THE NEW DEAL SHOW—October 22—Betty Boop

†EDUCATED FISH—October 29—Color Classic

PROTECK THE WEAKERIST—November 19—Popeye

THE FOXY HUNTER—November 26—Betty Boop

MAGIC ON BROADWAY—November 26—Screen Song (with Jay Freeman and orchestra)

*POPEYE THE SAILOR MEETS ALI BABA'S FORTY THIEVES—November 26—Popeye special

FOWL PLAY—December 17—Popeye

ZULA HULA—December 24—Betty Boop

LITTLE LAMBY—December 31—Color Classic

1938

LET'S CELEBRAKE—January 21—Popeye

RIDING THE RAILS—January 28—Betty Boop

YOU TOOK THE WORDS RIGHT OUT OF MY HEART—January 28—Screen Song (with Jerry Blaine and orchestra)

LEARN POLIKNESS—February 18—Popeye

BE UP TO DATE—February 25—Betty Boop

THE TEARS OF AN ONION—February 26—Color Classic

THE HOUSE BUILDER UPPER—March 18—Popeye

HONEST LOVE AND TRUE—March 25—Betty Boop

THANKS FOR THE MEMORY—March 25—Screen Song (with Bert Block and his orchestra)

OUT OF THE INKWELL—April 22—Betty Boop

BIG CHIEF UGH-AMUGH-UGH—April 25—Popeye

HOLD IT!—April 29—Color Classic

SWING SCHOOL—May 27—Betty Boop

YOU LEAVE ME BREATHLESS—May 27—Screen Song (with Jimmy Dorsey and orchestra)

I YAM LOVE SICK—May 29—Popeye

PLUMBING IS A PIPE—June 17—Popeye

†HUNKY AND SPUNKY—June 24—Color Classic

PUDGY AND THE LOST KITTEN—June 24—Betty Boop

THE JEEP—July 15—Popeye

BUZZY BOOP—July 29—Betty Boop

BESIDE A MOONLIT STREAM—July 29—Screen Song (with Frank Dailey and orchestra)

PUDGY THE WATCHMAN—August 12—Betty Boop

BULLDOZING THE BULL—August 19—Popeye

ALL'S FAIR AT THE FAIR—August 26—Color Classic

BUZZY BOOP AT THE CONCERT—September 16—Betty Boop

MUTINY AIN'T NICE—September 23—Popeye

SALLY SWING—October 14—Betty Boop

GOONLAND—October 21—Popeye

THE PLAYFUL POLAR BEARS—October 28—Color Classic

A DATE TO SKATE—November 18—Popeye

ON WITH THE NEW—December 2—Betty Boop

*In color.

PUDGY IN THRILLS AND CHILLS—December 23—Betty Boop

COPS IS ALWAYS RIGHT—December 29—Popeye

1939

ALWAYS KICKIN'—January 26—Color Classic

MY FRIEND THE MONKEY—January 27—Betty Boop

CUSTOMERS WANTED—January 27—Popeye

SO DOES AN AUTOMOBILE—March 31—Betty Boop

*ALADDIN AND HIS WONDERFUL LAMP—April 7—Popeye special

SMALL FRY—April 21—Color Classic

LEAVE WELL ENOUGH ALONE—April 28—Popeye

MUSICAL MOUNTAINEERS—May 12—Betty Boop

WOTTA NIGHTMARE—May 19—Popeye

THE SCARED CROWS—June 9—Betty Boop

GHOSKS IS THE BUNK—June 14—Popeye

BARNYARD BRAT—June 30—Color Classic

RHYTHM ON THE RESERVATION—July 7—Betty Boop

HELLO, HOW AM I—July 14—Popeye

IT'S THE NATURAL THING TO DO—July 30—Popeye

YIP, YIP, YIPPY—August 11—(officially released as a Betty Boop cartoon, though she does not appear)

THE FRESH VEGETABLE MYSTERY—September 29—Color Classic

NEVER SOCK A BABY—November 3—Popeye

GULLIVER'S TRAVELS—December 22—Feature-length cartoon

1940 (Copyright dates marked by ©)

SHAKESPEARIAN SPINACH—January 19—Popeye

WAY BACK WHEN A TRIANGLE HAD ITS POINTS—© January 26—Stone Age

LITTLE LAMBKIN—© February 2—Color Classic

WAY BACK WHEN A NIGHTCLUB WAS A STICK—© March 15—Stone Age

FEMALES IS FICKLE—March 8—Popeye

WAY BACK WHEN A NIGHTCLUB WAS A STICK— March 15—Stone Age

ANTS IN THE PLANTS—March 15—Color Classic

STEALIN' AIN'T HONEST—March 22—Popeye

ME FEELIN'S IS HURT—April 12—Popeye

GRANITE HOTEL—April 26—Stone Age

A KICK IN TIME—May 17—Color Classic

ONION PACIFIC—May 24—Popeye

THE FOUL BALL PLAYER—May 24—Stone Age

WIMMEN IS A MYSKERY—June 7—Popeye

THE UGLY DINO—June 14—Stone Age

NURSE MATES—June 20—Popeye

WEDDING BELTS—July 5—Stone Age

FIGHTIN' PALS—July 12—Popeye

SNUBBED BY A SNOB—July 19—Color Classic

WAY BACK WHEN A RAZZBERRY WAS A FRUIT—July 26—Stone Age

DOING IMPOSSIKIBLE STUNTS—August 2—Popeye

THE FULLA BLUFF MAN—August 9—Stone Age

WIMMIN HADN'T OUGHTA DRIVE—August 16—Popeye

YOU CAN'T SHOE A HORSEFLY—August 23—Color Classic

PUTTIN' ON THE ACT—August 30—Popeye

SPRINGTIME IN THE ROCK AGE—August 30—Stone Age

PEDAGOGICAL INSTITUTION (COLLEGE TO YOU)—September 13—Stone Age

POPEYE MEETS WILLIAM TELL—September 20—Popeye

THE DANDY LION—September 20—Animated Antics

WAY BACK WHEN WOMEN HAD THEIR WEIGH—September 26—Stone Age

MY POP, MY POP—© October 18—Popeye

KING FOR A DAY—October 18—Gabby

SNEAK, SNOOP AND SNITCH—October 25—Animated Antics

THE CONSTABLE—November 15—Gabby

WITH POOPDECK PAPPY—November 15—Popeye

MOMMY LOVES PUPPY—November 29—Animated Antics

POPEYE PRESENTS EUGENE THE JEEP—December 13—Popeye

BRING HIMSELF BACK ALIVE—December 20—Animated Antics

1941 *(Copyright dates marked by* © *)*

PROBLEM PAPPY—January 10—Popeye

ALL'S WELL—January 17—Gabby

QUIET! PLEASE—February 7—Popeye

ZERO, THE HOUND—© February 14—Animated Antics

TWO FOR THE ZOO—February 21—Gabby

OLIVE'S SWEEPSTAKES TICKET—March 7—Popeye

TWINKLETOES GETS THE BIRD—March 14—Animated Antics

FLIES AIN'T HUMAN—April 4—Popeye

SWING CLEANING—April 11—Gabby

RAGGEDY ANN AND RAGGEDY ANDY—April 11—Two-reel special

SNEAK, SNOOP AND SNITCH IN TRIPLE TROUBLE—May 9—Animated Antics

POPEYE MEETS RIP VAN WINKLE—May 9—Popeye

OLIVE'S BOITHDAY PRESINK—June 13—Popeye

FIRE CHEESE—June 20—Gabby

TWINKLETOES—WHERE HE GOES NOBODY KNOWS—June 27—Animated Antics

CHILD PSYKOLOJIKY—July 11—Popeye

COPY CAT—July 18—Animated Antics

GABBY GOES FISHING—July 18—Gabby

THE WIZARD OF ANTS—August 8—Animated Antics

PEST PILOT—August 8—Popeye

IT'S A HAP-HAP-HAPPY DAY—August 15—Gabby

VITAMIN HAY—© August 22—Color Classic

TWINKLETOES IN HAT STUFF—August 29—Animated Antics

I'LL NEVER CROW AGAIN—September 19—Popeye

†SUPERMAN—September 26—Superman

THE MIGHTY NAVY—November 14—Popeye

THE MECHANICAL MONSTERS—November 21—Superman

NIX ON HYPNOTRICKS—December 19—Popeye

MR. BUG GOES TO TOWN (a.k.a. HOPPITY GOES TO TOWN)—© December 4—Feature-length cartoon

1942 *(Copyright date marked by* © *)*

BILLION DOLLAR LIMITED—January 9—Superman

KICKIN' THE CONGA 'ROUND—January 17—Popeye

BLUNDER BELOW—February 13—Popeye

THE ARCTIC GIANT—February 26—Superman

FLEETS OF STREN'TH—March 13—Popeye

THE BULLETEERS—March 26—Superman

THE RAVEN—April 3—Two-reel special

PIP-EYE, PUP-EYE, POOP-EYE AND PEEP-EYE—April 10—Popeye

THE MAGNETIC TELESCOPE—April 24—Superman

OLIVE OYL AND WATER DON'T MIX—May 8—Popeye

MANY TANKS—May 15—Popeye

ELECTRIC EARTHQUAKE—May 15—Superman

BABY WANTS A BOTTLESHIP—July 3—Popeye

VOLCANO—July 10—Superman

TERROR ON THE MIDWAY—August 30—Superman

Terrytoons

Following is a complete list of Terrytoons produced for theatrical release. They were first distributed by Fox Pictures (on behalf of Educational Pictures) and then by 20th Century-Fox.

All Terrytoons carried the slogan "by Paul Terry and Frank Moser" until Moser's departure in 1936, at which time Terry began assigning specific director credits. When applicable, we give the series title, the main (and in some cases, subsidiary) characters in parentheses, and, starting in 1936, the names of the directors. Beginning in the 1940s, Terrytoons incorporated character names into its official cartoon titles (HECKLE AND JECKLE, THE TALKING MAGPIES, IN FISHING BY THE SEA; MIGHTY MOUSE IN THROWING THE BULL; and the like). For the sake of simplicity we have eliminated those prefixes and listed the title itself, with separate character identification.

Except where noted, Terrytoons were released in black and white until 1943, when the studio switched to full-color production.

In the 1960s, Terrytoons began releasing, alongside its new theatrical shorts, cartoons originally made for television. These include the DEPUTY DAWG, ASTRONUT, and POSSIBLE POSSUM titles on this list, and also later entries in the HECTOR HEATHCOTE, SIDNEY, and HASHIMOTO series.

Although 20th Century-Fox has continued to release twelve Terrytoons a year to theaters, 1968 was the last year in which new theatrical cartoons appeared on the schedule. Therefore, our filmography ends at that point; everything released since then was originally shown on television.

One dagger next to a title (†) indicates an Academy Award nominee.

1930

CAVIAR—February 23

PRETZELS—March 9

SPANISH ONIONS—March 23

INDIAN PUDDING—April 6

ROMAN PUNCH—April 20

HOT TURKEY—May 4

HAWAIIAN PINEAPPLE—May 4

SWISS CHEESE—May 18

CODFISH BALLS—June 1

HUNGARIAN GOULASH—June 15

BULLY BEEF—July 13

KANGAROO STEAK—July 27

MONKEY MEAT—August 10

CHOP SUEY—August 24

FRENCH FRIED—September 7

DUTCH TREAT—September 21

IRISH STEW—October 5

FRIED CHICKEN—October 19

JUMPING BEANS—November 2

SCOTCH HIGHBALL—November 16

SALT WATER TAFFY—November 30

GOLF NUTS—December 14

PIGSKIN CAPERS—December 28

1931

POPCORN—January 11

CLUB SANDWICH (on studio records as DANCING MICE)—January 25—Farmer Al Falfa

RAZZBERRIES—February 8—Farmer Al Falfa

GO WEST, BIG BOY—February 22

QUACK QUACK—March 8

THE EXPLORER—March 22—Farmer Al Falfa

CLOWNING—April 5

SING SING PRISON—April 19

THE FIREMAN'S BRIDE—May 3

THE SULTAN'S CAT—May 17—Farmer Al Falfa

A DAY TO LIVE—May 31

2000 B.C.—June 14

BLUES—June 28

BY THE SEA—July 12

HER FIRST EGG—July 26

JAZZ MAD—August 9

CANADIAN CAPERS—August 23—Farmer Al Falfa

JESSE AND JAMES—September 6

THE CHAMP—September 20—Farmer Al Falfa

AROUND THE WORLD—October 4

JINGLE BELLS—October 18

THE BLACK SPIDER—November 1

CHINA—November 15

THE LORELEI—November 29

SUMMERTIME—December 13

ALADDIN'S LAMP—December 27

1932

THE VILLAIN'S CURSE—January 10

NOAH'S OUTING—January 24—Farmer Al Falfa

THE SPIDER TALKS—February 7

PEG LEG PETE—February 21

PLAY BALL—March 6

YE OLDE SONGS—March 20—Farmer Al Falfa

BULL-ERO—April 3

RADIO GIRL—April 17

WOODLAND—May 1—Farmer Al Falfa

ROMANCE—May 15

BLUEBEARD'S BROTHER—May 29

FARMER ALFALFA'S BEDTIME STORY—June 12—Farmer Al Falfa

THE MAD KING—June 26

COCKY COCKROACH—July 10

SPRING IS HERE—July 24—Farmer Al Falfa

FARMER ALFALFA'S APE GIRL—August 7—Farmer Al Falfa

SHERMAN WAS RIGHT—August 21

BURLESQUE—September 4

SOUTHERN RHYTHM—September 18

FARMER ALFALFA'S BIRTHDAY PARTY—October 2—Farmer Al Falfa

COLLEGE SPIRIT—October 16

HOOK AND LADDER NUMBER ONE—October 30

THE FORTY THIEVES—November 13

TOYLAND—November 27

HOLLYWOOD DIET—December 11

IRELAND OR BUST—December 25

1933

JEALOUS LOVER—January 8

ROBIN HOOD—January 22

HANSEL AND GRETEL—February 5

TALE OF A SHIRT—February 19

DOWN ON THE LEVEE—March 5

WHO KILLED COCK ROBIN?—March 19

OH SUSANNA—April 2

ROMEO AND JULIET—April 16

PIRATE SHIP—April 30

TROPICAL FISH—May 14—Farmer Al Falfa

CINDERELLA—May 28

KING ZILCH—June 11

THE BANKER'S DAUGHTER—June 25 (Fanny Zilch, Oil Can Harry)

THE OIL CAN MYSTERY—July 9 (Fanny, Oil Can, Strongheart)

FANNY IN THE LION'S DEN—July 23 (Fanny, Oil Can, Strongheart)

HYPNOTIC EYES—August 11 (Fanny, Oil Can, Strongheart)

GRAND UPROAR—August 25

PICK-NECKING—Farmer Al Falfa—September 22

FANNY'S WEDDING DAY—October 6 (Fanny, Strongheart)

A GYPSY FIDDLER—October 6

BEANSTALK JACK—October 20

THE VILLAGE BLACKSMITH—November 3—Farmer Al Falfa

ROBINSON CRUSOE (copyrighted as SHIPWRECKED BROTHERS)—November 17—Farmer Al Falfa

LITTLE BOY BLUE—November 30

IN VENICE—December 15

THE SUNNY SOUTH—December 29

1934

HOLLAND DAYS—January 12

THE THREE BEARS—January 26

RIP VAN WINKLE—February 9

THE LAST STRAW—February 23

THE OWL AND THE PUSSYCAT—March 9—Farmer Al Falfa

A MAD HOUSE—March 23

JOE'S LUNCH WAGON—April 6

JUST A CLOWN—April 20

THE KING'S DAUGHTER—May 4

THE LION'S FRIEND—May 18

PANDORA—June 1

SLOW BUT SURE—June 15

SEE THE WORLD—June 29

MY LADY'S GARDEN—July 13

IRISH SWEEPSTAKES—July 27

BUSTED BLOSSOMS—August 10

MICE IN COUNCIL—August 24

WHY MULES LEAVE HOME—September 7—Farmer Al Falfa

JAIL BIRDS—September 21

THE BLACK SHEEP—October 5

THE MAGIC FISH—October 17

HOT SANDS—November 2

TOM, TOM THE PIPER'S SON—November 16

JACK'S SHACK—November 30

SOUTH POLE OR BUST—December 14

THE DOG SHOW—December 28

1935

THE FIRST SNOW—January 11

WHAT A NIGHT—January 25—Farmer Al Falfa

THE BULLFIGHT—February 8

FIREMAN SAVE MY CHILD—February 22

THE MOTH AND THE SPIDER—March 8

OLD DOG TRAY—March 21—Farmer Al Falfa

FLYING OIL—April 5—Farmer Al Falfa

PEG LEG PETE, THE PIRATE—April 19

A MODERN RED RIDING HOOD—May 3

FIVE PUPLETS—May 17

OPERA NIGHT—May 31

KING LOONEY XIV—June 14

MOANS AND GROANS—June 28—Farmer Al Falfa

AMATEUR NIGHT—July 12

THE FOXY-FOX—July 26

CHAIN LETTERS—August 9

BIRDLAND—August 23

CIRCUS DAYS—September 6

HEY DIDDLE DIDDLE—September 20

FOILED AGAIN—October 14 (Oil Can, Fanny, Strongheart)

FOOTBALL—October 18

A JUNE BRIDE—November 1—Farmer Al Falfa

ALADDIN'S LAMP—November 15

SOUTHERN HORSE-PITALITY—November 29

YE OLDE TOY SHOP—December 13

THE MAYFLOWER—December 27

1936

THE FEUD—January 10

THE 19TH HOLE CLUB—January 24—Farmer Al Falfa

HOME TOWN OLYMPICS—February 7—Farmer Al Falfa

THE ALPINE YODELER—February 21—Farmer Al Falfa

BARNYARD AMATEURS—March 6—Farmer Al Falfa

OFF TO CHINA—March 20

THE WESTERN TRAIL—April 3—Farmer Al Falfa

A WOLF IN CHEAP CLOTHING—April 17

ROLLING STONES—May 1—Farmer Al Falfa

THE RUNT—May 15—Farmer Al Falfa

THE BUSY BEE—May 29

THE SAILOR'S HOME—June 12

A TOUGH EGG—June 26

THE HOT SPELL—July 10 (Farmer Al Falfa and Puddy the Pup)—Mannie Davis, George Gordon

PUDDY THE PUP AND THE GYPSIES—July 24—Farmer Al Falfa (Puddy)

FARMER AL FALFA'S PRIZE PACKAGE—July 31—Farmer Al Falfa (Kiko)

KIKO AND THE HONEY BEARS—August 21—Kiko—Mannie Davis, George Gordon

THE HEALTH FARM—September 4—Farmer Al Falfa—Mannie Davis, George Gordon

A BULLY FROG—September 18—Mannie Davis, George Gordon

KIKO FOILS A FOX—October 2—Kiko—Mannie Davis, George Gordon

SUNKEN TREASURE—October 16—Puddy—Mannie Davis, George Gordon

A BATTLE ROYAL—October 30—Kiko—Mannie Davis, George Gordon

ROBIN HOOD IN AN ARROW ESCAPE—November 13—Mannie Davis, George Gordon

FARMER AL FALFA'S TWENTIETH ANNIVERSARY—November 27—Farmer Al Falfa—Mannie Davis, George Gordon

CATS IN THE BAG—December 11—Puddy—Mannie Davis, George Gordon

SKUNKED AGAIN—December 25—Kiko—Mannie Davis, George Gordon

1937

SALTY MCGUIRE—January 8—Mannie Davis, George Gordon

THE TIN CAN TOURIST—January 22—Farmer Al Falfa—Mannie Davis, George Gordon

THE BOOK SHOP—February 5—Puddy—Mannie Davis, George Gordon

THE BIG GAME HUNT—February 19—Farmer Al Falfa—Mannie Davis, George Gordon

RED HOT MUSIC—March 5—Kiko—Mannie Davis, George Gordon

FLYING SOUTH—March 19—Farmer Al Falfa—Mannie Davis, George Gordon

THE HAY RIDE—April 12—Kiko—Mannie Davis, George Gordon

BUG CARNIVAL—April 16—Mannie Davis, George Gordon

SCHOOL BIRDS—April 30—Mannie Davis, George Gordon

PUDDY'S CORONATION—May 14—Puddy—Mannie Davis, George Gordon

OZZIE OSTRICH COMES TO TOWN—May 28—Kiko—Mannie Davis, George Gordon

PLAY BALL—June 11—Kiko—Mannie Davis

THE MECHANICAL COW—June 25—Farmer Al Falfa—Jack Zander

PINK ELEPHANTS—July 9—Farmer Al Falfa—Dan Gordon

THE HOMELESS PUP—July 23—Puddy—George Gordon

THE PAPER HANGERS—July 30—Mannie Davis

TRAILER LIFE—August 20—Farmer Al Falfa

THE VILLAIN STILL PURSUED HER—September 3—Oil Can Harry

KIKO'S CLEANING DAY—September 17—Kiko—George Gordon

A CLOSE SHAVE—October 1—Farmer Al Falfa, Ozzie—Mannie Davis

THE DANCING BEAR—October 15—Farmer Al Falfa

THE SAW MILL MYSTERY—October 29—Oil Can Harry—Connie Rasinski

THE DOG AND THE BONE—November 12—Puddy—George Gordon

THE TIMID RABBIT—November 26—Mannie Davis

THE BILLY GOAT WHISKERS—December 10—John Foster

THE BARNYARD BOSS—December 24—Connie Rasinski

1938

THE LION HUNT—January 7—Mannie Davis

BUGS BEETLE AND HIS ORCHESTRA—January 21—John Foster

HIS OFF DAY—February 4—Puddy—Connie Rasinski

JUST ASK JUPITER—February 18—Mannie Davis

GANDY THE GOOSE—March 4—John Foster

HAPPY AND LUCKY—March 18—Puddy—Connie Rasinski

A MOUNTAIN ROMANCE—April 1—Mannie Davis

ROBINSON CRUSOE'S BROADCAST—April 15—John Foster

MAID IN CHINA—April 29—Connie Rasinski

THE BIG TOP—May 12—Puddy—Mannie Davis

DEVIL OF THE DEEP—May 27—John Foster

HERE'S TO GOOD OLD JAIL—June 10—Eddie Donnelly

THE LAST INDIAN—June 24—Connie Rasinski

MILK FOR BABY—July 8—Mannie Davis

MRS. O'LEARY'S COW—July 22—Eddie Donnelly

ELIZA RUNS AGAIN—July 29—Connie Rasinski (last Educational)

CHRIS COLUMBO—August 12—Ed Donnelly (first 20th Century Fox)

STRING BEAN JACK—August 26—John Foster (first in color)

GOOSE FLIES HIGH—September 9—Gandy Goose—John Foster

WOLF'S SIDE OF THE STORY—September 23—Connie Rasinski

THE GLASS SLIPPER—October 7—Mannie Davis

THE NEWCOMER—October 21—Panda Bear—Mannie Davis

THE STRANGER RIDES AGAIN—November 4—Mannie Davis

HOUSEWIFE HERMAN—November 18—Eddie Donnelly

VILLAGE BLACKSMITH—December 2—Mannie Davis

DOOMSDAY—December 16—Gandy Goose—Connie Rasinski

THE FRAME-UP—December 30—Gandy Goose—Connie Rasinski

1939

*THE OWL AND THE PUSSY CAT—January 13—Eddie Donnelly

*In color.

ONE GUN GARY IN NICK OF TIME—January 27—Eddie Donnelly

*THE THREE BEARS—February 10—Mannie Davis

FROZEN FEET—February 24—Connie Rasinski

G-MAN JITTERS—March 10—Gandy Goose—Eddie Donnelly

*THE NUTTY NETWORK—March 24—Mannie Davis

THE CUCKOO BIRD—April 7—Mannie Davis

THEIR LAST BEAN—April 21—Eddie Donnelly

BARNYARD EGGCITEMENT—May 5—Connie Rasinski

NICK'S COFFEE POT—May 19—Connie Rasinski

THE PRIZE GUEST—June 2—Mannie Davis

A BULLY ROMANCE—June 16—Gandy Goose—Eddie Donnelly

AFRICA SQUAWKS—June 30—Connie Rasinski

BARNYARD BASEBALL—July 14—Gandy Goose—Mannie Davis

OLD FIRE HORSE—July 28—Eddie Donnelly

TWO HEADED GIANT—August 11—Connie Rasinski

THE GOLDEN WEST—August 25—Mannie Davis

SHEEP IN THE MEADOW—September 22—Mannie Davis

*HOOK, LINE AND SINKER—September 28—Gandy Goose—Eddie Donnelly

THE ORPHAN DUCK—October 6—Dinky—Connie Rasinski

THE WATCHDOG—October 20—Eddie Donnelly

ONE MOUSE IN A MILLION—November 3—Connie Rasinski

A WICKY-WACKY ROMANCE—November 17—Mannie Davis

THE HITCHHIKER—December 1—Gandy Goose—Eddie Donnelly

THE ICE POND—December 15—Mannie Davis

*THE FIRST ROBIN—December 29—Connie Rasinski

1940

A DOG IN A MANSION—January 12—Eddie Donnelly

EDGAR RUNS AGAIN—January 26—Mannie Davis

*HARVEST TIME—February 9—Connie Rasinski

THE HARE AND THE HOUNDS—February 23—Eddie Donnelly

ALL'S WELL THAT ENDS WELL—March 8—Mannie Davis

MUCH ADO ABOUT NOTHING—March 22—Dinky—Connie Rasinski

*In color.

IT MUST BE LOVE—April 5—Gandy Goose—Connie Rasinski

*JUST A LITTLE BULL—April 19—Eddie Donnelly

WOT'S ALL TH' SHOOTIN' FER—May 3—Volney White

SWISS SKI YODELERS—May 17—Eddie Donnelly

CATNIP CAPERS—May 31—Mannie Davis

PROFESSOR OFFKEYSKI—June 14—Connie Rasinski·

ROVER'S RESCUE—June 28—Volney White

RUPERT THE RUNT—July 12—Mannie Davis

LOVE IN A COTTAGE—July 28—Volney White

*BILLY MOUSE'S AKWAKADE—August 9—Eddie Donnelly

CLUB LIFE IN STONE AGE—August 23—Mannie Davis

*THE LUCKY DUCK—September 6—Dinky—Connie Rasinski

TOUCHDOWN DEMONS—September 20—Volney White

HOW WET WAS MY OCEAN—October 4—Eddie Donnelly

HAPPY HAUNTING GROUNDS—October 18

LANDING OF THE PILGRIMS—November 1—Connie Rasinski

THE MAGIC PENCIL—November 15—Gandy Goose—Volney White

PLANE GOOFY—November 29—Eddie Donnelly

SNOWMAN—December 13—Mannie Davis

*TEMPERAMENTAL LION—December 27—Connie Rasinski

1941

WHAT A LITTLE SNEEZE WILL DO—January 10—Eddie Donnelly

HAIRLESS HECTOR—January 24—Volney White

*MISSISSIPPI SWING—February 7—Connie Rasinski

FISHING MADE EASY—February 21—Gandy Goose—Eddie Donnelly

*THE HOME GUARD—March 7—Gandy Goose—Mannie Davis

WHEN KNIGHTS WERE BOLD—March 21—Volney White

THE BABY SEAL—April 10—Connie Rasinski

*UNCLE JOEY—April 18—Mannie Davis

THE DOG'S DREAM—May 2—Eddie Donnelly

THE MAGIC SHELL—May 16—Mannie Davis

WHAT HAPPENS AT NIGHT—May 30—Connie Rasinski

HORSE FLY OPERA—June 13—Eddie Donnelly

GOOD OLD IRISH TUNES—June 27—Connie Rasinski

BRINGING HOME THE BACON—July 11—Aesop's Fables—Mannie Davis

TWELVE O'CLOCK AND ALL AIN'T WELL—July 25—Eddie Donnelly

THE OLD OAKEN BUCKET—August 8—Connie Rasinski

THE ICE CARNIVAL—August 22—Eddie Donnelly

*THE ONE MAN NAVY—September 5—Gandy Goose—Mannie Davis

UNCLE JOEY COMES TO TOWN—September 19—Mannie Davis

WELCOME LITTLE STRANGER—October 3—Dinky—Connie Rasinski

THE FROZEN NORTH—October 17—Connie Rasinski

*SLAP HAPPY HUNTERS—October 31—Gandy Goose—Eddie Donnelly

BACK TO THE SOIL—November 14—Eddie Donnelly

*THE BIRD TOWER—November 28—Mannie Davis

A YARN ABOUT YARN—December 12—Connie Rasinski

FLYING FEVER—December 26—Gandy Goose—Mannie Davis

1942

*THE TORRID TOREADOR—January 9—Eddie Donnelly

*HAPPY CIRCUS DAYS—January 23—Connie Rasinski

FUNNY BUNNY BUSINESS—February 6—Eddie Donnelly

*CAT MEETS MOUSE—February 20—Mannie Davis

EAT ME KITTY, EIGHT TO THE BAR—March 6—Mannie Davis

*SHAM BATTLE SHENANIGANS—March 20—Gandy Goose—Connie Rasinski

OH GENTLE SPRING—April 3—Connie Rasinski

*LIGHTS OUT—April 17—Gandy Goose—Eddie Donnelly

TRICKY BUSINESS—May 1—Gandy Goose—Eddie Donnelly

*NECK AND NECK—May 15—Mannie Davis

THE STORK'S MISTAKE—May 29—Eddie Donnelly

*ALL ABOUT DOGS—June 12—Connie Rasinski

WILFUL WILLIE—June 26—Connie Rasinski

THE OUTPOST—July 10—Gandy Goose—Mannie Davis

TIRE TROUBLE—July 24—Gandy Goose—Eddie Donnelly

*†ALL OUT FOR "V"—August 7—Mannie Davis

*LIFE WITH FIDO—August 21—Dinky—Connie Rasinski

THE BIG BUILD-UP—September 4—Puddy—Mannie Davis

*SCHOOL DAZE—September 18—Nancy—No credits

*NIGHT LIFE IN THE ARMY—October 12—Gandy Goose—Mannie Davis

*THE MOUSE OF TOMORROW—October 16—Super Mouse—Eddie Donnelly

*DOING THEIR BIT—October 30—Nancy—No credits

ICKLE MEETS PICKLE—November 13—Connie Rasinski

*FRANKENSTEIN'S CAT—November 27—Super Mouse—Mannie Davis

*BARNYARD WAAC—December 11—Eddie Donnelly

*SOMEWHERE IN THE PACIFIC—December 25—Mannie Davis

1943 *(All cartoons in color from this time on)*

SCRAP FOR VICTORY—January 22—Gandy Goose—Connie Rasinski

HE DOOD IT AGAIN—February 5—Super Mouse—Eddie Donnelly

BARNYARD BLACKOUT—March 5—Mannie Davis

SHIPYARD SYMPHONY—March 19—Eddie Donnelly

PATRIOTIC POOCHES—April 9—Connie Rasinski

THE LAST ROUND-UP—Mav 14—Mannie Davis

PANDORA'S BOX—June 11—Super Mouse—Connie Rasinski

MOPPING UP—June 25—Eddie Donnelly

KEEP 'EM GROWING—July 28—Mannie Davis

SUPER MOUSE RIDES AGAIN (retitled MIGHTY MOUSE RIDES AGAIN)—August 6—Mannie Davis

CAMOUFLAGE—August 27—Gandy Goose—Eddie Donnelly

SOMEWHERE IN EGYPT—September 17—Gandy Goose—Mannie Davis

DOWN WITH CATS—October 7—Super Mouse—Connie Rasinski

ALADDIN'S LAMP—October 22—Gandy Goose—Eddie Donnelly

LION AND THE MOUSE—November 12—Super Mouse—Mannie Davis

YOKEL DUCK MAKES GOOD—November 26—Eddie Donnelly

THE HOPEFUL DONKEY—December 17—Mannie Davis

1944

THE BUTCHER OF SEVILLE—January 7—Eddie Donnelly

*In color.

THE HELICOPTER—January 21—Eddie Donnelly

WRECK OF THE HESPERUS—February 11—Mighty Mouse—Mannie Davis

A DAY IN JUNE—March 3—Eddie Donnelly

THE CHAMPION OF JUSTICE—March 17—Mighty Mouse—Mannie Davis

THE FROG AND THE PRINCESS—April 7—Gandy Goose—Eddie Donnelly

MIGHTY MOUSE MEETS JECKYLL AND HYDE CAT—April 28—Mannie Davis

†MY BOY JOHNNY—May 12—Eddie Donnelly

ELIZA ON THE ICE—June 16—Mighty Mouse—Connie Rasinski

WOLF! WOLF!—June 22—Mighty Mouse—Mannie Davis

THE GREEN LINE—July 7—Mighty Mouse—Eddie Donnelly

CARMEN'S VERANDA—July 28—Mannie Davis

THE CAT CAME BACK—August 18—Connie Rasinski

THE TWO BARBERS—September 1—Mighty Mouse—Eddie Donnelly

THE GHOST TOWN—September 22—Gandy Goose—Mannie Davis

SULTAN'S BIRTHDAY—October 13—Mighty Mouse—Bill Tytla

A WOLF'S TALE—October 27—Connie Rasinski

AT THE CIRCUS—November 17—Mighty Mouse—Eddie Donnelly

GANDY'S DREAM GIRL—December 8—Gandy Goose—Mannie Davis

DEAR OLD SWITZERLAND—December 22—Eddie Donnelly

1945

MIGHTY MOUSE AND THE PIRATES—January 12—Connie Rasinski

PORT OF MISSING MICE—February 2—Mighty Mouse—Eddie Donnelly

ANTS IN YOUR PANTRY—February 16—Mannie Davis

RAIDING THE RAIDERS—March 9—Mighty Mouse—Connie Rasinski

POST WAR INVENTIONS—March 23—Gandy Goose—Connie Rasinski

FISHERMAN'S LUCK—March 23—Gandy Goose—Eddie Donnelly

MIGHTY MOUSE AND THE KILKENNY CATS—April 13—Mannie Davis

MOTHER GOOSE NIGHTMARE—May 4—Gandy Goose—Connie Rasinski

SMOKEY JOE—May 25—Connie Rasinski

THE SILVER STREAK—June 8—Mighty Mouse—Eddie Donnelly

AESOP'S FABLE: THE MOSQUITO—June 29—Gandy Goose—Mannie Davis

MIGHTY MOUSE AND THE WOLF—July 20—Eddie Donnelly

†GYPSY LIFE—August 3—Mighty Mouse—Connie Rasinski

THE FOX AND THE DUCK—August 24—Mannie Davis

SWOONING THE SWOONERS—September 14—Connie Rasinski

THE WATCH DOG—September 28—Eddie Donnelly

WHO'S WHO IN THE JUNGLE—October 19—Gandy Goose—Eddie Donnelly

MIGHTY MOUSE MEETS BAD BILL BUNION—November 9—Mannie Davis

THE EXTERMINATOR—November 23—Gandy Goose—Eddie Donnelly

MIGHTY MOUSE IN KRAKATOA—December 4—Connie Rasinski

1946 *(Copyright date marked by ©)*

THE TALKING MAGPIES—January 4—Mannie Davis

SVENGALI'S CAT—January 18—Mighty Mouse—Eddie Donnelly

THE FORTUNE HUNTERS—February 8—Gandy Goose—Connie Rasinski

THE WICKED WOLF—March 8—Mighty Mouse—Mannie Davis

MY OLD KENTUCKY HOME—March 29—Mighty Mouse—Eddie Donnelly

IT'S ALL IN THE STARS—April 12—Gandy Goose—Connie Rasinski

THROWING THE BULL—May 3—Mighty Mouse—Connie Rasinski

THE GOLDEN HEN—May 24—Gandy Goose—Mannie Davis

DINKY FINDS A HOME—June 7—Dinky Duck—Eddie Donnelly

THE JOHNSTOWN FLOOD—June 28—Mighty Mouse—Connie Rasinski

PEACE-TIME FOOTBALL—July 19—Gandy Goose—Mannie Davis

THE TROJAN HORSE—July 26—Mighty Mouse—Mannie Davis

THE TORTOISE WINS AGAIN—August 9—Connie Rasinski

WINNING THE WEST— © August 16—Mighty Mouse—Eddie Donnelly

THE ELECTRONIC MOUSE TRAP—September 6—Mighty Mouse—Mannie Davis

THE JAIL BREAK—September 20—Mighty Mouse—Eddie Donnelly

THE SNOW MAN—October 11—Connie Rasinski

THE HOUSING PROBLEM—October 25—Mannie Davis

THE CRACKPOT KING—November 15—Mighty Mouse—Eddie Donnelly

THE UNINVITED PESTS—November 29—Heckle and Jeckle—Connie Rasinski

THE HEPCAT—December 6—Mighty Mouse—Mannie Davis

BEANSTALK JACK—December 20—Eddie Donnelly

1947 *(Copyright date marked by ©)*

CRYING WOLF—January 10—Mighty Mouse—Connie Rasinski

MC DOUGAL'S REST FARM—January 31—Heckle and Jeckle—Mannie Davis

DEADEND CATS—February 14—Mighty Mouse—Eddie Donnelly

HAPPY GO LUCKY—February 28—Heckle and Jeckle—Connie Rasinski

MEXICAN BASEBALL—March 14—Gandy Goose—Mannie Davis

ALADDIN'S LAMP—March 28—Mighty Mouse—Eddie Donnelly

CAT TROUBLE—April 11—Heckle and Jeckle—Connie Rasinski

THE SKY IS FALLING—April 25—Mighty Mouse—Mannie Davis

THE INTRUDERS—May 9—Heckle and Jeckle—Eddie Donnelly

MIGHTY MOUSE MEETS DEADEYE DICK—May 30—Connie Rasinski

FLYING SOUTH—August 15—Heckle and Jeckle—Mannie Davis

A DATE FOR DINNER—August 29—Mighty Mouse—Eddie Donnelly

FISHING BY THE SEA—September 19—Heckle and Jeckle—Connie Rasinski

THE FIRST SNOW—October 10—Mighty Mouse—Mannie Davis

ONE NOTE TONY— © October 22—Connie Rasinski

SUPER SALESMAN—October 24—Heckle and Jeckle—Eddie Donnelly

A FIGHT TO THE FINISH—November 14—Mighty Mouse—Connie Rasinski

THE WOLF'S PARDON—December 5—Eddie Donnelly

HITCH HIKERS—December 12—Heckle and Jeckle—Connie Rasinski

SWISS CHEEZE FAMILY ROBINSON—December 19—Mighty Mouse—Mannie Davis

LAZY LITTLE BEAVER—December 26—Mighty Mouse—Eddie Donnelly

1948

FELIX THE FOX—January —Mannie Davis

TAMING THE CAT—January—Heckle and Jeckle—Connie Rasinski

MIGHTY MOUSE AND THE MAGICIAN—March—Eddie Donnelly

GANDY GOOSE AND THE CHIPPER CHIPMUNK—March—Mannie Davis

HOUNDING THE HARES—April—Eddie Donnelly

THE FEUDING HILLBILLIES—April—Mighty Mouse—Connie Rasinski

MYSTERY IN THE MOONLIGHT—May—Eddie Donnelly

SEEING GHOSTS—June—Mannie Davis

SLEEPLESS NIGHT—June—Heckle and Jeckle—Connie Rasinski

THE WITCH'S CAT—July—Mighty Mouse—Mannie Davis

MAGPIE MADNESS—July—Heckle and Jeckle—Eddie Donnelly

LOVE'S LABOR WON—September—Mighty Mouse—Mannie Davis

THE HARD BOILED EGG—October—Connie Rasinski

THE MYSTERIOUS STRANGER—October—Mighty Mouse—Eddie Donnelly

TRIPLE TROUBLE—November—Mighty Mouse—Eddie Donnelly

OUT AGAIN, IN AGAIN—November—Heckle and Jeckle—Connie Rasinski

FREE ENTERPRISE—November—Heckle and Jeckle—Mannie Davis

MAGIC SLIPPER—December—Mighty Mouse—Mannie Davis

GOONEY GOLFERS—December—Heckle and Jeckle—Connie Rasinski

1949

THE WOODEN INDIAN—January—Connie Rasinski

POWER OF THOUGHT—January—Heckle and Jeckle—Eddie Donnelly

RACKET BUSTER—February—Mighty Mouse—Mannie Davis

DINGBAT LAND—February—Gandy Goose, Sourpuss

LION HUNT—March—Heckle and Jeckle—Eddie Donnelly

STOWAWAYS—April—Heckle and Jeckle—Connie Rasinski

COLD ROMANCE—April—Mighty Mouse—Mannie Davis

THE KITTEN SITTER—May—Eddie Donnelly

HAPPY LANDING—June—Heckle and Jeckle

THE CATNIP GANG—July—Mighty Mouse—Eddie Donnelly

HULA HULA LAND—July—Heckle and Jeckle—Mannie Davis

THE LYIN' LION—August—Connie Rasinski

MRS. JONES REST FARM—August—Eddie Donnelly

THE COVERED PUSHCART—September—Sourpuss—Mannie Davis

A TRUCKLOAD OF TROUBLE—October—Connie Rasinski

PERILS OF PEARL PUREHEART—October—Mighty Mouse—Eddie Donnelly

DANCING SHOES—November—Heckle and Jeckle—Mannie Davis

FLYING CUPS AND SAUCERS—November—Connie Rasinski

PAINT POT SYMPHONY—December—Connie Rasinski

STOP, LOOK AND LISTEN—December—Mighty Mouse—Eddie Donnelly

1950

COMIC BOOK LAND—January—Gandy Goose—Mannie Davis

FOX HUNT—February—Heckle and Jeckle—Connie Rasinski

BETTER LATE THAN NEVER—March—Victor the Volunteer—Eddie Donnelly

ANTI-CATS—March—Mighty Mouse—Mannie Davis

AESOP'S FABLE: FOILING THE FOX—April—Connie Rasinski

THE BEAUTY SHOP—April—Dinky Duck—Eddie Donnelly

MERRY CHASE—May—Heckle and Jeckle—Mannie Davis

DREAM WALKING—May—Gandy Goose—Connie Rasinski

LAW AND ORDER—June—Mighty Mouse—Eddie Donnelly

THE RED HEADED MONKEY—July—Mannie Davis

ALL THIS AND RABBIT STEW—July—Dingbat—Connie Rasinski

THE DOG SHOW—August—Eddie Donnelly

KING TUT'S TOMB—August—Heckle and Jeckle—Mannie Davis

CAT HAPPY—September—Little Roquefort—Connie Rasinski

IF CATS COULD SING—October—Eddie Donnelly

MOUSE AND GARDEN—October—Little Roquefort—Mannie Davis

BEAUTY ON THE BEACH—November—Mighty Mouse—Connie Rasinski

WIDE OPEN SPACES—November—Gandy Goose—Eddie Donnelly

SOUR GRAPES—December—Dingbat—Mannie Davis

MOTHER GOOSE'S BIRTHDAY PARTY—December—Mighty Mouse—Connie Rasinski

1951

RIVAL ROMEOS—January—Heckle and Jeckle—Eddie Donnelly

SQUIRREL CRAZY—January—Nutsy—Mannie Davis

THREE IS A CROWD—February—Little Roquefort—Connie Rasinski

WOODMAN SPARE THAT TREE—February—Eddie Donnelly

STAGE STRUCK—February—Half Pint—Mannie Davis

SUNNY ITALY—March—Mighty Mouse—Connie Rasinski

SONGS OF ERIN—March—Gandy Goose—Connie Rasinski

BULLDOZING THE BULL—March—Heckle and Jeckle—Eddie Donnelly

SPRING FEVER—April—Gandy Goose—Mannie Davis

GOONS FROM THE MOON—April—Mighty Mouse—Connie Rasinski

MUSICAL MADNESS—May—Little Roquefort—Eddie Donnelly

THE ELEPHANT MOUSE—May—Half Pint—Mannie Davis

THE RAIN MAKERS—June—Heckle and Jeckle—Connie Rasinski

INJUN TROUBLE—June—Mighty Mouse—Eddie Donnelly

SEASICK SAILORS—July—Little Roquefort—Mannie Davis

TALL TIMBER TALE—July—Terry Bears—Connie Rasinski

AESOP'S FABLES: GOLDEN EGG GOOSIE—August—Eddie Donnelly

A SWISS MISS—August—Mighty Mouse—Mannie Davis

STEEPLE JACKS—September—Heckle and Jeckle—Connie Rasinski

LITTLE PROBLEMS—September—Terry Bears—Eddie Donnelly

PASTRY PANIC—October—Little Roquefort—Mannie Davis

THE HELPFUL GENIE—October—Connie Rasinski

'SNO FUN—November—Heckle and Jeckle—Eddie Donnelly

A CAT'S TALE—November—Mighty Mouse—Mannie Davis

BEAVER TROUBLE—December—Connie Rasinski

THE HAUNTED CAT—December—Little Roquefort—Eddie Donnelly

1952

PAPA'S LITTLE HELPERS—January—Terry Bears—Mannie Davis

MOVIE MADNESS—January—Heckle and Jeckle—Connie Rasinski

MECHANICAL BIRD—February—Eddie Donnelly

SEASIDE ADVENTURE—February—Heckle and Jeckle—Mannie Davis

CITY SLICKER—March—Little Roquefort—Mannie Davis

PREHISTORIC PERILS—March—Mighty Mouse—Connie Rasinski

PAPA'S DAY OF REST—March—Terry Bears—Mannie Davis

FLAT FOOT FLEDGLING—April—Dinky—Mannie Davis

TIME GALLOPS ON—April—Mannie Davis

OFF TO THE OPERA—May—Heckle and Jeckle—Connie Rasinski

THE HAPPY COBBLERS—May—Mannie Davis

HYPNOTIZED—June—Little Roquefort—Mannie Davis

HANSEL AND GRETEL—June—Mighty Mouse—Connie Rasinski

FLIPPER FROLICS—July—Connie Rasinski

LITTLE ANGLERS—July—Terry Bears—Connie Rasinski

FOOLISH DUCKLING—August—Dinky—Mannie Davis

HOUSE BUSTERS—August—Heckle and Jeckle—Connie Rasinski

MYSTERIOUS COWBOY—September—Mannie Davis

HAPPY VALLEY—September—Aesop's Fables—Eddie Donnelly

GOOD MOUSE KEEPING—October—Little Roquefort—Mannie Davis

NICE DOGGY—October—Terry Bears—Eddie Donnelly

HAPPY HOLLAND—November—Mighty Mouse—Eddie Donnelly

MOOSE ON THE LOOSE—November—Heckle and Jeckle—Mannie Davis

SINK OR SWIM—November—Dinky—Connie Rasinski

FLOP SEACRET—December—Little Roquefort—Eddie Donnelly

PICNIC WITH PAPA—December—Terry Bears—Mannie Davis

1953

SOAPY OPERA—January—Mighty Mouse—Connie Rasinksi

THRIFTY CUBS—January—Terry Bears—Mannie Davis

HAIR CUT-UPS—February—Heckle and Jeckle—Eddie Donnelly

WISE QUACKS—February—Dinky—Mannie Davis

MOUSE MEETS BIRD—March—Little Roquefort—Connie Rasinski

SNAPPY SNAP SHOTS—March—Terry Bears—Eddie Donnelly

HERO FOR A DAY—April—Mighty Mouse—Mannie Davis

PILL PEDDLERS—April—Heckle and Jeckle—Connie Rasinski

FEATHERWEIGHT CHAMP—May—Dinky—Eddie Donnelly

PLAYFUL PUSS—May—Little Roquefort—Mannie Davis

PLUMBER'S HELPERS—May—Terry Bears—Connie Rasinski

HOT RODS—June—Mighty Mouse—Eddie Donnelly

TEN PIN TERRORS—June—Heckle and Jeckle—Connie Rasinski

THE ORPHAN EGG—July—Dinky—Eddie Donnelly

FRIDAY THE 13TH—July—Little Roquefort—Mannie Davis

WHEN MOUSEHOOD WAS IN FLOWER—July—Mighty Mouse—Connie Rasinski

OPEN HOUSE—August—Terry Bears—Eddie Donnelly

BARGAIN DAZE—August—Heckle and Jeckle—Mannie Davis

SPARKY THE FIREFLY—September—Aesop's Fables—Connie Rasinski

MOUSE MENACE—September—Little Roquefort—Eddie Donnelly

THE RELUCTANT PUP—October—Terry Bears—Mannie Davis

HOW TO KEEP COOL—October—Dimwit—Connie Rasinski

THE TIMID SCARECROW—November—Dinky—Eddie Donnelly

LOG ROLLERS—November—Heckle and Jeckle—Mannie Davis

GROWING PAINS—December—Terry Bears—Eddie Donnelly

1954

SPARE THE ROD—January—Mighty Mouse—Connie Rasinski

RUNAWAY MOUSE—January—Little Roquefort—Mannie Davis

HOW TO RELAX—February—Dimwit—Connie Rasinski

BLIND DATE—February—Heckle and Jeckle—Eddie Donnelly

NONSENSE NEWSREEL—March—Mannie Davis

HELPLESS HIPPO—March—Mighty Mouse—Connie Rasinski

PET PROBLEMS—April—Terry Bears—Eddie Donnelly

PRESCRIPTION FOR PERCY—April—Little Roquefort—Mannie Davis

SATISFIED CUSTOMERS—May—Heckle and Jeckle—Connie Rasinski

TALL TALE TELLER—May—Phoney Baloney—Connie Rasinski

ARCTIC RIVALS—June—Willie the Walrus—Mannie Davis

HOWLING SUCCESS—July—Terry Bears—Connie Rasinski

PRIDE OF THE YARD—August—Percival Sleuthhound—Eddie Donnelly

CAT'S REVENGE—September—Little Roquefort—Mannie Davis

REFORMED WOLF—October—Mighty Mouse—Connie Rasinski

BLUE PLATE SYMPHONY—Heckle and Jeckle—Connie Rasinsky

1955

BARNYARD ACTOR—January—Gandy Goose—Connie Rasinski

A YOKOHAMA YANKEE—January—Connie Rasinski

DUCK FEVER—February—Terry Bears—Connie Rasinski

THE FIRST FLYING FISH—February—Aesop's Fables—Connie Rasinski

NO SLEEP FOR PERCY—March—Little Roquefort—Connie Rasinski

AN IGLOO FOR TWO—March—Willie the Walrus—Connie Rasinski

*GOOD DEED DAILY—April—Connie Rasinski

*BIRD SYMPHONY—April—Connie Rasinski

PHONEY NEWS FLASHES—May—Connie Rasinski

FOXED BY A FOX—May—Connie Rasinski

LAST MOUST OF HAMLIN—June—Connie Rasinski

*LITTLE RED HEN—July—Connie Rasinski

1956

CLOCKMAKERS DOG—January—Connie Rasinski

*PARK AVENUE PUSSYCAT—January—Connie Rasinski

MIAMI MANIACS—February—Heckle and Jeckle—Connie Rasinski

*URANIUM BLUES—March—Connie Rasinski

HEP MOTHER HUBBARD—March—Connie Rasinski

SCOUTS TO THE RESCUE—April—Good Deed Daily—Connie Rasinski

BAFFLING BUNNIES—April—Terry Bears—Connie Rasinski

*OCEANS OF LOVE—May—Connie Rasinski

*LUCKY DOG—June—Connie Rasinski

*POLICE DOGGED—July—Clancy the Bull—Connie Rasinski

*THE BRAVE LITTLE BRAVE—July—Mannie Davis

*CLOAK AND STAGGER—August—Good Deed Daily—Connie Rasinski

1957

PIRATE'S GOLD—January—Heckle and Jeckle—Eddie Donnelly

*TOPSY TV—January—John Doormat—Connie Rasinski

*GAG BUSTER—February—Spoofy—Connie Rasinski

A HARE BREADTH FINISH—February—Connie Rasinski

AFRICAN JUNGLE HUNT—March—Phoney Baloney—Connie Rasinski

*A BUM STEER—March—Beefy—Mannie Davis

*THE BONE RANGER—April—Sniffer—Connie Rasinski

DADDY'S LITTLE DARLING—April—Dimwit—Connie Rasinski

LOVE IS BLIND—May—Mannie Davis

*GASTON IS HERE—May—Gaston Le Crayon—Connie Rasinski

*SHOVE THY NEIGHBOR—June—John Doormat—Connie Rasinski

*CLINT CLOBBER'S CAT—July—Clint Clobber—Connie Rasinski

*FLEBUS—August—Ernest Pintoff

1958 *(All in CinemaScope)*

SPRINGTIME FOR CLOBBER—January—Clint Clobber—Connie Rasinski

IT'S A LIVING—February—Dinky Duck—Win Hoskins

GASTON'S BABY—March—Gaston Le Crayon—Connie Rasinski

THE JUGGLER OF OUR LADY—April—Al Kouzel

GASTON, GO HOME—May—Gaston Le Crayon—Connie Rasinski

DUSTCAP DOORMAT—June—John Doormat—Al Kouzel

CAMP CLOBBER—July—Clint Clobber—Dave Tendlar

SICK, SICK SIGNEY—August—Sidney—Art Bartsch

OLD MOTHER CLOBBER—September—Clint Clobber—Connie Rasinski

GASTON'S EASEL LIFE—October—Gaston Le Crayon—Dave Tendlar

SIGNED, SEALED AND CLOBBERED—November—Clint Clobber—Connie Rasinski

†SIDNEY'S FAMILY TREE—December—Sidney—Art Bartsch

1959 *(All in CinemaScope)*

CLOBBER'S BALLET ACHE—January—Clint Clobber—Connie Rasinski

A TALE OF A DOG—February—Dave Tendlar

ANOTHER DAY, ANOTHER DOORMAT—March—John Doormat—Al Kouzel

THE FLAMBOYANT ARMS—April—Clint Clobber—Connie Rasinski

FOOFLE'S TRAIN RIDE—May—Foofle—Dave Tendlar

GASTON'S MAMA LISA—June—Gaston Le Crayon—Connie Rasinski

THE MINUTE AND A $\frac{1}{2}$ MAN—July—Hector Heathcoate—Dave Tendlar

THE FABULOUS FIREWORK FAMILY—August—Al Kouzel

WILD LIFE—September—Heckle and Jeckle—Martin B. Taras

HASHIMOTO SAN—October—Hashimoto—Bob Kuwahara, Dave Tendlar

OUTER SPACE VISITOR—November—Mighty Mouse—Dave Tendlar

THE LEAKY FAUCET—December—Martin B. Taras

1960 *(Releases not dated by studio from here on in)*

*HIDE AND GO SIDNEY—January—Sidney—Art Bartsch

THOUSAND SMILE CHECKUP—January—Heckle and Jeckle—Martin B. Taras

*THE MISUNDERSTOOD GIANT—February—Connie Rasinski

*FOOFLE'S PICNIC—March—Foofle—Dave Tendlar

AESOP'S FABLES: THE TIGER KING—March—Connie Rasinski

*THE FAMOUS RIDE—April—Hector Heathcoate—Connie Rasinski

TUSK TUSK—Sidney—Martin B. Taras

MINT MEN—Heckle and Jeckle—Dave Tendlar

*HEARTS AND GLOWERS—Martin B. Taras

*THE WAYWARD HAT—Foofle—Dave Tendlar

TRAPEZE PLEASE—Heckle and Jeckle—Connie Rasinski

*THE LITTLEST BULLY—Sidney—Martin B. Taras

*TWO TON BABY SITTER—Sidney—Dave Tendlar

*TIN PAN ALLEY CAT—Dave Tendlar

DEEP SEA DOODLE—Heckle and Jeckle—Dave Tendlar

*HOUSE OF HASHIMOTO—Hashimoto—Connie Rasinski

STUNT MEN—Heckle and Jeckle—Martin B. Taras

*DANIEL BOONE, JR.—Hector Heathcoate—Dave Tendlar

*CinemaScope.

1961

THE MYSTERIOUS PACKAGE—Mighty Mouse—Mannie Davis

*NIGHT LIFE IN TOKYO—Hashimoto—Mannie Davis

CAT ALARM—Mighty Mouse—Connie Rasinski

*SO SORRY, PUSSYCAT—Hashimoto—Art Bartsch

DRUM ROLL—Hector Heathcoate—Dave Tendlar

*SON OF HASHIMOTO—Hashimoto—Connie Rasinski

*STRANGE COMPANION—Hashimoto—Mannie Davis

RAILROADED TO FAME—Hector Heathcoate—Dave Tendlar

THE FIRST FAST MAIL—Hector Heathcoate—Dave Tendlar

*HONORABLE CAT STORY—Hashimoto—Connie Rasinski

*CROSSING THE DELAWARE—Hector Heathcoate—Art Bartsch

1962

KLONDIKE STRIKE OUT—Hector Heathcoate—Dave Tendlar

WHERE THERE'S SMOKE—Deputy Dawg—Bob Kuwahara

HE-MAN SEAMAN—Hector Heathcoate—Art Bartsch

*HONORABLE FAMILY PROBLEM—Hashimoto—Bob Kuwahara

NOBODY'S GHOUL—Deputy Dawg—Dave Tendlar

*PEANUT BATTLE—Sidney—Connie Rasinski

RIVERBOAT MISSION—Hector Heathcoate—Dave Tendlar

*LOYAL ROYALTY—Hashimoto—Bob Kuwahara

REBEL TROUBLE—Deputy Dawg—Dave Tendlar

*SEND YOUR ELEPHANT TO CAMP—Sidney—Art Bartsch

BIG CHIEF, NO TREATY—Deputy Dawg—Bob Kuwahara

FIRST FLIGHT UP—Hector Heathcoate—Bill Tytla

*HOME LIFE—Sidney—Connie Rasinski

A FLIGHT TO THE FINISH—Hector Heathcoate—Dave Tendlar

1963

*TEA HOUSE MOUSE—Hashimoto—Bob Kuwahara

*TO BE OR NOT TO BE—Sidney—Connie Rasinski

ASTRONUT—Deputy Dawg—Connie Rasinski

THE MISSING GENIE—April—Luno—Connie Rasinski

TEA PARTY—Hector Heathcoate—Dave Tendlar

*CinemaScope.

*PEARL CRAZY—Hashimoto—Bob Kuwahara

SIDNEY'S WHITE ELEPHANT—Sidney—Art Bartsch

TROUBLE IN BAGHDAD—Luno—Connie Rasinski

A BELL FOR PHILADELPHIA—Hector Heathcoate—Bob Kuwahara

*CHERRY BLOSSOM FESTIVAL—Hashimoto—Bob Kuwahara

DRIVEN TO EXTRACTION—Sidney—Art Bartsch

THE BIG CLEAN-UP—Hector Heathcoate—Dave Tendlar

*SPOOKY-YAKI—Hashimoto—Bob Kuwahara

1964

ROC-A-BYE SINBAD—Luno—Connie Rasinski

THE RED TRACTOR—Duckwood—Dave Tendlar

BROTHER FROM OUTER SPACE—Astronut—Connie Rasinski

SEARCH FOR MISERY—Pitiful Penelope—Bob Kuwahara

KING ROUNDER—Luno—Connie Rasinski

SHORT TERM SHERIFF—Donkey Otie, Duckwood—Dave Tendlar

KISSER PLANT—Astronut—Connie Rasinski

ADVENTURE BY THE SEA—Luno—Art Bartsch

OIL THRU THE DAY—Duckwood—Dave Tendlar

OUTER GALAXY GAZETTE—Astronut—Connie Rasinski

THE GOLD DUST BANDIT—Luno—Art Bartsch

MOLECULAR MIXUP—Astronut—Dave Tendlar

1965

GADMOUSE THE APPRENTICE GOOD FAIRY—January—Sad Cat—Ralph Bakshi

THE SKY'S THE LIMIT—February—Astronut—Dave Tendlar

FREIGHT FRIGHT—March—Possible Possum—Connie Rasinski

DON'T SPILL THE BEANS—April—Sad Cat—Ralph Bakshi

WEATHER MAGIC—May—Astronut—Cosmo Anzilotti

DARN BARN—June—Possible Possum—Connie Rasinski

DRESS REVERSAL—July—Sad Cat—Ralph Bakshi

ROBOTS IN TOYLAND—August—Astronut—Connie Rasinski

GET THAT GUITAR—September—Possible Possum—Art Bartsch

THE THIRD MUSKETEER—October—Sad Cat—Ralph Bakshi

TWINKLE, TWINKLE LITTLE TELSTAR—November—Astronut—Art Bartsch

THE TOOTHLESS BEAVER—December—Possible Possum—Connie Rasinski

1966

GEMS FROM GEMINI—January—Astronut—Dave Tendlar

DR. HA HA HA—February—James Hound—Ralph Bakshi

MESSED UP MOVIE MAKERS—March—Heckle and Jeckle—George Bakes, Al Chiarito

CHAMPION CHUMP—April—Martian Moochers—Bob Kuwahara

HAUNTED HOUSECLEANING—May—Astronut—Connie Rasinski

SCUBA DUBA DO—June—Sad Cat—Ralph Bakshi

THE MONSTER MAKER—July—James Hound—Ralph Bakshi

THE COWARDLY WATCHDOG—August—Martian Moochers—Bob Kuwahara

RAIN DRAIN—September—James Hound—Ralph Bakshi

WATCH THE BUTTERFLY—October—Possible Possum—Dave Tendlar

DREAM-NAPPING—November—James Hound—Ralph Bakshi

THE PHANTOM SKYSCRAPER—December—James Hound—Ralph Bakshi

1967

A VOODOO SPELL—January—James Hound—Ralph Bakshi

MR. WIN LUCKY—February—James Hound—Ralph Bakshi

IT'S FOR THE BIRDS—March—James Hound—Ralph Bakshi

THE HEAT'S OFF—April—James Hound—Ralph Bakshi

TRAFFIC TROUBLE—May—James Hound—Ralph Bakshi

BUGGED BY A BUG—June—James Hound—Ralph Bakshi

FANCY PLANTS—July—James Hound—Ralph Bakshi

GIVE ME LIBERTY—August—James Hound—Ralph Bakshi

WHICH IS WITCH—September—James Hound—Ralph Bakshi

DR. RHINESTONE'S THEORY—October—James Hound—Ralph Bakshi

FROZEN SPARKLERS—November—James Hound—Ralph Bakshi

BARON VON GO-GO—December—James Hound—Ralph Bakshi

1968

DRIBBLE DRABBLE—January—Sad Cat—Art Bartsch

BIG GAME FISHING—February—Sad Cat—Art Bartsch

GRAND PRIX WINNER—March—Sad Cat—Art Bartsch

BIG BAD BOBCAT—April—Possible Possum—Cosmo Anzilotti

COMMANDER GREAT GUY—May—Sad Cat—Art Bartsch

ALL TEED OFF—June—Sad Cat—Art Bartsch

SURPRISIN' EXERCISIN'—July—Possible Possum—Cosmo Anzilotti

JUDO KUDOS—August—Sad Cat—Art Bartsch

THE ABOMINABLE MOUNTAINEERS—September—Sad Cat—Art Bartsch

THE ROCK HOUNDS—October—Possible Possum—Dave Tendlar

LOOPS AND SWOOPS—November—Sad Cat—Art Bartsch

MOUNT PINEY—December—Possible Possum—Art Bartsch

The Walter Lantz Cartoons

Following is a complete list of sound cartoons produced for theatrical release by Walter Lantz. Series title and/or starring character is indicated after each film's release date. With the exception of the 1948–49 product, they were all distributed by Universal Pictures.

Lantz and Bill Nolan shared production and directing credits from 1929 to 1935, but there is no way to determine who actually directed each cartoon. Lantz only began awarding director credits to his staff in 1938.

There is no director credited on screen for most

of Lantz's 1951–52 releases, which the producer claims to have directed himself.

Copyright dates are listed when it was impossible to ascertain definite release dates. In the 1960s Universal stopped assigning release dates altogether, and the last yearly entries in this list are not tallied in any particular release order.

We have attempted to list the home movie titles assigned to various Lantz cartoons by Castle Films, as prints still circulate under those names.

One dagger (†) next to a film title indicates an Academy Award nominee.

1929 *(Copyright date marked by ©)*

WEARY WILLIES—August 5—Oswald the Rabbit
SAUCY SAUSAGES—August 19—Oswald
RACE RIOT—September 2—Oswald
OIL'S WELL—September 16—Oswald
PERMANENT WAVE—September 30—Oswald
COLD TURKEY—October 14—Oswald
PUSSY WILLIE—October 14—Oswald
AMATEUR NIGHT—November 11—Oswald
SNOW USE—November 25—Oswald
NUTTY NOTES—December 9—Oswald
KOUNTY FAIR— © December 17—Oswald

1930 *(Copyright dates marked by ©)*

HURDY GURDY— © January 3—Oswald
CHILE CON CARMEN—January 15—Oswald
KISSES AND KURSES— © February 3—Oswald
BROADWAY FOLLY— © February 19—Oswald
BOWERY BIMBOS—March 18—Oswald
HASH SHOP—April 12—Oswald
PRISON PANIC—April 30—Oswald
TRAMPING TRAMPS—May 6—Oswald
HOT FOR HOLLYWOOD—May 19—Oswald
HELL'S HEELS—June 2—Oswald
MY PAL PAUL—June 16—Oswald
SONG OF THE CABALLERO—June 29—Oswald
NOT SO QUIET—June 30—Oswald
SPOOKS—July 14—Oswald

SONS OF THE SADDLE—July 20—Oswald
COLD FEET— © August 13—Oswald
SNAPPY SALESMAN— © August 18—Oswald
HENPECKED— © August 20—Oswald
SINGING SAP—September 8—Oswald
FANNY THE MULE—September 15—Oswald
DETECTIVE—September 22—Oswald
THE FOWL BALL—October 13—Oswald
STRANGE AS IT SEEMS—October 27—Oswald
THE NAVY—November 3—Oswald
MEXICO—November 17—Oswald
AFRICA—December 1—Oswald
ALASKA—December 15—Oswald
MARS—December 29—Oswald

1931 *(Copyright dates marked by ©)*

CHINA—January 12—Oswald
COLLEGE—January 27—Oswald
SHIPWRECK—February 9—Oswald
THE FARMER—March 23—Oswald
FIREMAN—April 6—Oswald
SUNNY SOUTH—April 20—Oswald
COUNTRY SCHOOL—May 5—Oswald
THE BANDMASTER— © May 27—Oswald
NORTH WOODS—June 1—Oswald
STONE AGE—July 15—Oswald
RADIO RHYTHM—July 27—Oswald
KENTUCKY BELLE—September 2—Oswald
HOT FEET—September 14—Oswald
THE HUNTER— © September 30—Oswald
IN WONDERLAND—October 26—Oswald
TROLLEY TROUBLES—November 23—Oswald
HARE MAIL—November 30—Oswald
FISHERMAN—December 7—Oswald
THE CLOWN—December 21—Oswald

1932

MECHANICAL COW—January 4—Oswald
GRANDMA'S PET—January 18—Oswald
OH, TEACHER—February 1—Oswald

MECHANICAL MAN—February 15—Oswald

GREAT GUNS—February 29—Oswald

WINS OUT—March 14—Oswald

BEAUS AND ARROWS—March 28—Oswald

MAKING GOOD—April 11—Oswald

LET'S EAT—April 21—Oswald

FOILED AGAIN—April 25—Oswald

WINGED HORSE—May 9—Oswald

TO THE RESCUE—May 23—Oswald

CATNIPPED—May 23—Oswald

A WET KNIGHT—June 20—Oswald

A JUNGLE JUMBLE—July 4—Oswald

DAY NURSE—August 1—Oswald

THE ATHLETE—August 29—Pooch the Pup

BUSY BARBER—September 12—Oswald

THE BUTCHER BOY—September 26—Pooch

CARNIVAL CAPERS—October 10—Oswald

THE CROWD SNORES—October 24—Pooch

THE UNDERDOG—November 7—Pooch

WILD AND WOOLLY—November 21—Oswald

CATS AND DOGS—December 5—Pooch

TEACHER'S PEST—December 19—Oswald

1933

MERRY DOG—January 2—Pooch

OSWALD THE PLUMBER—January 16—Oswald

THE TERRIBLE TROUBADOR—January 30—Pooch

THE SHRIEK—February 27—Oswald

THE LUMBER CHAMP—March 13—Pooch

GOING TO BLAZES—April 10—Oswald

S.O.S. ICICLE—May 8—Pooch

BEAU BEST—May 22—Oswald

NATURE'S WORKSHOP—June 5—Pooch

HAM AND EGGS—June 19—Oswald

PIN-FEATHERS—July 3—Pooch

A NEW DEAL—July 17—Oswald

CONFIDENCE—July 31—Oswald

HOT AND COLD—August 14—Pooch

KING KLUNK—September 4—Pooch

FIVE AND DIME—September 18—Oswald

SHE DONE HIM RIGHT—October 9—Pooch

IN THE ZOO—November 6—Oswald

†MERRY OLD SOUL—November 27—Oswald

PARKING SPACE—December 18—Oswald

1934

CHICKEN REEL—January 1—Oswald

THE CANDY HOUSE—January 15—Oswald

COUNTY FAIR—February 5—Oswald

THE TOY SHOPPE—February 19—Oswald

KINGS UP—March 12—Oswald

WOLF, WOLF—April 2—Oswald

GINGERBREAD BOY—April 16—Oswald

ANNIE MOVED AWAY—May 28—Oswald

GOLDILOCKS AND THE THREE BEARS—May 14—Oswald

THE WAX WORKS—June 25—Oswald

WILLIAM TELL—July 9—Oswald

CHRIS COLUMBO JR.—July 23—Oswald

DIZZY DWARF—August 6—Oswald

HAPPY PILGRIMS—September 3—Oswald

†*JOLLY LITTLE ELVES—October 1—Cartune Classic

SKY LARKS—October 22—Oswald

SPRING IN THE PARK—November 12—Oswald

*TOYLAND PREMIERE—December 10—Cartune Classic

1935

ROBINSON CRUSOE ISLE—January 7—Oswald

HILL BILLYS—February 1—Oswald

TWO LITTLE LAMBS—March 11—Oswald

DO A GOOD DEED—March 25—Oswald

*CANDY LAND—April 22—Cartune Classic

ELMER THE GREAT DANE—April 29—Oswald

GOLD DUST OSWALD—May—Oswald

*SPRINGTIME SERENADE—May 27—Cartune Classic

TOWNE HALL FOLLIES—June 3—Oswald

AT YOUR SERVICE—July 8—Oswald

*THREE LAZY MICE—July 15—Cartune Classic

BRONCO BUSTER—August 5—Oswald

AMATEUR BROADCAST—August 26—Oswald

*THE QUAIL HUNT—September 23—Oswald

*In color.

THE FOX AND THE RABBIT—September 30—Cartune Classic

MONKEY WRETCHES—November 11—Oswald

CASE OF THE LOST SHEEP—December 9—Oswald

DOCTOR OSWALD—December 30—Oswald

1936 (Copyright date marked by ©)

SOFTBALL GAME—January 27—Oswald

ALASKA SWEEPSTAKES—February 17—Oswald

SLUMBERLAND EXPRESS—March 9—Oswald

BEAUTY SHOPPE—March 30—Oswald

BARNYARD FIVE—April 20—Oswald

THE FUN HOUSE—May 4—Oswald

FARMING FOOLS—© May 19—Oswald

BATTLE ROYAL—June 22—Oswald

MUSIC HATH CHARMS—September 7—Oswald

KIDDIE REVUE—September 21—Oswald

BEACHCOMBERS—October 5—Oswald

NIGHT LIFE OF THE BUGS—October 19—Oswald

PUPPET SHOW—November 2—Oswald

UNPOPULAR MECHANIC—November 6—Oswald

TURKEY DINNER—November 30—Meany, Miny, Moe

GOPHER TROUBLE—November 30—Oswald

KNIGHTS FOR A DAY—December 25—Meany, Miny, Moe

1937

THE GOLFERS—January 11—Meany, Miny, Moe

HOUSE OF MAGIC—February 8—Meany, Miny, Moe

EVERYBODY SINGS—February 22—Oswald

THE BIG RACE—March 3—Meany, Miny, Moe

DUCK HUNT—March 8—Oswald

LUMBER CAMP—March 15—Meany, Miny, Moe

THE BIRTHDAY PARTY—March 29—Oswald

STEEL WORKERS—April 26—Meany, Miny, Moe

TRAILER THRILLS—May 3—Oswald

THE STEVEDORES—May 24—Meany, Miny, Moe

THE WILY WEASEL—June 7—Oswald

COUNTRY STORE—July 5—Meany, Miny, Moe

THE PLAYFUL PUP—July 12—Oswald

FIREMAN'S PICNIC—August 16—Meany, Miny, Moe

REST RESORT—August 23—Meany, Miny, Moe

OSTRICH FEATHERS—September 6—Meany, Miny, Moe

AIR EXPRESS—September 20—Meany, Miny, Moe

LOVE SICK—October 4—Oswald

KEEPER OF THE LIONS—October 18—Oswald

MECHANICAL HANDYMAN—November 8—Oswald

FOOTBALL FEVER—November 15—Oswald

THE MYSTERIOUS JUG—November 29—Oswald

DUMB CLUCK—December 20—Oswald

1938 (Copyright dates marked by ©)

THE LAMPLIGHTER—January 10—Oswald

MAN HUNT—February 7—Oswald

YOKEL BOY MAKES GOOD—February 21—Oswald

TRADE MICE—February 28—Oswald

FEED THE KITTY—March 14—Oswald

NELLIE, THE SEWING MACHINE GIRL—April 11—Cartune

TAIL END—April 25—Cartune

THE PROBLEM CHILD—May 16—Oswald

MOVIE PHONEY NEWS—May 30—Cartune

NELLIE, THE INDIAN CHIEF'S DAUGHTER—June 6—Cartune

HAPPY SCOUTS—June 20—Oswald

CHEESE NAPPERS—July 4—Baby Face Mouse—Alex Lovy

SILLY SEALS— © July 12—Les Kline

VOODOO IN HARLEM—July 18—Cartune

BARNYARD ROMEO—August 1—Oswald

QUEEN'S KITTENS—August 8—Oswald

THE BIG CAT AND THE LITTLE MOUSIE—August 15—Baby Face Mouse

GHOST TOWN FROLICS—September 5—Oswald

PIXIELAND—September 12—Oswald

THE CAT AND THE BELL—October 3—Baby Face Mouse

HOLLYWOOD BOWL— © October 5—Elmer Perkins

RABBIT HUNT—October 10—Oswald

THE SAILOR MOUSE—November 7—Baby Face Mouse—Alex Lovy

DISOBEDIENT MOUSE—November 28—Baby Face Mouse—Les Kline

BABY KITTENS—December 19—Cartune—Alex Lovy

LITTLE BLUE BLACKBIRDS—December 26—Cartune—Patrick Lenihan

1939

SOUP TO MUTTS—January 9—Cartune—Les Kline

I'M JUST A JITTERBUG—January 23—Cartune—Alex Lovy

MAGIC BEANS—February 13—Nertsery Rhyme—Les Kline

BIRTH OF A TOOTHPICK—February 27—Cartune—Burt Gillett

LITTLE TOUGH MICE—March 13—Cartune—Alex Lovy

ONE-ARMED BANDIT—March 27—Cartune—Alex Lovy

CRACKPOT CRUISE—April 10—Cartune—Alex Lovy

CHARLIE CUCUKOO—April 24—Cartune—Elmer Perkins

NELLIE OF THE CIRCUS—May 8—Cartune—Alex Lovy

BOLO MOLA LAND—May 28—Cartune—Alex Lovy

THE BIRD ON NELLIE'S HAT—June 19—Cartune—Alex Lovy

STUBBORN MULE—July 3—Li'l Eightball—Burt Gillett

ARABS WITH DIRTY FEZZES—July 31—Cartune—Alex Lovy

SNUFFY SKUNK'S PARTY—August 7—Cartune—Elmer Perkins

SLAP HAPPY VALLEY—August 21—Cartune—Alex Lovy

SILLY SUPERSTITION—August 28—Li'l Eightball—Burt Gillett

*A-HAUNTING WE WILL GO—September 4—Cartune—Burt Gillett

*LIFE BEGINS FOR ANDY PANDA—September 9—Andy Panda—Alex Lovy

*SCRAMBLED EGGS—November 20—Peterkin—Alex Lovy

*THE SLEEPING PRINCESS—December 4—Nertsery Rhyme—Burt Gillett

1940 (All cartoons in color from this time on)

ANDY PANDA GOES FISHING—January 22—Andy Panda—Burt Gillett

KITTEN MITTENS—February 12—Cartune—Alex Lovy

ADVENTURES OF TOM THUMB JR.—March 4—Cartune—Burt Gillett

100 PIGMIES AND ANDY PANDA—April 22—Andy Panda—Alex Lovy

CRAZY HOUSE—September 23—Andy Panda—Walter Lantz

RECRUITING DAZE—October 28—Cartune—Alex Lovy

KNOCK KNOCK—November 25—Andy Panda (Woody Woodpecker's debut)—Walter Lantz

SYNCOPATED SIOUX—December 30—Cartune—Walter Lantz

1941

MOUSE TRAPPERS—January 27—Andy Panda—Alex Lovy

FAIR TODAY—February 24—Cartune—Walter Lantz

SCRUB ME MAMA WITH A BOOGIE BEAT—March 28—Cartune—Walter Lantz

HYSTERICAL HIGH SPOTS IN AMERCIAN HISTORY—March 31—Cartune—Walter Lantz

DIZZY KITTY—May 26—Andy Panda—Walter Lantz

SALT WATER DAFFY—June 9—Cartune—Walter Lantz

WOODY WOODPECKER (a.k.a. THE CRACKED NUT)—July 7—Woody Woodpecker—Walter Lantz

ANDY PANDA'S POP—July 28—Andy Panda—Alex Lovy

THE SCREWDRIVER—August 11—Woody Woodpecker—Walter Lantz

†THE BOOGIE WOOGIE BUGLE BOY OF COMPANY B—September 1—Cartune—Walter Lantz

MAN'S BEST FRIEND—October 20—Cartune—Walter Lantz

WHAT'S COOKIN'? (a.k.a. PANTRY PANIC)—November 24—Woody Woodpecker—Walter Lantz

$21.00 A DAY ONCE A MONTH—December 1—Swing Symphonies—Walter Lantz

1942

UNDER THE SPREADING BLACKSMITH'S SHOP—January 12—Andy Panda—Alex Lovy

HOLLYWOOD MATADOR—February 9—Woody Woodpecker—Walter Lantz

THE HAMS THAT COULDN'T BE CURED—March 4—Swing Symphonies—Walter Lantz

MOTHER GOOSE ON THE LOOSE—April 13—Cartune—Walter Lantz

GOODBYE MR. MOTH—May 11—Andy Panda—Walter Lantz

NUTTY PINE CABIN—June 1—Andy Panda—Alex Lovy

ACE IN THE HOLE—June 22—Woody Woodpecker—Alex Lovy

†JUKE BOX JAMBOREE—July 27—Swing Symphonies—Alex Lovy

PIGEON PATROL—August 3—Homer Pigeon—Alex Lovy

ANDY PANDA'S VICTORY GARDEN—September 7—Andy Panda—Alex Lovy

*In color.

YANKEE DOODLE SWING SHIFT—September 21—Swing Symphonies—Alex Lovy

THE LOAN STRANGER—October 19—Woody Woodpecker—Alex Lovy

BOOGIE WOOGIE SIOUX—November 30—Swing Symphonies—Alex Lovy

AIR RADIO WARDEN—December 21—Cartune—Alex Lovy

1943

COW COW BOOGIE—January 3—Swing Symphonies—Alex Lovy

THE SCREWBALL—February 15—Woody Woodpecker—Alex Lovy

EGG CRACKER SUITE—March 22—Swing Symphonies (Oswald)—Ben Hardaway, Emery Hawkins

SWING YOUR PARTNER—April 26—Swing Symphonies (Homer Pigeon)—Alex Lovy

†THE DIZZY ACROBAT—May 31—Woody Woodpecker—Alex Lovy

CANINE COMMANDOS—June 28—Cartune—Alex Lovy

RATION BORED—July 26—Woody Woodpecker—Emery Hawkins, Milt Schaffer

PASS THE BISCUITS MIRANDY—August 23—Swing Symphonies—James Culhane

BOOGIE WOOGIE MAN—September 27—Swing Symphonies—James Culhane

MEATLESS TUESDAY—October 25—Andy Panda—James Culhane

1944

THE GREATEST MAN IN SIAM—March 27—Swing Symphonies—James Culhane

BARBER OF SEVILLE—April 10—Woody Woodpecker—James Culhane

JUNGLE JIVE—May 15—Swing Symphonies—James Culhane

†FISH FRY—June 19—Andy Panda—James Culhane

ABOU BEN BOOGIE—September 18—Swing Symphonies—James Culhane

THE BEACH NUT—October 16—Woody Woodpecker—James Culhane

SKI FOR TWO (a.k.a. WOODY PLAYS SANTA)—November 13—Woody Woodpecker—James Culhane

THE PAINTER AND THE POINTER—December 18—Andy Panda—James Culhane

1945

THE PIED PIPER OF BASIN STREET—January 15—Swing Symphonies—James Culhane

CHEW-CHEW BABY—February 5—Woody Woodpecker—James Culhane

THE SLIPHORN KING OF POLAROO—March 19—Swing Symphonies—Dick Lundy

WOODY DINES OUT—May 14—Woody Woodpecker—James Culhane

CROW CRAZY—July 9—Andy Panda—Dick Lundy

DIPPY DIPLOMAT—August 27—Woody Woodpecker—James Culhane

LOOSE NUT—December 17—Woody Woodpecker—James Culhane

1946

†THE POET AND PEASANT—March 18—Andy Panda—Dick Lundy

MOUSIE COME HOME—April 15—Andy Panda—James Culhane

APPLE ANDY—May 20—Andy Panda—Dick Lundy

WHO'S COOKIN' WHO?—June 24—Woody Woodpecker—Dick Lundy

BATHING BUDDIES—July 1—Woody Woodpecker—Dick Lundy

THE RECKLESS DRIVER—August 26—Woody Woodpecker—James Culhane

FAIR WEATHER FRIENDS—November 18—Woody Woodpecker—James Culhane

THE WACKY WEED—December 16—Andy Panda—Dick Lundy

1947

†MUSICAL MOMENTS FROM CHOPIN—February 24—Musical Miniatures (Andy Panda, Woody Woodpecker)—Dick Lundy

SMOKED HAMS—April 28—Woody Woodpecker—Dick Lundy

COO-COO BIRD—June 9—Woody Woodpecker—Dick Lundy

OVERTURE TO WILLIAM TELL—June 16—Musical Miniature (Wally Walrus)—Dick Lundy

WELL OILED—June 30—Woody Woodpecker—Dick Lundy

SOLID IVORY—August 25—Woody Woodpecker—Dick Lundy

WOODY THE GIANT KILLER—December 15—Woody Woodpecker—Dick Lundy

THE BAND MASTER—December—Andy Panda—Dick Lundy (this and subsequent releases into 1949 released by United Artists)

1948 *(Copyright dates marked by* © *)*

THE MAD HATTER—February—Woody Woodpecker—Dick Lundy

BANQUET BUSTERS—March (Woody Woodpecker, Andy Panda)—Dick Lundy

KIDDIE KONCERT—April—Cartune (Wally Walrus)—Dick Lundy

WACKY-BYE BABY—May—Woody Woodpecker—Dick Lundy

PIXIE PICNIC—May—Musical Miniatures—Dick Lundy

WET BLANKET POLICY—August 27—Woody Woodpecker—Dick Lundy

PLAYFUL PELICAN—October 8—Andy Panda—Dick Lundy

DOG TAX DODGERS— © November 26—Andy Panda—Dick Lundy

WILD AND WOODY—December 31—Woody Woodpecker—Dick Lundy

1949

SCRAPPY BIRTHDAY—February 11—Andy Panda—Dick Lundy

DROOLER'S DELIGHT—March 25—Woody Woodpecker—Dick Lundy

1951

PUNY EXPRESS—January 22—Woody Woodpecker—Walter Lantz

SLEEP HAPPY—March 26—Woody Woodpecker—Walter Lantz

WICKET WACKY— © May 28—Woody Woodpecker—Walter Lantz

SLING SHOT 6 7/8—July 23—Woody Woodpecker—Walter Lantz

REDWOOD SAP—October 1—Woody Woodpecker—Walter Lantz

DESTINATION MEATBALL—December 24—Woody Woodpecker—Walter Lantz

1952

BORN TO PECK—February 25—Woody Woodpecker—Walter Lantz

STAGE HOAX—April 21—Woody Woodpecker—Walter Lantz

WOODPECKER IN THE ROUGH—June 16—Woody Woodpecker—Walter Lantz

SCALP TREATMENT—September 18—Woody Woodpecker—Walter Lantz

THE GREAT WHO DOOD IT—October 20—Woody Woodpecker—Don Patterson

TERMITES FROM MARS—December 8—Woody Woodpecker—Don Patterson

1953

WHAT'S SWEEPIN'?—January 5—Woody Woodpecker—Don Patterson

THE DOG THAT CRIED WOLF—March 23—Cartune—Paul J. Smith

BUCCANEER WOODPECKER—April 20—Woody Woodpecker—Don Patterson

THE MOUSE AND THE LION—May 11—Foolish Fable—Paul J. Smith

OPERATION SAWDUST—June 15—Woody Woodpecker—Don Patterson

THE FLYING TURTLE—June 29—Foolish Fable—Paul J. Smith

WRESTLING WRECKS—July 20—Woody Woodpecker—Don Patterson

MAW AND PAW—August 10—Maw and Paw—Paul J. Smith

BELLE BOYS—September 14—Woody Woodpecker—Don Patterson

*HYPNOTIC HICK—September 26—Woody Woodpecker—Don Patterson

PLYWOOD PANIC—September 28—Maw and Paw—Paul J. Smith

HOT NOON—October 12—Woody Woodpecker—Paul J. Smith

CHILLY WILLY—December 21—Chilly Willy—Alex Lovy

1954

SOCKO IN MOROCCO—January 18—Woody Woodpecker—Don Patterson

A HORSE'S TALE—February 15—Sugarfoot—Paul J. Smith

*In 3-D.

ALLEY TO BALI—March 15—Woody Woodpecker—Don Patterson

DIG THAT DOG—April 12—Cartune—Ray Patterson

UNDER THE COUNTER SPY (a.k.a. SECRET AGENT F.O.B.)—May 10—Woody Woodpecker—Don Patterson

HAY RUBE—June 7—Sugarfoot—Paul J. Smith

HOT ROD HUCKSTER—July 5—Woody Woodpecker—Paul J. Smith

BROADWAY BOW WOWS—August 2—Cartune—Ray Patterson

PIG IN A PICKLE—August 30—Maw and Paw—Paul J. Smith

REAL GONE WOODY—September 20—Woody Woodpecker—Paul J. Smith

FINE FEATHERED FRENZY—October 25—Woody Woodpecker—Don Patterson

CONVICT CONCERTO—November 20—Woody Woodpecker—Don Patterson

I'M COLD (a.k.a. SOME LIKE IT NOT)—December 20—Chilly Willy—Tex Avery

1955

HELTER SHELTER—January 17—Woody Woodpecker—Paul J. Smith

†CRAZY MIXED-UP PUP—February 14—Cartune—Tex Avery

WITCH CRAFTY—March 14—Woody Woodpecker—Paul J. Smith

†THE LEGEND OF ROCKABYE POINT (a.k.a. ROCKABYE LEGEND)—April 11—Chilly Willy—Tex Avery

PRIVATE EYE POOCH—May 9—Woody Woodpecker—Paul J. Smith

SH-H-H-H—June 6—Cartune—Tex Avery

BEDTIME BEDLAM—July 4—Woody Woodpecker—Paul J. Smith

FLEA FOR TWO—July 20—Cartune—Ray Patterson

PAW'S NIGHT OUT—August 1—Maw and Paw—Paul J. Smith

SQUARE SHOOTING SQUARE—September—Woody Woodpecker—Paul J. Smith

HOT AND COLD PENGUIN—October 24—Chilly Willy—Alex Lovy

BUNCO BUSTERS—November 21—Woody Woodpecker—Paul Smith

THE TREE MEDIC—December 9—Woody Woodpecker—Alex Lovy

1956

PIGEON HOLED—January 16—Homer Pigeon—Alex Lovy

AFTER THE BALL—February 13—Woody Woodpecker—Paul J. Smith

GET LOST—March 12—Woody Woodpecker—Paul J. Smith

THE OSTRICH EGG AND I—April 9—Maggie and Sam—Alex Lovy

CHIEF CHARLIE HORSE—May 7—Woody Woodpecker—Paul J. Smith

ROOM AND WRATH—June 4—Chilly Willy—Alex Lovy

WOODPECKER FROM MARS—July 2—Woody Woodpecker—Paul J. Smith

HOLD THAT ROCK—July 30—Chilly Willy—Alex Lovy

TALKING DOG—August 27—Maggie and Sam—Alex Lovy

CALLING ALL CUCKOOS—September 24—Woody Woodpecker—Paul J. Smith

NIAGARA FOOLS—October 22—Woody Woodpecker—Paul J. Smith

ARTS AND FLOWERS—November 19—Woody Woodpecker—Paul J. Smith

WOODY MEETS DAVY CREWCUT—December 17—Woody Woodpecker—Alex Lovy

1957

FOWLED-UP PARTY—January 14—Maggie and Sam—Alex Lovy

RED RIDING HOODLUM—February 11—Woody Woodpecker—Paul J. Smith

THE PLUMBER OF SEVILLE—March 11—Cartune—Alex Lovy

BOX CAR BANDIT—April 8—Woody Woodpecker—Paul J. Smith

OPERATION COLD FEET—May 6—Chilly Willy—Alex Lovy

UNBEARABLE SALESMAN—June 3—Woody Woodpecker—Paul J. Smith

INTERNATIONAL WOODPECKER—July 1—Woody Woodpecker—Paul J. Smith

TO CATCH A WOODPECKER—July 29—Woody Woodpecker—Alex Lovy

GOOFY GARDENER—August 26—Cartune—Alex Lovy

THE BIG SNOOZE—August 30—Chilly Willy—Alex Lovy

ROUND TRIP TO MARS—September 23—Woody Woodpecker—Paul J. Smith

DOPEY DICK AND THE PINK WHALE—Woody Wood-pecker—Paul J. Smith

FODDER AND SON—November 4—Woody Woodpecker—Paul J. Smith

SWISS MISS-FIT—December 2—Chilly Willy—Alex Lovy

THE BONGO PUNCH—December 30—Pepito Chickeeto—Alex Lovy

1958

MISGUIDED MISSILE—January 27—Woody Wood-pecker—Paul J. Smith

WATCH THE BIRDIE—February 24—Woody Wood-pecker—Alex Lovy

SALMON YEGGS—March 24—Windy—Paul J. Smith

HALF-EMPTY SADDLES—April 21—Woody Woodpecker—Paul J. Smith

POLAR PESTS—May 19—Chilly Willy—Alex Lovy

A CHILLY RECEPTION—June 16—Chilly Willy—Alex Lovy

HIS BETTER ELF—July 14—Woody Woodpecker—Paul J. Smith

EVERGLADE RAID—August 11—Woody Woodpecker—Paul J. Smith

TREE'S A CROWD—September 8—Woody Woodpecker—Paul J. Smith

THREE-RING FLING—October 6—Windy—Alex Lovy

JITTERY JESTER—November 3—Woody Woodpecker—Paul J. Smith

LITTLE TELLEVILLAIN—December 8—Chilly Willy—Alex Lovy

1959 (Copyright date marked by ©)

TRUANT STUDENT—January 5—Windy and Breezy—Paul J. Smith

ROBINSON GRUESOME—February 2—Chilly Willy—Paul J. Smith

TOM CAT COMBAT—March—Woody Woodpecker—Paul J. Smith

YUKON HAVE IT—April—Chilly Willy—Alex Lovy

LOG JAMMED—April—Woody Woodpecker—Paul J. Smith

PANHANDLE SCANDAL—May—Woody Woodpecker—Alex Lovy

BEE BOPPED—June—Windy and Breezy—Jack Hannah

WOODPECKER IN THE MOON—July—Woody Wood-pecker—Alex Lovy

THE TEE BIRD—July 13—Woody Woodpecker—Paul J. Smith

ROMP IN A SWAMP—August 7—Woody Woodpecker—Paul J. Smith

SPACE MOUSE— © September 7—Space Mouse—Alex Lovy

KIDDIE LEAGUE—November 3—Woody Woodpecker—Paul J. Smith

MOUSE TRAPPED—December 8—Hickory, Dickory and Doc—Alex Lovy

1960

BILLION-DOLLAR BONER—January 5—Woody Wood-pecker—Alex Lovy

WITTY KITTY—February 2—Doc—Alex Lovy

PISTOL-PACKIN' WOODPECKER—March 2—Woody Wood-pecker—Paul J. Smith

HEAP BIG HEPCAT—March 30—Woody Woodpecker—Paul J. Smith

BALLYHOOEY—April 20—Woody Woodpecker—Alex Lovy

HOW TO STUFF A WOODPECKER—May 18—Woody Wood-pecker—Paul J. Smith

BATS IN THE BELFRY—June 16—Woody Woodpecker—Paul J. Smith

OZARK LARK—July 13—Woody Woodpecker—Paul J. Smith

FISH HOOKED—August 10—Chilly Willy—Paul J. Smith

FREELOADING FELINE—September 7—Cartune—Jack Hannah

HUNGER STRIFE—October 5—Cartune—Jack Hannah

SOUTHERN FRIED HOSPITALITY—November 28—Woody Woodpecker—Jack Hannah

FOWLED-UP FALCON—December 20—Woody Wood-pecker—Paul J. Smith

1961

ROUGH AND TUMBLEWEED—January—Inspector Wil-loughby—Paul J. Smith

POOP DECK PIRATE—January—Woody Woodpecker—Jack Hannah

EGGNAPER—February—Cartune—Jack Hannah

THE BIRD WHO CAME TO DINNER—March—Woody Woodpecker—Jack Hannah

GABBY'S DINER—April—Woody Woodpecker—Jack Hannah

PAPOOSE ON THE LOOSE—April—Cartune—Paul J. Smith

CLASH AND CARRY—May—Chilly Willy—Jack Hannah

ST. MORITZ BLITZ—May—Chilly Willy—Paul J. Smith

BEARS AND THE BEES—May—Cartune—Jack Hannah

SUFFERIN' CATS—June—Woody Woodpecker—Paul J. Smith

MISSISSIPPI SLOW BOAT—July—Inspector Willoughby—Paul J. Smith

FRANKENSTYMIED—July—Woody Woodpecker—Jack Hannah

BUSMAN'S HOLIDAY—August—Woody Woodpecker—Paul J. Smith

TRICKY TROUT—September—Chilly Willy—Paul J. Smith

PHANTOM OF THE HORSE OPERA—October—Woody Woodpecker—Paul J. Smith

TIN CAN CONCERT—October—Cartune—Jack Hannah

DOC'S LAST STAND—November—Doc—Jack Hannah

WOODY'S KOOK-OUT—November—Woody Woodpecker—Jack Hannah

CASE OF THE RED-EYED RUBY—December—Inspector Willoughby—Paul J. Smith

1962

HOME SWEET HOMEWRECKER—January—Woody Woodpecker—Paul J. Smith

ROCK-A-BYE GATOR—January—Woody Woodpecker—Jack Hannah

PEST OF SHOW—February—Doc and Champ—Jack Hannah

ROOM AND BORED—March—Woody Woodpecker—Paul J. Smith

MACKEREL MOOCHER—March—Chilly Willy—Jack Hannah

FOWLED-UP BIRTHDAY—April—The Beary Family—Jack Hannah

ROCKET RACKET—April—Woody Woodpecker—Jack Hannah

PHONEY EXPRESS—May—Insepctor Willoughby—Paul J. Smith

CARELESS CARETAKER—May—Woody Woodpecker—Paul J. Smith

MOTHER'S LITTLE HELPER—June—The Beary Family—Paul J. Smith

TRAGIC MAGIC—July—Woody Woodpecker—Paul J. Smith

HYDE AND SNEAK—July—Inspector Willoughby—Paul J. Smith

VOODOO BOO-HOO—August—Woody Woodpecker—Jack Hannah

CROWIN' PAINS—September—Woody Woodpecker—Paul J. Smith

PUNCHY POOCH—September—Doc and Champ—Jack Hannah

LITTLE WOODY RIDING HOOD—October—Woody Woodpecker—Paul J. Smith

CORNY CONCERTO—October—Doc and Champ—Jack Hannah

1963

FISH AND CHIPS—January—Chilly Willy—Jack Hannah

GREEDY GABBY GATOR—January—Woody Woodpecker—Sid Marcus

COMING-OUT PARTY—February—Inspector Willoughby—Paul J. Smith

CASE OF THE COLD-STORAGE YEGG—March—Inspector Willoughby—Paul J. Smith

ROBIN HOODY WOODY—March—Woody Woodpecker—Paul J. Smith

CHARLIE'S MOTHER-IN-LAW—April—The Beary Family—Paul J. Smith

STOWAWAY WOODY—May—Woody Woodpecker—Sid Marcus

HI-SEAS HI-JACKER—May—Inspector Willoughby—Sid Marcus

SHUTTER BUG—June—Woody Woodpecker—Paul J. Smith

SALMON LOAFER—June—Chilly Willy—Sid Marcus

COY DECOY—July—Woody Woodpecker—Sid Marcus

GOOSE IN THE ROUGH—August—The Beary Family—Paul J. Smith

THE TENANTS' RACKET—August—Woody Woodpecker—Sid Marcus

SHORT IN THE SADDLE—September—Woody Woodpecker—Paul J. Smith

PESKY PELICAN—September—Chilly Willy—Sid Marcus

TEEPEE FOR TWO—October—Woody Woodpecker—Sid Marcus

THE GOOSE IS WILD—October—The Beary Family—Paul J. Smith

SCIENCE FRICTION—November—Woody Woodpecker—Sid Marcus

CALLING DR. WOODPECKER—December—Woody Woodpecker—Paul J. Smith

1964

DUMB LIKE A FOX—January—Woody Woodpecker—Sid Marcus

THE CASE OF THE MALTESE CHICKEN—February—Inspector Willoughby

DEEP-FREEZE SQUEEZE—March—Chilly Willy

SADDLE-SORE WOODY—April—Woody Woodpecker—Paul J. Smith

WOODY'S CLIP JOINT—May—Woody Woodpecker—Sid Marcus

RAH RAH RUCKUS—June—The Beary Family—Paul J. Smith

SKINFOLKS—July—Woody Woodpecker—Sid Marcus

LIGHTHOUSE-KEEPING BLUES—August—Chilly Willy—Sid Marcus

GET LOST! LITTLE DOGGY—September—Woody Woodpecker—Sid Marcus

FREEWAY FRACAS—September—Woody Woodpecker—Paul J. Smith

ROOFTOP RAZZLE DAZZLE—October—The Beary Family—Paul J. Smith

SKI-NAPPER—November—Chilly Willy—Sid Marcus

ROAMIN' ROMAN—December—Woody Woodpecker—Paul J. Smith

1965

THREE LITTLE WOODPECKERS—January—Woody Woodpecker—Sid Marcus

THE CASE OF THE ELEPHANT'S TRUNK—January—Inspector Willoughby—Paul J. Smith

WOODPECKER WANTED—February—Woody Woodpecker—Paul J. Smith

FRACTURED FRIENDSHIP—February—Chilly Willy—Sid Marcus

BIRDS OF A FEATHER—March—Woody Woodpecker—Sid Marcus

GUEST WHO?—March—The Beary Family—Paul J. Smith

CANNED DOG FEUD—April—Woody Woodpecker—Paul J. Smith

HALF-BAKED ALASKA—April—Chilly Willy—Sid Marcus

JANIE GET YOUR GUN—May—Woody Woodpecker—Paul J. Smith

DAVEY CRICKET—May—The Beary Family—Paul J. Smith

SIOUX ME—June—Woody Woodpecker—Sid Marcus

PESTY GUEST—June—Chilly Willy—Sid Marcus

WHAT'S PECKIN'?—July—Woody Woodpecker—Paul J. Smith

1966

ROUGH RIDING HOOD—January—Woody Woodpecker—Sid Marcus

FOOT BRAWL—January—The Beary Family—Paul J. Smith

LONESOME RANGER—February—Woody Woodpecker—Sid Marcus

SNOW PLACE LIKE HOME—February—Chilly Willy—Paul J. Smith

WOODY AND THE BEANSTALK—March—Woody Woodpecker—Paul J. Smith

SOUTH POLE PALS—March—Chilly Willy—Paul J. Smith

HASSLE IN A CASTLE—April—Woody Woodpecker—Paul J. Smith

POLAR FRIGHT—April—Chilly Willy—Paul J. Smith

THE BIG BITE—April—Woody Woodpecker—Paul J. Smith

ASTRONUT WOODY—May—Woody Woodpecker—Paul J. Smith

TEENY WEENY MEANY—May—Chilly Willy—Sid Marcus

PRACTICAL YOKE—May—Woody Woodpecker—Paul J. Smith

MONSTER OF CEREMONIES—May—Woody Woodpecker—Paul J. Smith

1967

OPERATION SHANGHAI—Chilly Willy—Paul J. Smith

SISSY SHERIFF—Woody Woodpecker—Paul J. Smith

WINDOW PAINS—The Beary Family—Paul J. Smith

VICIOUS VIKING—Chilly Willy—Paul J. Smith

HAVE GUN—CAN'T TRAVEL—Woody Woodpecker—Paul J. Smith

THE NAUTICAL NUT—Woody Woodpecker—Paul J. Smith

HOT TIME ON ICE—Chilly Willy—Paul J. Smith

HOT DIGGITY DOG—Woody Woodpecker—Paul J. Smith

MOUSE ON THE HOUSE—The Beary Family—Paul J. Smith

HORSE PLAY—Woody Woodpecker—Paul J. Smith

CHILLY AND THE WOODCHOPPER—Chilly Willy—Paul J. Smith

SECRET AGENT WOODY—Woody Woodpecker—Paul J. Smith

CHILLY CHUMS—Chilly Willy—Paul J. Smith

1968

LOTSA LUCK—Woody Woodpecker—Paul J. Smith

UNDERSEA DOGS—Chilly Willy—Paul J. Smith

JERKY TURKEY—The Beary Family—Paul J. Smith

FAT IN THE SADDLE—Woody Woodpecker—Paul J. Smith

FEUDIN, FIGHTIN' 'N' FUSSIN'—Woody Woodpecker—Paul J. Smith

PASTE MAKES WASTE—The Beary Family—Paul J. Smith

A PECK OF TROUBLE—Woody Woodpecker—Paul J. Smith

A LAD IN BAGDAD—Woody Woodpecker—Paul J. Smith

HIWAY HECKLERS—Chilly Willy—Paul J. Smith

ONE HORSE TOWN—Woody Woodpecker—Paul J. Smith

BUGGED IN A RUG—The Beary Family—Paul J. Smith

CHILLER DILLERS—Chilly Willy—Paul J. Smith

WOODY THE FREELOADER—Woody Woodpecker—Paul J. Smith

1969

HOOK LINE AND STINKER—Woody Woodpecker—Paul J. Smith

GOPHER BROKE—The Beary Family—Paul J. Smith

LITTLE SKEETER—Woody Woodpecker—Paul J. Smith

PROJECT REJECT—Chilly Willy—Paul J. Smith

WOODY'S KNIGHTMARE—Woody Woodpecker—Paul J. Smith

CHARLIE'S CAMPOUT—The Beary Family—Paul J. Smith

TUMBLEWEED GREED—Woody Woodpecker—Paul J. Smith

CHILLY AND THE LOONEY GOONEY—Chilly Willy—Paul J. Smith

SHIP AHOY, WOODY—Woody Woodpecker—Paul J. Smith

PREHISTORIC SUPER SALESMAN—Woody Woodpecker—Paul J. Smith

COOL IT, CHARLIE—The Beary Family—Paul J. Smith

PHONY PONY—Woody Woodpecker—Paul J. Smith

SLEEPYTIME BEAR—Chilly Willy—Paul J. Smith

1970

CHARLIE IN HOT WATER—The Beary Family—Paul J. Smith

CHARLIE'S GOLF CLASSIC—The Beary Family—Paul J. Smith

THE UNHANDY MAN—The Beary Family—Paul J. Smith

THE BUNGLING BUILDER—The Beary Family—Paul J. Smith

GOONEY'S GOOFY LANDING—Chilly Willy—Paul J. Smith

CHILLY'S ICE FOLLY—Chilly Willy—Paul J. Smith

CHILLY'S COLD WAR—Chilly Willy—Paul J. Smith

SEAL ON THE LOOSE—Woody Woodpecker—Paul J. Smith

WILD BILL HICCUP—Woody Woodpecker—Paul J. Smith

COO COO NUTS—Woody Woodpecker—Paul J. Smith

HI-RISE WISE GUYS—Woody Woodpecker—Paul J. Smith

BUSTER'S LAST STAND—Woody Woodpecker—Paul J. Smith

ALL HAMS ON DECK—Woody Woodpecker—Paul J. Smith

1971

A GOONEY IS BORN—Chilly Willy—Paul J. Smith

SLEEPY TIME CHIMES—Woody Woodpecker—Paul J. Smith

RELUCTANT RECRUIT—Woody Woodpecker—Paul J. Smith

CHARLIE THE RAINMAKER—The Beary Family—Paul J. Smith

HOW TO TRAP A WOODPECKER—Woody Woodpecker—Paul J. Smith

AIRLIFT A LA CARTE—Chilly Willy—Paul J. Smith

WOODY'S MAGIC TOUCH—Woody Woodpecker—Paul J. Smith

THE BUNGLING BUILDER—The Beary Family—Paul J. Smith

KITTY FROM THE CITY—Woody Woodpecker—Paul J. Smith

CHILLY'S HIDE-AWAY—Chilly Willy—Paul J. Smith

SNOOZIN' BRUIN WOODY—Woody Woodpecker—Paul J. Smith

MOOCHIN' POOCH—The Beary Family—Paul J. Smith

SHANGHAI WOODY—Woody Woodpecker—Paul J. Smith

1972

LET CHARLIE DO IT—The Beary Family—Paul J. Smith

A FISH STORY—The Beary Family—Paul J. Smith

RAIN RAIN, GO AWAY—The Beary Family—Paul J. Smith

UNLUCKY POTLUCK—The Beary Family—Paul J. Smith

THE RUDE INTRUDER—Chilly Willy—Paul J. Smith

INDIAN CORN—Woody Woodpecker—Paul J. Smith

GOLD DIGGIN' WOODPECKER—Woody Woodpecker—Paul J. Smith

PECKING HOLES IN POLES—Woody Woodpecker—Paul J. Smith

CHILI CON CORNY—Woody Woodpecker—Paul J. Smith

SHOW BIZ BEAGLE—Woody Woodpecker—Paul J. Smith

FOR THE LOVE OF PIZZA—Woody Woodpecker—Paul J. Smith

THE GENIE WITH THE LIGHT TOUCH—Woody Woodpecker—Paul J. Smith

BYE BYE BLACKBOARD—Woody Woodpecker—Paul J. Smith

The Ub Iwerks Cartoons

Following is a complete list of cartoons produced by Ub Iwerks for Celebrity Productions in the 1930s. It does not include his work for Walt Disney, Warner Brothers, or Columbia Pictures, which is listed separately under those company headings. Series titles are listed where applicable.

Because there is such confusion regarding production order and release dates on FLIP THE FROG, we have listed all entries for this series with copyright dates for the sake of uniformity. Copyright dates are given for the other series only when the definite release dates were not available.

FLIP THE FROG and WILLIE WHOPPER were released by MGM, while the Comicolor shorts were distributed independently by producer Pat Powers. All Comicolor shorts were filmed in Cinecolor, as were three WILLIE WHOPPER cartoons, which are noted in the listing.

Credits on Iwerks' cartoons ranged from sparse to nonexistent, but the word "director" was never used; therefore, no such credits appear on this filmography.

1931 *(Copyright dates marked by* ©*)*

*FIDDLESTICKS— © April 24—Flip the Frog

FLYING FISTS— © April 24—Flip the Frog

THE VILLAGE BARBER— © April 27—Flip the Frog

THE CUCKOO MURDER CASE— © April 27—Flip the Frog

LAUGHING GAS— © May 1—Flip the Frog

RAGTIME ROMEO— © May 4—Flip the Frog

THE VILLAGE SMITTY— © May 11—Flip the Frog

THE SOUP SONG— © May 25—Flip the Frog

MOVIE MAD— © August 29—Flip the Frog

THE NEW CAR— © December 21—Flip the Frog

PUDDLE PRANKS—Date unknown—Flip the Frog

1932 *(Copyright dates marked by* ©*)*

JAIL BIRDS— © February 15—Flip the Frog

AFRICA SQUEAKS— © February 19—Flip the Frog

THE VILLAGE SPECIALIST— © March 28—Flip the Frog

STORMY SEAS— © April 19—Flip the Frog

WHAT A LIFE— © April 19—Flip the Frog

THE MILKMAN— © April 20—Flip the Frog

SPOOKS— © May 5—Flip the Frog

FIRE! FIRE!— © May 5—Flip the Frog

PUPPY LOVE— © May 9—Flip the Frog

SCHOOL DAYS— © May 26—Flip the Frog

THE BULLY— © June 23—Flip the Frog

THE OFFICE BOY— © July 28—Flip the Frog

*In color.

ROOM RUNNERS— © August 15—Flip the Frog

CIRCUS— © September 7—Flip the Frog

THE GOAL RUSH— © October 3—Flip the Frog

THE PHONEY EXPRESS— © October 27—Flip the Frog

THE MUSIC LESSON— © November 28—Flip the Frog

THE NURSE MAID— © December 19—Flip the Frog

1933 (Copyright dates marked by ©)

FUNNY FACE— © January 30—Flip the Frog

COO-COO, THE MAGICIAN— © March 6—Flip the Frog

FLIP'S LUNCHROOM— © April 3—Flip the Frog

TECHNOCRACKED— © May 8—Flip the Frog

BULLONEY— © May 30—Flip the Frog

A CHINAMAN'S CHANCE— © June 27—Flip the Frog

PALEFACE— © August 12—Flip the Frog

PLAY BALL—September 16—Willie Whopper

SODA SQUIRT— © October 12—Flip the Frog

SPITE FLIGHT—October 14—Willie Whopper

STRATOS FEAR—November 11—Willie Whopper

**JACK AND THE BEANSTALK—December 23

1934 (Copyright dates marked by ©)

*DAVY JONES LOCKER—January 13—Willie Whopper

**THE LITTLE RED HEN—February 16

*HELL'S FIRE—February 17—Willie Whopper

**ROBIN HOOD, JR.—March 10—Willie Whopper

**THE BRAVE TIN SOLDIER—April 7

INSULTIN' THE SULTAN—April 14—Willie Whopper

**PUSS IN BOOTS—May 17

REDUCING CREME—May 19—Willie Whopper

RASSLIN' ROUND— © June 1—Willie Whopper

**THE QUEEN OF HEARTS—June 25

THE CAVE MAN— © July 6—Willie Whopper

JUNGLE JITTERS- © July 24—Willie Whopper

**ALADDIN AND HIS WONDERFUL LAMP—August 10

GOOD SCOUT— © September 1—Willie Whopper

VIVA WILLIE— © September 20—Willie Whopper

**THE HEADLESS HORSEMAN—October 1

**THE VALIANT TAILOR—October 29

**DON QUIXOTE—November 26

**JACK FROST—December 24

1935 (All Comicolor shorts)

LITTLE BLACK SAMBO—February 6

BREMEN TOWN MUSICIANS—March 6

OLD MOTHER HUBBARD—April 3

MARY'S LITTLE LAMB—May 1

SUMMERTIME—June 15

SINBAD THE SAILOR—July 30

THE THREE BEARS—August 30

BALLOONLAND (a.k.a. THE PINCUSHION MAN)—September 30

SIMPLE SIMON—November 15

HUMPTY DUMPTY—December 30

1936 (All Comicolor shorts)

ALI BABA—January 30

TOM THUMB—March 30

DICK WHITTINGTON'S CAT—May 30

LITTLE BOY BLUE—July 30

HAPPY DAYS—September 30

The Van Beuren Cartoons

Following is a complete list of cartoons produced by the Van Beuren Corporation, beginning with its first sound release. These shorts were released by Pathé, which in the early 1930s was absorbed by RKO Radio Pictures. RKO continued to release the Van Beuren product until the cartoon studio's demise in 1936.

Many of these films were retitled for home-movie and television release; we have listed as many of these alternate titles as it was possible to

*In color.

**A Comicolor short.

determine. Although we have listed only the originals, series titles and character names were also changed: Tom and Jerry became Dick and Larry, and Cubby Bear was renamed Brownie Bear.

Copyright dates are listed where it was impossible to ascertain accurate release dates for the cartoons.

The first Van Beuren cartoon to be released with sound was DINNER TIME, copyrighted December 17, 1928. It was five months later that the next sound film was made, accounting for the gap in time on this list.

1928 *(Copyright dates marked by* © *)*

DINNER TIME—© December 17—Aesop's Fables—Paul Terry

1929 *(All copyright dates)*

THE FAITHFUL PUP—May 4—Aesop's Fables—Paul Terry

CONCENTRATE—May 4—Aesop's Fables—Paul Terry

THE JAIL BREAKERS—May 6—Aesop's Fables—Paul Terry

WOODCHOPPERS—May 9—Aesop's Fables—Paul Terry

PRESTO CHANGO—May 20—Aesop's Fables—Paul Terry

SKATING HOUNDS—May 27—Aesop's Fables—Paul Terry

STAGE STRUCK—June 25—Aesop's Fables—Paul Terry

BUG HOUSE COLLEGE DAYS—July 23—Aesop's Fables—Paul Terry

HOUSE CLEANING TIME—July 23—Aesop's Fables—John Foster

A STONE AGE ROMANCE—August 1—Aesop's Fables—No credits

THE BIG SCARE—August 15—Aesop's Fables—Paul Terry

JUNGLE FOOL—September 15—Aesop's Fables—John Foster, Mannie Davis

FLY'S BRIDE—September 21—Aesop's Fables—John Foster

SUMMER TIME—October 11—Aesop's Fables—John Foster

MILL POND—October 18—Aesop's Fables—John Foster

BARNYARD MELODY—November 1—Aesop's Fables—John Foster

TUNING IN—November 7—Aesop's Fables—No credits

NIGHT CLUB—December 1—Aesop's Fables—John Foster, Mannie Davis

CLOSE CALL—December 1—Aesop's Fables—Harry Bailey

1930

THE IRON MAN—January 4—Aesop's Fables—John Foster

SHIP AHOY—January 7—Aesop's Fables—John Foster

SINGING SAPS—February 7—Aesop's Fables—John Foster, Mannie Davis

SKY SKIPPERS—February 14—Aesop's Fables—John Foster, Harry Bailey

GOOD OLD SCHOOLDAYS—March 7—Aesop's Fables—John Foster, Mannie Davis

FOOLISH FOLLIES—March 7—Aesop's Fables—John Foster, Harry Bailey

DIXIE DAYS—April 8—Aesop's Fables—John Foster, Mannie Davis

WESTERN WHOOPEE—April 10—Aesop's Fables—John Foster, Harry Bailey

THE HAUNTED SHIP—April 27—Aesop's Fables—John Foster, Mannie Davis

NOAH KNEW HIS ARK—May 25—Aesop's Fables—John Foster, Mannie Davis

OOM PAH PAH—May 30—Aesop's Fables—John Foster, Harry Bailey

A ROMEO ROBIN—June 22—Aesop's Fables—John Foster, Mannie Davis

JUNGLE JAZZ—July 6—Aesop's Fables—John Foster, Harry Bailey

SNOW TIME—July 20—Aesop's Fables—John Foster, Mannie Davis

HOT TAMALE—August 3—Aesop's Fables—John Foster

LAUNDRY BLUES—August 17—Aesop's Fables—John Foster, Mannie Davis

FROZEN FROLICS—August 31—Aesop's Fables—John Foster, Harry Bailey

FARM FOOLERY—September 14—Aesop's Fables—John Foster

CIRCUS CAPERS—September 28—Aesop's Fables—John Foster, Harry Bailey

MIDNIGHT—October 12—Aesop's Fables—John Foster, Mannie Davis

THE BIG CHEEZE—October 26—Aesop's Fables—John Foster

GYPPED IN EGYPT—November 9—Aesop's Fables—John Foster, Mannie Davis

THE OFFICE BOY—November 23— Aesop's Fables—John Foster, Harry Bailey

STONE AGE STUNTS—December 7—Aesop's Fables—John Foster

KING OF THE BUGS—December 21—Aesop's Fables—John Foster, Harry Bailey

1931

TOY TOWN TALES (a.k.a. TOYLAND ADVENTURE)—January 4—Aesop's Fables—John Foster, Mannie Davis

RED RIDING HOOD—January 18—Aesop's Fables—John Foster, Harry Bailey

THE ANIMAL FAIR—February 1—Aesop's Fables—John Foster, Mannie Davis

COWBOY BLUES—February 15—Aesop's Fables—John Foster, Harry Bailey

RADIO RACKET—March 1—Aesop's Fables—John Foster

COLLEGE CAPERS—March 15—Aesop's Fables—John Foster, Harry Bailey.

OLD HOKUM BUCKET—March 29—Aesop's Fables—No credits

CINDERELLA BLUES—April 12—Aesop's Fables—John Foster, Harry Bailey

MAD MELODY—April 26—Aesop's Fables—John Foster, Mannie Davis

THE FLY GUY—May 10—Aesop's Fables—John Foster, Harry Bailey

PLAY BALL—May 24—Aesop's Fables—John Foster, Mannie Davis

FISHERMAN'S LUCK—June 13—Aesop's Fables—John Foster, Harry Bailey

PALE FACE PUP—June 22—Aesop's Fables—John Foster, Mannie Davis

MAKING 'EM MOVE (a.k.a. IN A CARTOON STUDIO)—July 5—Aesop's Fables—John Foster, Harry Bailey

FUN ON THE ICE—July 19—Aesop's Fables—John Foster, Mannie Davis

WOT A NIGHT—August 1—Tom and Jerry—John Foster, George Stalling

BIG GAME—August 3—Aesop's Fables—No credits

LOVE IN A POND—August 17—Aesop's Fables—John Foster, Mannie Davis

FLY HI—August 31—Aesop's Fables—John Foster, Harry Bailey

POLAR PALS—September 5—Tom and Jerry—John Foster, George Rufle

THE FAMILY SHOE—September 14—Aesop's Fables—John Foster, Mannie Davis

FAIRYLAND FOLLIES—September 28—Aesop's Fables—John Foster, Harry Bailey

TROUBLE—October 10—Tom and Jerry—John Foster, George Stallings

HORSE COPS—October 12—Aesop's Fables—John Foster, J. J. McManus

COWBOY CABARET—October 26—Aesop's Fables—John Foster, Mannie Davis

IN DUTCH—November 9—Aesop's Fables—John Foster, Harry Bailey

JUNGLE JAM—November 14—Tom and Jerry—John Foster, George Rufle

THE LAST DANCE—November 23—Aesop's Fables—No credits

A SWISS TRICK—December 19—Tom and Jerry—John Foster, George Stallings

1932 *(Copyright dates marked by* ©*)*

TOY TIME—January 27—Aesop's Fables—John Foster, Harry Bailey

ROCKETEERS—January 30—Tom and Jerry—John Foster, George Rufle

A ROMEO MONK—February 20—Aesop's Fables—John Foster, Mannie Davis

RABID HUNTERS—February 27—Tom and Jerry—John Foster, George Stallings

FLY FROLIC—March 5—Aesop's Fables—John Foster, Harry Bailey

THE CAT'S CANARY—March 26—Aesop's Fables—John Foster, Mannie Davis

IN THE BAG—March 26—Tom and Jerry—John Foster, George Rufle

JOINT WIPERS—April 23—Tom and Jerry—John Foster, George Stallings

MAGIC ART—April 25—Aesop's Fables—John Foster, Harry Bailey

POTS AND PANS—May 14—Tom and Jerry—John Foster, George Rufle

HAPPY POLO—May 14—Aesop's Fables—No credits

SPRING ANTICS—May 21—Aesop's Fables—John Foster, Mannie Davis

THE TUBA TOOTER—June 4—Tom and Jerry—John Foster, George Stallings

CIRCUS ROMANCE—June 25—John Foster, Harry Bailey

PLANE DUMB—June 25—Tom and Jerry—John Foster, George Rufle

FARMERETTE— © June 28—Aesop's Fables—No credits

STONE AGE ERROR—July 9—Aesop's Fables—John Foster, Mannie Davis

REDSKIN BLUES—July 23—Tom and Jerry—John Foster, George Stallings

CHINESE JINKS—July 23—Aesop's Fables—John Foster, Mannie Davis

THE BALL GAME—July 30—Aesop's Fables—John Foster, George Rufle

WILD GOOSE CHASE—August 12—Aesop's Fables—John Foster, Mannie Davis

JOLLY FISH—August 19—Tom and Jerry—John Foster, George Stallings

NURSERY SCANDAL—August 26—Aesop's Fables—John Foster, Harry Bailey

BRING 'EM BACK HALF-SHOT—September 9—Aesop's Fables—John Foster, Mannie Davis

BARNYARD BUNK—September 16—Tom and Jerry—John Foster, George Rufle

DOWN IN DIXIE—September 23—Aesop's Fables—John Foster, Harry Bailey

CATFISH ROMANCE—October 7—Aesop's Fables—John Foster, Mannie Davis

A SPANISH TWIST—October 7—Tom and Jerry—John Foster, George Stallings

FEATHERED FOLLIES—October 21—Aesop's Fables—No credits

VENICE VAMP—November 4—Aesop's Fables—John Foster, Mannie Davis

PIANO TOONERS—November 11—Tom and Jerry—John Foster, George Rufle

HOKUM HOTEL—November 18—Aesop's Fables—John Foster, Harry Bailey

PENCIL MANIA—December 9—Tom and Jerry—John Foster, George Stallings

PICKANINNY BLUES— © December 12—Aesop's Fables —John Foster, Mannie Davis

A YARN OF WOOL— © December 16—Aesop's Fables—John Foster, Harry Bailey

BUGS AND BOOKS— © December 30—Aesop's Fables—John Foster, Mannie Davis

1933 *(Copyright dates marked by* © *)*

TIGHT ROPE TRICKS—January 6—Tom and Jerry—John Foster, George Rufle

SILVERY MOON— © January 13—Aesop's Fables—John Foster, Mannie Davis

A.M. TO P.M.— © January 20—Aesop's Fables—No credits

TUMBLE DOWN TOWN— © January 27—Aesop's Fables—John Foster, Harry Bailey

THE MAGIC MUMMY—February 7—Tom and Jerry—John Foster, George Stallings

OPENING NIGHT— © February 10—Cubby Bear—No credits

PANICKY PUP—February 24—Tom and Jerry—John Foster, Harry Bailey

LOVE'S LABOR WON— © March 10—Aesop's Fables—John Foster, Mannie Davis

THE LAST MAIL— © March 24—Cubby—Mannie Davis

HAPPY HOBOES—March 31—Tom and Jerry—George Stallings, George Rufle

PUZZLED PALS— © March 31—Tom and Jerry—George Stallings, Frank Sherman

RUNAWAY BLACKIE— © April 7—Cubby—Harry Bailey

HOOK AND LADDER HOKUM (a.k.a. FIRE FIRE)—April 28—Tom and Jerry—George Stallings, Tish Tash (Frank Tashlin)

BUBBLES AND TROUBLES— © April 28—Cubby—Mannie Davis

A DIZZY DAY— © May 5—Aesop's Fables—Harry Bailey

BARKING DOGS— © May 18—Aesop's Fables—Mannie Davis

IN THE PARK— © May 26—Tom and Jerry—Frank Sherman, George Rufle

THE BULLY'S END— © June 16—Aesop's Fables—Harry Bailey

INDIAN WHOOPEE— © July 7—Aesop's Fables—Mannie Davis

DOUGHNUTS— © July 10—Tom and Jerry—Frank Sherman, George Rufle

FRESH HAM— © July 12—Aesop's Fables—No credits

ROUGH ON RATS— © July 14—Aesop's Fables—Harry Bailey

THE PHANTOM ROCKET—July 31—Tom and Jerry—Frank Sherman, George Rufle

THE NUT FACTORY—August 11—Cubby—Mannie Davis

CUBBY'S WORLD FLIGHT—August 25—Cubby—Hugh Harman, Rudolf Ising

THE FATAL NOTE—September 29—The Little King—No credits

CUBBY'S PICNIC (a.k.a. PICNIC PROBLEMS)—October 6—Cubby—Steve Muffati, Eddie Donnelly

MARCHING ALONG—October 27—The Little King—James Tyer

THE GAY GAUCHO—November 3—Cubby—Rollin Hamilton, Tom McKimson

ON THE PAN—November 24—The Little King—No credits

GALLOPING FANNY (a.k.a. GALLOPING HOOVES)—December 1—Cubby—Steve Muffati, Eddie Donnelly

PALS (a.k.a. CHRISTMAS NIGHT)—December 22—The Little King—James Tyer

CROON CRAZY—December 29—Cubby—Steve Muffati

1934

THE RASSLIN' MATCH—January 5—Amos n' Andy—George Stallings

JEST OF HONOR—January 19—The Little King—George Stallings

SINISTER STUFF (a.k.a. VILLAIN PURSUES HER)—January 26—Cubby—Steve Muffati

THE LION TAMER—February 2—Amos n' Andy—George Stallings

JOLLY GOOD FELONS—February 16—The Little King—George Stallings

GOODE KNIGHT—February 23—Cubby—George Stallings

SULTAN PEPPER—March 16—The Little King—George Stallings

HOW'S CROPS? (a.k.a. BROWNIE'S VICTORY GARDEN)—March 23—Cubby—George Stallings

A ROYAL GOOD TIME—April 13—The Little King—George Stallings

CUBBY'S STRATOSPHERE FLIGHT—April 20—Cubby—George Stallings

ART FOR ART'S SAKE—May 11—The Little King—George Stallings

MILD CARGO (a.k.a. BROWNIE BUCKS THE JUNGLE)—May 18—Cubby—George Stallings

CACTUS KING—June 8—The Little King—George Stallings

FIDDLIN' FUN—June 15—Cubby—George Stallings

GRANDFATHER'S CLOCK—June 29—Toddle Tales—Burt Gillett, Jim Tyer

PASTRY TOWN WEDDING—July 27—Rainbow Parade—Burt Gillett, Ted Eshbaugh

ALONG CAME A DUCK—August 10—Toddle Tales—Burt Gillett, Steve Muffati

A LITTLE BIRD TOLD ME—September 7—Toddle Tales—Burt Gillett, Jim Tyer

THE PARROTVILLE FIRE DEPARTMENT—September 14—Rainbow Parade—Burt Gillett, Steve Muffati

1935

THE SUNSHINE MAKERS—January 11—Rainbow Parade—Burt Gillett, Ted Eshbaugh

PARROTVILLE OLD FOLKS—January 25—Rainbow Parade—Burt Gillett, Tom Palmer

JAPANESE LANTERNS—March 8—Rainbow Parade—Burt Gillett, Ted Eshbaugh

SPINNING MICE—April 5—Rainbow Parade—Burt Gillett, Tom Palmer

PICNIC PANIC—May 3—Rainbow Parade—Burt Gillett, Tom Palmer

THE FOXY TERRIER—May 31—Rainbow Parade—Burt Gillett

THE MERRY KITTENS—May 31—Rainbow Parade—Burt Gillett, James Culhane

PARROTVILLE POST OFFICE—June 28—Rainbow Parade—Burt Gillett, Tom Palmer

RAG DOG—July 19—Rainbow Parade—Burt Gillett

THE HUNTING SEASON—August 19—Rainbow Parade—Burt Gillett, Tom Palmer

SCOTTIE FINDS A HOME—August 23—Rainbow Parade—Burt Gillett

BIRD SCOUTS—September 20—Rainbow Parade—Burt Gillett, Tom Palmer

MOLLY MOO COW AND THE INDIANS—November 15—Rainbow Parade—Burt Gillett, Tom Palmer

MOLLY MOO COW AND THE BUTTERFLIES—November 15—Rainbow Parade—Burt Gillett, Tom Palmer

MOLLY MOO COW AND RIP VAN WINKLE—December 17—Rainbow Parade—Burt Gillett, Tom Palmer

1936

TOONERVILLE TROLLEY—January 17—Rainbow Parade—Burt Gillett, Tom Palmer

FELIX THE CAT AND THE GOOSE THAT LAID THE GOLDEN EGGS—February 7—Rainbow Parade (Felix the Cat)—Burt Gillett, Tom Palmer

MOLLY MOO COW AND ROBINSON CRUSOE—February 28—Rainbow Parade—Burt Gillett, Tom Palmer

NEPTUNE NONSENSE—March 20—Rainbow Parade (Felix the Cat)—Burt Gillett, Tom Palmer

BOLD KING COLE—May 29—Rainbow Parade (Felix the Cat)—Burt Gillett

A WAIF'S WELCOME—June 19—Rainbow Parade—Tom Palmer

TROLLEY AHOY—July 3—Rainbow Parade (Toonerville Trolley)—Burt Gillett

CUPID GETS HIS MAN—July 24—Rainbow Parade—Tom Palmer

IT'S A GREEK LIFE—August 2—Rainbow Parade—Dan Gordon

TOONERVILLE PICNIC—October 2—Rainbow Parade (Toonerville Trolley)—Burt Gillett

The Columbia/Screen Gems Cartoons

Following is a complete list of theatrical cartoons produced and/or distributed by Columbia Pictures, from the beginning of the sound era until 1948, when the company affiliated with UPA. It does *not* include the Walt Disney cartoons Columbia released from 1929 to 1932.

As explained in chapter 8, the majority of Charles Mintz's cartoons carried no director credit. Ben Harrison and Manny Gould were responsible for virtually every Krazy Kat cartoon through the late 1930s. Dick Huemer, Sid Marcus, and Art Davis supervised the first Scrappy shorts, with Marcus and Davis staying on the series after Huemer left in 1933. When the COLOR RHAPSODIES commanded the attention of Harrison, Gould, Marcus, and Davis in the latter part of the decade, Allen Rose and Harry Love assumed greater responsibility for the Scrappy and Krazy series. Official director credits were only assigned from the late thirties onward.

Columbia produced black-and-white cartoons longer than any other Hollywood studio. In the following list, distinctions between black-and-white and color cartoons can be made by series title. The COLOR RHAPSODIES and BARNEY GOOGLE cartoons were the only color releases in the 1930s. In the 1940s the FOX AND CROW, LI'L ABNER, and FLIPPY cartoons were also made in color. Everything else was in black and white until 1947.

In 1941 Columbia released three films produced by Cartoon Films Ltd. as part of a topical series called THIS CHANGING WORLD. THE CARPENTERS, BROKEN TREATIES, and HOW WAR CAME (an Academy Award nominee) were all directed by Paul Fennell.

The films below are listed in order of release; copyright dates are used only when it was impossible to ascertain a definite release date. Series titles are also given throughout.

One dagger next to the film title (†) indicates an Academy Award nominee.

1929

RATSKIN—August 15—Krazy Kat

CANNED MUSIC—September 12—Krazy Kat

PORT WHINES—October 10—Krazy Kat

SOLE MATES—November 7—Krazy Kat

FARM RELIEF—December 30—Krazy Kat

1930

THE CAT'S MEOW—January 2—Krazy Kat

SPOOK EASY—January 30—Krazy Kat

SLOW BEAU—February 27—Krazy Kat

DESERT SUNK—March 27—Krazy Kat

AN OLD FLAME—April 24—Krazy Kat

ALASKAN KNIGHTS—May 23—Krazy Kat

JAZZ RHYTHM—June 19—Krazy Kat

HONOLULU WILES—July 17—Krazy Kat

CINDERELLA—August 14—Krazy Kat

THE BAND MASTER—September 8—Krazy Kat

THE APACHE KID—October 9—Krazy Kat

LAMBS WILL GAMBLE—November 1—Krazy Kat

THE LITTLE TRAIL—December 3—Krazy Kat

1931

TAKEN FOR A RIDE—January—Krazy Kat

RODEO DOUGH—February 13—Krazy Kat

SWISS MOVEMENTS—April 4—Krazy Kat

DISARMAMENT CONFERENCE—April 27—Krazy Kat

SODA POPPA—May 29—Krazy Kat

THE STORK MARKET—July 11—Krazy Kat

YELP WANTED—July 16—Scrappy

SVENGARLIC—August 3—Krazy Kat

THE LITTLE PEST—August 15—Scrappy

THE WEENIE ROAST—September 14—Krazy Kat

SUNDAY CLOTHES—September 15—Scrappy

THE DOG SNATCHER—October 15—Scrappy

BARS AND STRIPES—October 15—Krazy Kat

HASH HOUSE BLUES—November 2—Krazy Kat

SHOWING OFF—November 11—Scrappy

MINDING THE BABY—November 16—Scrappy

THE RESTLESS SAX—December 1—Krazy Kat

1932 *(Copyright dates marked by ©)*

CHINATOWN MYSTERY—January 4—Scrappy

PIANO MOVER—January 4—Krazy Kat

LOVE KRAZY—© January 30—Krazy Kat

HOLLYWOOD GOES KRAZY—February 13—Krazy Kat

TREASURE RUNT—February 25—Scrappy

WHAT A KNIGHT—March 14—Krazy Kat

RAILROAD WRETCH—© March 31—Scrappy

SOLDIER OLD MAN—April 2—Krazy Kat

BIRTH OF JAZZ—April 13—Krazy Kat

THE PET SHOP—April 28—Scrappy

RITZY HOTEL—May 9—Krazy Kat

STEPPING STONES—May 17—Scrappy

HIC-CUPS THE CHAMP—May 28—Krazy Kat

BATTLE OF THE BARN—May 31—Scrappy

THE PAPER HANGER—June 21—Krazy Kat

FARE-PLAY—July 2—Scrappy

CAMPING OUT—August 10—Scrappy

LIGHTHOUSE KEEPING—August 15—Krazy Kat

SEEING STARS—September 12—Krazy Kat

THE BLACK SHEEP—September 17—Scrappy

PROSPERITY BLUES—October 8—Krazy Kat

THE GREAT BIRD MYSTERY—October 20—Scrappy

THE CRYSTAL GAZEBO—November 7—Krazy Kat

FLOP HOUSE—November 9—Scrappy

THE MINSTREL SHOW—November 21—Krazy Kat

SHOW TIME—November 30—Krazy Kat

THE BAD GENIUS—December 1—Scrappy

THE WOLF AT THE DOOR—December 29—Scrappy

1933

WEDDING BELLS—January 10—Krazy Kat

SASSY CATS—January 25—Scrappy

THE MEDICINE SHOW—February 7—Krazy Kat

SCRAPPY'S PARTY—February 13—Scrappy

WOODEN SHOES—February 25—Krazy Kat

THE BEER PARADE—March 4—Scrappy

BUNNIES AND BONNETS—March 29—Krazy Kat

THE BROADWAY MALADY—April 18—Krazy Kat

THE FALSE ALARM—April 22—Scrappy

RUSSIAN DRESSING—May 1—Krazy Kat

THE MATCH KID—May 9—Scrappy

TECHNORACKET—May 20—Scrappy

HOUSE CLEANING—June 1—Krazy Kat

THE WORLD'S AFFAIR—June 5—Scrappy

ANTIQUE ANTICS—June 14—Krazy Kat

OUT OF THE ETHER—September 5—Krazy Kat

MOVIE STRUCK—September 8—Scrappy

WHACKS MUSEUM—September 29—Krazy Kat

SANDMAN TALES—October 6—Scrappy

KRAZY SPOOKS—October 13—Krazy Kat

HOLLYWOOD BABIES—November 10—Scrappy

STAGE KRAZY—November 13—Krazy Kat

THE BILL POSTER—November 24—Krazy Kat

AUTO SHOW—December 8—Scrappy

THE CURIO SHOP—December 15—Krazy Kat

1934

THE AUTOGRAPH HUNTER—January 5—Krazy Kat

SCRAPPY'S ART GALLERY January 12—Scrappy

SCRAPPY'S TELEVISION—January 29—Scrappy

SOUTHERN EXPOSURE—February 5—Krazy Kat

TOM THUMB—February 16—Krazy Kat

AW, NURSE—March 9— Scrappy

CINDER ALLEY—March 9—Krazy Kat

BOWERY DAZE—March 30—Krazy Kat

SCRAPPY'S TOY SHOP—April 13—Scrappy

BUSY BUS—April 20—Krazy Kat

THE MASQUERADE PARTY—May 11—Krazy Kat

SCRAPPY'S DOG SHOW—May 18—Scrappy

SCRAPPY'S THEME SONG—June 15—Scrappy

SCRAPPY'S RELAY RACE—July 7—Scrappy

THE GREAT EXPERIMENT—July 27—Scrappy

SCRAPPY'S EXPEDITION—August 27—Scrappy

THE TRAPEZE ARTIST—September 1—Krazy Kat

KATNIPS OF 1940—October 12—Krazy Kat

CONCERT KID—November 2—Scrappy

†HOLIDAY LAND—November 9—Color Rhapsodies (Scrappy)

KRAZY'S WATERLOO—November 16—Krazy Kat

BABES AT SEA—November 30—Color Rhapsodies

HAPPY BUTTERFLY—December 20—Scrappy

GOOFY GONDOLAS—December 21—Krazy Kat

1935

THE GLOOM CHASERS—January 18—Scrappy

THE SHOEMAKER AND THE ELVES—January 20—Color Rhapsodies

THE BIRD MAN—February 1—Krazy Kat

THE GOLD GETTERS—March 1—Scrappy

HOTCHA MELODY—March 15—Krazy Kat

THE MAKE-BELIEVE REVUE—March 22—Color Rhapsodies

GRADUATION EXERCISES—April 12—Scrappy

THE PEACE CONDFERENCE—April 26—Krazy Kat

A CAT, A MOUSE AND A BELL—May 10—Color Rhapsodies

THE KING'S JESTER—May 20—Krazy Kat

SCRAPPY'S GHOST STORY—May 24—Scrappy

THE PUPPET MURDER CASE—June 21—Scrappy

LITTLE ROVER—June 28—Color Rhapsodies

SCRAPPY'S BIG MOMENT—July 28—Scrappy

GARDEN GAIETIES—August 1—Krazy Kat

NEIGHBORS—August 15—Color Rhapsodies

SCRAPPY'S TRAILER—August 29—Scrappy

MONKEY LOVE—September 12—Color Rhapsodies

A HAPPY FAMILY—September 27—Krazy Kat

BON BON PARADE—October 10—Color Rhapsodies

*TETCHED IN THE HEAD—October 24—Barney Google

LET'S RING DOORBELLS—November 7—Scrappy

PATCH MAH BRITCHES—December 19—Barney Google

KANNIBAL KAPERS—December 27—Krazy Kat

1936

SCRAPPY'S BOY SCOUTS—January 2—Scrappy

THE BIRD STUFFER—February 1—Krazy Kat

DOCTOR BLUEBIRD—February 5—Color Rhapsodies

SCRAPPY'S PONY—February 27—Scrappy

LI'L ANJIL—March 19—Krazy Kat

SPARK PLUG—April 12—Barney Google

FOOTBALL BUGS—April 29—Color Rhapsodies

MAJOR GOOGLE—May 24—Barney Google

SCRAPPY'S CAMERA TROUBLES—June 5—Scrappy

GLEE WORMS—June 24—Color Rhapsodies

PLAYING POLITICS—July 8—Scrappy

THE UNTRAINED SEAL—July 26—Color Rhapsodies

HIGHWAY SNOBBERY—August 9—Krazy Kat

THE NOVELTY SHOP—August 15—Color Rhapsodies

IN MY GONDOLA—September 3—Color Rhapsodies

LOONEY BALLOONISTS—September 24—Scrappy

MERRY MUTINEERS—October 2—Color Rhapsodies

KRAZY'S NEWSREEL—October 24—Krazy Kat

BIRDS IN LOVE—October 28—Color Rhapsodies

TWO LAZY CROWS—November 26—Color Rhapsodies

DIZZY DUCKS—November 28—Scrappy

A BOY AND HIS DOG—December 23—Color Rhapsodies

MERRY CAFE—December 26—Krazy Kat

*All Barney Googles in color.

1937

GIFTS FROM THE AIR—January 1—Color Rhapsodies

SKELETON FROLIC—January 29—Color Rhapsodies—Ub Iwerks

THE LYIN' HUNTER—February 12—Krazy Kat

MERRY MANNEQUINS—March 19—Color Rhapsodies—Ub Iwerks

PUTTIN' OUT THE KITTEN—March 26—Scrappy

LET'S GO—April 10—Color Rhapsodies

SCRAPPY'S BAND CONCERT—April 29—Scrappy

KRAZY'S RACE OF TIME—May 6—Krazy Kat

MOTHER HEN'S HOLIDAY—May 7—Color Rhapsodies

THE FOXY PUP—May 21—Color Rhapsodies

SCRAPPY'S MUSIC LESSON—June 4—Scrappy

THE STORK TAKES A HOLIDAY—June 11—Color Rhapsodies

THE MASQUE RAID—June 25—Krazy Kat

INDIAN SERENADE—July 16—Color Rhapsodies

I WANT TO BE AN ACTRESS—July 18—Scrappy

SPRING FESTIVAL—August 6—Color Rhapsodies

SCARY CROWS—August 20—Color Rhapsodies

SWING MONKEY SWING—September 10—Color Rhapsodies

CANINE CAPERS—September 16—Scrappy

THE FIRE PLUG—October 16—Scrappy

THE AIR HOSTESS—October 22—Color Rhapsodies

THE LITTLE MATCH GIRL—November 5—Color Rhapsodies

THE CLOCK GOES ROUND AND ROUND—November 6—Scrappy

RAILROAD RHYTHM—November 20—Krazy Kat

SCRAPPY'S NEWS FLASHES—December 8—Scrappy

HOLLYWOOD PICNIC—December 18—Color Rhapsodies

1938 *(Most shorts without director credits)*

THE NEW HOMESTEAD—January 7—Scrappy

BLUEBIRD'S BABY—January 21—Color Rhapsodies

SCRAPPY'S TRIP TO MARS—February 4—Scrappy

THE HORSE ON THE MERRY-GO-ROUND—February 17—Color Rapsodies—Ub Iwerks

SAD LITTLE GUINEA PIGS—February 22—Krazy Kat

THE AUTO CLINIC—March 4—Krazy Kat

THE FOOLISH BUNNY—March 26—Color Rhapsodies—Art Davis

SCRAPPY'S PLAYMATES—March 27—Scrappy

LITTLE BUCKAROO—April 11—Krazy Kat

SHOWTIME—April 14—Color Rhapsodies—Ub Iwerks

THE BIG BIRDCAST—May 13—Color Rhapsodies

KRAZY MAGIC—May 20—Krazy Kat

WINDOW SHOPPING—June 3—Color Rhapsodies—Sid Marcus

KRAZY'S TRAVEL SQUAWKS—July 4—Krazy Kat

POOR LITTLE BUTTERFLY—July 4—Color Rhapsodies—Ben Harrison

THE CITY SLICKER—July 8—Scrappy

POOR ELMER—July 22—Color Rhapsodies—Sid Marcus

THE FROG POND—August 12—Color Rhapsodies—Ub Iwerks

HOLLYWOOD GRADUATION—August 26—Color Rhapsodies—Art Davis

GYM JAMS—September 9—Krazy Kat

THE EARLY BIRD—September 16—Scrappy

ANIMAL CRACKER CIRCUS—September 23—Color Rhapsodies—Ben Harrison

HAPPY BIRTHDAY—October 7—Scrappy

HOT DOGS ON ICE—October 21—Krazy Kat

LITTLE MOTH'S BIG FLAME—November 3—Color Rhapsodies—Sid Marcus

MIDNIGHT FROLICS—November 24—Color Rhapsodies—Ub Iwerks

THE LONE MOUNTIE—December 10—Krazy Kat

THE KANGAROO KID—December 23—Color Rhapsodies—Ben Harrison

1939

SCRAPPY'S ADDED ATTRACTION—January 13—Scrappy

PEACEFUL NEIGHBORS—January 26—Color Rhapsodies—Sid Marcus

KRAZY'S BEAR TALE—January 27—Krazy Kat

THE GORILLA HUNT—February 24—Color Rhapsodies—Ub Iwerks

SCRAPPY'S SIDE SHOW—March 3—Scrappy

THE HAPPY TOTS—March 31—Color Rhapsodies—Ben Harrison

GOLF CHUMPS—April 6—Krazy Kat

THE HOUSE THAT JACK BUILT—April 14—Color Rhapsodies—Sid Marcus

A WORM'S EYE VIEW—April 28—Scrappy

KRAZY'S SHOE SHOP—May 12—Krazy Kat

LUCKY PIGS—May 26—Color Rhapsodies—Ben Harrison

SCRAPPY'S RODEO—June 2—Scrappy

NELL'S YELLS—June 30—Color Rhapsodies—Ub Iwerks

HOLLYWOOD SWEEPSTAKES—July 28—Rhapsodies—Ben Harrison

JITTERBUG KNIGHTS—August 11—Rhapsodies—Sid Marcus

THE CHARM BRACELET—September 1—Phantasies (Scrappy)

CROP CHASERS—September 22—Rhapsodies—Ub Iwerks

LITTLE LOST SHEEP—October 6—Fables (Krazy Kat)

DREAMS ON ICE—October 20—Rhapsodies—Sid Marcus

MOUNTAIN EARS—November 3—Rhapsodies—Manny Gould

MILLIONAIRE HOBO—November 24—Phantasies (Scrappy)

MOTHER GOOSE IN SWINGTIME—December 18—Rhapsodies—Manny Gould

PARK YOUR BABY—December 22—Fables (Scrappy)

1940 *(Most shorts without director credits)*

A BOY, A GUN AND BIRDS—January 12—Rhapsodies—Ben Harrison

THE MOUSE EXTERMINATOR—January 26—Phantasies (Krazy Kat)

THE HAPPY TOTS' EXPEDITION—February 9—Rhapsodies—Ben Harrison

MAN OF TIN—February 23—Phantasies (Scrappy)

BLACKBOARD REVUE—March 15—Rhapsodies—Ub Iwerks

PRACTICE MAKES PERFECT—April 5—Fables (Scrappy)

THE GREYHOUND AND THE RABBIT—April 19—Rhapsodies

FISH FOLLIES—May 10—Phantasies

THE EGG HUNT—May 31—Rhapsodies—Ub Iwerks

BARNYARD BABIES—June 14—Fables

YE OLDE SWAP SHOPPE—June 28—Rhapsodies—Ub Iwerks

NEWS ODDITIES—July 19—Phantasies

POOCH PARADE—July 19—Fables (Scrappy)

THE TIMID PUP—August 1—Rhapsodies—Ben Harrison

A PEEP IN THE DEEP—August 23—Fable (Scrappy)

TANGLED TELEVISION—August 30—Rhapsodies—Sid Marcus

SCHOOLBOY DREAMS—September 24—Phantasies (Scrappy)

FARMER TOM THUMB—September 27—Fables

MR. ELEPHANT GOES TO TOWN—October 4—Rhapsodies—Art Davis

HAPPY HOLIDAYS—October 25—Phantasies

MOUSE MEETS LION—October 25—Fables

THE MAD HATTER—November 3—Rhapsodies—Sid Marcus

WISE OWL—December 6—Rhapsodies—Ub Iwerks

PAUNCH 'N' JUDY—December 13—Fables

1941 *(Most shorts without director credits)*

A HELPING PAW—January 7—Rhapsodies—Sid Marcus

THE STREAMLINED DONKEY—January 17—Fables

THE LITTLE THEATRE—February 7—Phantasies (Scrappy)

WAY OF ALL PESTS—February 28—Rhapsodies—Art Davis

IT HAPPENED TO CRUSOE—March 14—Fables

THERE'S MUSIC IN YOUR HAIR—March 28—Phantasies

THE LAND OF FUN—April 18—Rhapsodies—Sid Marcus

THE CUTE RECRUIT—May 2—Phantasies

TOM THUMB'S BROTHER—June 12—Rhapsodies—Sid Marcus

KITTY GETS THE BIRD—June 13—Fables

THE WALL FLOWER—July 3—Phantasies

THE CUCKOO I.Q.—July 3—Rhapsodies—Sid Marcus

DUMB LIKE A FOX—July 18—Fables

PLAYING THE PIED PIPER—August 8—Fables

THE MERRY MOUSE CAFE—August 15—Phantasies

THE CRYSTAL GAZER—September 26—Phantasies

WHO'S ZOO IN HOLLYWOOD—October 17—Rhapsodies—Art Davis

THE GREAT CHEEZE MYSTERY—October 27—Fables—Art Davis

*THE FOX AND THE GRAPES—December 5—Rhapsodies (Fox and Crow)—Frank Tashlin

RED RIDING HOOD RIDES AGAIN—December 5—Rhapsodies—Sid Marcus

THE TANGLED ANGLER—December 26—Fables—Frank Tashlin

*All Fox and Crow shorts in color.

1942

A HOLLYWOOD DETOUR—January 23—Rhapsodies—Frank Tashlin

UNDER THE SHEDDING CHESTNUT TREE—February 22—Fables—Bob Wickersham

WACKY WIGWAMS—February 22—Rhapsodies—Alec Geiss

DOG MEETS DOG—March 6—Phantasies—Frank Tashlin

CONCERTO IN B-FLAT MINOR—March 20—Rhapsodies—Frank Tashlin

WOLF CHASES PIG—April 20—Fables—Frank Tashlin

THE WILD AND WOOZY WEST—April 30—Phantasies—Allen Rose

CINDERELLA GOES TO A PARTY—May 3—Rhapsodies—Frank Tashlin

A BATTLE FOR A BOTTLE—May 29—Phantasies—Frank Tashlin

WOODMAN SPARE THAT TREE—July 2—Rhapsodies—Bob Wickersham

THE BULLDOG AND THE BABY—July 3—Fables—Alec Geiss

OLD BLACKOUT JOE—August 27—Phantasies—Paul Sommer

SONG OF VICTORY—September 4—Rhapsodies—Bob Wickersham

THE GULLIBLE CANARY—September 18—Phantasies—Alec Geiss

THE DUMB CONSCIOUS MIND—October 23—Phantasies—Paul Sommer, John Hubley

TITO'S GUITAR—October 30—Rhapsodies—Bob Wickersham

MALICE IN SLUMBERLAND—November 20—Phantasies—Alec Geiss

TOLL BRIDGE TROUBLES—November 27—Rhapsodies (Fox and Crow)—Bob Wickersham

CHOLLY POLLY—December 18—Phantasies—Alec Geiss

KING MIDAS JUNIOR—December 18—Rhapsodies—Paul Sommer, John Hubley

1943

SLAY IT WITH FLOWERS—January 8—Rhapsodies (Fox and Crow)—Bob Wickersham

THE VITAMIN G MAN—January 22—Phantasies—Paul Sommer, John Hubley

*All Li'l Abner shorts in color.

THERE'S SOMETHING ABOUT A SOLDIER—February 26—Rhapsodies—Alec Geiss

KINDLY SCRAM—March 5—Phantasies—Alec Geiss

PROFESSOR SMALL AND MISTER TALL—March 26—Rhapsodies—Paul Sommer, John Hubley

WILLOUGHBY'S MAGIC HAT—April 30—Phantasies—Bob Wickersham

PLENTY BELOW ZERO—May 14—Rhapsodies (Fox and Crow)—Bob Wickersham

DUTY AND THE BEAST—May 28—Phantasies—Alec Geiss

HE CAN'T MAKE IT STICK—June 11—Rhapsodies—Paul Sommer, John Hubley

REE FOR TWO—June 21—Rhapsodies (Fox and Crow)—Bob Wickersham

MASS MOUSE MEETING—June 25—Phantasies—Alec Geiss

THE FLY IN THE OINTMENT—July 23—Phantasies—Paul Sommer

A HUNTING WE WON'T GO—August 23—Rhapsodies (Fox and Crow)—Bob Wickersham

DIZZY NEWSREEL—August 27—Phantasies—Alec Geiss

THE ROCKY ROAD TO RUIN—September 16—Rhapsodies—Paul Sommer

ROOM AND BORED—September 30—Fox and Crow—Bob Wickersham

NURSERY CRIMES—October 8—Phantasies—Alec Geiss

†IMAGINATION—October 29—Rhapsodies—Bob Wickersham

THE COCKY BANTAM (a.k.a. BLACK AND BLUE MARKET)—November 12—Phantasies—Paul Sommer

WAY DOWN YONDER IN THE CORN—November 25—Fox and Crow—Bob Wickersham

THE PLAYFUL PEST—December 3—Phantasy—Paul Sommer

THE HERRING MURDER MYSTERY—December 30—Rhapsodies—Don Roman

1944

POLLY WANTS A DOCTOR—January 6—Phantasy—Howard Swift

MAGIC STRENGTH—February 4—Phantasy—Bob Wickersham

THE DREAM KIDS—February 5—Fox and Crow—Bob Wickersham

*AMOOZIN BUT CONFOOZIN'—March 3—Li'l Abner

LIONEL LION—March 3—Phantasy—Paul Sommer

GIDDY YAPPING—April 7—Phantasy—Howard Swift

SADIE HAWKINS DAY—May 4—Li'l Abner—Bob Wickersham

DISILLUSIONED BLUEBIRD—May 26—Rhapsodies—Howard Swift

TANGLED TRAVELS—June 9—Phantasies—Alec Geiss

MR. FORE BY FORE—July 7—Phantasies—Howard Swift

CASE OF THE SCREAMING BISHOP—August 4—Phantasy—No Credits

A PEEKOOLYAR SITCHEEAYSHUN—August 11—Li'l Abner—Sid Marcus

MUTT'N BONES—August 25—Phantasies—Paul Sommer

MR. MOOCHER—September 8—Fox and Crow—Bob Wickersham

PORKULIAR PIGGY—October 13—Li'l Abner—Bob Wickersham

BE PATIENT, PATIENT—October 27—Fox and Crow—Bob Wickersham

AS THE FLY FLIES—November 17—Phantasies—Howard Swift

KICKAPOO JUICE—December 1—Li'l Abner—Howard Swift

THE EGG YEGG—December 8—Fox and Crow—Bob Wickersham

1945

DOG, CAT AND CANARY—January 5—Rhapsodies—Howard Swift

KU-KUNUTS—March 30—Fox and Crow—Bob Wickersham

FIESTA TIME—April 4—Rhapsodies—Bob Wickersham

GOOFY NEWS VIEWS—April 27—Phantasy—Sid Marcus

RIPPLING ROMANCE—June 21—Rhapsodies—Bob Wickersham

BOOBY SOCKS—July 12—Phantasy—Howard Swift, Bob Wickersham

HOT FOOT LIGHTS—August 2—Rhapsodies—Howard Swift

TREASURE JEST—August 30—Fox and Crow—Howard Swift

CARNIVAL COURAGE—September 6—Rhapsodies—Howard Swift

PHONEY BALONEY—September 13—Fox and Crow—Bob Wickersham

SIMPLE SIREN—September 20—Phantasy—Paul Sommer

RIVER RIBBER—October 4—Rhapsodies—(Prof. Small and Mr. Tall)—Paul Sommer

1946

*CATNIPPED—February 14—Flippy—Bob Wickersham

FOXEY FLATFOOTS—April 11—Fox and Crow—Bob Wickersham

KONGO-ROO—April 18—Phantasies—Howard Swift

POLAR PLAYMATES—April 25—Rhapsodies—Howard Swift

UNSURE RUNTS—May 16—Fox and Crow—Howard Swift

SNAP HAPPY TRAPS—June 6—Phantasies—Bob Wickersham

PICNIC PANIC—June 20—Rhapsodies—Bob Wickersham

THE SCHOONER THE BETTER—July 4—Phantasies—Howard Swift

CAGEY BIRD—July 18—Flippy—Howard Swift

MYSTO FOX—August 29—Fox and Crow—Bob Wickersham

SILENT TWEETMENT—September 19—Flippy—Bob Wickersham

1947 (All cartoons in color from this time on)

LOCO LOBO—January 9—Rhapsodies—Howard Swift

FOWL BRAWL—January 19—Phantasies—Howard Swift

UNCULTURED VULTURE—February 6—Phantasies—Bob Wickersham

COCKATOOS FOR TWO—February 13—Rhapsodies—Bob Wickersham

BIG HOUSE BLUES—March 6—Rhapsodies (Flippy)—Howard Swift

WACKY QUACKY—March 20—Phantasies—Alex Lovy

LEAVE US CHASE IT—May 15—Phantasies—Howard Swift

MOTHER HUBBA-HUBBA HUBBARD—May 29—Rhapsodies—Bob Wickersham

TOOTH OR CONSEQUENCES—June 5—Phantasies—Howard Smith

UP'N ATOM—July 10—Rhapsodies—Sid Marcus

SWISS TEASE—September 11—Rhapsodies—Sid Marcus

KITTY CADDY—November 6—Phantasies—Sid Marcus

BOSTON BEANY—December 4—Rhapsodies—Sid Marcus

*All Flippy shorts in color.

1948

TOPSY TURKEY—February 5—Phantasies—Sid Marcus

FLORA—March 18—Rhapsodies—Alex Lovy

SHORT SNORTS ON SPORTS—June 3—Phantasies—Alex Lovy

PICKLED PUSS—September 2—Rhapsodies—Howard Swift

LO, THE POOR BUFFAL—November 4—Rhapsodies—Alex Lovy

1949

COO-COO BIRD DOG—February 3—Phantasies—Sid Marcus

GRAPE NUTTY—April 14—Rhapsodies (Fox and Crow)—Alex Lovy

CAT-TASTROPHY—June 30—Rhapsodies—Sid Marcus

The Warner Brothers Cartoons

Following is a complete list of theatrical cartoons produced and/or released by Warner Brothers. Throughout the list, MM Stands for the Merrie Melodies series, and LT for Looney Tunes. When applicable, the starring character is also given in parentheses. Copyright dates are used when it was impossible to ascertain a definite release date.

This list does not include Warners' nontheatrical cartoons (such as the Private Snafu series), sponsored films, or feature-film work, most of which is cited by title in Chapter 9. In 1961 the company released its only extended-length short subject, THE ADVENTURES OF THE ROAD RUNNER, which combined new and old footage; the new footage was later adapted for the television shorts called ROAD RUNNER A GO GO and ZIP, ZIP, HURRAY.

There is one disputed title from 1931 called BOSKO'S ORPHANS, which was probably a working title for BIG-HEARTED BOSKO. These early cartoons were neither copyrighted nor assigned specific release dates; therefore, the 1930–32 shorts are grouped under reported year of release without further information.

The Looney Tunes series was produced in black and white until 1943; the Merrie Melodies experimented with color in 1934, then switched to color production full-time in 1935.

Because of the variation between directors' full names, which usually appeared on screen, and their more familiar nicknames, we have decided to list both, with the nickname in parentheses—for example, Charles M. (Chuck) Jones.

One dagger (†) next to a film title indicates an Academy Award nominee; a double dagger (‡) indicates an Academy Award winner.

1930 (No release dates or copyright dates)

SINKING IN THE BATHTUB—LT (Bosko)—Harman/Ising

CONGO JAZZ—LT (Bosko)—Harman/Ising

HOLD ANYTHING—LT (Bosko)—Harman/Ising

THE BOOZE HANGS HIGH—LT (Bosko)—Harman/Ising

BOX CAR BLUES—LT (Bosko)—Harman/Ising

BIG MAN FROM THE NORTH—LT (Bosko)—Harman/Ising

AIN'T NATURE GRAND—LT (Bosko)—Harman/Ising

UP'S N' DOWN'S—LT (Bosko)—Harman/Ising

THE DUM PATROL—LT (Bosko)—Harman/Ising

YODELING YOKELS—LT (Bosko)—Harman/Ising

BOSKO'S HOLIDAY—LT (Bosko)—Harman/Ising

THE TREE'S KNEE—LT (Bosko)—Harman/Ising

BOSKO SHIPWRECKED—LT (Bosko)—Harman/Ising

1931–1932 (No release dates or copyright dates)

BOSKO THE DOUGHBOY—LT (Bosko)—Hugh Harman

BOSKO'S SODA FOUNTAIN—LT (Bosko)—Hugh Harman

BOSKO'S FOX HUNT—LT (Bosko)—Hugh Harman

BOSKO'S ZOO—LT (Bosko)—Hugh Harman

BATTLING BOSKO—LT (Bosko)—Hugh Harman

BIG HEARTED BOSKO—LT (Bosko)—Hugh Harman

BOSKO'S PARTY—LT (Bosko)—Hugh Harman

BOSKO AND BRUNO—LT (Bosko)—Hugh Harman

BOSKO AND HONEY—LT (Bosko)—Hugh Harman

BOSKO'S DOG RACE—LT (Bosko)—Hugh Harman

BOSKO AT THE BEACH—LT (Bosko)—Hugh Harman

BOSKO'S STORE—LT (Bosko)—Hugh Harman

BOSKO THE LUMBERJACK—LT (Bosko)—Hugh Harman

LADY PLAY YOUR MANDOLIN—MM—Rudolf Ising

SMILE DARN YA SMILE—MM (Foxy)—Rudolf Ising

YOU DON'T KNOW WHAT YOU'RE DOING—MM (Piggy)—Rudolf Ising

HITTING THE TRAIL TO HALLELUJAH LAND—MM (Piggy)—Rudolf Ising

ONE MORE TIME—MM (Foxy)—Rudolf Ising

RED-HEADED BABY—MM—Rudolf Ising

PAGAN MOON—MM—Rudolf Ising

FREDDIE THE FRESHMAN—MM—Rudolf Ising

CROSBY-COLUMBO-VALLEE—MM—Rudolf Ising

GOOPY GEAR—MM (Goopy Gear)—Rudolf Ising

†IT'S GOT ME AGAIN—MM—Rudolf Ising

MOONLIGHT FOR TWO—MM (Goopy Gear)—Rudolf Ising

THE QUEEN WAS IN THE PARLOR—MM—Rudolf Ising

1933

I LOVE A PARADE—no date available—MM—Rudolf Ising

A GREAT BIG BUNCH OF YOU—January 9—MM—Rudolf Ising

RIDE HIM, BOSKO—January 16—LT (Bosko)—Hugh Harman

YOU'RE TOO CARELESS WITH YOUR KISSES—January 16—MM—Rudolf Ising

I WISH I HAD WINGS—January 16—MM—Rudolf Ising

THREE'S A CROWD—January 17—MM—Rudolf Ising

BOSKO'S DIZZY DATE—February 6—LT (Bosko)—Hugh Harman

THE SHANTY WHERE OLD SANTA CLAUS LIVES—February 6—MM—Rudolf Ising

BOSKO THE DRAWBACK—February 24—LT (Bosko)—Hugh Harman

BOSKO THE SPEED KING—March 22—LT (Bosko)—Hugh Harman

BOSKO'S WOODLAND DAZE—March 22—LT (Bosko)—Hugh Harman

BOSKO IN DUTCH—March 25—LT (Bosko)—I. (Friz) Freleng

BOSKO IN PERSON—April 10—LT (Bosko)—I. (Friz) Freleng

ONE STEP AHEAD OF MY SHADOW—April 12—MM—Rudolf Ising

YOUNG AND HEALTHY—April 19—MM—Rudolf Ising

BOSKO'S KNIGHT-MARE—June 8—LT (Bosko)—Hugh Harman

BOSKO THE SHEEPHERDER—June 14—LT (Bosko)—Hugh Harman

THE ORGAN GRINDER—June 19—MM—Rudolf Ising

WAKE UP THE GYPSY IN ME—June 19—MM—Rudolf Ising

BEAU BOSKO—July 1—LT (Bosko)—I. (Friz) Freleng

I LIKE MOUNTAIN MUSIC—August 3—MM—Rudolf Ising

SHUFFLE OFF TO BUFFALO—August 3—MM—I. (Friz) Freleng

BUDDY'S DAY OUT—September 9—LT (Buddy)—Jack King

BOSKO THE MUSKETEER—September 16—LT (Bosko)—Hugh Harman

BOSKO'S PICTURE SHOW—September 18—LT (Bosko)—I. (Friz) Freleng

WE'RE IN THE MONEY—September 19—MM—Rudolf Ising

I'VE GOT TO SING A TORCH SONG—September 23—MM—Tom Palmer

THE DISH RAN AWAY WITH THE SPOON—September 24—MM—Rudolf Ising

BOSKO'S MECHANICAL MAN—September 27—LT (Bosko)—Hugh Harman

BUDDY'S BEER GARDEN—November 11—LT (Buddy)—Earl Duval

BUDDY'S SHOWBOAT—December 9—LT (Buddy)—Jack King

SITTIN' ON A BACKYARD FENCE—December 16—MM—Earl Duval

1934

BUDDY THE GOB—January 13—LT (Buddy)—I. (Friz) Freleng

PETTIN' IN THE PARK—January 27—MM—Bernard Brown

*HONEYMOON HOTEL—February 17—MM—Earl Duval

BUDDY AND TOWSER—February 24—LT (Buddy)—I. (Friz) Freleng

*In color.

*BEAUTY AND THE BEAST—April 14—MM—I. (Friz) Freleng

BUDDY'S GARAGE—April 14—LT (Buddy)—Earl Duval

THOSE WERE WONDERFUL DAYS—April 26—MM—Bernard Brown

BUDDY'S TROLLEY TROUBLES—May 5—LT (Buddy)—I. (Friz) Freleng

GOIN' TO HEAVEN ON A MULE—May 19—MM—I. (Friz) Freleng

BUDDY OF THE APES—May 26—LT (Buddy)—Ben Hardaway

HOW DO I KNOW IT'S SUNDAY?—June 9—MM—I. (Friz) Freleng

BUDDY'S BEARCATS—June 23—LT (Buddy)—Jack King

WHY DO I DREAM THOSE DREAMS—June 30—MM—I. (Friz) Freleng

THE GIRL AT THE IRONING BOARD—August 23—MM—I. (Friz) Freleng

THE MILLER'S DAUGHTER—October 13—MM—I. (Friz) Freleng

SHAKE YOUR POWDER PUFF—October 17—MM—I. (Friz) Freleng

BUDDY THE DETECTIVE—October 17—LT (Buddy)—Jack King

BUDDY THE WOODSMAN—October 20—LT (Buddy)—Jack King

BUDDY'S CIRCUS—November 8—LT (Buddy)—Jack King

VIVA BUDDY—December 12—LT (Buddy)—Jack King

1935 (Copyright date marked by ©)

**RHYTHM IN THE BOW—February 1—MM—Ben Hardaway

COUNTRY BOY—February 18—MM—I. (Friz) Freleng

POP GOES MY HEART—MM—March 4—I. (Friz) Freleng

BUDDY'S ADVENTURES—March 5—LT (Buddy)—Ben Hardaway

BUDDY THE DENTIST—© March 5—LT (Buddy)—Ben Hardaway

BUDDY'S PONY EXPRESS—March 9—LT (Buddy)—Ben Hardaway

BUDDY'S THEATRE—April 1—LT (Buddy)—Ben Hardaway

ALONG FLIRTATION WALK—April 6—MM—I. (Friz) Freleng

THOSE BEAUTIFUL DAMES—April 6—MM—I. (Friz) Freleng

BUDDY OF THE LEGION—April 6—LT (Buddy)—Ben Hardaway

MY GREEN FEDORA—May 4—MM—I. (Friz) Freleng

BUDDY'S LOST WORLD—May 18—LT (Buddy)—Jack King

MR. AND MRS. IS THE NAME—June 3—MM—I. (Friz) Freleng

INTO YOUR DANCE—June 8—MM—I. (Friz) Freleng

BUDDY'S BUG HUNT—June 22—LT (Buddy)—Jack King

I HAVEN'T GOT A HAT—July 1—MM—(Porky and Beans)—I. (Friz) Freleng

BUDDY IN AFRICA—July 6—LT (Buddy)—Ben Hardaway

THE COUNTRY MOUSE—July 13—MM—I. (Friz) Freleng

BUDDY STEPS OUT—July 20—LT (Buddy)—Jack King

MERRY OLD SOUL—August 17—MM—I. (Friz) Freleng

BUDDY THE GEE MAN—August 24—LT (Buddy)—Jack King

THE LADY IN RED—September 21—MM—I. (Friz) Freleng

A CARTOONIST'S NIGHTMARE—September 21—LT (Beans)—Jack King

LITTLE DUTCH PLATE—October 19—MM—I. (Friz) Freleng

HOLLYWOOD CAPERS—October 19—LT (Beans)—Jack King

1936 (Copyright dates marked by ©)

GOLDDIGGERS OF '49—January 6—LT (Beans, with Porky)—Fred (Tex) Avery

I WANNA PLAY HOUSE—January 18—MM—I. (Friz) Freleng

BILLBOARD FROLICS—© January 27—MM—I. (Friz) Freleng

THE PHANTOM SHIP—February 1—LT—Jack King

THE CAT CAME BACK—February 8—MM—I. (Friz) Freleng

BOOM, BOOM—February 29—LT (Porty Pig)—Jack King

PAGE MISS GLORY—March 7—MM—Fred (Tex) Avery

ALPINE ANTICS—© March 9—LT—Jack King

THE FIRE ALARM—© March 9—LT (Ham and Ex)—Jack King

THE BLOW-OUT—April 4—LT (Porky Pig)—Fred (Tex) Avery

FLOWERS FOR MADAME—April 6—MM—I. (Friz) Freleng

I'M A BIG SHOT NOW—April 11—MM—I. (Friz) Freleng

WESTWARD WHOA!—April 25—LT (Porky Pig)—Jack King

*In color
**Last MERRIE MELODIE filmed in black and white.

PLANE DIPPY—April 30—LT (Porky Pig)—Fred (Tex) Avery

LET IT BE ME—May 2—MM—I. (Friz) Freleng

I'D LOVE TO TAKE ORDERS FROM YOU—May 16—MM—Fred (Tex) Avery

FISH TALES—May 23—LT—Jack King

BINGO CROSBYANA—May 30—MM—I. (Friz) Freleng

SHANGHAIED SHIPMATES—June 20—LT—Jack King

WHEN I YOO HOO—June 27—MM—I. (Friz) Freleng

PORKY'S PET—July 11—LT (Portky Pig)—Jack King

I LOVE TO SINGA—July 18—MM—Fred (Tex) Avery

PORKY THE RAINMAKER—August 1—LT (Porky Pig)—Fred (Tex) Avery

SUNDAY, GO TO MEETIN' TIME—August 8—MM—I. (Friz) Freleng

PORKY'S POULTRY PLANT—August 22—LT (Porky Pig)—Frank Tashlin

AT YOUR SERVICE, MADAME—August 29—MM—I. (Friz) Freleng

TOY TOWN HALL—September 19—MM—I. (Friz) Freleng

MILK AND MONEY—October 3—LT—Porky Pig—Fred (Tex) Avery

PORKY'S MOVING DAY—October 7—LT (Porky Pig)—Jack King

BOULEVARDIER FROM THE BRONX—October 10—MM—I. (Friz) Freleng

LITTLE BEAU PORKY—October 24—LT (Porky Pig)—Frank Tash (Tashlin)

DON'T LOOK NOW—November 7—MM—Fred (Tex) Avery

THE VILLAGE SMITHY—November 14—LT (Porky Pig)—Fred (Tex) Avery

COO-COO NUT GROVE—November 29—MM—I. (Friz) Freleng

PORKY IN THE NORTHWOODS—December 19—LT (Porky Pig)—Frank Tash (Tashlin)

1937

HE WAS HER MAN—January 2—MM—I. (Friz) Freleng

PORKY THE WRESTLER—January—LT (Porky Pig)—Fred (Tex) Avery

PIGS IS PIGS—January 30—MM—I. (Friz) Freleng

PORKY'S ROAD RACE—February 6—LT (Porky Pig)—Frank Tash (Tashlin)

I ONLY HAVE EYES FOR YOU—March 6—MM—Fred (Tex) Avery

PICADOR PORKY—March 13—LT (Porky Pig)—Fred (Tex) Avery

THE FELLA WITH THE FIDDLE—March 27—MM—I. (Friz) Freleng

SHE WAS AN ACROBAT'S DAUGHTER—April 10—MM—I. (Friz) Freleng

PORKY'S ROMANCE—April 17—LT (Porky Pig)—Frank Tash (Tashlin)

PORKY'S DUCK HUNT—April 17—LT (Porky Pig)—Fred (Tex) Avery

AIN'T WE GOT FUN—May 1—MM—Fred (Tex) Avery

PORKY AND GABBY—May 15—LT (Porky Pig)—Ub Iwerks

CLEAN PASTURES—May 22—MM—I. (Friz) Freleng

PORKY'S BUILDING—June 19—LT (Porky Pig)—Frank Tash (Tashlin)

STREAMLINED GRETA GREEN—June 19—MM—I. (Friz) Freleng

SWEET SIOUX—June 26—MM—I. (Friz) Freleng

PORKY'S SUPER SERVICE—July 3—LT (Porky Pig)—Ub Iwerks

UNCLE TOM'S BUNGALOW—July 12—MM—Fred (Tex) Avery

EGGHEAD RIDES AGAIN—July 17—MM (Egghead)—Fred (Tex) Avery

PORKY'S BADTIME STORY—July 24—LT (Porky Pig)—Robert Clampett

PLENTY OF MONEY AND YOU—July 31—MM—I. (Friz) Freleng

PORKY'S RAILROAD—August 7—LT (Porky Pig)—Frank Tashlin

A SUNBONNET BLUE—August 21—MM—Fred (Tex) Avery

GET RICH QUICK PORKY—August 28—LT (Porky Pig)—Robert Clampett

SPEAKING OF THE WEATHER—September 4—MM—Frank Tashlin

PORKY'S GARDEN—September 11—LT (Porky Pig)—Fred (Tex) Avery

DOG DAZE—September 18—MM—I. (Friz) Freleng

I WANNA BE A SAILOR—September 25—MM—Fred (Tex) Avery

ROVER'S RIVAL—October 9—LT (Porky Pig)—Robert Clampett

THE LYIN' MOUSE—October 16—MM—I. (Friz) Freleng

THE CASE OF THE STUTTERING PIG—October 30—LT (Porky Pig)—Frank Tashlin

LITTLE RED WALKING HOOD—November 6—MM (Egghead)—Fred (Tex) Avery

PORKY'S DOUBLE TROUBLE—November 13—LT (Porky Pig)—Frank Tashlin

THE WOODS ARE FULL OF CUCKOOS—December 4—MM—Frank Tashlin

PORKY'S HERO AGENCY—December 4—LT (Porky Pig)—Robert Clampett

SEPTEMBER IN THE RAIN—December 18—MM—I. (Friz) Freleng

1938 *(Copyright dates marked by ©)*

DAFFY DUCK AND EGGHEAD—January 1—MM (Daffy Duck, Egghead)—Fred (Tex) Avery

PORKY'S POPPA—January 15—LT (Porky Pig)—Robert Clampett

MY LITTLE BUCKAROO—January 29—MM—I. (Friz) Freleng

PORKY AT THE CROCADERO—February 5—LT (Porky Pig)—Frank Tashlin

JUNGLE JITTERS—February 19—MM—I. (Friz) Freleng

WHAT PRICE PORKY—February 26—LT (Porky Pig)—Robert Clampett

SNEEZING WEASEL—March 12—MM—Fred (Tex) Avery

PORKY'S PHONEY EXPRESS—March 19—LT (Porky Pig)—Cal Dalton, Cal Howard

A STAR IS HATCHED—April 2—MM—I. (Friz) Freleng

PORKY'S FIVE AND TEN—April 16—LT (Porky Pig)—Robert Clampett

PENGUIN PARADE—April 23—MM—Fred (Tex) Avery

PORKY'S HARE HUNT—April 30—LT (Porky Pig)—Ben Hardaway, Cal Dalton

NOW THAT SUMMER IS GONE—May 14—MM—Frank Tashlin

INJUN TROUBLE—May 21—LT (Porky Pig)—Robert Clampett

THE ISLE OF PINGO PONGO—May 28—MM (Egghead)—Fred (Tex) Avery

PORKY THE FIREMAN—June 4—LT (Porky Pig)—Frank Tashlin

KATNIP KOLLEGE—June 11—MM—Ben Hardaway, Cal Dalton

PORKY'S PARTY—June 25—LT (Porky Pig)—Robert Clampett

HAVE YOU GOT ANY CASTLES?—June 25—MM—Frank Tashlin

LOVE AND CURSES—July 9—MM—Ben Hardaway, Cal Dalton

CINDERELLA MEETS FELLA—July 23—MM (Egghead)—Fred (Tex) Avery

PORKY'S SPRING PLANTING—July 25—LT (Porky Pig)—Frank Tashlin

PORKY AND DAFFY—August 6—LT (Porky Pig, Daffy Duck)—Robert Clampett

THE MAJOR LIED TILL DAWN—August 13—MM—Frank Tashlin

WHOLLY SMOKE—August 27—LT (Porky Pig)—Frank Tashlin

A FEUD THERE WAS—September 24—MM—Egghead (Elmer Fudd)—Fred (Tex) Avery

PORKY IN WACKYLAND—September 24—LT (Porky Pig)—Robert Clampett

LITTLE PANCHO VANILLA—October 8—MM—Frank Tashlin

PORKY'S NAUGHTY NEPHEW—October 15—LT (Porky Pig)—Robert Clampett

JOHNNY SMITH AND POKER HUNTAS—October 22—MM (Egghead)—Fred (Tex) Avery

PORKY IN EGYPT—November 5—LT (Porky Pig)—Robert Clampett

YOU'RE AN EDUCATION—November 5—MM—Frank Tashlin

THE NIGHT WATCHMAN—November 19—MM—Charles M. (Chuck) Jones

THE DAFFY DOC—November 26—LT (Daffy Duck)—Robert Clampett

DAFFY DUCK IN HOLLYWOOD—December 12—MM (Daffy Duck)—Fred (Tex) Avery

A LAD IN BAGDAD—© December 15—MM—Ben Hardaway, Cal Dalton

CRACKED ICE—© December 16—MM—Frank Tashlin

PORKY THE GOB—December 17—LT (Porky Pig)—Ben Hardaway, Cal Dalton

COUNT ME OUT—December 17—MM—Ben Hardaway, Cal Dalton

MICE WILL PLAY—December 31—MM—Fred (Tex) Avery

1939

THE LONE STRANGER AND PORKY—January 7—LT (Porky Pig)—Robert Clampett

DOG GONE MODERN—January 14—MM—Charles M. (Chuck) Jones

IT'S AN ILL WIND—January 28—LT (Porky Pig)—Ben Hardaway, Cal Dalton

HAMATEUR NIGHT—January 28—MM (Egghead)—Fred (Tex) Avery

ROBIN HOOD MAKES GOOD—February 11—MM—Charles M. (Chuck) Jones

PORKY'S TIRE TROUBLE—February 18—LT (Porky Pig)—Robert Clampett

GOLD RUSH DAZE—February 25—MM—Ben Hardaway, Cal Dalton

PORKY'S MOVIE MYSTERY—March 11—LT—Porky Pig, Robert Clampett

A DAY AT THE ZOO—March 11—MM (Egghead)—Fred (Tex) Avery

PRESTO CHANGE-O—March 25—MM (formative Bugs Bunny)—Charles M. (Chuck) Jones

BARS AND STRIPES FOREVER—April 8—MM—Ben Hardaway, Cal Dalton

CHICKEN JITTERS—April 22—LT (Porky Pig)—Robert Clampett

DAFFY DUCK AND THE DINOSAUR—April 22—MM (Daffy Duck)—Charles M. (Chuck) Jones

PORKY AND TEABISCUIT—May 1— LT (Porky Pig)—Ben Hardaway, Cal Dalton

THUGS WITH DIRTY MUGS—May 6—MM—Fred (Tex) Avery

KRISTOPHER KOLUMBUS, JR.—May 13—LT (Porky Pig)—Robert Clampett

NAUGHTY BUT MICE—May 20—MM (Sniffles)—Charles M. (Chuck) Jones

POLAR PALS—June 3—LT (Porky Pig)—Robert Clampett

BELIEVE IT OR ELSE—June 3—MM (Egghead)—Fred (Tex) Avery

HOBO GADGET BAND—June 17—MM—Ben Hardaway, Cal Dalton

SCALP TROUBLE—June 24—LT (Porky Pig, Daffy Duck)—Robert Clampett

OLD GLORY—July 1—MM (Porky Pig)—Charles M. (Chuck) Jones

PORKY'S PICNIC—July 15—LT (Porky Pig)—Robert Clampett

DANGEROUS DAN MCFOO—July 15—MM—Fred (Tex) Avery

SNOW MAN'S LAND—July 29—MM—Charles M. (Chuck) Jones

WISE QUACKS—August 5—LT (Daffy Duck)—Robert Clampett

HARE-UM SCARE-UM—August 12—MM (formative Bugs Bunny)—Ben Hardaway, Cal Dalton

†DETOURING AMERICA—August 25—MM—Fred (Tex) Avery

PORKY'S HOTEL—September 2—LT (Porky Pig)—Robert Clampett

LITTLE BROTHER RAT—September 2—MM (Sniffles)—Charles M. (Chuck) Jones

SIOUX ME—September 9—MM—Ben Hardaway, Cal Dalton

JEEPERS CREEPERS—September 23—LT (Porky Pig)—Robert Clampett

LAND OF THE MIDNIGHT FUN—September 23—MM—Fred (Tex) Avery

THE LITTLE LION HUNTER—October 7—MM (Inki)—Charles M. (Chuck) Jones

THE GOOD EGG—October 21—MM—Charles M. (Chuck) Jones

NAUGHTY NEIGHBORS—November 4—LT (Porky Pig)—Robert Clampett

FRESH FISH—November 4—MM—Fred (Tex) Avery

PIED PIPER PORKY—November 4—LT (Porky Pig)—Robert Clampett

FAGIN'S FRESHMEN—November 18—MM—Ben Hardaway, Cal Dalton

PORKY THE GIANT KILLER—November 18—LT (Porky Pig)—I. (Friz) Freleng

SNIFFLES AND THE BOOKWORM—December 2—MM (Sniffles)—Charles M. (Chuck) Jones

THE FILM FAN—December 16—LT (Porky Pig)—Robert Clampett

SCREWBALL FOOTBALL—December 16—MM—Fred (Tex) Avery

THE CURIOUS PUPPY—December 30—MM—Charles M. (Chuck) Jones

1940 *(Copyright date marked by ©)*

PORKY'S LAST STAND—January 6—LT (Porky Pig)—Robert Clampett

EARLY WORM GETS THE BIRD—January 13—MM—Fred (Tex) Avery)

AFRICA SQUEAKS—January 27—LT (Porky Pig)—Robert Clampett

MIGHTY HUNTERS—January 27—MM (Canyon Kiddies)—Charles M. (Chuck) Jones

ALI BABA BOUND—February 10—LT (Porky Pig)—Robert Clampett

BUSY BAKERS—February 10—MM—Ben Hardaway, Cal Dalton

ELMER'S CANDID CAMERA—March 2—MM (Elmer Fudd, with formative Bugs Bunny)—Charles M. (Chuck) Jones

PILGRIM PORKY—March 16—LT (Porky Pig)—Robert Clampett

CROSS COUNTRY DETOURS—March 16—MM—Fred (Tex) Avery

CONFEDERATE HONEY—March 30—MM—I. (Friz) Freleng

SLAP HAPPY PAPPY—April 13—LT (Porky Pig)—Robert Clampett

THE BEAR'S TALE—April 13—MM—Fred (Tex) Avery

THE HARDSHIP OF MILES STANDISH—April 13—MM (Elmer Fudd)—I. (Friz) Freleng

YOU OUGHT TO BE IN PICTURES—April 27—LT (Porky Pig, Daffy Duck)—I. (Friz) Freleng

PORKY'S POOR FISH—© April 27—LT (Porky Pig)—Robert Clampett

SNIFFLES TAKES A TRIP—May 11—MM (Sniffles)—Charles M. (Chuck) Jones

A GANDER AT MOTHER GOOSE—May 25—MM—Fred (Tex) Avery

THE CHEWIN' BRUIN—June 8—LT (Porky Pig)—Robert Clampett

TOM THUMB IN TROUBLE—June 8—MM—Charles M. (Chuck) Jones

CIRCUS TODAY—June 22—MM—Fred (Tex) Avery

PORKY'S BASEBALL BROADCAST—July 6—LT (Porky Pig)—I. (Friz) Freleng

LITTLE BLABBERMOUSE—July 6—MM—I. (Friz) Freleng

THE EGG COLLECTOR—July 20—MM (Sniffles)—Charles M. (Chuck) Jones

†A WILD HARE—July 27—MM (Bugs Bunny, Elmer Fudd)—Fred (Tex) Avery

GHOST WANTED—August 10—MM—Charles M. (Chuck) Jones

PATIENT PORKY—August 24—LT (Porky Pig)—Robert Clampett

CEILING HERO—August 24—MM—Fred (Tex) Avery

MALIBU BEACH PARTY—September 14—MM—I. (Friz) Freleng

CALLING DR. PORKY—September 21—LT (Porky Pig)—I. (Friz) Freleng

STAGE FRIGHT—September 28—MM—Charles M. (Chuck) Jones

PREHISTORIC PORKY—October 12—LT (Porky Pig)—Robert Clampett

HOLIDAY HIGHLIGHTS—October 12—MM—Fred (Tex) Avery

GOOD NIGHT ELMER—October 26—MM (Elmer Fudd)—Charles M. (Chuck) Jones

SOUR PUSS—November 2—LT (Porky Pig)—Robert Clampett

WACKY WILDLIFE—November 9—MM—Fred (Tex) Avery

BEDTIME FOR SNIFFLES—November 23—MM (Sniffles)—Charles M. (Chuck) Jones

PORKY'S HIRED HAND—November 30—LT (Porky Pig)—I. (Friz) Freleng

OF FOX AND HOUNDS—December 7—MM—Fred (Tex) Avery

TIMID TOREADOR—December 21—LT—Norman McCabe, Robert Clampett

SHOP, LOOK AND LISTEN—December 21—MM (Little Blabbermouse)—I. (Friz) Freleng

1941

ELMER'S PET RABBIT—January 4—MM (Bugs Bunny, Elmer Fudd)—Charles M. (Chuck) Jones

PORKY'S SNOOZE REEL—January 11—LT (Porky Pig)—Norman McCabe, Robert Clampett

THE FIGHTING 69½TH—January 18—MM—I. (Friz) Freleng

SNIFFLES BELLS THE CAT—February 1—MM (Sniffles)—Charles M. (Chuck) Jones

THE HAUNTED MOUSE—February 15—LT—Fred (Tex) Avery

THE CRACKPOT QUAIL—February 15—MM—Fred (Tex) Avery

THE CAT'S TAIL—March 1—MM—I. (Friz) Freleng

JOE GLOW, THE FIREFLY—March 8—LT—Charles M. (Chuck) Jones

TORTOISE BEATS HARE—March 15—MM (Bugs Bunny)—Fred (Tex) Avery

PORKY'S BEAR FACTS—March 29—LT (Porky Pig)—I. (Friz) Freleng

GOOFY GROCERIES—March 29—MM—Robert Clampett

TOY TROUBLE—April 12—MM (Sniffles)—Charles M. (Chuck) Jones

PORKY'S PREVIEW—April 19—LT (Porky Pig)—Fred (Tex) Avery

THE TRIAL OF MR. WOLF—April 26—MM—I. (Friz) Freleng

PORKY'S ANT—May 10—LT (Porky Pig)—Charles M. (Chuck) Jones

FARM FROLICS—May 10—MM—Robert Clampett

†HOLLYWOOD STEPS OUT—May 24—MM—Fred (Tex) Avery

A COY DECOY—June 7—LT (Porky Pig, Daffy Duck)—Robert Clampett

†HIAWATHA'S RABBIT HUNT—June 7—MM—I. (Friz) Freleng

PORKY'S PRIZE PONY—June 21—LT (Porky Pig)—Charles M. (Chuck) Jones

THE WACKY WORM—June 21—MM—I. (Friz) Freleng

MEET JOHN DOUGHBOY—July 5—LT—Robert Clampett

THE HECKLING HARE—July 5—MM (Bugs Bunny)—Fred (Tex) Avery

INKI AND THE LION—July 19—MM—(Inki)—Charles M. (Chuck) Jones

AVIATION VACATION—August 2—MM—Fred (Tex) Avery

WE, THE ANIMALS, SQUEAK—August 9—LT (Porky Pig)—Robert Clampett

SPORTS CHUMPIONS—August 16—MM—I. (Friz) Freleng

HENPECKED DUCK—August 30—LT (Porky Pig, Daffy Duck)—Robert Clampett

SNOW TIME FOR COMEDY—August 30—MM—Charles M, (Chuck) Jones

ALL THIS AND RABBIT STEW—September 13—MM (Bugs Bunny)—Fred (Tex) Avery

NOTES TO YOU—September 20—LT (Porky Pig)—I. (Friz) Freleng

THE BRAVE LITTLE BAT—September 27—MM (Sniffles)—Charles M. (Chuck) Jones

ROBINSON CRUSOE, JR.—October 11—LT (Porky Pig)—Norman McCabe

THE BUG PARADE—October 11—MM—Fred (Tex) Avery

ROOKIE REVUE—October 25—MM—I. (Friz) Freleng

PORKY'S POOCH—November 1—LT (Porky Pig)—Robert Clampett

SADDLE SILLY—November 8—MM—Charles M. (Chuck) Jones

THE CAGEY CANARY—November 22—MM—Fred (Tex) Avery

PORKY'S MIDNIGHT MATINEE—November 22—LT (Porky Pig)—Charles M. (Chuck) Jones

†RHAPSODY IN RIVETS—December 6—MM—I. (Friz) Freleng

WABBIT TWOUBLE—December 20—MM (Bugs Bunny, Elmer Fudd)—Wobert Cwampett

1942

HOP, SKIP AND A CHUMP—January 3—MM—I. (Friz) Freleng

PORKY'S PASTRY PIRATES—January 17—LT (Porky Pig)—I. (Friz) Freleng

THE BIRD CAME C.O.D.—January 17—MM (Conrad Cat)—Charles M. (Chuck) Jones

ALOHA HOOEY—January 24—MM—Fred (Tex) Avery

WHO'S WHO IN THE ZOO—January 31—LT—Norman McCabe

CONRAD THE SAILOR—February 14—MM (Conrad Cat)—Charles M. (Chuck) Jones

PORKY'S CAFE—February 21—LT (Porky Pig)—Charles M. (Chuck) Jones

CRAZY CRUISE—February 28—MM—Fred (Tex) Avery

THE WABBIT WHO CAME TO SUPPER—March 28—MM (Bugs Bunny, Elmer Fudd)—I. (Friz) Freleng

SAPS IN CHAPS—April 11—LT—I. (Friz) Freleng

HORTON HATCHES THE EGG—April 11—MM—Robert Clampett

DOG TIRED—April 25—MM—Charles M. (Chuck) Jones

DAFFY'S SOUTHERN EXPOSURE—May 2—LT (Daffy Duck)—Norm McCabe

THE WACKY WABBIT—May 2—MM (Bugs Bunny, Elmer Fudd)—Robert Clampett

THE DRAFT HORSE—May 9—MM—Charles M. Jones

NUTTY NEWS—May 23—LT—Robert Clampett

LIGHTS FANTASTIC—May 33—MM—I. (Friz) Freleng

HOBBY HORSE LAFFS—June 6—LT—Norm McCabe

HOLD THE LION, PLEASE—June 6—MM (Bugs Bunny—Charles M. (Chuck) Jones

GOPHER GOOFY—June 20—LT—Norman McCabe

DOUBLE CHASER—June 20—MM—I. (Friz) Freleng

WACKY BLACKOUTS—July 4—LT—Robert Clampett

BUGS BUNNY GETS THE BOID—July 4—/MM (Bugs Bunny)—Robert Clampett

FONEY FABLES—July 18—MM—I. (Friz) Freleng

THE DUCKTATOR—August 1—LT—Norman McCabe

THE SQUAWKIN' HAWK—August 1—MM (Henry Hawk)—Charles M. (Chuck) Jones

EATIN' ON THE CUFF—August 15—LT—Robert Clampett

FRESH HARE—August 15—MM (Bugs Bunny, Elmer Fudd)—I. (Friz) Freleng

THE IMPATIENT PATIENT—August 29—LT (Daffy Duck)—Norman McCabe

FOX POP—August 29—MM—Charles M. (Chuck) Jones

THE DOVER BOYS—Septebmer 19—MM—Charles M. (Chuck) Jones

THE HEP CAT—October 3—LT—Robert Clampett

THE SHEEPISH WOLF—October 17—MM—I. (Friz) Freleng

THE DAFFY DUCKAROO—October 24—LT (Daffy Duck)—Norman McCabe

THE HARE-BRAINED HYPNOTIST—October 31—MM (Bugs Bunny, Elmer Fudd)—I. (Friz) Freleng

A TALE OF TWO KITTIES—November 21—MM (Tweety)—Robert Clampett

MY FAVORITE DUCK—December 5—LT (Daffy Duck, Porky Pig)—Charles M. (Chuck) Jones

DING DOG DADDY—December 5—MM—I. (Friz) Freleng

CASE OF THE MISSING HARE—December 12—MM (Bugs Bunny)—Charles M. (Chuck) Jones

CONFUSIONS OF A NUTZY SPY—December 26—LT (Porky Pig)—Norman McCabe

COAL BLACK AND DE SEBBEN DWARFS—December 26—MM—Robert Clampett

1943 (Copyright date marked by ©)

†PIGS IN A POLKA—January 9—MM—I. (Friz) Freleng

TO DUCK OR NOT TO DUCK—January 9—LT (Daffy Duck, Elmer Fudd)—Charles M. (Chuck) Jones

TORTOISE WINS BY A HARE—January 23—MM (Bugs Bunny)—Robert Clampett

HOP AND GO—February 6—LT (Claude Hopper)—Norman McCabe

FIFTH COLUMN MOUSE—February 6—MM—I. (Friz) Freleng

FLOP GOES THE WEASEL—February 20—MM—Charles M. (Chuck) Jones

SUPER RABBIT—April 3—MM (Bugs Bunny)—Charles M. (Chuck) Jones

THE UNBEARABLE BEAR—April 17—MM (Sniffles)—Charles M. (Chuck) Jones

THE WISE QUACKING DUCK—© May 12—LT (Daffy Duck)—Robert Clampett

†GREETINGS BAIT—May 15—MM (Wacky Worm)—I. (Friz) Freleng

TOKIO JOKIO—May 15—LT—Norman McCabe

JACK RABBIT AND THE BEANSTALK—May 29—MM (Bugs Bunny)—I. (Friz) Freleng

YANKE DOODLE DAFFY—June 5—LT (Daffy Duck)—I. (Friz) Freleng

THE ARISTO CAT—June 12—MM (Hubie and Bertie)—Charles M. (Chuck) Jones

SCRAP HAPPY DAFFY—June 19—LT (Daffy Duck)—Frank Tashlin

TIN PAN ALLEY CATS—June 26—MM—Robert Clampett

WACKIKI WABBIT—July 3—MM (Bugs Bunny)—Charles M. (Chuck) Jones

PORKY PIG'S FEAT—July 17—LT (Porky Pig, Daffy Duck)—Frank Tashlin

HISS AND MAKE UP—September 11—MM—I. (Friz) Freleng

CORNY CONCERTO—September 25—MM (Bugs Bunny, Porky Pig, Elmer Fudd)—Robert Clampett

FIN' 'N CATTY—October 9—MM—Charles M. (Chuck) Jones

FALLING HARE—October 23—MM (Bugs Bunny)—Robert Clampett

DAFFY THE COMMANDO—October 30—LT (Daffy Duck)—I. (Friz) Freleng

INKI AND THE MINAH BIRD—November 6—MM (Inki)—Charles M. (Chuck) Jones

AN ITCH IN TIME—November 20—MM (Elmer Fudd)—Robert Clampett

PUSS 'N BOOTY—December 11—LT—Robert Clampett

LITTLE RED RIDING RABBIT—December 18—MM (Bugs Bunny)—I. (Friz) Freleng

1944

WHAT'S COOKIN', DOC?—January 1—MM (Bugs Bunny)—Robert Clampett

MEATLESS FLYDAY—January 29—MM—I. (Friz) Freleng

TOM TURK AND DAFFY—February 12—LT (Daffy Duck)—Charles M. (Chuck) Jones

BUGS BUNNY AND THE THREE BEARS—February 26—MM (Bugs Bunny)—Charles M. (Chuck) Jones

I GOT PLENTY OF MUTTON—March 11—LT—Frank Tashlin

THE WEAKLY REPORTER—March 25—MM—Charles M. (Chuck) Jones

TICK TOCK TUCKERED—April 8—LT (Porky Pig, Daffy Duck)—Robert Clampett

BUGS BUNNY NIPS THE NIPS—April 22—MM (Bugs Bunny)—I. (Friz) Freleng

†THE SWOONER CROONER—May 6—LT (Porky Pig)—Frank Tashlin

RUSSIAN RHAPSODY—May 20—MM—Robert Clampett

DUCK SOUP TO NUTS—May 27—LT (Daffy Duck)—I. (Friz) Freleng

ANGEL PUSS—June 3—LT—Charles M. (Chuck) Jones

SLIGHTLY DAFFY—June 17—MM (Daffy Duck)—I. (Friz) Freleng

HARE RIBBIN—June 24—MM (Bugs Bunny)—Robert Clampett

BROTHER BRAT—July 15—LT (Porky Pig)—Frank Tashlin

HARE FORCE—July 22—MM (Bugs Bunny)—I. (Friz) Freleng

FROM HAND TO MOUSE—August 5—LT—Charles M. (Chuck) Jones

BIRDY AND THE BEAST—August 19—MM (Tweety)—Robert Clampett

BUCKAROO BUGS—August 26—LT (Bugs Bunny)—Robert Clampett

PLANE DAFFY—September 16—LT (Daffy Duck)—Frank Tashlin

GOLDILOCKS AND THE JIVIN' BEARS—September 24—MM—I. (Friz) Freleng

LOST AND FOUNDLING—September 30—MM (Sniffles)—Charles M. (Chuck) Jones

BOOBY HATCHED—October 14—LT—Frank Tashlin

THE OLD GREY HARE—October 28—MM (Bugs Bunny, Elmer Fudd)—Robert Clampett

THE STUPID CUPID—November 25—LT (Elmer Fudd, Daffy Duck)—Frank Tashlin

STAGE DOOR CARTOON—December 30—MM (Bugs Bunny, Elmer Fudd)—I. (Friz) Freleng

1945

ODOR-ABLE KITTY—January 5—LT (Pepe LePew)—Charles M. (Chuck) Jones

HERR MEETS HARE—January 13—MM (Bugs Bunny)—I. (Friz) Freleng

DRAFTEE DAFFY—January 27—LT (Daffy Duck)—Robert Clampett

UNRULY HARE—February 10—MM (Bugs Bunny, Elmer Fudd)—Frank Tashlin

TRAP HAPPY PORKY—February 24—LT (Porky Pig)—Charles M. (Chuck) Jones

†LIFE WITH FEATHERS—March 24—MM (Sylvester)—I, (Friz) Freleng

BEHIND THE MEAT BALL—April 7—LT—Frank Tashlin

HARE TRIGGER—April 21—MM (Bugs Bunny, Yosemite Sam)—I. (Friz) Freleng

AIN'T THAT DUCKY—May 19—LT (Daffy Duck)—I. (Friz) Freleng

GRUESOME TWOSOME—June 9—MM (Tweety)—Robert Clampett

A TALE OF TWO MICE—June 9—LT (Babbit, Catstello)—Frank Tashlin

WAGON HEELS—July 28—MM (Porky Pig)—Robert Clampett

HARE CONDITIONED—August 11—LT (Bugs Bunny)—Charles M. (Chuck) Jones

THE BASHFUL BUZZARD—September 15—LT (Beaky Buzzard)—Robert Clampett

FRESH AIREDALE—© September 24—MM—Charles M. (Chuck) Jones

PECK UP YOUR TROUBLES—October 20—MM—I. (Friz) Freleng

HARE TONIC—November 10—LT (Bugs Bunny, Elmer Fudd)—Charles M. (Chuck) Jones

NASTY QUACKS—December 1—MM—Frank Tashlin

1946

BOOK REVUE—January 5—LT (Daffy Duck)—Robert Clampett

BASEBALL BUGS—February 2—LT (Bugs Bunny)—I. (Friz) Freleng

HOLIDAY FOR SHOESTRINGS—February 23—MM—I. (Friz) Freleng

QUENTIN QUAIL—March 2—MM—Charles M. (Chuck) Jones

BABY BOTTLENECK—March 16—LT (Porky Pig, Daffy Duck)—Robert Clampett

HARE REMOVER—March 23—MM (Bugs Bunny, Elmer Fudd)—Frank Tashlin

DAFFY DOODLES—April 6—LT (Daffy Duck, Porky Pig)—Robert McKimson

HOLLYWOOD CANINE CANTEEN—April 20—MM—Robert McKimson

HUSH MY MOUSE—May 4—LT—Charles M. (Chuck) Jones

HAIR RAISING HARE—May 25—MM (Bugs Bunny)—Charles M. (Chuck) Jones

KITTY KORNERED—June 8—LT (Porky Pig)—Robert Clampett

HOLLYWOOD DAFFY—June 22—MM (Daffy Duck)—I. (Friz) Freleng

ACROBATTY BUNNY—June 29—LT (Bugs Bunny)—Robert McKimson

THE EAGER BEAVER—July 13—MM—Charles M. (Chuck) Jones

THE GREAT PIGGY BANK ROBBERY—July 27—LT (Daffy Duck)—Robert Clampett

BACALL TO ARMS—August 3—MM—Robert Clampett

OF THEE I STING—August 17—LT—I. (Friz) Freleng

†WALKY TALKY HAWKY—August 31—MM (Foghorn Leghorn)—Robert McKimson

RACKETEER RABBIT—September 14—LT (Bugs Bunny)—I. (Friz) Freleng

FAIR AND WORMER—September 28—MM—Charles M. (Chuck) Jones

THE BIG SNOOZE—October 5—LT (Bugs Bunny, Elmer Fudd)—Robert Clampett

THE MOUSE-MERIZED CAT—October 19—MM (Babbit, Catstello)—Robert McKimson

MOUSE MENACE—November 2—LT (Porky Pig)—Arthur Davis

RHAPSODY RABBIT—November 9—MM (Bugs Bunny)—I. (Friz) Freleng

ROUGHLY SQUEAKING—November 28—LT (Hubie and Bertie)—Charles M. (Chuck) Jones

1947

ONE MEAT BRAWL—January 18—MM (Porky Pig)—Robert McKimson

GOOFY GOPHERS—January 25—LT—Arthur Davis

THE GAY ANTIES—February 15—MM—I. (Friz) Freleng

PAYING THE PIPER—February 15—LT (Porky Pig)—Robert McKimson

A HARE GROWS IN MANHATTAN—March 22—MM (Bugs Bunny)—I. (Friz) Freleng

BIRTH OF A NOTION—April 12—LT (Daffy Duck)—Robert McKimson

‡TWEETIE PIE—May 3—MM (Tweety and Sylvester)—I. (Friz) Freleng

SCENT-IMENTAL OVER YOU—May 8—LT (Pepe LePew)—Charles M. (Chuck) Jones

RABBIT TRANSIT—May 10—LT (Bugs Bunny)—I. (Friz) Freleng

HOBO BOBO—May 17—MM (Bobo)—Robert McKimson

ALONG CAME DAFFY—June 14—LT (Daffy Duck)—I. (Friz) Freleng

INKI AT THE CIRCUS—June 21—MM (Inki)—Charles M. (Chuck) Jones

EASTER YEGGS—June 28—LT (Bugs Bunny, Elmer Fudd)—Robert McKimson

THE UPSTANDING SITTER—July 3—LT (Daffy Duck)—Robert McKimson

CROWING PAINS—July 12—LT (Foghorn Leghorn)—Robert McKimson

A PEST IN THE HOUSE—August 2—MM (Daffy Duck, Elmer Fudd)—Charles M. (Chuck) Jones

THE FOXY DUCKLING—August 23—MM—Arthur Davis

LITTLE ORPHAN AIREDALE—October 4—LT (Charlie Dog, Porky Pig)—Charles M. (Chuck) Jones

SLICK HARE—November 1—MM (Bugs Bunny, Elmer Fudd)—I. (Friz) Freleng

MEXICAN JOYRIDE—November 29—LT (Daffy Duck)—Arthur Davis

DOGGONE CATS—November 30—MM—Arthur Davis

CATCH AS CATS CAN—December 6—MM—Arthur Davis

1948 *(Copyright dates marked by* ©*)*

GORILLA MY DREAMS—January 3—LT (Bugs Bunny)—Robert McKimson

HARE-DO—January 15—MM (Bugs Bunny, Elmer Fudd)—I. (Friz) Freleng

A FEATHER IN HIS HARE—February 7—LT (Bugs Bunny)—Charles M. (Chuck) Jones

WHAT MAKES DAFFY DUCK—February 14—LT (Daffy Duck)—Arthur Davis

MISSISSIPPI HARE—February 26—LT (Bugs Bunny)—Charles M. (Chuck) Jones

WHAT'S BREWIN', BRUIN?—February 28—LT—Three Bears—Charles M. (Chuck) Jones

DAFFY DUCK SLEPT HERE—March 6—MM (Daffy Duck, Porky Pig)—Robert McKimson

BACK ALLEY OPROAR—March 27—MM (Sylvester, Elmer Fudd)—I. (Friz) Freleng

RABBIT PUNCH—April 10—MM (Bugs Bunny)—Charles M. (Chuck) Jones

HOP, LOOK AND LISTEN—April 17—LT (Hippety Hopper)—I. (Friz) Freleng

NOTHING BUT THE TOOTH—May 1—MM (Porky Pig)—Arthur Davis

BUCCANEER BUNNY—May 8—LT (Bugs Bunny, Yosemite Sam)—I. (Friz) Freleng

BONE, SWEET BONE—May 22—MM—Arthur Davis

BUGS BUNNY RIDES AGAIN—June 12—MM (Bugs Bunny, Yosemite Sam)—I. (Friz) Freleng

THE RATTLED ROOSTER—June 26—LT—Arthur Davis

THE SHELL-SHOCKED EGG—July 10—MM—Robert McKimson

HAREDEVIL HARE—July 24—LT (Bugs Bunny)—Charles M. (Chuck) Jones

YOU WERE NEVER DUCKIER—August 7—MM (Daffy Duck)—Charles M. (Chuck) Jones

DOUGH RAY ME-OW—August 14—MM—Arthur Davis

HOT CROSS BUNNY—August 21—MM (Bugs Bunny)—Robert McKimson

THE PEST THAT CAME TO DINNER—September 11—LT (Porky Pig)—Arthur Davis

HARE SPLITTER—September 25—MM (Bugs Bunny)—I. (Friz) Freleng

ODOR OF THE DAY—October 2—LT—Arthur Davis

HOUSE HUNTING MICE—© October 7—LT (Hubie and Bertie)—Charles M. (Chuck) Jones

THE FOGHORN LEGHORN—October 9—MM (Foghorn Leghorn)—Robert McKimson

DAFFY DILLY—ⓒ October 21—MM (Daffy Duck)—Charles M. (Chuck) Jones

A LAD IN HIS LAMP—October 23—LT (Bugs Bunny)—Robert McKimson

KIT FOR CAT—November 6—LT (Sylvester, Elmer Fudd)—I. (Friz) Freleng

STUPOR SALESMAN—November 20—LT (Daffy Duck)—Arthur Davis

RIFF RAFFY DAFFY—November 27—MM (Daffy Duck)—Arthur Davis

MY BUNNY LIES OVER THE SEA—December 4—MM (Bugs Bunny)—Charles M. (Chuck) Jones

A HORSEFLY FLEAS—December 13—LT—Robert McKimson

SCAREDY CAT—December 18—MM (Porky Pig, Sylvester)—Charles M. (Chuck) Jones

A HICK, A SLICK AND A CHICK—December 27—MM—Arthur Davis

TWO GOPHERS FROM TEXAS—ⓒ December 27—MM (Goofy Gophers)—Arthur Davis

1949

WISE QUACKERS—January 1—LT (Daffy Duck)—I. (Friz) Freleng

HARE DO—January 15—MM (Bugs Bunny, Elmer Fudd)—I. (Friz) Freleng

HOLIDAY FOR DRUMSTICKS—January 22—MM (Daffy Duck)—Arthur Davis

AWFUL ORPHAN—January 29—MM (Charlie Dog, Porky Pig)—Charles M. (Chuck) Jones

PORKY CHOPS—February 12—LT (Porky Pig)—Arthur Davis

I TAW A PUTTY TAT—ⓒ March 5—MM (Tweety and Sylvester)—I. (Friz) Freleng

DAFFY DUCK HUNT—March 26—LT (Daffy Duck)—Robert McKimson

REBEL RABBIT—April 9—MM (Bugs Bunny)—Robert McKimson

†MOUSE WRECKERS—April 23—LT (Hubie, Bertie, and Claude Cat)—Charles M. (Chuck) Jones

HIGH DIVING HARE—April 30—LT (Bugs Bunny, Yosemite Sam)—I. (Friz) Freleng

THE BEE-DEVILED BRUIN—May 14—MM (Three Bears)—Charles M. (Chuck) Jones

CURTAIN RAZOR—May 21—LT (Porky Pig)—I. (Friz) Freleng

BOWERY BUGS—June 4—MM (Bugs Bunny)—Arthur Davis

MOUSE MAZURKA—June 11—MM—I. (Friz) Freleng

LONG-HAIRED HARE—June 25—LT (Bugs Bunny)—Charles M. (Chuck) Jones

HENHOUSE HENERY—July 2—LT (Foghorn Leghorn, Henery Hawk)—Robert McKimson

KNIGHTS MUST FALL—July 16—MM (Bugs Bunny)—I. (Friz) Freleng

BAD OL' PUTTY TAT—July 23—MM (Tweety and Sylvester)—I. (Friz) Freleng

THE GRAY HOUNDED HARE—August 6—LT (Bugs Bunny)—Robert McKimson

OFTEN AN ORPHAN—August 13—LT (Charlie Dog)—Charles M. (Chuck) Jones

THE WINDBLOWN HARE—August 27—LT (Bugs Bunny)—Robert McKimson

DOUGH FOR THE DO-DO—September 2—MM (Porky Pig)—I. (Friz) Freleng

FAST AND FURRY-OUS—September 16—LT (Roadrunner)—Charles M. (Chuck) Jones

EACH DAWN I CROW—September 23—MM (Elmer Fudd)—I. (Friz) Freleng

FRIGID HARE—October 7—MM (Bugs Bunny)—Charles M. (Chuck) Jones

SWALLOW THE LEADER—October 14—LT—Robert McKimson

BYE, BYE BLUEBEARD—October 21—LT (Porky Pig)—Arthur Davis

†FOR SCENT-IMENTAL REASONS—November 12—LT (Pepe LePew)—Charles M. (Chuck) Jones

HIPPETY HOPPER—November 19—MM (Hippety Hopper)—Robert McKimson

WHICH IS WITCH?—December 3—LT (Bugs Bunny)—I. (Friz) Freleng

BEAR FEAT—December 10—LT (Three Bears)—Charles M. (Chuck) Jones

A HAM IN A ROLE—December 13—LT (Goofy Gophers)—Robert McKimson

RABBIT HOOD—December 24—MM (Bugs Bunny)—Charles M. (Chuck) Jones

1950

HOME TWEET HOME—January 14—MM (Tweety and Sylvester)—I. (Friz) Freleng

HURDY GURDY HARE—January 21—MM (Bugs Bunny)—Robert McKimson

BOOBS IN THE WOOD.—January 28—LT (Porky Pig & Daffy Duck—Robert McKimson

MUTINY ON THE BUNNY—February 18—LT (Bugs Bunny, Yosemite Sam)—I. (Friz) Freleng

THE LION'S BUSY—February 18—LT (Beaky Buzzard)—I. (Friz) Freleng

THE SCARLET PUMPERNICKEL—March 4—LT (Daffy Duck and an All-Star Cast)—Charles M. (Chuck) Jones

HOMELESS HARE—March 11—MM (Bugs Bunny)—Charles M. (Chuck) Jones

STRIFE WITH FATHER—April 1—MM (Beaky Buzzard)—Robert McKimson

THE HYPO-CHONDRI-CAT—April 15—MM (Claude Cat, Hubie and Bertie)—Charles M. (Chuck) Jones

BIG HOUSE BUNNY—April 22—MM (Bugs Bunny)—I. (Friz) Freleng

THE LEGHORN BLOWS AT MIDNIGHT—May 6—LT (Foghorn Leghorn)—Robert McKimson

HIS BITTER HALF—May 20—MM (Daffy Duck)—I. (Friz) Freleng

AN EGG SCRAMBLE—May 27—MM (Porky Pig)—Robert McKimson

WHAT'S UP, DOC?—June 17—LT (Bugs Bunny, Elmer Fudd)—Robert McKimson

ALL ABIR-R-RD—June 24—LT (Tweety and Sylvester)—I. (Friz) Freleng

8 BALL BUNNY—July 8—LT (Bugs Bunny)—Charles M. (Chuck) Jones

IT'S HUMMER TIME—July 22—LT—Robert McKimson

GOLDEN YEGGS—August 5—MM (Daffy Duck)—I. (Friz) Freleng

HILLBILLY HARE—August 12—MM (Bugs Bunny)—Robert McKimson

DOG GONE SOUTH—August 26—MM (Charlie Dog)—Charles M. (Chuck) Jones

THE DUCKSTERS—September 2—LT (Daffy Duck)—Charles M. (Chuck) Jones

BUNKER HILL BUNNY—September 9—MM (Bugs Bunny, Yosemite Sam)—I. (Friz) Freleng

A FRACTURED LEGHORN—September 16—MM (Foghorn Leghorn)—Robert McKimson

CANARY ROW—October 7—MM (Tweety and Sylvester)—I. (Friz) Freleng

STOOGE FOR A MOUSE—October 21—MM—I. (Friz) Freleng

POP 'IM POP—October 28—LT (Sylvester and Junior)—Robert McKimson

BUSHY HARE—November 18—LT (Bugs Bunny)—Robert McKimson

CAVEMAN INKI—November 25—LT (Inki)—Charles M. (Chuck) Jones

DOG COLLARED—December 5—MM (Porky Pig)—Robert McKimson

RABBIT OF SEVILLE—December 16—LT (Bugs Bunny, Elmer Fudd)—Charles M. (Chuck) Jones

TWO'S A CROWD—December 30—LT (Claude Cat)—Charles M. (Chuck) Jones

1951

HARE WE GO—January 6—MM (Bugs Bunny)—I. (Friz) Freleng

A FOX IN A FIX—January 20—MM—Robert McKimson

CANNED FEUD—February 3—LT (Sylvester)—I. (Friz) Freleng

RABBIT EVERY MONDAY—February 10—LT (Bugs Bunny)—I. (Friz) Freleng

PUTTY TAT TROUBLE—February 24—LT (Tweety)—I. (Friz) Freleng

CORN PLASTERED—March 3—MM—Robert McKimson

BUNNY HUGGED—March 10—MM (Bugs Bunny)—Charles M. (Chuck) Jones

SCENT-IMENTAL ROMEO—March 24—MM (Pepe LePew)—Charles M. (Chuck) Jones

A BONE FOR A BONE—April 7—LT (Goofy Gophers)—I. (Friz) Freleng

FAIR-HAIRED HARE—April 14—LT (Bugs Bunny, Yosemite Sam)—I. (Friz) Freleng

A HOUND FOR TROUBLE—April 28—LT (Charlie Dog)—Charles M. (Chuck) Jones

EARLY TO BET—May 5—MM—Robert McKimson

RABBIT FIRE—May 9—LT (Bugs Bunny, Daffy Duck, Elmer Fudd)—Charles M. (Chuck) Jones

ROOM AND BIRD—June 2—MM (Tweety and Sylvester)—I. (Friz) Freleng

CHOW HOUND—June 16—LT—Charles M. (Chuck) Jones

FRENCH RAREBIT—June 30—MM (Bugs Bunny)—Robert McKimson

WEARING OF THE GRIN—July 28—LT (Porky Pig)—Charles M. (Chuck) Jones

LEGHORN SWOGGLED—July 28—MM (Foghorn Leghorn)—Robert McKimson

HIS HARE RAISING TALE—August 11—LT (Bugs Bunny)—I. (Friz) Freleng

CHEESE CHASERS—August 25—MM (Claude Cat, Hubie and Bertie)—Charles M. (Chuck) Jones

LOVELORN LEGHORN—September 8—LT (Foghorn Leghorn)—Robert McKimson

TWEETY'S S.O.S.—September 22—MM (Tweety and Sylvester)—I. (Friz) Freleng

BALLOT BOX BUNNY—October 6—MM (Bugs Bunny, Yosemite Sam)—I. (Friz) Freleng

A BEAR FOR PUNISHMENT—October 20—LT (Three Bears)—Charles M. (Chuck) Jones

SLEEPY TIME POSSUM—November 3—MM—Robert McKimson

DRIP-ALONG DAFFY—November 17—MM (Porky Pig, Daffy Duck)—Charles M. (Chuck) Jones

BIG TOP BUNNY—December 12—MM (Bugs Bunny)—Robert McKimson

TWEET, TWEET, TWEETY—December 15—LT (Tweety and Sylvester)—I. (Friz) Freleng

THE PRIZE PEST—December 22—LT (Daffy Duck)—Robert McKimson

1952

WHO'S KITTEN WHO?—January 5—LT (Sylvester, Hippety Hopper)—Robert McKimson

OPERATION: RABBIT— January 19—LT (Bugs Bunny, Wile E. Coyote)—Charles M. (Chuck) Jones

FEED THE KITTY—February 2—MM (Marc Anthony)—Charles M. (Chuck) Jones

LITTLE BEAU PEPE—February 9—MM (Pepe LePew)—Charles M. (Chuck) Jones

GIFT WRAPPED—February 16—LT (Tweety and Sylvester)—I. (Friz) Freleng

FOXY BY PROXY—February 23—MM (Bugs Bunny)—I. (Friz) Freleng

THUMB FUN—March 1—LT (Porky Pig, Daffy Duck)—Robert McKimson

14 CARROT RABBIT—March 15—LT (Bugs Bunny, Yosemite Sam)—I. (Friz) Freleng

KIDDIN' THE KITTEN—April 5—MM—Robert McKimson
WATER, WATER EVERY HARE—April 19—LT (Bugs Bunny)—Charles M. (Chuck) Jones

LITTLE RED RODENT HOOD—May 3—MM—I. (Friz) Freleng

SOOK-A-DOODLE-DO—May 10—LT (Foghorn Leghorn)—Robert McKimson

BEEP BEEP—May 24—LT (Road Runner)—Charles M. (Chuck) Jones

HASTY HARE—June 7—LT (Bugs Bunny)—Charles M. (Chuck) Jones

AIN'T SHE TWEETY—June 21—LT (Tweety and Sylvester)—I. (Friz) Freleng

THE TURN-TALE WOLF—June 28—MM—Robert McKimson

CRACKED QUACK—July 5—MM (Daffy Duck)—I. (Friz) Freleng

OILY HARE—July 26—MM (Bugs Bunny)—Robert McKimson

HOPPY GO LUCKY—August 9—MM (Sylvester, Hippety Hopper)—Robert McKimson

GOING! GOING! GOSH—August 23—MM (Road Runner)—Charles M. (Chuck) Jones

BIRD IN A GUILTY CAGE—August 30—LT (Tweety and Sylvester)—I. (Friz) Freleng

MOUSE WARMING—September 8—LT (Hubie and Bertie)—Charles M. (Chuck) Jones

RABBIT SEASONING—September 20—MM (Bugs Bunny, Daffy Duck, and Elmer Fudd)—Charles M. (Chuck) Jones

THE EGG-CITED ROOSTER—October 4—MM (Foghorn Leghorn)—Robert McKimson

TREE FOR TWO—October 18—MM (Sylvester, Spike and Chester)—I. (Friz) Freleng

SUPER SNOOPER—November 1—LT (Daffy Duck)—Robert McKimson

RABBIT'S KIN—November 15—MM (Bugs Bunny)—Robert McKimson

TERRIER STRICKEN—November 29—MM (Claude Cat)—Charles M. (Chuck) Jones

FOOL COVERAGE—December 13—LT (Daffy Duck, Porky Pig)—Robert McKimson

HARE LIFT—December 20—LT (Bugs Bunny, Yosemite Sam)—I. (Friz) Freleng

1953

DON'T GIVE UP THE SHEEP—January 3—LT (Wolf and Sheepdog)—Charles M. (Chuck) Jones

SNOW BUSINESS—January 17—LT (Tweety and Sylvester)—I. (Friz) Freleng

A MOUSE DIVIDED—January 31—MM (Sylvester)—I. (Friz) Freleng

FORWARD MARCH HARE—February 14—LT (Bugs Bunny)—Charles M. (Chuck) Jones

KISS ME CAT—February 21—LT (Marc Anthony)—Charles M. (Chuck) Jones

DUCK AMUCK—February 28—MM (Daffy Duck)—Charles M. (Chuck) Jones

UPSWEPT HARE—March 14—MM (Bugs Bunny, Elmer Fudd)—Robert McKimson

A PECK O' TROUBLE—March 28—LT (Foghorn Leghorn)—Robert McKimson

FOWL FEATHER—April 4—MM (Tweety and Sylvester)—I. (Friz) Freleng

MUSCLE TUSSLE—April 18—MM (Daffy Duck)—Robert McKimson

SOUTHERN FRIED RABBIT—May 2—LT (Bugs Bunny, Yosemite Sam)—I. (Friz) Freleng

ANT PASTED—May 9—LT (Elmer Fudd)—I. (Friz) Freleng

MUCH ADO ABOUT NUTTING—May 23—MM—Charles M. (Chuck) Jones

THERE AUTO BE A LAW—June 6—LT—Robert McKimson

HARE-TRIMMED—June 20—MM (Bugs Bunny, Yosemite Sam)—I. (Friz) Freleng

TOM-TOM TOMCAT—June 27—MM (Tweety and Sylvester)—I. (Friz) Freleng

WILD OVER YOU—July 11—LT—Charles M. (Chuck) Jones

DUCK DODGERS IN THE 24½TH CENTURY—July 25—MM (Daffy Duck, Porky Pig)—Charles M. (Chuck) Jones

BULLY FOR BUGS—August 9—LT (Bugs Bunny)—Charles M. (Chuck) Jones

PLOP GOES THE WEASEL—August 22—LT—Robert McKimson

CAT-TAILS FOR TWO—August 29—MM (Speedy Gonzales)—Robert McKimson

A STREET CAT NAMED SYLVESTER—September 5—LT (Tweety and Sylvester)—I. (Friz) Freleng

ZIPPING ALONG—September 19—MM (Road Runner)—Charles M. (Chuck) Jones

DUCK, RABBIT, DUCK—October 3—MM (Bugs Bunny, Daffy Duck, Elmer Fudd)—Charles M. (Chuck) Jones

EASY PECKIN'S—October 17—LT (Foghorn Leghorn)—Robert McKimson

CATTY CORNERED—October 31—MM (Sylvester)—I. (Friz) Freleng

OF RICE AND HEN—November 14—LT (Foghorn Leghorn)—Robert McKimson

CATS A-WEIGH—November 28—MM (Sylvester, Hippety Hopper)—Robert McKimson

ROBOT RABBIT—December 12—LT (Bugs Bunny, Elmer Fudd)—I. (Friz) Freleng

PUNCH TRUNK—December 19—LT—Charles M. (Chuck) Jones

1954

DOG POUNDED—January 2—LT (Tweety and Sylvester)—I. (Friz) Freleng

I GOPHER YOU—February 3—MM (Goofy Gophers)—I. (Friz) Freleng

FELINE FRAME-UP—February 13—LT (Claude Cat, Marc Anthony)—Charles M. (Chuck) Jones

CAPTAIN HAREBLOWER—February 16—MM (Bugs Bunny, Yosemite Sam)—I. (Friz) Freleng

WILD WIFE—February 20—MM—Robert McKimson

NO BARKING—February 27—MM (Claude Cat)—Charles M. (Chuck) Jones

BUGS AND THUGS—March 13—LT (Bugs Bunny)—I. (Friz) Freleng

THE CAT'S BAH—March 20—LT (Pepe LePew)—Charles M. (Chuck) Jones

DESIGN FOR LEAVING—March 27—LT (Daffy Duck, Elmer Fudd)—Robert McKimson

BELL HOPPY—April 17—MM (Sylvester, Hippety Hopper)—Robert McKimson

NO PARKING HARE—May 1—LT (Bugs Bunny)—Robert McKimson

DOCTOR JERKYLE'S HIDE—May 8—LT (Spike and Chester, Sylvester)—I. (Friz) Freleng

CLAWS FOR ALARM—May 22—MM (Porky Pig, Sylvester)—Charles M. (Chuck) Jones

LITTLE BOY BOO—June 5—LT (Foghorn Legorn)—Robert McKimson

DEVIL MAY HARE—June 19—LT (Bugs Bunny, Tasmanian Devil)—Robert McKimson

MUZZLE TOUGH—June 26—MM (Tweety and Sylvester)—I. (Friz) Freleng

THE OILY AMERICAN—July 10—MM—Robert McKimson

BEWITCHED BUNNY—July 24—LT (Bugs Bunny)—Charles M. (Chuck) Jones

SATAN'S WAITIN'—August 7—LT (Tweety and Sylvester)—I. (Friz) Freleng

STOP, LOOK AND HASTEN!— August 14—MM (Road Runner)—Charles M. (Chuck) Jones

YANKEE DOODLE BUGS—August 28—LT (Bugs Bunny)—I. (Friz) Freleng

GONE BATTY—September 4—LT (Bobo)—Robert McKimson

GOO GOO GOLIATH—September 18—MM—I. (Friz) Freleng

BY WORD OF MOUSE—October 2—LT (Sylvester)—I. (Friz) Freleng

†FROM A TO Z-Z-Z-Z—October 16—LT (Ralph Phillips)—Charles M. (Chuck) Jones

QUACK SHOT—October 30—MM (Daffy Duck)—Robert McKimson

*LUMBER JACK RABBIT—November 13—LT (Bugs Bunny)—Charles M. (Chuck) Jones

*In 3-D.

MY LITTLE DUCKAROO—November 27—MM (Daffy Duck)—Charles M. (Chuck) Jones

SHEEP AHOY—December 11—MM (Wolf and Sheepdog)—Charles M. (Chuck) Jones

BABY BUGGY BUNNY—December 18—MM (Bugs Bunny)—Charles M. (Chuck) Jones

1955

PIZZICATO PUSSYCAT—January 1—MM—I. (Friz) Freleng

FEATHER DUSTER—January 15—MM (Foghorn Leghorn)—Robert McKimson

PESTS FOR GUESTS—January 30—MM (Elmer Fudd, Goofy Gophers)—I. (Friz) Freleng

BEANSTALK BUNNY—February 12—MM (Bugs Bunny, Daffy Duck, Elmer Fudd)—Charles M. (Chuck) Jones

ALL FOWLED UP—Feburary 19—LT (Foghorn Leghorn)—Robert McKimson

STORK NAKED—February 26—MM (Daffy Duck)—I. (Friz) Freleng

LIGHTHOUSE MOUSE—March 12—MM (Sylvester, Hippety Hopper)—Robert McKimson

SAHARA HARE—March 26—LT (Bugs Bunny, Yosemite Sam)—I. (Friz) Freleng

†SANDY CLAWS—April 2—LT (Tweety and Sylvester)—I. (Friz) Freleng

READY, SET, ZOOM—April 30—LT (Road Runner)—Charles M. (Chuck) Jones

THE HOLE IDEA—April 30—LT—Robert McKimson

HARE BRUSH—© May 7—MM (Bugs Bunny, Elmer Fudd)—I. (Friz) Freleng

PAST PERFUMANCE—May 21—MM (Pepe LePew)—Charles M. (Chuck) Jones

TWEETY'S CIRCUS—June 4—MM (Tweety and Sylvester)—I. (Friz) Freleng

RABBIT RAMPAGE—June 11—LT (Bugs Bunny, Elmer Fudd)—Charles M. (Chuck) Jones

LUMBER JERKS—June 25—LT (Goofy Gophers)—I. (Friz) Freleng

THIS IS A LIFE?—July 9—MM (Bugs Bunny, Daffy Duck, Elmer Fudd, Yosemite Sam)—I. (Friz) Freleng

DOUBLE OR MUTTON—July 23—LT (Wolf and Sheepdog)—Charles M. (Chuck) Jones

JUMPIN' JUPITER—August 6—MM (Porky Pig, Sylvester)—Charles M. (Chuck) Jones

A KIDDIE'S KITTY—August 20—MM (Sylvester)—I. (Friz) Freleng

HYDE AND HARE—August 27—LT (Bugs Bunny)—I. (Friz) Freleng

DIME TO RETIRE—September 3—LT (Porky Pig, Daffy Duck)—Robert McKimson

†SPEEDY GONZALES—September 17—MM (Speedy Gonzales)—I. (Friz) Freleng

KNIGHT-MARE HARE—October 1—MM (Bugs Bunny)—Charles M. (Chuck) Jones

TWO SCENTS WORTH—October 15—MM (Pepe LePew)—Charles M. (Chuck) Jones

RED RIDING HOODWINKED—October 29—LT (Tweety and Sylvester)—I. (Friz) Freleng

ROMAN LEGION HARE—November 12—LT (Bugs Bunny, Yosemite Sam)—I. (Friz) Freleng

HEIR CONDITIONED—November 26—LT (Sylvester, Elmer Fudd)—I. (Friz) Freleng

GUIDED MUSCLE—December 10—LT (Road Runner)—Charles M. (Chuck) Jones

PAPPY'S PUPPY—December 17—MM (Sylvester)—I. (Friz) Freleng

ONE FROGGY EVENING—December 31—MM—Charles M. (Chuck) Jones

1956

BUGS BONNETS—January 14—MM (Bugs Bunny, Elmer Fudd)—Charles M. (Chuck) Jones

TOO HOP TO HANDLE—January 28—LT (Sylvester, Hippety Hopper)—Robert McKimson

WEASEL STOP—February 11—LT (Foghorn Leghorn)—Robert McKimson

THE HIGH AND THE FLIGHTY—February 18—MM (Foghorn Leghorn, Daffy Duck)—Robert McKimson

BROOMSTICK BUNNY—February 25—LT (Bugs Bunny)—Charles M. (Chuck) Jones

ROCKET SQUAD—March 10—MM (Daffy Duck, Porky Pig)—Charles M. (Chuck) Jones

TWEET AND SOUR—March 24—LT (Tweety and Sylvester)—I. (Friz) Freleng

HEAVEN SCENT—March 31—MM (Pepe LePew)—Charles M. (Chuck) Jones

MIXED MASTER—April 14—LT—Robert McKimson

RABBITSON CRUSOE—April 28—LT (Bugs Bunny, Yosemite Sam)—I. (Friz) Freleng

GEE WHIZ-Z-Z-z—May 15—LT (Road Runner)—Charles M. (Chuck) Jones

TREE CORNERED TWEETY—May 19—MM (Tweety and Sylvester)—I. (Friz) Freleng

UNEXPECTED PEST—June 2—MM (Sylvester)—Robert McKimson

NAPOLEON BUNNY-PART—June 16—MM (Bugs Bunny)—I. (Friz) Freleng

TUGBOAT GRANNY—June 23—MM (Tweety and Sylvester)—I. (Friz) Freleng

STUPOR DUCK—July 7—LT (Daffy Duck)—Robert McKimson

BARBARY COAST BUNNY—July 21—LT (Bugs Bunny)—Charles M. (Chuck) Jones

ROCKET BYE BABY—August 4—MM—Charles M. (Chuck) Jones

HALF-FARE HARE—August 18—MM (Bugs Bunny)—Robert McKimson

RAW! RAW! ROOSTER—August 25—LT (Foghorn Leghorn)—Robert McKimson

THE SLAP-HOPPY MOUSE—September 1—MM (Sylvester, Hippety Hopper)—Robert McKimson

A STAR IS BORED—September 15—LT (Bugs Bunny, Daffy Duck)—I. (Friz) Freleng

DEDUCE YOU SAY—September 29—LT (Daffy Duck, Porky Pig)—Charles M. (Chuck) Jones

YANKEE DOOD IT—October 13—MM (Elmer Fudd)—I. (Friz) Freleng

WIDEO WABBIT—October 27—MM (Bugs Bunny, Elmer Fudd)—Robert McKimson

THERE THEY GO-GO-GO—November 10—LT (Road Runner)—Charles M. (Chuck) Jones

TWO CROWS FROM TACOS—November 24—MM (Speedy Gonzales)—I. (Friz) Freleng

THE HONEY-MOUSERS—December 8—LT—Robert McKimson

TO HARE IS HUMAN—December 15—MM (Bugs Bunny, Wile E. Coyote)—Charles M. (Chuck) Jones

1957

THE THREE LITTLE BOPS—January 5—LT—I. (Friz) Freleng

TWEET ZOO—January 12—MM (Tweety and Sylvester)—I. (Friz) Freleng

SCRAMBLED ACHES—January 26—LT (Road Runner)—Charles M. (Chuck) Jones

ALI BABA BUNNY—February 9—MM (Bugs Bunny, Daffy Duck)—Charles M. (Chuck) Jones

GO FLY A KIT—February 16—LT—Charles M. (Chuck) Jones

TWEETY AND THE BEANSTALK—March 16—MM (Tweety and Sylvester)—I. (Friz) Freleng

BEDEVILED RABBIT—April 13—MM (Bugs Bunny, Tasmanian Devil)—Robert McKimson

BOYHOOD DAZE—April 20—MM (Ralph Phillips)—Charles M. (Chuck) Jones

CHEESE IT, THE CAT—May 4—LT (Honey-Mousers)—Robert McKimson

FOX TERROR—May 11—MM (Foghorn Leghorn)—Robert McKimson

PIKER'S PEAK—May 25—LT (Bugs Bunny, Yosemite Sam)—I. (Friz) Freleng

STEAL WOOL—June 8—LT (Wolf and Sheepdog)—Charles M. (Chuck) Jones

BOSTON QUACKIE—June 22—LT (Daffy Duck)—Robert McKimson

WHAT'S OPERA, DOC?—July 6—MM (Bugs Bunny, Elmer Fudd)—Charles M. (Chuck) Jones

†TABASCO ROAD—July 20—LT (Speedy Gonzales)—Robert McKimson

‡BIRDS ANONYMOUS—August 10—MM (Sylvester and Tweety)—I. (Friz) Freleng

DUCKING THE DEVIL—August 17—MM (Daffy Duck, Tasmanian Devil)—Robert McKimson

BUGSY AND MUGSY—August 31—LT (Bugs Bunny)—I. (Friz) Freleng

ZOOM AND BORED—September 14—LT (Road Runner)—Charles M. (Chuck) Jones

GREEDY FOR TWEETY—September 28—LT (Tweety and Sylvester)—I. (Friz) Freleng

TOUCHÉ AND GO—October 12—MM (Pepe LePew)—Charles M. (Chuck) Jones

SHOW BIZ BUGS—November 2—LT (Bugs Bunny, Daffy Duck)—I. (Friz) Freleng

MOUSE TAKEN IDENTITY—November 16—MM (Sylvester, Hippety Hopper)—I. (Friz) Freleng

GONZALES' TAMALES—November 30—LT (Speedy Gonzales)—I. (Friz) Freleng

RABBIT ROMEO—December 14—MM (Bugs Bunny, Elmer Fudd)—Robert McKimson

1958 (Copyright dates marked by ©)

DON'T AXE ME—January 4—MM (Daffy Duck, Elmer Fudd)—Robert McKimson

TORTILLA FLAPS—January 18—LT (Speedy Gonzales)—I. (Friz) Freleng

HARELESS WOLF—February 1—MM (Bugs Bunny)—I. (Friz) Freleng

A PIZZA TWEETY PIE—February 22—LT (Tweety and Sylvester)—I. (Friz) Freleng

ROBIN HOOD DAFFY—March 8—MM (Daffy Duck)—Charles M. (Chuck) Jones

HARE-WAY TO THE STARS—March 29—LT (Bugs Bunny)—Charles M. (Chuck) Jones

WHOA, BE GONE—April 12—MM (Road Runner)—Charles M. (Chuck) Jones

A WAGGILY TALE—April 26—LT—I. (Friz) Freleng

FEATHER BLUSTER—May 10—MM (Foghorn Leghorn)—Robert McKimson

NOW HARE THIS—May 31—LT (Bugs Bunny)—Robert McKimson

TO ITCH HIS OWN—June 28—MM—Charles M. (Chuck) Jones

DOG TALES—July 26—LT—Robert McKimson

‡KNIGHTY-KNIGHT BUGS—August 23—LT (Bugs Bunny, Yosemite Sam)—I. (Friz) Freleng

WEASEL WHILE YOU WORK—© September 6—MM (Foghorn Leghorn)—Robert McKimson

A BIRD IN A BONNET—© September 27—MM (Tweety and Sylvester)—I. (Friz) Freleng

HOOK, LINE AND STINKER—© October 11—LT (Road Runner)—Charles M. (Chuck) Jones

PRE-HYSTERICAL HARE—November 1—LT (Bugs Bunny, Elmer Fudd)—Robert McKimson

GOPHER BROKE—November 15—LT (Goofy Gophers)—Robert McKimson

HIP, HIP-HURRY!—December 6—MM (Road Runner)—Charles M. (Chuck) Jones

CAT FEUD—December 20—MM—Charles M. (Chuck) Jones

1959

BATON BUNNY—January 10—LT (Bugs Bunny)—Charles M. (Chuck) Jones

MOUSE PLACED KITTEN—January 24—MM—Robert McKimson

CHINA JONES—February 14—LT (Daffy Duck, Porky Pig)—Robert McKimson

HARE-ABIAN NIGHTS—February 28—MM (Bugs Bunny, Yosemite Sam)—Ken Harris

TRICK OR TWEET—March 21—MM (Tweety and Sylvester)—I. (Friz) Freleng

THE MOUSE THAT JACK BUILT—April 4—MM—Robert McKimson

APES OF WRATH—April 18—MM (Bugs Bunny)—I. (Friz) Freleng

HOT ROD AND REEL—May 9—LT (Road Runner)—Charles M. (Chuck) Jones

A MUTT IN A RUT—May 23—LT (Elmer Fudd)—Robert McKimson

BACKWOODS BUNNY—June 13—MM (Bugs Bunny)—Robert McKimson

REALLY SCENT—June 27—MM (Pepe LePew)—Charles M. (Chuck) Jones

†MEXICALI SHMOES—July 4—LT (Speedy Gonzales)—I. (Friz) Freleng

TWEET AND LOVELY—July 18—MM (Tweety and Sylvester)—I. (Friz) Freleng

WILD AND WOOLY HARE—August 1—LT (Bugs Bunny, Yosemite Sam)—I. (Friz) Freleng

CAT'S PAW—August 15—LT (Sylvester)—Robert McKimson

HERE TODAY, GONE TAMALE—August 29—LT (Speedy Gonzales)—I. (Friz) Freleng

BONANZA BUNNY—September 5—MM (Bugs Bunny)—Robert McKimson

A BROKEN LEGHORN—September 26—LT (Foghorn Leghorn)—Robert McKimson

WILD ABOUT HURRY—October 10—MM (Road Runner)—Charles M. (Chuck) Jones

A WITCH'S TANGLED HARE—October 31—LT (Bugs Bunny)—Abe Levitow

UNNATURAL HISTORY—November 14—MM—Abe Levitow

TWEET DREAMS—December 5—LT (Tweety and Sylvester)—I. (Friz) Freleng

PEOPLE ARE BUNNY—December 19—MM (Bugs Bunny, Daffy Duck)—Robert McKimson

1960 *(Copyright dates marked by ©)*

FASTEST WITH THE MOSTEST—January 9—LT (Road Runner)—Charles M. (Chuck) Jones

WEST OF THE PESOS—January 23—MM (Speedy Gonzales)—I. (Friz) Freleng

HORSE HARE—February 3—LT (Bugs Bunny)—I. (Friz) Freleng

WILD WILD WORLD—February 27—MM—Robert McKimson

GOLDIMOUSE AND THE THREE CATS—March 19—LT (Sylvester)—I. (Friz) Freleng

PERSON TO BUNNY—April 2—MM (Bugs Bunny)—I. (Friz) Freleng

WHO SCENT YOU?—April 23—LT (Pepe LePew)—Charles M. (Chuck) Jones

HYDE AND GO TWEET—May 14—MM (Tweety and Sylvester)—I. (Friz) Freleng

RABBIT'S FEAT—June 4—LT (Bugs Bunny, Wile E. Coyote)—Charles M. (Chuck) Jones

CROCKETT-DOODLE-DO—June 25—MM (Foghorn Leghorn)—Robert McKimson

†MOUSE AND GARDEN—July 16—LT (Sylvester)—I. (Friz) Freleng

READY WOOLEN AND ABLE—July 30—MM (Wolf and Sheepdog)—Charles M. (Chuck) Jones

MICE FOLLIES—August 20—LT (Honey-mousers)—Robert McKimson

FROM HARE TO HEIR—September 3—MM (Bugs Bunny, Yosemite Sam)—I. (Friz) Freleng

THE DIXIE FRYER—September 24—MM (Foghorn Leghorn)—Robert McKimson

HOPALONG CASUALTY—October 8—MM (Road Runner)—Charles M. (Chuck) Jones

TRIP FOR TAT—October 29—MM (Tweety and Sylvester)—I. (Friz) Freleng

DOGGONE PEOPLE—November 12—MM (Elmer Fudd)—Robert McKimson

†HIGH NOTE—© December 3—LT—Charles M. (Chuck) Jones

LIGHTER THAN HARE—© December 17—MM (Bugs Bunny, Yosemite Sam)—I. (Friz) Freleng

1961

CANNERY WOE—January 7—LT (Speedy Gonzales)—I. (Friz) Freleng

ZIP 'N SNORT—January—MM (Road Runner)—Charles M. (Chuck) Jones

HOPPY DAZE—February—LT (Sylvester, Hippety Hopper)—Robert McKimson

THE MOUSE ON 57TH STREET—February—MM—Charles M. (Chuck) Jones

STRANGLED EGGS—March—MM (Foghorn Leghorn)—Robert McKimson

BIRDS OF A FATHER—April—MM (Sylvester and Junior)—Robert McKimson

D' FIGHTING ONES—April 22—MM (Sylvester)—I. (Friz) Freleng

THE ABOMINABLE SNOW RABBIT—May—LT (Bugs Bunny, Daffy Duck)—Charles M. (Chuck) Jones

LICKETY SPLAT—June—LT (Road Runner)—Charles M. (Chuck) Jones

A SCENT OF THE MATTERHORN—June—LT (Pepe LePew)—Charles M. (Chuck) Jones

THE REBEL WITHOUT CLAWS—July 15—LT (Tweety and Sylvester)—I. (Friz) Freleng

†THE PIED PIPER OF GUADALUPE—August 19—LT (Speedy Gonzales)—I. (Friz) Freleng

COMPRESSED HARE—August—MM (Bugs Bunny)—Charles M. (Chuck) Jones

PRINCE VIOLENT—September 2—LT (Bugs Bunny and Yosemite Sam)—I. (Friz) Freleng

DAFFY'S INN TROUBLE—September 23—LT (Daffy Duck)—Robert McKimson

WHAT'S MY LION?—October 21—LT (Elmer Fudd)—I. (Friz) Freleng

†BEEP PREPARED—November 11—MM (Road Runner)—Charles M. (Chuck) Jones

THE LAST HUNGRY CAT—December—MM (Tweety and Sylvester)—I. (Friz) Freleng

†NELLY'S FOLLY—December—MM—Charles M. (Chuck) Jones

1962

WET HARE—January—LT (Bugs Bunny)—Robert McKimson

A SHEEP IN THE DEEP—February—MM (Wolf and Sheepdog)—Charles M. (Chuck) Jones

FISH AND SLIPS—March—LT (Sylvester, Junior)—Robert McKimson

QUACKODILE TEARS—March—MM (Daffy Duck)—I. (Friz) Freleng

CROW'S FEAT—April 21—MM (The Two Crows)—I. (Friz) Freleng

MEXICAN BOARDERS—May 22—LT (Speedy Gonzales, Sylvester)—I. (Friz) Freleng

BILL OF HARE—June 9—MM (Bugs Bunny and Tasmanian Devil)—Robert McKimson

ZOOM AT THE TOP—June 30—MM (Road Runner)—Charles M. (Chuck) Jones

THE SLICK CHICK—July 21—LT (Foghorn Leghorn)—Robert McKimson

LOUVRE COME BACK TO ME—August 18—LT (Pepe LePew)—Charles M. (Chuck) Jones

HONEY'S MONEY—September 1—MM (Yosemite Sam)—I. (Friz) Freleng

THE JET CAGE—September 22—LT (Tweety and Sylvester)—I. (Friz) Freleng

MOTHER WAS A ROOSTER—October—MM (Foghorn Leghorn)—Robert McKimson

GOOD NOOSE—November—LT (Daffy Duck)—Robert McKimson

SHISHKABUGS—December 8—LT (Bugs Bunny)—I. (Friz) Freleng

MARTIAN THRU GEORGIA—December—LT (Bugs Bunny)—Charles M. (Chuck) Jones

1963

DEVIL'S FEUD CAKE—February 9—MM—I. (Friz) Freleng

I WAS A TEENAGE THUMB—March—MM—Charles M. (Chuck) Jones

FAST BUCK DUCK—March—MM—Robert McKimson, Ted Bonnicksen

MEXICAN CAT DANCE—April 20—LT—I. (Friz) Freleng

THE MILLION-HARE—April—LT (Bugs Bunny)—Robert McKimson

†NOW HEAR THIS—April—LT—Charles M. (Chuck) Jones

WOOLEN UNDER WHERE—May—MM (Wolf and Sheepdog)—Charles M. (Chuck) Jones

HARE-BREADTH HURRY—June—LT (Bugs Bunny, Wile E. Coyote)—Charles M. (Chuck) Jones

BANTY RAIDS—June—MM (Foghorn Leghorn)—Robert McKimson

CHILI WEATHER—August 17—MM (Speedy Gonzales)—I. (Friz) Freleng

THE UNMENTIONABLES—September 7—MM (Bugs Bunny)—I. (Friz) Freleng

AQUA DUCK—September—MM (Daffy Duck)—Robert McKimson

MAD AS A MARS HARE—October—MM (Bugs Bunny)—Charles M. (Chuck) Jones

CLAWS IN THE LEASE—November 9—MM (Sylvester, Junion)—Robert McKimson

TRANSYLVANIA 6-5000—November MM (Bugs Bunny)—Charles M. (Chuck) Jones

TO BEEP OR NOT TO BEEP—December—MM (Road Runner)—Charles M. (Chuck) Jones

1964

DUMB PATROL—January—LT (Bugs Bunny, Yosemite Sam)—Gerry Chiniquy

A MESSAGE TO GRACIAS—February 8—LT (Speedy Gonzales, Sylvester)—Robert McKimson

BARTHOLOMEW VERSUS THE WHEEL—February 29—MM—Robert McKimson

FREUDY CAT—March 14—LT (Sylvester)—Robert McKimson

DR. DEVIL AND MR. HARE—March 28—MM (Bugs Bunny)—Robert McKimson

NUTS AND VOLTS—April 25—LT (Speedy Gonzales, Sylvester)—I. (Friz) Freleng

THE ICEMAN DUCKETH—May 16—LT (Daffy Duck, Bugs Bunny)—Phil Monroe

WAR AND PIECES—June 6—LT (Road Runner)—Charles M. (Chuck) Jones

HAWAIIAN AYE AYE—June 27—MM (Tweety and Sylvester)—Gerry Chiniquy

FALSE HARE—July 18—LT (Bugs Bunny)—Robert McKimson

SENORELLA AND THE GLASS HUARACHE—August—LT—I. (Friz) Freleng

PANCHO'S HIDEAWAY—October 24—LT (Speedy Gonzales, Yosemite Sam)—I. (Friz) Freleng

ROAD TO ANDALAY (working title: TEQUILA MOCKING BIRD)—December 26—MM (Speedy Gonzales)—I. (Friz) Freleng

1965

IT'S NICE TO HAVE A MOUSE AROUND THE HOUSE—January 16—LT (Speedy Gonzales, Daffy Duck)—I. (Friz) Freleng

CATS AND BRUISES—January 30—MM (Speedy Gonzales, Sylvester)—I. (Friz) Freleng

THE WILD CHASE—February 27—MM (Road Runner, Speedy Gonzales, Sylvester)—Hawley Pratt

MOBY DUCK—March 27—LT (Daffy Duck, Speedy Gonzales)—Robert McKimson

ASSAULT AND PEPPERED—April 24—MM (Daffy Duck, Speedy Gonzales)—Robert McKimson

WELL WORN DAFFY—May 22—LT (Daffy Duck, Speedy Gonzales)—Robert McKimson

SUPPRESSED DUCK—June 26—MM (Daffy Duck, Porky Pig)—Robert McKimson

CORN ON THE COP—July 24—MM (Porky Pig, Daffy Duck)—Irv Spector

RUSHING ROULETTE—July 31—MM (Road Runner)—Robert McKimson

RUN, RUN SWEET ROAD RUNNER—August 21—MM (Road Runner)—Rudy Larriva

TEASE FOR TWO—August 28—LT (Daffy Duck, Goofy Gophers)—Robert McKimson

TIRED AND FEATHERED—September 18—MM (Road Runner)—Rudy Larriva

BOULDER WHAM—October 9—MM (Road Runner)—Rudy Larriva

CHILI CON CORNY—October 23—LT (Speedy Gonzales, Daffy Duck)—Robert McKimson

JUST PLANE BEEP—October 30—MM (Road Runner)—Rudy Larriva

HARRIED AND HURRIED—November 13—MM (Road Runner)—Rudy Larriva

GO GO AMIGO—November 20—MM (Speedy Gonzales, Daffy Duck)—Robert McKimson

HIGHWAY RUNNERY—December 11—LT (Road Runner)—Rudy Larriva

CHASER ON THE ROCKS—December 25—MM (Road Runner)—Rudy Larriva

1966

ASTRODUCK—January 1—LT (Daffy Duck, Speedy Gonzales)—Robert McKimson

SHOT AND BOTHERED—January 8—LT (Road Runner)—Rudy Larriva

OUT AND OUT ROUT—January 29—MM (Road Runner)—Rudy Larriva

MUCHO LOCOS—February 5—MM (Speedy Gonzales, Daffy Duck)—Robert McKimson

THE SOLID TIN COYOTE—February 19—LT (Road Runner)—Rudy Larriva

MEXICAN MOUSEPIECE—February 26—MM (Speedy Gonzales, Daffy Duck)—Robert McKimson

CLIPPETY CLOBBERED—March 12—LT (Road Runner)—Rudy Larriva

DAFFY RENTS—March 26—LT (Daffy Duck, Speedy Gonzales)—Robert McKimson

A HAUNTING WE WILL GO—April 16—LT (Speedy Gonzales, Daffy Duck)—Robert McKimson

SNOW EXCUSE—May 21—MM (Speedy Gonzales, Daffy Duck)—Robert McKimson

A SQUEAK IN THE DEEP—July 9—LT (Daffy Duck, Speedy Gonzales)—Robert McKimson

FEATHER FINGER—August 20—MM (Speedy Gonzales, Daffy Duck)—Robert McKimson

SWING DING AMIGO—September 17—LT (Speedy Gonzales, Daffy Duck)—Robert McKimson

SUGAR AND SPIES—November 5—LT (Road Runner)—Robert McKimson

A TASTE OF CATNIP—December 3—MM (Speedy Gonzales, Daffy Duck)—Robert McKimson

1967

DAFFY'S DINER—January 21—MM (Speedy Gonzales, Daffy Duck)—Robert McKimson

THE QUACKER TRACKER—April 29—LT (Speedy Gonzales, Daffy Duck)—Rudy Larriva

THE MUSIC MICE-TRO—May 27—MM (Speedy Gonzales, Daffy Duck)—Rudy Larriva

THE SPY SWATTER—June—LT (Speedy Gonzales, Daffy Duck)—Rudy Larriva

SPEEDY GHOST GOES TO TOWN—July—MM (Speedy Gonzales, Daffy Duck)—Alex Lovy

RODENT TO STARDOM—August—LT (Speedy Gonzales, Daffy Duck)—Alex Lovy

GO AWAY STOWAWAY—September—MM (Speedy Gonzales, Daffy Duck)—Alex Lovy

COOL CAT—October—LT (Cool Cat)—Alex Lovy

MERLIN THE MAGIC MOUSE—November—MM (Merlin the Magic Mouse)—Alex Lovy

FIESTA FIASCO—December 9—LT (Speedy Gonzales, Daffy Duck)—Alex Lovy

1968

HOCUS POCUS POWWOW—January 13—LT (Merlin the Magic Mouse)—Alex Lovy

NORMAN NORMAL—February 3—MM—Alex Lovy

BIG GAME HAUNT—February 10—MM (Cool Cat)—Alex Lovy

SKYSCPAPER CAPER—March 9—MM (Speedy Gonzales, Daffy Duck)—Alex Lovy

HIPPYDROME TIGER—March 30—MM (Cool Cat)—Alex Lovy

A FEUD WITH A DUDE—May 4—MM (Merlin the Magic Mouse)—Alex Lovy

SEE YA LATER GLADIATOR—May 25—LT (Daffy Duck, Speedy Gonzales)—Alex Lovy

THE DOOR—June 1—MM—Ken Mundie

3-RING WING-DING—July 13—LT (Cool Cat)—Alex Lovy

FLYING CIRCUS—September 14—LT—Alex Lovy

CHIMP AND ZEE—October 12—MM—Alex Lovy

BUNNY AND CLAUDE—November 9—MM (Bunny and Claude)—Robert McKimson

1969

THE GREAT CARROT TRAIN ROBBERY—January 25—MM (Bunny and Claude)—Robert McKimson

FISTIC MYSTIC—February 22—LT (Merlin the Magic Mouse)—Robert McKimson

RABBIT STEW AND RABBITS TOO—March 15—MM (Rapid Rabbit)—Robert McKimson

SHAMROCK AND ROLL—MM (Merlin the Magic Mouse)—Robert McKimson

BUGGED BY A BEE—MM (Cool Cat)—Robert McKimson

INJUN TROUBLE—MM—Robert McKimson

The MGM Cartoons

Following is a complete list of cartoons produced and/or distributed by Metro-Goldwyn-Mayer. All are in color unless otherwise noted; two-color technicolor was used until the release of THE OLD PLANTATION in 1935. The series title for each short subject is given whenever applicable.

The Happy Harmonies series of 1934–38 were jointly credited to Harman and Ising, but we have been able to identify which director worked on each short. Later discrepancies between official screen billing and acknowledged credits have been noted in the filmography.

In addition to the short subjects listed here, the MGM cartoon department contributed sequences to the feature-films ANCHORS AWEIGH (1945), HOLIDAY IN MEXICO (1946), DANGEROUS WHEN WET (1953), and INVITATION TO THE DANCE (1957).

From 1948–50 the studio released a handful of propaganda-type shorts made by John Sutherland Productions (MAKE MINE FREEDOM, MEET KING JOE, WHY PLAY LEAP FROG?, ALBERT IN BLUNDERLAND, FRESH LAID PLANS, INSIDE CACKLE CORNERS), which were not part of any regular series. These are not included in our list.

The final series of Tom and Jerry cartoons made by Chuck Jones in the mid- and late 1960s are grouped by year, but not necessarily in the order of their release.

One dagger next to a film title (†) indicates an Academy Award nominee; a double dagger (‡) indicates an Academy Award winner.

1934

THE DISCONTENTED CANARY—September 1—Happy Harmonies—Rudolf Ising

THE OLD PIONEER—September 29—Happy Harmonies—Rudolf Ising

A TALE OF THE VIENNA WOODS—October 27—Happy Harmonies—Hugh Harman

BOSKO'S PARLOR PRANKS—November 24—Bosko—Hugh Harman

TOYLAND BROADCAST—December 22—Happy Harmonies—Rudolf Ising

1935

HEY, HEY FEVER—January 9—Bosko—Hugh Harmon

WHEN THE CAT'S AWAY—February 16—Happy Harmonies—Rudolf Ising

THE LOST CHICK—March 9—Happy Harmonies—Hugh Harman

THE CALICO DRAGON—March 30—Happy Harmonies—Rudolf Ising

THE GOOD LITTLE MONKEYS—April 13—Happy Harmonies—Hugh Harman

THE CHINESE NIGHTINGALE—April 27—Happy Harmonies—Rudolf Ising

POOR LITTLE ME—May 11—Happy Harmonies—Hugh Harman

BARNYARD BABIES—May 25—Happy Harmonies—Rudolf Ising

THE OLD PLANTATION—September 21—Happy Harmonies—Rudolf Ising

HONEYLAND—October 19—Happy Harmonies—Rudolf Ising

ALIAS ST. NICK—November 16—Happy Harmonies—Rudolf Ising

RUN, SHEEP, RUN—December 14—Happy Harmonies—Hugh Harman

1936

BOTTLES—January 11—Happy Harmonies—Hugh Harman

THE EARLY BIRD AND THE WORM—February 8—Happy Harmonies—Rudolf Ising

THE OLD MILL POND—March 7—Happy Harmonies—Hugh Harman

TWO LITTLE PUPS—April 4—Happy Harmonies—Rudolf Ising

THE OLD HOUSE—May 2—Happy Harmonies—Hugh Harman

PUPS' PICNIC—May 30—Happy Harmonies—Rudolf Ising

TO SPRING—June 20—Happy Harmonies—William Hanna

LITTLE CHEEZER—July 11—Happy Harmonies—Rudolf Ising

THE PUPS' CHRISTMAS—December 12—Happy Harmonies—Rudolf Ising

1937

CIRCUS DAZE—January 16—Bosko—Hugh Harman

SWING WEDDING—February 13—Happy Harmonies—Hugh Harman

BOSKO'S EASTER EGGS—March 20—Bosko—Hugh Harman

BOSKO AND THE PIRATES—May 1—Bosko—Hugh Harman

THE HOUND AND THE RABBIT—May 29—Happy Harmonies—Rudolf Ising

WAYWARD PUPS—July 10—Happy Harmonies—Rudolf Ising

BOSKO AND THE CANNIBALS—August 28—Happy Harmonies—Hugh Harman

LITTLE BUCK CHEEZER—December 15—Little Cheezer—Rudolf Ising

1938

BOSKO IN BAGDAD—January 1—Bosko—Hugh Harman

PIPE DREAM—February 5—Happy Harmonies—Hugh Harman

*CLEANING HOUSE—February 19—Captain and the Kids—Robert Allen

LITTLE BANTAMWEIGHT—March 12—Happy Harmonies—Rudolf Ising

*BLUE MONDAY—April 2—Captain and the Kids—William Hanna

*POULTRY PIRATES—April 16—Captain and the Kids—Friz Freleng

*CAPTAIN'S PUP—April 30—Captain and the Kids—Robert Allen

*A DAY AT THE BEACH—June 25—Captain and the Kids—Friz Freleng

*WHAT A LION!—July 16—Captain and the Kids—William Hanna

*THE PYGMY HUNT—August 6—Captain and the Kids—Friz Freleng

*OLD SMOKEY—September 3—Captain and the Kids—No credits

*BURIED TREASURE—September 17—Captain and the Kids—Robert Allen

*THE WINNING TICKET—October 1—Captain and the Kids—No credits

*HONDURAS HURRICANE—October 15—Captain and the Kids—sepiatone—No credits

THE CAPTAIN'S CHRISTMAS—December 17—Captain and the Kids—No credits

*In sepiatone.

1939

PETUNIA NATURAL PARK—January 14—Captain and the Kids—No credits

*SEAL SKINNERS—January 28—Captain and the Kids—No credits

*MAMA'S NEW HAT—February 11—Captain and the Kids—Friz Freleng

*JITTERBUG FOLLIES—February 25—Milt Gross

*WANTED: NO MASTER—March 18—Milt Gross

THE LITTLE GOLDFISH—April 15—Rudolf Ising

ART GALLERY—May 13—Hugh Harman

THE BEAR THAT COULDN'T SLEEP—June 10—Barney Bear—Rudolf Ising

GOLDILOCKS AND THE THREE BEARS—July 15—Hugh Harman

THE BOOKWORM—August 26—Friz Freleng

ONE MOTHER'S FAMILY—September 30—Rudolf Ising

THE BLUE DANUBE—October 28—Hugh Harman

†PEACE ON EARTH—December 9—Hugh Harman

THE MAD MAESTRO—December 30—Hugh Harman

1940

THE FISHING BEAR—January 20—Barney Bear—Rudolf Ising

PUSS GETS THE BOOT—February 10—Tom and Jerry—William Hanna, Joseph Barbera (credited to Rudolf Ising)

HOME ON THE RANGE—March 23—Rudolf Ising

A RAINY DAY—April 20—Hugh Harman

SWING SOCIAL—May 18—William Hanna, Joseph Barbera (credited to Rudolf Ising)

TOM TURKEY AND HIS HARMONICA HUMDINGERS—June 8—Hugh Harman

‡THE MILKY WAY—June 22—Rudolf Ising

ROMEO IN RHYTHM—August 10—Rudolf Ising

PAPA GETS THE BIRD—September 7—Hugh Harman

THE HOMELESS FLEA—October 12—Rudolf Ising

GALLOPIN' GALS—October 26—Hanna-Barbera

LONESOME STRANGER—November 23—Hugh Harman

MRS. LADYBUG—December 21—Rudolf Ising

1941

ABDUL THE BULBUL AMEER—February 22—Hugh Harman

THE PROSPECTING BEAR—March 8—Barney Bear—Rudolf Ising

THE LITTLE MOLE—April 5—Hugh Harman

THE GOOSE GOES SOUTH—April 26—Hanna-Barbera

†ROOKIE BEAR—May 17—Barney Bear—Rudolf Ising

DANCE OF THE WEED—June 7—Rudolf Ising

THE ALLEY CAT—July 5—Hugh Harman

THE MIDNIGHT SNACK—July 19—Tom and Jerry—Hanna-Barbera

LITTLE CAESARIO—August 30—Bob Allen

OFFICER POOCH—September 6—Hanna-Barbera

THE FLYING BEAR—November 1—Barney Bear—Rudolf Ising

†THE NIGHT BEFORE CHRISTMAS—December 6—Tom and Jerry—Hanna-Barbera

THE FIELD MOUSE—December 27—Hugh Harman

1942

FRAIDY CAT—January 17—Tom and Jerry—Hanna-Barbera

THE HUNGRY WOLF—February 21—Hugh Harman

THE FIRST SWALLOW—March 14—Jerry Brewer (credited to Rudolf Ising)

THE BEAR AND THE BEAVERS—March 28—Barney Bear—Rudolf Ising

DOG TROUBLE—April 18—Tom and Jerry—Hanna-Barbera

LITTLE GRAVEL VOICE—May 16—Rudolf Ising

PUSS N' TOOTS—May 30—Tom and Jerry—Hanna-Barbera

BATS IN THE BELFRY—July 4—Jerry Brewer (credited to Rudolf Ising)

THE BOWLING ALLEY CAT—July 18—Tom and Jerry—Hanna-Barbera

‡THE BLITZ WOLF—August 22—Tex Avery

THE EARLY BIRD DOOD IT—August 29—Tex Avery

CHIPS OFF THE OLD BLOCK—September 12—Robert Allen

FINE FEATHERED FRIEND—October 10—Tom and Jerry—Hanna-Barbera

WILD HONEY—November 7—Barney Bear—Rudolf Ising

BARNEY BEAR'S VICTORY GARDEN—December 26—Barney Bear—Rudolf Ising

1943

SUFFERIN' CATS—January 16—Tom and Jerry—Hanna-Berbera

BAH WILDERNESS—February 13—Barney Bear—Rudolf Ising

DUMB HOUNDED—March 20—Droopy—Tex Avery

THE BOY AND THE WOLF—April 24—Rudolf Ising

RED HOT RIDING HOOD—May 8—Tex Avery

THE LONESOME MOUSE—May 22—Tom and Jerry—Hanna-Barbera

WHO KILLED WHO?—June 5—Tex Avery

‡YANKEE DOODLE MOUSE—June 26—Tom and Jerry—Hanna-Barbera

THE UNINVITED PEST—July 17—Barney Bear—Rudolf Ising

ONE HAM'S FAMILY—August 14—Tex Avery

WAR DOGS—October 9—Hanna-Barbera

STORK'S HOLIDAY—October 23—George Gordon

WHAT'S BUZZIN' BUZZARD—November 27—Tex Avery

BABY PUSS—December 25—Tom and Jerry—Hanna-Barbera

1944

INNERTUBE ANTICS—January 22—George Gordon

ZOOT CAT—February 26—Tom and Jerry—Hanna-Barbera

SCREWBALL SQUIRREL—April 1—Screwy Squirrel—Tex Avery

BATTY BASEBALL—April 22—Tex Avery

MILLION DOLLAR CAT—May 6—Tom and Jerry—Hanna-Barbera

THE TREE SURGEON—June 3—George Gordon

HAPPY GO NUTTY—June 24—Screwy Squirrel—Tex Avery

THE BODYGUARD—July 22—Tom and Jerry—Hanna-Barbera

BEAR RAID WARDEN—September 9—Barney Bear—George Gordon

BIG HEEL WATHA—October 21—Screwy Squirrel—Tex Avery

PUTTIN' ON THE DOG—October 28—Tom and Jerry—Hanna-Barbera

*MOUSE TROUBLE—December 23—Tom and Jerry—Hanna-Barbera

BARNEY BEAR'S POLAR PEST—December 30—Barney Bear—George Gordon

1945

SCREWY TRUANT—January 13—Screwy Squirrel—Tex Avery

UNWELCOME GUEST—February 17—Barney Bear—George Gordon

SHOOTING OF DAN MCGOO—March 3—Droopy—Tex Avery

JERKY TURKEY—April 7—Tex Avery

THE MOUSE COMES TO DINNER—May 5—Tom and Jerry—Hanna-Barbera

MOUSE IN MANHATTAN—July 7—Tom and Jerry—Hanna-Barbera

TEE FOR TWO—July 21—Tom and Jerry—Hanna-Barbera

SWING SHIFT CINDERELLA—August 25—Tex Avery

FLIRTY BIRDY—September 22—Tom and Jerry—Hanna-Barbera

WILD AND WOLFY—November 3—Droopy—Tex Avery

‡QUIET PLEASE—December 22—Tom and Jerry—Hanna-Barbera

1946

LONESOME LENNY—March 9—Screwy Squirrel—Tex Avery

SRINGTIME FOR THOMAS—March 30—Tom and Jerry—Hanna-Barbera

THE MILKY WAIF—May 18—Tom and Jerry—Hanna-Barbera

THE HICK CHICK—June 15—Tex Avery

TRAP HAPPY—June 29—Tom and Jerry—Hanna-Barbera

NORTHWEST HOUNDED POLICE—August 3—Droopy—Tex Avery

SOLID SERENADE—August 31—Tom and Jerry—Hanna-Barbera

HENPECKED HOBOES—October 26—George and Junior—Tex Avery

1947

CAT FISHIN'—March 15—Tom and Jerry—Hanna-Barbera

PART TIME PAL—March 15—Tom and Jerry—Hanna-Barbera

HOUND HUNTERS—April 12—George and Junior—Tex Avery

‡THE CAT CONCERTO—April 26—Tom and Jerry—Hanna-Barbera

RED HOT RANGERS—May 31—George and Junior—Tex Avery

†DR. JEKYLL AND MR. MOUSE—June 14—Tom and Jerry—Hanna-Barbera

SALT WATER TABBY—July 12—Tom and Jerry—Hanna-Barbera

UNCLE TOM'S CABANA—July 19—Tex Avery

A MOUSE IN THE HOUSE—August 30—Tom and Jerry—Hanna-Barbera

SLAP HAPPY LION—September 20—Tex Avery

THE INVISIBLE MOUSE—September 27—Tom and Jerry—Hanna-Barbera

KING-SIZE CANARY—December 6—Tex Avery

1948

THE BEAR AND THE BEAN—January 31—Barney Bear—Michael Lah, Preston Blair

WHAT PRICE FLEADOM—April 24—Tex Avery

KITTY FOILED—June 1—Tom and Jerry—Hanna-Barbera

LITTLE TINKER—June 15—Tex Avery

THE BEAR AND THE HARE—June 26—Barney Bear—Michael Lah, Preston Blair

THE TRUCE HURTS—July 17—Tom and Jerry—Hanna-Barbera

HALF-PINT PIGMY—August 17—Tex Avery

OLD ROCKIN' CHAIR TOM—September 18—Tom and Jerry—Hanna-Barbera

LUCKY DUCKY—October 9—Tex Avery

PROFESSOR TOM—October 30—Tom and Jerry—Hanna-Barbera

THE CAT THAT HATED PEOPLE—November 20—Tex Avery

‡MOUSE CLEANING—December 11—Tom and Jerry—Hanna-Barbera

1949

GOGGLE FISHING BEAR—January 15—Barney Bear—Michael Lah, Preston Blair

BAD LUCK BLACKIE—January 22—Tex Avery

POLKA DOT PUSS—February 26—Tom and Jerry—Hanna-Barbera

SENOR DROOPY—April 9—Droopy—Tex Avery

THE LITTLE ORPHAN—April 30—Tom and Jerry—Hanna-Barbera

†HATCH UP YOUR TROUBLES—May 14—Tom and Jerry—Hanna-Barbera

HOUSE OF TOMORROW—June 11—Tex Avery

HEAVENLY PUSS—July 9—Tom and Jerry—Hanna-Barbera

DOGGONE TIRED—July 30—Tex Avery

WAGS TO RICHES—August 13—Tex Avery

CAT AND MERMOUSE—September 13—Tom and Jerry—Hanna-Barbera

LITTLE RURAL RED RIDING HOOD—September 17—Tex Avery

LOVE THAT PUP—October 1—Tom and Jerry (with Spike and Tyke)—Hanna-Barbera

JERRY'S DIARY—October 22—Tom and Jerry—Hanna-Barbera

OUT-FOXED—November 5—Droopy—Tex Avery

TENNIS CHUMPS—December 10—Tom and Jerry—Hanna-Barbera

COUNTERFEIT CAT—December 24—Spike—Tex Avery

1950

LITTLE QUACKER—January 7—Tom and Jerry—Hanna-Barbera

SATURDAY EVENING PUSS—January 19—Tom and Jerry—Hanna-Barbera

TEXAS TOM—March 11—Tom and Jerry—Hanna-Barbera

JERRY AND THE LION—April 8—Tom and Jerry—Hanna-Barbera

VENTRILOQUIST CAT—May 27—Tex Avery

THE CUCKOO CLOCK—June 10—Tex Avery

SAFETY SECOND—July 1—Tom and Jerry—Hanna-Barbera

TOM AND JERRY IN THE HOLLYWOOD BOWL—September 16—Tom and Jerry—Hanna-Barbera

GARDEN GOPHER—September 30—Spike—Tex Avery

THE FRAMED CAT—October 21—Tom and Jerry—Hanna-Barbera

THE CHUMP CHAMP—November 4—Droopy—Tex Avery

CUEBALL CAT—November 25—Tom and Jerry—Hanna-Barbera

THE PEACHY COBBLER—December 9—Tex Avery

1951

CASANOVA CAT—January 6—Tom and Jerry—Hanna-Barbera

COCKADOODLE DOG—February 10—Spike—Tex Avery

JERRY AND THE GOLDFISH—March 3—Tom and Jerry—Hanna-Barbera

DAREDEVIL DROOPY—March 31—Droopy—Tex Avery

JERRY'S COUSIN—April 7—Tom and Jerry—Hanna-Barbera

DROOPY'S GOOD DEED—May 5—Droopy—Tex Avery

SLEEPY TIME TOM—May 26—Tom and Jerry—Hanna-Barbera

SYMPHONY IN SLANG—June 6—Tex Avery

HIS MOUSE FRIDAY—July 7—Tom and Jerry—Hanna-Barbera

SLICKED-UP PUP—September 8—Tom and Jerry (with Spike and Tyke)—Hanna-Barbera

CAR OF TOMORROW—September 22—Tex Avery

NIT WITTY KITTY—October 6—Tom and Jerry—Hanna-Barbera

DROOPY'S DOUBLE TROUBLE—November 17—Droopy—Tex Avery

CAT NAPPING—December 8—Tom and Jerry—Hanna-Barbera

1952

FLYING CAT—January 12—Tom and Jerry—Hanna-Barbera

MAGICAL MAESTRO—February 9—Tex Avery

DUCK DOCTOR—February 16—Tom and Jerry—Hanna-Barbera

‡TWO MOUSEKETEERS—March 15—Tom and Jerry—Hanna-Barbera

SMITTEN KITTEN—April 12—Tom and Jerry—Hanna-Barbera

TRIPLET TROUBLE—April 19—Tom and Jerry—Hanna-Barbera

ONE CAB'S FAMILY—May 15—Tex Avery

LITTLE RUNAWAY—June 14—Tom and Jerry—Hanna-Barbera

ROCK-A-BYE BEAR—July 26—Tex Avery

FIT TO BE TIED—July 26—Tom and Jerry—Hanna-Barbera

PUSH-BUTTON KITTY—September 6—Tom and Jerry—Hanna-Barbera

CABALLERO DROOPY—September 27—Droopy—Dick Lundy

CRUISE CAT—October 18—Tom and Jerry—Hanna-Barbera

LITTLE WISE QUACKER—November 8—Barney Bear—Dick Lundy

THE DOG HOUSE—November 29—Tom and Jerry—Hanna-Barbera

BUSYBODY BEAR—December 20—Barney Bear—Dick Lundy

1953

THE MISSING MOUSE—January 10—Tom and Jerry—Hanna-Barbera

BARNEY'S HUNGRY COUSIN—January 31—Barney Bear—Dick Lundy

JERRY AND JUMBO—February 21—Tom and Jerry—Hanna-Barbera

COBS AND ROBBERS—March 14—Barney Bear—Dick Lundy

‡JOHANN MOUSE—March 21—Tom and Jerry—Hanna-Barbera

LITTLE JOHNNY JET—April 18—Tex Avery

THAT'S MY PUP—April 25—Tom and Jerry (with Spike and Tyke)—Hanna-Barbera

HEIR BEAR—May 30—Barney Bear—Dick Lundy

T.V. OF TOMORROW—June 6—Tex Avery

WEE WILLIE WILDCAT—June 20—Barney Bear—Dick Lundy

JUST DUCKY—September 5—Tom and Jerry—Hanna-Barbera

HALF-PINT PALOMINO—September 26—Barney Bear—Dick Lundy

TWO LITTLE INDIANS—October 17—Tom and Jerry—Hanna-Barbera

LIFE WITH TOM—November 21—Tom and Jerry—Hanna-Barbera

THREE LITTLE PUPS—December 26—Droopy—Tex Avery

1954

PUPPY TALE—January 23—Tom and Jerry—Hanna-Barbera

POSSE CAT—January 30—Tom and Jerry—Hanna-Barbera

DRAG-ALONG DROOPY—February 20—Droopy—Tex Avery

IMPOSSIBLE POSSUM—March 28—Barney—Dick Lundy

HIC-CUP PUP—April 17—Tom and Jerry (with Spike and Tyke)—Hanna-Barbera

BILLY BOY—May 8—Tex Avery

LITTLE SCHOOL MOUSE—May 29—Tom and Jerry—Hanna-Barbera

SLEEPY-TIME SQUIRREL—June 19—Barney Bear—Dick Lundy

HOMESTEADER DROOPY—July 10—Droopy—Tex Avery

BIRD-BRAIN BIRD DOG—July 30—Barney Bear—Dick Lundy

BABY BUTCH—August 14—Tom and Jerry—Hanna-Barbera

MICE FOLLIES—September 4—Tom and Jerry—Hanna-Barbera

FARM OF TOMORROW—September 18—Tex Avery

NEOPOLITAN MOUSE—October 2—Tom and Jerry—Hanna-Barbera

THE FLEA CIRCUS—November 6—Tex Avery

DOWNHEARTED DUCKLING—November 13—Tom and Jerry—Hanna-Barbera

*PET PEEVE—November 20—Tom and Jerry—Hanna-Barbera

*DIXIELAND DROOPY—December 4—Droopy—Tex Avery

*TOUCHÉ PUSSY CAT—December 18—Tom and Jerry—Hanna-Barbera

1955

SOUTHBOUND DUCKLING—March 12—Tom and Jerry—Hanna-Barbera

*PUP ON A PICNIC—April 30—Tom and Jerry (with Spike and Tyke)—Hanna-Barbera

FIELD AND SCREAM—April 30—Tex Avery

MOUSE FOR SALE—May 21—Tom and Jerry—Hanna-Barbera

DESIGNS ON JERRY—September 2—Tom and Jerry—Hanna-Barbera

*TOM AND CHERIE—September 9—Tom and Jerry—Hanna-Barbera

THE FIRST BAD MAN—September 30—Tex Avery

SMARTY CAT—October 14—Tom and Jerry—Hanna-Barbera

DEPUTY DROOPY—October 28—Droopy—Tex Avery, Michael Lah

PECOS PEST—November 11—Tom and Jerry—Hanna-Barbera

*In CinemaScope.

*THAT'S MY MOMMY—November 19—Tom and Jerry—Hanna-Barbera

CELLBOUND—November 25—Tex Avery, Michael Lah

†GOOD WILL TO MEN—December 23—Hanna-Barbera

1956 *(All in CinemaScope)*

THE FLYING SORCERESS—January 27—Tom and Jerry—Hanna-Barbera

THE EGG AND JERRY—March 23—Tom and Jerry—Hanna-Barbera

BUSY BUDDIES—May 4—Tom and Jerry—Hanna-Barbera

MUSCLE BEACH TOM—September 7—Tom and Jerry—Hanna-Barbera

MILLIONAIRE DROOPY—September 21—Tex Avery

DOWNBEAT BEAR—October 21—Tom and Jerry—Hanna-Barbera

BLUE CAT BLUES—November 16—Tom and Jerry—Hanna-Barbera

BARBECUE BRAWL—December 14—Tom and Jerry—Hanna-Barbera

1957 *(All in CinemaScope)*

CAT'S MEOW—January 25—Tex Avery

TOPS WITH POPS—February 22—Tom and Jerry—Hanna-Barbera

GIVE AND TYKE—March 29—Spike and Tyke—Hanna-Barbera

TIMID TABBY—April 19—Tom and Jerry—Hanna-Barbera

GRIN AND SHARE IT—May 17—Droopy—Michael Lah

FEEDIN' THE KIDDIE—June 7—Tom and Jerry—Hanna-Barbera

SCAT CATS—July 26—Spike and Tyke—Hanna-Barbera

MUCHO MOUSE—September 6—Tom and Jerry—Hanna-Barbera

BLACKBOARD JUMBLE—October 4—Droopy—Michael Lah

TOM'S PHOTO FINISH—November 1—Tom and Jerry—Hanna-Barbera

†ONE DROOPY KNIGHT—December 6—Droopy—Michael Lah

1958 *(All in CinemaScope)*

HAPPY GO DUCKY—January 3—Tom and Jerry—Hanna-Barbera

*In CinemaScope

SHEEP WRECKED—February 7—Droopy—Michael Lah

ROYAL CAT NAP—March 7—Tom and Jerry—Hanna-Barbera

MUTTS ABOUT RACING—April 4—Droopy—Michael Lah

VANISHING DUCK—May 2—Tom and Jerry—Hanna-Barbera

ROBIN HOODWINKED—June 6—Tom and Jerry—Hanna-Barbera

DROOPY LEPRECHAUN—July 4—Droopy—Michael Lah

TOT WATCHERS—August 1—Tom and Jerry—Hanna-Barbera

1961

SWITCHIN' KITTEN—September 7—Tom and Jerry—Gene Deitch

DOWN AND OUTING—October 26—Tom and Jerry—Gene Deitch

IT'S GREEK TO ME-OW—December 7—Tom and Jerry—Gene Deitch

1962

HIGH STEAKS—January—Tom and Jerry—Gene Deitch

MOUSE INTO SPACE—February—Tom and Jerry—Gene Deitch

LANDING STRIPLING—April—Tom and Jerry—Gene Deitch

CALYPSO CAT—June—Tom and Jerry—Gene Deitch

DIKIE MOE—July—Tom and Jerry—Gene Deitch

THE TOM AND JERRY CARTOON KIT—August—Tom and Jerry—Gene Deitch

TALL IN THE TRAP—September—Tom and Jerry—Gene Deitch

SORRY SAFARI—October—Tom and Jerry—Gene Deitch

BUDDIES THICKER THAN WATER—November—Tom and Jerry—Gene Deitch

CARMEN GET IT—December—Tom and Jerry—Gene Deitch

1963

PENTHOUSE MOUSE—Tom and Jerry—Chuck Jones

1964

THE CAT ABOVE, THE MOUSE BELOW—Tom and Jerry—Chuck Jones

IS THERE A DOCTOR IN THE MOUSE?—Tom and Jerry—Chuck Jones

MUCH ADO ABOUT MOUSING—Tom and Jerry—Chuck Jones

SNOWBODY LOVES ME—Tom and Jerry—Chuck Jones

UNSHRINKABLE JERRY MOUSE—Tom and Jerry—Chuck Jones

1965

‡THE DOT AND THE LINE—MGM Cartoon—Chuck Jones

AH—SWEET MOUSE STORY OF LIFE—Tom and Jerry—Chuck Jones

TOM-IC ENERGY—Tom and Jerry—Chuck Jones

BAD DAY AT CAT ROCK—Tom and Jerry—Chuck Jones

THE BROTHERS CARRY-MOUSE-OFF—Tom and Jerry—Jim Pabian

HAUNTED MOUSE—Tom and Jerry—Chuck Jones

I'M JUST WILD ABOUT JERRY—Tom and Jerry—Chuck Jones

OF FELINE BONDAGE—Tom and Jerry—Chuck Jones

TOM THUMP—Tom and Jerry—Chuck Jones

THE YEAR OF THE MOUSE—Tom and Jerry—Chuck Jones

THE CAT'S ME-OUCH—Tom and Jerry—Chuck Jones

JERRY-GO-ROUND—Tom and Jerry—Abe Levitow

1966

DUEL PERSONALITY—Tom and Jerry—Chuck Jones

JERRY JERRY QUITE CONTRARY—Tom and Jerry—Chuck Jones

LOVE ME, LOVE MY MOUSE—Tom and Jerry—Chuck Jones

PUSS 'N' BOATS—Tom and Jerry—Abe Levitow

FILET MEOW—Tom and Jerry—Abe Levitow

MATINEE MOUSE—Tom and Jerry—Tom Ray

A-TOMINABLE SNOWMAN—Tom and Jerry—Abe Levitow

CATTY CORNERED—Tom and Jerry—Abe Levitow

1967

THE BEAR THAT WASN'T—MGM Cartoon—Chuck Jones

CAT AND DUPLICAT—Tom and Jerry—Chuck Jones

O SOLAR MEOW—Tom and Jerry—Abe Levitow

GUIDED MOUSE-ILLE—Tom and Jerry—Abe Levitow

ROCK 'N' RODENT—Tom and Jerry—Abe Levitow

CANNERY RODENT—Tom and Jerry—Chuck Jones

THE MOUSE FROM H.U.N.G.E.R—Tom and Jerry—Abe Levitow

SURF BORED CAT—Tom and Jerry—Abe Levitow

SHUTTER BUGGED CAT—Tom and Jerry—Tom Ray

ADVANCE AND BE MECHANIZED—Tom and Jerry—Ben Washam

PURR CHANCE TO DREAM—Tom and Jerry—Ben Washam

The Paramount/Famous Studios Cartoons

Following is a complete list of cartoons produced and released by Paramount Pictures. Not included are later independent cartoons acquired for release by Paramount, which were not part of any regular series.

Where applicable, series title and starring character are indicated in parentheses, followed by the director's name. In some instances the director credits were not available, and research among Paramount's records and those of the U.S. Copyright Office proved futile. On several 1940s cartoons no director was credited on screen.

With the exception of the Popeye shorts released in 1942 and almost all cartoons released in 1943, all Paramount cartoons were filmed in color. Copyright dates are listed for these films only when it was impossible to ascertain a definite release date.

1942

YOU'RE A SAP, MR. JAP—August 7—Popeye—Dan Gordon

ALONA ON THE SARONG SEAS—September 4—Popeye—I. Sparber

JAPOTEURS—September 18—Superman—Seymour Kneitel

A HULL OF A MESS—October 16—Popeye—I. Sparber

SHOWDOWN—October 16—Superman—I. Sparber

SCRAP THE JAPS—November 20—Popeye—Seymour Kneitel

ELEVENTH HOUR—November 20—Superman—Dan Gordon

ME MUSICAL NEPHEWS—December 25—Popeye—Seymour Kneitel

DESTRUCTION, INC.—December 25—Superman—I. Sparber

1943

SPINACH FER BRITAIN—January 22—Popeye—I. Sparber

THE MUMMY STRIKES—February 19—Superman—I. Sparber

SEEIN' RED WHITE 'N' BLUE—February 19—Popeye—Dan Gordon

TOO WEAK TO WORK—March 19—Popeye—I. Sparber

JUNGLE DRUMS—March 26—Superman—Dan Gordon

A JOLLY GOOD FURLOUGH—April 23—Popeye—Dan Gordon

RATION FER THE DURATION—May 28—Popeye—Seymour Kneitel

UNDERGROUND WORLD—June 18—Superman—Seymour Kneitel

THE HUNGRY GOAT—June 25—Popeye—Dan Gordon

HAPPY BIRTHDAZE—July 16—Popeye—Dan Gordon

SECRET AGENT—July 30—Superman—Seymour Kneitel

WOOD PECKIN'—August 6—Popeye—I. Sparber

*CARTOONS AIN'T HUMAN—September 3—Popeye—Seymour Kneitel

HER HONOR THE MARE—November 26—Popeye—I. Sparber

NO MUTTON FOR NUTTIN'—November 26—Noveltoon (Blackie)—No credits

EGGS DON'T BOUNCE—December 24—Little Lulu—I. Sparber

MARRY-GO-ROUND—December 31—Popeye—Seymour Kneitel

1944

HENPECKED ROOSTER—February 18—Noveltoon—Seymour Kneitel

HULLABA-LULU—February 25—Little Lulu—Seymour Kneitel

CILLY GOOSE—March 24—Noveltoon—Seymour Kneitel

LULU GETS THE BIRDIE—March 31—Little Lulu—I. Sparber

WE'RE ON OUR WAY TO RIO—April 21—Popeye—I. Sparber

SUDDENLY IT'S SPRING!—April 28—Noveltoon (Raggedy Ann)—Seymour Kneitel

LULU IN HOLLYWOOD—May 19—Little Lulu—I. Sparber

ANVIL CHORUS GIRL—May 26—Popeye—I. Sparber

LUCKY LULU—June 30—Little Lulu—Seymour Kneitel

SPINACH-PACKIN' POPEYE—July 21—Popeye—I. Sparber

PUPPET LOVE—August 11—Popeye—Seymour Kneitel

IT'S NIFTY TO BE THRIFTY—August 18—Little Lulu—Seymour Kneitel

PITCHING WOO AT THE ZOO—September 1—Popeye—I. Sparber

I'M JUST CURIOUS—September 8—Little Lulu—Seymour Kneitel

MOVING AWEIGH—September 22—Popeye—No credits available

INDOOR OUTING—September 29—Little Lulu—I. Sparber

LULU AT THE ZOO—November 17—Little Lulu—I. Sparber

YANKEE DOODLE DONKEY—November 27—Noveltoon (Spunky)—I. Sparber

SHE-SICK SAILORS—December 8—Popeye—Seymour Kneitel

GABRIEL CHURCH KITTEN—December 15—Noveltoon—Seymour Kneitel

BIRTHDAY PARTY—December 29—Little Lulu—I. Sparber

1945

POP-PIE A LA MODE—January 26—Popeye—I. Sparber

WHEN G.I. JOHNNY COMES HOME—February 2—Noveltoon—Seymour Kneitel

MAGICALULU—March 2—Little Lulu—Seymour Kneitel

TOPS IN THE BIG TOP—March 16—Popeye—I. Sparber

SCRAPPILY MARRIED—March 30—Noveltoon—Seymour Kneitel

BEAU TIES—April 20—Little Lulu—Seymour Kneitel

SHAPE AHOY—April 27—Popeye—I. Sparber

*Last black-and-white release.

A LAMB IN A JAM—May 4—Noveltoon (Blackie)—I. Sparber

DAFFYDILLY DADDY—May 25—Little Lulu—Seymour Kneitel

FOR BETTER OR NURSE—June 8—Popeye—I. Sparber

SNAP HAPPY—June 22—Little Lulu—Bill Tytla

A SELF-MADE MONGREL—June 29—Noveltoon—No credits available

MESS PRODUCTION—August 24—Popeye—Seymour Kneitel

THE FRIENDLY GHOST—November 16—Noveltoon (Casper)—I. Sparber

MAN'S PEST FRIEND—November 30—Little Lulu—Seymour Kneitel

OLD MACDONALD HAD A FARM—December 28—Noveltoon—Seymour Kneitel

1946

BARGAIN COUNTER ATTACK—January 11—Little Lulu—I. Sparber

CHEESE BURGLAR—February 22—Noveltoon—I. Sparber

BORED OF EDUCATION—March 1—Little Lulu—Bill Tytla

HOUSE TRICKS—March 15—Popeye—Seymour Kneitel

SERVICE WITH A GUILE—April 19—Popeye—Bill Tytla

KLONDIKE CASANOVA—May 31—Popeye—I. Sparber

PEEP IN THE DEEP—June 7—Popeye—Seymour Kneitel

SHEEP SHAPE—June 28—Noveltoon (Blackie)—I. Sparber

ROCKET TO MARS—August 9—Popeye—Bill Tytla

CHICK AND DOUBLE CHICK—August 16—Little Lulu—Seymour Kneitel

RODEO ROMEO—August 16—Popeye—I. Sparber

GOAL RUSH—September 27—Noveltoon—I. Sparber

SUDDEN FRIED CHICKEN—October 18—Noveltoon—Bill Tytla

SPREE FOR ALL—October 18—Noveltoon—Seymour Kneitel

THE FISTIC MYSTIC—November 29—Popeye—Seymour Kneitel

THE ISLAND FLING—December 27—Popeye—Bill Tytla

1947

MUSICA-LULU—January 24—Little Lulu—I. Sparber

A SCOUT WITH THE GOUT—March 24—Little Lulu—Bill Tytla

ABUSEMENT PARK—April 25— Popeye—I. Sparber

STUPIDSTITIOUS CAT—April 25—Noveltoon—Seymour Kneitel

THE ENCHANTED SQUARE—May 9—Noveltoon (Raggedy Ann)—Seymour Kneitel

LOOSE IN THE CABOOSE—May 23—Little Lulu—Seymour Kneitel

I'LL BE SKIING YA—June 13—Popeye—I. Sparber

MADHATTAN ISLAND—June 27—Noveltoon—Seymour Kneitel

CAD AND CADDY—July 18—Little Lulu—I. Sparber

MUCH ADO ABOUT MUTTON—July 25—Noveltoon—I. Sparber

THE WEE MEN—August 8—Noveltoon—Bill Tytla

THE MILD WEST—August 22—Noveltoon—Seymour Kneitel

POPEYE AND THE PIRATES—September 12—Popeye—Seymour Kneitel

ROYAL FOUR FLUSHER—September 12—Popeye—Seymour Kneitel

A BOUT WITH A TROUT—October 10—Little Lulu—I. Sparber

NAUGHTY BUT MICE—October 10—Noveltoon—Seymour Kneitel

WOTTA KNIGHT—October 24—Popeye—I. Sparber

SAFARI SO GOOD—November 7—Popeye—I. Sparber

SUPER LULU—November 21—Little Lulu—Bill Tytla

THE BABY SITTER—November 28—Little Lulu—Seymour Kneitel

SANTA'S SURPRISE—December 5—Noveltoon—Seymour Kneitel

ALL'S FAIR AT THE FAIR—December 19—Popeye—Seymour Kneitel

THE CIRCUS COMES TO CLOWN—December 26—Screen Song—I. Sparber

1948

CAT O'NINE AILS—January 9—Noveltoon—Seymour Kneitel

BASE BRAWL—January 23—Screen Song—No credits available

THE DOG SHOW-OFF—January 30—Litlle Lulu—Seymour Kneitel

OLIVE OYL FOR PRESIDENT—January 30—Popeye—I. Sparber

FLIP FLAP—February 13—Noveltoon—I. Sparber

LITTLE BROWN JUG—February 20—Screen Song—Seymour Kneitel

WIGWAM WHOOPEE—February 27—Popeye—I. Sparber

THE GOLDEN STATE—March 12—Screen Song—No credits available

WE'RE IN THE HONEY—March 19—Noveltoon—No credits available

WINTER DRAWS ON—March 19—Screen Song—No credits available

PRE-HYSTERICAL MAN—March 26—Popeye—Seymour Kneitel

THE BORED CUKOO—April 9—Noveltoon—Bill Tytla

THERE'S GOOD BOOS TONIGHT—April 23—Noveltoon (Casper)—I. Sparber

THE LAND OF THE LOST—June 7—Noveltoon—I. Sparber

SING OR SWIM—June 16—Screen Song—Seymour Kneitel

POPEYE MEETS HERCULES—June 18—Popeye—Bill Tytla

BUTTERSCOTCH AND SODA—July 6—Noveltoon (Little Audrey)—No credits available

CAMPTOWN RACES—July 30—Screen Song—Seymour Kneitel

WOLF IN SHEIK'S CLOTHING—July 30—Popeye—I. Sparber

THE LONE STAR STATE—August 20—Screen Song—I. Sparber

SPINACH VS. HAMBURGERS—August 27—Popeye—Seymour Kneitel

SNOW PLACE LIKE HOME—September 3—Popeye—Seymour Kneitel

THE MITE MAKES RIGHT—October 15—Noveltoon—Bill Tytla

READIN', RITIN', AND RHYTHMETIC—October 22—Screen Song—Seymour Kneitel

ROBIN HOOD WINKED—November 12—Popeye—Seymour Kneitel

HECTOR'S HECTIC LIFE—November 19—Noveltoon—Bill Tytla

THE OLD SHELL GAME—December 17—Noveltoon—Seymour Kneitel

SYMPHONY IN SPINACH—December 31—Popeye—Seymour Kneitel

1949

THE FUNSHINE STATE—January 7—Screen Song—Seymour Kneitel

THE LITTLE CUTUP—January 21—Noveltoon—I. Sparber

HEP CAT SYMPHONY—February 4—Noveltoon—Seymour Kneitel

THE EMERALD ISLE—February 25—Screen Song—Seymour Kneitel

COMIN' ROUND THE MOUNTAIN—March 11—Screen Song—I. Sparber

THE LOST DREAM—March 18—Noveltoon (Little Audrey)—Bill Tytla

POPEYE'S PREMIERE—March 25—Popeye—No credits available

THE STORK MARKET—April 8—Screen Song—Seymour Kneitel

LITTLE RED SCHOOL MOUSE—April 15—Noveltoon—No credits available

A-HAUNTING WE WILL GO—May 13—Noveltoon (Casper)—Seymour Kneitel

LUMBER JACK AND JILL—May 27—Popeye—Seymour Kneitel

A MUTT IN A RUT—May 27—Noveltoon—I. Sparber

SPRING SONG—June 24—Screen Song—I. Sparber

HOT AIR ACES—June 24—Popeye—I. Sparber

THE SKI'S THE LIMIT—June 24—Screen Song—I. Sparber

CAMPUS CAPERS—July 1—Noveltoon—Bill Tytla

TOYS WILL BE TOYS—July 15—Screen Song—Seymour Kneitel

A BALMY SWAMI—July 22—Popeye—I. Sparber

FARM FOOLERY—August 5—Screen Song—Seymour Kneitel

TAR WITH A STAR—August 12—Popeye—Bill Tytla

OUR FUNNY FINNY FRIENDS—August 26—Screen Song—Seymour Kneitel

SILLY HILLBILLY—September 9—Popeye—I. Sparber

MARRIAGE VOWS—September 16—Screen Song—I. Sparber

THE BIG FLAME-UP—September 30—Screen Song—I. Sparber

LEPRECHAUN'S GOLD—October 14—Noveltoon—Bill Tytla

BARKING DOGS DON'T FITE—October 28—Popeye—I. Sparber

STROLLING THRU THE PARK—November 4—Screen Song—Seymour Kneitel

SONG OF THE BIRDS—November 18—Noveltoon (Little Audrey)—Bill Tytla

THE BIG DRIP—November 25—Screen Song—I. Sparber

SNOW FOOLIN'—December 16—Screen Song—I. Sparber

THE FLY'S LAST FLIGHT—December 23—Popeye—Seymour Kneitel

1950

LAND OF THE LOST JEWELS—January 6—Noveltoon—I. Sparber

BLUE HAWAII—January 13—Screen Song—Seymour Kneitel

HOW GREEN IS MY SPINACH—January 27—Popeye—Seymour Kneitel

DETOURING THRU MAINE—February 17—Screen Song—Seymour Kneitel

QUACK A DOODLE DO—March 3—Noveltoon (Baby Huey)—I. Sparber

GYM JAM—March 17—Popeye—I. Sparber

SHORTENIN' BREAD—March 24—Screen Song—I. Sparber

TEACHER'S PEST—March 31—Noveltoon—I. Sparber

WIN, PLACE AND SHOWBOAT—April 28—Screen Song—I. Sparber

BEACH PEACH—May 12—Popeye—Seymour Kneitel

JINGLE, JANGLE, JUNGLE—May 19—Screen Song—Seymour Kneitel

TARTS AND FLOWERS—May 26—Noveltoon (Little Audrey)—Bill Tytla

UPS AND DOWNS DERBY—June 9—Noveltoon (Lightning)—Seymour Kneitel

JITTERBUG JIVE—June 23—Popeye—Bill Tytla

HEAP, HEP INJUNS—June 30—Screen Song—I. Sparber

PLEASED TO EAT YOU—July 21—Noveltoon—I. Sparber

GOBS OF FUN—July 28—Screen Song—I. Sparber

POPEYE MAKES A MOVIE—August 11—Popeye—Seymour Kneitel

GOOFY GOOFY GANDER—August 18—Noveltoon (Little Audrey)—Bill Tytla

HELTER SWELTER—August 25—Screen Song—Seymour Kneitel

SAVED BY THE BELL—September 15—Noveltoon—Seymour Kneitel

BOOS IN THE NIGHT—September 22—Screen Song—I. Sparber

BABY WANTS SPINACH—September 29—Popeye—Seymour Kneitel

QUICK ON THE VIGOR—October 6—Popeye—Seymour Kneitel

CASPER'S SPREE UNDER THE SEA—October 13—Casper—Bill Tytla

MICE MEETING YOU—November 10—Noveltoon (Herman and Katnip)—Seymour Kneitel

VOICE OF THE TURKEY—November 10—Noveltoon—Bill Tytla

RIOT IN RHYTHM—November 10—Popeye—Seymour Kneitel

FIESTA TIME—November 17—Screen Song—Seymour Kneitel

FRESH YEGGS—November 17—Screen Song—Seymour Kneitel

FARMER AND THE BELLE—December 1—Popeye—Seymour Kneitel

SOCK-A-BYE KITTY—December 2—Noveltoon (Buzzy)—Seymour Kneitel

ONCE UPON A RHYME—December 20—Casper—I. Sparber

1951

ONE QUACK MIND—January 12—Noveltoon (Baby Huey)—I. Sparber

VACATION WITH PLAY—January 19—Popeye—I. Sparber

TWEET MUSIC—February 9—Screen Song—I. Sparber

MICE PARADISE—March 9—Noveltoon—I. Sparber

BOO-HOO BABY—March 30—Casper—Seymour Kneitel

DRIPPY MISSISSIPPI—April 13—Screen Song—Seymour Kneitel

THRILL OF FAIR—April 20—Popeye—Seymour Kneitel

HOLD THE LION PLEASE—April 27—Noveltoon (Little Audrey)—I. Sparber

LAND OF LOST WATCHES—May 4—Noveltoon—Seymour Kneitel

ALPINE FOR YOU—May 18—Popeye—I. Sparber

MINERS FORTY-NINERS—May 18—Screen Song—I. Sparber

AS THE CROW LIES—June 1—Noveltoon (Buzzy)—Seymour Kneitel

TO BOO OR NOT TO BOO—June 8—Casper—I. Sparber

DOUBLE CROSS COUNTRY RACE—June 15—Popeye—Seymour Kneitel

SING AGAIN OF MICHIGAN—June 29—Screen Song—I. Sparber

SLIP US SOME REDSKIN—July 6—Noveltoon—Seymour Kneitel

PILGRIM POPEYE—July 13—Popeye—I. Sparber

BOO SCOUT—July 27—Casper—I. Sparber

PARTY SMARTY—August 3—Noveltoon (Baby Huey)—Seymour Kneitel

CASPER COMES TO CLOWN—August 10—Casper—I. Sparber

CAT-CHOO—October 12—Noveltoon (Buzzy)—Seymour Kneitel

LET'S STALK SPINACH—October 19—Popeye—Seymour Kneitel

AUDREY THE RAINMAKER—October 26—Noveltoon (Little Audrey)—I. Sparber

CAT TAMALE—November 9—Noveltoon (Herman and Katnip—Seymour Kneitel

VEGETABLE VAUDEVILLE—November 9—Kartune—I. Sparber

PUNCH AND JUDO—November 16—Popeye—I. Sparber

CASPER TAKES A BOW-WOW—December 7—Casper—I. Sparber

BY LEAPS AND HOUNDS—December 14—Noveltoon (Herbert)—I. Sparber

SCOUT FELLOW—December 21—Noveltoon (Baby Huey)—Seymour Kneitel

SNOOZE REEL—December 28—Kartune—Seymour Kneitel

1952 *(Copyright date marked by* © *)*

POPEYE'S PAPPY—January 25—Popeye—Seymour Kneitel

DEEP BOO SEA—February 15—Casper—Seymour Kneitel

OFF WE GLOW—February 29—Kartune—I. Sparber

LUNCH WITH A PUNCH—March 14—Popeye—I. Sparber

CAT CARSON RIDES AGAIN—April 4—Noveltoon (Herman and Katnip)—Seymour Kneitel

GHOST OF THE TOWN—April 11—Capser—I. Sparber

THE AWFUL TOOTH—May 2—Noveltoon (Buzzy)—Seymour Kneitel

FUN AT THE FAIR—May 9—Kartune—I. Sparber

SWIMMER TAKE ALL—May 16—Popeye—Seymour Kneitel

LAW AND AUDREY—May 23—Noveltoon (Little Audrey)—I. Sparber

SPUNKY SKUNKY—May 30—Casper—I. Sparber

FRIEND OR PHONY—June 30—Popeye—I. Sparber

DIZZY DINOSOURS—July 4—Kartune—Seymour Kneitel

CITY KITTY—July 18—Noveltoon (Katnip)—I. Sparber

CAGE FRIGHT—August 8—Casper—Seymour Kneitel

GAG AND BAGGAGE—August 8—Kartune—I. Sparber

TOTS OF FUN—August 15—Popeye—Seymour Kneitel

CLOWN ON THE FARM—August 22—Noveltoon (Baby Huey)—Seymour Kneitel

POPALONG POPEYE—©August 29—Popeye—Seymour Kneitel

PIG-A-BOO—September 12—Casper—I. Sparber

SHUTEYE POPEYE—October 3—Popeye—I. Sparber

MICE-CAPADES—October 3—Herman and Katnip—Seymour Kneitel

TRUE BOO—October 24—Casper—I. Sparber

FOREST FANTASY—November 14—Kartune—Seymour Kneitel

BIG BAD SINBAD—December 12—Popeye—Seymour Kneitel

THE CASE OF THE COCKEYED CANARY—December 19—Noveltoon (Little Audrey)—Seymour Kneitel

FEAST AND FURIOUS—December 26—Noveltoon (Finny the Goldfish)—I. Sparber

1953

HYSTERICAL HISTORY—January 23—Kartune—Seymour Kneitel

ANCIENT FISTORY—January 30—Popeye—Seymour Kneitel

FRIGHTDAY THE 13TH—February 13—Casper—I. Sparber

OF MICE AND MAGIC—February 20—Herman and Katnip—I. Sparber

STARTING FROM HATCH—March 6—Noveltoon (Baby Huey)—Seymour Kneitel

SPOOK NO EVIL—March 13—Casper—Seymour Kneitel

CHILD SOCKOLOGY—March 27—Popeye—I. Sparber

PHILHARMANIACS—April 3—Kartune—Seymour Kneitel

WINNER BY A HARE—April 17—Noveltoon (Tommy Tortoise and Moe Hare)—I. Sparber

AERO-NUTICS—May 8—Kartune—Seymour Kneitel

HERMAN THE CATOONIST—May 15—Herman and Katnip—I. Sparber

POPEYE'S MIRTHDAY—May 22—Popeye—Seymour Kneitel

NORTH PAL—May 29—Casper—I. Sparber

BETTER BAIT THAN NEVER—June 5—Noveltoon (Buzzy)—Seymour Kneitel

TOREDORABLE—June 12—Popeye—Seymour Kneitel

INVENTION CONVENTION—June 10—Kartune—I. Sparber

BY THE OLD MILL SCREAM—July 3—Casper—Seymour Kneitel

SURF BORED—July 17—Noveltoon (Little Audrey)—I. Sparber

BABY WANTS A BATTLE—July 24—Popeye—Seymour Kneitel

NO PLACE LIKE ROME—July 31—Kartune—I. Sparber

FIREMAN'S BRAWL—August 21—Popeye—I. Sparber

LITTLE BOO PEEP—August 28—Casper—Seymour Kneitel

DRINKS ON THE MOUSE—August 28—Herman and Katnip—Dave Tendlar

*POPEYE, THE ACE OF SPACE—October 2—Popeye—Seymour Kneitel

SHAVING MUGS—October 9—Popeye—Seymour Kneitel

DO OR DIET—October 16—Casper—I. Sparber

HUEY'S DUCKY DADDY—November 20—Noveltoon (Baby Huey)—I. Sparber

BOO'S AND SADDLES—December 25—Casper—I. Sparber

NORTHWEST MOUSIE—December 28—Herman and Katnip—Seymour Kneitel

1954

FLOOR FLUSHER—January 1—Popeye—I. Sparber

*BOO MOON—January 1—Casper—Seymour Kneitel

THE SEAPREME COURT—January 29—Noveltoon (Little Audrey)—Seymour Kneitel

CRAZY TOWN—February 26—Noveltoon—I. Sparber

SURF AND SOUND—March 5—Herman and Katnip—Dave Tendlar

ZERO THE HERO—March 26—Casper—Seymour Kneitel

POPEYE'S 20TH ANNIVERSARY—April 2—Popeye—I. Sparber

HAIR TODAY, GONE TOMORROW—April 16—Noveltoon (Buzzy)—Seymour Kneitel

CASPER GENIE—May 28—Casper—Seymour Kneitel

TAXI-TURVY—June 4—Popeye—Seymour Kneitel

CANDY CABARET—June 11—Noveltoon—Dave Tendlar

OF MICE AND MENACE—June 25—Herman and Katnip—Seymour Kneitel

BRIDE AND GLOOM—July 2—Popeye—I. Sparber

PUSS 'N' BOOS—July 16—Casper—Seymour Kneitel

THE OILY BIRD—July 30—Noveltoon (Inchy the Worm)—I. Sparber

GREEK MIRTHOLOGY—August 13—Popeye—Seymour Kneitel

SHIP-A-HOOEY—August 20—Herman and Katnip—I. Sparber

*In 3-D.

FRIGHT TO THE FINISH—August 27—Popeye—Seymour Kneitel

BOOS AND ARROWS—October 15—Casper—Seymour Kneitel

FIDO BETA KAAPA—October 29—Noveltoon (Fido)—I. Sparber

PRIVATE-EYE POPEYE—November 12—Popeye—Seymour Kneitel

RAIL-RODENTS—November 26—Herman and Katnip—Dave Tendlar

BOO RIBBON WINNER—December 3—Casper—I. Sparber

GOPHER SPINACH—December 10—Popeye—Seymour Kneitel

NO IF'S, AND OR BUTTS—December 17—Noveltoon (Buzzy)—I. Sparber

1955

COOKING WITH GAGS—January 14—Popeye—I. Sparber

HIDE AND SHRIEK—January 28—Casper—Seymour Kneitel

DIZZY DISHES—February 4—Noveltoon (Little Audrey)—I. Sparber

NURSE TO MEET YA—February 11—Popeye—I. Sparber

ROBIN RODENTHOOD—February 25—Herman and Katnip—Dave Tendlar

KEEP YOUR GRIN UP—March 4—Casper—I. Sparber

PENNY ANTICS—March 11—Popeye—Seymour Kneitel

GIT ALONG LIL' DUCKIE—March 25—Noveltoon (Baby Huey)—Dave Tendlar

A BICEP BUILT FOR TWO—April 8—Herman and Katnip—Seymour Kneitel

BEAUS WILL BE BEAUS—May 20—Popeye—I. Sparber

SPOOKING WITH A BROGUE—May 27—Casper—Seymour Kneitel

GIFT OF GAG—May 27—Popeye—Seymour Kneitel

NEWS HOUND—June 10—Noveltoon (Snapper)—I. Sparber

POOP GOES THE WEASEL—July 8—Noveltoon (Wishbone and Waxey the Weasel)—Dave Tendlar

BULL FRIGHT—July 15—Casper—Seymour Kneitel

CAR-RAZY DRIVERS—July 22—Popeye—Seymour Kneitel

MOUSE TRAPEZE—August 5—Herman and Katnip—I. Sparber

RABBIT PUNCH—September 30—Noveltoon (Tommy Tortoise and Moe Hare)—Dave Tendlar

MISTER AND MISTLETOE—September 30—Popeye—I. Sparber

LITTLE AUDREY RIDING HOOD—October 14—Noveltoon (Little Audrey)—Seymour Kneitel

RED, WHITE AND BOO—October 21—Casper—I. Sparber

COPS IS TOPS—November 4—Popeye—I. Sparber

MOUSIER HERMAN—November 25—Herman and Katnip—Dave Tendlar

A JOB FOR A GOB—December 9—Popeye—Seymour Kneitel

BOO KIND TO ANIMALS—December 23—Casper—I. Sparber

KITTY CORNERED—December 30—Noveltoon (Kitty Cuddles)—Dave Tendlar

1956

HILLBILLING AND COOING—January 13—Popeye—Seymour Kneitel

GROUND HOG PLAY—February 10—Casper—Seymour Kneitel

MOUSEUM—February 24—Herman and Katnip—Seymour Kneitel

SLEUTH BUT SURE—March 23—Noveltoon (Tommy Tortoise and Moe Hare)—Dave Tendlar

POPEYE FOR PRESIDENT—March 30—Popeye—Seymour Kneitel

DUTCH TREAT—April 20—Casper—I. Sparber

SWAB THE DUCK—May 11—Noveltoon (Baby Huey)—Dave Tendlar

OUT TO PUNCH—June 8—Popeye—Seymour Kneitel

PENGUIN FOR YOUR THOUGHTS—June 15—Casper—Seymour Kneitel

WILL DO MOUSEWORK—June 29—Herman and Katnip—Seymour Kneitel

ASSAULT AND FLATTERY—July 6—Popeye—I. Sparber

PEDRO AND LORENZO—July 13—Noveltoon—Dave Tendlar

MOUSETRO HERMAN—August 10—Herman and Katnip—I. Sparber

INSECT TO INJURY—August 10—Popeye—Dave Tendlar

LINE OF SCREAMMAGE—August 17—Casper—Seymour Kneitel

PARLEZ-VOUZ WOO—September 12—Popeye—Seymour Kneitel

SIR IRVING AND JEAMES—October 19—Noveltoon—Seymour Kneitel

FLIGHT FROM WRONG—November 2—Casper—Seymour Kneitel

I DON'T SCARE—November 16—Popeye—I. Sparber

HIDE AND PEAK—December 7—Herman and Katnip—Dave Tendlar

A HAUL IN ONE—December 14—Popeye—I. Sparber

LION IN THE ROAR—December 21—Noveltoon (Louis the Lion)—Seymour Kneitel

1957

SPOOKING ABOUT AFRICA—January 4—Casper—Seymour Kneitel

PEST PUPIL—January 25—Noveltoon (Baby Huey)—Dave Tendlar

NEARLY WEDS—February 8—Popeye—Seymour Kneitel

CAT IN THE ACT—February 22—Herman and Katnip—Dave Tendlar

HOOKY SPOOKY—March 1—Casper—Seymour Kneitel

FISHING TACKLER—March 29—Noveltoon (Little Audrey)—I. Sparber

THE CRYSTAL BRAWL—April 5—Popeye—Seymour Kneitel

PATRIOTIC POPEYE—May 10—Popeye—Seymour Kneitel

PEEKABOO—May 24—Casper—Seymour Kneitel

MR. MONEY GAGS—June 7—Noveltoon (Tommy Tortoise and Moe Hare)—I. Sparber

SKY SCRAPPERS—June 14—Herman and Katnip—Dave Tendlar

SPREE LUNCH—June 21—Popeye—Seymour Kneitel

L'AMOUR THE MERRIER—July 5—Noveltoon—Seymour Kneitel

GHOST OF HONOR—July 19—Casper—I. Sparber

SPOOKY SWABS—August 9—Popeye—I. Sparber

FROM MAD TO WORSE—August 16—Herman and Katnip—Seymour Kneitel

ICE SCREAM—August 30—Casper—Seymour Kneitel

POSSUM PEARL—September 20—Noveltoon—Seymour Kneitel

JUMPING WITH TOY—October 4—Noveltoon (Baby Huey)—Dave Tendlar

JOLLY THE CLOWN—October 25—Noveltoon—Seymour Kneitel

BOO BOP—November 11—Casper—Seymour Kneitel

ONE FUNNY KNIGHT—November 22—Herman and Katnip—Dave Tendlar

COCK-A-DOODLE DINO—December 6—Noveltoon—I. Sparber

1958

DANTE DREAMER—January 3—Noveltoon—I. Sparber

HEIR RESTORER—January 24—Casper—Isadore Sparber

SPORTICLES—February 14—Noveltoon—Seymour Kneitel

SPOOK AND SPAN—February 28— Casper—Seymour Kneitel

GRATEFUL GUS—March 7—Noveltoon—Dave Tendlar

FRIGHTY CAT—March 14—Herman and Katnip—I. Sparber

FINNEGAN'S FLEA—April 4—Noveltoon—I. Sparber

GHOST WRITERS—April 25—Casper—Seymour Kneitel

WHICH IS WITCH—May 2— Casper—Seymour Kneitel

OKEY DOKEY DONKEY—May 16—Noveltoon (Spunky)—I. Sparber

CHEW CHEW BABY—August 15—Noveltoon—I. Sparber

TRAVELAFFS—August 22—Noveltoon—I. Sparber

YOU SAID A MOUSEFUL—August 29—Herman and Katnip—Seymour Kneitel

STORK RAVING MAD—October 3—Noveltoon—Seymour Kneitel

RIGHT OFF THE BAT—November 7—Modern Madcap—Seymour Kneitel

DAWG GAWN—December 12—Noveltoon (Little Audrey)—Seymour Kneitel

1959

OWLY TO BED—January 2—Herman and Katnip—Seymour Kneitel

DOING WHAT'S FRIGHT—January 16—Casper—Seymour Kneitel

THE ANIMAL FAIR—January 30—Noveltoon—Seymour Kneitel

FIT TO BE TOYED—February 6—Modern Madcap—Seymour Kneitel

FELINEOUS ASSAULT—February 20—Herman and Katnip—Seymour Kneitel

LA PETITE PARADE—March 6—Modern Madcap—Seymour Kneitel

DOWN TO MIRTH—March 20—Casper—Seymour Kneitel

FUN ON FURLOUGH—April 3—Herman and Katnip—Seymour Kneitel

HOUNDABOUT—April 10—Noveltoon—Seymour Kneitel

HUEY'S FATHER'S DAY—May 8—Noveltoon (Baby Huey)—Seymour Kneitel

NOT GHOULTY—June 5—Casper—Seymour Kneitel

SPOOKING OF GHOSTS—June 12—Modern Madcap—Seymour Kneitel

CASPER'S BIRTHDAY PARTY—July 31—Casper—Seymour Kneitel

TALKING HORSE SENSE—September 11—Modern Madcap—Seymour Kneitel

T.V. FUDDLEHEAD—October 16—Modern Madcap—Seymour Kneitel

KATNIP'S BIG DAY—October 30—Herman and Katnip—Seymour Kneitel

OUT OF THIS WHIRL—November 13—Noveltoon—Seymour Kneitel

1960

MIKE THE MASQUERADER—January 1—Modern Madcap—Seymour Kneitel

THE BOSS IS ALWAYS RIGHT—January 15—Jeepers and Creepers—Seymour Kneitel

BE MICE TO CATS—February 5—Noveltoon (Skit and Skat)—Seymour Kneitel

FIDDLE FADDLE—February 26—Modern Madcap—Seymour Kneitel

TROUBLE DATE—March 11—Jeepers and Creepers—Seymour Kneitel

FROM DIME TO DIME—March 25—Modern Madcap—Seymour Kneitel

MONKEY DOODLES—April—Noveltoon—Seymour Kneitel

TRIGGER TREAT—April—Modern Madcap—Seymour Kneitel

SILLY SCIENCE—May—Noveltoon—Seymour Kneitel

PECK YOUR OWN HOME—May—Noveltoon—Seymour Kneitel

BUZY BUDDIES—June—Jeepers and Creepers—Seymour Kneitel

THE SHOE MUST GO ON—June—Modern Madcap—Seymour Kneitel

COUNTER ATTACK—July—Noveltoon—Seymour Kneitel

TOPCAT—The Cat—Seymour Kneitel

ELECTRONICA—July—Modern Madcap—Seymour Kneitel

TURNING THE FABLES—August—Noveltoon—Seymour Kneitel

SHOOTIN' STARS—August—Modern Madcap (The Cat)—Seymour Kneitel

FINE-FEATHERED FIEND—September—Noveltoon—Seymour Kneitel

SCOUTING FOR TROUBLE—September—Jeepers and Creepers—Seymour Kneitel

DISGUISE THE LIMIT—September—Modern Madcap—Seymour Kneitel

GALAXIA—October—Modern Madcap—Seymour Kneitel

PLANET MOUSEOLA—October—Noveltoon—Seymour Kneitel

BOUNCING BENNY—November—Modern Madcap—Seymour Kneitel

NORTHERN MITES—November—Noveltoon—Seymour Kneitel

TERRY THE TERROR—December—Modern Madcap—Seymour Kneitel

MICENIKS—December—Noveltoon—Seymour Kneitel

1961

COOL CAT BLUES—January—The Cat—Seymour Kneitel

PHANTOM MOUSTACHER—January—Modern Madcap—Seymour Kneitel

THE LION'S BUSY—February—Noveltoon—Seymour Kneitel

THE KID FROM MARS—February—Modern Madcap—Seymour Kneitel

GOODIE THE GREMLIN—April—Noveltoon—Seymour Kneitel

THE MIGHTY THERMITE—April—Modern Madcap—Seymour Kneitel

ALVIN'S SOLO FLIGHT—April—Noveltoon (Little Lulu)—Seymour Kneitel

HOUND ABOUT THAT—April—Noveltoon—Seymour Kneitel

IN THE NICOTINE—June—Modern Madcap—Seymour Kneitel

TRICK OR TREE—July—Noveltoon—Seymour Kneitel

THE INQUISIT VISIT—July—Modern Madcap—Seymour Kneitel

BOPIN' HOOD—August—The Cat—Seymour Kneitel

CAPE KIDNAVERAL—August—Noveltoon—Seymour Kneitel

MUNRO—September—Noveltoon—Gene Deitch

TURTLE SCOOP—October—Noveltoon—Seymour Kneitel

CANE AND ABLE—October—The Cat—Seymour Kneitel

ABNER, THE BASEBALL—November—Special, two reels—Seymour Kneitel

KOZMO GOES TO SCHOOL—November—Noveltoon—Seymour Kneitel

THE PLOT SICKENS—December—Modern Madcap—Seymour Kneitel

1962

PERRY POPGUN—January—Noveltoon—Seymour Kneitel

CRUMLEY COGWELL—January—Modern Madcap—Seymour Kneitel

WITHOUT TIME OR REASON—January—Noveltoon—Seymour Kneitel

POPCORN AND POLITICS—February—Modern Madcap—Seymour Kneitel

GOOD AND GUILTY—February—Noveltoon—Seymour Kneitel

GIDDY GADGETS—March—Modern Madcap—Seymour Kneitel

HI-FI JINX—March—Modern Madcap—Seymour Kneitel

T.V. OR NO T.V.—March—Noveltoon—Seymour Kneitel

FUNDERFUL SUBURBIA—March—Modern Madcap—Seymour Kneitel

SAMSON SCRAP—March—Modern Madcap—Gene Deitch

FROG'S LEGS—April—Comic Kings (Little Lulu)—Seymour Kneitel

HOME SWEET SWAMPY—May—Comic Kings (Beetle Bailey)—Seymour Kneitel

HERO'S REWARD—May—Comic Kings (Beetle Bailey)—Seymour Kneitel

PSYCHOLOGICAL TESTING—June—Comic Kings (Beetle Bailey)—Seymour Kneitel

SNUFFY'S SONG—June—Comic Kings (Snuffy Smith)—Seymour Kneitel

THE HAT—June—Comic Kings (Snuffy Smith)—Seymour Kneitel

ET TU OTTO—September—Comic Kings (Beetle Bailey)—Seymour Kneitel

ANATOLE—September—Noveltoon—Gene Deitch

A TREE IS A TREE IS A TREE?—October—Comic Kings (Beetle Bailey)—Seymour Kneitel

THE METHOD AND MAW—October—Comic Kings (Snuffy Smith)—Seymour Kneitel

PENNY PALS—October—Modern Madcap—Seymour Kneitel

TAKE ME TO YOUR GEN'RUL—October—Comic Kings (Snuffy Smith)—Seymour Kneitel

YULE LAFF—October—Noveltoon—Seymour Kneitel

KEEPING UP WITH KRAZY—October—Comic Kings (Krazy Kat)—Gene Deitch

ROBOT RINGER—November—Modern Madcap—Seymour Kneitel

IT'S FOR THE BIRDIES—November—Noveltoon—Seymour Kneitel

MOUSE BLANCHE—November—Comic Kings (Krazy Kat)—Gene Deitch

ONE OF THE FAMILY—December—Modern Madcap—Seymour Kneitel

FIDDLIN' AROUND—December—Noveltoon—Seymour Kneitel

1963

RINGADING KID—January—Modern Madcap—Seymour Kneitel

OLLIE THE OWL—January—Noveltoon—Seymour Kneitel

DRUM UP A TENANT—February—Modern Madcap—Seymour Kneitel

GOOD SNOOZE TONIGHT—February—Noveltoon—Seymour Kneitel

ONE WEAK VACATION—March—Modern Madcap—Seymour Kneitel

A SIGHT FOR SQUAW EYES—March—Noveltoon—Seymour Kneitel

TRASH PROGRAM—April—Modern Madcap—Seymour Kneitel

GRAMPS TO THE RESCUE—September—Noveltoon—Seymour Kneitel

HARRY HAPPY—September—Modern Madcap—Seymour Kneitel

HOBO'S HOLIDAY—October—Noveltoon—Seymour Kneitel

TELL ME A BADTIME STORY—October—Modern Madcap—Seymour Kneitel

HOUND FOR POUND—October—Noveltoon—Seymour Kneitel

THE PIG'S FEAT—October—Modern Madcap—Seymour Kneitel

SOUR GRIPES—October—Modern Madcap—Seymour Kneitel

THE SHEEPISH WOLF—November—Noveltoon—Seymour Kneitel

GOODIE'S GOOD DEED—November—Modern Madcap—Seymour Kneitel

HICCUP HOUND—November—Noveltoon—Seymour Kneitel

MUGGY-DOO BOYCAT—December—Modern Madcap—Seymour Kneitel

1964

WHIZ QUIZ KID—February—Noveltoon—Seymour Kneitel

PANHANDLING ON MADISON AVENUE—April—Swifty and Shorty—Seymour Kneitel

FIZZICLE FIZZLE—April—Swifty and Shorty—Seymour Kneitel

SAILING ZERO—April—Swifty and Shorty—Seymour Kneitel

FIX THAT CLOCK—May—Swifty and Shorty—Seymour Kneitel

A FRIEND IN TWEED—May—Swifty and Shorty—Seymour Kneitel

THE ONCE-OVER—June—Swifty and Shorty—Seymour Kneitel

SERVICE WITH A SMILE—Swifty and Shorty—Seymour Kneitel

CALL ME A TAXI—July—Swifty and Shorty—Seymour Knietel

HIGHWAY SNOBBERY—July—Swifty and Shorty—Seymour Kneitel

HIP HIP OLE—September—Swifty and Shorty—Seymour Kneitel

ROBOT RIVAL—September—Modern Madcap—Seymour Kneitel

LADDY AND HIS LAMP—September—Noveltoon—Seymour Kneitel

ACCIDENTS WILL HAPPEN—September—Swifty and Shorty—Seymour Kneitel

AND SO TIBET—October—Modern Madcap—Seymour Kneitel

THE BUS WAY TO TRAVEL—October—Swifty and Shorty—Seymour Kneitel

READIN', WRITHING AND 'RITHMETIC—November—Modern Madcap—Seymour Kneitel

NEAR SIGHTED AND FAR OUT—November—Modern Madcap—Seymour Kneitel

A TIGER'S TAIL—December—Noveltoon—Seymour Kneitel

HOMER ON THE RANGE—December—Noveltoon—Seymour Kneitel

1965

HORNING IN—January—Noveltoon—Howard Post

A HAIR-RAISING TALE—January—Noveltoon—Howard Post

CAGEY BUSINESS—February—Modern Madcap—Howard Post

THE STORY OF GEORGE WASHINGTON—February—Noveltoon—Jack Mendelsohn

A LEAK IN THE DIKE—March—Noveltoon—Jack Mendelsohn

POOR LITTLE WITCH GIRL—April—Modern Madcap (Honey Halfwitch)—Howard Post

THE ITCH—May—Modern Madcap—Howard Post

INFERIOR DECORATOR—June—Swifty and Shorty—Howard Post

HERE'S NUDNIK—August—Nudnik—Gene Deitch

SOLITARY REFINEMENT—September—Modern Madcap—Howard Post

OCEAN BRUISE—September—Swifty and Shorty—Howard Post

SHOEFLIES—October—Honey Halfwitch—Howard Post

TALLY-HOKUM—October—Noveltoon—Howard Post

THE OUTSIDE DOPE—November—Modern Madcap—Howard Post

DRIVE ON NUDNIK—November—Nudnik—Gene Deitch

GETTING AHEAD—December—Swifty and Shorty—Howard Post

HOME SWEET NUDNIK—December—Nudnik—Gene Deitch

LES BOYS—December—Swifty and Shorty—Howard Post

GERONIMO & SON—December—Noveltoon—Howard Post

1966

OP POP WHAM AND BOP—January—Noveltoon—Howard Post

SICK TRANSIT—January—Noveltoon—Howard Post

SPACE KID—February—Noveltoon—Howard Post

WELCOME NUDNIK—February—Nudnik—Gene Deitch

BAGGIN' THE DRAGON—February—Honey Halfwitch—Howard Post

FROM NAGS TO WITCHES—February—Honey Halfwitch—Howard Post

TRICK OR CHEAT—March—Honey Halfwitch—Howard Post

I WANT MY MUMMY—March—Modern Madcap—Howard Post

THE ROCKET RACKET—March—Honey Halfwitch—Howard Post

NUDNIK ON THE ROOF—May—Nudnik—Gene Deitch

A BALMY KNIGHT—June—Modern Madcap—Shamus Culhane

THE DEFIANT GIANT—June—Honey Halfwitch—Howard Post

FROM NUDNIK WITH LOVE—June—Nudnik—Gene Deitch

THRONE FOR A LOSS—July—Honey Halfwitch—Howard Post

POTIONS AND NOTIONS—August—Honey Halfwitch—Shamus Culhane

A WEDDING KNIGHT—August—Modern Madcap—Howard Post

WHO NEEDS NUDNIK?—August—Nudnik—Gene Deitch

NUDNIK ON THE BEACH—September—Nudnik—Gene Deitch

GOOD NEIGHBOR NUDNIK—November—Nudnik—Gene Deitch

TWO BY TWO—January—Modern Madcap—Howard Post

1967

BLACK SHEEP BLACKSMITH—January—Modern Madcap—Howard Post

NUDNIK ON A SHOWCASE—January—Nudnik—Gene Deitch

THE SPACE SQUID—January—Go-Go Toons—Shamus Culhane

NOWHERE WITH NUDNIK—March—Nudnik—Gene Deitch

THINK OR SINK—March—Merry Makers—Shamus Culhane

MY DADDY THE ASTRONAUT—April—Fractured Fable—Shamus Culhane

THE TRIP—April—Noveltoon—Shamus Culhane

GOODNIGHT SWEET NUDNIK—April—Nudnik—Gene Deitch

ALTER EGOTIST—April—Honey Halfwitch—Shamus Culhane

THE SQUAW PATH—May—Go-Go Toons—Shamus Culhane

THE PLUMBER—May—Go-Go Toons—Shamus Culhane

HALT, WHO GROWS THERE?—May—Merry Makers—Shamus Culhane

ROBIN HOODWINKED—June—Noveltoon—Shamus Culhane

CLEAN SWEEP—June—Honey Halfwitch—Chuck Harriton

FROM ORBIT TO OBIT—June—Merry Makers—Shamus Culhane

HIGH BUT NOT DRY—August—Honey Halfwitch—Shamus Culhane

BROTHER BAT—August—Honey Halfwitch—Shamus Culhane

FORGET-ME-NUTS—August—Merry Makers—Shamus Culhane

THE STUCK-UP WOLF—September—Fractured Fable—Shamus Culhane

NUDNIK ON A SHOESTRING—October—Nudnik—Gene Deitch

A BRIDGE GROWS IN BROOKLYN—October—Go-Go Toons—Chuck Harriton

THE STUBBORN COWBOY—October—Fractured Fable—Shamus Culhane

NUDNIK'S NUDNICKEL—November—Nudnik—Gene Deitch

I REMEMBER NUDNIK—November—Nudnik—Gene Deitch

THE OPERA CAPER—November—Go-Go Toons—Shamus Culhane (Finished by Ralph Bakshi)

KEEP THE COOL BABY—November—Go-Go Toons—Chuck Harriton

THE FUZ—December—Fractured Fable—Ralph Bakshi

THE MINI-SQUIRTS—December—Fractured Fable—Ralph Bakshi

MARVIN DIGS—December—Go-Go Toons—Ralph Bakshi

MOUSE TREK—© December 31—Fractured Fable—Ralph Bakshi

The UPA Cartoons

The following is a complete list of UPA's theatrical short subjects, all of which were made in color and released by Columbia Pictures. We include the release date, series title, and director for each short.

UPA produced two theatrical feature films, 1001 ARABIAN NIGHTS (1959), which was released by Columbia, and GAY PURR-EE (1962), which was released by Warner Brothers. UPA animation appeared in other films as well, including THE FOURPOSTER (1952) and DREAMBOAT (1952).

One dagger next to a film title (†) indicates an Academy Award nominee. A double dagger (‡) indicates an Academy Award Winner.

1948

†ROBIN HOODLUM—December 23—Fox and Crow—John Hubley

1949

THE MAGIC FLUKE—March 27—Fox and Crow—John Hubley

RAGTIME BEAR—September 8—Jolly Frolics (Mr. Magoo)—John Hubley

1950

PUNCHY DE LEON—January 12—Jolly Frolics (Fox and Crow)—John Hubley

SPELLBOUND HOUND—March 16—Mr. Magoo—John Hubley

THE MINER'S DAUGHTER—May 25—Jolly Frolics—Robert Cannon

GIDDYAP—July 27—Jolly Frolics—Art Babbitt

†TROUBLE INDEMNITY—September 14—Mr. Magoo—Pete Burness

THE POPCORN STORY—November 30—Jolly Frolics—Art Babbitt

BUNGLED BUNGALOW—December 28—Mr. Magoo—Pete Burness

1951

GERALD MCBOING BOING—January 25—Jolly Frolics—Robert Cannon

THE FAMILY CIRCUS—January 25—Jolly Frolics—Art Babbitt

BARE FACED FLATFOOT—April 26—Mr. Magoo—Pete Burness

GEORGIE AND THE DRAGON—September 27—Jolly Frolics—Robert Cannon

FUDDY DUDDY BUDDY—October 18—Mr. Magoo—John Hubley

WONDER GLOVES—November 29—Jolly Frolics—Robert Cannon

GRIZZLY GOLFER—December 20—Mr. Magoo—Pete Burness

1952

THE OOMPAHS—January 24—Jolly Frolics—Robert Cannon

SLOPPY JALOPY—February 21—Mr. Magoo—Pete Burness

‡ROOTY TOOT TOOT—March 27—Jolly Frolics—John Hubley

DOG SNATCHER—May 29—Mr. Magoo—Pete Burness

WILLIE THE KID—June 26—Jolly Frolics—Robert Cannon

†PINK AND BLUE BLUES—August 28—Mr. Magoo—Pete Burness

PETE HOTHEAD—September 25—Jolly Frolics—Ted Parmelee

HOTSY FOOTSY—October 23—Mr. Magoo—William Hurtz

†MADELINE—November 27—Jolly Frolics—Robert Cannon

CAPTAINS OUTRAGEOUS—December 25—Mr. Magoo—Pete Burness

1953

LITTLE BOY WITH A BIG HORN—March 26—Jolly Frolics—Robert Cannon

THE EMPEROR'S NEW CLOTHES—April 30—Jolly Frolics—Ted Parmelee

SAFETY SPIN—May 21—Mr. Magoo—Pete Burness

†CHRISTOPHER CRUMPET—June 25—Jolly Frolics—Robert Cannon

GERALD MCBOING BOING'S SYMPHONY—July 15—Robert Cannon

MAGOO'S MASTERPIECE—July 30—Mr. Magoo—Pete Burness

A UNICORN IN THE GARDEN—September 24—William Hurtz

MAGOO SLEPT HERE—November 19—Mr. Magoo—Pete Burness

THE TELL-TALE HEART—December 27— Ted Parmelee

1954

BRINGING UP MOTHER—January 14—William Hurtz

BALLET-OOPS—February 11—Robert Cannon

MAGOO GOES SKIING—March 11—Mr. Magoo—Pete Burness

THE MAN ON THE FLYING TRAPEZE—April 8—Ted Parmelee

FUDGET'S BUDGET—June 17—Robert Cannon

KANGAROO COURTING—July 22—Pete Burness

HOW NOW BOING BOING—September 9—Robert Cannon

DESTINATION MAGOO—December 16—Mr. Magoo—Pete Burness

1955

*‡WHEN MAGOO FLEW—January 6—Mr. Magoo—Pete Burness

SPARE THE CHILD—January 27—Abe Liss

FOUR WHEELS AND NO BRAKE—January 27—Ted Parmelee

MAGOO'S CHECK-UP—February 24—Mr. Magoo—Pete Burness

BABY BOOGIE—May 19—Paul Julian

MAGOO'S EXPRESS—May 19—Mr. Magoo—Pete Burness

MADCAP MAGOO—June 23—Mr. Magoo—Pete Burness

CHRISTOPHER CRUMPET'S PLAYMATE—September 8—Robert Cannon

STAGE DOOR MAGOO—October 6—Mr. Magoo—Pete Burness

RISE OF DUTON LANG—December 1—Osmond Evans

*MAGOO MAKES NEWS—December 12—Mr. Magoo—Pete Burness

*In CinemaScope.

1956

†GERALD MCBOING BOING ON THE PLANET MOO—February 9—Robert Cannon

MAGOO'S CAINE MUTINY—March 8—Mr. Magoo—Pete Burness

*MAGOO GOES WEST—April 19—Mr. Magoo—Pete Burness

*CALLING DR. MAGOO—May 24—Mr. Magoo—Pete Burness

†THE JAYWALKER—May 31—Robert Cannon

*MAGOO BEATS THE HEAT—June 21—Mr. Magoo—Pete Burness

*‡MAGOO'S PUDDLE JUMPER—July 26—Mr. Magoo—Pete Burness

*TRAILBLAZER MAGOO—September 13—Mr. Magoo—Pete Burness

*MAGOO'S PROBLEM CHILD—October 18—Mr. Magoo—Pete Burness

*MEET MOTHER MAGOO—December 27—Mr. Magoo—Pete Burness

1957

*MAGOO GOES OVERBOARD—February 21—Mr. Magoo—Pete Burness

*MATADOR MAGOO—March 30—Mr. Magoo—Pete Burness

*MAGOO BREAKS PAR—June 27—Mr. Magoo—Pete Burness

*MAGOO'S GLORIOUS FOURTH—July 25—Mr. Magoo—Pete Burness

*MAGOO'S MASQUERADE—August 15—Mr. Magoo—Rudy Larriva

*MAGOO SAVES THE BANK—September 26—Mr. Magoo—Pete Burness

ROCK HOUND MAGOO—October 24—Mr. Magoo—Pete Burness

MAGOO'S MOOSE HUNT—November 28—Mr. Magoo—Robert Cannon

*In CinemaScope.

MAGOO'S PRIVATE WAR—December 19—Mr. Magoo—Rudy Larriva

1958

†TREES AND JAMAICA DADDY—January 30—Ham and Hattie—Lew Keller

SAILING AND VILLAGE BAND—February 27—Ham and Hattie—Lew Keller

MAGOO'S YOUNG MANHOOD—March 13—Mr. Magoo—Pete Burness

SCOUTMASTER MAGOO—April 10—Robert Cannon

THE EXPLOSIVE MR. MAGOO—May 8—Mr. Magoo—Pete Burness

MAGOO'S THREE-POINT LANDING—June 5—Mr. Magoo—Pete Burness

MAGOO'S CRUISE—September 11—Mr. Magoo—Rudy Larriva

LOVE COMES TO MAGOO—October 2—Mr. Magoo—Tom McDonald

SPRING AND SAGANAKI—October—Ham and Hattie—Lew Keller

GUMSHOE MAGOO—November—Mr. Magoo—Gil Turner

1959

BWANA MAGOO—January 9—Mr. Magoo—Tom McDonald

PICNICS ARE FUN AND DINO'S SERENADE—January 16—Ham and Hattie—Lew Keller

MAGOO'S HOMECOMING—March 5—Mr. Magoo—Gil Turner

MERRY MINSTREL MAGOO—April 9—Mr. Magoo—Rudy Larriva

MAGOO'S LODGE BROTHER—May 7—Mr. Magoo—Rudy Larriva

TERROR FACES MAGOO—July 9—Mr. Magoo—Chris Ishii

Academy Award Nominees and Winners

1931–32

*FLOWERS AND TREES, Walt Disney
MICKEY'S ORPHANS, Walt Disney
IT'S GOT ME AGAIN, Warner Brothers

1932–33

BUILDING A BUILDING, Walt Disney
THE MERRY OLD SOUL, Walter Lantz
THE THREE LITTLE PIGS, Walt Disney

1934

HOLIDAY LAND, Charles Mintz/Columbia
JOLLY LITTLE ELVES, Walter Lantz
*THE TORTOISE AND THE HARE, Walt Disney

1935

THE CALICO DRAGON, MGM
*THREE ORPHAN KITTENS, Walt Disney
WHO KILLED COCK ROBIN? Walt Disney

1936

*COUNTRY COUSIN, Walt Disney
OLD MILL POND, MGM
SINBAD THE SAILOR, Max Fleischer

1937

EDUCATED FISH, Max Fleischer
THE LITTLE MATCH GIRL, Charles Mintz/Columbia
*THE OLD MILL, Walt Disney

1938

BRAVE LITTLE TAILOR, Walt Disney
MOTHER GOOSE GOES HOLLYWOOD, Walt Disney
*FERDINAND THE BULL, Walt Disney
GOOD SCOUTS, Walt Disney
HUNKY AND SPUNKY, Max Fleischer

1939

DETOURING AMERICA, Warner Brothers
PEACE ON EARTH, MGM
THE POINTER, Walt Disney
*THE UGLY DUCKLING, Walt Disney

1940

*MILKY WAY, MGM
PUSS GETS THE BOOT, MGM
A WILD HARE, Warner Brothers

1941

BOOGIE WOOGIE BUGLE BOY OF COMPANY B, Walter Lantz
HIAWATHA'S RABBIT HUNT, Warner Brothers
HOW WAR CAME, Columbia
*LEND A PAW, Walt Disney
THE NIGHT BEFORE CHRISTMAS, MGM
RHAPSODY IN RIVETS, Warner Brothers
THE ROOKIE BEAR, MGM

*An asterisk represents an Academy Award winner.

RHYTHM IN THE RANKS, George Pal Puppetoon

SUPERMAN NO. 1, Max Fleischer

TRUANT OFFICER DONALD, Walt Disney

1942

ALL OUT FOR V, Terrytoons

THE BLITZ WOLF, MGM

*DER FUEHRER'S FACE, Walt Disney

JUKE BOX JAMBOREE, Walter Lantz

PIGS IN A POLKA, Warner Brothers

TULPIS SHALL GROW, George Pal Puppetoon

1943

THE DIZZY ACROBAT, Walter Lantz

THE FIVE HUNDRED HATS OF BARTHOLONEW CUBBINS, George Pal Puppetoon

GREETINGS, BAIT, Warner Brothers

IMAGINATION, Columbia

REASON AND EMOTION, Walt Disney

*YANKEE DOODLE MOUSE, MGM

1944

AND TO THINK I SAW IT ON MULBERRY STREET, George Pal Puppetoon

THE DOG, CAT AND CANARY, Columbia

FISH FRY, Walter Lantz

HOW TO PLAY FOOTBALL, Walt Disney

*MOUSE TROUBLE, MGM

MY BOY, JOHNNY, Terrytoons

SWOONER CROONER, Warner Brothers

1945

DONALD'S CRIME, Walt Disney

JASPER AND THE BEANSTALK, George Pal Puppetoon

LIFE WITH FEATHERS, Warner Brothers

MIGHTY MOUSE IN GYPSY LIFE, Terrytoons

POET AND PEASANT, Walter Lantz

*QUIET PLEASE, MGM

RIPPLING ROMANCE, Columbia

1946

*THE CAT CONCERTO, MGM

CHOPIN'S MUSICAL MOMENTS, Walter Lantz

JOHN HENRY AND THE INKY POO, George Pal Puppetoon

SQUATTER'S RIGHTS, Walt Disney

WALKY TALKY HAWKY, Warner Brothers

1947

CHIP AN' DALE, Walt Disney

DR. JEKYLL AND MR. MOUSE, MGM

PLUTO'S BLUE NOTE, Walt Disney

TUBBY THE TUBA, George Pal Puppetoon

*TWEETIE PIE, Warner Brothers

1948

*THE LITTLE ORPHAN, MGM

MICKEY AND THE SEAL, Walt Disney

MOUSE WRECKERS, Warner Brothers

ROBIN HOODLUM, UPA

TEA FOR TWO HUNDRED, Walt Disney

1949

*FOR SCENT-IMENTAL REASONS, Warner Brothers

HATCH UP YOUR TROUBLES, MGM

MAGIC FLUKE, UPA

TOY TINKERS, Walt Disney

1950

*GERALD MCBOING-BOING, UPA

JERRY'S COUSIN, MGM

TROUBLE INDEMNITY, UPA

1951

LAMBERT, THE SHEEPISH LION, Walt Disney

ROOTY TOOT TOOT, UPA

*TWO MOUSEKETEERS, MGM

1952

*JOHANN MOUSE, MGM

LITTLE JOHNNY JET, MGM

MADELINE, UPA

PINK AND BLUE BLUES, UPA

ROMANCE OF TRANSPORTATION, National Film Board of Canada

1953

CHRISTOPHER CRUMPET, UPA

FROM A TO Z-Z-Z-Z, Warner Brothers

RUGGED BEAR, Walt Disney

THE TELL-TALE HEART, UPA

*TOOT, WHISTLE, PLUNK AND BOOM, Walt Disney

1954

CRAZY MIXED-UP PUP, Walter Lantz
PIGS IS PIGS, Walt Disney

SANDY CLAWS, Warner Brothers

TOUCHÉ, PUSSY CAT, MGM

*WHEN MAGOO FLEW, UPA

1955

GOOD WILL TO MEN, MGM

THE LEGEND OF ROCK-A-BYE-POINT, Walter Lantz

NO HUNTING, Walt Disney

*SPEEDY GONZALES, Warner Brothers

1956

GERALD MCBOING-BOING ON PLANET MOO, UPA

THE JAYWALKER, UPA

*MR. MAGOO'S PUDDLE JUMPER, UPA

1957

*BIRDS ANONYMOUS, Warner Brothers

ONE DROOPY KNIGHT, MGM

TABASCO ROAD, Warner Brothers

TREES AND JAMAICA DADDY, UPA

THE TRUTH ABOUT MOTHER GOOSE, Walt Disney

1958

*KNIGHTY KNIGHT BUGS, Warner Brothers

PAUL BUNYAN, Walt Disney

SIDNEY'S FAMILY TREE, Terrytoons

1959

MEXICALI SHMOES, Warner Brothers

*MOONBIRD, Storyboard, Inc.

NOAH'S ARK, Walt Disney

THE VIOLINIST, Pintoff Productions

1960

GOLIATH II, Walt Disney

HIGH NOTE, Warner Brothers

MOUSE AND GARDEN, Warner Brothers

*MUNRO, Rembrandt Films (released by Paramount)

A PLACE IN THE SUN, George K. Arthur-Go Pictures, Inc

1961

AQUAMANIA, Walt Disney

BEEP PREPARED, Warner Brothers

*ERSATZ (The Substitute), Zagreb Film

NELLY'S FOLLY, Warner Brothers

THE PIED PIPER OF GUADALUPE, Warner Brothers

1962

*THE HOLE, Storyboard Inc.

ICARUS MONTGOLFIER WRIGHT, Format Films

NOW HEAR THIS, Warner Brothers

SELF DEFENSE—FOR COWARDS, Rembrandt Films

SYMPOSIUM ON POPULAR SONGS, Walt Disney

1963

AUTOMANIA 2000, Halas and Batchelor Productions

*THE CRITIC, Pintoff-Crossbow Productions

*An asterisk represents an Academy Award winner.

THE GAME (IGRA), Zagreb Film

MY FINANCIAL CAREER, National Film Board of Canada

PIANISSIMO, Cinema 16

1964

CHRISTMAS CRACKER, National Film Board of Canada

HOW TO AVOID FRIENDSHIP, Rembrandt Films

NUDNIK NO. 2, Rembrandt Films

*THE PINK PHINK, DePatie-Freleng

1965

CLAY OR THE ORIGIN OF SPECIES, Eliot Noyes

*THE DOT AND THE LINE, MGM

THE THIEVING MAGPIE, Giulio Gianini–Emanuele Luzzati

1966

THE DRAG, National Film Board of Canada

*HERB ALPERT AND THE TIJUANA BRASS DOUBLE FEATURE, Hubley Studio (released by Paramount)

THE PINK BLUEPRINT, DePatie-Freleng

1967

*THE BOX, Murakami-Wolf Films

HYPOTHESE BETA, Films Orzeaux

WHAT ON EARTH! National Film Board of Canada

1968

THE HOUSE THAT JACK BUILT, National Film Board of Canada

THE MAGIC PEAR TREE, Murakami-Wolf Productions

WINDY DAY, Hubley Studio (released by Paramount)

*WINNIE THE POOH AND THE BLUSTERY DAY, Walt Disney

1969

*IT'S TOUGH TO BE A BIRD, Walt Disney

OF MEN AND DEMONS, Hubley Studio (released by Paramount)

WALKING, National Film Board of Canada

1970

THE FURTHER ADVENTURES OF UNCLE SAM: PART TWO, The Haboush Company

*IS IT ALWAYS RIGHT TO BE RIGHT? Stephen Bosustow Productions

THE SHEPHERD, Cameron Guess and Associates

1971

*THE CRUNCH BIRD, Maxwell-Petok-Petrovich Productions

EVOLUTION, National Film Board of Canada

THE SELFISH GIANT, Potterton Productions

1972

*THE CHRISTMAS CAROL, Richard Williams

KAMA SUTRA RIDES AGAIN, Bob Godfrey Films

TUP TUP, Zagreb Film

1973

*FRANK FILM, Frank Mouris

THE LEGEND OF JOHN HENRY, Stephen Bosustow–Pyramid Films Production

PULCINELLA, Luzzati-Gianini

1974

*CLOSED MONDAYS, Lighthouse Productions

THE FAMILY THAT DWELT APART, National Film Board of Canada

HUNGER, National Film Board of Canada

VOYAGE TO NEXT, Hubley Studio

WINNIE THE POOH AND TIGGER TOO, Walt Disney

*An asterisk represents an Academy Award winner.

Glossary of Animation Terms

Background The backdrop or setting of a scene, usually painted and then placed underneath the cels.

Cel Familiar term for "celluloid," the transparent sheet on which characters are inked (on the front) and painted (on the back).

Cleanup The process in which rough pencil animation is refined.

Effects Animation Usually done by a specialist, this term encompasses most *non*-character animation: wind, rain, fire, explosions, and the like.

Exposure Sheet The animator's blueprint, on which the action and dialogue are indicated frame-by-frame.

Extreme Generally the beginning or end of a specific action by a character, preceding or following movement in-between. Also known as the "key pose."

Field Indicates camera position in relation to the animation being photographed; for instance, 12-field is a long shot, 4-field a closeup.

Full Animation The traditional theatrical animation in which every frame or every other frame is animated.

In-between A transitional animation drawing in a cycle of motion between extremes.

In-betweener The person whose job it is to draw in-betweens, usually the first step toward becoming an animator.

Inker The person who traces penciled animation drawings onto the cels, a process now handled in many cases by Xeroxing.

Layout The physical mapping-out of a film, including the art direction, composition, and relationship of characters to the background.

Limited Animation A process developed in the television era to cut down the number of drawings in animation by using less movement.

Model Sheet A reference chart on which a particular character is visually analyzed in different postures and moods, at different angles, and the like, to which all drawings conform.

Movieola A film viewing/editing machine generally used to watch a work in progress.

Multiplane Camera An elaborate animation camera developed by the Disney studio, for which each shot is separated into as many as 14 layers; when the camera shoots through these layers an illusion of depth is created.

Nitrate The highly flammable material of which both cels and motion picture film were made until the late 1940s

Overlay A stationary drawing, cut-out, or mask laid over the cels to shoot a particular scene.

Painter The person whose job it is to paint the cel once it is inked.

Pan A gradual camera movement, from side to side or up and down a frame.

Peg A standard knob on an animator's drawing board over which pre-punched paper is laid in order to hold it in place.

451

Pencil Test A test film of preliminary pencil animation before it is cleaned up, inked, and painted.

Pose Reel A test film, much like a filmstrip, consisting of storyboard sketches or animators' extremes in sequence, which are set to a prerecorded soundtrack before they have been animated. Like a pencil test, this serves as a blueprint for the finished film.

Registration The steadiness of the moving image from one frame to the next, insured by the use of pre-punched paper and cels which are laid over standard-sized pegs.

Rotoscope The device patented by Max Fleischer that enables an animator to trace over live-action filmed movement frame by frame.

Rough A loose pencil drawing, for animation or storyboard purposes.

Storyboard A sequence of drawings pinned on a wall that serves as a visual script for a film.

Truck The movement of a camera toward or away from a scene.

Xerox The photocopying process that has, in most cases, replaced the hand-inking of cels from pencil drawings.

Sources for Renting and Purchasing Cartoons

16MM RENTAL AND SALE; SALES ON SUPER 8MM

The following companies and institutions have particularly strong selections in the areas cited:

Silent animation:

Museum of Modern Art
Department of Film Circulating Programs
11 West 53rd Street
New York, New York 10019

(for educational and cultural institutions only; one excellent program on the beginnings of animation and another on Winsor McCay; many experimental and avant-garde films as well)

Glenn Photo Supply
(formerly known as Em Gee
   Film Library)
6924 Canby Avenue
Reseda, California 91335

(probably the largest collection of rare animated films in the country; also offers prints for sale)

Walt Disney:

The Disney company franchises 16mm rental of many short subjects and feature films to a number of well-known rental firms (Films Inc., Macmillan Audio Brandon, Twyman Films, Swank Motion Pictures, Select Films, etc.). A wide selection of films is available for Super 8mm purchase through camera stores and film dealers. The Disney home office to contact is at 800 Sonora Avenue, Glendale, California 91201. Unfortunately, many important Disney shorts are not available for sale or rental, but schools may obtain some key 1930s cartoons on long-term lease.

Max Fleischer:

Many public-domain Fleischer cartoons, both silent and sound, are available from various dealers, but the single largest sources are:

Kit Parker Films
Carmel Valley, California 93924

(new 16mm prints of many rare Inkwell cartoons as well as many of the Color Classics are now available for rent)

Ivy Films/16
165 West 46th Street
New York, New York 10036

(virtually every Fleischer short, except the Superman & Popeye series, from 1927–1941. Beware of newly colored prints of the Betty Boop cartoons, in Super 8 and 16mm)

United Artists 16mm
729 Seventh Avenue
New York, New York 10019

(has the entire theatrical Popeye library, many of the shorts being arranged according to thematic programs)

Terrytoons:

Black-and-white Terrytoons, both silent and sound, have been offered for many years through dealers, but are difficult to locate on a specific-title basis. Color Terrytoons are offered for sale and rental through a large number of dealers, all of whom are licensed by Viacom, 1211 Avenue of the Americas, New York, New York 10036.

Walter Lantz:

Lantz cartoons have long been available on 8mm and 16mm through Castle Films (now Universal 8); many dealers still rent these prints, and camera stores sell new Super 8mm copies. The original sources remain Universal 8 and Universal 16, 445 Park Avenue, New York, New York 10022.

Ub Iwerks:

Many Iwerks cartoons in public domain are widely offered, but the main source for brand-new sale prints from original negatives is Blackhawk Films, 1235 West 5th Street, Davenport, Iowa 52808.

Van Beuren:

There is no one source for these cartoons, but the largest supplier of black-and-white Van Beuren titles is Select Films, 115 West 31st Street, New York, New York 10001. Blackhawk Films offers new prints for sale of some later color titles.

Columbia/Mintz:

Until recently one could find these cartoons only by chance, mainly in older rental catalogues. Now Kit Parker Films, Carmel Valley, California 93924, has made up new 16mm prints of many Columbia titles for rent.

Warner Brothers:

Prints of Warner Brothers cartoons have been franchised to rental libraries for many years and are still widely available. The official source for all color, pre-1950 cartoons is United Artists 16mm, 729 Seventh Avenue, New York, New York 10019.

MGM:

Harman-Ising titles were distributed for many years by a now-defunct company called Pictoreels; some of these prints still appear in older rental catalogues. Otherwise, the exclusive distributor for all MGM titles is Films Incorporated, which has offices in many cities; main office is 4420 Oakton Street, Skokie, Illinois 60076. Super 8mm prints are offered through many dealers by Ken Films.

Paramount/Famous:

Popeye titles are distributed exclusively by United Artists 16mm. Other 1940s titles are offered by Ivy Films. (See Max Fleischer above.) The 1950s and 60s titles are available in erratic fashion through Films Incorporated. (See MGM above.)

UPA:

UPA cartoons have been franchised to many rental libraries through Columbia Pictures. Columbia also sells some excellent titles on Super 8mm, through dealers and from its home office at 711 Fifth Avenue, New York, New York 10022.

GENERAL SOURCES FOR RENTING

Select Films
115 West 31st Street
New York, New York 10001

Kit Parker Films
P.O. Box 227
Carmel Valley, California 93924

Macmillan/Audio Brandon
34 MacQuesten Parkway South
Mount Vernon, New York 10550

Budget Films
4590 Santa Monica Boulevard
Los Angeles, California 90029

Swank Motion Pictures
201 South Jefferson Avenue
St. Louis, Missouri 63166

Twyman Films
329 Salem Avenue
Dayton, Ohio 45401

GENERAL SOURCES FOR PURCHASING

Festival Films
4445 Aldrich Avenue South
Minneapolis, Minnesota 55409

Blackhawk Films
1235 West 5th Street
Davenport, Iowa 52808

Reel Images
456 Monroe Turnpike
Monroe, Connecticut 06468

Cinema Concepts
91 Main Street
Chester, Connecticut 06412

National Cinema Service
333 West 57th Street
New York, New York 10019

VIDEO PURCHASING

Many film dealers are now selling cartoons on videotape. Among the leaders in this new field are:

Video Dimensions
43 East 10th Street
New York, New York 10003

Video Images
456 Monroe Turnpike
Monroe Connecticut 06468

Index

NOTE: References in *italics* are to illustrations. When a reference is to text and illustration on the same page, the page number is in roman type.

About Ben Boogie (Lantz), 178
Abrams, Ray, Lantz animator, 161, 173, 180
Academy Awards (*see specific studios*)
Ace in the Hole (Lantz), 165
Ace of Space, The (Famous), 310
Admission Free (Fleischer), 97
Aesop's Fables (Terry), 27, 31, 36, 125–127, 195
Aesop's Fables series (Van Beuren), 196
Ain't That Ducky (Warner), 252
Aladdin and His Wonderful Lamp (Iwerks), 162, 163, 191
Alice in Cartoonland series, 30–32
Alice in Wonderland (Disney), 42, 73
All Out for "V" (Terry), 135–136
Allegro Non Troppo, 342
Allen, Bob, director for MGM, 277
Allen, Dayton:
    voice of Deputy Dawg, 149
    voices of Heckle and Jeckle, 141
Allen, Heck, Lantz writer for Tex Avery, 176*n*.
Alley to Bali (Lantz), 174
Amos 'n' Andy (Van Beuren), 200
Anchors Aweigh (MGM), 293–294
Anderson, Carl, Bray animator, 20*n*.
Anderson, Eddie "Rochester," in *The Mouse That Jack Built*, 269
Anderson, Fred, joins Terry as animator-director, 126
Anderson, Ken, Disney art director and character designer, 75
Anderson, "Vet," editorial cartoonist, 13, 20*n*.
Andrews, Julie, *Mary Poppins*, 76
Andriot, Lucien, photographer on Terry medical film (WWI), 125
Andy Gump series (Universal), 157
Andy Panda, 163–164, 171–172
Andy Panda series (Lantz), 163–164
Animated Antics (Fleischer), 116
Animated cartoons:
    feature films, 340–342
    indifference to, 122
    shorts, demise of, 337, 338
    (*See also* Silent era; *specific studios*)
Animated Grouch Chasers (Barré; 1915–16), 12
Animated Hair cartoons (Fleischer), 89
Another Day, Another Doormat (Terry), 145
Anzilotti, Cosmo:
    Paramount designer/layout man, 316
    Terrytoons director-animator, 151
Aqua Duck (Warner), 271
Aristo-cat, The (Warner), 244
Artistocats, The (Disney), 76, 77
Arlen, Harold, score for *Gay Purr-ee*, 336
Armstrong, Joe, animator, *18*
Armstrong, Louis, caricatured in *Clean Pastures*, 234

Army First Motion Picture Unit, 318
Associated Animators, 205
Astronut (Terry), 150
At Your Service, Madam (Warner), 234
Audio Cinema, backs Moser-Terry-Coffman, 127–128
Augustson, Cliff, assistant at Famous Studios, 308
Autry, Gene, 172
Avery, Tex:
    Lantz animator, 155, 160, 161
    Lantz director, 176–177
    MGM director, 285–291, 294–299
    Warner director, 219, 225–227, 230, 232, 234–237, 242–244

Babbitt, Art:
    Disney animator, 41, 44, 61
    defines Goofy as a character, 46, 48–49
    leaves Disney for UPA, 64
    Terry animator, 128, 129
    UPA director, 331
Baby Huey, 309, 310
Baby Sitter, The (Famous), 306
Baby Wants Spinach (Famous), 312
Back Alley Oproar (Warner), 253
Background artist, distinction between layout man and, 260
Backus, Jim, voice for Mister Magoo, 323
Bad Luck Blackie (MGM), 289, 290
Bad Ol' Pretty Tat (Warner), 25
Bailey, Harry:
    joins Terry as director-animator, 126
    stays with Van Beuren, 195
Baker, Wee Bonnie, sings for Chilly Willy, 168*n*.
Bakes, George, assistant at Famous Studios, 308
Bakshi, Ralph:
    director of feature-length cartoons, 341–342
    producer-director for Paramount, 316
    Terrytoons animator-director, 150, 151
    leaves Terrytoons for Paramount, 151
Balloon Land (Pincushion Man; Iwerks), 191
Balukas, Mike, inker for *Krazy Kat*, 206
Bambi (Disney), 65–66
Band Concert, The (Disney), 42, 49, 169
Bandmaster, The (Lantz), 171–172
Banquet Busters (Lantz), 171
Barbecue Brawl (MGM), 298
Barber of Seville, The (Lantz), 166, 182
Barbera, Joe:
    background, 282
    at MGM, 277
        and Hanna, 282–285, 291–295, 297, 299–300
        leaves MGM to open studio with Hanna, 300

Barbera, Joe (*Cont.*):
    Terry animator, 130
        leaves Terry for MGM, 132
    at Van Beuren studio, 200
    (*See also* Hanna-Barbera)
Barbetta, Dante, Famous Studios animator, 308
Barge, Ed, MGM animator, 292, *293*
Barks, Carl, Disney writer, 69
Barney Bear, 279–280, 282, 296–297
Barney Google (Columbia), 211
Barré, Raoul, 11–12, 14, *25*
    acquisition and animation of Mutt and Jeff, 12–15, 156
    developments by studio, 11, 14
    joins Messmer at Sullivan studio, 25
    studio opened, 11, 12
Barrier, Mike, animation historian, 50
Bartsch, Art:
    Terry background artist, 142
    Terrytoons director-animator, 151
Batchelder, Warren, Warner animator, 269
Bathing Buddies (Lantz), 171
Battaglia, Aurie, UPA artist, 332
Bauer, Eli, 150
    Paramount story man, 315, 316
    Terrytoons writer, 144, 151
    creates Hector Heathcote, 149
Bear and the Bean, The (MGM), 296
Bear and the Beavers, The (MGM), 280
Bear and the Hare, The (MGM), 206
Bear for Punishment, A (Warner), 259–260
Bear That Couldn't Sleep, The (MGM), 279–280
Bear That Wasn't, The (MGM), 302
Beary's Family Album, The (Lantz), 181, 182
Beatles, *Yellow Submarine* (1968), 340–341
Beck, Jackson, voice for Bluto, 309
Beckerman, Howard:
    assistant at Famous Studios, 308
    free-lance writer for Paramount, 315
    UPA/New York animator, 333
Bedknobs and Broomsticks (Disney), 76
Bedtime (Fleischer), 83, *84*
Beezy Bear (Disney), 72
Belabour Thy Neighbor, 149
Bemelmans, Ludwig, author of *Madeline*, 328
Ben and Me (Disney), 72
Benedict, Ed:
    Lantz animator, 161
    at MGM, 299
Benny, Jack, in *The Mouse That Jack Built*, 269
Bentley, Robert, Lantz animator, 175
Bertino, Al (writer):
    for Lantz, 179
    for Terrytoons, 150
Betty Boop, 96–102, 109, 110
Betty Boop and Grampy (Fleischer), 102
Betty Boop and the Little King (Fleischer), 110

Betty Boop's Big Boss (Fleischer), 97
Betty Boop's Crazy Inventions (Fleischer), 101
Betty Boop's Museum (Fleischer), 98
Betty Boop's Ups and Downs (Fleischer), 101
Bickenbach, Dick:
   Iwerks animator, 190, *193*
   MGM layout man, *293*, 299
Big Bad Wolf, 40
Billion Dollar Limited, The (Fleischer), 118
Billy Boy (MGM), 299
Bimbo, *95*–97, *99*–101
Bimbo's Initiation (Fleischer), 98
Binder, Henry, joins Screen Gems, 217
Birds Anonymous (Warner), 207
Birdy and the Beast (Warner), 225
Blackburn, Norm:
   Iwerks animator, 190, *193*
   Warner animator, 220
Blackton, J. Stuart, (early animator), 3
   Enchanted Drawing, The (1900), 1
   Humorous Phases of Funny Faces (1906), 2
Blair, Preston (animator):
   for Disney, 60, *62*
   for Lantz, 159
   for MGM, 287–289, *296, 297*
   for Mintz, 210
Blanc, Mel:
   character voices for Warner, 232, 241, 253, 254, 264, 270
   Woody Woodpecker voice, 165
Blechman, R. O., translates book into cartoon, *The Juggler of Our Lady*, 146
Bletcher, Billy:
   voice in *Boy Meets Dog*, 163
   for *Little Boy Blue*, 191
Blow Me Down (Fleischer), 104
Blowout, The (Warner), 232
Blue Cat Blues (MGM), 292, 300
Bluto, 104, 106, 309
Bobby Bumps (1915), 19–21
Bold King Cole (Van Beuren), 203
Bone Trouble (Disney), 69
Bonnicksen, Ted, Warner animator, 269
Boo Moon (Famous), 310, *311*
Boogie Woogie Bugle Boy of Company B, The (Lantz), 167
Boomer Bill, 22
Boop-Oop-A-Doop (Fleischer), 97
Bootleg Pete, 32
Bosko, 220–223
   taken to MGM by Harman-Ising, 224, 276
Bosko in Dutch (Warner), 223
Bosko's Holiday (Warner), 222
Bosustow, Steve, *319*
   control of UPA, 321, *327*, 329, 334
   Iwerks animator, 190, *193*
   Lantz animator, 161
   leaves Disney for UPA, 64
   partnership in UPA, 320
   sells UPA to Saperstein, 335
   starts studio with Schwartz and Hilberman, 318–320
   and UPA take over Fox and Crow from Screen Gems, 217
Bouncing Ball series, 87–89, 94–96
Bounds, Phyllis, Disney artist, 65
Bourne, Larz, 150

Bourne, Larz *(Cont.)*:
   creates *Deputy Dawg* series, 149
   Famous Studios writer, 309
Bowers, Charles, 12–13
   joins Barré, 12
   opens own studio, 15
   takes over Barré studio, 14–15
Bowling Alley Cat (MGM), 284
Bowsky, Willard, Fleischer animator, *113*
Boy Meets Dog (Lantz), 163
Boy Named Charlie Brown, A, 342
Boyle, Jack, 25
Bradley, Scott, MGM music director, 284–285
Brave Little Tailor, The (Disney), 50
Bray, John Randolph, 6–12, 17–22, 81–82, 156–157
   closes studio, 157
   commissions Fleischer for Army training films, 81
   experiments by, 20–21
   instructional films, 20, 21
   Lantz creations for, 21, 156–157
   meets Max Fleischer, 80
   Paramount-Bray Pictograph, The (1916), 20, 22
   patents by, 7–11
Bray-Hurd Patent Trust, 19
Brewster Color, 21
Brice, Fanny, and Betty Boop films, 97
Brightman, Homer:
   Lantz writer, 175
   MGM writer, 300
Broadway Malady (Columbia), 207
Bromides, 156
Bronis, Jimmy, production manager for Screen Gems, 213
Brother Brat (Warner), 248
Brotherhood of Man (UPA), 321
Brotherly Love (Fleischer), 107
Brown, Treg, sound-effects work at Warner, 232, 262
Bruehl, Anton, photographer, 157
Bryan, Arthur Q., voice for Elmer Fudd, 242, 264, 270
Buccaneer Bunny (Warner), 256
Buchwald, Sam:
   in charge of Famous Studios, 305, 309, 310
   Fleischer business manager, 120
Budd, Leighton:
   Bray animator, 20
   with Terry, 125
Buddy, 224
Buddy the Gee-Man (Warner), 224
Buddy's Garage (Warner), 224
Buddy's Theatre (Warner), 224
Buell, Marjorie Henderson (Marge), creator of *Little Lulu*, 306
Buena Vista, 39*n*.
Bugs Bunny, 70, 219, 237, 241–246, 250–252, 256–259, 264–268, 270–272, 342
Bugs Bunny Nips the Nips (Warner), 250
Bugs Bunny Rides Again (Warner), 256, 268
Bugs Bunny Show (TV show), 270–271
Bugs Bunny Superstar, 342
Bugs Bunny and the Three Bears (Warner), 244
Bulleteers, The (Fleischer), 118
Bully, The (Iwerks), 188

Bunny and Claude, 272
Bunny Hugged (Warner), 258
Buñuel, Louis, creator of film *Un Chien Andalou* (1929), 98
Burks, John, inventor of 3-D system used by Fleischer, 109
Burness, Pete, 335
   UPA director, 331–332, 335
   at Van Beuren studio, 200
   Warner animator, 253
Burton, John:
   live-action cameraman at Warner, 238
   3-D simulation at Warner, 266
Busy Body Bear (MGM), 297
Busy Buddies (MGM), 300
Butler, Daws:
   voice in Chilly Willy cartoons, 177
   wolf voice for MGM, 299
Buzzy the Crow, 309, 310
Byrne, Tom, Sullivan animator, 25

Calico Dragon, The (MGM), 276
California Institute of the Arts, 77
Calker, Darrell:
   composer for Screen Gems, 217
   Lantz musical director, 167–168
Calloway, Cab:
   in Betty Boop films, 98
   caricatured in *Clean Pastures*, 234
Calpini, Orestes, Famous Studios animator, 308
Candy Land (Lantz), 161
Cannata, George (animator):
   for Famous Studios, 308
   for Fleischer, 96
   for Sullivan, 24, *25*
Cannon, Bob "Bobe":
   UPA director-animator, 321, 325–327, 332
   Warner animator, 225, 244
Cannon, Johnny, Disney animator, 35
Capp, Al, creator of *Li'l Abner*, 216
Captain and the Kids, The (MGM), 277–278
Captains Outrageous (UPA), 331
Carey, John, Warner animator, 269
Carlson, Bob, Disney animator, 72
Carlson, Wallace, Bray animator, 20
Carney, Art, imitated in *The Honey Mousers*, 269
Carr, Jack, *Krazy Kat* staff, 206, *208*
Cartoon Classics series (Lantz), 161
Cartoon renaissance, 342
Cartoonland Mysteries (Lantz), 178
Cartoons Ain't Human (Famous), 306, 311
Case of the Cold Storage Yegg (Lantz), 179
Casper, 307–310
Casper, The Friendly Ghost series (Famous), 307, 309
Cat Above and the Mouse Below, The (MGM), 302
Cat Concerto (MGM), *290*, 291
Cat Tails for Two (Warner), 266
Celluloid (cel-and-background technique), 9, 21, 92, 124
Centaurs, The (McCay), 5
Champion, Marge, poses for *Snow White*, 56
Chaplin, Charlie, animated cartoons, 22
Charlotte's Web, 342

457

Cheese It the Cat (Warner), 269
Cheese Nappers (Lantz), 162
Chevalier, Maurice, and Betty Boop films, 97
Chien Andalou, Un (Buñuel and Dali), 98
Child Sock-ology (H-B), *338*
Chilly, Willy, 168*n.*, 176–177, 181
China Jones (Warner), 269
Chiniquy, Gerry, Warner director-animator, 271
Chouinard Art School, Los Angeles, 43
Chow Hound (Warner), 260
Christmas Comes but Once a Year (Fleischer), 110
Christmas Night (Pals; Van Beuren), 199
Christopher Crumpet (UPA), 328
Churchill, Frank (musician):
　for Disney, 40
　for Lantz, 163
Cinderella (Disney), 73
Cinecolor, 190, 224–225, 253
CinemaScope, 72
　first Disney feature in, 74
　at MGM, 280, 298–300
　Terrytoons in, 142, 146, *149*
　at UPA, 332
Circus Capers (Van Beuren), 196
Clampett, Bob, 338
　Harman-Ising animator, 219
　Screen Gems director, 217
　Warner animator, 224–227
　Warner director, 232–234, 236, 237, 243, 245–248, 251–253, 268*n.*
Clark, Les, Disney animator, 35, 44, 75
Claws in the Lease (Warner), 253
Clean Pastures (Warner), 234
Clock Cleaners (Disney), 50
Clock Goes Round and Round (Columbia), 213
Close Call, A (Terry), *127*
Close Call, A (Van Beuren), 197
Coal Black and De Sebben Dwarfs (Warner; spoof of *Snow White*), 246–248
Cobean, Sam:
　Disney animator, 44, 74
　at Screen Gems, 214
Cockatoos for Two, 217
Coe, Al, Lantz animator, 179
Coffman, Joseph, forms company with Moser and Terry, 127
Cohen, Herman R., Lantz animator, 175
Cohl, Emile (early French animator), 3
　Drame chez les Fantoches (1908), 3
　and metamorphosis on film, 91
Colonel Heeza Liar in Africa (Bray), 7–8, 20, 21
Colonel Heeza Liar series (Bray), 156
Color (*see* Brewster Color; Cinecolor; DeLuxe color; Technicolor; *specific studios*)
Color Classics (Fleischer), 110
Color Rhapsodies (Columbia), 211–212
Columbia Pictures, 38, 205–213, 322, 333
　and Screen Gems, 214–217
Colvig, Pinto, 40
　Goofy's voice, 40
　leaves Disney for Fleischer, 70, *111*, 116
　and Pluto's laugh, 48
Comic Book Land (Terry), 135

Comicolor Cartoons (Iwerks), 189–192
Confidence (Lantz), 160
Confusions of a Nutzy Spy (Warner), 250
Congdon, Leadora, art-deco designs for *Miss Glory*, 235
Contest (Fleischer), 85
Convict Concerto (Lantz), 170*n.*
Coo-Coo Bird Dog, 216
Coo-Coo Nut Grove (Warner), 234
Cook, Robert, Disney sound engineer, 62
Cool Cat, 272
Coonskin, 342
Corny Concerto (Warner; spoof of *Fantasia*), 246
Correll, Charles, and Freeman Gosden, *Amos 'n' Andy* voices for Van Beuren, 200
Cosgriff, Jack, at Screen Gems, 214
Costello, William (Red Pepper Sam), Popeye's voice, 104
Costs (*see specific studios*)
Count Screwlouse from Toulousse, 278
Country Cousin, The (Disney), 44, 51
Country School, The (Lantz), 159
Cowboy Needs a Horse, A (Disney), 72
Coy Decoy, A (Warner), 237
Craig, Anderson, Terry artist, 142
Crandall, Roland "Doc," Fleischer animator, 84
Crane, Doug, Paramount animator, 315
Crazy Mixed-up Pup (Lantz), 176
Crippen, Fred, joins UPA, 332
Crosby, Bing:
　Paul Whiteman voice in *The King of Jazz*, 158
　song in Popeye Film
Crystal Gazebo, The (Columbia), 207
Cubby Bear, 199
Cubby's World Flight (Van Beuren), 199
Cuckoo Murder Case, The (Iwerks), 187
Cueball Cat (MGM), 291
Culhane, Jimmie (Shamus):
　Bray animator, 21, 157
　Disney animator, 46, 58
　Fleischer animator, 92, 94, 96, 112
　head of Paramount Cartoon Studios, 315
　Iwerks animator, 187, *193*
　leaves Iwerks for Van Beuren, 192, 200, 203
　Krazy Kat inker and assistant animator, 206
　Lantz animator, 155
　Lantz director, 166–169
　Warner animator, 244
Curious Puppy (Warner), 239
Customers Wanted (Fleischer), 105

Dachsund and the Sausage, The (*The Artist's Dream*; Bray), 6
Daffy Doc (Warner), 237
Daffy Doodles (Warner), 251
Daffy Duck, 219, 236–238, *248*–252, 256, 258–259, 269–272
Daffy Duck and the Dinosaur (Warner), 269
Daffy Duck and Egghead (Warner), 236
Dali, Salvador, creates film *Un Chien Andalou* (1929), 98
Dalton, Cal, Warner director, 242

Dance Contest, The (Fleischer), 105, 106
Danch, Bill, writes stories for Lantz, 179
Dangerous When Wet (MGM), 294
Dante Dreamer (Famous), 311
Darling Nellie Gray (Fleischer), 89
David, Tissa, UPA/New York animator, 333
Davis, Art:
　in-betweener for Huemer at Fleischer studio, 86
　Lantz animator, 179, 180
　Mintz animator, 206, 208, 209, 211, 212
　Screen Gems animator, 213
　Warner director, 252
Davis, Mannie:
　Barré/Bowers animator, 13
　Fleischer animator, 84
　Terry animator and director, 126, 127, 130, 133
　Van Beuren animator, 195, 198
Davis, Marc, 44
　Snow White animation, 56
Davy Jones' Locker (Iwerks), 189
Dazzo, Jack, assistant at Famous Studios, 308
DeBeck, Billy, creator of *Barney Google* comic strip, 211
Debut of Thomas Cat (Bray), 21
Deduce You Say (Warner), 259
DeForest, Lee, creates synchronization process (*Phonofilms*), 89
De Guard, Philip (background artist):
　for Tower 12 Productions, 301
　for Warner, 257, 260
De Hartog, Jan, playwright for *The Four-poster*, 328
Deitch, Gene:
　director: creates cartoons for MGM, 300, 301
　creates shorts for Paramount, 313
　joins UPA/New York, 333
　Terrytoons artistic director at CBS, 143–144
DeLara, Phil, Warner animator, 269
DeLuxe color, used for Terrytoons, 148
DeNat, Joe (musician):
　for *Krazy Kat*, 206–208
　for Scrappy, 211
DePatie, David H., leases Warner animation plant, 271–272
　(*See also* DePatie-Freleng Enterprises)
Depatie-Freleng Enterprises, 271–272, 339
Deputy Dawg, 149, *150*
Der Fuehrer's Face (Disney), 66, 70
De Seversky, Maj. Alexander, aviation expert, 67
Designs on Jerry (MGM), 299
Diamonds in the Rough (Terry), 150
Dick Tracy, 336
Dietrich, James, Lantz music director, 158
Dingbat Land (Terry), 135
Dinky Doodle series (Bray), 21, 156–157
Dinner Time (Terry), 127
Dirks, Rudolph, Hearst cartoonist, 17
Dirty Duck, 342
Disney, Roy, business manager for Disney Studios, 30, 33–35, 37, 39, 60
Disney, Walt, 3, 27, 29–78, 327

Disney, Walt (Cont.):
  Academy Awards, 36, 39
  animation, perfection of, in 1950s, 73
  animation department continued after
    death of, 77
  and art of animation, 43, 45
  as artist, 32
  background of, 30
  California Institute of the Arts founded
    by, 77
  color: creative uses of, 40
    introduction of, 39, 41–42
  costs: of films, 34, 38, 42, 57, 60, 66, 72, 74
    of multiplane camera, 51
  effect of WWII on studio, 63–64
  effects department established, 52–53
  films made by, 27, 30–36, 38–44, 46,
    49–51, 53–77, 157–158, 169, 194,
    199, 200, 341
  live-action film, 74–75
  multiplane camera introduced, 51–52
  personality of, as director of studio, 29
  photographic processes developed, 68
  seeks challenges other than film, 75
  short subjects vs. feature films, 69–72
  sound: introduction of, 34–35
    stereophonic, 72
  as story man, 33
  storyboards used by, 30
  studio established in California, 30
  studio strike (mid-1941), 64
  and television films, 72, 77
  Xerox process, 75
Disneyland television series, 72
Dizzy Dishes (Fleischer), 96
Dizzy Red Riding Hood (Fleischer), 94
Dockstader, Tod, joins Terrytoons staff,
  144
Dr. Jerkyl's Hyde (Warner), 253
Dog Gone Modern (Warner), 239
Dog Trouble (MGM), 292
Doing Their Bit (Terry), 135
Donald Duck, 49–51, 69–72
Donald's Dilemma (Disney), 69
Donald's Dream Voice (Disney), 69
Donnelly, Eddie, Terry animator-director,
  133
Dorgan, Tad (author):
  Silk Hat Harry, 17
  Tad's Indoor Sports, 17
D'Orsi, Ugo, Disney effects animator, 61
Dot and the Line, The (MGM), 302
Double Dribble (Disney), 71
Double or Mutton (Warner), 263
Dough for the Do-Do (Porky in Wackyland;
  Warner), 253
Dover Boys, The (Warner), 244
Draftee Daffy (Warner), 251
Drame chez les Fantoches (Cohl), 3
Dranko, Robert, UPA art director, 331, 335
Dream Walking, A (Fleischer), 105
Dripalong Daffy (Warner), 259
Droopy, 286, 299
Duck Amuck (Warner), 26, 238–259
Duck Dodgers in the 24½th Century
  (Warner), 259, 261
Duck! Rabbit! Duck! (Warner), 258
Ducktators, The (Warner), 250
Dumbo (Disney), 65–66

Duncan, Phil, at Screen Gems, 214
Dunn, John, 339
  writer for Warner, 270
Dunning, George, 341
  director for Yellow Submarine, 341
  UPA animator-director, 332
Durante, Jimmy, inspiration for Sourpuss,
  135
Dyson, Russ, Famous Studios animator,
  308

Eastman, Phil:
  UPA writer, 319, 321, 325, 334
  writer for Snafu films, 250
Easy Winners, 147–148
Edelman, Heinz, designer for Yellow Sub-
  marine, 314
Edouarde, Carl, Van Beuren music direc-
  tor, 195
Educational Pictures:
  complains about quality of Moser-Terry
    films, 130
  distributes Moser-Terry-Coffman films,
    128
Effects department established at Disney,
  52–53
Egghead, 235–237
Eggnapper (Lantz), 179
Eisenberg, Harvey, MGM animator, 283
Elmer Fudd, 219, 237, 242, 246, 253, 259,
  264, 268, 270
Elmer's Candid Camera (Warner), 242
Elmer's Pet Rabbit (Warner), 257
Enchanted Drawing, The (1900), 1
Enchanted Square, The (Famous), 307
Enemy Bacteria (Lantz), 172
Engel, Jules:
  designer for UPA, 321, 326
  Disney animator, 61
  leaves UPA to create Format Films, 335
Englander, Otto:
  Iwerks writer, 190
  leaves Iwerks for Disney, 192
Eshbaugh, Ted, Van Beuren animator-
  director, 200, 201
Estabrook, Howard, writer, Aesop's Fa-
  bles idea presented to Terry, 125
Eugster, Al (animator):
  for Disney, 44, 58
  for Famous Studios, head animator, 308
  for Fleischer, 29, 92, 96, 111, 112
  for Iwerks, 187, 193
    leaves Iwerks for Disney, 192
  for Mintz, 210
  for Paramount, 314
  for Sullivan, 24, 25
Evolution (Fleischer), 87

Fables Pictures Inc. (see Fables Studio)
Fables Studio, 126
  taken over by Van Beuren Productions,
    127
Fadiman, Edwin Miles, forms distribution
  firm with Fleischer, 89
Fair Weather Friends (Lantz), 167
Fallaice, Sal, assistant at Famous Studios,
  308
Family Circus, The (UPA), 331

Famous Adventures of Mr. Magoo, The
  (UPA), 336
Famous Studios, 26, 305–316
  dissolved, name changed to Paramount
    Cartoon Studios, 311
  films made by, 305–312
  formula cartoons, 309–310
  methods of producing cartoons, 308–
    309
  new name for Fleischer's studio after
    Fleischer's departure, 120
  puns and violence in cartoons, 309
  remakes of old cartoons and characters,
    306, 309
  schedule, 308
  Technicolor, 306, 310
  3-D cartoons, 310
Fantasia (Disney), 59–64, 341
Fantasound, 63
Fantastic Animation Festival, 342
Fantastic Planet, 342
Faringer, Ray, Iwerks staff, 193
Farmer, The (Lantz), 159
Farmer Al Falfa, 124–126, 129, 134, 197
Farmer Al Falfa's Prize Package (Terry), 129
Farmerette (Van Beuren), 198
Farrish, Ben, assistant at Famous Studios,
  308
Fast and Furry-ous (Warner), 261
Fatso Bear, 179
Feature films, 340–342
  (See also specific studios)
Feed the Kitty (Warner), 260
Feiffer, Jules:
  contributes stories to Tom Terrific, 147
  creates pilot, Easy Winners, 147–148
  joins CBS Terrytoons staff, 144
Feline Frame-up (Warner), 260
Felix the Cat, 22–25, 203, 204
Felix the Cat, and the Goose that Laid the Gold-
  en Egg (Van Beuren), 203
Felix the Cat series (Van Beuren), 203, 204
Females Is Fickle (Fleischer), 107
Ferdinand the Bull (Disney), 51
Ferguson, Norman "Fergy":
  Disney animator, 41, 46–48
  establishes Pluto, 46
  Disney director, 62
  Terry animator, 129
Fetchit, Stepin, caricatured in Clean Pas-
  tures, 234
Fiddlesticks (Iwerks), 186
Field Mouse, The (MGM), 280–281
Fields, W. C., caricatured in At Your Ser-
  vice, Madam, 234
Fifth Column Mouse (Warner), 250
Fight On for Old (UPA), 332
Filmation, 339
Finding His Voice (Fleischer), 91
Fire Alarm (Warner), 226n.
Fischinger, Oskar, and The Sorcerer's Ap-
  prentice, 60–61
Fish Fry (Lantz), 167
Fisher, Bud, Mutt and Jeff cartoonist,
  12–15, 124
  (See also Barré, Raoul; Bowers, Charles)
Fitz, 85, 88, 90, 91
Fitzsimmons, John A., assistant to McCay,
  4

Flat Hatting (UPA), 321
Flebus (Terry), 144
Fleischer, Dave, 26, 81, 84, 85, 94, 113
  as film cutter, 81
  opens studio with Max, 88
  Screen Gems production supervisor, 215
  troubleshooter for Universal after Paramount break, 120
  works for Columbia Pictures after Paramount break, 120
Fleischer, Joe, works with Max on rotoscope, 80–81
Fleischer, Lou, supervises sound and music at Fleischer studio, 92
Fleischer, Max, 79–120
  background of, 80
  Bray animator, 20
  commissioned to make Army training films, 81
  leaves Bray to start own studio with Dave, 21, 82
  returns to Bray after Paramount break, 120
  cel-and-background technique, 92
  costs, advertising shorts, 95, 116
  decline after break with Paramount, 120
  and DeForest's sound synchronization process, 89
  distribution firm, 84, 89–90
  experimental film projects, 86
  films made by, 80–110, 112–119
    advertising shorts, *88*, 95, 96, 116
    educational, 86–87, 91
    feature-length, 80, 111–119
  fortunes begin to sink, 110
  live-and-cartoon combination, 82–83, 90
  loses studio, 80
  mechanical genius of, 79, 81, 82
  meets Bray, 80
  metamorphosis on film, 91
  moderate success with short-subject films, 116
  Paramount breaks with, 119–120
  Paramount distributes cartoons, 90
  rotograph invention, 84
  rotoscope patented by, 80–81, 114
  "slash" system used by, 85–86
  sound, introduction of, 89, 91–95
  special effects, 83
  studio expansion for feature films, 111–112
  3-D, 109–110
  turntable camera, 110
  unsung hero in animation, 79–80
  works for Jam Handy Company after Paramount break, 120
Fleury, Eugene, layout background artist for Warner, 244
Flip the Frog, 186–188
Flip the Frog series (Iwerks), 186–188
Flippy, 216
Flirty Birdy (MGM), 292
Flowers and Trees (Disney), 39–40
Flying Mouse, The (Disney), 41–42, 50
Foghorn Leghorn, 219, *254*, 255, 269–270
Follett, F. M., Bray animator, 20
Foolish Fables (Lantz), 175

For Better or Worser (Fleischer), 109
For Scent-Imental Reasons (Warner), 254
Format Films, 335
Foster, John (animator), *18*
  joins Terry and director-animator, 126
  becomes head of story department, 132–134, 137
  Van Beuren director, 195
  fired, 198
Foster, Warren, Warner writer, 236, 246, *255*, 267–270
Fourposter, The (UPA), 328–329
Fox, Fontaine, creator of *Toonerville Trolley* comic strip, 203
Fox and Crow, 214–217, 322
Fox Films, 13, 14
Fox and the Grapes (Columbia), 214
Fox Pop (Warner), 244
Foxy, 221–222
Franklin, Sidney, director, worked with Terry on medical films (WWI), 125
Franklyn, Milt, music director for Warner, 270
Freberg, Stan, jazz singer in *The Three Little Bops*, 269
Frees, Paul, voices for *The Beary's Family Album*, 182
Freleng, Isadore "Friz," 158
  and beginning of Warner studio, 219–220
  DePatie-Freleng Enterprises, 271–272, 339
  Disney animator, 33, 185
  joins MGM, 277
  leaves MGM for Warner, 278
  leaves Warner, 271–272
  Warner animator, 219
  Warner animator-director, 223–225, 234–238, 243–245, 253, 256, 257, 260, 265–268, 270, 271
Frenchy Discovers America, 21
Fresh Vegetable Mystery, The (Fleischer), 110
Friel, Dick, Barré-Bowers animator, 15
Fritz the Cat, 316, 341
From A to Z-Z-Z (Warner), 260
From Rags to Rags (Columbia), 215
Fuddy Duddy Buddy (UPA), 323
Fuller, Bing animator, *18*
Fun and Fancy Free (Disney), 68
Funny Face (Iwerks), 188

Gabby Gator, 179
Gabby's Diner (Lantz), 179
Gable, Clark, caricatured in *Coo-coo Nut Grove*, 234
Gable, Fred, UPA writer, 329
Gadmouse the Apprentice Good Fairy (Terry), 151
Gamer, A. C., effects animator for Warner, 262
Gandy Goose, 134, 135
Garbo, Greta, caricatured in *Coo-coo Nut Grove*, 234
Garity, William E., sound track for *Musical Miniatures*, 169
Garland, Judy, voice in *Gay Purr-ee*, 336
Gaston, Guy, animator, *18*
Gay Gaucho (Van Beuren), 199
Gay Purr-ee (UPA), 336

Geisel, Ted (Dr. Seuss), 245, 250, 325
Geiss, Alec:
  Bray animator, 21
  at Screen Gems, 214
Gentilella, Johnny (animator):
  at Famous Studios, 308
  at Terry studio, 142
  at Van Beuren studio, 200
Georgie and the Dragon (UPA), 327–328
Gerald McBoing Boing (UPA), 317, 323–326
Gerald McBoing Boing on the Planet Moo (UPA), 326, 332
Gerald McBoing Boing Show (TV; UPA), 332
Gerald McBoing Boing's Symphony (UPA), 326
Germanetti, George, Famous Studios animator, 308
Geronimi, Clyde "Gerry":
  Bray animator, 21
  Disney director, 69, 70, 72, 74
Gershman, Ed:
  business manager for UPA, 320, 322
  Disney staff, 62
Gerstein, Mordi, joins UPA, 332
Gertie the Dinosaur (McCay; 1914), 4–5, 123
Ghosks Is the Bunk (Fleischer), 104
Ghost of Honor (Famous), 310
Giant Killer, The (Lantz), 171
Giddy Yapping (Columbia), 215
Giddyap (UPA), 331
Gifts from the Air (Columbia), 211
Gilbert, C. Allen, introduction of animation and live action to Bray, 20–21
Gillett, Burt, 13, 15, 17, 40
  Fleischer animator, 84
  Hearst animator, 156
  Lantz director, 163
  leaves Disney, 69
  Van Beuren director, 200–203
Glackens, Louis, animator, 20*n*.
Glass disk, 11–12
Gleason, Jackie, imitated in *The Honey Mousers*, 269
Glee Worms (Columbia), 211
Gloom Chasers (Columbia), *209*
G-Man Jitters (Terry), 134
Godwin, Frank, illustrator, worked with Terry on medical films (WWI), 125
Goin' to Heaven on a Mule (Warner), 225
Gold, Ernest, musical composer for UPA, 330
Gold Diggers of '49 (Warner), 226–227, 232
Goldberg, Rube, 6
Goldilocks and the Three Bears (Lantz), 161, 178
Goldman, Les, forms Tower 12 Productions with Chuck Jones, 301–302
Goodbye Mr. Moth (Lantz), 164
Goodford, Jack, artistic supervisor for UPA/New York, 333
Goodwill to Men (remake of *Peace on Earth*; MGM), 280
Goofy, 40, 46–51, 70
Goonland (Fleischer), 108
Gopher Broke (Warner), 270
Gordon, Dan:
  joins MGM, 277
  leaves Terry for MGM, 132
  Terry animator, 130
  at Van Beuren studio, 200

460

Gordon, George:
  at MGM, 277, 296
  Terry director, 130
  leaves Terry, 132
  works freelance for Terrytoons, 150
Gordon, Mack, and Harry Revel, song
  used in Popeye film, 105
Gosden, Freeman, and Charles Correll,
  Amos 'n' Andy voices for Van Beuren
  cartoon, 200
Gould, Al, painter on staff of *Krazy Kat*, 206
Gould, Ira, painter on staff of *Krazy Kat*,
  206
Gould, Manny:
  Barré-Bowers animator, 13
  Mintz animator-director, 205–208, 211
Goulet, Robert, voice in *Gay-Purr-ee*, 336
Graduation Exercises (Columbia), 211
Graham, Don, teaches at Disney Studios,
  43, 45
Grampy, 102
Grampy's Indoor Outing (Fleischer), 102
Gran' Pop series (Iwerks), 192
Grand Uproar (Fleischer), 95
Grandpre, George:
  Lantz animator, 161
  Warner animator, 269
Grant, Joe, Disney writing team for
  Dumbo, 65
Grape Nutty (Columbia), 215
Grasshopper and the Ant, The (Disney), 42
Great Piggy Bank Robbery, The (Warner),
  248, 252
Green, Bert, animator, cartoons for *Pathé
  News*, 6
Greene, Walter, Lantz music director,
  180–181
Gribbroek, Robert, Warner layout man,
  257, 260
Grin and Bear It (Disney), 72
Gross, Milt:
  Barré-Bowers animator, 13
  cartoonist, 6, 21
  comic artist, joins MGM, 278
Gruelle, Johnny, creator of Raggedy Ann
  and Andy, 116
Guarnier, Lu, UPA/New York animator,
  333
Gulf and Western purchases Paramount
  Cartoon Studios, 315
Gulliver's Travels (Fleischer), 80, 112, *113*,
  114–115
Gunning, F. C. "Wid," 27
Gypped in Egypt (Van Beuren), *196*

Habousch, Victor, UPA art director, 336
Hair Raising Hare (Warner), 252
Halee, Roy, singing voice of Mighty
  Mouse, 139
Half-Baked Alaska (Lantz), 179–181
Hall, Dick, Iwerks staff, *193*
Ham and Ex, 226
Ham and Hattie series (UPA), 334–335
Hamateur Night (Warner), 237
Hamilton, Rollin "Ham," Warner
  animator, 220
Hammer, Barbara, UPA writer, 332
Hand, David:
  Bray animator, 21

Hand, David *(Cont.)*:
  Disney director, 69
Hanna, William "Bill":
  background, 282
  director for MGM, 277
    and Barbera, 282–285, 291–295, 297,
    299–300
    leaves MGM to open studio with
    Barbera, 300
  (See also Hanna-Barbera)
Hanna-Barbera, 302–303, 337, *338*
  limited animation, 337–338
Hannah, Jack:
  Disney animator, 43, 47
  Disney director, 69–72
  Disney television director, 77
  Disney writer, 69
  Lantz director, 155
  Lantz television director, 178
  leaves Lantz, 179
Hansen, Bernice, voice of Little Cheezer, 276
Happy Go Ducky (MGM), 30
Happy Harmony series, 275–276
Happy Hoboes (Van Beuren), *198*
Happy Hooligan, 15, 17
Harburg, E. Y. "Yip":
  lyrics for *Hell Bent for Election*, 320
  score for *Gay Purr-ee*, 336
Hardaway, Ben "Bugs":
  Iwerks writer, 190
  Lantz writer, 166, 173
    and Woody Woodpecker creator, 164
  Warner writer, 192, 224, 236, 237, 241
Harding, La Verne, Lantz animator, 161,
  166, 173
Hare Brush (Warner), 267, 268
Hare Grows in Manhattan, A (Warner),
  249, 268
Hare Trigger (Warner), 256
Hare-um Scare-um (Warner), 237, 242
Harline, Leigh, music score for *Mr. Bug
  Goes to Town*, 119
Harman, Hugh, 158, 199
  and beginning of Warner studio, 219–
  220
  Disney animator, 30–32
  Lantz animator, 155, *170n.*
  Warner supervisor/director, 222
    break with Warner, 224, 276
  works for MGM, 275–276, 278–282
Harman, Walker, Disney animator, 30
Harris, Ken, Warner animator, *246*, 257,
  260
Harris, Phil, voice in Disney films, 76
Harrison, Ben:
  Barré-Bowers animator, 13
  Mintz animator-director, 205–208, 211
Harrison, Paul, 53
Harrison, Rex, in *The Fourposter*, 328–329
Harriton, Chuck:
  Famous Studios animator, 308
  Paramount animator-director, 315
Harvey Company buys Paramount car-
  toons, 312
Harveytoons, 312
Hashimoto San (Terry), 149
Haul in One, A (Famous), 312
Hausner, Jerry, voice for Waldo, 323

Hawkins, Emery:
  Lantz animator, 166
  MGM animator, 277
  Mintz animator, 210, 212
  at Screen Gems, 214
He Can't Make It Stick (Columbia), 215
Headless Horseman, The (Iwerks), 191, 192
Health Farm, The (Terry), *132*
Hearst, Randolph, 12, 124
Hearst International Film Service, 12, 15,
  156
Heavenly Puss (MGM), 292–293
Heavy Traffic, 341
Heckle and Jeckle, 140, 141, 148
Heckle and Jeckle series (Terry), 140, 141
Hector Heathcote, 149
Hector Heathcote Show, 149
Hee, T.:
  caricaturist for Warner, 234–235
  Disney director, 62
  UPA art director and writer, 331
  writes stories for Terrytoons, 150
Heinemann, Art:
  Lantz layout man and color stylist, 166
  UPA art director, 331
Hell Bent for Election (UPA), 318–321
Helter Shelter (Lantz), 175
Hendricks, Bill, producer of Warner car-
  toons, 272
Henery Hawk, 254
Herbert, Hugh, comedian, 237
Herman the Catoonist (Famous), 310
Herman the Mouse, 308–310
Herr Meets Hare (Warner), 250
Herriman, George, creator of *Krazy Kat*
  comic strip, 17, 205
Hershfield, Harry, newspaper cartoonist
  joins MGM staff, 278
Hey Good Lookin', 342
Hey There, It's Yogi Bear (H-B), 338n.
High and the Flighty, The, 254, 269–270
High Note (Warner), 271
Hilberman, Dave, *319*
  leaves Disney for UPA, 64
  partnership with UPA, 320
    sells out interest, 321
  at Screen Gems, 214
  starts studio with Zack Schwartz, 318–
  320
Hiltz, Jim, joins UPA, 332
Hippity Hopper (Warner), 255
Hoban, Walter, *Jerry on the Job*, 17
Hockey Homicide (Disney), 70
Hocus Pocus Powwow (Warner), 271
Hogan, Rich, writer for Warner, 255
Hole Idea (Warner), 269
Holidayland (Columbia), 211
Hollywood Daffy (Warner), 269
Hollywood Picnic (Columbia), 211
Hollywood Production Code, 61
Homeless Hare (Warner), 225
Honey Halfwitch series (Paramount), 314
Honey-Mousers (Warner), 268, 269
Honeymoon Hotel (Warner), 225
Horton Hatches the Egg (Warner), 245
Hoskins, Win, Fleischer animator, *111*
Hot and Cold (Lantz), 161
Hot Dog (Bray), 21, 157
Housecleaning Blues (Fleischer), 102, *109*

How Now McBoing Boing (UPA), 326
Howard, Cal:
  Fleischer animator, *111*
  Lantz story man, 161, 179
  Screen Gems writer, 217
  Warner writer, 217
  writes stories for Terrytoons, 150
How's Crops (Van Beuren), 199
Hubley, John, 319
  Disney animator, 43
    leaves Disney for UPA, 64
  influence of Warner cartoons on UPA,
    244
  at Screen Gems, 214, 318
  at UPA, 321, 334
    supervising director, 322–326, 328,
      331
Hudson, Bill, Famous Studios animator,
  308
Huemer, Dick, 27, 30, 32
  Barré-Bowers animator, 13, 14
  Disney director, 69, 70, 72
  Fleischer animator, 84, *85*, 87
    use of in-betweener, 86
  Mintz story man, 208, 209
    leaves Mintz for Disney, 210
  writing team for *Dumbo*, 65
Huffine, Ray, Lantz layout/background
  man, 179
Hugo the Hippo, 342
Humorous Phases of Funny Faces (1906), 2
Humpty Dumpty Jr. (Iwerks), 191
Hunger Strife (Lantz), 179
Hunn, Dan, assistant at Famous Studios,
  308
Hurd, Earl (animator):
  inventor of cels, 19
  leaves Bray, 21
  patents by, 9–10
  Terry association, 125
  visual ideas in *Bobby Bumps*, 19–21
Hurter, Albert:
  Barré-Bowers animator, 13, 14
  Big Bad Wolf creator at Disney, 40
  Three Little Pigs creator at Disney, 40
Hurtz, William (Bill), 335
  designer for UPA, 319, 321, 325
  director for UPA, 329
  leaves Disney for UPA, 64
Hypnotic Hick (Lantz), 175

I Eats My Spinach (Fleischer), 104
I Haven't Got a Hat (Warner), 226
I Like Babies and Infinks (Fleischer), 107
I Taw a Putty Tat (Warner), 254
I Was a Teen-aged Thumb (Warner), 271
I Yam What I Yam (Fleischer), 104
Ichabod and Mr. Toad (Disney), 68
Ickle and Pickle (Terry), 140
I'm Forever Blowing Bubbles (Fleischer), 93
Impossible Possum, The (MGM), 297
In My Merry Oldsmobile (Fleischer), *88*, 96
In the Good Old Summertime (Fleischer), 89
Industrial Films and Poster Service, 320
  film, *Hell Bent for Election*, 320
Inki, 244
Inki at the Circus (Warner), 244
Inki and the Minah Bird (Warner), 244
Inkwell series (Fleischer), 81–82, 84

Inspector Willoughby, 179
International Film Service (Hearst Interna-
  tional Film Service), 12, 15, 156
Invitation to the Dance (*Sinbad the Sailor*
  segment; MGM), 294
Is My Palm Red? (Fleischer), 97
Ishii, Chris, artistic supervisor for UPA/
  New York, 333
Ising, Rudolf, 158, 199
  and beginning of Warner studio, 219–
    220
  break with Warner, 224, 276
  Disney animator, 30, *31*
  Warner supervisor/director, 222
  works for MGM, 275–276, 278–280, 282
Isle of the Pingo Pongo (Warner), 235
It's the Natural Thing To Do (Fleischer), 106
It's Tough To Be a Bird (Disney), 76
Iwerks, Ub, 44, 51, 185–194
  Academy Awards for technical
    achievements, 194
  background, 185
  color, 191
    Cinecolor, 190
    Technicolor, 186, 189
  contract with Mintz, 192
  costs of multiplane camera, 192
  Disney animator, 27, 34–38, 43, 186
    leaves Disney, 36
    returns to Disney to develop photo-
      graphic processes, 68, 192–194
    visual innovations, 133
  expands studio, 187, 190
  films made by, 186–192
  mechanical genius, 188
  and MGM, 275
  and Mintz, 212
  multiplane camera developed, 192
  starts own studio, 186
  studio closes (1936), 192
  technical achievements, 194
  Warner Brothers, help from, 192
  works for Warner, 227

Jack and the Beanstalk (Iwerks), 191
Jackson, Wilfred:
  Disney director, 69, 72
  Disney sound department, 34, 35
James Hound series (Terry), 151
Jay Ward Productions, 335, 338
Jaywalker, The (UPA), 332
Jefferson Film Corporation, 15
Jenkyns, Chris, writes stories for Terry-
  toons, 150
Jerry on the Job, 17, 156
Jitterbug Follies (MGM), 278
Joe Glow the Firefly (Warner), 239, 240
Johnny Appleseed (Disney), 68
Johnson, Tom, Famous Studios head
  animator, 308
Johnston, Ollie, Disney animator, 44, 75
Johnstown Flood, The (Terry), 138
Jolly Little Elves (Lantz), 161
Jolson, Al, caricatured in *Clean Pastures*,
  234
Jolt for General Germ (Fleischer), 96
Jones, Chuck, 40, 270, 338
  creator of *Duck Amuck*, 26
  director for *Hell Bent for Election*, 320

Jones, Chuck *(Cont.)*:
  forms Tower 12 Productions with Les
    Goldman, 301–302
  Iwerks cel washer, 187
  Lantz writer, 175
  story for *Gay Purr-ee*, 336
  Warner animator, 219, 225–227
  Warner director, 236–244, 247, 254,
    257–266, 268, 270, 271
Jones, Dorothy, story for *Gay Purr-ee*, 336
Jones, Volus, at Screen Gems, 214
J. R. the Wonder Dog, 278
Juggler of Our Lady, The (Terry), 146
Julian, Paul, designer for UPA, 321, 328
Jungle Book, The (Disney), 76
Juster, Norton, author, 302
J. Wellington Wimpy, 106

Kahl, Milt, Disney animator, 44, 75
Kane, Helen, model for Betty Boop, 96
Kansas City Film Ad Company, 30
Karloff, Boris, narrates *The Juggler of Our
  Lady*, 146
Karp, Hubie, Warner gag man, *248*
Katnip the cat, 309, 310
Katz, Ray, joins Screen Gems, 217
Kaufman, Millard, writer for UPA, 323
Kay, Arthur, voice for Gandy Goose, 134
Kaye, Buddy, theme song for *Little Lulu*, 306
Keith-Albee, controlling interest in
  Aesop's Fables Studio, 195
Keith-Albee Theatre circuit, backing for
  Terry *Fables*, 126
Keller, Lew,
  UPA art director, 331, 335
Kelly, Gene, 293–294
Kelly, Ray:
  joins MGM, 277
  Terry animator, 130
    leaves Terry for MGM, 132
  at Van Beuren studio, 200
Kelly, Walt, Disney animator, 44
Kelsey, Dick, Disney art director, 61
Ketcham, Hank, Disney animator, 44
Kimball, Ward, 75
  Disney animator, 43, 44, 67
  Disney director, 72, 76
Kimmelman, Phil, assistant at Famous
  Studios, 308
King, Jack, *18*
  Bray animator, 21
  Disney director, 69, 71
  Hearst animator, 156
  returns to Disney, 227
  Terry/Hearst animator, 17
  Warner director, 224, 226n.
King, John, Paramount producer, 22, 23
King Features Syndicate, 15
  Krazy Kat cartoons, 211
  sells Popeye rights to Fleischer, 102
King of Jazz, The (Lantz), 158
King Size Canary (MGM), 289–290
King's Tailor, The (Iwerks), 192
Kings Up (Lantz), *160*, 161
Kinney, Dick:
  Disney writer, 70
  UPA writer, 335
  writes stories: for Lantz, 179
    for Terrytoons, 150

Kinney, Jack:
  Disney director, 69–72
  Disney television show, 77
  UPA director, 335
Klein, Earl, layout man for Warner, 240
Klein, I., 1, 13
  Disney animator, 52
  Famous Studios writer, 309
  Hearst animator, 156
  Mintz animator, 210
  Terry story man, 137
  Van Beuren animator, 200
Klein, Phil:
  Famous Studios animator, 308
  at Screen Gems, 214
  at Van Beuren studio, 200
Kley, Heinrich, 61
Kline, Les, Lantz director, 163
Klynn, Herb:
  designer for UPA, 321
  leaves UPA to create Format Films, 335
Kneitel, Seymour:
  Famous Studios supervisor, 305, 310
  Fleischer animator, 113
  head of Paramount Cartoon Studios, 312–313
Knighty Knight Bugs (Warner), 267–268
Knock Knock (Lantz), 164, 237, color
Koko the Clown, 26, 81, 82, 85, 87, 90, 91, 97, 99–101
Koko Gets Egg-cited (Fleischer), 85
Koko the Kid (Fleischer), 91
Koko the Kop (Fleischer), 90, 91
Koko Squeals (Fleischer), 91
Koko's Catch (Fleischer), 85
Koko's Earth Control (Fleischer), 90
Kopietz, Fred:
  Iwerks animator, 187
  Lantz animator, 161
Kouzel, Al, Terrytoons writer, 144, 151
Krakatoa (Terry), 138
Krantz, Steve:
  producer for Fritz the Cat, 341
  producer for The Mighty Thor and Spiderman, 315
Krazy Kat, 16, 25, 205, 206, 207, 208, 209–211, 213
Kuwahara, Bob, 151
  creates Hashimoto for Terrytoons, 149

La Paloma (Fleischer), 93
LaCava, Gregory:
  director, My Man Godfrey, 15
  Hearst animator, 12
  Hearst production chief, 156
  with John Terry studio
  leaves Hearst for live-action films, 15, 16
Lady and the Tramp (Disney), 74
Laemmle, Carl, Universal founder and president, 157
Lah, Michael:
  MGM animator, 294
  MGM director, 296, 297, 299
Lantz, Grace Stafford (see Stafford, Grace)
Lantz, Michael, sculptor, 155–156
Lantz, Walter, 18, 44, 155–183
  animation taught by Lundy, 170–171
  background, 155–156
  Barré-Bowers animator, 156

Lantz, Walter (Cont.):
  Bray animator, 20, 156
    becomes studio manager, 21, 156
    series creator, 21, 156–157
  budget problems, 181
  cartoons succeed by default, 181
  classical music in films, 166, 168–169
  closes studio, 182
  commercial and industrial films, 163, 172
  costs, 158, 159, 162, 163, 170, 172, 188
  distributes through United Artists, 172
  expands studio, 175
  films made by, 157–179, 182, 237
  financial difficulty, 172
  government commissions during WWII, 172
  Hearst animator, 11n., 16, 156
  leaves Universal, 161
  live-action/animation film technique, 162
  moves to California, 27, 157
  new characters, 162, 179
  quality: decline in, 175, 181
    improvement in, 179–181
    lacking in cartoons, 173
  and rotoscoping, 163
  and Sennett, Mack, studio, 157
  sets up studio at Universal, 157–158
  sound, 161
    early technique, 158
    films based on classical music, 166, 168–169
    prescored music, 169
  starts own studio, 161–162
  survivor in industry, 155
  and television, cartoons released on, 178, 181–182
  with Terry studio, 17
  3-D, 175
Lardner, Ring, Jr., script for Brotherhood of Man (UPA), 321
Larriva, Rudy:
  UPA animator, 325
  UPA director, 335
  Warner animator, 272
Larson, Eric, Disney animator, 44, 75
Last Hungry Cat, The (Warner), 254
Laurie, Joe, Jr., gag collection purchased by Terry, 126
Lava, William, music director for Warner, 270
Lawrence, Eddie, voices for Swifty and Shorty series, 314
Layout, term explained, 260
Legend of Rockabye Point, The (Lantz), 177
Lerner, Sammy (songwriter):
  for Betty Boop, 97
  for Popeye, 107
Let's Celebrake (Fleischer), 107
Let's Get Movin' (Famous), 312
Let's You and Him Fight (Fleischer), 104
Leventhal, J. F., mechanical draftsman with Bray, 20, 21
Levitow, Abe:
  MGM animator, 302
  UPA director, 336
  Warner animator, 257
Life Begins for Andy Panda (Lantz), 164

Life with Tom (MGM), 298
Li'l Abner series (Columbia), 216
Li'l Anjil (Columbia), 211
Limited animation, 65, 338
Lion Hunt (UPA), 332
Lion Hunter, The (Warner), 244
Lion Tamer, The (Van Beuren), 200
Lippman, Sidney, theme song for Little Lulu, 306
Liss, Abe, creative director of UPA/New York, 333
Little Audrey, 306, 309, 310
Little Boy Blue (Iwerks), 191
Little Buck Cheeser (MGM), 282
Little Cheeser, 276
Little Dutch Mill, The (Fleischer), 110
Little Herman (Thanhauser), 122–124
Little Hiawatha (Disney), 51
Little King, 199–200
Little Lulu, 306, 307
Little Lulu, 306
Little Match Girl, The (Columbia), 212–213
Little Mole, The (MGM), 281
Little Nemo (McCay), 3, 4
Little Nibbles, 297
Little Pest, The (Columbia), 209
Little Red Hen, The (Iwerks), 191
Little Roquefort, 143
Little Rural Riding Hood (MGM), 287, 295
Little Swee' Pea (Famous), 312
Little Tinker (MGM), 289
Littlejohn, Bill:
  MGM animator, 277, 278, 281
  at Van Beuren Studio, 200
Live-action/animation films:
  Disney, 74–75
  Fleischer, 82–83
  MGM, 293–295
  Mintz, 213
  Warner, 237–238, 245, 248
Livingstone, Mary, in The Mouse That Jack Built, 269
Lonesome Ghosts (Disney), 50
Lonesome Lenny (MGM), 289
Looney Tunes (Warner), 220, 225, 252, 272
Loopy de Loop series (H-B), 338
Lord of the Rings, The, 342
Lorre, Peter, caricatured in Cockatoos for Two, 217
Lounsbery, John, Disney animator, 44, 75
Love, Ed, Lantz animator, 172
Love, Harry:
  effects animator for Warner, 262
  Krazy Kat animator, 206, 208
  Scrappy animator, 211
Love's Labor Won (Terry), 139
Lovy, Alex:
  directs at Screen Gems, 217
  joins Hanna-Barbera, 179
  Lantz director, 163, 165, 176–178
  at Van Beuren studio, 200
  Warner director, 272
Lucky Ducky (MGM), 286
Lugosi, Bela, as Black God in Night on Bald Mountain, 62
Lulu in Hollywood (Famous), 306
Lulu's Birthday Party (Famous), 306
Lumber Jack Rabbit (Warner), 265–266
Lundy, Dick, 49

463

Lundy, Dick *(Cont.)*:
Disney animator, 41
leaves Disney, 69
Lantz animator, 155
Lantz director, 169–172, 176n.
MGM director, 296–297
Luske, Hamilton, Disney director, 72, 76
Lutz, Edward, 1920 handbook on animation, 27
Lyman, Abe, bandleader featured in *Merrie Melodies*, 222

Ma and Pa Kettle movies, *Maw and Paw* cartoons based on, 175
McCabe, Norman, animator with Warner, 250
McCay, Winsor (early animator), 1, 3–6, 123
registration techniques, 11
McCollum, Hugh, general manager for Screen Gems, 215
McCormack, Don, production manager of UPA/New York, 333
Macdonald, Jim, sound wizard at Disney, 59
McDonald, Tom, UPA director, 335
McGraw, John, layout background artist for Warner, 244
McIntosh, Bob, UPA artist, 332
McKee, Donald, Terry story man, 137
McKennon, Dal, Inspector Willoughby's voice, 179
McKimson, Charles, Warner animator, 269
McKimson, Robert, Warner animator-director, 243, 252–255, 257, 260, 266, 268–270, 272
McKimson, Tom, Warner animator, *248*
McLeish (Ployardt), John, Screen Gems designer, 318
McLeod, Victor, Lantz animator, 161
McManus, Don, effects animator at Disney, 52
McManus, George (cartoonist), 6
Bringing Up Father, 17
Mad Hatter, The (Lantz), 171
Madeline (UPA), 328
Magic Fluke, The (UPA), 322
Magic Pencil, The (Terry), 135
Magnetic Telescope, The (Fleischer), 118
Magoo's Puddle Jumper (UPA), 332
Maimone, Sal, Famous Studios animator, 308
Maine Stein Song, The (Fleischer), 94
Major Lied Till Dawn, The (Warner), 231
Make Mine Music (Disney), 66, 68
Making 'em Move (Van Beuren), 196
Malibu Beach Party (Warner), 269
Maltese, Michael:
Lantz writer, 175, 177
Warner writer, 236, 245, 256–258, 260, 262, 264, 265, 268, 270
works for Screen Gems, 217
writer for Tower 12 Productions, 301, 302
Mama's New Hat (MGM), 278
Man Called Flinstone, The (H-B), 338n.
Manne, Maurice, sound mixer for Popeye, *312*

Manuel, George, Iwerks writer, 190, *193*
Marcus, Sid:
joins Lantz as director, 179
Mintz animator, 29, *206*, 208, 209, 211, 212
Screen Gems animator, 213
Marge (Marjorie Henderson Buell), creator of *Little Lulu* comic strip, 306
Marriner, William F., cartoonist, 22
Mars (Lantz), 159
Marshall, Lewis, MGM animator, 300
Marvels of Motion (Fleischer), 89
Marvin Digs (Paramount), 316
Mary Poppins (Disney), 68, 76, 194
Mason, James, narrator for *The Tell-Tale Heart*, 329
Masquerade Party, The (Columbia), 207
Mass Mouse Meeting (Columbia), 215
Matte process, 194, 238
Matthews, Pat, UPA animator, 325
Maw and Paw series (Lantz), 175
Maxwell, Carmen "Max":
Disney animator, 30
MGM production manager, 277
Warner animator, 220
Mayer, Henry (Hy):
illustrator for comics on-screen for Universal Weekly (from 1913), 6
Travelaughs series, 6
Meador, Joshua, effects animator at Disney, 52
Mechanical Doll (Fleischer), 85
Mechanical Monsters (Fleischer), 118
Melendez, Bill, producer-director, 338
UPA animator, 325, 326
Melendez, J. C., Warner animator, 269
Melody (Disney), 72
Melody Time (Disney), 66, 68
Mendelsohn, Jack, newspaper cartoonist at Paramount, 74
Mercer, Jack:
Famous Studios writer, 308, 309
Popeye's voice, 104, 309
writes stories for Terrytoons, 150
Merman, Ethel, in Fleischer Bouncing Ball films, 95
Merrie Melodies (Warner), 222, 224, 234, 252
Merry Old Soul (Lantz), 160
Messmer, Otto, 22–25, 27
animator with Henry Mayer, 6
joins Famous Studios, 26, 308–309
joins Sullivan, 22
Sullivan animator, *25*
Metro-Goldwyn-Mayer (*see* MGM)
Meyer, Carl "Mike":
animator/story man leaves Terry, 132
Famous Studios writer, 309
joins MGM, 277
at Van Beuren studio, 200
MGM, 70, 72, 202–205, 275–303
Academy Awards, 282, 285, 291, 293, 302
nominations, 280, 283, 299
becomes interested in cartoons, 275–276
budgets, 277, 278, 298–301
CinemaScope, 280, 298–300
closes cartoon studio, 300, 302–303
develops own cartoon studio, 277

MGM *(Cont.)*:
distributes Iwerks cartoons, 186–187
Iwerks loses MGM distribution, 192
films made by, 30, 269, 275–302
Harman and Ising produce cartoons for, 275–276, 278
hires Milt Gross, 278
hires Harry Hershfield, 278
hires Terry animators, 132
live-action/animation films, 293–295
musical scores for films, 284
pose reels, 296
releases new cartoons, 300
rotoscoping, 294
television specials, 302
Tiffany's of motion picture studios, 275
Tower 12 Productions, 301–302
MGM Animation Visual Arts (formerly Tower 12 Productions), 301–302
Mice Meeting You (Famous), 309
Michigan J. Frog, 264
Mickey Mouse, 27, 34–36, 39, 46, 48, 49, 197
Mickey's Fire Brigade (Disney), 50
Mickey's Garden, color
Mickey's Pal Pluto (Disney), 46
Mickey's Service Station (Disney), 50
Mickey's Trailer (Disney), 50
Midnight Frolics (Columbia), 212
Midnight Snack, The (MGM), 283
Mighty Heroes, The (Terry), 151, 152
Mighty Hunters (Warner), 240–241
Mighty Mouse, 136, 138–139, 148, *149*
Mighty Thor, The (Paramount), 315
Milky Waif, The (MGM), 297
Milky Way, The (MGM), 292
Millar, Tubby:
joins Warner Brothers, 224
writer for Warner, 236
Miller, Jack, writer for Warner, 236
Mills Brothers in Fleischer Bouncing Ball films, 95
Mini-Squirts (Paramount), 316
Minnie the Moocher (Fleischer), 98
Mintz, Charles, 34, 157–158, 205–213
behind in ideas and technique, 207
and color, 211
distributor for Disney, 33–34
films made by, 207–213
formulas in films, 207
live-action/animation cartoon, failure of, 213
loses studio, 213
potential of staff untapped, 210
studio, 29, 44
Minute and a Half Man, The (Terry), 149
Mishkin, Lee, assistant at Famous Studios, 308
Miss Glory (Warner), 235
Mr. Bug Goes to Town (Fleischer), 80, 116–119
Mister Magoo, 322–323, 331–336
Modeling (Fleischer), 82–83
Monahan, Dave:
Screen Gems writer, 217
writer for Warner, 235
Monroe, Phil:
Warner animator, 257
Warner director, 271
Montage, 240, 245

Moore, Fred, Disney animator, 41, 61
  reestablishes Mickey Mouse, 46, 48
Moore, Phil, jazz score for *Rooty Toot Toot*, 328
Moore, Victor, caricatured in *Ain't That Ducky*, 252
Moreno, George, Lantz animator, 159, 161
Moreno, Manuel, Lantz animator, 161
Morley, Robert, narrator for *The Dot and the Line*, 302
Morrison, Tommy:
  story supervisor for Terrytoons, 150, 151
  Terry animator, 121, 128
  Terry story man, 132, 133, 137, 139
Moser, Frank:
  Barré-Bowers animator, 12, 13
  and color, 129
  cost of Terrytoons, 130
  joins Hearst, 12, 15
  joins Terry: as director-animator, 126, 127
    as partner, 121, 125, 127
  relocates after fall of Audio Cinema, 129
  share in company bought by Terry, 130
Mother Goose Goes to Hollywood (Disney), 51
Mouse Cleaning (MGM), 291–292
Mouse and His Child, The, 342
Mouse Mazurka (Warner), 268
Mouse That Jack Built, The (Warner), 269
Mouse of Tomorrow, The (Terry), 137–138
Mouse Trapped (Lantz), 177
Movement, illusion of, 2
Movie Mad (Iwerks), 187
Moving Day (Disney), 50
Muchos Locos (Warner), 272
Muffati, Steve, Famous Studios head animator, 308
Multiplane camera:
  developed by Disney, 51–52
  developed by Iwerks, 192
Multiplane cranes and *Fantasia*, 63
Multitrack, multispeaker sound system for *Fantasia* (Fantasound), 63
Munro (Paramount), 313
Murikami, Jimmy, joins UPA, 332
Muscle Beach Tom (MGM), 299
Muse, Ken, MGM animator, 292, *293*
Museum of Natural History, New York, and Fleischer's film on Darwin, 87
Music Land (Disney), 51
Musical Miniatures series (Lantz), 169, 170
Musical Moments from Chopin (Lantz), 169
Mutt and Jeff, 12–15, 124, 156
Mutt and Jeff films, 13, 14
My Daddy, the Astronaut (Paramount), 315
My Dream Is Yours (Warner), 257
My Little Duckaroo (Warner), 259
My Man Godfrey, 15
My Old Kentucky Home (Fleischer), 89

Nancy and Sluggo, 135
Nash, Clarence, voice of Donald Duck, 49
Natwick, Grim, 11, 15–16, *18*
  Disney animator, 29
    Snow White animator, 56–57
  Fleischer animator, 96, 112
    creates Betty Boop, 96
  Hearst animator, 156

Natwick, Grim (*Cont.*):
  Iwerks animator, 187, 190, *193*
    leaves Iwerks for Disney, 192
  joins John Terry studio, 17
  Lantz animator, 155
  UPA/New York animator, 333
Naughty but Mice (Warner), 239
Neiberg, Al, composed songs for *Gulliver's Travels*, 114
Neighbors (Columbia), 211
Nellie, the Sewing Machine Girl (Lantz), 162
Nelly's Folly (Warner), 271
Neptune Nonsense (Van Beuren), 203
Newman's Laugh-O-Grams (Disney), 30
Nicholas, George, Lantz animator, 161
Nichols, Charles "Nick":
  Disney director, 70, 72
  Disney television show, 77
Nielson, Kay, Disney storyboard illustrator, 62
Night on Bald Mountain, 62
Night Before Christmas, The (MGM), 283
Night Watchman, The (Warner), 239
Nine Lives of Fritz the Cat, The, 342
Nit Witty Kitty (MGM), 292
No Barking (Warner), 253
No Sail (Disney), 71
Noah's Ark (Disney), 72
Noble, Maurice:
  layout man and co-director for Tower 12 Productions, 301
  Warner layout man, 257, 260–261, 264
    co-director credit, 270
Nolan, Bill (animator), *18*, 56, 185
  invents moving backgrounds, 11
  joins Hearst, 12
  joins Messmer at Sullivan studio, 24
  joins John Terry studio, 17
  Krazy Kat animator, 205
  Lantz's partner at Universal, 158, 159
  leaves Lantz, 161
  moves to California, 27
  on own with *Krazy Kat*, 25
  studio opened with Barré, 11
Novagraph Company, 89
Noveltoons series (Famous), 306
Novros, Les, *Snow White* animator, 56
Nudnick (Paramount), 313

O'Brien, Dave, in *TV of Tomorrow*, 295
O'Brien, Ken, Lantz animator, 172
O'Connor, Ken, Disney art director, 62
Odor-able Kitty, The (Warner), 254
Office Boy, The (Iwerks), *187*, 188
Oh Mabel (Fleischer), 87
Old Glory (Warner), 239
Old Mill, The (Disney), 51
Old Rockin' Chair (MGM), 292
Olive Oyl, 104, 309
Olive's Birthday Presink (Fleischer), 115
One Droopy Knight (MGM), 299
One Froggy Evening (Warner), 264–265
101 Dalmatians (Disney), 75
One More Time (Warner), 222
One Step Ahead of My Shadow (Warner), 222
1001 Arabian Nights (UPA), 335, color
Oompahs, The (UPA), 328
Opening Night (Van Beuren), 199
Opper, Frederick, Hearst cartoonist, 17

Optical printers, 194
Oriolo, Joe, Famous Studios animator, 307
Orphans' Benefit (Disney), 49
Osborne, Robert, designer for *Flat Hatting*, 321
Oswald, 32, 33, 157–162, 206
Oswald the Lucky Rabbit (Disney), 32–34
Out of the Inkwell series (Fleischer), 81–85, 90–91, 94, 115, 120
Owl and the Pussycat, The (Terry), 135

Pabian, Jim, MGM animator, 302
Paint, problems with, 21–22
Palmer, Lilli, in *The Fourposter*, 328–329
Palmer, Tom:
  at Van Beuren studio, 200, 203
  Warner director, 224
Pantry Panic (Lantz), 167
Paramount-Bray Pictograph, The (1916), 20, 21
Paramount Cartoon Studios, 311, 312
  buys shorts from Deitch, 313
  buys shorts from Snyder, 313
  cost of shorts, 313
  films made by, 313–316
  hired by King Features for television, 313
  improvement at, 315
  Mendelsohn, Jack, writes and directs for, 314
  purchased by Gulf and Western, 315
  sells cartoons to Harvey Company, 312
Paramount Pictures:
  breaks with Fleischer, 119–120
  distributes Fleischer cartoons, 90
  Famous Studios (*see* Famous Studios)
  introduces Mae West, 101
  (*See also* Paramount Cartoon Studios)
Parker, Dana, 24, *25*
Parker, Ralph, Disney writer, *67*
Parker, Sam, model for Gulliver, 114
Parmelee, Ted, 335
  director for UPA, 329
  Screen Gems designer, 318
Parrotville Post Office (Van Beuren), 202
Parsons, Louella, 36
Partch, Virgil "Vip," Disney animator, 44
Patents:
  Bray, 7–11
  Hurd, 9–10
Pathé, Charles, 7
  distributes Terry's *Fables*, 127
Pathé News, 6
Pattengill, Bill:
  Famous Studios animator, 308
  Paramount animator, 314
Patterson, Don:
  Lantz animator, 173
  Lantz director, 173–175
  Mintz animator, 210
Patterson, Ray:
  MGM animator, 292
  Mintz animator, 210
Paul Bunyan (Disney), 72
Peace on Earth (MGM), 280, 281
Peanut Vendor, The (Fleischer), 94
Peanuts films, 342
Peg Leg Pete, 32, 37
"Peg system," 11
Penner, Ed, Disney writer, 74

Penner, Joe, voice imitated for Egghead, 236
People Are Bunny (Warner), 269
Pepe le Pew, 219, 254
Perils of Pearl Pureheart, The (Terry), 139
"Persistence of vision," 2
Peter Pan (Disney), 73–74
Petunia Pig, 230
Phables series, 12, 17
Phantom Tollbooth, The (MGM), 302
Piano Tooners (MGM), 197, 198
Pickford, Mary, 42
Pierce, Tedd:
  gagman rotoscoped for *Thugs with Dirty Mugs*, 235
  works for Screen Gems, 217
  writer: for Lantz, 179
    for UPA, 332
    for Warner, 235, 269
Pigs Is Pigs (Disney), 72
Pigs in a Polka (Warner), 244
Pike, Miles, effects animation at Disney, 60–61
Pincushion Man (*Balloon Land*; Iwerks), 191
Pink Panther shorts (De Patie-Freleng), 339
Pink Phink, The (De Patie-Freleng), 339
Pinocchio (Disney; 1940), 57–59
Pintoff, Ernest:
  joins CBS Terrytoons staff, 144
  joins UPA, 332
Pitts, ZaSu, voice imitated for Olive Oyl, 104
Pizzicato Puzzy Cat (Warner), 266
Plane Crazy (Iwerks), 186
Plane Daffy (Warner), 250
Play Ball (Iwerks), 188–189
Playful Pelican (Lantz), 172
Ployardt, John (McLeish), at Screen Gems, 214
Plumber of Seville, The (Lantz), 177
Plummer, Elmer, Disney colorist, 61
Pluto, 37, 46, 48, 50, 66, 69, 70
Plutopia (Disney), 66, 70
Poddany, Eugene:
  Lantz music director, 177n.
  music copyist for Stalling, 270
Poe, Edgar Allan, author of *The Tell-Tale Heart*, 329
Poet and Peasant (Lantz), 169
Pogany, Willy, Lantz artist, 163
Polifka, Bernyce, layout background artist for Warner, 244
Pooch the Pup, 160, 161
Poor Cinderella (Fleischer), 110
Poor Little Me (MGM), 276
Pop 'im Pop (Warner), 253
Popcorn Story, The (UPA), 313
Popeye, 102–109, 115, 306, 309, 311–312
Popeye Meets Aladin and His Wonderful Lamp (Fleischer), 109
Popeye Meets Ali Baba and His 40 Thieves (Fleischer), 108
Popeye Presents Eugene the Jeep (Fleischer), 115
Popeye for President (Famous), 311–312
Popeye the Sailor (Fleischer), 103–104
Popeye the Sailor Meets Sinbad the Sailor (Fleischer), 108
Popeye's 20th Anniversary (Famous), 312, 313

Porky and Beans, 226
Porky Pig, 219, 226, 230, 232–234, 237–240, 248–251, 259
Porky Pig's Feat (Warner), 248–250
Porky in Wackyland (Warner), 233
Porky's Ant (Warner), 239
Porky's Duck Hunt (Warner), 236, 241, 242
Porky's Five and Ten (Warner), 233–134
Porky's Hare Hunt (Warner), 237, 241
Porky's Preview (Warner), 244
Porky's Romance (Warner), 228–229, 230
Possible Possum (Terry), 151
Post, Howard:
  head of Paramount Cartoon Studios, 313–315
  in-betweener at Famous Studios, 308
Powers, Pat:
  finances Iwerks studio, 186
  producer: for Disney, 38
    for Iwerks, 190, 192
Powers, Tom E., *Phables* series cartoonist, 12, 17
Pratt, Hawley:
  director for DePatie-Freleng, 339
  Warner layout man, 256, 260
  co-director credit, 270
Praxinoscope, 3
Prescored music for cartoons:
  Lantz, 169
  Terry, 128, 131
Prima, Louis, voice in *The Jungle Book*, 76
Private Snafu (Warner), 250
Production Code (1934), 101, 178
Professor Small and Mr. Tall (Columbia), 214
"Progress projection," 68
Puddle Pranks (Iwerks), 186
Pudgy, 102
Punch Trunk (Warner), 260
Puny Express (Lantz), 176n.
Puppet Show, The (Lantz), 161
Puppetoons series, 305
Pups' Picnic (MGM), 276
Puss Gets the Boot (MGM), 282–283, 291, 292
Puss 'n' Toots (MGM), 283
Pyle, Willis, UPA animator, 325

Questel, Mae:
  voice for Betty Boop, 97
  voice for Little Audrey and Popeye, 309
  voice for Olive Oyl, 104, 309
Quimby, Fred, head of new animation department at MGM, 277–299

Rabbit Fire (Warner), 258
Rabbit Rampage (remake of *Duck Amuck*; Warner), 259
Rabbit Seasoning (Warner), 258
Raggedy Ann and Andy, 116, 307
Raggedy Ann and Andy (feature-length film), 342
Raggedy Ann and Raggedy Andy (Fleischer), 116
Ragtime Bear (UPA), 322–323
Rainbow Parade (Van Beuren), 201, 202, 204
Rainger, Ralph, and Leo Robin, music score for *Gulliver's Travels*, 113
Rainy Day, A (MGM), 281
Raksin, David, music composer for UPA, 330

Rapf, Maurice, script for *Brotherhood of Man*, 321
Rapid Rabbit, 272
Rasinski, Connie, Terry animator-director, 132–133, 139, 140, 151
Rasinski, Joe, Terry cameraman, 133
Rasslin' Match, The (Van Beuren), 200, 204
Raven, The (Fleischer), 116
Ray, Tom (animator):
  for MGM, 302
  for Tower 12 Productions, 301
  for Warner, 269
Raymond, Sid, voice for Katnip and Baby Huey, 309
Ready, Set, Zoom (Warner), 262
Ready, Woolen and Able (Warner), 263
Rebner, Ed, pianist in *Musical Moments from Chopin*, 169
Red Hot Riding Hood (MGM), 285–289
Red Pepper Sam (William Costello), Popeye's voice, 104
Red Seal Pictures, 89–90
Reden, Morey:
  Famous Studios animator, 308
  Paramount animator, 314
Registration of drawings, 11
Reitherman, Wolfgang (Woolie):
  Disney animator, 44, 72
  Disney director, 75–77
Reluctant Dragon, The (Disney), 64, 70, 74
Rescuers, The (Disney), 77
Revel, Harry, and Mack Gordon, song used in Popeye film, 105
Rhapsody in Rivets (Warner), 244
Ride Him, Bosko! (Warner), 223
Riding the Rails (Fleischer), 102
Riley, Larry, Famous Studios writer, 308
Rip Van Winkle (Disney), 42
Rivera, Tony, at Screen Gems, 214
RKO, 39n., 127
  distributes *Toonerville* and *Felix* cartoons, 203
Roach, Hal, 157
Road Runner, The, 219, 261–264, 272
Road Runner series (Warner), 262
Roberts, Bill, Disney animator, 61
Robin, Leo, and Ralph Rainger, music score for *Gulliver's Travels*, 113
Robin Hood (Disney), 76
Robin Hood Daffy (Warner), 259
Robin Hoodlum (UPA), 322
Robinson, Bill "Bojangles," caricatured in *Clean Pastures*, 234
Robinson, Earl, music for *Hell Bent for Election*, 320
Rocket to Mars (Famous), 311
Rocket Racket (Lantz), 180
Rocky and Bullwinkle (Jay Ward), 335
Rodemich, Gene, Van Beuren music director, 196
Rogers, Shorty, music for *The Three Little Bops*, 269
Rogers, Will, 42
Rogers and Hart music used in Fleischer *Talkartoons*, 95
Roman, Dun, UPA artist, 332
Romay, Lina, in *Señor Droopy*, 295
Room and Bored (Columbia), 216
Room and Wrath (Lantz), 177
Rooty Toot Toot (UPA), 328

Rose, Allen (animator):
  for Famous Studios, 308
  for Iwerks, 190, *193*
  for Mintz, 206, *208*, 211
  for Screen Gems, 213
Ross, Virgil:
  Lantz animator, 161
  Warner animator, 225
Roth, Lillian, in Fleischer Bouncing Ball films, 95
Rotograph, invented by Max Fleischer, 84
Rotoscope:
  patented by Max Fleischer, 80–81
  used in *Gulliver's Travels*, 114
Rotoscoping, 56, 162, 163, 235, 240, 272, 294
Rowley, George, effects animator at Disney, 52
Royal Cat Nap (MGM), 300
Rufle, George, 13
  Barré-Bowers animator, 13
  Famous Studios animator, 308
  Hearst animator, 156
  joins Van Beuren, 197
Rugged Bear (Disney), 72
Russian Rhapsody (Warner), 251

Sabo, Joe, free-lance writer for Paramount, 315
Saidenberg, Ted, pianist in *Musical Moments from Chopin*, 169
Salkin, Leo, UPA, story man, 332
Saludos Amigos (Disney), 67
Sammy Johnsin (Sullivan), 22
Sanborn, Nellie, timing on talkies at Fleischer studio, 93
Sanders, George, voice in *The Jungle Book*, 76
Saperstein, Henry G., buys UPA, 335–336
Sasanoff, Michael, Warner animator, *248*
Save Old Piney (Terry), 150
Scaredy Cat (Warner), 260
Schaffer, Milt, Lantz writer, 166, 179
Scheib, Philip A., *142*, 149
  music scores for Moser-Terry films, 128
  prescored Terrytoons, 131
  scores for Terry musical spoofs, 139
Schlesinger, Leon, and Warner cartoons, 220
  sells out interest in studio to Warner Brothers, 252
  in *You Ought to Be in Pictures*, 237–238
Schnerk, Jack, Paramount animator, 315
School Daze (Terry), 135
Schultz, Seymour, business manager for Famous Studios, *312*
Schuster, Joe, creator of *Superman* with Jerry Siegel, 116
Schwalb, Ben, Screen Gems general manager, 213
Schwartz, Zack, *319*
  Disney art director, 45, 61
  partnership in UPA, 320
  sells out interest, 321
  at Screen Gems, 214, 318
  starts studio with Dave Hilberman, 318–320
Scott, Bill, 335
  UPA writer, 325, 328, 329, 332

Scott, Bill *(Cont.)*:
  Warner writer, 253
Scrap Happy Daffy (Warner), 250
Scrap the Japs (Famous), 311
Scrappy, 208–211, 213
Scrappy's Ghost Story (Columbia), 211
Scrappy's Party (Columbia), 209
Screen Gems, 213–217, 318
  ahead of time in cartoons, 215
  changes in managers, 215
  dissolved by Columbia, 217
  films made by, 214–216
  hires talented and creative people, 214, 217
Screen Song series (Famous), 309
Screwy Squirrel, 289
Scribner, Rod, Warner animator, 251, 269
Searl, Leon, *Krazy Cat* animator, *16*
Sears, Ted, 13
  Fleischer animator, 96
  heads story department at Disney studio, 38, 40, 46
Seely, John, music director for Warner, 270
Segar, Elzie, creator of Popeye comic strip, 103, 106
Selzer, Edward, head of Warner cartoons, 252, *255*, 270
Selznick, Lewis J., indifference to animated cartoons, 122
Señor Droopy (MGM), 295
Serviss, Prof. Garrett P., works with Fleischer on Einstein film, 86
Seuss, Dr. (Ted Geisel), 245, 250, 325
Sham Battle Shenanigans (Terry), *136*
Sharples, Winston:
  composed song for *Gulliver's Travels*, 114
  music director: for Famous Studios, 310
    for Van Beuren, 201
Sharpsteen, Ben:
  Barré-Bowers animator, 13
  Disney director, 69
  Fleischer animator, 84
  Hearst animator, 156
  Terry/Hearst animator, 17
Shaw, Dick, UPA writer, 332
She Reminds Me of You (Fleischer), 95
Sheep Ahoy (Warner), 263
Sheep in the Deep, A (Warner), 263
Sherman, Frank, animator, *18*
Sh-h-h-h-h (Lantz), 177
Shields, Hugh (Jerry):
  animator, collaborates with Terry, 123
  director-animator for Terry, 126
Shove Thy Neighbor (Terry), 144
Show Biz Bugs (Warner), 268, 271
Show Biz Whiz (Terry), 150
Shull, William at Screen Gems, 214
Sick, Sick Sidney (Terry), 146
Sidney's Family Tree (Terry), 146
Siegel, Jerry, creator of *Superman* with Joe Schuster, 116
Silent era, 1–28
  American animation, beginnings, 3–6
  animation studios: Barré, 11–12, 14
    Bowers, 12–15
    Bray, 6–12, 17–22
    Disney, 27
    Fleischer, 26
    Hearst, 12, 15
    McKay, 1, 3–6, 11
    Sullivan, 22–25

Silent era, animation studios *(Cont.)*:
    Terry, J., 17
  animation as trade, 1
  assembly-line animation, 7–10
  development during teens, 12
  developments, Barré studio (*see* Barré, Raoul)
  first animated cartoon, 2
  first commercial cartoon, 7
  French animation, 3
  "glass disk," 11
  introduction of sound, 27
  labor-saving patents, 7–10
  naiveté of audiences, 4
  zoetrope, 2
Silk Hat Harry, 17
Silly Symphony series (Disney), 35, 39–41, 49, 51, 59
Silverman, Fred, children's programming for CBS, 151
Silverman, Larry:
  Terry animator, 142
  at Van Beuren studio, 200
Simmons, Grant, at Screen Gems, 214
Sinking in the Bathtub (first *Looney Tune*; Warner), 220
Sinking of the Lusitania, The (McCay), 5
Sioux City Sue (Lantz sequence), 172
16mm filmstrips and projectors introduced, 21
Skeleton Dance, The (Disney), 35–36
Skeleton Frolic (Columbia), 212
Ski for Two (*Woody Plays Santa*; Lantz), 166–167
Skyscraping (Fleischer), 96
"Slash" system, 11
  used by Fleischer, 85–86
Sleeping Beauty (Disney), 74
Sleepy-Time Squirrel (MGM), 297
Smile Darn Ya, Smile (Warner), 222
Smith, Claude:
  Disney animator, 44
  MGM model designer, 287–289
  Mintz animator, 210
Smith, Frank, UPA animator, 325
Smith, Paul:
  Lantz animator, 173
  Lantz director, 175–176, 181–182
  Warner animator, 220
Smith, Sidney, cartoonist, 6
Smith, Webb:
  Lantz writer, 172
  and storyboard at Disney studio, 38
Smitten Kitten, The (MGM), 298
Snafu films (Warner), 250
Snow White (Fleischer), 98–101
Snow White and the Seven Dwarfs (Disney), 53–57
Snyder, William:
  creates shorts for Paramount, 313
  producer for Deitch cartoons, 300
So Much for So Little (Warner), 265
Socko in Morocco (Lantz), 174
Soglow, Otto, creator of comic strip *The Little King*, 199
Somewhere in Dreamland (Fleischer), 110
Sommer, Paul:
  joins MGM, 277
  at Screen Gems, 214
Song of the Birds (Fleischer), 110
Song Car-Tunes, 87–89, 94–96

Song of the South (Disney), 68, 194
Sound:
introduction of: by Disney, 34—35
by Fleischer, 89, 91—95
by Lantz, 158, 161, 169
by Terry, 127
by Van Beuren, 127, 195—196
stereophonic, 72
Sound system for *Fantasia*, 63
Sourpuss, 135
Southbound Duckling (MGM), 297
Southern Fried Hospitality (Lantz), 179
Southworth, Ken:
Lantz animator, 175
MGM animator, 300
Sparber, Isadore (Izzy):
Fleischer story man, 120
supervision of Famous Studios, 305,
310, 312
Sparring Partner (Fleischer), 83
Special effects, 83
(*See also* Live-action/animation films)
Spector, Irv:
Famous Studios writer, 309
UPA/New York animator, 333
Speedy Gonzales, 219, *266, 267, 272*
Spellbound Hound (UPA), 323
Spence, Irven:
Iwerks animator, 187, *193*
MGM animator, 284, 292, *293, 299*
Spencer, Fred, animator, character
analysis of Donald Duck, 49
Spiderman, 315
Spike and Tyke, 298, *299*
Spree Lunch (Famous), 312
Square Shooting Square (Lantz), 175
Squawkin' Hawk (Warner), 254
Stafford, Grace:
voices for *The Beary's Family Album*, 182
Woody Woodpecker's voice, 165, 173
Stage Door Cartoon (Warner), 268
Stage Hoax (Lantz), 173, 174
Stahl, Al, Terry story man, 137
Stalling, Carl:
composer-arranger for Disney, 35, 231
Iwerks music director, 187, *193*
Warner music director, 192, 231—232,
240, 269, 270
Stallings, George, *18*
Barré-Bowers animator, 13
Bray supervisor, 21
glass disk inventor, 11—12
Hearst animator, 156
joins Van Beuren, 197
Van Beuren director, 198
Stang, Arnold, voice for Herman the
mouse, 309
Star Is Born, A (Warner), 234
Starlighters, The, sing for *The Woody
Woodpecker Polka*, 168*n*.
Steamboat Willie (Disney; 1928), 27, 34—35,
38, 43
Stein, Milt, assistant at Famous Studios,
308
Step on It (Fleischer), 96
Stimson, Sammy, animator, *18*
Stokes, Bob, Iwerks staff, *193*
Stone Age Cartoons (Fleischer), 115
Stoopnocracy (Fleischer), 95

Stopping the Show (Fleischer), 97
Story of George Washington, The
(Paramount), 314
Story of a Mosquito, The (McCay), 4
Storyboards at Disney studio, 30, 38
Stratos Fear (Iwerks), 189
String Bean Jack (Terry), 134
Stultz, Joe, Famous Studios writer, 308
Sturtevant, Sterling, UPA art director, 331
Suddenly It's Spring (Famous), 307
Suited to a T (Fleischer), 96
Sullivan, Pat:
animator, 22—26
newspaper cartoonist, 22
Sultan Pepper (Van Beuren), 199
Sultan's Daughter, The (Terry), 136—137
Sunday Clothes (Columbia), 209
Sunshine Makers (Van Beuren), 201, 202
Super Mouse, 137—138
Super Rabbit (Warner), 251
Superman (Fleischer), 116—118
Superman (Famous), 306
Surry, Cecil, Lantz animator, 161, 175
Sutherland, Sid:
Lantz animator, 161
Warner animator, 225
"Sweatbox" at Disney studio, 55
Swift, Howard:
Disney animator, 62
Screen Gems director, 214, 215
Swifty and Shorty series (Paramount), 314
Swing Shift Cinderella (MGM), 287
Swing Symphonies series (Lantz), 166, 167
Swing You Sinners (Fleischer), 96
Swinnerton, Jimmy:
creator of *The Canyon Kiddies* comic strip,
240
creator of *Little Jimmy* comic strip, 17
Swiss Miss-fit (Lantz), 177
Swojak, Jon, assistant at Famous Studios,
308
Swooner Crooner (Warner), 248
Sword and the Stone, The (Disney), 75
Sylvester, 219, 253—254, *267, 272*

Tad's Indoor Sports, 17
Tafuri, Nick:
Famous Studios animator, 308
Paramount animator, 314
Tale of Two Kitties (Warner), 249, 253
Talkartoons (Fleischer), 92—110, 115
Talkies at Fleischer studio, 91—96
Taras, Marty:
Famous Studios animator, 308
Paramount animator, 314
at Van Beuren studio, 200
Tash, Frank (*see* Tashlin, Frank)
Tash, Tish (*see* Tashlin, Frank)
Tashlin, Frank:
author of *The Bear That Wasn't*, 302
Disney animator, 74
Iwerks animator, 190, *193*
Screen Gems writer and production
supervisor, 213, 215, 318
Van Beuren writer, 200
Warner director, 219, 227—232, 241, 243,
248—250
live-action writer-director, 231
Tasmanian Devil, 255—256

Taylor, Deems, and *Fantasia*, 63
Technicolor, 39, 108, 110, 186, 189, 201,
202, 211, 253, 306, 310, 336
Technirama process and *Sleeping Beauty*,
74
Techno-Cracked (Iwerks), 187
Tee Bird, The (Lantz), 182
Television films (*see specific studios*)
Tell-Tale Heart, The (UPA), 329—330
Tempo Production, 321
Tendlar, Dave:
Famous Studios head animator, 308
Krazy Kat inker and assistant animator,
206
Terrytoons director-animator, 151
Termites from Mars (Lantz), 173—174
Terror Faces Magoo (UPA), 333, 334
Terry, John:
forms company with Paul Terry, 125
studio, 17
Terry, Paul, 121—153
assembly-line production, 124
background, 122—123
and Bray, 20, 124
budget studio, 121
buys out Moser, 130
and color, 129, 134
comic strip *Alonzo* creator, 123
company formed, short-lived, 125
compared to Disney, 121
cost of Terrytoons, 130
double-exposure filming by, 11*n*.
early matte system devised by, 123
expands business, 130
and feature-length cartoons, 135
film credit to animators, 133
filmed medical procedures during WWI,
125
films made by, 27, 31, 122—141
formula cartoons, 135
gag file and collection, 126
indifference to animated cartoons encountered by, 122
lack of quality in product, 128—129
loses key men, 132
Moser-Terry-Coffman company
formed, 127
prescored music for cartoons, 128, 131
relocates after fall of Audio Cinema, 129
repetition and simplicity in films, 121—
122, 141—142
sells studio and properties to CBS,
142—143
simplicity and repetition in films, 121—
122, 141—142
and sound, 127
prescored music, 128, 131
(*See also* Scheib, Philip A.)
and starring characters in cartoons, 141
starts own studio, 21, 22, 125
and television, sells all assets to, 142—
143
unionization of studio, 133—134
unresponsive to new ideas, 132
watercolor backgrounds, 142
Terrytoons, 143—152
changes in design and color styling
under Deitch, 144
Deitch hired as artistic director, 144—146

468

Terrytoons (Cont.):
distributed by Viacom, 152
films, 144–152
free-lancers hired for, 149–150
new characters created, 149, 151
new stars in, 144–146
production ceases, 152
Terry assets purchased, 142–143
Terry staff retained, 143
20th Century Fox association, 152, 153
Weiss assumes control of, 148–149
Terrytoons (Terry), 122, 132, 135, 138
Tex in 1999 (Fleischer), 96
Thanhouser film company, Little Herman sold to, 124
That Little Big Fellow (Fleischer), 91
Theatrical cartoon short, demise of, 337, 338
There They Go-Go-Go (Warner), 262
There's Good Boos Tonight (Famous), 307
This Little Piggy Went to Market (Fleischer), 95
Thomas, Frank, Disney animator, 44, 73, 75
Thompson, Bill, voice for Droopy, 286
Thompson, Richard:
animator for Tower 12 Productions, 301
Warner animator, 257
Thorsen, Charlie, first model sheet for Bugs Bunny, 242
Thousand Smile Checkup (Terry), 148
1001 Arabian Nights (UPA), 335, color
Three Caballeros, The (Disney), 66–68, 194
3-D:
Disney, 72
Famous Studios, 310
Fleischer, 109–110
Lantz, 175
UPA, 330
Warner, 265–266
Three Little Bops, The (Warner), 269
Three Little Pigs, 40
Three Little Pigs, The (Disney), 40, 41, 43, 199, 200, 269
Three Little Pups (MGM), 299
Three Little Woodpeckers (Lantz), 179
Thrill of Fair (Famous), 312
Thru the Mirror (Disney), 50
Thugs with Dirty Mugs (Warner), 235
Thurber, Alfred, cameraman, 25
Thurber, James, author of A Unicorn in the Garden, 329
Tight Rope Tricks (Van Beuren), 198
Timberg, Sammy, songwriter for Fleischer films, 97, 107, 114, 116
Timmens, Jim, replaces Scheib to write scores for Terrytoons, 149
Tin Pan Alley Cats (Warner), 247
Tish Tash (see Tashlin, Frank)
To Have Is Human (Warner), 261
Toby the Pup, 208
Toddle Tales (Van Beuren), 201
Tokio Jokio (Warner), 250
Tom and Jerry, 70, 197–198, 282–285, 290–293, 297–301, 302
Tom and Jerry Festival of Fun, The (MGM), 301
Tom and Jerry in the Hollywood Bowl (MGM), 291

Tom and Jerry series (for television; H-B), 303
Tom Terrific (Terry), 146, 147
Tom Thumb (Iwerks), 191
Tom Thumb in Trouble (Warner), 239, 240
Too Hop to Handle (Warner), 253
Toonerville cartoons, 203
Toot, Whistle, Plunk, and Boom (Disney), 72
Topsy TV (Terry), 146
Tortoise Beats Hare (Warner), 245
Tortoise and the Hare, The (Disney), 42, 51
Tortoise Wins by a Hare (Warner), 245
Tot Watchers (MGM), 300
Touché Pussy Cat (MGM), 297
Tower 12 Productions, 301–302
Toy Shoppe, The (Lantz), 161
Toyland Broadcast (MGM), 276
Toyland Premiere (Lantz), 161
Transylvania 6-5000 (Warner), 271
Travelaughs series, 6
Trees and Jamaica Daddy (UPA), 335
Triple Trouble (Terry), 139
Trouble Indemnity (UPA), 234
Tubby the Tuba, 342
Turkisher, Art, Iwerks staff, 193
Turner, Bill:
Famous Studios writer, 308
Fleischer story man on talkies, 92–94, 116
Turner, Gil:
Lantz animator, 175
UPA director, 335
Turntable camera, 110
TV of Tomorrow (MGM), 295
Tweetie Pie (Warner), 253
Tweety, 219, 252–254, 257, 267
Two Guys from Texas (Warner), 257
Two Little Indians (MGM), 297
Two Little Pups (MGM), 276
Two Mouseketeers (MGM), 297, 298, 300
Tyer Jim:
Famous Studios animator, 308
Terrytoons animator, 142, 143, 147
Tytla, Bill:
Barré-Bowers animator, 13
director of Famous Studios, 311
Disney animator, 45, 53, 56, 62
leaves Disney for UPA, 64
Terry director-animator, 126, 128–129, 136–137
works free lance for Terrytoons, 150

UAW
sponsors Brotherhood of Man, 321
sponsors Hell Bent for Election, 318–320
Ugly Duckling, The (Disney), 51
Uncle Tom's Cabana (MGM), 287
Unicorn in the Garden, A (UPA), 329
United Artists, 39, 207
distributes Lantz cartoons, 172
United Productions of America (see UPA)
Universal:
becomes Universal International, 172
distributes Lantz cartoons, 157
Unnatural History (Bray), 21, 157
UPA, 72, 317–336
Academy Awards, 324, 332
nominations, 322, 335
beginnings, 318–320

UPA (Cont.):
budgets, 326–327
and CBS television, 332
CinemaScope, 332
color used by, 325–326, 336
commercial work, 327, 333
demise of, 334–336
distributed by Columbia Pictures, 322
early achievements, 320–321
films made by, 317, 331–336
growth of, 330–331
and "limited animation," 65
New York studio (see UPA/New York)
praised, 324–325
problems, 326
receives top animators from Disney studio, 64
under Saperstein, 335–336
success of, 317
takes over Fox and Crow from Screen Gems, 217
3-D, 330
TV commercials and survival of studio, 327
variety of films, 330
(See also UPA/New York)
UPA/New York, 333–335
Bert and Harry Piel campaign, 333
closes, 335
commercial work, 333–334
(See also UPA)
Urbano, Carl, MGM animator, 279

Vallee, Rudy, in Fleischer Bouncing Ball films, 95
Van Beuren, Amadee J., 195–204
break with Terry, 195
changes to studio operation by Gillett, 200–201
color: introduced, 201
misused, 202
films made by, 196–204
purchases Fontaine Fox's Toonerville Trolley comic strip, 203
sound, introduction of, at Fables Studio, 127, 195–196
studio, 26
demise of, 130, 203–204
outgrowth of Aesop's Fables Studio, 127, 195
Van Dyke, Dick, Mary Poppins, 76
Vaughn, Lloyd, Warner animator, 257
Vegetable Vaudeville (Famous), 309
Victory through Air Power (Disney), 66
Vinci, Carlo, Terry animator, 142
Voodoo in Harlem (Lantz), 162

Wabbit Twouble (Warner), 245
Waldman, Myron:
Famous Studios animator, 307–308
Fleischer animator, 94, 102, 112
Waldo, 323
Walker, Harold (Hal), Sullivan animator, 24, 25
Walky Talky Hawky (Warner), 254
Waller, Fats, caricatured in Clean Pastures, 234
Wanted: No Master (MGM), 278

Ward, Jack:
  Famous Studios writer, 308
  Van Beuren music assistant, 196
Warner, Harry, 252
Warner, Jack L., 252, 272
Warner Brothers, 70, 72, 219–273
  Academy Awards, 253, 254, 265, 266, 267
  animators giants in field, 219
  break with Harman-Ising, 224
  budget restrictions, 247, 263–264, 272, 273
  caricatures of Hollywood stars in cartoons, 234
  cartoons best in business, 231
  character matchups, 269, 271, 272
  cinematic techniques developed through Tashlin, 227–230
  and color, 224–225, 234, 252, 253
  comic nuance, 258
  cute animal characters, 260
  decline in quality, 270
  dismal quality of DePatie-Freleng films, 272
  Disney plagiarized, 223
  distinctive style of films, 219
  effective animated speed, 227
  films made by, 220, 222–227, 230, 232–272
  formula cartoons under Harman-Ising, 223
  government assignments, 257
  graphic design, 261
  "jam sessions," 236
  kidding self-reference initiated by Tashlin, 230
  last years of production, 270–271
  live-action/animation film, 237–238, 245, 248, 257
  miniaturization in films, 239
  montage, 240, 245
  new star character needed, 224
  new talent, 224
  reorganizes animation department, 272
  returns to cartoon releases, 272
  Schlesinger retires, 252
  Schlesinger's cartoon department: accepts free-lance assignments from other studios, 238–239
  stepchild of Warner, 238
Selzer, Edward, new head of cartoon studio, 252
  star characters, 219
  stops distributing short subjects, 272–273
  stylized and formalized backgrounds, 244, 246
  3-D film, 265–266
  transitions in cartoon department, 266
  vivid graphics, 270
  yearly schedule, 244, 247, 252

Washam, Ben (animator):
  for MGM, 302
  for Tower 12 Productions, 301
  for Warner, 257
Watership Down, 342
Way Down Yonder in Corn (Columbia), 216
We Aim to Please (Fleischer), 105, 106, 312
Webster, Dorothy, Iwerks staff, 193
Weir, Joyce, UPA animator, 321
Weiss, Alfred, 90
Weiss, Bill:
  business manager for Terrytoons, 143, 152
  controller for Moser-Terry, 129
We're on Our Way to Rio (Famous), 311
Western Whoopee (Van Beuren), 197
Wet Blanket Policy (Lantz), 168
What Makes Daffy Duck? (Warner), 253
What! No Spinach? (Famous), 312
What's Brewin' Bruin? (Warner), 259
What's Cookin', Doc? (Warner), 245, color
What's New, Mr. Magoo (UPA), 336
What's Opera, Doc? (Warner), 261, 263, 264
"Wheel of life" (zoetrope), 2
Wheeler, Clarence, music director, 177
When Magoo Flew (UPA), 332
White, Volney, Terry director, 135
Whiteman, Paul, and The King of Jazz, 158
Whittier, Gordon, Famous Studios animator, 308
Who Killed Cock Robin? (Disney), 51
Who Killed Who? (MGM), 289
Who's Cookin' Who? (Lantz), 167
Wickersham, Bob:
  Mintz animator, 210
  Screen Gems director, 214, 215
Wickie, Gus, Bluto's voice, 104
Wild Hare, A (Warner), 242–243
Wild Wild World (Warner), 269
Wild and Woody (Lantz), 176n.
Wild and Woolfy (MGM), 287
Wile E. Coyote, 219, 261–263, 272
Williams, Esther, in Dangerous When Wet, 294
Williams, Roy:
  Disney animator, 67
  Disney writer, 69
Willie the Operatic Whale (Disney), 68
Willie Whopper, 188–189, 192
Willoughby Wren, 217
Wilson, Don, in The Mouse That Jack Built, 269
Wilson, Lionel, voices for Tom Terrific, 147
Wimmin Hadn't Oughta Drive (Fleischer), 115
Windley, Al, cameraman for Krazy Kat, 206
Winkler, George:
  Mintz staff, 208
  production manager for Screen Gems, 213
Winkler, Margaret J., film distributor, 30, 32, 33, 205

Winnie the Pooh (Disney), 77
Winnie the Pooh and Tigger Too (Disney), 77
Wise, Fred, theme song for Little Lulu, 306
Wise Flies (Fleischer), 96
With Poopdeck Pappy (Fleischer), 115
Wizards, 342
Wolf, The, 286–287, 299
Wolf, Berny:
  inker for Krazy Kat, 206
  Iwerks animator, 190, 193
  leaves Iwerks for Disney, 192
Woodpecker from Mars (Lantz), 174
Woodpecker in the Moon (Lantz), 174
Woody Dines Out (Lantz), 167
Woody Plays Santa (Ski for Two; Lantz), 166–167
Woody Woodpecker, 16, 164–168, 171, 173–174, 179–182, 241
Woody Woodpecker (Lantz), 165
Woody Woodpecker Polka, The (Lantz), 168n.
Woody Woodpecker series (Lantz), 164–168, 171, 173–174, 179–182
Woolery, Adrian:
  leaves Disney for UPA, 64
  production manager of UPA, 322, 327
World's Affair, The (Columbia), 210
Worth, Paul, general manager for Screen Gems, 215
Wot a Nite (Van Beuren), 197–198
Wright, Ralph, new Goofy format, 70
Wynken, Blynken and Nod (Disney), 52
Wynn, Ed, inspiration for Gandy Goose, 134

Xerox process, 101 Dalmatians, 75

Yakky Doodle, 297–298
Yankee Doodle Mouse (MGM), 285
Yellow Submarine (1968), 340–341
Yelp Wanted (Columbia), 208
Yosemite Sam, 219, 256
You Ought to Be in Pictures (Warner), 237–238
Young, Cy, 21
  Disney effects animator, 52
You're Driving Me Crazy (Fleischer), 95

Zagreb Animation Studio, 329
Zamora, Rudy (animator):
  for Fleischer, 94, 96
  for Iwerks, 187
  for Sullivan, 24
Zander, Jack:
  MGM animator, 277, 292
  Terry animator, 121, 130
  leaves Terry for MGM, 132
  at Van Beuren studio, 200
  Warner animator, 221
Zipping Along (Warner), 262
Zoetrope (wheel of life), 2
Zoom and Bored (Warner), 262
Zukor, Lou, Iwerks animator, 190, 193